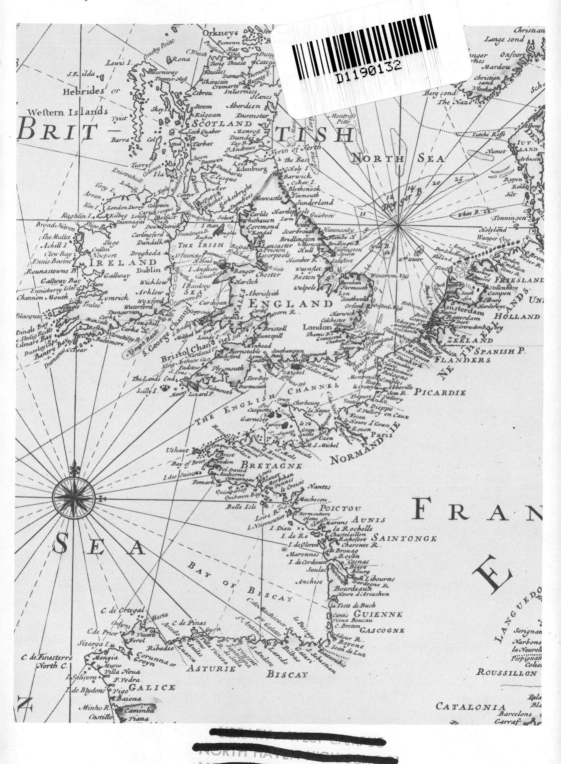

SEA OF GLORY

*The Continental Navy Fights
for Independence
1775–1783*

Sea of Glory

THE CONTINENTAL NAVY FIGHTS
FOR INDEPENDENCE
1775–1783

by

Nathan Miller

DAVID McKAY COMPANY, INC., NEW YORK

SEA OF GLORY

LIBRARY OF CONGRESS CATALOG CARD NUMBER: 72–92647

MANUFACTURED IN THE UNITED STATES OF AMERICA

ISBN: 0–679–50392–7

Contents

To
Jeanette

Without Her
There Would Have Been
No Book

Foreword

Historians have lingered over the American Revolution, examining in exhaustive detail its military and political aspects, its diplomatic and social overtones. Yet the naval side of the conflict has been almost completely neglected. Except for a few perfunctory—and often inaccurate—lines on John Paul Jones and perhaps a casual mention of the contribution of the French fleet to the victory at Yorktown, most writers have ignored the vital role of seapower in the winning of American independence. George Washington knew better. "Whatever efforts are made by the land armies, the navy must have the casting vote in the present contest," he declared. True, this statement was made in the afterglow of Cornwallis's surrender, but Washington had in fact refused to commit his army to the Yorktown campaign until assured of a "decisive naval superiority."

From the very beginning, the American War of Independence was a maritime conflict. The high-handed manner adopted by the Royal Navy in enforcing the laws against smuggling helped bring on the war. And after it had begun, both the Americans and British depended on supplies transported from across the sea to maintain their armies in the field. Britain had undisputed control of American waters and should have had no difficulty in snuffing out the rebellion by choking off the tools of war destined for the rebels from abroad. That this was not done was the result of muddled planning and the courage and skill of Yankee seamen. The Continental Navy, the privateers, and the navies of the individual states evaded the Royal Navy's blockade. For three years they provided the sinews of war until the intervention of France guaranteed the eventual independence of the American colonies.

The Continental Navy played a multi-faceted role in the winning of independence. It supplied Washington's army with sorely needed munitions by either capturing British vessels or carrying supplies from France and the West Indies. The increasing disenchantment of the British people with a long-standing and unpopular war was gradually brought to fever heat by the growing depredations of American naval vessels and privateers upon British commerce. And the infant navy helped draw a considerable part of the British fleet to the Western Hemisphere, dividing the Royal Navy at a time when it was confronted by the combined naval power of the European nations. What had begun as a minor struggle between the British and their North American colonies developed after 1778 into a world-wide maritime conflict. Britain's failure to strangle the rebellion in its infancy resulted in a war in which the fleets of France, Spain, and Holland were ranged against her and which spread from the coastal waters of America to the West Indies, Europe, and the Indian Ocean. It was a war Britain could not win.

No effort has been made to relate that story since 1913 when Gardner W. Allen published his *Naval History of the American Revolution* and Alfred T. Mahan wrote *Major Operations of the Navies in the War of American Independence*. These were pioneering works which attempted to present an objective account of the naval side of the American Revolution without patriotic bias. Both books have serious shortcomings, however. Allen deals almost entirely with the Continental Navy and fails to mesh its operations with the maneuvers of the European fleets. Mahan, on the other hand, dismisses the Continental Navy out of hand and concentrates on the great fleets. I have tried to deal with the naval war as a conceptual whole, placing proper emphasis on all its aspects. Unfortunately, limitations of space have prevented discussion of the activities of the various state navies except for operations that were intertwined with those of the Continental Navy.

The most serious problem faced by writers dealing with the early history of our navy is that of sources. Time, war, weather, and carelessness have deprived us of essential documentation. There are great gaps in our knowledge that will probably never be filled. Many of the surviving narratives are one-sided and partisan, so conclusions drawn from them must of necessity be mere informed guesses. As J. Fenimore Cooper pointed out more than a century and a quarter ago when he was writing his own *Naval History of the United States*: "The documents connected with the early history of the navy . . . were never kept with sufficient method, and the few that did exist have been scattered and lost." One of the most fortunate results of the bicentennial of American independence has been the decision of the Naval History Division of the Navy Department to correct this deficiency. Surviving source materials on the naval history of the American Revolution are at last being gathered from public and private archives around the world and made available to the interested public. Since 1964, the massive volumes of the *Naval Documents of the American Revolution* have flowed one by one from the press at a steady pace. The debt of gratitude owed the compilers can only be acknowledged, not repaid.

Official records, reports, logbooks, letters, and journals buttressed by modern analyses provide the basic framework of this book. Although I have abstained from detailed citations, the reader is assured that documentary support exists for every quotation or statement of fact. I have not presumed to tamper with the splendors of eighteenth-century spelling or syntax except in cases where meaning might be obscured.

I would like to express my appreciation to Dan Catlin for his careful and intelligent editing which has made this a better book than it might have been. Thanks are also due to friends who read parts of the manuscript and offered many useful suggestions: Ernest B. Furguson, Stanley Weiss, and Max Parrish. A special debt is owed Shirley Jack and Shirley Kranz for their patience and industry in typing what must have been a particularly difficult and trying manuscript.

One thing more. In writing this book, I have tried to focus the spotlight on the ordinary seamen of the great age of fighting sail. Except in rare cases, they did not write letters or keep journals and have vanished without casting a shadow across the pages of history. But they struggled and fought and died that America might be free. This book is intended as their memorial.

SEA OF GLORY
*The Continental Navy Fights
for Independence
1775–1783*

Prologue

Sliding away from a wharf at the foot of Walnut Street in the gray morning mist of December 3, 1775, the small boat dropped down past a line of ships anchored off the Philadelphia waterfront. A bulky man with a heavy undershot jaw and an aggressive, domineering look about him huddled in the stern against the wind whipping in off Delaware Bay. Gazing over the straining backs of the oarsmen, he searched for his destination with the narrowed eye of an experienced seaman. There she lay—dead ahead amid bobbing chunks of ice—a bluff-bowed vessel of some three hundred tons. The ship's newly painted yellow topsides had been pierced for twenty-four guns but she was slab-sided and square-sterned in an age when graceful quarter galleries set off men-of-war. Even here in harbor, her cannon rode only a few feet above the water, pointing out from her sides like stubby black fingers.

Esek Hopkins, commander of the tiny fleet being fitted out by order of the Continental Congress to challenge the naval might of Great Britain, had arrived to take up his post. Both the commodore and his squadron were new to the ways of war. Nearly eight months had passed since news of the fighting at Lexington and Concord had

I

raced through the colonies like fire in a ship's rigging—and it had taken that long to convince the Americans of the need for a navy. Up and down the Atlantic shore, militiamen had shouldered muskets, left anxious wives twisting their aprons and marched off on the road to Boston. Protected by hastily built fortifications and the cannon of the Royal Navy, a British army of six thousand men nursed wounds inflicted, to their surprise, by Middlesex farmers and villagers and sullenly awaited reinforcements from home. The presence of this garrison led to the immediate mobilization of a colonial army, but few Americans could conceive of resisting the most powerful navy the world had ever seen.

Just a few weeks before, Hopkins, an old merchant skipper whose naval experience was limited to privateering in the wars against France, had been a landlocked brigadier general in charge of his native Rhode Island's military forces. And until almost the same time, his flagship had been the stolid Philadelphia merchantman *Black Prince.* Now, along with three smaller cargo ships, she had been purchased by Congress and was being transformed by the dockyards into the *Alfred,* pride of the new navy of the United Colonies. Her hull had been swept clean, new masts had been stepped, and the vessel re-rigged under the direction of Captain John Barry, her former master, with the hope of improving her sailing qualities. But she would remain "clumsey and crank."

Hopkins's boat bumped to a stop against the wooden hull of the *Alfred.* Hand over hand, the commodore went up his flagship's side and through an entry port with a deliberation befitting his rank and fifty-seven years. Boatswain's pipes twittered a shrill salute in the best tradition of the Royal Navy as his foot hit the deck. He swept off his hat as green-coated marines—recruited at the drumhead in front of a waterfront tavern only a few weeks before—snapped to a semblance of attention. The salute was completed with a swish of swords. In the absence of Captain Dudley Saltonstall, who had not yet arrived from his home in Connecticut, the *Alfred*'s first lieutenant stepped forward. He was a sharp-featured, bantam cock of a man who called himself John Paul Jones. Hopkins probably regarded him with interest, for more than a little mystery surrounded this man. Gossip in the harborside grog shops and in the committee rooms of Congress had it that Jones was not his real name and he had been a pirate—or at least a slaver. Some whispered that he had killed a man

while master of a ship in the West Indies and had been on the run
from the law.

Lying nearby, crews drawn up at attention on deck or manning
the yards, was the rest of Hopkins's fleet. Equal in size to the *Alfred*
and also armed with twenty-four guns was the *Columbus*, which had
begun life as the *Sally*. There were also the brigs *Cabot* and *Andrew
Doria*, both of fourteen guns. John Adams, who had as much to do
with the creation of the Continental Navy as any man, was to recall
that the *Columbus* was named "after the discoverer of this quarter of
the globe"; the *Cabot* "for the discoverer of this northern part of the
continent," and the *Doria* "in memory of the great Genoese admiral." The *Black Prince* had been rechristened *Alfred* to honor the
founder of the British navy—"the greatest navy that had ever existed." No one seemed to have noted that it would be the task of the
Alfred's officers and men to cause that navy as much trouble as possible. The name change required no alteration to the flagship's figurehead, however. It was a knight holding a sword, who could be
either Edward, Black Prince of Wales, or King Alfred.

After reading his orders, the commodore nodded to Lieutenant
Jones, who raised what he later called "the Flag of Freedom" to the
top of its staff. Cheers rang out from the crews of the ships and were
answered by the crowds lining the shore. A ball of white smoke
puffed on the side of the *Alfred* and salutes thundered over the river.
The design of the new flag that appeared through the clouds of
smoke remains a subject of debate, but modern researchers are convinced it was the Grand Union flag—the British Union Jack in the
upper left corner, with thirteen alternating red and white stripes.
Like the symbolic name of the flagship, the ensign of the United Colonies was one more sign of the reluctance of the Americans to make
the final break with the mother country. They were fighting tyranny
—and considered themselves loyal subjects of the Crown.

News of the commissioning of the fleet was not long in reaching
London. An informant, known only as "B.P.," wrote the Earl of
Dartmouth, the secretary of state for the American Department,
from Maryland on December 20, 1775, that "an Admiral is
appointed . . . and on the 3d instant, the Continental flag on board
the *Black Prince*, opposite Philadelphia, was hoisted." By spring, he
predicted, American ports "will swarm with privateers. . . . Many of
the Captains of these vessels, in the last war, proved their intrepidity

to the world by their prizes, and some of them have already taken valuable prizes. . . ." The Americans, his Lordship was warned, would be no "contemptible enemy at sea."

I

The Gathering Storm

His Majesty's Frigate *Scarborough*, nearly six weeks out from Plymouth Sound, turned easily in the brisk offshore wind as the echoes of her salute reverberated across the naval anchorage off Boston. With his ship safely at anchor, Captain Andrew Barkley ordered his gig swung out. When the boat had been brought around to the entry port, he gathered up a packet of dispatches sealed in oilskins and lowered himself into the craft. "Let fall!" ordered the coxwain. Oars were dipped and the gig skimmed away over the water toward the tall, black sides of the *Preston*, flagship of Samuel Graves, Vice Admiral of the Blue and commander of the British fleet in North American waters. Heavy with the weight of official seals, the pouch contained orders that were to result in the first shots of the American Revolution—five months before the fighting at Lexington and Concord.

For the first time, Barkley had a chance to look about him. From where he sat, Boston appeared almost an island, attached to the mainland by a thin, mile-long neck of mud flats. The town itself was a jumble of roofs topped with chimneys from which fluttered tatters of smoke. Bristling steeples punctuated the skyline. Skirting the town was a complex of piers, shipyards, stages for drying fish, distilleries, warehouses, and wharves. The waterfront seemed strangely silent and deserted. Not a topsail could be seen in the wide harbor except those of Graves's warships and a few transports.

Though it was December 3, 1774—exactly a year before the morning Esek Hopkins assumed command of the Continental Navy —the tide of rebellion was already running high. Five months before, on June 1, Lord North, the prime minister, had ordered the port of Boston closed to all seaborne commerce until the town paid for three shiploads of tea that had been unceremoniously dumped in the harbor in protest against a tax on it. Civilian control of the government of the colony had been superseded and General Thomas Gage appointed military governor. The narrow streets echoed to the heavy clumping of army boots and the thumping of drums. With their seaborne trade cut off, the citizenry had plenty of time to stand about and watch as the number of occupying Redcoats increased until there were nearly five thousand of them—almost a third of the town's normal population.

For months, the Americans had been gathering gunpowder and arms against the day when they felt they would be forced to defend their liberties. As there were few powder mills in the colonies, large amounts of ammunition and other military supplies were brought in from England, the European continent, and the West Indies. Alarmed, the British government had finally decided to break up the trade. Captain Barkley brought with him an Order in Council approved by King George III on October 19, prohibiting the export of powder to the colonies. Royal governors were ordered to join in enforcing the embargo.

Government secrets have a way of getting out—no matter what the era. The documents intended for Rhode Island's governor fell into the hands of the General Assembly, which had them printed in the *Providence Gazette* on December 10. The news quickly reached Boston, and the Committee of Public Safety sent Paul Revere, a silversmith and dispatch rider, off to Portsmouth, New Hampshire, to urge the local Sons of Liberty to seize the powder and guns at Fort William and Mary while there was still time. Leaving his young second wife and their newborn son at his house on North Square near the waterfront, Revere galloped off over snowy and icy roads. Saddlebags bulging with dispatches and newspaper accounts, he rode into Portsmouth on December 13. Late that same night, about four hundred men set out from the town by barge, boat, and scow for the fort at the mouth of the Piscataqua River. Although surprised and surrounded, the post's commander warned them off. He was ignored. "I immediately ordered three 4-pounders to be fired at them and then the small arms," he reported. "Before we could be ready to fire again, we were stormed on all quarters."

For several hours, the raiders waded back and forth, waist-deep in icy water, carrying nearly a hundred kegs of powder from the fort to their boats. They dared not wear shoes during the loading, fearing they might strike a spark and blow up the whole place. Nearly frozen but triumphant, the Sons of Liberty hid their prize in a pit under the pulpit of a meeting house. Then they dispersed to their homes. General Gage was angered—and resolved immediately to seize all rebel gunpowder. Lexington and Concord, a world-wide maritime conflict, and the end of the old British Empire resulted.

The war at sea had been a long time coming. British policy in the dozen years between the end of the Seven Years' War in 1763 and the outbreak of the Revolution transformed the Royal Navy from a welcome symbol of imperial defense to one of colonial oppression. Successive ministries used the navy to enforce the collection of revenue and to suppress smuggling in America. They hoped to ease the burden of debt resulting from the defense of the newly won North American empire. Quite naturally the Americans, who had expected less interference—not more—now that the French had been expelled from North America, were increasingly drawn into conflict with the King's ships and officers.

New England became the storm center of the struggle because Britain's restrictive colonial policies severely threatened her considerable commercial and maritime interests. From the time of the earliest settlement, a century and a half before, the Yankees had developed a strong blue-water tradition. The thin, boulder-strewn soil of the northern colonies was difficult to farm profitably, and, unlike in Virginia, there was no staple crop such as tobacco that could be readily sold in England. The Yankees had become sailors, shipbuilders, fishermen, whalers, and slavers. Despite the strict limitations placed on colonial commerce by Britain's economic policies, great fleets of trading vessels sailed from New England ports for the sugar islands of the West Indies, the slave coast of Africa, and the Mediterranean.

This maritime tradition was not limited to peaceful pursuits. During the century of wars between the British and the Dutch, French and Spanish, hundreds of American privateers—swift-sailing, privately owned commerce raiders licensed by the Crown— slipped out of North American inlets and rivers in search of prizes. Colonial-manned ships had taken part in the great campaigns against Quebec, Louisburg, and Havana. Thousands of American seamen had learned the man-of-war's trade. Lamenting the brewing conflict with the colonies, one member of the House of Lords declared that America had been "a great nursery where seamen are raised, trained, and maintained in time of peace to serve their country in time of war." A French diplomat estimated that as many as thirty thousand Americans had served in the Royal Navy during the Seven Years' War.

Britain emerged financially exhausted from this Great War for Empire. In seven years, the national debt had nearly doubled from 72 million pounds to 132 million pounds. Trade showed few signs of immediate revival, and money was tight. Everyday living costs reflected the effects of inflation. A four-pound loaf of bread, once sold for a penny, had increased two-and-a-half times in price. Beef and mutton, which had cost about four pence a pound, now commanded up to three times as much. Mobs of English countrymen who rioted against a new tax on cider gave Americans a vivid lesson in how to nullify an unpopular tax.

With other avenues to solvency seemingly blocked, the cool, appraising eye of George Grenville, the prime minister, fell upon the Acts of Trade and Navigation. It was a fatal mistake. Dating back to the mid-seventeenth century, these laws were aimed at subordinating the economic interests of the colonies to that of the mother country by tying their trade to Britain. Before 1763, there was little opposition in the colonies because both sides were prospering, and enforcement was lax. For decades, Britain's economic policy in America had been "salutory neglect." Sir Robert Walpole, who headed the government for two decades, had declined to tax the colonies. He believed unrestricted trade would bring more gold to England than taxes or customs duties.

After rebellion flared in America, one historian[1] has pointed out, it became customary among Englishmen to forget the long-running series of political quarrels with the colonies that had troubled their relationship for a century and to look back on the period before 1763 as a golden age in imperial relations. "Our prime minister's grey-goose quill governed," it was said, " 'til that fatal hour when the evil Genius of Britain whispered in the ear of George Grenville, 'George! erect thyself into a great financier.' " Grenville was humorless and without spark but he had some reputation as a financier. He was truly horrified by the cost of the just-concluded war.

The defense establishment was ordered cut, and within a year after Grenville came to power, the army had been reduced from one hundred twenty thousand men to thirty thousand. The powerful fleet built by Lord Anson to fight the French was allowed to dissipate. By April 1764, there were only seventeen ships of the line ready for service at sea. The cost in human terms cannot be computed. The Earl of Chatham, who as William Pitt had been the architect of victory, was to say: "The bravest men the world ever saw were sent to starve in country villages." Well might the sailors who had fought with Sir Edward Hawke against the French Admiral Conflans at the decisive battle of Quiberon Bay in 1759 sing:

> Ere Hawke did Bang
> Mounseer Conflang
> You gave us beef and beer:
> Now Mounseer's beat,
> We've nought to eat,
> Since you have nought to fear.

But Grenville was deaf to such appeals. The immediate problem was to find the 350,000 pounds a year it cost to maintain ten thousand men in America. He turned his attention to the collection of customs duties in the colonies, where graft and corruption were rife. To net 2,000 pounds cost the British government 8,000 pounds. For generations, the colonists had practiced a left-handed form of free trade. Smuggling was openly ignored by British officials, and the col-

[1] John C. Miller, *Origins of the American Revolution* (Boston 1943).

onies soaked up contraband like a sponge. Ranking posts in the customs service were sinecures for political appointees who never left
England. Their poorly paid agents were discovered by the colonial
merchants to be "needy Wretches who found it easier and more
profitable, not only to wink but to sleep in their own beds; the
Merchants' Pay being more generous than the King's." James Otis,
the Massachusetts lawyer, allowed that "a very small office in the
customs in America has raised a man a fortune. . . ."

With all his economies, all his careful prunings of expenses insufficient to meet his designs, Grenville moved to put an end to the
700,000-pounds-a-year smuggling trade by ordering the Royal Navy
to enforce the Navigation Acts. When attempts to suppress smuggling did little to ease the burden on the Treasury, Grenville and his
successors resorted to such additional measures as the Stamp Tax,
the Sugar Act, the Townshend duties and other levies. To the colonial merchants, in the grip of a postwar recession, tighter controls on
trade were decidedly unwelcome. Colonial commerce depended not
so much upon violation of the trade laws as ignoring them because
they had not been enforced.

The presence of the Royal Navy sent a shudder of apprehension
through the colonial merchants. "Men of war, cutters, marines with
their bayonets fixed, judges of admiralty, collectors, comptrollers,
searchers, tide waiters, land waiters, with a whole catalogue of pimps
are sent hither, not to protect our trade but to distress it," objected a
memorial from Boston. Governor Francis Bernard of Massachusetts
declared that the navy's antismuggling campaign "caused greater
alarm than the taking of Fort William Henry in 1757." The editor of
the *Providence Gazette* inveighed against "insulting Captains Bash-
aws, I mean captains of warships."

Twenty-one ships, the second-largest fleet of the British navy,
took up station at major ports from Nova Scotia to Florida to put
teeth into Grenville's revenue measures. They were a varied lot. The
largest, known as a ship of the line, corresponded to the battleship of
a later age. These were armed with from 60 to 120 guns, mounted on
two or three gun decks. Royal Navy ships were rated according to
their gunpower with a first-rate carrying 100 guns or more; a
second-rate 90 to 98 guns; a third-rate 64 to 80 guns and a
fourth-rate 50 guns. Frigates carried from 20 to 44 guns. Of less

power were sloops, schooners, cutters, brigs, and bomb ketches, all mounting a variety of small guns. A typical first-rate, Lord Nelson's flagship *Victory*, a 100-gun ship of the line launched in 1765, and still on display at Portsmouth, England, was 226 feet long, 52 feet in beam, and drew about 22 feet of water. Ready for sea, she carried a complement of 850 officers and men and cost about 57,000 pounds—the modern equivalent of $1.5 million.

As first- and second-rates were dull sailers, the workhorse of the battle line was the 74-gun ship. Cheaper to build and requiring a smaller crew (about 650 men) than a three-decker, the 74 had timbers heavy enough to stand up to terrific pounding and sufficient armament on her two gun decks to make herself felt. By the end of the Revolutionary War, almost half the 174 ships of the line carried on the Royal Navy's roster were 74s. Next in number were the 64-gun two-deckers which had been laid down as an economy move. Four 64s could be built for the same amount of money and material it cost to send three 74s to sea. They were also manned by smaller crews. The 64 turned out to be false economy, however. Her firepower was only two-thirds that of a 74 and her hull was too light to withstand extensive battering. By the end of the war, this class of ship had fallen out of favor.

Perhaps the best-known wooden fighting ship was the graceful frigate, the equivalent of the modern cruiser. Her armament, ranging upward to 44 guns, was carried on one deck. Lighter guns were also mounted on the quarterdeck or rear part of the ship. From a distance, it was difficult to tell a frigate from a ship of the line. The difference in length was negligible, the sail plan identical. Not until the 74 came over the horizon so that her high sides and double rows of gun ports became visible, could the difference be made out. Nevertheless, the purposes of the two ships were different. The 74 was built to fight anything that floated. She was much higher, deeper, and broader than the frigate—and much slower and less maneuverable. Ships of the line usually operated in squadrons of less than ten ships or fleets of more than ten; if a single ship of the line was detached, it was almost always because no frigate was available for the special duty.

The frigate, on the other hand, was only called upon to fight ships of her own class. When attached to a fleet, she served as the admiral's eyes and ears, scouring the sea while the larger ships plowed

onward in line one ahead of the other. During a battle, frigates were
usually stationed on the unengaged side of the fleet, ready to repeat
signals from the flagship, take a disabled friendly ship in tow, or harass a disabled enemy. The duty most prized by frigate captains was
detached service. This assignment might take a ship anywhere in the
world to attack enemy commerce, to protect the nation's own trade,
or to hunt down privateers and pirates. With this kind of leeway,
dashing frigate captains could make their reputations and fortunes in
prize money.

Sloops of war carried from eight to twenty guns. They were
ship-rigged, that is, three-masted like the larger ships, and carried
their armament on one deck. Brigs were two-masted, square-rigged
ships. A brigantine was a two-masted vessel with a square-rig on the
foremast and a fore-and-aft rig on the mainmast. Schooners, carrying fore-and-aft rigs on two masts, were the most common of the
smaller craft. Many of a frigate's duties were performed by these
ships though they seldom operated with the battle fleet. Bomb
ketches, or "bombs" as they were called, were specially designed to
carry two heavy sea mortars throwing hollow, powder-packed shells
a foot or more in diameter. With their two masts set well aft so there
would be enough room for the mortars they had a distinctive appearance.

Like all fleets in the age of fighting sail, the one sent from England to America was more powerful on paper than in the water. It
suffered a chronic manpower shortage. During the years the Royal
Navy operated as a floating customs service in North America, sailors constantly deserted. This steady draining away of seamen had, as
Neil R. Stout has written, "a marked effect upon the events that led
up to the Revolution." [2]

Ship's logs of the fleet repeat a wearying refrain, according to
Stout: "Swam away 4 men," or "5 sailers ran off with the
whaleboat." The smugglers had a free hand as the navy's vessels lay
harmlessly in port because so many of their men had deserted—or
"run"—as it was entered on the books. Admiral Alexander Colvill,
the station commander, showered the Admiralty with reports of

---

[2] See Neil R. Stout, "Manning the Royal Navy in North America, 1763–1775," *The
American Neptune*, XXIII (July 1963) and *The Royal Navy in American Waters 1760–1775*
(unpublished doctoral dissertation, University of Wisconsin 1962). Microfilm in Library of
Congress.

vessels unable to sail because their crews had jumped ship. The *Jamaica*, which was to patrol the waters off Rhode Island, the center of the smuggling trade, could not leave New York during the winter of 1763–1764. In June 1764, Colvill reported that three ships, otherwise ready for sea, could not sail because they were short of hands. Less than a year later, he informed the Admiralty that a sizable portion of the fleet was unfit for service due to the loss of so many men. When the *Coventry* paid off in 1768, notes Stout, it was found that from the time she had sailed from Spithead five years before, the vessel had spent only 10 percent of her time at sea—and about half that had been consumed by the round trip from England to America.

Stout blames rum and the deliberate enticement of seamen away from the Royal Navy by the colonial merchants for the high desertion rate. Sailors received a daily ration of a half-pint of rum but were not content with it. They also patronized the numerous grog shops located in every port. Colvill tried everything to halt the drunkenness that prevailed among his men. Attempts to close the grog shops next to the dockyard at Halifax and a suggestion that the shore headquarters of the New York station be moved from the temptations of Lower Manhattan to Turtle Bay were in vain. "The sailors consumed such large quantities of drink that decent liquor would have been bad enough for health and morals," suggests Stout, "but New England Kill-Devil," which was the most generally available liquor, was especially vile stuff.

Writing to the Earl of Sandwich, First Lord of the Admiralty, Major John Pitcairn of the marines—who was to be second in command at Lexington and Concord and who was killed at Bunker Hill —painted a particularly vivid picture of conditions:

> The battalion of Marines are getting the better of their drunkeness . . . I assure you my Lord I have had a disagreeable time of it: I have lived almost night and day amongst the men in their barracks for these five or six weeks past, on purpose to keep them from the pernicious rum. I would not have your Lordship think from this that we are worse than the other battalions here, the rum is so cheap that it debauches both navy and army, and kills many of them. Depend on it, my Lord, it will destroy more of us than the Yankees will.

Royal Navy officers also charged that the merchants were deliberately enticing men from the King's service by dangling offers of higher wages and better living conditions. "It was to the merchants' advantage to keep the navy ships immobile and unable to examine vessels for illicit molasses, tea and wines," Stout observes. After 1774, these illegal cargos included an ever-mounting supply of gun-powder and muskets—"arms [which] helped to establish American Independence." Not only did navy captains bitterly complain that their men were being bribed to desert to merchant ships with offers of three pounds a month—more than triple the navy wage which had not been raised in a century—their efforts to enlist replacements were frustrated.[3]

To solve its manning problem, the Royal Navy resorted to the same remedy it used at home—impressment. And impressment, in turn, resulted in more desertion as the pressed men fled. Press gangs swept the streets and alleys of the coastal towns and boarded mer-chant or fishing vessels in search of likely hands. When the supply of prime seamen was inadequate, landsmen were caught in the nets spread by the press gangs. As Dr. Samuel Johnson observed: "No man will be a sailor who has contrivance enough to get himself into a jail; for being in a ship is being in a jail with the chance of being drowned. . . . A man in jail has more room, better food, and com-monly better company." Shortly after Colvill's ships arrived in American waters, notes Stout, the Admiral reported: "The most se-vere punishments I ever knew have been inflicted, even to six and seven hundred lashes a man having been given from ship to ship." To stem the hemorrhage of manpower resulting from desertion, cap-tains often transferred entire crews from ship to ship without letting them set foot on land. One historian states that as late as 1811, some ships had been away from home for as long as fifteen years without the men having been paid as much as a shilling.[4]

Historians have traditionally ignored the widespread unrest created by impressment in colonial America when assessing the causes of the American Revolution. They have regarded it as significant only in relation to the War of 1812. But Jesse Lemisch, who has analyzed the role of the merchant seaman as part of a study

---

[3] The pay of an Ordinary Seaman had been fixed at nineteen shillings a month under Charles II and was not raised until after the mutinies of 1797.

[4] Christopher Lloyd, *The British Seaman* (London 1968).

of the Revolution "from the bottom up," thinks otherwise. "Impressment angered and frightened the seamen, but it pervaded and disrupted all society, giving other elements and groups cause to share a common grievance with the press gang's more direct victims," he says.[5]

Pitched battles between press gangs and sailors were not uncommon in colonial America. Periodically, rioting exploded in the seaports in response to "hot presses," or large-scale sweeps for manpower. Boston was disrupted by widespread turmoil in November 1747, following the navy's seizure of sailors from merchantmen lying in the harbor. "For some days government was at an end in the Bay Town," writes one historian.[6] Several thousand seamen, unruly apprentices and blacks raged through the city. Only the frantic pleas of the authorities dissuaded Commodore Charles Knowles, the navy commander whose high-handed methods had touched off the troubles, from bombarding the town to put down the insurrection.

The return of peace in 1763 did not end anti-impressment riots—perhaps because impressment now lacked even the cloak of patriotism. "Seamen took to the woods or fled town altogether, dreading the appearance of a man-of-war's boat—in the words of one—as a flock of sheep dreaded a wolf's appearance," states Lemisch. "If they offered to work at all, they demanded inflated wages and refused to sail to ports where there was a danger of impressment." Boats carrying press gangs were burned and landing parties were mobbed. Press gangs soon discovered that their prey often had sympathetic allies ashore. Not only were the commonfolk likely to join seamen in violent resistance, but they also often had the assistance of those higher up on the economic and social scale. Colonial juries would not indict seamen who resisted press gangs, Lemisch adds. In some cases, he notes, officers were prevented from seizing men by the threat of prosecution.

The most widely publicized incident occurred in 1769, when Lieutenant Henry Panton, of the frigate *Rose*, was killed as he was trying to take four sailors from the Marblehead brigantine *Pitt Packet*, homeward bound from Europe. James Otis, Boston's fore-

---

[5] "Jack Tar in the Streets," *The William and Mary Quarterly*, XXV (July 1968), and "The American Revolution Seen from the Bottom Up," in Barton J. Bernstein, ed., *Towards a New Past: Dissenting Essays in American History* (New York 1969).

[6] Carl Bridenbaugh, *Cities in Revolt: Urban Life in America 1743–1776* (New York 1971).

most lawyer, was engaged as senior counsel for the sailors who were
to be tried by a special court of vice admiralty on charges of piracy
and murder on the high seas. At this time, Otis, who had once been
hit on the head with a cutlass by a customs official, was undergoing
what John Adams cailed "one of his unlucid intervals" and could
not be persuaded even to discuss the case, let alone appear in court.
The burden of the defense fell upon young Adams, his assistant. It
looked like an open and shut case.

Armed with knives and a harpoon, the seamen chosen for impressment had retreated to the forepeak of the brigantine where they
swore they would never be taken alive. "I know who you are!"
Adams reported one of them, Michael Corbet, as having shouted to
the advancing Panton. "You are a lieutenant of a man-of-war, come
with a press-gang to deprive me of my liberty. You have no right to
impress me. I have retreated from you as far as I can. I can go no
further. I and my companions are determined to stand upon our defense. Stand off!" Marking a line on the deck, Corbet ordered the
officer to keep back. Panton, disdaining this warning, stepped forward. Blood gushed from his neck and he fell; Corbet's harpoon had
severed his jugular vein.

Reminiscing nearly a half-century later, Adams recalled:

> I had taken more pains in that case than any other, before or since.
> . . . All my books were on the table before me, and I vainly felt as if I
> could shake the town and the world. A crowded audience attending,
> still as midnight, in eager expectation. I had scarcely risen and said—
> May it please your Excellencies, and your Honors, my defense of the
> prisoners is, that the melancholy action for which they stand accused is
> justifiable homicide, and therefore no crime at all—and produced one
> authority very plump to the purpose when Hutchinson [Thomas
> Hutchinson, the Chief Justice of Massachusetts] darted up and moved
> that the court should adjourn to the council chamber! No reason was
> given; not a word was said. . . .

Adams was astounded. What lay behind Hutchinson's attempt
to silence defense counsel? That night he relentlessly turned the
scene over in his mind, searching for a clue. He recalled that on the
table before him lay a volume of *The British Statutes at Large* with
the page turned down to a statute known as the Sixth of Anne—
approved by Parliament in 1708 in the sixth year of Queen Anne's
reign. Adams was prepared to contend this law made impressment il-

legal in America. There was considerable disagreement as to the meaning of the statute and its existence was not widely known in the colonies. It was "almost the only British statute that included the word or idea of impressment," Adams wrote. "I was determined that if the law of God, of nature, of nations, of the common law of England could not preserve the lives of my clients, that statute should, if it could."

Next morning, Adams and the defendants were back in the courtroom. "Never was [there] a more gloomy set of countenances, painted with horror and terror, than the audience showed, expecting a sentence of death," he reported. "The Court appeared; the prisoners were ordered to the bar. The President arose, and pronounced the unanimous sentence of the court—that the killing of Lieutenant Panton was justifiable homicide in necessary defense. . . . and not another word was said."

Adams was elated at having saved the lives of his clients, but he never forgave Hutchinson for denying him the opportunity to argue what he was convinced would have been a momentous case that would "have accelerated the Revolution." He believed the motive for preventing him from speaking was "first and last . . . fear" that he would publicize the existence of the Sixth of Anne.

Arguments over the legality of impressment might rage among the lawyers, but law or no law, the navy continued to grab men where it could find them. Lemisch contends that impressment began to be used as a political weapon. For example, Admiral Graves wrote the Admiralty on February 20, 1775: "Necessity obliges me, contrary to my inclination, to use this method to man the King's Ships, and it shall be done with all possible moderation, though at a place extremely violent in supporting and carrying into execution the Resolutions and Directions of the Continental Congress." In September, Parliament repealed the Sixth of Anne, ending, Lemisch notes, whatever uncertainty that had prevailed about the legality of impressment in America.

Lemisch estimates that perhaps as many as twenty thousand seamen and fishermen were deprived of their livelihoods by the post-1763 trade restrictions. When this economic blow is combined with their anger at the injustice of impressment—which the vast majority of Americans considered a direct violation of seamen's rights—a volatile, unruly population was created, ready to take action against other supposed oppressions by the King's ministers. Viewed in this light, states Lemisch, the riotous and undisciplined conduct of the American merchant seaman cannot be dismissed as blind and irrational. "The pattern of political expression, established as a response to impressment, was now adapted and broadened" to become an accepted form of political expression, he argues.

Smoldering anger among the seamen at impressment and the loss of berths led to bloodshed—the so-called Boston Massacre of March 5, 1770—Lemisch contends. British soldiers seeking off-duty work on the waterfront to eke out their miserable pay were brought into direct confrontation with jobless American seamen. When the smoke had cleared, five Bostonians lay dying in the street. But while such firebrands as Samuel Adams, a second cousin to the younger John Adams, and John Hancock were rallying the mob, Parliament repealed the Townshend Acts, except for a three-pence-a-pound levy on tea, which was maintained as a symbol of Britain's right to tax the colonies. Trade began to show signs of recuperating. Rhode Island had 150 slavers at work, and 123 whaling vessels cleared Nantucket. For the next three years, Lord North was little disposed to renew the quarrel with the colonies. Easy-going and good humored, he spent many happy hours dozing in his seat in Commons, prompting one agitated member to wish the prime minister had "some one at his elbow, to pull him every now and then by the ear . . . to keep him awake to the affairs of America."

The American radicals lay becalmed, and they waited impatiently for a fresh breeze. The lull was not broken until March 1772, when the schooner *Gaspée*, armed with four 3-pounders and commanded by Lieutenant William Dudingston, appeared off the Rhode Island coast. Dudingston began aggressively patrolling Narragansett Bay, arousing the hatred of the Providence and Newport smugglers, who, until then, had violated the Navigation Acts with impunity. Two years before, the customs collector at Newport had been mobbed and the colony's Superior Court had refused to issue writs of assistance, or general search warrants, to the customs-house officers. The obnoxious Dudingston was something new in the Rhode Islanders' experience—a naval officer who was determined to stamp out smuggling without regard for the sensibilities of the Americans. He was reported to have said that he would be delighted to see Newport burn about the heads of its inhabitants.

Tension increased. Newport buzzed with rumors that an armed ship would be fitted out by the merchants to rescue any vessel taken by the *Gaspée* for violating the antismuggling laws. The opportunity presented itself on June 9. The New York to Providence packet *Hannah* sailed from Newport to Providence and the schooner followed, ordering her to heave-to for examination. Instead, the *Hannah*'s skipper refused, and as the freshening breeze carried the packet out of gunshot, the *Gaspée* gave chase. With both ships crowding on sail, the *Hannah* led the schooner up the bay and lured her into shoal water where she ran aground.

By sunset, all Providence knew that the hated *Gaspée* lay helpless, at least until midnight when the tide would float her clear. Shortly after nightfall, a drummer paraded through the streets of the town urging citizens to join an expedition to dispose of the schooner once and for all. Under the command of Abraham Whipple, an old privateersman linked to some of the colony's leading families, eight longboats, their oars muffled and crews armed with staves, stones, and a few firearms, slipped silently down the bay to where the *Gaspée* lay stranded, about seven miles from town.

"Who comes there?" demanded Dudingston. Whipple answered: "I am the sheriff of the county of Kent. God damn you; so surrender, God damn you!" The officer refused and Joseph Bucklin, one of the men in the boats, turned to a neighbor and said: "Ephe, reach me your gun and I can kill that fellow." Drawing a bead on the officer he fired. "Good God, I am done for!" Dudingston cried out as he fell to his deck with wounds in the groin and arm. "I have killed the rascal!" shouted Bucklin, and the Americans stormed aboard the ship. After having stripped the schooner of all valuables and put its painfully wounded captain adrift in a small boat with his crew, the raiders set fire to the *Gaspée*. She blew up when the flames reached her magazine. Dudingston survived to fight in the Revolution and died a rear admiral.

Despite an earnest desire to play down the American problem, the British government could not tamely ignore this outrage. A thousand pounds' reward was promptly offered for the arrest of the leader of the raiding party and 500 pounds for any of his accomplices. A special Commission of Inquiry was established to search out the culprits and send them to London for trial. As it happened, no Americans were to decorate the gallows at Tyburn. The commissioners were handicapped by the blank memories displayed by the citizens of Providence. Nevertheless, Whipple found it wise to depart on a long ocean voyage. Esek Hopkins, Whipple's uncle by marriage, cautioned him to stay away until the storm subsided: "There is now setting a Court of Commissioners . . . in order to take up and send home to England for trial all those that were concerned in the burning of the schooner *Gaspée*. . . . What will be the consequences I can't tell you, but I hope all those concerned will not come by water into this port before the times alter."

Disgusted by the turn of events, Admiral Sir James Montagu, then the commander in North American waters, declared: "So farewell *Gaspée*! Farewell Justice! I am prepared for the consequences, I know what they will be. Here is an end to security for government servants, here is an end to collecting revenue and enforcing the Acts of Trade." The admiral was quite right. The destruction of the *Gaspée* breathed new life into the patriot cause.

To keep the East India Company from bankruptcy resulting from mismanagement by its own directors, Parliament granted it a monopoly in 1773 for supplying tea to the American colonies. Part of the company's problem lay in the refusal of the Yankees to buy British tea because it was taxed; they drank instead an immense amount of smuggled Dutch tea, depriving both the East India Company and the Crown of revenue. Believing that the colonists would prize cheap tea more than principle, Lord North gave the Company the right to sell its product directly to the Americans, cutting out the middlemen. This made the price lower than that charged by the smugglers, even with the 3-pence-a-pound tax still in effect. It was obvious that Lord North and most other British leaders did not know their Americans, for it soon became apparent that the Americans were more interested in brewing trouble than tea.

The tea monopoly succeeded in uniting the smugglers, the legal merchants, and the radical Sons of Liberty. The smugglers were afraid of being driven out of business by cheap tea; the lawful businessmen feared the East India Company's monopoly might be extended to other goods; and the radicals regarded the ministry's decision to retain the tea tax as one more violation of their rights as

British citizens. Tea became the symbol of imperial domination of colonial affairs. In some ports it was landed and allowed to rot in damp cellars. It was not even permitted ashore in Philadelphia and New York. In Annapolis a mob forced the merchant to whom the offending tea had been consigned to put the torch not only to the cargo but to the ship that had brought it into the harbor. And in Boston on the night of December 16, 1773, a group of men sketchily disguised as Mohawk Indians boarded the tea ships and emptied the chests into the water.

The events that led to war followed in quick succession. Lord North ordered the port of Boston closed until the tea had been paid for and appointed General Gage military governor of the colony. Alarmed, the colonies rallied to the support of the Bostonians and sent delegates to the First Continental Congress, which met in Philadelphia on September 5, 1774. It approved the formation of a Continental Association—a pledge by the colonies to embargo the importation of British goods beginning on December 1. Two days later, the *Scarborough* arrived at Boston with the Order in Council prohibiting the export of gunpowder to the American colonies—touching off a frantic race between the colonists and the Royal authorities to the magazines and arsenals.

All over the countryside during the mild winter of 1774–1775, New Englanders hoarded both arms and powder, and when the early spring came they practiced military exercises and sharpshooting on their village greens. They spoke of resisting a French invasion but it was strongly suspected that these Frenchmen wore scarlet coats. Even the children played, not at hunting Indians, as was their normal custom, but at mowing down British regulars. General Gage's well-organized system of informers soon told him where the arms and powder were being stockpiled—and an order for a secret march was given. Shortly after ten o'clock on the night of April 18, 1775, about seven hundred men pushed off in longboats from the foot of Boston Common. With muffled oars, they were rowed across the black waters of the Charles River and waded ashore near Cambridge. Early next morning, the troops, tired and chilled, their feet sloshing in their boots, were streaming along the road to Lexington and Concord.

II

"What Is the Admiral Doing?"

Strongly built and rugged-looking, Admiral Samuel Graves, the British naval commander in America, gave the appearance of steadiness and resourcefulness. At sixty-two he had reached midpoint in the Royal Navy's complicated grades of admiral, and he had seen a great deal of war. As a young lieutenant, he had been in the disastrous expedition against Cartagena in 1742. He had commanded ships in the Channel Fleet under Hawke, and had taken part in the decisive defeat of the French at Quiberon Bay in 1759. With his bluff manner and rough exterior, the admiral appeared to be just the type of old sea dog to teach the rebels a lesson.

Indeed, Viscount Barrington, the secretary at war, suggested that the army be completely withdrawn from the colonies, leaving the task of subduing the rebellious Yankees entirely to the navy. In a series of letters to Lord Dartmouth, the American secretary, extending from late 1774 well into the following year, Barrington declared that the army would be unable to subjugate the rebels. Even if it managed to do so, a permanent occupation force would be required, further embittering relations between the colonies and the mother country. "A conquest by land is unnecessary," he wrote on Christmas Eve, 1774, "when the country can be reduced first by distress and then to obedience by our Marines totally interrupting all commerce and fishery, and even seizing all the ships in ports, with very little expense and bloodshed." As late as August 8, 1775, well after the Ministry had decided to send an additional twenty thousand men to America, Barrington wrote Lord North: "My opinion always has been and still is, that the Americans may be reduced by the fleet, but never can be by the army."

Just such a blockade was feared by the wiser American leaders, so little did they suppose at the outset of the conflict that the colonies could make any headway against Britain's naval might. Coastal shipping provided the major link between the colonies due to the primitiveness of the roads. Unable to produce sufficient arms and munitions to supply an army, the Americans were completely dependent on supplies that came in by sea. Severing these lines of communication would strangle the patriot cause. They needn't have worried. Barrington was regarded as an old woman, and no consideration ap pears to have been given his suggestion. And even if it had, there is serious doubt whether Graves would have been the man to carry out an aggressive blockade.

The image projected by Graves—like that of his fleet—was far more forceful than the reality. He had never achieved a record as a fighter or as an administrator—and during his years in America failed to show either imagination or determination. In the twilight between peace and war that followed Lexington and Concord, he avoided the responsibility thrust upon him by events. Because he did not receive direct orders from the Admiralty to act offensively against colonial shipping and colonial ports until September, Graves remained semi-neutral. This astonishing attitude, as if the army were at war while the navy was not, could hardly have been anticipated by the government in London—or by the colonists.[1]

From the very beginning, Admiral Graves failed to live up to his responsibilities. Reeling back into Boston before the attacks of the aroused Yankee militiamen, the Redcoats were cooped up in the town, as the British admitted, "Like a parcel of Chickens." Supplies, if not scant, were far from enough to satisfy General Gage. He fully

---

[1] The most readily available account of Graves's operations is Allen French, *The First Year of the American Revolution* (New York 1968).

expected Graves's ships to lay a heavy toll on colonial commerce to provision the garrison, to guard British supply ships on the three-thousand-mile voyage from home, and to prevent the Americans from obtaining guns and powder abroad. Unfortunately, the pinch-penny economies of Grenville and his successors had had their effect on the Royal Navy. While Graves's squadron was adequate for peace, it was too weak for war. As Admiral Alfred T. Mahan was to observe:[2] "The opening conflict between Great Britain and her North American Colonies teaches clearly the necessity, too rarely recognized in practice, that when a State has decided to use force, the force provided should be adequate from the first." The force applied by the British in North America in 1775 was clearly inadequate.

During twelve years of peace, the navy had been honeycombed with parsimony and corruption. The Earl of Sandwich, First Lord of the Admiralty since 1771, was contemptuous of the Americans and seemingly oblivious to the crisis brewing in the colonies. He reviled the colonists as "the most treacherous, infamous, worthless race of men on earth." "Shall we," he asked, "be afraid of a body of fanatics in New England, who will bluster and swell when danger is at a distance, but when it comes near, will like all other mobs throw down their arms and run away?" The Ministry was so convinced that a sizable force would not be needed to deal with such rabble that it sought almost a half million pounds less for the navy in 1775 than it had in 1774. The estimates called for only eighteen thousand seamen as compared to twenty thousand on the books the year before—even though the Boston Port Bill and its companion measures made it obvious that force would be required to suppress the growing unrest in North America.

Even more serious was the condition of the navy's ships. Large sums were appropriated for the repair of vessels that lay rotting in harbor with not a penny spent on them. Accounts were never audited, estimates were falsified, and ships counted twice on official reports. Some ships were placed in commission to please political supporters of the King when there was no intention of fitting them out for active service. Authorities differ over the number of vessels ready to fight, because the official lists were swollen by those used as

---

[2] Alfred T. Mahan, *Major Operations of the Navies in the War of American Independence* (Boston 1913).

hulks or not fitted to serve in the line of battle—but whatever the number, it was inadequate for war.

Furthermore, the American rebellion had cost the Royal Navy a valued source of timber and such naval stores as tar, pitch, rosin, and turpentine. Unprecedented demands had been made on the forests of England during the Seven Years' War, denuding them of seasoned timber for ship construction. The result was a shortage of sound oak for both new construction and repairs. Another serious handicap was the shortage of masts. For well over a century, practically all the great masts for ships of the line had come from the pine forests of New England. As the war went on, the dockyards of Portsmouth and Plymouth were gradually depleted of the "great sticks" used in the larger ships. For want of tall New England pine many vessels were crippled at the most critical phase of the struggle. Their spars were due for replacement every ten years, but because the supply was exhausted, they had to be fitted out with old masts whose natural strength and resiliency had long since departed. Eventually great masts began to be shipped in from the Baltic and New Brunswick—but by then the damage had been done.[3]

Admiral Hugh Palliser, a member of the Board of Admiralty, calculated in July 1775 that at least fifty men-of-war would be needed on the American station. "A less number of ships than the above will be insufficient to perform the services expected," he told Sandwich without apparent effect. At that time Graves had only twenty-nine ships under his command. He kept three large men-of-war, the *Boyne*, of 70 guns, the *Somerset*, 64, as well as his 50-gun flagship, the *Preston*, at Boston. The *Asia*, 64, was sent to New York and the frigate *Rose*, 20, to Newport. Smaller ships, mostly of less than 20 guns, were stationed off Portsmouth, Marblehead, and other important harbors. They were not enough. The siege of Boston was no more than a few weeks old before various Royal governors were appealing to Graves for ships; first for support, then as refugees in flight. Worse still was the endless succession of orders from the Admiralty. Within one typical September week, Graves received three letters from their Lordships. One ordered him "to visit every harbour

---

[3] The definitive work on the influence of masts on American independence is Robert G. Albion, *Forests and Seapower: The Timber Problem of the Royal Navy 1652–1862* (Cambridge 1926).

in said colonies to disable ships fitting out"; the second instructed
him "to convey transports to the ports to demand provisions"; the
third pressed him "to examine the ballast of all vessels arriving in
North America to see if their masters have ballasted with flint
stones."

With this handful of ships Graves was responsible for patrolling
some 1,800 miles of coast running from the mouth of the St. Lawrence to Cape Florida and out to the Bahamas. Boston Harbor could
be entered by various inlets and not all of them could be blocked.
The *Rose* and her auxiliaries could not completely control the waters
of Narragansett Bay. There were creeks and rivers everywhere with a
perplexity of narrow and dangerous channels known only to Yankee
seamen where light craft could easily lie hidden from the King's
ships. Supplies were scarce, the vessels available were—as always—
shorthanded and often in poor condition. The vagaries of wind and
water kept a sizable part of the fleet in the dockyards undergoing repairs.

From southern waters, the captain of the *Tamer*, 16, wrote Admiral Graves that "her Sheathing is dropping off forward and as the
Worms bite so much am fearful that her Plank will soon be eat thro.
. . . As to my Sails I have but one Suit that can be depended on,
most other Stores I am Short of." Ordered to cruise along the New
England coast and to send any ships taken into Boston under prize
crews, the captain of the *Viper* told Graves:

> I am very much distressed for petty Officers as well as Warrants; my
> Carpenter is infirm and past Duty; my Gunner made from a Livery
> Servant, neither Seaman nor Gunner; my Master a man in Years,
> never an officer before, made from A.B. on Board one of the Guard
> Ships, he then keeping a publick House at Gosport: Petty Officers I
> have but one, who owns himself mad at times. A Masters Mate I have
> not, nor anyone [who] can make a Boatswains Mate. I have not one
> person I could trust with the Charge of a Vessel I might bring in.

Despite the difficulties confronting him, Graves might not have
failed so completely if he had shown the persistence of the typical
British sea captain, in the opinion of Allen French. He knew, of
course, the business of his profession and was careful and voluminous in his reports. In fact, he was so fond of writing that he left an
exhaustive record of his weakness and mediocrity for later genera-

tions. The admiral was quick to detect and criticize the errors committed by the land forces, while playing it safe unless and until he was pressured into action by the army. Suffering from the aftereffects of a stroke, Graves was a harbor admiral, content to alternate between his flagship and his house ashore. Fond of issuing orders "under his hand," he was content to administrate instead of taking his flagship to sea and providing an example for his men.

Graves's main passion seems not to have been putting down the rebellion but insuring the advancement of his three nephews. Having no son of his own to establish, he transferred his solicitude to his relatives, who served under him as lieutenants. At one point he tried to have them all assigned to his flagship so that their careers could be better propelled by the breeze of patronage. When Sandwich finally replaced Graves with what he hoped was a more aggressive and imaginative commander, he relieved the blow by assuring the admiral that he would "provide" for his ubiquitous nephews. Obviously, Graves was hardly the sort of commander to impress the Americans with the superiority of Britain at sea.

The Yankees did not take long to discover that the admiral was not even supreme in the waters surrounding Boston. Studding the harbor were several small islands planted with pasturage and stocked with cattle. Instead of clearing the herds off the outer islands and allowing the cattle to fatten under the cannon of his ships, Graves left them largely unmolested, despite the besieged garrison's demands for fresh meat. Presented with this opportunity to seize the grazing herds, the Americans called upon their most readily available means of offense: whaleboats. Six days after the Battle of Lexington, on April 25, orders went out from the Massachusetts Committee of Public Safety to concentrate such craft in the Boston area. Shortly, more than a hundred fast-darting whaleboats, manned by willing oarsmen, swarmed out of creeks and pulled around rocky headlands to harass the British fleet.

Outdistancing the heavier British longboats, the rebels burned lighthouses, removed navigational aids, and swept cattle and forage from the islands. Graves was so harried that he claimed the Yankees had amassed three hundred boats. He openly feared that some of his larger ships, shorthanded and at anchor, might be taken by surprise or burned. "These nocturnal movements of the Whale Boats about the harbour, and the knowledge of there being some hundreds of them, capable of carrying from 10 to 16 men each, with Ease, began to cause some apprehension in the large men of war, particularly in those stationed some distance from the Town," the admiral wrote.

Perhaps the most successful—and mortifying to the British—attack was a commando-style raid on May 27. The day had begun cheerfully for Graves. For the first time, he raised his flag [4] as Vice Admiral of the White, word of his promotion from Vice Admiral of the Blue having arrived two days before. "The Squadron Saluted with 13 Guns," states the log of the *Preston*. "Returned 13." But at 2 P.M. a more ominous signal streamed from a yardarm of the flagship. Rebel whaleboats were out again, this time trying to steal cattle and hogs grazing on Noddle's Island on the northeast side of Boston Harbor near Chelsea. A column of smoke from the island indicated that the hay stored there had been put to the torch. Boatloads of marines and the schooner *Diana*, commanded by Lieutenant Thomas Graves, one of the admiral's nephews, were ordered to get behind the Yankees and cut off their line of retreat. A brisk skirmish developed and it was joined in by the American artillery batteries on the mainland. The *Diana* ran aground in the shallows, and before the British could refloat her, the Yankees set the schooner afire. They made off with her four 6-pound guns and a number of smaller weapons—as well as four hundred head of cattle that were supposed to grace the mess tables of the garrison.[5]

While Graves was hard-pressed to deal with the daring whale-

---

[4] In the eighteenth-century Royal Navy, flag officers—admirals, vice admirals and rear admirals—were ranked in order of seniority in squadrons of the red, white, and blue. A captain newly promoted to flag rank would be a Rear Admiral of the Blue. Then he would become a Rear Admiral of the White and finally Rear Admiral of the Red. His next promotion would make him Vice Admiral of the Blue and so on. A Vice Admiral of the White would fly the white ensign and so would all ships of his command.

The news of Graves's promotion was brought by H.M.S. *Cerberus*, which carried a distinguished cargo—Major Generals William Howe, Henry Clinton, and John Burgoyne. Her sailing was hailed by a London wit with a bit of verse:

Behold the *Cerberus* the Atlantic plough,
Her precious cargo, Burgoyne, Clinton, Howe.
Bow, wow, wow!

[5] Ever protective of the interests of his relatives, Graves made haste to inform the Admiralty that the younger Graves had acquitted himself well despite the loss of his ship. He wrote: "The concurrent Testimony of those immediately concerned, of the nearest Spectators, and indeed the general Voice, authorize me to assure their Lordships of the perseverance and good Conduct of Lieut. Graves, the Commander of the *Diana* in this action." Such timely intervention made it possible for the younger Graves to survive defeat and eventually to hoist his own flag as Lord Nelson's second-in-command at Copenhagen.

boats playing havoc in his own fleet anchorage, some of his captains adopted more vigorous and aggressive tactics. British cruisers ranged along the New England coast at will, blockading ports and harassing colonial trading vessels. "The seacoasts are kept in constant apprehension of being made miserable by the once proud navy of Britain, now degraded to a level with the corsairs of Barbary," Mercy Warren, the wife of James Warren, president of the Massachusetts Provincial Congress, complained to John Adams. Coastal towns and villages expected marauding warships to loom over the horizon with all guns blazing. Local committees of public safety bombarded the army with demands for the return of men who had marched off behind rattling drums to the siege of Boston. The militia company from Durham, New Hampshire, got only as far as Exeter before heading homeward. "Six or seven expresses arrived at Durham the night after our return, some desiring us to march to Kittery; some to Hampton; some to Ipswich," related one militiaman. "The whole country was in a continual alarm."

The high-handed methods of some of the British captains quickly aroused the anger of Yankee seamen. They awaited an opportunity to strike back—and it presented itself early in May. Patrolling Buzzard's Bay off Cape Cod, Captain John Linzee, of the 16-gun sloop-of-war *Falcon*, was lying in wait for a vessel from the West Indies with a rich cargo when he fell in with an empty timber sloop. Linzee learned from the sloop's master that his intended prey had already reached Dartmouth, Massachusetts. The British captain put his men and guns aboard the sloop and sent her into the port. Finding the Indiaman riding at anchor and her crew ashore, the British sailors boarded her, hoisted sail, and made for the open sea. "The Bedford people resented this conduct in such manner as to immediately fit out two sloops with thirty men on board," states a contemporary account, and went in search of the "royal pirates." After a sharp hand-to-hand struggle, the Yankee seamen retook both ships —along with fifteen of the *Falcon*'s crew—and lodged them in the Taunton jail.

The most significant of the early clashes—the naval Lexington —took place off Machias, in the eastern district of Massachusetts, as

Maine was known at the time of the Revolution. Situated at the head
of a winding bay, Machias was remote from the rest of the colony
and was short of provisions after a severe winter. At the same time,
the British army was so short of wood for fortifications and fuel that
General Gage quickly endorsed a proposal by Captain Ichabod
Jones, a wealthy Loyalist merchant, to secure lumber from the
Maine settlements in exchange for the badly needed supplies. Jones,
who had been commercial agent for the settlers, saw a chance to
make a tidy profit for himself as well as help the King's troops. As a
precaution, Admiral Graves sent the 100-ton schooner *Margaretta*,
armed with four 3-pounders and several swivels, or light guns, under
the command of Midshipman James Moore to convoy the timber
sloops *Unity* and *Polly* to Machias.

Arriving off the town on the evening of June 2, 1775, Jones
began negotiating for an exchange the next day. He found the people
of Machias a singularly stiff-necked and uncooperative lot—even for
Yankees. They had a reputation for independence reaching back to
the settlement of the colony. The Treaty of Paris in 1763 had thrown
open the northern part of Maine to settlers and one historian has observed that "many perennial troublemakers, roughnecks, unscrupulous profiteers, restless and adventurous individuals" were attracted
to the area by its remoteness. Without a second thought, the settlers
took trees suitable for masts for the ships of the Royal Navy and
sawed them up into boards for sale in Boston, some three hundred
sailing miles away. There was also considerable anger among the settlers over the failure of the Crown's agents to confirm land grants,
leaving in doubt the ownership of property they had worked for
years and considered rightfully theirs.

The news of Lexington and Concord had been received with enthusiasm in Machias. It arrived almost simultaneously with an order
from the Provincial Congress "authorizing and requiring preparations and efforts incident to a state of hostility." The bolder spirits of
the town immediately set up a "liberty pole" as a symbol of freedom,
a tall Maine pine denuded of all foliage except for a green tuft at the
very top. Amid shouts and a flurry of musket shots, the tree was installed on high ground overlooking the settlement. Gathering around
it, the townspeople pledged themselves to resist British oppression,
and, if necessary, to sacrifice their property and blood in defense of
the town. With the *Margaretta* lying offshore, gun ports raised and

cannon run out, ready for action, the challenge had come far quicker than anyone had expected.

Bad weather and political turmoil had cut Machias off from the outside world, so most of the inhabitants, curious for news, were on the town wharf when Jones was rowed ashore. He circulated a contract for signature by the settlers. Before he would order the stores unloaded they had to agree to allow him to load lumber for the British in Boston. Unless they promised to protect him while the task was underway, there would be no distribution of provisions.

An unhappy murmur swept over the crowd. Just eight days before, the settlement's leading citizens had written the Provincial Congress begging for supplies. "A very severe drought last fall prevented our laying in of sufficient stores," they declared. "Nor have we this spring been able to procure provisions sufficient for carrying on our business. . . . Some of our mills stand still; almost all our vessels have forsaken us; our lumber lies in heaps." Supplies on hand would be adequate for only three more weeks. While Jones insisted he was collecting firewood, the settlers surmised from the type of pickets and plank sought that the lumber would be used for fortifications. There was strong resistance to signing the contract.

Unsatisfied with the number of signatures he had been able to gather, Jones prevailed upon the local authorities to call a town meeting so the matter could be put to a vote. At the meeting on June 6, Jones declared that Admiral Graves had allowed him to sail with the provisions only on condition that he return with a cargo of lumber. Nevertheless there was considerable opposition to any action that would help the Redcoats. As the Reverend James Lyon, chairman of the Machias Committee of Public Safety, later reported to the Provincial Congress, "the people . . . seemed so adverse to the measures proposed" that Jones secretly asked Midshipman Moore to bring the *Margaretta* closer inshore so "that her Guns would reach the Houses." The vote went in favor of signing Jones's contract. Apologizing later for the action, Lyon reported that the settlers considered themselves "nearly as prisoners of war, in the hands of the common enemy."

Jones ordered the *Unity* and the *Polly* alongside the wharf and began distributing his provisions—but only to those who had voted in his favor at the town meeting. This aroused the anger of those denied supplies and together with like-minded men from the backwoods settlements of Mispecka and Pleasant River, they resolved that the British should not have any lumber. They agreed they would attempt to seize Jones and Midshipman Moore that Sunday while they attended services at the Reverend Lyon's meeting house.

While one part of the group attended the services on the morning of June 11 to keep an eye on the intended victims, a larger armed party started across the Machias River on logs. Glancing out an open window, London Atus, Lyon's black servant, saw the armed men and concluded they were British troops—of whom he had heard much in recent days—bent on attacking the town. He gave a loud yell and with a single bound leaped out the window and made for the nearby forest. Instantly sizing up the situation, Moore and Jones did the same. The merchant escaped into the woods while the officer, with a mob brandishing fowling pieces, scythes, and pitchforks at his heels, raced to the wharf where the schooner's boat awaited him. Safely aboard the *Margaretta*, Moore got her underway down river, but not before passing the word that he would burn the town if any harm came to Jones.

Flushed with success, the settlers vowed to capture the schooner. One group set to work stripping the *Unity* while another piled into small boats and canoes and swarmed along the river bank to the British anchorage where they demanded that the schooner "surrender to America." "Fire and be damn'd!" Moore shouted back. A sharp exchange of small arms fire took place before the *Margaretta* withdrew farther downstream to escape the harassing fire. During the night, according to a British account, the rebels "endeavoured to Board us with a Number of Boats & Canoes." They were "beat off by a brisk fire."

The next day, in haste to be out of confining waters, where his ship was a target for firing from the shore, Moore ordered all sail to be made, but the *Margaretta*'s boom and gaff were carried away by accident as she came about. Boarding a timber sloop, the British refitted from her spars and took her master, Captain Robert Avery, to serve as pilot. Forty men, including Jeremiah O'Brien, a thirty-one-year-old firebrand, and five of his brothers, armed with "guns, swords, axes & pick forks," hoisted sail in the *Unity* and made off after the crippled *Margaretta*. Another twenty men, led by Benjamin Foster, a prosperous sawmill owner, joined the chase in the *Polly*; they ran aground, however, and took no part in the rest of the action.

The *Unity*'s new crew, using the pine boards that had been loaded aboard the sloop, fell to work building breastworks to screen themselves from heavier British firepower.

Despite the hour's lead held by the *Margaretta*, the distance between the two craft closed rapidly. In their eagerness to get at the enemy, the Americans had sailed without appointing a captain. O'Brien was nominated and, amid cheers from the crew, was unanimously elected. His first official act was to allow three men, who in the cold light of reflection had decided not to see the adventure through, to depart in a small boat. When the *Unity* came within hailing distance of the *Margaretta*, Moore demanded that the Yankees veer off, and threatened to open fire. "In America's name, I demand you surrender!" replied O'Brien. Realizing that he could not escape, Moore brought the schooner about and fired a broadside into the *Unity*, cutting up her sails and rigging. Then a backwoods moosehunter named Thomas Knight picked off the *Margaretta*'s helmsman with a ball through the head.

Out of control, the *Margaretta* became entangled in the *Unity*'s rigging, and the two vessels momentarily hung together. John O'Brien, the captain's younger brother, leaped to the schooner's deck, only to see the ships part, leaving him stranded among the enemy. A bayonet charge convinced young O'Brien of the foolhardiness of his position, and he jumped overboard. Once again, however, Jeremiah O'Brien skillfully maneuvered the *Unity* alongside her foe. This time the craft were lashed together. While his men slashed frantically at the lashings with cutlass and axe, Midshipman Moore lobbed several hand grenades onto the crowded deck of the Yankee vessel to keep off boarders. Joseph Wheaton, one of the *Unity*'s men, said the explosions "threw our crew into great disorder, they having killed and wounded nine men. . . ." But O'Brien rallied his men and they leaped onto the deck of the schooner. ". . . With clubed Muskets [we] drove the crew from their quarters, from the waist into the hold of the *Margarette*," Wheaton reported. "Thus ended this bloody affray."

Moore, mortally wounded in the breast, was carried below and asked why he had not surrendered. He looked up and whispered that "he preferred Death before yielding to such a sett of Villains." Another victim was the unlucky Captain Avery who had been taken from his timber sloop. Eight other British marines and sailors were killed while fourteen Americans died or were wounded—heavy casualties considering the size of the forces involved. For the first time, a ship of the Royal Navy had been forced to strike its colors to the rebellious colonists. News of the victory spread rapidly, and it did much to boost the morale of men about to battle the world's most powerful navy.

Aware of the revenge they had invited, and knowing their own weakness, the citizens of Machias took the *Margaretta*'s guns and transferred them to the *Unity*, renamed the *Machias Liberty*. Placed under O'Brien's command, she became the first American armed cruiser of the Revolution. Presumably, she was chosen rather than the schooner for this role because of her superior sailing qualities. The guns were scarcely transferred before two small British ships appeared in the lower bay to take soundings for an atlas of the American coast. The British commander knew nothing of the events that had taken place in Machias, and he was captured when he came ashore. His two vessels, the armed schooner *Diligent* and the tender *Tattamagouche*, were taken by O'Brien and Benjamin Foster without a gun being fired.

Thirsting for more victories, O'Brien and his crew carried their prisoners, who now included Ichabod Jones, to Watertown, where the Massachusetts legislature was meeting. That body resolved: "The thanks of this Congress be, and they are hereby given, to Capt. Jeremiah O'Brien and Capt. Benjamin Foster and the other brave men under their command, for the courage and good conduct in taking one of the tenders belonging to our enemies. . . ." The men from Machias arrived as the legislature was debating whether the colony should establish a sea defense force. Early in June it had extensively debated a proposal to maintain armed vessels, only to finally order it "to subside." No reason was given for the inaction but such an enterprise probably appeared hopeless against the British fleet. A letter from Governor Nicholas Cooke, of Rhode Island, had no effect, even though he pointed out that British transports and store ships were only lightly manned and armed and sailed from England without convoy.

The situation of Machias was critical. The town was defenseless unless allowed to defend itself on the seas. Moreover, Machias now had two armed vessels taken from the British. If their American crews were captured, they were liable to be treated as pirates unless their enterprise was legalized. So the Assembly voted to support O'Brien and Foster, to pay their previous expenses, to commission the two vessels, and to supply them with powder and other ammunition. O'Brien was named "Commander of the Armed Schooner *Diligent*, and of the sloop *Machias Liberty*, now lying in the Harbour of Machias, fixed for the purpose of guarding the Sea-Coast."

Thus, in late August 1775, Massachusetts acquired at one stroke a navy-in-being. The British were alarmed and the two tiny vessels were magnified to five or six. "Massachusetts took these steps because no help was to be expected from the Continental Congress," explains French. That body had voted on July 18 that the colonies should provide for their own defense by armed vessels or otherwise. For his part, George Washington, the army's new commander-in-chief, pointed out that in deference to the orders of Congress he was prevented from helping the coastal towns. In fact, he consistently refused to detach men from the army at Cambridge to meet real or rumored descents upon the coast. "Massachusetts had therefore to provide for itself."

The Bay Colony was only the second to support a navy. The first was Rhode Island. Angered by the energetic activities of Captain James Wallace, commander of the *Rose*, which in company with smaller ships patrolled Narragansett Bay, seizing boats and provisions without formal warrant, the Assembly voted on June 12, 1775, to commission two armed vessels. The largest of the two craft was the *Katy*, armed with ten 4-pounders and manned by a crew of eighty men; the smaller was named *Washington* and had a crew of thirty. Both were placed under the command of Abraham Whipple, who three years before had led the party that burned the *Gaspée*. He was "required and enjoined in His Majesty's Name" to "encounter expulse expel and resist by Force of Arms . . . all and every such Person and Persons as Shall attempt or enterprize the Destruction, Invasion Detrimant or Annoyance of the Inhabitants of this Colony. . . ."

On June 15, the same day he received his commission, Whipple reported that he put to sea and captured one of the *Rose*'s tenders—believed to be the Revolution's "first authorized capture" at sea of a British vessel. Moreover, Whipple took not a merchantman but a vessel properly commissioned. Thus his action may be considered the first official act of war committed by any colony on the water. Captain Wallace had clear warning that his command of Rhode Island waters was to be disputed henceforth. Infuriated, Wallace, who had not forgotten the *Gaspée* affair, wrote: "You Abraham Whipple on the 10th of June 1772 burned his majesty's vessel the *Gaspée* and I will hang you at the yard arm." Whipple was understood to have answered: "Sir, Always catch a man before you hang him."

Although most of the Revolution's early naval activity occurred in New England, South Carolina participated in the spontaneous attempts to obtain gunpowder. Learning that a powder-ship was expected to arrive at St. Augustine in Florida, a sloop was dispatched from Beaufort, South Carolina, to intercept her. The American vessel arrived almost too late. The British ship, in order to cross the bar, had unloaded much of her volatile cargo into lighters. Nevertheless, the sloop "commanded by one Clement Lempriere, run alongside the said Brigantine, and in a hostile and violent manner instantly boarded her with twenty-six men, some armed with Muskets and Bayonets fixed, and others with Swords and Pistols . . . and then, in an audacious and piratical-like manner, opened the hatches and took out of said Brigantine, and put aboard said Sloop, one hundred and eleven barrels of Gunpowder belonging to His Majesty." So wrote Governor Patrick Tonyn in a proclamation offering two hundred pounds reward for Lempriere. The attack was a bold one, for it was made within sight of a Royal Navy man-of-war. Luckily, she was aground. The sloop, which had a "Letter or Commission from Henry Laurens, styling himself President of the Council of Safety in Charles Town," was pursued but got safely back to Beaufort.

In the shadows, the bitter price of admiralty—a price that Britons had long before learned to pay—was being exacted. The American and British seamen wounded during the fight between the *Unity* and *Margaretta* had been taken to the shop of Jonas Farnsworth, a tradesman and Machias's part-time schoolmaster, which had been turned into a hospital. Bleeding and suffering from lack of adequate care, the wounded lingered for weeks. On June 23, Farnsworth wrote in his journal that a British sailor had bled to death and "John Berry's wounds got a bleeding and bled very much." Four days later, Farnsworth noted: "This morning, a young man, John Lennon, belonging to the tender, died of his wounds. He fairly bled to death having a wound through the arm: not hurting the Bone. He was accordingly buried about sunset."

Although the Americans were flexing their muscles at sea, Admiral Graves planned no attacks and directed no reprisals. He showed little energy in finding supplies and did not squeeze the rebels as he might have. Instead, he wielded his busy pen in verbose reports, bitterly criticizing Gage and expressing astonishment and regret at each misfortune. The navy's failure to produce supplies brought upon it the wrath of the hungry British soldiers in Boston. In the officers' mess, Graves and the navy were blamed for the inactivity, disgrace, and distress of the army. Some accused the admiral of operating a black market—"miserable lean mutton may now and then be bought in Boston at eighteen-pence a pound," it was said, "and slander does not scruple to hint at the Admiral as the seller." Graves was even accused of appropriating for his own table some turtles and pineapples sent to British officers by friends in the West Indies. Some angry officers suggested that Graves should be strung up from his own yardarm. The admiral and Gage quarreled openly—Graves and the general's father had been enemies—and the bad blood extended downward to the lower ranks, a state of affairs that was to grow worse as the siege dragged on.

Even Sandwich was finally moved to remonstrate with Graves. "I cannot omit this opportunity of repeating to you my earnest recommendation to exert yourself to the utmost towards crushing the daring rebellion that [has] now extended itself almost over the whole continent of America. . . . You may be blamed for doing little but can never be censured for doing too much." Scathingly summarizing Graves's activities—or lack of them—General Burgoyne drafted the following indictment:

> It may be asked in England—what [is] the Admiral doing? I wish I was able to answer that question satisfactorily. But I can only say what he is *not* doing.
> That He is not supplying the troops with sheep & oxen, the dinners of the best of us bear meager testimony—the want of broth in the Hospitals bears a more melancholy one.
> He is *not* defending his own flocks & herds, for the enemy has re-

peatedly and in the most insulting manner, plundered his own appropriated islands.

He is *not* defending the other islands in the harbour; for the enemy landed in force, burned the lighthouse at noon day, & killed and took a party of marines almost under the guns of two or three men of war.

He is *not* employing his ships to keep up communications & intelligence with the servants & friends of the Government at different parts of the Continent, for I do not believe General Gage had received a letter from any correspondent out of Boston these six weeks.

He is surely intent upon greater objects you will think—supporting in material points the dignity & terror of the British flag—& where a number of boats have been built for the rebels, privateers fitted out, prizes carried in, the King's armed vessels sunk, the crews made prisoners, the officers killed—He is doubtless enforcing instant restitution & reparations by the voice of his Cannon, and laying the towns in ashes which refuse his terms—

Alas! He is *not*.

On September 17, 1775, the Ministry finally decided that it had had enough of Graves. Sandwich informed him that he would be replaced at the end of the year. "You may . . . be assured that I shall in every place, both public and private, do you the justice you deserve and declare my opinion that it has been more owing to accident than to misconduct that the operations of the fleet during this summer have not carried that importance with them that the nation expected," the First Lord wrote in an attempt to soften the blow. But Graves was never employed in an important post again.

Graves's failure was to be Britain's failure. Because of his passivity and lack of initiative—as well as the inadequate fleet supplied him—the American Revolution was not strangled in its cradle. As Captain William M. James has suggested, it is interesting to speculate on what might have been the result if an efficient fleet commanded by an energetic admiral had been sent to American waters early in the conflict.[6] Undoubtedly, the British ships would have effectively closed the port of Boston, controlled the whole seaboard, and solidly supported the Royal governors in their efforts to uphold the Crown. "Complete command of the tradeways and communications, coupled with a strong show of force in the various harbours, would have given a very different turn to the course of events," he states. Britain was to pay dearly for the miscalculation.

---

[6] William M. James, *The British Navy in Adversity* (New York 1926).

III

Birth of a Navy

"What think you of an American Fleet?" Sitting ramrod-straight at his writing table, John Adams wrote hastily to his old friend, James Warren. "I don't Mean 100 ships of the Line, but I suppose this Term might be applied to any naval force consisting of several Vessels, tho the Number, the Weight of Metal, or the Quantity of Tonnage may be small." Pleading and cajoling, debating on the floor of the Continental Congress and intriguing behind the scenes, Adams had been working for months for the creation of a fleet. But as he sat writing in his room at Mrs. Yard's boardinghouse, a modest place on Arch Street not far from the Philadelphia waterfront, the prospects for organization of a Continental Navy were still uncertain.

Short, portly, and round-faced, Adams did not regard himself as one of the more imposing members of Congress. With the capacity for self-flagellation that was to become renowned in his family, he often despaired of exercising any influence on his fellow delegates. But he was a tenacious and determined fighter. In his old age, few of the honors that had come to him were to mean as much as being the real father of the American navy. To all who would listen, he expounded on the need for a fleet. An army had been quickly organ-

ized, and Washington named its commander. Why shouldn't there
be a navy? A fleet would defend the seacoast towns, protect vital
trade, retaliate against British raiders, and make it possible to seek
out among the neutral nations of the world the arms and stores that
made resistance possible. Had not America sufficient material and
men to build ships and fight them? With the combatants separated
by the broad Atlantic and both having important maritime interests,
who could doubt that the struggle would be a naval conflict?

As early as June 7, 1775, Adams was busily at work trying to
drum up support for a navy. Eagerly, he noted that Christopher
Gadsden, a South Carolina delegate who as a young man had served
as an officer in the British navy, "has several Times taken Pains to
convince me that the Fleet is not so formidible to America as we
fear. . . . He thinks, the Men would not fight on board the large
ships with their fellow subjects but would certainly kill their own
officers." And from his home in Braintree, Massachusetts, Josiah
Quincy wrote Adams on July 11 to suggest that armed row-galleys
might be the best way to protect colonial shipping from marauding
British men-of-war. "As the whole Continent is so firmly united why
might not a number of Vessels of War be fitted out & judiciously stationed so as to intercept and prevent any supplies going to our Enemies," he wrote, quill racing across the page as he warmed to the
idea. "Consequently, unless they can make an Impression inland,
they must leave the country or starve."

Yet, Congress balked all during the hectic summer of 1775 at
taking any steps to defend the coast. There were at least two major
reasons for this reluctance to act. To Southerners, a navy smacked
too much of being a New England venture. Except for the merchants
of Charleston, they had few ships of their own, and most of their produce was carried in English bottoms. "They agree that a Fleet would
protect and secure the Trade of New England but deny that it would
that of the Southern colonies," observed Adams. Moreover, a majority of the delegates did not regard the break with Britain as final. Organization of a navy would denote sovereignty, and therefore independence. Such a move was still a year off and conservatives had the
dominant voice in Congress. Stubbornly, they refused to consider
where the rebellion would eventually lead—and viewed the formation of a navy as a hasty and unwise challenge to the mightiest fleet
the world had ever seen.

The first formal movement in behalf of a Continental Navy came from Rhode Island, the same colony that had been in the lead in organizing a state navy. Increasingly angered at the aggressiveness of Captain Wallace in the *Rose*, the Rhode Island Assembly took an important step on August 26. It passed a resolution declaring "that the building and equiping of an American fleet, as soon as possible, would greatly and essentially conduce to the preservation of the lives, liberty and property of the good people of these colonies." Rhode Island's two delegates to Congress, then in recess, former Governors Samuel Ward and Stephen Hopkins, were instructed "to use their whole influence at the ensuing Congress for building at the Continental expense a fleet of sufficient force, for the protection of these colonies, and for employing them in such manner and places as will most effectively annoy our enemies, and contribute to the common defense of these colonies. . . ." After having duly approved this revolutionary act—and raising the monthly pay of Abraham Whipple from seven pounds ten shillings to nine pounds—the Assembly shouted "God Save the King!" and went home.

Unknown to the Rhode Islanders, steps were being taken on another front. By late summer, George Washington, hoping to capture desperately needed munitions from the British, had ordered a small armed vessel fitted out and sent in pursuit of enemy store ships and transports sailing without convoy along the New England coast.[1] Washington was attempting to end the military stalemate at Boston. James Warren summed up the situation there, saying the British "want courage to attack us and we want Powder to attack them so there is no attack on either side."

Congress reconvened in Philadelphia on September 5, but because of a failure to get a quorum and other delays, the Rhode Island naval resolution was not introduced, probably by Ward, until October 3. One by one, the members of the Continental Congress straggled back to the Pennsylvania State House during those autumn days. Presiding over the assembly was John Hancock. The millionaire smuggler's love of display would soon have a Philadelphia newspaper observing: "John Hancock of Boston appears in public with all the state and pageantry of an Oriental prince; he rides in an ele-

---

[1] See Chapters IV and V for an account of the activities of Washington's navy in New England waters.

gant chariot . . . attended by four servants dressed in superb livery, mounted on fine horses richly caparisoned; and escorted by fifty horsemen with drawn sabres, the half of which proceeds and the other follows his carriage." The patriarch of the half-hundred delegates was a benevolent old gentleman of seventy who had a habit of napping during the afternoon sessions. John Adams, an assiduous diarist, left this pen portrait of Benjamin Franklin:

> His conduct has been composed and grave, and in the opinion of many gentlemen, very reserved. He has not assumed anything, nor affected to take the lead: but he seemed to choose that the Congress should pursue their own sentiments, and to adopt their own plans. . . . He does not hesitate at our boldest measures, but rather seems to think us too irresolute and backward.

Adams was less respectful of some of the other delegates, especially the Southerners who often opposed New England's designs. Samuel Chase, of Maryland, "is violent and boisterous," he confided to his diary. Edward Rutledge, of South Carolina, "is a very uncouth and ungraceful speaker; he shrugs his shoulders, distorts his body, nods and wriggles his head, and looks about with his eyes from side to side. . . . His brother John dodges his head too, rather disagreeably, and both of them spout out their language in a rough and rapid torrent but without much force or effect." South Carolina's Arthur Middleton "had little information and less argument; in rudeness and sarcasm his forte lay, and he played off his artillery without reserve." Adams was equally severe with his fellow New Englanders. Eliphalet Dyer, of Connecticut, was "long-winded and roundabout, obscure and cloudy." Roger Sherman, also of Connecticut, had an "air . . . the reverse of grace. . . . Generally he stands upright, with his hands before him, the fingers of his left hand clenched into a fist and the wrist of it grasped in his right. He has a clear head and judgement; but when he moves a hand in anything like action, Hogarth's genius could not have invented a motion more opposite to grace." Caesar Rodney, of Delaware, was "the oddest looking man in the world; he is tall, thin and slender as a reed; His face is not bigger than a large apple, yet there is sense and fire, spirit, wit and humor in his countenance."

Unready, or perhaps unwilling, to consider the organization of a navy at this point, Congress postponed discussion of the Rhode

Island proposal for three days. The next day, October 4, was devoted to a debate on trade. The question was whether to adhere to the embargo entailed in the Continental Association, or to relax it so exports of tobacco and lumber could be sent abroad to relieve the distress of various sections of the country. Should trade be allowed in exchange for munitions? Should goods be exported? Or should the colonies wait until the need of the Europeans for American goods forced them to come to colonial ports seeking trade?

Midway in this debate, on October 5, letters arrived from London, reporting that two unarmed brigs loaded with arms, powder, and other military stores had sailed for Quebec on August 11 without convoy. Grasping the importance of the news, the navy's supporters moved at once that a committee of three be named to prepare a plan for intercepting the store ships and that it "proceed on this business immediately." These valuable cargoes should not be allowed to remain in British hands when they could provide a windfall for Washington's army, they argued. Once again, debate divided along sectional lines—New England against the South.

"The opposition to [the motion] was very loud and Vehement," Adams recalled in his *Autobiography* many years later. "It was . . . represented as the most wild, visionary, mad project that had ever been imagined. It was an Infant, taking a mad Bull by his horns. And what was more profound and remote, it was said it would ruin the Character and corrupt the morals of all our Seamen. It would make them selfish, piratical, mercenary, bent wholly upon plunder, &c. &c. &c." The last objection was more foresighted than it seemed, although it did not distinguish between a navy and privateering. Later, the temptation of prize money from free enterprise commerce-raiding was to make it exceedingly difficult to man the navy's ships.

Long into the afternoon the debate continued, with Adams taking the lead in support of the motion. The State House clock, checked twice a day by David Rittenhouse, the astronomer, boomed out the hours. The great white paneled meeting room, which had been brilliant with October sunshine, grew dark. Both sides sensed that the decision taken on this resolution might well determine the fate of the rising demand for a Continental Navy.

The minute any American captain was authorized to fire so much as a popgun from his deck, the greatest navy that had ever sailed the sea would turn its guns upon ports from Falmouth to Savannah, declared the opposition. "Mr. Edward Rutledge never displayed so much eloquence as against it," Adams wrote. "He never appeared to me to discover so much information and sagacity, which convinced me that he had been instructed out-of-doors by some of the most knowing Merchants and Statesmen in Philadelphia. . . . These formidible Arguments and this terrible Rhetoric, were answered by Us by the best Reasons We could alledge, and the great Advantages of distressing the Enemy, supplying ourselves and beginning a System of maritime and naval Operations, were represented in colours as glowing and animating."

All of Adams's forty-one years had been spent on the coast of Massachusetts among seamen and merchants, shipbuilders, and fishermen. He drew upon this experience to speak of "the Activity, Enterprize, Patience, Perserverance, and daring Intrepidity of our Seamen. . . . If they were once let loose upon the Ocean, they would contribute greatly to the relief of our Wants as well as to the distress of the Enemy." Finally, a vote was taken and the resolution carried by a small margin. Adams, Silas Deane of Connecticut, and John Langdon of New Hampshire—"three members who had expressed much zeal in favor of the motion"—were appointed the committee. They obviously had some prior understanding, for the committee met only briefly before presenting a plan for dealing with the supply ships.

The committee recommended that a letter be sent to Washington informing him of the sailing of the brigs and suggested that he apply to Massachusetts for permission to use the colony's armed ships to intercept them. Hancock added in a letter dispatched that same day that if the Massachusetts ships were unavailable, "you will Employ such as soonest can be fitted out"—which could have been used by the general as authority for forming his own little navy if he had not already done so. Hancock's letter is a clear indication that Congress had no prior knowledge of Washington's naval activities. Similar letters were also sent to Governors Cooke of Rhode Island and Jonathan Trumbull of Connecticut, asking them to dispatch their armed ships in search of the supply vessels. All ships involved in the operation were to be "on the Continental Risque and pay during their being thus Employ'd," and officers and men would be "entitled to one half of the value of the Prizes by them taken." Washington did send two of his schooners northward to the Gulf of

St. Lawrence in search of the munitions ships without finding them. Out of this tentative and reluctant beginning was to grow an American navy.

To understand the evolution of the Continental Navy, it must be kept in mind that two proposals, each aiming at a single purpose, proceeded simultaneously through the meetings of Congress. Although they were similar in purpose, they were never considered jointly. The first was the Rhode Island resolution; the second the plan to intercept the Quebec munitions ships. The reason for separate consideration is that the first was regarded as a permanent measure, the second as an expedient.

The committee which had been appointed to prepare a plan for intercepting the vessels bound to Canada made another report on October 6, but it was ordered tabled "for the perusal of the members for a week." While the *Journal* of the Continental Congress is vague about the contents of the report, later events indicate that it called for the fitting out of two armed vessels. In the meantime, heated debate on the Rhode Island resolution took place on October 7. The walls of the State House resounded to the attacks of the hulking Samuel Chase of Maryland. Notes taken by Adams provide a lively account of the arguments. "It is the maddest idea in the World, to think of building an American Fleet," thundered Chase. "Its Latitude is wonderful. We should mortgage the whole Continent." But he was willing to go along with the procurement of two swift sailing vessels "for gaining Intelligence."

Georgia's Dr. John J. Zubly declared: "If the Plans of some Gentlemen are to take Place, an American Fleet must be Part of it—extravagant as it is." Christopher Gadsden of South Carolina temperately favored the plan to secure armed vessels, saying it was "absolutely necessary that some Plan of Defence by Sea should be adopted." Although he opposed the "Extensiveness of the Rhode Island Plan," he thought it worthy of serious consideration. The navy's supporters, obviously aware that the hour for action had not yet arrived, bided their time. "Lightly skirmishing" with their opponents, in Adams's words, they agreed to postpone action on the proposal until October 16, and then again for a further month.

Congress resolved upon a historic step on October 13. Acting upon the recommendation made a week before by the special committee, it ordered the fitting out "with all possible dispatch" of two armed vessels, one of ten guns and the other of fourteen guns, to cruise for three months to the eastward "for intercepting such transports as may be laden with warlike stores and other supplies for our enemies." The smaller of these vessels was to become the *Cabot*; the larger the *Andrew Doria*. A separate three-man committee was chosen to estimate the cost of operating these ships. Once again, Silas Deane and John Langdon were chosen, but Adams was replaced by Gadsden, apparently a bid for Southern support of the project without sacrificing New England's control.

Each day, the gap between Britain and her colonies widened, and on both sides there was growing conviction that a war that must be fought to a victorious conclusion had begun. Marauding expeditions along the coast of Maryland and Virginia by a small armada commanded by Lord Dunmore, Virginia's Royal Governor, brought the Southern delegates into line, making the passage of naval legislation possible. The decision of Admiral Graves—stirred into action by the complaints that he was doing nothing to suppress the rebellion—to send out ships to punish the coastal towns that had given the greatest offense also played a major role in gaining support for the Continental Navy.

Falmouth [now Portland], Maine, had held Captain Henry Mowat, one of Graves's officers, prisoner until he escaped. Machias had seized four British ships, Gloucester had fired on the *Falcon* and Portsmouth on a boat from the *Scarborough*, Newburyport had worked with Falmouth to secure supplies for the rebels. All were slated by Graves for destruction. The British expedition was placed under Mowat's command, and he was given the *Canceaux*, of eight guns, the *Halifax*, of six guns, and two armed transports carrying about a hundred soldiers. "You are to go to all or as many of the above named Places as you can, and make the most vigorous Efforts to burn the Towns, and destroy the Shipping in the Harbours," he was told.

After struggling with a gale, Mowat's squadron arrived off Gloucester. Upon review, he decided that the scattered houses and his shortage of ammunition would make it difficult to burn the town. Mowat decided to press on to Falmouth, anchoring there late in the day on October 16. A lieutenant was sent ashore with a letter that was read to the inhabitants gathered in the meeting house. Because

of the premeditated attacks by the townspeople "on the legal Peroga-
tives of the best of Soverigns," Mowat had orders "to execute a just
Punishment on the Town of Falmouth." The people were warned to
remove "without delay the Human Species out of the said town"
within two hours when the punishment would begin. The signal to
open fire would be "a red pendant" at the main masthead of the
Canceaux, accompanied by the firing of a single gun.

"It is impossible to describe the amazement which prevailed
upon reading this alarming declaration," wrote the Reverend Jacob
Bailey. "A frightful consternation ran through the assembly, every
heart was seized with terror, every countenance changed color, and a
profound silence ensued for several moments." In spite of nearly six
months of war, the inhabitants of Falmouth had not yet learned that
squabbles with the King's officers might lead to violence. Frantic
parleys were held, and a committee went out to the *Canceaux* to beg
Mowat not to open fire "with the night approaching." He replied
that he would hold off the attack and refer the matter back to Boston
if all arms and ammunition in the town were turned over to him.
Stalling for time, the committee sought a delay to obtain the opinion
of the inhabitants. As a symbol of good faith, the British captain demanded that a quantity of arms be delivered by eight o'clock that
night. Only eight or ten muskets were handed over.

In the morning, the townspeople were bold enough to refuse the
British demand. The committee was again sent out to the ship, with
the hope of extending the grace period, but Mowat quickly sent the
group ashore, allowing them only until nine o'clock to clear the area.
"Perceiving women and children still in the town, I made it forty
minutes after nine before the Signal was hoisted," he reported. As
the blood-red flag streamed out in the wind, a gun was fired. Moments later, the sides of the British ships were lined with smoke and
fire.

"The firing began from all the vessels with all possible briskness,
discharging on all parts of the town, which lay on a regular descent
toward the harbor, a horrible shower of balls from three to nine
pounds weight, bombs, carcasses [incendiary shells], live shells,
grapeshot and musket balls," reported Enoch Freeman, chairman of
the Committee of Public Safety. "The firing lasted, with little cessa-
tion, until six o'clock. . . ." Flaming shells plunged among the
buildings but the wind was adverse and some of the inhabitants

could be seen trying to extinguish the fires. Mowat sent landing parties ashore to put the remaining buildings to the torch. There was some skirmishing and two of the British sailors were slightly wounded. By evening, as he drew off, "the body of the town was in one flame," the British commander reported. "Falmouth, with the Blockhouse and battery, the principal wharfs and storehouses, with eleven sail of vessels . . . several of which with cargoes" were "all laid into ashes." Four other ships were taken as prizes. Only about a third of the some three hundred houses, "the refuse of the town," and damaged by the flames, remained standing.

The people of Falmouth were left to face the winter in the ashes of their homes, with little clothing and few provisions. A month after the bombardment a visitor reported there was "no lodging, eating or housekeeping in Falmouth." To Americans, the burning of the town without warning at the start of winter was an atrocity, and they cited it as an example of British ruthlessness toward defenseless civilians. An outraged George Washington declared:

> The Ministry have begun the Destruction of our Sea Port Towns, by burning a flourishing Town of about 300 Houses to the Eastward called Falmouth. This they Effected with every Circumstance of Cruelty and Barbarity, which Revenge and Malice could suggest. We expect every Moment to hear other Places have been attempted and have been better prepared for their Reception.

The destruction of Falmouth and the prospect of attacks upon other coastal towns—although none were launched—was one more reason for broadened congressional support for the Continental Navy. Sensing the change in atmosphere, Samuel Ward, sponsor of the still-to-be-acted-upon Rhode Island resolution, noted: "Our instruction for an American fleet has been long upon the table. When it was first presented, it was looked upon as perfectly chimerical; but the gentlemen now consider it in a very different light . . . I have great hopes of carrying it. Dr. Franklin, Colonel Lee, the two Adamses, and many others will support it. . . ."

Having cleared the first barrier, the navy's supporters now moved forward with more certainty. Two additional ships, one not to mount more than twenty guns and the other not more than thirty-six guns, were authorized by Congress on October 30. They became the *Columbus* and the *Alfred*. These vessels were not limited to intercepting transports. They were "to be employed . . . for the protection and defense of the united Colonies, as the Congress shall hereafter direct." By this action, Congress committed itself to building a navy. To carry out this objective, four additional members were named to what became known as the Naval Committee, raising the membership from three to seven. The new members were John Adams, Stephen Hopkins, Richard Henry Lee of Virginia, and Joseph Hewes of North Carolina—making the total membership four New Englanders and three Southerners.

By the end of October, five months after Lexington and Concord, the American colonies had definitely embarked on a policy of naval warfare. Adams's notes on the debate, tantalizingly incomplete as they are, provide some reasons for the changed attitude. Trade must be had, a whole continent could not be blockaded by the British fleet with only a few ships here and there, "a navy consisting of a cutter" riding triumphantly between the Virginia capes. "Why should not America have a navy?" asked Virginia's George Wythe. "No maritime power near the sea-coast can be safe without it. It is no chimera. The Romans suddenly built one in their Carthaginian War. Why may not we lay a foundation for it? We abound with firs, iron ore, tar, pitch, turpentine; we have all the materials for the construction of a navy."

The city where Congress lived and labored was the colonial metropolis. With its 38,000 people, it far surpassed New York and Boston, its two nearest rivals, in size and was the second city of the British Empire. Visitors were fascinated not so much by the size of the metropolis as by the way it was laid out. America's other cities had retained many characteristics of the Old World towns—narrow and winding streets huddled about a central green as if there were no room to expand. Philadelphia, with its checkerboard streets, was the first planned city. "The regularity and elegance of this city are very striking," wrote John Adams. Neat, red-brick buildings fronted on tree-lined avenues, many of them paved in the middle and bordered by brick sidewalks. Streams of carriages and sedan chairs bustled along the streets, carrying the delegates from their boardinghouses to the State House, and on to the taverns and great homes at night.

During the early days of the Revolution, the Spartan virtues of self-denial were still being extolled. "Let us eat potatoes and drink water," Adams declared in a virtuous mood. "Let us wear canvas, and undressed sheepskins, rather than submit to the unrighteous and ignominious domination that is prepared for us." Despite such protestations, silk stockings and velvet waistcoats continued to be the dress of the delegates and imported wines their refreshment. Nevertheless, they put in long working hours. "My time was never more fully employed," wrote Dr. Franklin to a friend in England. "In the morning at six, I am at the Committee of Public Safety . . . which holds till nine, when I am at the Congress, and that sits till after four in the afternoon." Early in the session, Delaware's George Read found it necessary to apologize to his wife for not writing more often. "I prepare in the morning for the meeting at nine o'clock, and often do not return to my lodgings till after that time at night," he said.

Anyone out for an early evening stroll that winter would have seen a small group of men making their way through the descending twilight to a waterfront tavern. There in a private room they met as the Naval Committee to realize the decision to arm ships and send them to sea with all possible speed. Within a few weeks they accomplished a remarkable amount of work—and laid the foundation for an American navy. Merchant ships were purchased and their modification into men-of-war was begun; the first officers were chosen; policies and regulations for administering the Continental Navy were promulgated; and the enlistment of marines and seamen was authorized. It was decided to hold the meetings after six o'clock in the evening so there would be no conflict with the regular sessions of Congress "in order to dispatch this business with all possible celerity." Often the meetings continued to midnight, as the members were stimulated by rich conversation and a generous flow of wine and Jamaica rum.

Once again, John Adams provides a glimpse into the relaxed atmosphere in which the committee operated. He was to remember his service on it as "the pleasantest part of my Labours for the four Years I spent in Congress." Lee and Gadsden "were sensible Men and veary chearful: But Governor Hopkins of Rhode Island, above seventy Years of Age kept us all alive. Upon Business his Experience and Judgement were very Usefull. But when the Business of the Evening was over, he kept Us in Conversation till Eleven and sometimes twelve O Clock. His Custom was to drink nothing all day nor till Eight O Clock in the Evening, and then his Beveredge was Jamaica

Spirit and Water. It gave him Wit, Humour, Anecdotes, Science and Learning. He had read Greek, Roman and British history: and was familiar with English Poetry particularly Pope, Tompson [Thomson] and Milton. And the flow of His Soul made all his reading our own, and seemed to bring to recollection in all of Us all We had ever read. I could neither eat nor drink in those days. The other Gentlemen were very temperate. Hopkins never drank to excess, but all he drank was immediately not only converted into Wit, Sense, Knowledge and good humour, but inspired Us all with similar qualities."

On November 2, Congress authorized the Naval Committee to spend up to $100,000 to purchase and fit out the four vessels already approved, and empowered it "to agree with such officers and seamen as are proper to man and command" them. Congress also fixed the "encouragement" of these officers and men at "one-half of all ships of war made prize by them, and one-third of all transport vessels." Initially, the Naval Committee, dominated as it was by New Englanders, looked north for suitable ships. Silas Deane was sent to New York and Connecticut in search of two ships suitable for conversion and men and powder for them. Adams wrote almost identical letters on November 5, to James Warren and Elbridge Gerry, back home in Massachusetts, asking: "What Ships, Brigantines, Schooners, suitable for armed Vessells might be purchased or hired, and at what Price in our Province, what their Burthen, Depth of Water, Length of Keel, Breadth, hight between Decks, Age, etc. and to whom they belong?" Anticipating favorable action on the more extensive Rhode Island plan, Adams also questioned them concerning "What places are most suitable, that is safest and best accommodated, for building new Vessells, if any should be wanted? . . . But above all, what Persons, their Names, Ages, Places of Abode and Character may be found in our Province who might be qualified to serve as Commanders and Officers, etc."

As it turned out, the Naval Committee did not have to look any further than the Delaware River for its ships. All four were bought in Philadelphia, a move probably dictated by immediate availability and pressure from local shipowners. First to be purchased was the *Black Prince*, a vessel belonging to a syndicate headed by Robert Morris and John Nixon. Within a few weeks three other craft were added to the flotilla. Virtually nothing is known of these ships with the exception of those that became the *Columbus* and *Cabot*. Built by

Joshua Humphreys, a young shipbuilder and naval architect who later designed the frigates *Constitution* and *Constellation*, among others, the *Columbus* had a length along the keel of 75 feet, a beam of 27 feet and displaced about 288 tons. Both the *Columbus* and *Alfred* were originally armed with twenty-four 9-pound guns, but the flagship, at least, was later reduced to twenty guns. The *Cabot* and *Andrew Doria* were 14-gun brigs armed with 4-pounders. The *Cabot* was considered such a good vessel that when she was captured by the British in 1777 she was taken into the Royal Navy. She was about 75 feet long on deck, 25 feet in beam and displaced about 190 tons.

After selecting the ships to be converted into men-of-war in the absence of craft specially built for the purpose, the Naval Committee chose three men to oversee the operation. Each was well qualified for his post. For the structural work—the strengthening of beams, opening gunports, reinforcing timbers and bulwarks—young Humphreys was chosen. For re-rigging and outfitting, the committee turned to Captain John Barry, the *Black Prince*'s former skipper, who knew more about her sailing qualities than any other man. Captain Nathaniel Falconer, another Philadelphia shipmaster, was placed in charge of accumulating guns, powder, provisions, and other equipment.

Ship's carpenters began swarming over the *Alfred* and the other ships with Humphreys in constant attendance. The record still exists of the time spent working on the flagship—617 hours divided among thirty-four joiners, sawyers, caulkers, and laborers. The formidable catalogue of materials used included more than three thousand feet of planking, varying from two to six inches in thickness, fifty-four pounds of oakum and eight barrels of tar for caulking. The list included such details as "2 Sticking Candle sticks"—a reminder of how poorly lighted ships were between decks. These candlesticks were supplied with a spike at a right angle to the holder so they could be thrust into any upright piece of wood. While Humphreys' crews were strengthening the *Alfred*'s keel, cutting gunports in her sides and beefing up her timbers, Barry's team of riggers were also at work. They were surrounded by miles of rope of various thicknesses, lampblack, fathoms of cable and pounds of tallow for coating the rigging. Masts were re-stepped and new spars and sails sent aloft.

On November 10, Congress approved the raising of two battalions of marines. Officers were to include one colonel, two lieutenant colonels, two majors, and "other officers as usual in other regiments." Particular care was to be taken to ensure that "no persons be appointed to office, or inlisted into said Battalions, but such as are good seamen, or so acquainted with maritime affairs as to be able to serve to advantage by sea when required. . . ." They were to be known as the "first and second battalions of American Marines."

Fifteen days later, on November 25, Congress enacted legislation that, in Adams's recollection, was "the true origin and foundation of the American navy." This action began as an attempt to comply with repeated requests from Washington for the creation of procedures for handling prizes and the establishment of admiralty courts and ended as a justification for a naval war against Britain. Colonial vessels "have in a lawless manner, without even the semblance of just authority, been seized by his majesty's ships of war," the resolution declared. The burning of Falmouth was assailed, and it was charged that "hundreds of helpless women and children" had been "dispersed at a late season of the year . . . with a savage hope that those may perish under the approaching rigers of the season." As a result of these incidents "and other unprovoked injuries . . . the good people of these colonies . . . have at last determined to prevent as much as possible a repetition thereof, and to procure some reparation for the same, by fitting out armed vessels and ships of force."

All enemy men-of-war and transport vessels were to be fair game for colonial cruisers, and provisions were made for privateers.[2] Only captains holding commissions from Congress or its authorized agents would be permitted to take prizes, however. Congress recommended that the various colonies establish prize courts or use existing judicial machinery for the purpose. Congress also fixed the shares of the proceeds from the sale of prizes. In the case of privateers, the captors got everything; in the case of a vessel fitted out by a colony or Congress, two-thirds of the proceeds would go to the government and the rest to the captors, unless the prize were a ship of war. In that case the captors' share would be increased to one-half.

---

[2] As originally approved, the resolution stated that cargoes found on transports and supply ships would be seized but the ships would be released unless they were owned by American Loyalists. This restriction was dropped the following month.

While these important steps were being taken, Adams was at work drafting a set of rules and regulations for the new navy. Debated paragraph by paragraph, they were approved by Congress on November 28, with only minor changes. These regulations were an abridgment of the British naval statutes in effect in 1775, although Adams made them less stringent. More than half dealt with the care, feeding, rights, duties, and punishment of the ordinary seamen. Adams took his most extreme punishment from the Royal Navy— twelve lashes with the cat-o'-nine-tails. King's Regulations stated: "No Commander shall inflict any punishment upon a Seaman, beyond Twelve Lashes upon his bare Back with a Cat of Nine Tails, according to the ancient Practice of the Sea." Continental regulations read: "No Commander shall inflict any punishment upon a seamen beyond twelve lashes upon his bare back." But in the Royal Navy this injunction was more often ignored than obeyed. Captains ordered two or three dozen lashes at the gangway for trivial offenses, and the Admiralty ignored any complaints.

In the Continental Navy, sailors were to be punished for swearing by wearing a wooden collar "or some other shameful badge of distinction." Drunken sailors were to be put in irons until they sobered up, while officers guilty of the same offense were to forfeit two days' pay. For enlisted men, this was a flogging offense in the Royal Navy. American captains were also admonished "to take care that divine service be performed twice a day on board, and a sermon preached on Sundays, unless bad weather or other extraordinary accidents prevent it." In case a sailor deserved greater punishment than twelve lashes, he had to be tried by a court-martial which could impose the death penalty for desertion, mutiny, or murder.

Rations were fixed for each day of the week.[3] Each seaman was given a half-pint of rum per day "and descrestionary allowance on extra duty, and in time of engagement." A regular ration of vinegar was to be distributed to combat scurvy. In a thrifty Yankee touch, all ships were to be issued fishing tackle, and the catch distributed among the sick. If there was any surplus of fresh fish, it was to be given to the various messes to supplement regular rations.

Captains were to be paid $32.00 monthly and able seamen and marine privates $6.67. Later, when experience showed this was too

---

[3] See Appendix I for the complete text of the Rules for the Regulation of the Navy of the United Colonies, including the daily bill of fare.

low to attract hands, the sum was raised to $8.00 a month. The enlistment contract which accompanied the regulations provided that if a sailor were disabled, he would receive a bounty of $200; if he were killed, $200 was to go to his family. The man who first sighted an enemy ship that became a prize was to get double his share of prize money, while the man who first boarded her got a triple share. Ten shares were set aside to be distributed among those who performed their duty in an outstanding manner. With minor changes, Adams's regulations were in force throughout the Revolution and were re-adopted when the United States Navy was organized in 1798.

"You will perceive by a Letter from the [Naval] Committee, dated yesterday, that they have pitched upon you to take the Command of a small Fleet, which they and I hope will be but the Beginning of one much larger." So wrote Stephen Hopkins to his younger brother, Esek, on November 6.[4] In "pitching upon" Esek Hopkins, and a list of captains and lieutenants submitted to Congress on December 22, the committee followed the same principles of nepotism and political preferment that were the bane of the Royal Navy. Hopkins, whose pay was fixed at $125 a month, led the list as commander-in-chief. The senior captain was Dudley Saltonstall, of Connecticut, who was Silas Deane's brother-in-law. Then came Abraham Whipple, who was married to a niece of the committee chairman and the commodore. He was followed by Nicholas Biddle of Philadelphia, whose brother Edward was a member of the Pennsylvania congressional delegation, and John Burroughs Hopkins, the commodore's son. Paul Jones, who had the backing of Joseph Hewes, a North Carolina member of the Naval Committee, was named the senior lieutenant. Of the five juiciest naval plums, New England had plucked four—and the Hopkins family had three of these. The Yankees considered this only fair because the army's commander-in-chief was a Southerner; besides, New England exceeded the other colonies in the number of men with experience at sea.[5]

Esek Hopkins, who had divided his time between the sea and Rhode Island politics, was known as an aggressive and outspoken

---

[4] Although Hopkins was to be called commodore, this was a courtesy title, as there was no such formal rank in the Continental Navy.

[5] William J. Morgan provides a composite biography of the New England captains in the Continental Navy in his valuable *Captains to the Northward* (Barre, Mass. 1959).

man with an irascible temper. He had gone to sea at the age of twenty, had traveled to all parts of the globe and had successfully commanded privateers against the French. A surviving portrait shows him during what must have been a monumental carouse in Surinam. With glass in hand, he is shown conversing with a friend while other merchant captains in the group loll on the tavern floor in various stages of drunkenness. Hopkins had been on shore since 1772. When the Revolution broke out, he was pressed into service, along with other mariners familiar with cannon, to prepare a battery for the defense of Providence. Shortly thereafter, he was placed in charge of all the colony's military forces with the rank of brigadier general. He impressed General Henry Knox as "an antiquated figure, shrewd and sensible," and the enthusiastic Knox claimed he would "have mistaken him for an angel, only he swore now and then."

There has been considerable debate whether Congress, by appointing Hopkins as commander-in-chief, intended him to be equal in rank to George Washington, the army's commander-in-chief. The answer appears to be that he was to be given command only of the fleet fitting out at Philadelphia. Stephen Hopkins, in his letter of November 6, stated he was to be offered "Command of a Small Fleet." A congressional resolution of January 2, 1778, states that Hopkins "was appointed commander-in-chief of the fleet fitted out by the Naval Committee." Several other Continental ships were at sea in 1776 in addition to his own fleet, but they were not under his orders.

Dudley Saltonstall, the captain of the *Alfred*, was thirty-seven years old and, like the other New England captains, a member of an old family. Before the war, he had been a merchant captain and privateer. Like Esek Hopkins, he had been engaged in setting up artillery batteries at his hometown in New London when word of his appointment arrived. Nicholas Biddle, one of his fellow captains, described him as "a Sensible indefatigable, Morose man," but Paul Jones, Saltonstall's first lieutenant, complained of his "Rude Unhappy Temper," and called him "ill-natured and narrow-minded."

Little is known about John B. Hopkins, the commodore's thirty-three-year-old son, who was given command of the *Cabot*. He was one of ten children and followed his father to sea. Upon one of his visits home, young Hopkins took part in Abraham Whipple's expedition against the *Gaspée*. Whipple, himself, came to Philadelphia in the *Katy*, which was turned over to the Continental service and re-named the *Providence*. He was given command of the *Columbus*.

Nicholas Biddle, the only non-New Englander on the first list of captains, was to prove the most promising. He was also the only one with experience in the Royal Navy, having been appointed a mid-shipman in 1771, at the age of twenty-one. Before that, Biddle had had wide experience in the merchant service. The high point of his naval career was a polar expedition in which he gave up his warrant and went along as a captain's servant, so eager was he to take part in the adventure. Among his messmates was a sixteen-year-old mid-shipman named Horatio Nelson, who had also given up his rank to join the expedition. Returning to America after this voyage, Biddle was placed in charge of a ship sent by the Pennsylvania authorities to the French island of Santo Domingo, which then ran the blockade of Philadelphia with six and a half tons of badly needed gunpowder. He was given command of the row-galley *Franklin* in the Delaware River defenses and afterward, at the age of twenty-five, was posted as captain of the *Andrew Doria*.

Congress had still not acted upon the Rhode Island resolution but its long hesitation was coming to an end. All the postponements of the proposal make it clear that the members thought a commit-ment to build a fleet of frigates was something substantially more significant than the fitting out of a few small merchantmen as men-of-war to intercept British transports and supply ships. But the ear-lier proposal had served as an entering wedge. On December 11, Congress finally took up the Rhode Island Assembly's plea for a Continental Navy and referred it to a committee of twelve "to devise ways and means for furnishing these colonies with a naval arma-ment." Two days later, the committee returned with a report recom-mending the construction of thirteen frigates. Congress quickly ap-proved. The ships were to be "fitted for the sea" by the end of March, or in little more than three months, which would indeed have been record time.

Five ships of 32 guns, five of 28 guns, and three of 24 guns were authorized. These were to be warships built from the keel up. With what was probably more regard for the political influences involved than the shipbuilding capacities of the individual colonies, it was de-cided that two ships were to be built in Rhode Island, two in Massachusetts, two in New York, four in Pennsylvania, and one each in New Hampshire, Connecticut, and Maryland. The cost of each ship was estimated at $66,666.67, a total of $866,666.67—a not inconsiderable sum for that period.

The next day, a committee consisting of a member from each colony was chosen to oversee the building of the cruisers. Designated as the Marine Committee, it not only absorbed the members of the Naval Committee that was completing the outfitting of Hopkins's fleet, but took over its duties. From January 1776 until the end of 1779, the Marine Committee was the naval administration that supervised the rise and decline of the Continental Navy.

IV

Washington Sniffs the Sea

While Congress ponderously debated the organization of a navy, George Washington was sniffing the ocean breezes with the hope of capturing arms and ammunition from the enemy. Scarcity of gunpowder had haunted him from the moment he took command of the army. Supplies laboriously accumulated before Lexington and Concord were totally expended at Bunker Hill. Washington dared not fire a morning or sunset gun for fear it would touch off a British bombardment that couldn't be answered. "We are so exceedingly destitute," he said, "that our artillery will be of little use without a supply both large and seasonable." Shortly after his arrival at headquarters in Cambridge, he had ordered an accurate survey of the supply of powder on hand—only to be appalled by the final report. When it was presented, the general was "so struck that he did not utter a word for a half-hour." Aside from the supply the men already had in their horns, there was a reserve of only nine rounds for each soldier—with none for the artillery. Pickets guarding the roads leading out of Boston were often issued pikes and spears instead of muskets. Benjamin Franklin suggested that the army be supplied with

59

bows and arrows, reasoning that a man could shoot four arrows in the time it took to load and fire a musket just once.

From his camp, throughout the summer of 1775, Washington watched with growing desperation the steady and unhindered passage of supply ships and transports carrying the sinews of war to the enemy. What a temptation for a powder-starved army! It was enough to change his mind about the need for naval action. Only a short time before, he had opposed a plan broached by the Machias zealots to send their four ships on an expedition against Nova Scotia because not "a single ounce" of powder could be spared. Washington noted "our weakness and the Enemy's Strength at Sea." Now he wistfully observed: "A fortunate Capture of an Ordnance Ship would give new Life to our camp and an immediate Turn to the Issue of the Campaign."

So on September 2, 1775, orders were sent to Nicholson Broughton, an officer in Colonel John Glover's web-footed Marblehead regiment made up of sailors and fishermen: "You being appointed a Captain in the Army of the United Colonies of North America, are hereby directed to take Command of a Detachment of said Army and proceed on Board the Schooner *Hannah*, at Beverly, lately fitted out & equipp'd with Arms, Ammunition and Provisions at the Continental Expence." Broughton was ordered to immediately "Cruize against such Vessels as may be found on the High Seas and Elsewhere . . . in the service of the ministerial Army, and to take and seize all such Vessels, laden with Soldiers, Arms Ammunition or Provisions for or from s[ai]d Army. . . ."

Down through the years there has been considerable debate over who first suggested sending armed vessels to raid the British supply line. Some historians have said it was Glover; others credit John Manley, who was to become the most successful of Washington's captains. But neither side has been able to produce any evidence to back its claims. More than likely, Washington originated the plan himself. He had reconnoitered "the Sea Coast East of Boston Harbour" and had observed the activities of the whaleboats. It must have quickly occurred to him that if small craft could attack local installations with such success, bigger vessels could profitably attack the British store ships beating through Massachusetts Bay into Boston.

What legal right did Washington have to establish a fleet? Actually he had none—and he did not notify Congress of what he had done until a month after Broughton had spread his sails for the first time. Nevertheless, he found his commission as the army's commander-in-chief broad enough to cover any eventuality. Before sending out an entire fleet, Washington decided to experiment with one vessel to determine the validity of his idea. For this ship and crew, he turned to John Glover. Glover provided the *Hannah*, a coasting schooner named for his wife, which was moored to a pier he owned in nearby Beverly. The rental was to be "one Dollar pr Ton pr Month." Glover's regiment, later to gain fame for saving Washington's army after the Battle of Long Island and for ferrying it across the Delaware to Trenton, also furnished most of the fifty officers and men who were to go to sea aboard the *Hannah*. The Marbleheaders were selected because the commander-in-chief believed soldiers "who had been bred to the sea" could be quickly transformed into an efficient crew. Glover probably also had a hand in the selection of Nicholson Broughton to be the captain. Broughton, an old friend and business associate, had been a shipmaster for over twenty years and was thoroughly familiar with local waters. Unfortunately, Broughton, at fifty-one, turned out to be a contentious and avaricious man with a large opinion of himself.

Almost nothing certain is known of the *Hannah*—even though it is thought she was the first regularly commissioned ship fitted out by the United Colonies.[1] Her dimensions and rigging are guesswork, and her tonnage has been estimated from 40 to 78 tons. Work on converting her into an armed vessel began on August 4 as she lay at Glover's wharf. Carpenters cut gunports in her sides and strengthened her planking for several small cannon and a few swivels. The schooner was also supplied with a whaleboat and a larger cooking stove to meet the needs of her expanded crew. A month's provisions were stowed aboard, including salt beef, ship's bread, potatoes, and the inevitable rum—instead of the spruce beer that was doled out to the army.

Recruiting volunteers for the *Hannah*'s crew was an easy task.

---

[1] To add to the confusion, recent research has raised doubts about the reliability of the few facts that are known about the *Hannah*. For a full discussion, see Philip C. F. Smith and Russell W. Knight, "In Troubled Waters: The Elusive Schooner *Hannah*," in *American Neptune*, XXX (April 1970). The most complete account of the operations of *Hannah* and her successors is William B. Clark's trail-blazing *George Washington's Navy* (Baton Rouge 1960).

Drawn from several companies in Glover's Twenty-first Regiment—Broughton's own company provided a dozen privates—they were attracted by the prospect of prize money since, over and above their regular army wages, Washington promised the men one-third of the value of all captured cargoes, exclusive of military and naval stores. This provision did not apply to American ships recaptured from the enemy, but the general said he would suggest to the owners of such craft that they "make a Suitable Compensation" to those who had retaken them. As evidence of his confidence in the schooner's mission, Glover allowed his twenty-year-old son, John, Jr., to sail in her.

Washington's orders to Broughton were explicit. The *Hannah*'s mission was to attack only supply ships and transports; combat with British men-of-war was to be avoided because of the shortage of powder. Captured vessels, after being searched for important papers, were to be sent to the safest port near Cambridge so that enemy supplies could be placed at the disposal of the army as quickly as possible. Prisoners were to be treated with "Kindness and Humanity" and were to be sent to headquarters for interrogation.

Propelled by a fair wind, Broughton took the *Hannah* to sea on September 5. Late the same day, he sighted two vessels that turned out to be the British men-of-war *Lively*, 20 guns, and *Savage*, 8. They gave chase and the *Hannah* fled to Cape Ann, where Gloucester is located. Having no liking for unfamiliar waters after dark, the British vessels gave up the pursuit, although one of them hovered offshore during the night. The next day Broughton played a dangerous game of hide-and-seek with the warships, finally running into Gloucester Harbor for protection. About sunset he ventured out again, and the next morning his luck changed. He fell in with a large, unarmed ship and hailed her. She was the *Unity*, bound from Portsmouth to Boston. "I told him he must bear away and go into Cape Ann," Broughton reported to General Washington, "but being very loth I told him if he did not I should fire on him, on that he bore away and I have brought her safe into Cape Ann Harbour. . . ."

Visions of prize money soon vanished. The *Unity* turned out to be an American vessel belonging to John Langdon, one of New Hampshire's delegates to the Continental Congress. She had been captured earlier by the *Lively*. A British prize crew of six seamen commanded by a midshipman was taken with her. Bitterly disappointed at losing his very first prize, Broughton tried to make it appear that the *Unity* had been trading with the enemy. Writing to Washington on September 9, he maintained that the vessel was not bound to the West Indies as her skipper now claimed, but had been sent to loiter off Boston so the British could take her. Besides, reasoned Broughton, she carried more naval stores than was customary and a quantity of freshly salted cod and halibut whose export was forbidden by Massachusetts law. If Broughton could make his charges stick, he and his crew would receive one-third of the value of the *Unity*'s cargo as prize money. If not, they were dependent for compensation on the generosity of the ship's owners. Washington did not even bother to reply to Broughton's tale and ordered the recaptured vessel returned to John Langdon's agent.

Intoxicated with the prospects of prize money, Broughton's men reacted angrily to Washington's decision. Thirty-six of the *Hannah*'s crew, led by Joseph Searle, a soldier in Broughton's company, mutinied. Troops were sent to Gloucester to disarm them, and the mutineers were marched off to headquarters where an irate Washington awaited them. "The Rascals are brought down here and I hope they will meet their deserts," stated an observer in Cambridge. Similar sentiments were expressed by the commander-in-chief in a letter to Langdon recommending Broughton and his two lieutenants for a reward. "I should have done the same thing in behalf of the men . . . but for their exceeding ill behavior upon that occasion," he declared. "I hope to bestow a reward of a different kind upon them for their Mutinous behaviour."

Presented with the opportunity to show his raw and undisciplined army he meant business, Washington ordered a court-martial to try the prisoners on charges of "Mutiny, Riot and Disobedience of orders." All thirty-six were found guilty. Searle, the ringleader, was sentenced to "thirty-nine Lashes upon his bare back and be drumm'd out of the Army." Thirteen offenders were to be given twenty lashes each and were also to be drummed out of the service. Twenty-two prisoners were to be fined twenty shillings apiece, but three of them were found to be "proper objects of mercy." Their fines were remitted. At the last moment, as the troops were being lined up to witness punishment, Washington relented. Only Searle was flogged.

Because of these events, Washington developed an aversion to what he called "our rascally privateersmen" that endured as long as his association with them. A less determined commander might well have washed his hands of the whole seagoing experiment after this experience, William Clark points out, but Washington ordered more men from Glover's regiment to duty on the *Hannah* to bring her complement to full strength. His decision to continue the naval effort after the initial setback clearly emphasizes the importance he attached to the project.

Broughton got to sea again in late September, but his forays were not overly venturesome. He was content to remain in sight of land, and every evening he would put back into Marblehead so he and his crew could spend the night in their own beds. When Washington heard of the practice, he issued peremptory orders for more aggressive patrolling. "If our Cruizers find themselves watched at Marblehead and Cape Ann they must run out in the Night and Cruize further-off," he declared. On the night of October 6, Broughton sailed seaward and shortly after dawn gave chase to a British transport bound for Boston from Halifax. The *Hannah* fired several ranging shots at her, but the vessel was too close to Boston to be taken. Admiral Graves, informed of the attack, which he believed had been made by one of the armed schooners seized at Machias, acted with uncustomary energy. He immediately ordered the sloop *Nautilus*, 16, to sea "in quest of the Rebels."

Homeward bound, late on October 10, despite Washington's orders, Broughton was alarmed to see a sail approaching astern. One look convinced him that he had better forget his plans to reach Marblehead by nightfall and make for Beverly, which was closer. The distant sail was the *Nautilus*—and she was coming up fast to cut off the *Hannah* from shore. In a last-ditch effort to save his vessel, Broughton ran the *Hannah* aground on a sandbar just within Beverly harbor. Easing in as near as he dared, Captain John Collins, the skipper of the *Nautilus*, opened fire on the stranded schooner. Her officers and crew scrambled over the side and splashed ashore. Luckily, before the British could lower boats and row over to the *Hannah* to set her afire, the tide ebbed, leaving the *Hannah* high and dry on a wide mud flat. Crewmen and townspeople swarmed around and stripped the *Hannah* of her armament so that the British could not capture it.

Field pieces from nearby fortifications were trundled into place, and the townspeople opened fire on the *Nautilus*. "I was myself present," noted a diarist proudly as he described how the villagers "began to play their 4 lb guns & after making 8 or 10 shot apiece they levelled them well." The cannon fire was an unwelcome surprise for Captain Collins—especially since the guns were so well protected "as to put it out of my power to return the Compliment with that effect I could have wished." Collins exchanged a few shots with the battery "to no purpose." Unable to destroy the *Hannah* with gunfire, and with the tide still ebbing, he decided to abandon an unpleasant position. But the *Nautilus* drifted onto a mudbank and stuck there hard and fast.

For the next few hours, a hot battle raged between the trapped British warship and the local militiamen. Careened over on her side, the *Nautilus* could bring none of her guns to bear and was an inviting target for cannon and muskets. "For 4 hours we fired upon her constantly & tis supposed that she recd some of our shot," reported one of the gunners. But the British said the poor aim of the Americans saved the ship. " 'Tis very lucky they fired so high," said her captain. Even so, the *Nautilus* was badly knocked about. She was hit at least twenty times, her rigging was badly cut up, a gun was dismounted and two crewmen were wounded. The warship's ordeal ended with darkness and the turn of the tide. Finally floating free, the battered *Nautilus* cut her cable, leaving an anchor behind in her haste to be gone. Damage to the *Hannah* from enemy fire was slight, but her timbers had been strained by the grounding. She was removed from service later in the month. Broughton was laid up, too. He had caught a bad cold wading ashore from his ship.

Despite the inglorious career of the *Hannah*, Washington remained convinced of the soundness of his plan to send armed vessels to intercept British supply ships. Early in October, he decided to fit out two new craft and turned once again to Glover, who was ordered to procure the vessels in either Salem or Marblehead. "Let them be prime Sailors, put them into the best Order & loose no Time," wrote Colonel Joseph Reed, the general's military secretary, who was given the responsibility of directly overseeing the naval buildup. "A great Number of Transports are hourly expected at Boston from England and elsewhere." To help Glover, Colonel Stephen Moylan, Mustermaster General of the Army, was assigned to work with him. Moylan, a merchant-shipmaster from Philadelphia, was shrewd in the

ways of ship's carpenters and chandlers. "Associating him with . . .
Glover was a wise move, as the latter, having many friends and relatives in Marblehead, might prove inclined to softheartedness in dealing with kith and kin," remarks Clark.

Glover and Moylan proceeded quickly to Marblehead where
Glover persuaded two of his former business associates to lease their
vessels to the government. The larger of the two, the 72-ton schooner
Speedwell, owned by Thomas Grant, was rechristened *Hancock*. Archibald Selman's 60-ton schooner *Eliza* became the *Franklin*. The
transaction was not completed without some haggling. Both owners
balked at the extra expense of providing topsails for their ships,
which normally carried only a jib, foresail, and mainsail. The owners
finally agreed to bring the craft into condition for a normal peace-
time voyage, while the government assumed all other expenses.

In the meantime, Washington finally advised Congress, on October 5, what he was up to. A British supply ship carrying 1,900 barrels of flour had blundered into the hands of the Americans, and
Washington had ordered the flour brought to Cambridge for the use
of the army. Settlement of all claims arising from the case was left to
Congress. "I am the more induced to request this determination may
be speedy, as I have directed 3 Vessels to be equipped in order to cut
off the Supplies, and from a Number of Vessels arriving, it may become an Object of some Importance," he told John Hancock.
". . . I hope my Plan as well as the Execution will be favoured with
the Approbation of Congress." This was his first official reference to
his naval operations.

Before his dispatch was received in Philadelphia, an express
rider galloped into camp on the morning of October 11 with a letter
from Hancock, dated six days before. It was the message informing
Washington of the sailing of the two unarmed brigs loaded with
arms for the British garrison in Quebec. As has been seen, Washington was instructed to apply to Massachusetts authorities for the loan
of two of its armed vessels; if they were unavailable, the general was
empowered to fit out his own ships.

Reed quickly wrote to Glover and Moylan to galvanize them
into getting their ships to sea. "You will immediately set every Hand
to Work that can be procured & not a Moment of Time be lost . . .
getting them ready." The two schooners first completed should be
provisioned for six weeks and furnished with crews of seventy men

each. The instant they were ready, headquarters was to be advised. With this done, Washington informed Congress that its orders could be complied with by his own naval force "under the Command of Officers of the Continental Army, who are well recommended as Persons acquainted with the Sea, and capable of such Service."

But Glover and Moylan were having problems. "You Cannot Conceive the difficulty, the trouble & the delay there is in procureing the thousand things necessary for one of these vessels," complained Moylan to Reed. "I dare say one of them might be fitted in Philadelphia or New York in three days. . . . But here you must Search all over Salem, Marblehead, Danvers & Beverly for every Little thing is wanting." Supply problems were compounded by labor difficulties. The local carpenters "are to be sure the Idlest Scoundrels in Nature," added the exasperated Moylan. "If I could have procured others, I should have dismissed the whole Gang of them last Friday, & Such religious rascalls are they, that we Coud not prevail on them to work on the Sabbath. I have stuck very close to them since, & what by Scolding & Crying Shame for their torylike disposition in retarding the work, I think they mend something."

"Lose no Time," prodded an unsympathetic Reed. "Every Thing depends upon Expedition." In little more than two weeks, the ships were ready to take on their crews—excellent time considering the handicaps overcome by Glover and Moylan. Nicholson Broughton was given command of the *Hancock*, which carried six 4-pounders and ten swivels; John Selman, also a captain in the Twenty-first Regiment, was named master of the *Franklin*, armed with two 4-pounders, four 2-pounders and ten swivels. Each crowded with seventy of Glover's officers and men, the vessels sailed from Beverly on October 22. Broughton and Selman carried sealed orders from Washington that were not to be opened until they were at sea. These advised of the sailing of the unarmed munitions ships for Quebec and instructed the captains to set a course for the St. Lawrence, there to lie in wait for the craft. If the brigs were not sighted, the cruisers were to station themselves in such a position as to seize any other supply ships entering the area. After his initial experience with the erratic Broughton, Washington carefully stated that only ships actively serving the enemy were to be molested.

Convincing themselves that because of the lateness of the season they had missed the powder brigs—a not-too-difficult task—

Broughton and Selman set about seizing a number of small prizes. Just as he had in the case of the *Unity*, Broughton attempted to make it appear the vessels had been trading with the enemy. Washington, however, later ordered all of them returned to their rightful owners because they were not legitimate prizes. The pair also took it upon themselves to raid Charlottetown, capital of the Island of St. John [now Prince Edward Island], claiming they were preventing the concentration of recruits for a force to oppose the American invasion of Canada then underway.

Extensive looting took place. Philip Callbeck, the acting governor who was sent as a prisoner to Cambridge, complained bitterly to General Washington: "In Mrs. Callbeck's bedroom they broke open her drawers and Trunks, scatter'd her Cloaths about, read her Letters from her Mother and Sisters, took the Bed and window curtains, also the Bed & bedding . . . Some of the party took Mrs. Callbeck's Rings, Braclets, Buckles and Trinkets, also some of [her] Cloaths. After which they took the parlour window Curtains, Looking Glasses, Carpets and several articles of plate . . . They also took Mrs. Callbeck's little stores of Vinegar, Oil, Candles, Fruits, sweatmeats, Hams, Bacon &c." An embarrassed Washington immediately ordered Callbeck freed and his possessions restored.

It was at this inappropriate moment that the bumbling Broughton and Selman sailed into Beverly. While they were on their way to Cambridge, the angry commander-in-chief reported to Congress that they had failed to take the powder ships. "My fears that Broughton & Sillman woud not effect any good purpose were too well founded," he declared. "They are returned & brought with them three of the principal Inhabitants from the Island of St. Johns. . . . As the Captains Acted without an[y] Warrant for such Conduct, I have thought it but Justice to discharge these Gentlemen whose Famillys were Left in the utmost distress."

Washington resolved that he no longer wanted Broughton and Selman commanding his ships although he was willing to keep them in the army. "He met us on the steps" of his headquarters, recalled Selman. "We let his Excellency understand we had called to see him touching the Cruise. He appeared not pleased—he wanted not to hear any thing about it and broke off abruptly. . . ."

"Sir, will you stand again in Colonel Glover's regiment?" the General asked.

"I will not, Sir," replied Selman.

Washington then wheeled upon Broughton. "You, Sir, have said you would stand."

Broughton snapped: "I will not, Sir."

And so, as Selman later recalled, "thus ended the matter relative to the cruise"—a dismal conclusion to the first naval action formally authorized by the Continental Congress.

V

An Appeal to Heaven

With the sea chuckling under her bow, the armed schooner *Lee* bowled along, her topsail bellying taut in the whistling wind. She had been on patrol for several days without much success when, toward dusk on November 27, a lookout picked out the outlines of a large brig flying British colors and steering for Boston. Excitement raced along the deck of the schooner. Only a few days before, General Washington had notified the captains of his little fleet that just such a vessel, unarmed and loaded with arms and ammunition, had become separated from her convoy in a storm. Spies in Boston reported considerable anxiety among the British about the safety of the craft and her valuable cargo. Several frigates had been dispatched by Admiral Graves to search the sea lanes about Boston and bring her safely into port. One frigate had found the transport—only to lose her again. Now the seaborne game of hide-and-seek was over —and John Manley, the *Lee*'s skipper, was the winner.

Unlike the first captains chosen by the commander-in-chief, Manley was not an army officer, and had not been commissioned until he was selected to command the 74-ton schooner. Little is known of the early life of the man who finally realized Washington's hopes for his navy. One thing is certain, however: Manley had served for a time in the Royal Navy, though some of his detractors claimed he had risen only to boatswain's mate. At the time of his appointment, Manley was a forty-two-year-old, rough-and-ready Boston shipmaster of considerable experience living temporarily in Marblehead. His ship had been fitted out by Glover and Moylan at Beverly shortly after Broughton and Selman had departed on their northern cruise. The *Lee* was armed with four 4-pound guns and two 2-pounders. They had also prepared a smaller schooner, the *Warren*, at the same time, arming her with four 4-pounders.

Just a month after putting to sea for the first time, Manley fell in with the British brig he was looking for. In the failing light, he ran his schooner across her course and debated how to board her. To his surprise, the British resolved the problem. The brig lay back her sails and sent a string of signal flags fluttering aloft. The British had mistaken the *Lee* for a pilot boat come out to lead her into Boston. Manley quickly ordered eight men into a small boat. With their arms concealed, they rowed over to the brig. Battered by three weeks of gales and storms, her master heartily welcomed them to his deck. "No sooner had they got aboard," relates a British account, "than they drew their hangers and pistols." Surprise was complete and no resistance was offered. The prize was—as Manley and his crew had hoped—the long-sought ordnance transport *Nancy*.

Manley's eyes probably bulged when he read the manifest of her stores. Although there was little powder, the *Nancy* was a floating arsenal, carrying 2,000 muskets, 31 tons of musket shot, 30,000 round shot of various sizes, 100,000 musket flints, 11 mortar beds and—most imposing of all—a huge 13-inch mortar, which promised to be useful at the siege of Boston. An estimated value of 10,500 pounds was placed on the cargo, but its importance transcended mere price. Washington had just written to Congress asking for flints and here they were; he had been short of muskets for his men, and now at a stroke he had received a large supply, complete with bayonets. The wife of Dr. John Morgan, the new director general of hospitals, was having tea at headquarters when a messenger rushed in with a dispatch informing Washington of the capture of the *Nancy*. "What delighted me excessively," Mrs. Morgan wrote, "was seeing the pleasure which shown in every countenance, particularly General

[Horatio] Gates's: he was in ecstasy. And as General Washington was reading the invoice there was scarce an article he did not comment upon, and that with so much warmth as diverted everyone present."

Fearing that the British might make an attempt to regain the supplies that, along with the *Nancy*, had been taken into Gloucester, Washington ordered the local militia to help load it into wagons for transport to Cambridge. The monstrous brass mortar lead the way as the wagons creaked into camp on December 2. The troops shouted their exultation and felt "as if each grasped victory in his hand," noted Stephen Moylan. The mortar was fixed upon its mount and as the rank and file roared with laughter, Major General Israel Putnam —"Old Put" to the men—clambered upon it "with a bottle of rum in his hand, standing parson to christen, while godfather [Thomas] Mifflin gave it the name of Congress. The huzzahs on the occasion I dare say were heard through all the territories of our most gracious sovereign in this Province." As an extra fillip, the "R" in "G.R" emblazoned near the touch hole of the mortar was chiseled out, and a "W" struck for Washington. Then the monster was placed on display. Everyone agreed "it was the finest piece of ordnance ever landed in America."

The loss of the *Nancy* was a heavy blow to the British. Not only were the troops in Boston deprived of the equipment, but the rebels got a windfall that would have taken them at least eighteen months to produce on their own. Sir William Howe, who had replaced Gage as commander on the scene, declared with some understatement that it was "rather unfortunate." The Yankees, he said, "are now furnished with all the Requisites for setting the Town on Fire, having got a large Quantity of round Carcasses and other stores, with which they could not have been otherwise Supplied." In London, Lord Jeffrey Amherst, the army commander-in-chief, observed that "the loss was much resented in England, and occasioned some very severe animadversions upon the Admiralty, both within doors and without, for hazarding a cargo of such value and importance in a defenseless vessel." Lord Sandwich sourly observed that treachery had probably played a role in the loss of the transport. A lampoon circulated in Boston pointing out that Graves, "instead of sending his squadron to protect storeships and transports from England, has, with the utmost prudence, ordered the ships-of-war in this harbor to be secured with booms all around, to prevent their being boarded and taken by rebel whale-boats."

Washington had been correct in assuming that the capture of an enemy munitions ship "would give new Life to our camp." Nevertheless, his troubles were by no means over. Although Manley sent in several more valuable prizes, the commander-in-chief had his difficulties with the rest of his captains. By now his fleet had grown to six ships—the four outfitted at Beverly and two sent to sea from Plymouth. They were the *Harrison*, a 64-ton schooner armed with four 4-pound guns, and the *Washington*, a 160-ton brig that was the squadron's largest, most powerful craft. She carried six 6-pounders and 4-pounders and was commanded by Captain Sion Martindale, a Rhode Islander of broad experience who had sailed merchantmen out of Newport and Providence. Captain William Coit, of New London, a jovial, portly man who had divided his time between service at sea and the practice of law, was skipper of the *Harrison*.

"If you were where you could see me and did not laugh, all your risible faculties must perish," Coit wrote to a friend. "To see me strutting about on the quarterdeck of my schooner!—for she has a quarter-deck—Ah, and more than that too—four 4-pounders brought into this country by company of Lords Say and Seal, to Saybrook when they first came. A pair of cohorns[1] that Noah had in the Ark; one of which lacks touch-hole. . . . Six swivels, the first that were ever landed at Plymouth, and never fired since. . . . Her accommodations are fine: five of us in the cabin, and when there, are obliged to stow spoon fashion. Besides, she has a chimney in it, and the smoke serves for bedding, victuals, drink and choking." One of the masts was rotten and the deck in splinters. "If obliged to fire both guns of a side at a time, it would split her open from her gunwale to her keelson. . . . If there comes peace, I would recommend her and her apparatus, to be sent to the Royal Society: and I dare eat a red-hot gridiron if ever they have had, or will have, until the day of judgement, a curiosity equal to her."

Flying the pine-tree flag that Joseph Reed had suggested as the ensign of Washington's navy—a white field bearing a green pine tree and the words "An Appeal to Heaven"—the *Harrison* went to sea

---

[1] Cohorns were small mortars usually carried on the decks or in the fighting tops of ships.

early in November. Within a short time, Coit fell in with prey that suited his vessel: two provision ships piled high with crates from which stemmed the cackle of geese and chickens as well as the bleat, bellow, and squeal of sheep, cattle, and hogs destined for the garrison in Boston. Coit quickly made for Plymouth with his loot where a contemporary chronicler gleefully recorded that he "made the prisoners land upon the same rock our ancestors first trode when they landed in America, where they gave three cheers and wished success to American arms."

The rebellious spirit of the crews that manned Washington's ships was still evident. By mid-month, Coit's men were refusing to go to sea because of the severity of the weather, lack of warm clothes, and almost no pay. William Watson, the prize agent at Plymouth, analyzed the trouble: "Captain Coit has had much difficulty, and has been greatly perplexed with an uneasy set of fellows, who had got soured by the severity of the season and are longing for the leeks and onions of Connecticut." Similar problems occurred on board the *Washington.* After a brief and ineffectual maiden cruise, the crew, mostly Rhode Islanders, refused to obey orders. John Manvide, the ship's French surgeon, wrote in his journal: "As we were about to get under way and make for Cape Hand [Ann] our crew mutinied . . . and all said that they were willing to lend a hand to weigh anchor but that they refused to do any more." The men complained that they had "Inlisted to Serve in the Army & not as Marines."

Once again Watson acted as intermediary. Upon first hearing news of the revolt he called Martindale's crew "a set of the most unprincipled, abandoned fellows [I] ever saw." But after visiting the ship, he took a different view. A lack of warm clothing was all that was troubling the men. "After Supplying them with what was wanted, the whole Crew to a man gave three cheers & declared their readiness to go to Sea the next morning." On the same day Watson recorded his findings, December 4, Washington told Congress: "The plague, trouble and vexation I have had with the Crews of all the armed vessels is inexpressible; I do believe there is not on Earth a more disorderly set; every time they come into Port, we hear of nothing but mutinous Complaints. . . ."

Word of Manley's success in taking the *Nancy* and the visions of prize money—not the wrath of the commander-in-chief—sent Martindale's men to sea again. But less than thirty-six hours after sailing from Plymouth, the *Washington* was taken by the British frigate *Fowey*, 20. Not a shot was fired in her defense. Because the sea was running too high to send out a boat, the British waited until the next morning to board her. Martindale and his crew must have suffered the agonies of the damned. The *Washington* was the first American armed vessel to fall into British hands—and all had heard of the enemy's threats to hang from the nearest yardarm rebels taken under arms at sea. And think of the agonies of two of the *Washington*'s hands—deserters from the Royal Navy—as they awaited the dawn.

Taken before Admiral Graves, Martindale described the *Harrison* and the recognition signals he had agreed upon with Coit. The admiral resolved to place a crew aboard the *Washington* and send her out as a decoy with the idea of capturing other American cruisers. The condition of the ship quickly ended the idea. A survey team reported: "The guns and carriages totally unserviceable. The Small Arms many of them broke, and all out of repair . . . and we are of the opinion that she is not fit for war." So much for the largest and most powerful ship in Washington's navy. She was to end her career rotting beside a Boston wharf. Her crew was sent to England for trial, except for the two deserters who were remanded to the *Preston* for a court-martial. General Howe expressed the hope that the uncertainty about the fate of the *Washington*'s men would deter others from privateering. "Besides," he added in a letter to Lord Dartmouth, "I could wish a Distinction to be made between Prisoners taken on Shore and on Sea, which last Mode of War will hurt us more effectually than anything they can do by Land during our Stay at this Place."

Not all the *Washington*'s crew submitted as docilely as her officers. Although they were battened down in the main hold of the frigate taking them to England, some of the men, led by Israel Potter, a wounded veteran of Bunker Hill, plotted to take the ship. "We should undoubtedly have succeeded, as we had a number of resolute fellows on board, had it not been for the treachery of a renegade Englishman, who betrayed us," he reported. Potter was pointed out as the ringleader and spent the rest of the voyage in irons. None of the men who got to England were brought to trial. Smallpox carried off half of them. The officers were sent home to be exchanged for British prisoners, and the rest were pressed into the Royal Navy. Few saw their homes again.

The new year—1776—began with all five of Washington's remaining ships lying deserted at their piers. Winds howled among bare masts and whistled along empty decks. Four of the ships were at Beverly—the *Hancock*, the *Franklin*, the *Lee*, and the *Warren*—while the *Harrison* rested at Plymouth and the *Hannah* had been stricken off the books. Enlistments had run out with the old year and the crews had lost no time in abandoning ship. Moylan noted that "all the vessels are now in port, the officers and men quitted them; what a pity, as [British] vessels are every day arriving: indeed the chance of taking any, is pretty well over, as a man-of-war [the *Fowey*] is stationed so as to command the entrance of Beverly, Salem and Marblehead—we must have ships to cope with them." Washington agreed. What was needed were captains with the vigor and ability of Manley. While in the process of creating a new army to take the place of the militia force that had melted away with the old year, the commander-in-chief also concerned himself with his navy. Samuel Tucker of Marblehead was named skipper of the *Franklin*; William Burke, one of the few remaining officers of the *Warren*, became her commander, and Daniel Waters of Malden was given the *Lee*. Manley took over the *Hancock* and "for his great vigilance and industry" was appointed commodore "of our little fleet." The *Harrison* at Plymouth was dealt with too. Charles Dyar, who had been one of Coit's officers, was given command of her. A sixth schooner, the *Lynch*, was ordered outfitted at Beverly to replace the captured *Washington*. She was placed under the command of John Ayres, a Boston shipmaster.

Although Congress had sent him a number of blank commissions designed for the captains of the ships outfitting in the Delaware, Washington decided that he wanted to keep the New England fleet under his direct control. Unlike the earlier captains who had been given army commissions, the group appointed in 1776 were not of the army or the navy but were subject directly to Washington. The instructions sent to the new commanders made it clear that the commander-in-chief did not want a repetition of the "ill Success which attended the Major part of the Armed Vessels in former Cruzes." He blamed this on "the want of Industry & the inactivity of the Officers who commanded" and warned that any officers who failed to exert themselves "shall be dismissed the Service—& rendered incapable of Serveing there Country in any Honourable Station hereafter."

With this grim warning the six schooners put to sea in the bite of a New England winter. As to be expected, Manley got out first, eluding the waiting *Fowey* in dirty weather. He sailed almost to the entrance of Boston Harbor, where from his pitching deck he could see the tall masts of the British fleet, now under the command of Molyneux Shuldham, Vice Admiral of the Blue. Manley quickly took two supply ships and was convoying them into Plymouth on January 25, when he fell in with the *General Gage*, an 8-gun British schooner. The *Hancock*'s rigging was cut up and her gunner wounded before the fight was broken off after the prizes got clear. The Americans had but six powder charges left for their cannon. Although Washington was effusive in his praise for Manley's action, the commodore's thoughts were elsewhere. He pressed Washington for the command of a bigger and more powerful craft, no doubt influenced by the news that Congress had authorized the building of thirteen frigates. Assured that "every attention will be paid to any reasonable request of yours," Manley forced his way through the ice blocking Plymouth Harbor on January 30, only to be sighted by the 14-gun brig *Hope*, which had been specially sent out to track him down. The *Hancock* crowded on all sail. The brig still gained on her, so Manley ran his vessel ashore just south of Scituate in hopes that the British could not follow him. The *Hope* stood off shore pounding away at her. The *Boston Gazette* reported that the brig "fired not less than 400 times" and "the next day, 130 balls were found upon the adjacent shore." It was all a waste of ammunition, for no one was even wounded, although "one ball entered the stern [and] passed about six inches from Capt. Manley, who was confined by sickness to his cabin." The *Hope*'s captain claimed the *Hancock* was permanently disabled, but Manley refloated his vessel when the tide turned and took her into port for refitting.

In the meantime, Tucker and Waters, in the *Franklin* and *Lee*, were showing signs of the aggressive spirit that Washington desired in his captains. Slipping out of Beverly, they took several prizes in February after blustery weather drove the British blockaders from their stations. The *Harrison* made two short and fruitless cruises but was so badly in need of repair that Washington finally ordered her laid up. William Coit had the last laugh. Reduced to five vessels, Washington's navy undertook its first joint cruise under Manley's broad pennant at the beginning of March.

On the night of March 2, a strong wind carried the sound of a heavy bombardment at Boston to the ships lying at their rendezvous off Cape Ann. For three straight nights, Washington's army continued the shelling that was designed to draw enemy attention away from American efforts to fortify Dorchester Heights, which dominated the town and its harbor. On the second night, the 13-inch mortar captured by Manley blew up with a tremendous roar. The British, duped by the bombardment as Washington hoped, did not notice the Yankees digging in. When they did, it was too late. Admiral Shuldham told General Howe that with the Americans in possession of the Heights, the fleet would be shot to pieces if it remained in the harbor. There was nothing the British could do except evacuate Boston. By March 17, Howe had completed the embarkation of his troops and about a thousand dejected Loyalists. The fleet dropped down to Nantasket Road in the lower bay, where it remained for ten days awaiting stragglers. So massive an armada—Abigail Adams counted one hundred seventy sail—created much uneasiness among the Americans before it sailed for Halifax. "I shall order look-outs to be kept upon all the headlands, to discover their movements and courses," Washington advised Congress, "and moreover direct Commodore Manley, and his little squadron to dog them, as well for the same purpose, as for picking up any of their vessels, that may chance to depart their convoy."

Leaving Manley's ships under orders to harry the enemy convoy, the commander-in-chief moved the bulk of his army to New York where he expected the British to strike next. Responsibility for the tiny fleet was passed to the sickly and querulous General Artemas Ward, who was soon coping with the demands of the officers and crews for back pay and unpaid prize money. The men refused to take the schooners to sea, and their officers resigned. On April 17, Manley joined them, having achieved his commission as captain in the Continental Navy. He went ashore to await the completion of one of the two frigates building in Massachusetts. To replace the disaffected crews, John Glover's regiment, now the Fourteenth Continental, was combed once again. One group of grumbling men who hadn't been paid in months was thus substituted for another. Samuel Tucker was moved over from the *Franklin* to replace Manley in the *Hancock*, and James Mugford, her only remaining officer, assumed command of the *Franklin*.

With only a handful of men under his command, Mugford was cruising on May 17 outside Boston Harbor within sight of a British squadron when he observed a large vessel plodding in his direction. A boarding party from the *Franklin* quickly secured the ship, which proved to be the armed transport *Hope*, carrying 1,500 barrels of powder and other munitions. She was the most valuable prize taken since Manley had seized the *Nancy*. Fearing that British cruisers might retake the ship if he tried to send her into another, more distant port, Mugford decided upon a daring plan—he would take the *Hope* directly into Boston, passing through Pulling Point Gut, a shallow channel. This would avoid the guns of the waiting British men-of-war. That Friday had been proclaimed a day of prayer in the town and all Americans were urged to humbly petition "the Lord of Hosts, the God of Armies . . . to crown the continental arms by sea and land, with victory and success." The arrival of the *Hope*—valued at from 40,000 to 50,000 pounds—seemed an answer to these prayers.

Mugford stood out to sea two days later, planning to go to Beverly where he hoped to augment his seventeen-man crew with volunteers or a fresh draft from Glover's regiment. Accompanied by the privateer *Lady Washington*, which also needed hands, having only seven men on board, including Captain Joseph Cunningham, the *Franklin* sailed back out the Gut only to run aground. Anticipating a British attack—which was not long in developing—Mugford organized his men to meet it. Muskets, cutlasses, spears, and pistols were doled out to the men. The guns were charged with musket balls in lieu of grape shot, and the *Lady Washington* was anchored nearby.

The loss of the *Hope* had "intolerably vexed and chagrined" the British, reported the *New England Chronicle*, and they moved quickly to take advantage of the opportunity to retaliate. As many as thirteen boats were loaded with sailors and marines. The cutting-out expedition approached the stranded schooner after dark. Mugford hailed the lead boat, demanding to know who they were. Out of the dark came the answer: "From Boston." But Mugford was suspicious. "Keep off!" he warned. "Keep off, or we'll fire upon you."

"For God's sake, don't fire!" was the response. "We're coming on board."

Alarmed, Mugford fired his pistol into the craft, and the *Franklin* brought her broadside to bear on the attacking boats. The

Franklin's cannon sent a hail of musket balls flying into them. Screams tore the night. Before the schooner could fire her guns again, two or three of the British boats, each carrying more men than Mugford's entire crew, bumped against her side. With clubbed muskets, spears, and cutlasses, the Americans hacked at the heads and fingers of the boarders clutching at the gunwales. In the fitful light of musket flashes, the British lunged upward with lances and fired at the bobbing heads of the defenders. Other boats attacked the *Lady Washington*, but her tiny crew used their swivels, blunderbusses and muskets to such good effect that the enemy was unable to come to close quarters. The British probably thought the schooner was bigger and more powerful than she actually was. With unaccustomed enthusiasm, Artemas Ward told Washington that "after repeated efforts to board her they were beaten off by the intrepidity and exertions of the little company, who gloriously defended the *Lady* against the brutal ravishers of liberty."

Meantime, Mugford and his men were holding their own. One of the attacking boats capsized, catapulting its crew into the water. While floundering seamen and marines clung to the sides of the remaining craft, the fight raged over their heads. After about a half-hour, the British made a final assault. In repelling it, Mugford was fatally wounded by a lance. Thoroughly beaten, the remaining British boats drew off, and at dawn the rising tide floated the *Franklin*. Mugford was the only man killed aboard her, while the British lost at least seven dead. Informed of the gallant defense of the two schooners, George Washington expressed delight at the steadfastness of their crews. "It is only to be lamented that this affair was attended with the death of Captain Mugford," he wrote Ward. "He seemed to deserve a better fate."

A month after the evacuation of Boston—and well before the news had reached London—a convoy of thirty-five transports carrying three thousand Highland troops sailed from the Clyde for America. A few days out, the fleet was scattered by a storm. Most of the transports arrived in the Boston area while the British squadron was still in the lower harbor and joined with it. But several of the vessels appeared off the northern coast after the navy had left. They plopped into the Yankee net like codfish. First prey for Washington's fleet was the troopship *Anne*, taken by the *Lee*, *Lynch*, and *Warren* along with one hundred ten men from the Seventy-first Highland Regiment. Fired by the capture and reports that more transports were blindly on the way, the crews of the armed schooners eagerly scoured the sea lanes where they were expected. Several attacks were launched against the wallowing troopships but in each case Royal Navy frigates came up in time to end the fight.

On June 15, the transports *George* and *Arabella* sighted Cape Ann after a rough passage. Having no inkling that Howe had abandoned Boston, they were not surprised to see four schooners coming out to meet them. Lieutenant Colonel Archibald Campbell, who along with the staff of the second battalion of the Highland Regiment and a company of troops was on the *George*, took them to be "pilots or armed vessels in the service of his Majesty." To the shock of the Scotsmen, the schooners opened fire without warning, for they were the *Lee*, *Lynch*, *Warren*, and *Franklin*—the latter now commanded by John Skimmer, a Boston merchant skipper. Ordering the transport's 6-pounders to reply, Campbell pushed ahead. A "tolerable cannonade" followed that lasted until the schooners broke off the fight. Two soldiers and a sailor mortally wounded on the *George* and another man killed on the *Arabella*. "I thought it my duty . . . to push forward into the Harbour," reported Campbell, "not doubting I should receive protection either from a fort or some ship of force stationed there for the security of our fleet."

The sound of a roundshot whistling by his ear "was the first serious proof we had that there could scarcely be many friends of ours in Boston," the colonel continued with commendable restraint. A Yankee 18-pounder mounted on a headland had opened up on the *Arabella*, which ran aground in the direct line of fire. A mixed barrage of round and grape shot slammed into the transport and her flag was quickly hauled down. Then the Yankee gunners turned their attention to the *George*. There was no return fire, so in the descending darkness it was presumed that she, too, had struck. That was the last thing Campbell had in mind. Too far into the harbor to retreat, especially now that the wind had died away, he ordered the vessel anchored and prepared for action.

In the meantime, the four Yankee schooners had fallen in with the brig *Defence*, of the Connecticut Navy. Commanded by Captain Seth Harding, she carried sixteen 6-pounders, twenty swivels, and one hundred seventeen men. Joined by the *Hancock*, the ships moved past the stranded *Arabella* and eased along in the night until the stout hull of the *George* loomed ahead. Four of the schooners anchored under the bow of the transport, and the fifth on her stern, while the *Defence* took up station on her starboard side. From out of the night, Harding demanded to know from where the transport had come. "From Great Britain," came the reply.

"Then strike your colors to America."

"What brig is that?" asked a British officer.

"The Connecticut brig *Defence*," sang out Harding. "I do not want to kill your men, but have your ship I will. So strike your flag, or I'll open fire."

"Aye, I'll strike," was the derisive reply.

With that, the British 6-pounders unleashed a broadside into the brig. The compliment was returned, with the schooners joining in. The *George* concentrated on the Connecticut ship. Luckily, the transport's sides towered over her and the enemy's fire mostly cut up her sails and rigging. A few shots struck home, for nine of the *Defence*'s crew were wounded. Samuel Smedley, the brig's lieutenant, later accused the officers of the schooners of cowardice, charging they had refused to close with the transport. But some of the schooners must have taken part in the struggle because four of their crewmen were reported wounded.

The deck of the *George* was a shambles. Campbell reported that the seamen had refused to fight but "not an officer, noncommissioned officer, or private of the Seventy-first, but who stood to quarters with a ready and cheerful obedience." A major and seven soldiers were killed and another twelve Highlanders were wounded. The battle raged for an hour and a half and ended only when the gallant Scots had run out of ammunition. At sunrise the next day, they buried the Highland dead on an island in the harbor, as a lone bagpiper skirled a mournful and haunting farewell.

Three days later, the Americans captured another Scotch transport, the *Lord Howe*, carrying the grenadier company of the Seventy-first. She was taken without a fight. This brought the number of Highlanders captured to 354 men, plus another 83 women and children—the latter members of officers' families or their servants.[2] The

---

[2] Only upon one other occasion were large numbers of British troops captured at sea: in August 1780, when six companies of the Ninety-first Regiment en route to the West Indies were intercepted off Spain by a combined Franco-Spanish fleet.

capture of the transports was as disturbing to the British authorities as the taking of the *Nancy*. It was proposed that the government employ older warships to carry military equipment and ammunition across the Atlantic. The lower tier of guns could be removed from two-decked warships, leaving the deck empty to carry stores. The Admiralty rejected the proposal on technical grounds, but it seems likely that the real reason was an understandable aversion to having a large part of the Royal Navy converted into glorified army store ships.

This was the best testimony to the value of Washington's tiny fleet to the American cause. Throughout the rest of 1776 and into 1777, the armed schooners continued to cruise Massachusetts Bay, taking a considerable number of prizes, before the Marine Committee, which knew little about its operations, ordered the fleet disbanded. From the time that Nicholson Broughton first went to sea in the *Hannah* on September 5, 1775, until John Skimmer captured the rum- and sugar-laden brig *Dolphin* on October 25, 1777, William Clark estimates that Washington's schooners took fifty-five prizes. Of course, eleven of them had to be returned to their owners—including the seven taken by Broughton and Selman on their ill-fated cruise—but the rest included such important prizes as the *Nancy*, the *Hope* and the Scotch transports. The psychological effects of the capture of these vessels transcended their physical value. Weighing these achievements, one authority[3] has concluded that Washington's fleet was "quite as successful as any American fleet of equal size and force during the Revolution." It was quite an accomplishment for a band of "rascally privateersmen."

---

[3] Charles O. Paullin, *The Navy of the American Revolution* (Cleveland 1906).

VI

To Sea ... At Last

Hope had run high that Esek Hopkins could get the small squadron being fitted out in the Delaware ready for sea by late December 1775. He did not. A new year had begun, and winter had swept in. Ice was forming in the river and biting winds lashed the sailors as they worked at loading and stowing stores. Fearing that the ships might be frozen in if they remained much longer where they lay, the commodore and the Naval Committee of the Continental Congress agreed that the vessels should sail down the bay to Cape Henlopen. The remaining supplies could be carted to them later. On the morning of January 4, 1776, notices were posted in the coffeehouses and taverns along the Philadelphia waterfront summoning officers and men of the fleet to "immediately repair on board their respective Ships" to "avoid being deemed deserters." Until late in the afternoon, small boats filled with men and piled high with their dunnage pulled back and forth from Willing and Morris' Wharf to the four vessels anchored out in midstream.

"At 2 PM Cast off from ye Warf In Company with ye Commodore Ship *Alfred, Columbus* and *Cabot*," wrote James Josiah, first lieutenant of the *Andrew Doria*, at the top of the first page of the ship's canvas-bound journal. "Light airs from ye Westward & much Ice in ye River." Due to the delay in rounding up the crews, it was dark by the time the vessels had dropped the few miles down river to Mud Island—renamed Liberty Island in a burst of patriotic fervor—where they anchored. The night turned bitterly cold. By dawn, the Delaware was frozen from shore to shore, and the fleet was hemmed in by ice that was thickening by the hour. To Nicholas Biddle, skipper of the *Doria*, the scene must have been reminiscent of the icy wastes that had surrounded his ship during the polar expedition four years before. As long as the ice held—and for more than a week it showed no sign of breaking up—there was nothing for Hopkins and his officers to do except exercise their crews, maintain discipline, and guard against desertion now that the initial enthusiasm for the service was wearing off.

Shortages of seamen and supplies had been problems since Congress authorized the fleet. Sailors were reluctant to join a service with a fixed term of enlistment lasting a year. Even when Congress, at the commodore's urging, increased wages to $8 a month, the response was modest. The Naval Committee looked hungrily at the well-manned Pennsylvania row-galleys lying off Philadelphia, and Stephen Hopkins, its chairman, begged the local Committee of Safety for authority to recruit men among them. Permission was granted to enroll up to a hundred volunteers. As an extra bonus, the Pennsylvanians looked over the list of prisoners in the local jails, handpicking a few to whom freedom was offered on condition that they join the Continental Navy. At the commodore's suggestion, a request was also sent to Rhode Island to drum up hands and dispatch them by fast-sailing vessel for the Delaware.

No such difficulties were encountered recruiting the first two marine battalions authorized by Congress on November 10. Originally Congress had instructed George Washington to raise the men from the army besieging Boston, but the commander-in-chief replied that such a move would seriously deplete his already undersized force and disrupt its table of organization. So Congress decided to recruit Continental Marines in Philadelphia and other port towns. The first recruiting station appears to have been at the Tun Tavern on King Street, where Robert Mullan, the proprietor, was made a captain. Samuel Nicholas, owner of another popular Philadelphia tavern, the Conestoga Wagon, was also commissioned a captain. Marching along through the streets behind, merrily rattling drums, recruiting parties wearing new green and white uniforms and leather neck stocks, an accoutrement adopted from the Royal Marines, quickly attracted more than two hundred volunteers. This was enough to fill the marine complements of the waiting ships. One of the most successful recruiters was Lieutenant Isaac Craig, of the *Andrew Doria*. Within two weeks, the popular Irishman, who had lived in Philadelphia for ten years, signed up more than forty men. They ranged in age from nineteen to forty and included a doctor, a breeches maker, several carpenters, a baker, a barber, and a bricklayer.

Lying in the stream off Philadelphia, Hopkins's ships were a floating world unto themselves. Someone coming out to one of the vessels from shore would have found the entry port guarded by a young midshipman and a marine with musket and fixed bayonet.[1] After having been given permission to come aboard, the visitor found himself on the spar deck, just abaft, or to the rear, of the main-mast, the middle and tallest of the ship's three masts. Behind him—and slightly raised—was the quarterdeck, which overlooked the rest of the vessel. The highest and rearmost section was called the poop. Ranged on either side of the quarterdeck were the after guns, snugged down in their breachings with wooden tompions in their mouths to keep out seawater. Slightly forward of the mizzen, or rear-most mast, was the steering wheel and the binnacle, which housed the compass. Running along the top of the bulwarks, or rail, from the poop to bow, were canvas-covered rope nets supported by iron uprights. This was where the crew's hammocks were stowed when not in use.

The ship's waist extended from the quarterdeck to the forecas-tle. Several hatches covered by movable gratings led down into the interior of the vessel. Spare booms and spars were tightly lashed in position between the mainmast and foremast, resting amidships on the hatches. On top of these spars were the ship's boats—the long boat, the cutter, and the captain's gig—with their sails and oars stored inside. Often the boats housed a pen for sheep and pigs and a chicken coop so the officers could enjoy the luxury of fresh meat and eggs. The forecastle, or forward part of the ship, also carried several cannon, including a pair fixed to fire almost directly ahead, which were called bow chasers. There was also a carved wooden belfrey from which hung the ship's bell with the rope-plaited clapper for

---

[1] I am indebted to John Masefield's *Sea Life in Nelson's Time* (New York 1925), for the ng material. The late poet laureate's first book, it was originally published in 1905, and s the most complete and vivid description of life on an eighteenth-century man-of-war.

striking the hours.[2] The galley funnel, or the chimney of the ship's kitchen, jutted up through the forecastle deck.

The main deck lay below the spar deck. On a frigate or a smaller warship such as those in Hopkins's flotilla, it contained both the main battery of guns and the living quarters of the officers and men. Extending across the afterpart of the ship was the captain's quarters, lit by windows in the stern and along the side. On ships of the line, captains enjoyed private stern galleries, or verandahs overlooking the sea. A captain may have had a dining cabin, a day cabin, and a night cabin, but they were usually very bare. Besides a settee built in under the stern windows, his quarters might contain little more than a large fixed table, some heavy chairs, a cot, a wooden washstand, and a pair of guns. The only decoration might be a swinging lamp, a well-polished telescope hanging in a wall bracket, and perhaps a trophy of pistols and swords, or a stand of the ship's small arms in a rack about the mizzen-mast. A captain with a case of books and a pair of curtains to his windows was a rarity.

In these quarters, the captain lived an existence apart from the rest of his ship. He had his own cook, steward, clerk and coxswain, who served no one else. A marine sentry with a drawn sword stood at the door of his cabin day and night. Few men have had as much power over their subordinates as the captain of an eighteenth-century man-of-war. "He had the power to flog a man senseless and to break some of his officers," as Masefield points out. When he came up on the quarterdeck, the whole of the windward side was instantly cleared for his solitary promenade. "No man on board dared to address him, save on some questions relating to the duty of the day," Masefield continues. "No sailor could speak to him with his hat upon his head. One uncovered to one's captain as to one's God." When a captain returned after a visit ashore or to another vessel, he was received with all honors. Sideboys stood at attention at the gangway to await his arrival. The boatswain piped the side. The officers were drawn up on the quarterdeck. "As the captain stepped on board, all hands uncovered" and the only sound heard was the wailing of the boatswain's pipe. "The captain saluted the quarterdeck,

---

[2] One stroke was sounded for every half hour of a four-hour watch. For example, 12:30 A.M. was 1 bell; 1 A.M., 2 bells; 1:30 A.M., 3 bells; 2 A.M., 4 bells; 2:30 A.M., 5 bells; 3 A.M., 6 bells; 3:30 A.M., 7 bells; and 4 A.M., 8 bells. Then the process started over again for the next watch.

and passed aft to his cabin, generally paying not the very least attention to the assembled worshipers."

A captain did not stand watch or take part in the daily working
of the ship—unless action was in the offing or something had gone
wrong. Once or twice a week, he might ask the first lieutenant and a
few other officers to dine with him. Occasionally, a midshipman
might be invited in order to expose him to the company of his
betters. These dinners were formal affairs, for discipline was not
relaxed at any time. No one thought highly of a captain who was in
the least familiar with his officers. Although a white tablecloth might
be spread and the dishes served with more style, the food at the
captain's table was little different from that in the rest of the ship,
especially when the vessel had been at sea for some time and the
delicacies laid in by the captain for his own use had long since been
consumed.

A frigate might have four lieutenants and two marine officers.
The first lieutenant, the most senior, commanded in the absence of
the captain and was responsible for the day-to-day operation of the
ship. He stood no watches when the vessel was at sea but was on call
during the night. Junior lieutenants stood watches and made certain
that the ship's business was smartly carried on. In action, lieutenants
and senior midshipmen commanded batteries of guns, seeing to it
that their crews did not shirk their duty and fought with spirit. Lieutenants, when not dining with the captain, ate their meals in the
wardroom, forward of the captain's cabin. On either side of the
wardroom were the tiny cabins of the lieutenants and the marine
officers. They had barely enough space for a cot, desk, and clothes
chest. All partitions were light and removable; when the ship cleared
for action, the cabins and all their furnishings were cast into the
hold. The sailing master, who was in charge of navigating the ship,
the surgeon, the purser, and the chaplain, if any, were free to use the
wardroom, although they were warrant rather than commissioned
officers.

The gun deck was lined with cannon on both sides and was un-
obstructed as far forward as the foremast except for the capstan used
in raising the anchors. Just abaft of the foremast was the galley,
where the cook prepared the meals. The crew ate on tables between
the guns that were raised when not in use and slung their hammocks
at night from hooks in the overhead beams. The regulation distance

between hammocks was fourteen inches. This sounds worse than it was in practice, however, for half the men were usually on watch. The interior of the gun deck was usually painted bright red to lessen the psychological shock of the sight of blood, which was liberally splattered over it when the ship was in action. At night, the only lights allowed were candles encased in lanterns of thick horn. If a ship went into action at night, the sailors fought their guns by muzzle flashes and the fitful light cast by the battle lanterns placed beside each gun.

The orlop, the next deck down, was practically below the water-line. It was lit by a few tiny scuttles and by sputtering candles in tin sconces, called "purser's glims." The cockpit where the midshipmen, master's, and surgeon's mates were berthed lay aft. It was of considerable size although headroom was only about five feet. During a fight, the wounded were brought here for medical attention. The mess table at which the midshipmen made merry became the operating table where the surgeon performed amputations while his assistants held the writhing victims down by brute force. If the captain were wounded, he had to submit to the same primitive surgery as his rawest seaman. The same hot pitch that served to caulk the seams of the ship was used to seal the crude amputations. If shock did not kill the patient, the greatest danger after the operation was tetanus and gangrene resulting from the unsanitary conditions of the cockpit.

A midshipmen's mess was not a pleasant place. The occupants had to hunch over or bump their heads. The air was foul; the bilges reeked. Adding to the aroma was the nearby purser's storeroom where supplies of rancid butter and putrid cheese were doled out once or twice a week. At meals, the table was covered with a cloth or an old hammock that had to last a week. For seats, the young gentlemen used their sea chests. A feeble attempt to keep the berth clean was made by a messboy, usually a dirty, slow-witted lad unfitted for any other duty. He washed the weekly tablecloth and did the cooking for the midshipmen. Upon joining a ship, a youngster would pay a certain sum to the caterer of the mess, usually a master's mate, which was used to lay in a supply of luxuries such as potatoes, onions, coffee and sugar, to supplement the ship's limited rations.

Boys and men ranging in age from twelve to upward of forty were crammed into this fetid kennel. It was no place for innocents, with its casual cruelties and vices, especially when the rum began to flow. The older men seem to have understood this, for they usually stuck a fork in the table as a signal for the younger midshipmen to take to the hammocks. Youngsters who ignored the warning were given a few minutes' grace. If the "geese" had not flown by then, they were "colted," or whipped with a knotted cord. Then their elders passed the evening with cards, rum, and dirty stories.[3]

Midshipmen usually owed their appointments to patronage or "interest." Captains took them to sea to win the support of an influential family, to oblige a relative, or to settle a tradesman's debt. Often boys were entered on the muster rolls long before they were old enough to go to sea. For example, Lord Cochrane, the most dashing frigate captain of the Nelsonian age, was carried on the books of four ships at once to ensure his seniority when he finally donned a uniform. At sea, midshipmen were instructed every morning in navigation, nautical astronomy, and trigonometry. They were required to take the sun each noon with their quadrants, and were not allowed to eat until they had worked out the ship's position. When school hours were over, the midshipmen joined one of the watches to perfect the skills of their profession. They commanded small boats and went aloft with the men to learn how to bend and reef a sail. They directed the hoisting of supplies, mustered the men at night, commanded watering parties and supervised the stowing of hammocks in the nettings. They were always at the beck and call of the captain and first lieutenant. When a midshipman had reached the age of nineteen and had six years of service at sea, he was eligible to take the examination for lieutenant. A passing grade was no assur-

---

[3] Winston Churchill once defined the traditions of the Royal Navy as "rum, sodomy and the lash." Most accounts of the age of fighting sail are tight-lipped, however, in discussing the degree of homosexuality among officers and men. Michael Lewis, in his *Social History of the Navy* (London 1960), states that during the Napoleonic Wars there was "a considerable crop of homosexual offenses. The Courts Martial of the period include a good many cases of sodomy on the Lower Deck, in spite of the ferocious punishment of death inflicted upon those found guilty. The memoir-writers hardly ever mention the subject. . . . About officers, they are even more reticent; indeed, all but mute." Richard Hough, in *Captain Bligh and Mr. Christian* (London 1972), blames the cooling of a homosexual relationship between the two for the celebrated mutiny on the *Bounty* in 1789.

No data on homosexual offenses in the Continental Navy has been found and the subject is not mentioned in the Rules and Regulations adopted by Congress in 1775. But Harold D. Langley, in *Social Reform in the United States Navy, 1798–1862* (Urbana 1967), notes that there are a few recorded cases of punishment for homosexual offenses during this period—usually a dozen lashes and a discharge. This does not mean that such offenses were rare. "It seems likely that the offenses for which such punishment were administered were not always accurately described in the records. How often this happened and what circumlocutions were used it is impossible to say."

ance of promotion, for more than likely that depended on influence and luck.

Midshipmen were often mere children, but they were officers with power to maltreat and bully those under them. A midshipman had but to complain to a lieutenant to get a man a flogging at the gangway. Midshipmen were not free of the threat of punishment, however. The usual one was mastheading. The offending lad was sent aloft as far as he could go and ordered to remain there until told to come down. Often he stayed there for hours—missing meals and without anything to drink—sometimes for a full day and night. In winter, a few hours at the masthead, plunging and rolling with the ship in heavy seas, was enough to leave the victim nearly frozen to his perch. Some first lieutenants had a shorter way with disobedient midshipmen. They had them turned over a quarterdeck gun and given a taste of the "colt."

Cabins for the surgeon, purser, and master as well as the ship's tiny dispensary adjoined the cockpit. Up forward were racks for the seabags and chests of the men, to which access was allowed at certain fixed times. The sail-locker with its extra suits of sails was amidships. The cable tiers were nearby—the place where the anchor cables were stored after being hoisted in by the capstan. Then came the cubbyholes and storerooms of the boatswain, the carpenter, and the gunner. The carpenter, however, usually chose to work in the fresh air and daylight of the spar deck.

The hold, the lowest level of the ship, housed the fore and after magazines where the ship's ammunition was stored. Copper lids, secured by strong bars and padlocks, covered the magazines. A sentry stood at each hatch with a loaded musket. When the ship went into action, he was reinforced by a corporal's guard or a midshipman with a brace of pistols in his belt. No light was permitted in the magazines, which were lit from adjoining light-rooms or small cubicles built just forward of the magazine but separated from it by double glass windows. Lanterns placed behind these windows cast their feeble light into the magazine, where the gunner and his mates made cartridges by packing gunpowder into cloth bags. No one was allowed to enter a magazine unless he had put on thick felt slippers to prevent striking a spark. The magazine's deck and bulkheads were also covered with felt.

The ship's provisions and water casks were stowed between the magazines. The fish room, used for the storage of salt fish, lay forward of the after magazine. The spirit room, filled with casks of rum, brandy, and wine, was beside it. The bread room lay forward. It was lined with tin and packed with ship's biscuit that was supposed to be kept dry by hanging stoves. But nautical literature is filled with accounts of biscuit that was so moldy that seamen had to tap it before eating it to drive out the weevils. The rest of the hold was crowded with casks of peas, oatmeal, and salt meat—the staples of the sailor's diet. Regulations provided for the stowage of old provisions on top so they could be eaten first.

The day after Hopkins's squadron sailed downstream, the Naval Committee prepared its instructions for the commodore. These orders, which were in two parts, probably reached him on January 6. The first part consisted of general instructions relating to discipline and management of the fleet, which Hopkins passed on to his captains. The second part contained detailed orders for future operations which the commodore kept to himself. They set a surprisingly ambitious course for a handful of converted merchantmen manned by officers and men who were untried in the ways of war.

"You are instructed with the utmost diligence to proceed with the said Fleet to Sea and if the Wind and Weather will possibly admit of it to proceed directly for Chessepeak Bay in Virginia and when nearly arrived there you will send forward a small swift sailing Vessel to gain intelligence of the Enemies Situation and strength," Hopkins was told. "If by such intelligence you find they are not greatly superiour to your own you are immediately to Enter said bay, search out and attack, take or destroy all the Naval forces of our Enemies that you may find there. If you should be so fortunate as to execute this business successfully in Virginia you are to proceed immediately to the Southward and make yourself Master of such forces as the Enemy may have both in North and South Carolina. . . . Having compleated your Business in the Carolina's you are without delay to proceed Northward directly to Rhode Island, and attack, take and destroy all the Enemies Naval force that you find there."

These orders were a reminder that although New England officers might dominate the new navy, it had been created only with the support of the Southerners. As payment, they demanded first call upon the services of the fleet. Word had just been received in Philadelphia of the burning of Norfolk, Virginia, on New Year's Day on the orders of Lord Dunmore, the Royal Governor of Virginia. Christopher Gadsden, the South Carolina member of the Naval Committee who was shortly to return home to join his regiment as colonel, was probably responsible for the second part of Hopkins's orders. He painted a bright picture of the prospects for success off the Carolinas and suggested that a special signal be prepared to identify the fleet when it arrived off Charleston. In compliance with the request, Hopkins endorsed the letter in his own hand, "Som one of the Fleet if to gether or the Small Sloop if a lone will higst a Stripped Flagg half up the Flying Stay."

This statement can be interpreted to mean that as of the moment, Commodore Hopkins intended to comply with his orders. But he had been given considerable leeway. "Notwithstanding these particular Orders, which 'tis hoped you will be able to execute," he had been instructed by the Naval Committee, "if bad Winds or Stormy Weather, or any other unforseen accident or disaster disable you . . . You are then to follow such Courses as your best Judgement shall Suggest to you as most useful to the American Cause and to distress the Enemy by all means in your power." Taking advantage of this discretionary provision, Hopkins soon completely recast the mission of his small squadron.

By mid-January, the ice had thinned enough for the *Providence*, commanded by a Captain John Hazard,[4] to rejoin the fleet. Hazard brought a gift for the commodore from Gadsden in Philadelphia—a fine yellow flag emblazoned with a coiled serpent under which was inscribed "Don't Tread on Me." It was intended as his personal ensign. The *Providence*'s arrival also brought activity. Small boats from all the ships were manned with oarsmen and the five vessels were towed into the stream on January 17. Propelled by a fresh northwest breeze that billowed out their sails, they moved through the *chevaux-de-frise*—sunken iron spikes that had been emplaced to rip the bottom out of any British vessel attempting to attack Philadelphia—to Reedy Island where the ice closed in again. Realizing that the fleet was going to be delayed for some time, Hopkins wrote for the supplies that were still to be dispatched to his ships. Three wagons, containing everything from a case of cheese to a half-dozen swivels, soon rolled out of Philadelphia on their way to the anchorage. Despite the thickening ice, the little sloop *Fly*, carrying six 9-pounders and forty men who had been recruited in Rhode Island at Hopkins's sugges-

---

[4] Hazard, of whom little is known, was described by Nicholas Biddle as "A Stout Man Very Vain and Ignorant—as much low cunning as Capacity."

tion, managed to make its way up the bay at this time to join the squadron. Half the newcomers were distributed among the *Alfred, Columbus,* and *Cabot,* with the rest being retained on board the *Fly.* Using the power vested in him by Congress, Hopkins appointed Lieutenant Hoystead Hacker, the first lieutenant of the *Cabot* and a fellow Rhode Islander, skipper of the *Fly,* and took the craft into his fleet as a tender, or small dispatch vessel.

To keep the crews busy and out of mischief during the long process of getting to sea, Hopkins's captains continually exercised them at the guns. Over and over again, marine drummers stationed on the fleet's quarterdecks received the shouted command: "Beat to Quarters!" Thumping out a short, quick, and determined roll, the drums summoned the men to action. While the gun crews were still assembling, the gun captains, usually petty officers or experienced seamen, checked hurriedly to make certain that rammer, sponge, tub of water, horn of priming powder, and quoin, or elevating wedge, were in place. Ship's boys, or "powder monkeys," scurried up the ladders from the magazine deep in the ship's hold with shot and cartridges.

The guns of the period were mostly made of cast iron, and all were smooth-bore and muzzle-loading. Each was classified by the weight of the round (solid) shot it fired, the 9-pounder being the most common in Hopkins's fleet.[5] In computing the number of guns carried by a ship, only those ranged in broadside on the gundecks were counted, although men-of-war also carried several guns on their quarterdecks and others fitted to fire directly forward or aft. These were called bow and stern chasers. The cannon were mounted on wooden-wheeled carriages, or trucks, that were secured against the rolling and pitching of the ship—or recoil when they were in action—by breeching ropes and block and tackle. In bad weather, when the ship's rolling caused the guns to strain their fastenings, the tackles and breechings were doubled and wooden wedges were placed under the carriage wheels to prevent them from tearing loose. Besides the usual round shot for smashing hulls and masts, naval cannon were also loaded with grape shot, chain shot, and langrage,

---

[5] A 9-pound long gun had a point-blank range of 300 yards and an extreme range of 1,800 yards at 6 degrees elevation. An 18-pounder had a point-blank range of 265–300 yards and an extreme range of 2,500–2,870 yards at 10 degrees elevation. Point-blank range for a 32-pound long gun was 350 yards and 2,900 yards at extreme range.

among other projectiles. Grape consisted of small balls packed into canvas cylinders that would explode with ghastly effect among masses of men. Chain shot was made of two round shot fastened together with a piece of chain; this went spinning end-over-end through the air. Like langrage, a haphazard collection of old iron, nuts, bolts, scraps of chain, and bits of broken glass all tied up into a rough cylinder, it was a favorite weapon for tearing up sails and rigging. Because flying splinters were more terrible and more feared than solid shot in the age of wooden fighting ships, gunners did their best to produce them. Reducing powder charges when fighting at close range would cause the shot to tear off the biggest and most jagged splinters.

During training exercises the guns were loaded and fired by command. When the ship was in action the gun crews were expected to perform their tasks automatically. The first task of a gun crew was to throw off the lashings that secured the cannon and pull it in board as far as it would go for loading. A bag of powder and a wad was rammed in, to be followed by a round shot or other type of projectile which was rammed down on top the loose wad. Then the crew pulled upon the tackle until the carriage struck the side of the ship and the gun's muzzle stuck out as far as it would go. When the piece was loaded, the gun captain took out his priming iron—an implement like a needle with a corkscrew twist at the end—and thrust it down through the touch-hole and into the cartridge and pulled it out. From a box strapped about his waist, he took out a priming tube, made of goose quill, and placed it in the touch-hole so the sharp end entered the cartridge. If there were no priming tubes, the gun captain primed his piece from a powderhorn containing fine-milled powder. He poured powder down the touch-hole, laying a tiny train along a channel cut into the gun for that purpose. Sights were crude if available at all. When the gun was ready to be fired, it was aimed by elevating the quoin under the breech and manhandling the carriage to the right or left by handspikes, or wooden levers.

At "Fire!," a man who had been blowing upon a lighted match applied the red hot end to the touch-hole and smartly drew it back to avoid the "huff" or spit of flame from the vent at the moment of explosion. The match, a length of twisted cotton wick soaked in lye, burned very slowly, and once lit remained alight for hours. The matches were placed between the guns in tubs half-filled with sand and water. They were fixed in notches cut into the rims of each tub so the burning ends lay over the water and sand while the loose ends were coiled on the deck. After 1780, guns on some ships were fitted with flintlocks instead of matches. The trigger was pulled by a smart jerk on a lanyard. While the flintlock was more efficient and safer than a match, many seamen and officers, with the conservatism ingrained by their profession, resisted the changeover. Not until the Battle of the Nile in 1798, when one of the ships using flintlocks fired more rapidly than any other vessel in Nelson's fleet, were seamen convinced of their merit. Guns were fired on the upward roll if the intent was to dismantle the opponent, or on the start of the downward roll if the aim was to damage his hull. The decision was made by the ship's captain and passed to the gun crews by the lieutenants and midshipmen in charge of the various batteries.

When the gun fired, the recoil sent it flying back with terrific violence to the limit of the breeching. No sailor could predict from the course of the ship and the way the gun was pointed exactly how the gun would run back. Many men were killed or injured during battle by the recoil of their own weapons. They had to be alert and agile—or suffer the consequences. If the gun had fired successfully, it recoiled in position for reloading. Before a fresh cartridge was thrust down the muzzle, the barrel was wiped clean with a long-handled sponge dipped in a nearby tub of water. This was to prevent flaming scraps of the previous cartridge from prematurely igniting the new one. Sponge handles were usually made of heavy, flexible rope so that a sailor could bend it. Thus he would not have to lean out a gunport to pass it down the barrel, making himself a perfect target for the enemy's sharpshooters. The process of loading was complicated and clumsy—yet a well-trained gun crew could get off three shots in two minutes.

On the morning of February 11, Hopkins ordered his captains to recommence their slow progress toward the sea. "At 10 A M cast off from ye Pierse in Company with all ye Fleet," Lieutenant Josiah wrote in the *Doria*'s journal. It took two days to descend Delaware Bay to Whorekill Road just under Cape Henlopen, where reinforcements in the form of two small vessels from Baltimore awaited it. They were the sloop *Hornet*, armed with ten 4-pounders, commanded by a Baltimore merchant skipper, William Stone, and the schooner *Wasp*, of eight 4-pounders, under William Hallock, another Baltimorean. Both vessels had been fitted out by orders of Congress, and are believed to be the first vessels of the Continental Navy to get to sea. Named in the hope that they would carry a sting to the British, the "insect" ships were the first of a long line of vessels bearing those names that were to win fame in the American navy.

Once again, Hopkins was forced to await better weather before venturing to sea. The delays caused George Washington to observe to Joseph Reed, then working in Philadelphia: "I fear your fleet has been so long in fitting, and the destination of it so well known, that [in] the end [it] will be defeated, [even] if the vessels escape." Desertions were becoming more numerous among the men, as frostbite and hard work seemed the only rewards of the service. Some of the deserters were rounded up and lodged in the Lewes jail—among them a few of the prisoners who had been freed by the Pennsylvania Committee of Safety on the promise that they join the Continental Navy. Led by William Green, who had fled from the *Doria*, they secured arms and barricaded themselves in the jail and defied anyone to come and get them. The town militia surrounded the building, but no one was willing to go inside where the prisoners were threatening to shoot the first man who entered.

When a squad consisting of an officer and several marines returned to the *Doria* empty-handed, Captain Biddle decided to handle the matter himself. Accompanied only by a midshipman, he went ashore and strode up to the jail. From inside, Green and his companions were swearing they would never be taken. A ring of spectators and militiamen parted for Biddle.

"Green! Come out of there," he called. "Open the door or we'll break it in!"

"I'll not come out, and I'll shoot you if you try to come in!" Green shouted.

At the captain's orders the militia quickly produced a heavy log and swung it against the jail door. When it had splintered, Biddle stepped across the threshold as the militiamen dropped their makeshift battering ram and quickly moved out of the line of fire. Pistol in either hand, Biddle faced the ringleader, who pointed a musket at him.

"Now, Green," he said quietly, "if you do not take good aim, you are a dead man."

The deserter looked down the barrel of his weapon at Biddle. Instead of pulling the trigger, he hesitated. Then his hand began to shake. His musket clattered to the floor, and the militia rushed in to relieve the others of their arms. Biddle's coolness in the affair became the talk of the fleet, but he dismissed it in a letter to his sister, Lucy, saying: "Four Raskels stood on their defense, Barricaded their Room door which Obliged me to force it. Tell Cousin Clemmy I must owe him a letter till I can find Something worth telling." [6] Biddle returned to his ship in time to be summoned along with the other captains to the commodore's cabin aboard the *Alfred*.

One by one they were piped aboard the flagship—Whipple, of the *Columbus*; John B. Hopkins, of the *Cabot*; Hazard, of the *Providence*; Stone, of the *Hornet*; Hacker, of the *Fly*; Hallock, of the *Wasp*; and Biddle, of the *Andrew Doria*. Esek Hopkins presented each of his captains with long sheets of foolscap upon which his clerks had inscribed with a fair, round hand the "Signals for the American Fleet." Besides the general signals, there were specific ones for each ship. Those for the *Doria* were typical. Should the commodore wish to speak with Biddle, he would show a Dutch flag at the mizzen masthead of the *Alfred*. If he wished the brig to give chase, the Dutch flag would be flown at the fore masthead. If the chase were to the windward, the flagship would hoist its ensign and lower the commodore's pennant simultaneously; if it was to the leeward, the pennant would remain flying and the ensign would not be hoisted. A white pennant at the fore masthead would mean to break off the chase.

Then Hopkins issued orders that clearly indicate for the first time that he intended to disregard the instructions given him by the Naval Committee, namely, to proceed to the Chesapeake. "You are hereby Ordered to keep Company with me if possible and truly Observe the Signals give by the Ship I am in," he told his captains. "But in Case you should be Separated in a Gale of Wind or otherwise— You then are to use all possible Means to join the Fleet as soon as possible—But if you cannot in four days after you leave the Fleet You are to make the best of your way to the Southern port of Abaco, one of the Bahama Islands, and there wait for the Fleet fourteen

---

[6] As quoted in William B. Clark, *Captain Dauntless: The Story of Nicholas Biddle of the Continental Navy* (Baton Rouge 1949).

days—But if the Fleet does not join you in that time You are to Cruise in such place as you think will most annoy the Enemy. . . ." All British vessels or any vessels with supplies for the British Army in America were to be taken and sent into an American port. Finally, the captains were told that if their own ships should be taken, they should make certain that orders and signals were destroyed.

Sometime between January 5, the date he received his instructions, and February 14, when he set the rendezvous for the fleet in the Bahamas, Hopkins had decided to invoke the clause in his orders allowing him discretionary privileges. Although his captains were not informed of it yet, he planned a raid on the island of New Providence (now Nassau) in the Bahamas to capture gunpowder and ordnance stored there. As early as November 29, Congress had met in secret session to discuss a report of "a large quantity of powder" on the island and to instruct the Naval Committee to "take measures for securing and bring[ing] away" the powder. But there is no record of any orders being issued to Hopkins to do so.

Later, when Hopkins's conduct was being questioned, the commodore told John Hancock that the basis of his decision to go to Abaco was that the poor weather and large number of seamen sick with smallpox in the fleet had left it in no "Condition to keep on a Cold Coast." Obviously, the impression he was trying to create was that he had not changed his plans until after he put to sea. But his orders to his captains show that he had made up his mind in advance. Still later, he confided to his brother Stephen—the chairman of the Naval Committee and possibly Esek Hopkins's source of the information about Congress's interest in New Providence—that he had intended to sail to the Southern colonies after the raid. The intention faded because in his opinion the enemy off Virginia and south along the coast to Georgia was "too Strong for us." The lookout off the Charleston bar was to watch in vain for a ship with a "Stripped Flagg half up the Flying Stay."

Four days after the meeting in the commodore's cabin, the wind turned fair. Shortly before 1 P.M. on February 18, Hopkins gave the signal to weigh anchor by loosening the *Alfred*'s fore-topsail and sheeting it home. One after another, the ships of the fleet hoisted sail. Propelled by a freshening breeze, they followed the flagship around the Cape Henlopen lighthouse and over the horizon. Soon the smell of the land was gone and the wind was from the open sea.

VII

The New Providence Raid

Blowing weather shot with sudden squalls struck the fleet the second night after the low Delaware coast had dropped out of sight. "Hard gales & thick Weather," the laconic Lieutenant Josiah recorded in the *Doria*'s journal. "Lost sight of ye Sloop *Hornet* & *Fly* in the night." Masthead watches were set in hope of spotting the two small vessels but they remained unreported. Eventually the weather moderated, turning warm and balmy during the run south. Storms at sea do not occur as frequently as landsmen might think, and the ships' crews soon drifted into the traditional routine of a ship of war on a long ocean voyage.

The day of the man-of-war's man began at midnight, or at four in the morning, depending on the watch to which he had been assigned.[1] If he had the middle-watch, from midnight to 4 A.M., the work at night in fine weather was easy. The men had but to trim the sails and be ready for a call. Boatswain's mates and a midshipman or two kept watch forward. Lookouts were posted in the tops. The

[1] The following account of a ship's routine is based upon Masefield's *Sea Life in Nelson's Time.*

officer of the watch, the helmsman, a few marine sentries and a couple of midshipmen were on the quarterdeck. The only sound was the rhythmic creaking of the rigging and the gurgling of the waves as they bubbled past the hull. At eight bells, or 4 A.M., the boatswain's mates took their pipes to the fore and main hatchways and blew the prolonged, shrill call "All Hands!" This was followed by a shout of "Starboard [or Larboard] Watch, Ahoy! Rouse out there, you sleepers!" The watch below, who had been snug in their hammocks, turned out and bustled on deck to be mustered and sent to their stations. Laggards and sluggards were enlivened by the knotted ropes' ends wielded by the boatswain's mates. The lookouts and the helmsman were relieved. The log was heaved, and the speed of the ship marked. The men who had been on duty since midnight were now allowed to go below.

Under the direction of the first lieutenant, the crew was formed into divisions charged with performing the various tasks required to keep the ship operating. The older, more experienced seamen were stationed on the forecastle to work the anchor and the foresails. The topmen—those who manned the yards to bend sail and take it in—were chosen from among the younger, more active sailors. They were divided into three groups, one for each mast, and had the most dangerous job on the ship. They were called out in all weather to swarm high above the deck to work with the captain's eye on them because a ship's smartness was determined by how quickly her topmen could set or reef the sails. Some captains made it a practice to have the last topman on deck flogged so every man risked his neck to get down quickly. The afterguard handled the braces which trimmed the yards and were responsible for keeping the after part of the ship orderly. The largest and least respected group were the waisters, who performed the same duty in the middle of the ship and were composed of landsmen and the less bright seamen. The idlers—those who stood no watch, such as the cooper, the barber, the tailor, and the loblolly boys, or surgeon's assistants—formed the fifth division.

Shortly after four o'clock, the cook lit his fires in the galley, the carpenter and his mates came on deck, and the boatswain, a grizzled old sea dog who was responsible for running the ship, put the watch on duty to work. They rolled up their wide trousers, rigged the pumps, got out the scrubbers, holystone and buckets, and began to wash down the deck. "It was hard and often unpleasant work, scrubbing the deck in all weather, some fourteen hours after the last meal," notes Masefield. Following the holystoners came the broom and bucket men, who swilled and swept the dirty sand overboard. The deck was dried, brightwork polished, and lines coiled into place. By 7 A.M., when the first lieutenant came on deck to begin his long day of supervision, these chores had been completed.

A half-hour later, the boatswain's mates piped "All hands! Up hammocks!" With that, the watch below was up, lashing and carrying their hammocks on deck to the nettings where they were stowed under the eyes of the midshipmen. By 8 A.M., the captain had come on deck, and as eight bells was struck, the crew was piped to breakfast. Breakfast lasted a half-hour and was eaten at tables lowered into position between the guns. Each sailor had a knife, spoon, and earthenware bowl. For meals, sailors divided themselves into messes of four to eight men each, which were presided over by a mess cook. He received the provisions for the mess from the purser and delivered them to the cook in the galley for preparation. Breakfast consisted of "burgoo," or coarse oatmeal and water washed down with "Scotch coffee" made from burnt bread boiled in water and sweetened with a little sugar.

After breakfast the watch was called, and the lower deck was cleaned by the men who had just come off duty. It was never washed down with water except in fine weather when the gunports could be opened to dry the wet planking. Generally only holystones and sand were used, and the deck beams were sponged over with vinegar as a disinfectant. Wooden ships, often built of improperly seasoned timber, were always foul—no matter how clean the deck might appear. The ballast was dirty; the water in the bilges was putrid and sloshed with every roll of the ship; the hold badly ventilated and the gun deck packed with men who slung their hammocks only a few feet apart. The sailors were often flea-bitten and louse-ridden, rarely bathed and almost never removed their clothes. Ships smelled of an overpowering mixture of dry rot, bilge water, decaying stores, long-dead rats, and unwashed bodies.

Sailors who had the watch below could do as they wished—chat with their mates, mend their clothes or sleep if they could find space between the guns or a bit of the deck that was not being used by the carpenter, the cooper, or the sailmaker. "The watch and watch system, four hours on and four hours off, with the four hours off constantly broken in upon by the ship's routine, was severe and harassing," Masefield continues. "It meant that a sailor had but four hours sleep on one night and a bare seven hours the following night." The catnaps they managed during the day were too short, too uncertain to be counted upon. Even during their watches below at night they were liable to be rousted out by the boatswain's pipe to tack, to come about, to set or shorten sail. Once a month at least, they were drummed to general quarters in the middle of the night. Every Thursday, the hammocks were called up at 4 A.M., and the morning watch was spent washing clothes. A few captains tried a four- or quarter-watch system which was popular with their men because they could usually count on getting a full night in their hammocks.

By six bells, or eleven o'clock, the captain had breakfasted alone in his cabin, scanned the logs the midshipmen were required to keep, examined the accounts of the boatswain, purser, and carpenter, and had a talk with his first lieutenant. Frequently he came on deck with the black list of men awaiting punishment. "All hands to witness punishment!" bawled the boatswain's mates, and the master-at-arms, the ship's policeman, brought up the prisoners who were to be flogged with the cat-o'-nine-tails. The marines fell in upon the poop, with loaded muskets and sidearms. The junior officers gathered to the windward under the break of the poop while the captain and his lieutenants stood on the weather side of the quarterdeck. The ship's company gathered where they could in the waist. The first order issued by the captain was to "rig the gratings." The carpenter and his mates immediately dragged aft two of the wooden gratings that covered the hatches. One was placed flat on the deck, the other upright against the ship's side or the poop railings.

Writing under the pseudonym Jack Nastyface, one of the few seamen of the age of fighting sail to leave memoirs, charged that "in nineteen cases out of twenty cases [a sailor] is flogged for the most trifling offence or neglect, such as not hearing the watch called at night, not doing anything properly on deck or aloft . . . when, perhaps, he has been doing the best he could and at the same time ignorant of having done wrong, until he is pounced on and put in irons. So much for the legal process." [2] The captain read off the first

---

[2] Quoted in Henry Baynham, *From the Lower Deck* (Barre, Mass. 1970).

name on his list. The man was told he had broken the regulations of the service, fully knowing what the penalty would be. He was asked if he had anything to say in explanation and was expected to say "No"—nothing more. He had already been found guilty. The gratings were rigged. The cat was waiting. A wrong word now could only increase the number of strokes. The man stood at attention, awaiting the next order: "Strip." He flung off his shirt, and advanced bare shouldered to the gratings. The order was given to "Seize him up," and his arms were spread on the grating and his wrists bound to it. At this point, the captain produced a copy of the Articles of War and read the section which the offender had broken. The captain took off his hat and so did every man in the ship's company—not in sympathy with the man about to be flogged but in honor of the regulations. While the article was being read, one of the boatswain's mates undid a red baize bag in which the cat was kept.

At the order "Do your duty," the boatswain's mate advanced upon the man at the grating, and began to lay the whip on with the full strength and sweep of his arm. The force of the blow would have been enough to knock the victim down from sheer impact were he not supported by the grating. Boatswain's mates chosen to administer punishment were strong men, specially trained for the job. Classes were held to instruct a new mate in his duty, with lessons consisting of practice floggings on a cask. The mates knew that any sign of leniency or softheartedness could land them on the grating. Some seamen could take a dozen lashes, or as they expressed it, get a red checked shirt at the gangway, without crying aloud. But the force of each blow knocked the breath out of the victim with an involuntary "Ugh!" One blow was enough to produce blood and take off the skin where the lash fell. Six were enough to turn the victim's back raw. Twelve lashes—the normal minimum—turned it into a horrible red mess. Yet three dozen lashes was a usual punishment in the Royal Navy. Six dozen was frequent. Three hundred was unusual but not unknown. Five hundred was about as many as a man could take and survive. After each stroke, the mate drew the nine tails of the cat through his fingers to wipe off clotted flesh and blood that might cause them to stick together and prevent each one from having the maximum effect. A fresh boatswain's mate was put on to flog after each two dozen to insure maximum punishment. Left-handed boatswain's mates who could cross the cuts made by right-handed men were considered a prize.

Some men stood flogging better than others. To one man it was "nothing but an O, and a few O my Gods, and then you can put on your shirt." But another recalled that the first blow produced "an astounding sensation between the shoulders under my neck, which went to my toe-nails in one direction, and my finger nails in another, and stung me to the heart, as if a knife had gone through my body. . . . He came on a second time a few inches lower, and then I thought the former stroke was sweet and agreeable compared with that one. . . . I felt my flesh quiver in every nerve, from the scalp of my head to my toe-nails. The time between each stroke seemed so long as to be agonising, and yet the next came too soon. . . . The pain in my lungs was more severe, I thought, than on my back. I felt as if I would burst in the internal parts of my body. . . . I put my tongue between my teeth, held it there, and bit it almost in two pieces. What with the blood from my tongue and my lips, which I had also bitten, and the blood from my lungs, or some other internal part, ruptured by the writhing agony, I was almost choked, and became black in the face. . . . Only fifty had been inflicted. . . ." [3]

Courts-martial could—and did—order a thousand lashes, which was a death sentence and intended to be so. A sailor might receive such punishment for striking an officer and attempting to escape. It didn't matter that he might have been purposely and deliberately provoked—he was guilty and must be punished. The sentence was inflicted by flogging through the fleet. The victim was tied to a capstan bar and rowed in a longboat from his ship to all the vessels of the fleet, where a portion of the punishment was inflicted. Boats loaded with marines from each ship formed a procession which moved to the beat of a single drummer tapping out the "Rogue's March." If the man fainted, he was forcibly revived with rum or wine so he would miss nothing of his torture. A surgeon could order punishment halted and the man taken to the sick bay of his own ship

---

[3] The amount of flogging in a ship depended entirely on the captain. In some ships men were punished almost daily; in others it was a rarity. Such brutality was a direct cause of the naval mutinies of 1797. That same year, the crew of the British frigate *Hermione*, angered by the brutality of their officers, rebelled and murdered nine of them and turned the ship over to the Spaniards. Flogging was abolished in the U.S. Navy in 1850. It remained on the books of the Royal Navy until 1939, but had not been inflicted for decades.

where he rested until he had recovered enough strength to absorb more. The art was to keep him alive long enough to receive all the lashes ordered. There is at least one case of a captain ordering fifty lashes still due to be given to a dead man. His bones had been laid bare from neck to waist even before the cat had begun to swing again. Those who died during punishment were rowed ashore and silently buried in the mud below tidemark without religious rites. Jack Nastyface quotes one man facing such punishment as saying: "I would rather have been sentenced to be shot or hung at the yardarm." His offense was trying to escape after being impressed.

Punishment administered, the officers broke out their sextants and quadrants to fix the ship's position. Eight bells were struck and the boatswain's mate sounded his long, cheery "pipe to dinner." The crew went below for the pleasantest part of the day. Dinner, which lasted about a half-hour, was a merry meal with the prospect of the day's first ration of grog in the offing. At the tolling of one bell, the fifer struck up the lively "Nancy Dawson," or some other rollicking tune such as "Drops of Brandy," and the ship's company took it up. The cook of each mess went to the tubs where the grog had been prepared, carrying a flagon in which to bring the precious fluid back to his mates. The noon allowance was one gill of pure navy rum mixed with three gills of water. Another ration was issued at supper.[4]

At half-past one, when the last drops of grog had been drained, the watch on deck was called to duty. Frequently, the watch below was also summoned with the rest, to be drilled into smartness. Raw hands were taken below by the gunners to be trained at the guns. Other squads were sent aloft to learn the duties of topmen. At 4 P.M.

---

[4] The rum ration, which had been introduced in the Royal Navy in 1731, was abolished as of August 1, 1970. "There will be those who will mourn the passing," acknowledged Admiral Sir Michael LeFanu, the First Sea Lord and Chief of the Naval Staff. "But by and large I hope the fleet will see the rum issue is not appropriate for the modern, instant-response navy. I am not expecting to rocket to the top of the pops on this, but I am sure we are doing the right thing."

Prior to April 14, 1740, each man was issued a half pint of neat rum daily at a minimum. On that date, Vice Admiral Edward Vernon, commanding a squadron in the Caribbean, issued orders that added water to the rum ration and a new word to the English language—grog. Vernon, who wore a cloak made of a coarse-grained material called grogham, was affectionately known to his sailors as "Old Grog." They transferred the name to the new mixture.

Grog rations were abolished in the U.S. Navy in 1862, under pressure from temperance groups. At one point, battleships named after dry states were christened with lemonade rather than champagne.

the crew was piped to a supper of cheese and butter and wormy biscuits, and a second serving of grog. A sailor was not allowed to receive his rum ration neat, but with a little ingenuity and patience, he could obtain enough to slake his thirst. "A gill was not enough to turn an old seaman's head," writes Masefield, "but by saving up the gill till supper, and adding to it the second gill, with any third gill purchased or acquired from a shipmate, the oldest sailor found it possible to believe himself an admiral." Hence the word "groggy."

Just before sunset, the drummer beat to quarters and the sailors scampered to their battle stations. The guns were cast loose and the officers made an inspection of the ship. At this evening muster the master-at-arms made most of his arrests, concentrating on the men who had combined their dinner and supper grog. A little thickness of speech, a little too much gaiety, a little unsteadiness in gait was enough to win a date with the cat. After the guns had been secured, the hammocks were piped down from the nettings and slung into place. At 8 P.M., the first night watch was set, and the watch below was permitted to crawl into the hammocks until midnight. Lights were extinguished or covered so they would not show from a distance. Quiet settled over the ship only to be broken by an occasional "All's Well" from the sentries.

After a fast run south, Hopkins's fleet—now down to six ships— dropped anchor on March 1 in twelve fathoms off Grand Abaco Island in the Bahamas. For two days, the ships rocked in the lee of the island vainly awaiting the arrival of the *Hornet* and *Fly* and watering while the commodore perfected his plans. Water was carried to sea in wooden barrels and invariably became putrid and slimy from standing in the casks. At every opportunity, captains sent parties ashore, usually under command of a midshipman, to refill the casks with fresh water.

Two small sloops from New Providence were captured. From his prisoners, Hopkins learned that all British military and naval forces had been withdrawn from the island. Its two forts, which held a large quantity of gunpowder and a considerable number of heavy cannon, were defended by only a handful of militia. Hopkins summoned his captains to the flagship and for the first time informed them of the fleet's mission. Among the officers gathered in the *Alfred*'s great cabin was Lieutenant Thomas Weaver, of the *Cabot*, who was well acquainted with New Providence. He drew a rough map of the island, showing Nassau, the government seat, on the north shore and protected by Fort Nassau, just to the west of the town and now the site of a resort hotel, and the smaller Fort Montague, lying a few miles to the east. The harbor itself was protected by a long, low-lying island. To the west lay several small keys. Between the keys and the long island ran a narrow channel. Hopkins, who had sailed in this area during his merchant career, was thoroughly familiar with it. He proposed a surprise frontal attack, using the two captured sloops to carry marines directly into the harbor for an assault on Fort Nassau. No one there knew an enemy fleet lay about fifty miles away, the commodore reasoned. If the marines were concealed below deck, the sloops might be able to run in close under the fort and capture it before the alarm could be sounded. Then the fleet could sail through the channel into the harbor and, with the guns of the fort in the hands of the marines, command the town.

By nightfall of March 2, two companies of marines from the *Alfred* and *Columbus*, the half company from the *Cabot* and a detachment of 50 sailors—about 270 men in all—were packed aboard the sloops under the command of Captain Samuel Nicholas, the senior marine officer. The heavily laden craft weighed anchor late that night and several hours later the rest of the fleet followed them into the darkness. Because they were slow sailers, Hopkins planned to give the sloops a head start that would bring them off Fort Nassau at daybreak. The rest of the ships were to remain out of sight until the initial advantage of surprise had been secured. Unfortunately, the commodore blundered. Instead of keeping his ships below the horizon as the innocent-appearing sloops entered the harbor and the landing party secured the fort, he ordered his fleet to stand in toward the town. They were bowling along in the wake of the island sloops when a puff of smoke appeared at a gunport in the wall of Fort Nassau, followed by the bang of a heavy gun and the splash of a round shot. Another puff and splash followed and then a third.

All chance of surprise was lost. The small force of militia manning the fort had fired a signal for the rest of their fellows to turn out. Hopkins immediately sent a white flag fluttering to the top of the *Alfred*'s ensign staff—the signal for the captured sloops to return. A red pennant, the call for the captains to come aboard the flagship for consultation, followed the white flag. According to an account prepared later by Paul Jones for the King of France, the commodore proposed that the fleet sail around to the western end of the island, land the marines, and march upon Nassau from the rear. Jones, then the *Alfred*'s first lieutenant, said he protested against the plan because there was no anchorage to the westward and no road through the brush to Nassau. Instead, Jones allegedly suggested an alternate plan. He mentioned a fine anchorage just ten miles to the east of Nassau where the fleet could lie safely while the marines were landed closer to town. From there, they could march by a good road along the coast, outflank Fort Montague and capture Nassau. The local information on which the plan was based was said to have come to Jones from one of the pilots taken with the New Providence sloops. Hopkins liked the idea. With the *Alfred* in the van, and Jones and the captured pilot in the foretop, "from whence they could clearly see every danger," the fleet moved to the eastward, finally anchoring in Hanover Sound. It's a neat story—but it probably never happened.

For one thing, Jones was a stranger to the Bahamas, so it was highly unlikely that Hopkins and the other officers who knew them would entrust the safety of the fleet to Jones. For another, "no competent seamen would have sent the flagship, with the deepest draught of any vessel in the fleet, to spy out a channel through the shoals," observes Samuel Eliot Morison.[5] Interestingly, in a letter written a few weeks later to Joseph Hewes, his congressional patron, describing events at New Providence, Jones makes no mention of his plan. The little Scot, who had no small opinion of himself, would not have missed this chance to blow his own horn if there had been reason, so the later account must be so much embroidery.

At two o'clock in the afternoon of March 3, the marines and sailors stormed ashore through the surf under the guns of the *Wasp* and the *Providence*, in the first amphibious operation in American naval history. The ships' cannon were loaded and run out, but there was no opposition. Not a shot was fired. Forming up his men on the beach, Captain Nicholas moved rapidly along the coastal road toward Fort Montague, about halfway between the beachhead and the

---

[5] Samuel Eliot Morison, *John Paul Jones: A Sailor's Biography* (Boston 1959). This is by far the best and most readable of the many biographies of Paul Jones.

town. "The inhabitants were very much alarmed at our appearance, and supposed us to be Spaniards," he reported, "but were soon undeceived." A messenger from the governor, Montford Browne, asked the marine officer what his intentions were. He was told: "to take possession of all the warlike stores on the Island belonging to the Crown. . . ." If they were surrendered, no harm would be done to the Bahamians or their property. "As soon as the messenger was gone, I marched forward to take possession of Fort Montague," Nicholas continued.

"As we approached the fort (within about a mile, having a deep cove to go round, with a prodigious thicket on one side and the water on the other, entirely open to their view) they fired three 12-pound shot, which made us halt, and consult what was best to be done; we then thought it more prudent to send a flag [of truce] to let them know what our designs were in coming there." The garrison offered no further resistance, simply spiking their guns,[6] abandoning the fort, and withdrawing to the town.

Nicholas and his men found seventeen cannon—32-, 18-, and 12-pounders—from which the spikes were easily removed. The landing party, which had not had a chance to eat or rest since being loaded into the sloops the night before, settled down inside the fort. They planned to press on to the town the next day.

In the meantime, Governor Browne was doing his best to mobilize the island's population. A proclamation was issued offering a pistol to every free black who would join the militia, and other attempts were made to organize a defense—without much success. The volunteers melted away in the night and Browne's council told him it did not believe Fort Nassau could be defended with so few men. So the governor ordered the one hundred and sixty barrels of powder in the fort's magazines immediately loaded on a small sloop lying in the harbor. Stupidly, Hopkins had neglected to blockade the channel, so that the vessel easily escaped into the darkness to join the British forces at St. Augustine. The commodore's carelessness cost him the bulk of the powder that had brought him to New Providence in the first place.

Understandably, all resistance to the Americans collapsed the next morning. Nicholas's men entered Nassau, took possession of

---

[6] Guns were spiked by driving iron spikes into the touch-holes to make them inoperative.

Government House, which stood on a hill overlooking the town, and moved along the road to Fort Nassau, which surrendered without firing a shot. The loot surpassed that taken at Montague—raising the total number of guns captured to eighty-eight cannon of various sizes and fifteen mortars. There were also thousands of roundshot, a quantity of ordnance supplies, twenty-four barrels of powder that the British had not time to spirit away and "part of a Cask of Spirit"—which just might have been full when the landing party captured it. Owing to Hopkins's shortcomings, the amount of powder taken was far less than hoped. Nevertheless, the raid on New Providence can be considered the most successful American naval operation of the Revolution. Loading the booty onto the ships took two weeks. The amount was so large that the commodore had to press an island schooner into service to carry the surplus.

While the fleet was lying off Nassau, the schooner *Fly*, missing for almost a month, rejoined it. Lieutenant Hacker, her skipper, reported that his vessel had collided with the *Hornet* in a storm, carrying away "the boom and head of her Mast." The *Hornet* was blown off course toward the South Carolina coast but managed to limp back to Delaware Bay in early April. Hopkins had other problems. Sickness began to reach epidemic proportions in the fleet. Smallpox and fever raced from ship to ship. Actually, smallpox had been reported among the seamen even before the vessels had left the Delaware, and the inexperience of most of the officers in matters of health and sanitation had compounded the problem.

Biddle, remembering his training in the Royal Navy, had done his best to keep a clean ship. Because many of Biddle's crew had been inoculated against smallpox, Hopkins decided to transfer most of the sick to the *Doria*. Longboats full of sick men, surrounded by the stench of the disease, were rowed over to the brig. The sick lay in the bottom of the boats, terrible to look at because of the sores and swellings that made their faces unrecognizable. They croaked hoarsely for coolness and water. Every part of Biddle's ship was given over to accommodating the sick. Even Biddle gave up his own cot to a desperately ill midshipman. Although the *Doria* was immune to smallpox, its crew did not escape the ravages of fever. "While we lay here our people taking very Sickly with the fever, altho as much Care as possible was taking to prevent it," reported Lieutenant Josiah.

Having stowed all the seized cannon and supplies on his ships and having wooded and watered, Hopkins raised the signal to weigh anchor for home on the afternoon of March 16. Shortly before sailing, Governor Browne and two other officials who had been held under guard on shore were hustled aboard the flagship. In a hurriedly written note to Lord Dartmouth, the colonial secretary, smuggled past "innumerable Senterys" guarding him, Browne complained: "I have been cruelly treated by a few here." By dawn, the fleet was off Abaco again and a course was set to the north. The commodore's barge moved among the ships, distributing Hopkins's brief sailing instructions to his captains. He ordered them to keep company with the *Alfred.* If they should become separated, they were to lay a course for Block Island Channel, off the coast of Rhode Island, where they were to patrol for six days in hopes of making a rendezvous. If the flagship was not sighted in that time, they were on their own to "Cruise in such places as you think will most annoy the Enemy, or go in Port as you think fit. . . ."

The voyage was largely uneventful. Foul-bottomed, heavily laden, and slow, the fleet wallowed out of the blue tropic waters. As long as fair weather lasted the crews were exercised at the guns. A storm came up on March 22 and blew for three days. The *Wasp,* leaking badly, was separated from the rest of the ships. Taking in "20 Inches water an hour," according to her log, the schooner straggled into the Delaware with her pumps going and "a pees of Beef" stuffed into the leak. Fever and smallpox continued unabated in the rest of the fleet. The surgeon of the *Doria* and his mate were taken sick, leaving their patients in even more desperate straits. The routine of shortening and putting on sail began to be broken by funeral services and burials at sea.

As the fleet neared home waters, strange craft were sighted with increasing regularity. Hopkins sent the *Doria* and *Fly* off to chase a distant sail on March 27. The vessel was brought to with a shot across her bow and turned out to be a French schooner just out of New London for Haiti. She bore news that caused jubilation in the fleet—Boston had been evacuated by the British ten days before. Several small ships belonging to the British squadron cruising in Narragansett Bay were legitimate prey, however. Among the prizes were the armed schooner *Hawke,* the first British warship to be captured by a vessel of the Continental Navy, and the bomb brig *Bolton*, which carried two mortars as well as eight smaller guns. Both were taken without noticeable struggle. "At sunset we were twelve sail in all and had a very pleasant evening," wrote a satisfied Captain Nicholas on April 5. "At twelve o'clock went to bed. . . ."

The marine commander's dreams of prize money were soon punctured by the cry of "All hands to quarters!" Drums began to roll, the men were turned out of their hammocks and the deck of the *Alfred* rumbled as the guns were run out for action. The fleet was about twenty miles off Block Island when, shortly after the first hour of the mid-watch, a lookout on the *Doria* sighted two strange sail. Summoned on deck, Biddle made them out to be a full-rigged ship and a sloop—probably a British frigate and her tender. Signal lanterns were quickly hoisted to pass the information on to the *Alfred*. Although all the ships made ready for action, there was no command from Hopkins to form a line of battle or to engage the enemy. In fact, not one order was issued by the commodore during the engagement that ensued. He left each captain to his own devices. A general melee followed. "Away we all went Helter, Skelter, one flying here, another there," a disgusted Biddle wrote later.

With the *Cabot*, commanded by Captain John B. Hopkins, the commodore's son, in the van, the American fleet bore down on the larger of the two distant ships in two irregular divisions. The *Alfred* followed the *Cabot*, less than a hundred yards astern. The *Doria* led the leeward column—or the side away from the wind—and the *Columbus* and *Providence* were astern of her. The strange ship turned toward the advancing fleet. Within a half hour she was within pistol shot of the *Cabot* and was revealed as a 20-gun frigate.

"What ship is that?" asked the stranger.

"The *Cabot*, from Plymouth," Hopkins answered. "Who are you?"

"This is His Majesty's ship of war *Glasgow*, Tyringham Howe, commanding," was the reply. "What ships are in your company?"

Now the only sound was the running of the sea as the ships closed the distance between them.

"The *Columbus* and *Alfred*, a two-and-twenty-gun frigate!"

The silence did not last. From high in the *Cabot*'s fighting tops, an overzealous marine tossed a hand grenade on the *Glasgow*'s deck. Both the *Cabot* and the *Glasgow* opened up with broadsides. The

Cabot's 6-pounders were no match for the British ship's row of 9-pound guns. The *Cabot* sheered away, but was caught by a second broadside that poured fire and destruction into her, killing her sailing master and three others and wounding seven men, including Captain Hopkins. Biddle, in the *Doria*, had to turn quickly to port to escape a collision with the *Cabot*—a maneuver which saved the ships from fouling—but his vessel was carried away from the battle.

Then the *Alfred* attacked. Captain Saltonstall laid his ship broadside to broadside with the *Glasgow* and they pounded away at each other. With her main battery of twenty 9-pounders and an additional ten 6-pounders on her upper deck, the *Alfred* should have had the advantage. Down below on her gun deck, Lieutenant Jones urged his gun crews on. Suddenly, a lucky shot from the *Glasgow* carried away the *Alfred*'s wheelblock and tiller ropes. Unable to steer, she became unmanageable. The *Alfred* broached to, that is, she veered suddenly into the wind, so that the *Glasgow* could rake her by safely crossing the *Alfred*'s bow and firing into her without danger of being hit in return. "We received several shot under water, which made the ship very leaky," Jones wrote. "We had . . . the mainmast shot through and the upper works and rigging very considerably damaged." Several anxious minutes passed before the *Alfred*'s frenzied crew could rig a jury steering gear and get their ship back under control.

Meanwhile, Biddle was trying to get the *Doria* back into action. The fight had been underway for more than an hour before the brig could bring its guns to bear on the *Glasgow* without having to worry about hitting one of the American ships. The *Columbus* found herself blanketed by the other vessels. Her sails would not draw, which, as Whipple complained later, "put it out of my Power to get up with" the enemy craft. Hazard, commanding the *Providence*, seemed content to tack back and forth out of range.

Captain Howe and the *Glasgow*, having acquitted themselves brilliantly, decided at this point that an entire fleet was too much for a single frigate. Howe broke off the action, clapped on all sail, and headed for Newport, where a British fleet was waiting. The *Columbus*, which had just managed to get into the fight, maneuvered into position to rake the fleeing *Glasgow* by crossing her stern. The shots went high. Captain David Hawley, a Connecticut privateersman being held prisoner on the frigate, said "most of the shot went about 6 feet above the deck, whereas, if they had been properly levelled, must have soon cleared them of men." Nevertheless, the *Glasgow* had taken her share of punishment—Hawley reported she was "considerably damaged in her hull, had 10 shot through her main mast, 52 through her mizen stay sail, 110 thro' her main sail, 88 through her foresail, had her spars carried away and her rigging cut to pieces." Even so, she made good her escape from the disorganized American fleet, peppering her pursuers with shots from a pair of stern chasers run out of her cabin windows. A parting shot stove in the *Doria*'s quarterdeck arms chest and wounded a drummer in the leg.

Shortly after dawn—and after nearly four hours of fighting and pursuit—Hopkins made the signal for recall, breaking off the chase. He was worried about the safety of his prizes and the nearness of the British fleet, so he ordered a course set for New London. The sole success of the engagement for the Americans was the capture of the frigate's little tender by the *Hawke*, now manned by a prize crew. Considering the length and sharpness of the clash, the "butcher's bill" was small. Besides the casualties on the crippled *Cabot*, the *Alfred* had five men killed and seven wounded, while the *Doria* and *Columbus* each had one man hurt. As badly battered as she was, the *Glasgow* escaped with only one crewman killed and three wounded. All were hit by sharpshooters rather than cannon fire—proof that the American gunnery had been notably ineffective despite the long hours of drill. The night action made it all too clear that men, money, and ships alone do not make a navy. Tradition, training, discipline, and a heritage of victory are also required.

VIII

Neptune Resigns His Trident

New London's reaction to the arrival of the fleet was enthusiastic. Rocking at anchor in the harbor, heavy with the weight of the cannon and stores taken at New Providence, and accompanied by the prizes captured at sea, the ships were a brave sight to a people thirsting for victories. Few persons noticed the battered condition of the vessels. Talk about the humiliating encounter with the *Glasgow* was overshadowed by tales of the booty taken. But the first action of the commodore upon anchoring should have had a sobering effect. After he was rowed ashore in his barge, he pressed the local authorities to provide a hospital for the sick and wounded. Boat after boat left the ships filled with men suffering from fever and smallpox. Because there were more than two hundred, New London could not provide a building large enough to house them all. Sympathetic householders, moved by the plight of the seamen as they lay shivering in the bottom of the boats, with black-ringed eyes staring out of pallid faces, took the overflow into their homes.

With his ailing men taken care of, Hopkins sent off a report to Congress on his operations since leaving the Delaware. Of the fight with the *Glasgow*, he presented a carefully circumspect account that made no mention of the irregular manner in which the battle was fought. "The Officers all behaved well on board the *Alfred*, but too much Praise cannot be given to the Officers of the *Cabot* who gave and Sustain'd the whole Fire for some considerable time within pistol Shot," he wrote. Significantly, there was no mention of the other ships. At the same time, the commodore wrote Governor Trumbull of Connecticut and Governor Cooke of Rhode Island, offering them some of the captured cannon and part of the stores for the defense of their colonies. This move was to have serious repercussions since Hopkins's offer was made without consulting Congress on the disposition of what were Continental stores. A chain of events was set in motion that was to end with Hopkins's dismissal. But that was still in the future.

Congress instructed Hancock to offer official congratulations to the commodore. "Your Account of the Spirit and Bravery shown by the Men, affords them the greatest Satisfaction; and encourages them to expect similar Exertions of Courage on every future Occasion," he wrote. "Though it is to be regretted that the *Glasgow* Man of War made her Escape, yet it is not thro' any Misconduct, the Praise due to You and the other Officers, is undoubtedly the same." With an apparent view to getting the fleet to sea again as soon as possible, Hancock enclosed information that a British convoy would soon be leaving Antigua, apparently bound for New York under guard of "an old East India Ship, mounting 16 Guns." Hopkins's report was ordered published in the newspapers and a poet commemorated the triumph of the "Gallant Hopkins" in an ode that had Neptune resigning his trident and crown to Congress.

The men who had done the fighting knew better. Biddle told his brother that during the fight with the *Glasgow*, "I kept close to the Admiral that I might the sooner Receive his Orders. But he had none to give. And the *Cabot* Running off Obliged Me in order to Clear her to go a little out of my way. And before I could Regain My ground the *Alfred* had sheered off. Had I behaved as Capt. [John B.] Hopkins did, had I run on without Orders and brought on the Action in the Night I think I should have lost my Commission before now."

Paul Jones, writing to his Congressional patron, Joseph Hewes, was careful to praise the commodore but was sharply critical of his fellow officers. "I have the pleasure of Assuring you that the Commr in Chief is respected thro' the Fleet and I verily believe that the

Officers and men in general would go any length to execute his Orders. It is with pain that I confine this plaudit to an individual. I
should be happy in extending it to every Captain and Officer in the
Service—praise is certainly due to some—but Alas! there are Excep-
tions. It is certainly for the Interest of the Service that a Cordial in-
terchange of Civilities should Subsist between Superiour and Inferiour Officers—and therefore it is bad policy in Superiours to behave
towards their inferiours indiscriminately as tho they were of a lower
Species." He meant Captain Saltonstall—but as Admiral Morison
has noted, his own officers on the *Ranger* would soon be saying the
same thing about him. Later, Jones was not so charitable, saying: "It
is for the commander-in-chief and the captains to answer for the
escape of the *Glasgow*."

As the first burst of enthusiasm was dying away, criticism of the
handling of the fleet and individual ships during the action with the
Glasgow began to be heard in the waterside taverns of New London.
How was it that a mere 20-gun vessel could do so much damage to
an entire fleet and make good its escape? Rumors of cowardliness
circulated. The failure was emphasized by the news that on the same
day the *Glasgow* had escaped, Captain John Barry, commanding the
brigantine *Lexington*, had taken the British sloop *Edward* after a
sharp fight.

Abraham Whipple found the situation intolerable. He wrote
Hopkins on April 30, requesting a court-martial to inquire into his
conduct as commander of the *Columbus*. Hopkins granted his relative's request and the court-martial was held in the cabin of the *Alfred* on May 6, with Dudley Saltonstall presiding and eleven other
captains and lieutenants as members. They heard Whipple present
an emotional defense of his conduct and took evidence from several
witnesses from various ships of the fleet. The court quickly found his
"mode of attack on the *Glasgow* . . . preceded from Error in Judgement and not from Cowardice."

Two days later, another court-martial was convened on the *Alfred*—this time to try charges brought against Captain John Hazard
by the officers of the *Providence*. For the better part of a day, the
court listened to the evidence. The dozen officers found Hazard
guilty of breaches of orders, of neglect of duty in failing to prepare
his ship for action promptly on the night of the *Glasgow* fight, and of

embezzling part of his ship's stores. Although Hazard regarded the charges as "a Mear Triffle indeed," the court voted unanimously that he had "rendered himself unworthy of holding his Commission in the Navy of the United Colonies of North America." Hopkins endorsed the findings, and Hazard became the Continental Navy's first officer to be cashiered.

Command of the *Providence* passed to Lieutenant Paul Jones, along with a temporary appointment as captain. Jones accepted with alacrity, although he had refused the offer when the fleet had been anchored off Philadelphia because he "had never sailed in a sloop" and was unfamiliar with the fore-and-aft rig. He would "not have accepted it now," he declared, "had it not been for the Rude Unhappy Temper of my late Commander. I now reflect with Pleasure that I had Philosophy Sufficient to Avoid Quarreling with him—and that I even Obtained his blessing at Parting. May he soon become of an Affable even disposition, and may he find Pleasure in Communicating Happiness arround him."

Ominously, on the same day that Hazard's court-martial met, Congress ordered that the Naval Committee's instructions to Commodore Hopkins be reread on the floor. A special committee was named to inquire into the degree to which he had followed his orders. This was the opening gun in a long and bitter campaign that had its roots in the sectional conflict among the colonies. Not only were there sharp differences between Northerners and Southerners, but New England and the middle colonies argued over boundaries and western lands. Petty squabbles between soldiers from the various colonies were common and often damaged military efficiency. Sectional feuding extended right into the Continental Congress so that there were few periods during the Revolution when it was not divided into cliques. Unfortunately, Hopkins could not have done a better job of widening the existing rifts if he had tried. The Southern colonies were bitterly disappointed by his failure to come to their aid as instructed. They were annoyed that he had by-passed them on the homeward voyage for New England. To add to their irritation he had taken it upon himself to offer the booty from New Providence to Connecticut and Rhode Island without even consulting Congress, breeding resentment in the colonies not so well favored. The commodore was keenly aware of the uneasiness of the Southerners, but told his brother, Stephen, "If they think I am partial in favour of the Northern Colonies they are greatly mistaken."

Congressional bickering was sharpened by the fleet's inability to get to sea again despite persistent urgings from Philadelphia for it to either sail south or attack the Newfoundland fisheries. For once, the commodore can be absolved of most of the blame. The major reason that the fleet lay idle was because it could not recruit men to replace those discharged or sick. Even at this early date, privateering was draining off men from the navy. Wages paid on privateers were from one and one-half to twice those in the navy. Even more important, the crew's share in a prize taken by a privateer was half or more of her value while Congress had limited it to one-third of ships taken by the navy. Besides, sailors shipping on privateers often got advances against their shares of prize money before sailing so that a seaman had something to leave with his family or to use for one last fling on shore. Adding to the problem, hundreds of seamen had enlisted in the army before the navy had been established. Now they were unavailable for service at sea. To fill out his crews, Hopkins secured the temporary loan of 170 men from General Washington when the army commander passed through New London on his way to New York.

Word was received in New London that the British squadron commanded by Captain Wallace had been forced to abandon its station off Newport because local militia had erected batteries armed with 18-pound guns that could command the anchorage. For the first time in years, Narragansett Bay was free of British warships, so Hopkins decided to move his vessels to Providence where he thought it would be easier to prepare for a three- or four-month cruise. Using the men borrowed from Washington, the fleet put to sea on April 19—only to be delayed when the *Alfred* ran aground off Fisher's Island. She had to be lightened by the removal of stores and guns. When he arrived in Providence, a discouraging and disheartening situation confronted the commodore. Another hundred sick men had to put ashore. Hopkins observed "there is daily more taken down with some New Malignant fever." Because of his influence in his hometown, and in return for twenty-six guns he had brought for the defense of Newport, Hopkins expected permission to enlist men from among the troops there. But shortly after his arrival, he received orders from Congress to send twenty of the cannon to Philadelphia and Washington sent a peremptory demand for the return of the men he had loaned the fleet. The first duty assigned to Captain Jones and his new command was to convoy the troops to New York.

There were plenty of seamen in Providence but few of them would have anything to do with the Continental Navy. There were too many reports of slow pay and bad treatment. And when pay was forthcoming, it was given in already depreciated Continental paper currency. "When we wished to spend it," noted Marine Lieutenant John Trevett, of the *Columbus*, "it would not pay for a pair of shoes." There were also complaints of brutality and mistreatment from the men. Before Hazard was cashiered, the crew of the *Providence* pleaded with Hopkins for his dismissal. "Cannot bear with it," they told him. They charged that Hazard used a weighted cane or a knotted rope's end "to beat us with and [we] are kept from morning to night uppon deck and have scarce time to eat . . . we are used like dogs on Board the *Providence*, we hope that you will find us a new Captain or a new Vessel."

Politics and string-pulling for preferment among the officers also played a part in preventing the fleet from putting to sea. Hopkins's officers knew the thirteen frigates Congress had authorized were nearing completion, and most of them did not want to be away at sea when new commissions were being awarded. The officers were jealous of each other's rank and would not cooperate. Most had obtained their positions through influence in Congress and since they expected the same "interest" to gain them higher rank, they saw no need to work aboard ship. Hopkins realized that his officers had friends to protect them and was hesitant about ordering courts-martial for offenders. "I wish to God and for the good of my Country that no Officer in the Fleet depended on any Friend, but their own Merit," he fervently declared.

As for the fleet itself, only two vessels, the *Doria* and *Cabot*, were sufficiently manned to go to sea—and that feat was accomplished only by stripping the rest of the ships of available hands. During a brief cruise, the *Doria* captured two of the fleet of Scotch transports that had already encountered Washington's navy. Biddle said he had taken the unarmed ships "with the speaking trumpet." [1] The *Alfred* was disabled and unfit for duty at sea. The commodore reported, "She is tender sided . . . and her main mast has a 9 lb shot through it." Discouraged, Hopkins wrote Congress: "I am ready to follow any Instructions that you give at all times but am very much in doubt whether it will be in my power to keep the Fleet together with any credit to my Self or the Officers that belong to it. . . ."

While the ships swung idly at anchor off Providence, the complaints against Hopkins multiplied in Congress. Reports of insubordination among the officers and desertion among the men had poured into Philadelphia. The special committee that had been appointed to look into Hopkins's conduct took no action, but the Marine Committee—which had succeeded the Naval Committee—reported on June 13 that it had received complaints against the commodore and Captains Saltonstall and Whipple "for breach of orders and other mal-practices." All three were ordered to come to Philadelphia "to answer for their conduct."

Transmitting the order to Hopkins the next day, John Hancock, the Marine Committee's chairman, wrote: "As your Conduct in many Instances requires Explanation, you will of course be questioned with respect to your whole proceedings since you left this City. I give you this Notice that you may come prepared to answer for your general Conduct. . . ." The summons could hardly have come as a surprise to the commodore. His brother had written him at the end of May warning him of the rising tide of criticism, and he had replied that if Congress were able to persuade someone "more able to serve the common Cause than I am . . . in the difficult department I am placed in . . . he shall have all the assistance in my power to give."

Hancock was more frank in a letter to Washington. "The shameful Inactivity of our Fleet for some Time past; the frequent Neglect or Disobedience of Orders in Commodore Hopkins, the numberless Complaints exhibited to the Marine Committee ag[ains]t him, and also against Captains Saltonstal and Whipple, have in-

---

[1] One of the transports was the *Oxford*, carrying a company of the Black Watch (42nd) Regiment, while the other was the *Crawford*, with a company of the 71st Regiment. Prize crews were put aboard both but the transports became separated from the *Doria*. They were retaken by the British, only to fall once more into American hands.

duced the Congress . . . to order them to repair immediately to this City to answer for their Conduct," he told the commander-in-chief.

Command of the fleet passed to Nicholas Biddle as the senior officer remaining behind, but he was admonished to take no initiative without the express order of Congress—a strange order since one of the charges against Hopkins was the inactivity of the fleet.

Accompanied by Saltonstall and Whipple,[2] Hopkins arrived in Philadelphia as Congress was moving toward a final break with Britain. The naval officers arrived in the city on July 2. The temperature was exactly 70 degrees at six o'clock in the morning, a tall, red-headed Virginian noted, and during the next three hours it rose another 8 degrees. By midafternoon, the atmosphere inside the State House was stifling. These statistics were recorded by Thomas Jefferson, who took the readings with a newly purchased thermometer. Jefferson also remembered to the end of his long life the horseflies that buzzed through the open windows from a nearby livery stable, no doubt hastening a vote on the issue: "*Resolved,* That these United Colonies are, and, of right, ought to be, Free and Independent States. . . ."

Despite the dramatic events unfolding before Congress, the Marine Committee plunged ahead with its inquiry. Such officers of the *Alfred* and *Columbus* who were available were summoned to testify. On July 11, the committee reported "that the charge against Captain Saltonstal does not appear to the committee to be well founded, and that the charge against Captain Whipple amounts to nothing more than a rough, indelicate mode of behaviour to his marine officers." Both men were ordered to report back to their ships, although the committee admonished Whipple to "cultivate harmony with his officers." The charges against Hopkins were not disposed of so swiftly. He was kept dangling in uncertainty until the middle of August.

The commodore finally got the chance to tell his side of the story on August 12, when he appeared before Congress. The main point of his defense to the charge that he had disregarded his instruc-

---

[2] Whipple had taken the *Columbus* to sea on June 16, only to run into the British frigate *Cerberus*, 28. She fired three broadsides into the American ship, killing one man and cutting up her rigging rather badly. "I got in one broadside," Whipple reported, "but probably did her no damage."

tions was that conditions had changed between the time they were given him and the time he had sailed. Because of this change in situation, he had exercised the prerogative given him in his orders and had followed an alternate plan. As for turning the cannon over to the Rhode Island and Connecticut authorities, he contended that he had "no apprehension of the cannon being wanted more anywhere else, which was the reason of my delivering them to Governours Cooke and Trumbull."

The delegates questioned Hopkins at length, and quizzed two witnesses before going into closed session. With John Adams leading the defense, the debate was heated. Recognizing that the commodore had shortcomings and limitations, Adams frankly admitted them. But he also recognized that other influences besides the question of Hopkins's conduct were at work. "On this occasion I had a very laborious task against all the prejudices of the gentlemen from the Southern and Middle States and many from New England," he later recalled. "I thought, however, that Hopkins had done a great service, and made an important beginning of naval operations. It appeared to me that the Commodore was pursued and persecuted by that anti-New England spirit which haunted Congress in many other of their proceedings. . . .

"I saw nothing in the conduct of Hopkins, which indicated corruption or want of integrity. Experience and skill might have been deficient in several particulars: but where could we find greater experience or skill? I knew of none to be found," Adams continued. After the trial was over, William Ellery, who had succeeded Samuel Ward as a Rhode Island delegate, came over to Adams and told him: "You have made the old man your friend for life."

For all of Adams's efforts and eloquence, a strong case could be made against Hopkins. His explanations for failing to attack the enemy off the Southern coast were unsatisfactory to congressmen from that area. While there is no doubt that anti-New England feeling worked against him, Hopkins's own actions had helped to create the antagonism. He neither could nor would accept the concept that the navy had been created for the good of all the states, remarks a biographer.[3] He was also handicapped by his professional limitations. Although the New Providence raid was the most successful op-

---

[3] Morgan, *Captains to the Northward.*

eration carried out by the Continental Navy, he had almost botched it. And the night fight with the *Glasgow* illustrated all too well the commodore's inexperience in handling a fleet of fighting ships. Congress decided that blame for the failures of the navy had to be placed somewhere, and it fell naturally upon the shoulders of the commander-in-chief. If Congress were to exonerate Hopkins, some of the blame would have to be accepted by Congress itself. So, on August 16, Congress resolved "that the said conduct of Commodore Hopkins deserves the censure of this House and this house does accordingly censure him." Three days later he was ordered to return to Rhode Island to resume command of the fleet. Still, the sentence was not as severe as it might have been. Paul Jones, who was at sea in the *Providence* when he heard of the outcome of the trial, wrote a sympathetic note to his commander. "Your late trouble will tend to your future advantage by pointing out your friends and enemies," he wrote. "You will thereby be enabled to retain the one part while you guard against the other."

The fleet to which Commodore Hopkins returned, reduced in prestige, faced the same difficulty in the fall that had confronted it in the spring—the impossibility of recruiting enough seamen because of the competition of the privateers. Repeatedly, Hopkins urged Congress to increase the share of prize money allotted to the crews of naval vessels from the sale of captured ships and goods. Jones joined in, writing Robert Morris, a member of the Marine Committee, that it was impossible to engage seamen for the fleet as long as the privateers allotted them the full value of prizes while the navy was limited to one-third. Unless this was corrected, and "the private Emoluments of individuals in our Navy is made superior to that in Privateers it can never become respectable—it never will become formidible. And without a Respectable Navy—alas America! . . . If our Enemies, with the best established and most formidible Navy in the Universe, have found it expedient to assign all Prizes to the Captors —how much more is such policy essential to our infant Fleet."

For once, Congress listened. The captor's share of prize merchantman, storeship, or transport was increased to one-half, while they were given the entire proceeds if the prize were a man-of-war or a privateer. This was a step in the right direction although competition for crews from the privateers and squabbles over prize money continued to trouble the Continental Navy throughout the war. What was to be the proportion for each officer and man? And how should prize money be divided among a fleet? Should the crew of a sloop receive the same share as that of a frigate? Congress had tried to settle the question on January 6, 1776, by dividing the shares of a prize into twentieths after the government had received its half of the proceeds. Even this did not compare favorably with the British system, as the twentieths were really fortieths because the government took half the proceeds.

Prize money was a powerful incentive in the age of fighting sail. At a time when pay for both officers and the lower deck was pitiful, prize money was the dream of every captain and every ship's boy. On occasion, great sums were awarded. Admirals and captains were made rich for life by the proceeds of a single voyage. For example, after the British captured Havana in 1762, 736,000 pounds in prize money was divided—with the admiral's share reaching 122,697 pounds. A fourteen-year-old cabin boy earned $700 in prize money after a single month's cruise with Jones in the *Ranger* in 1779. He was also entitled to a ton of sugar, some thirty-five gallons of rum and twenty pounds each of cotton, ginger, logwood, and allspice.

A seaman's potential proceeds were still greater from a successful privateering voyage, so Hopkins desperately sought help from the General Assembly of Rhode Island to enlist men for the navy. He asked them to declare an embargo on the recruitment of seamen for privateers until the fleet was fully manned. The move failed by two votes. Too many of the members were deeply involved in privateering themselves. "I thought I had some Influence in the State I have lived so Long in, but find now that Private interest bears more Sway than I wish it did," he despaired in a letter to Hancock. "I am at a loss how we shall get the Ships mann'd." Fully one-third of the men who signed up for the navy took the month's pay advanced them and shipped on privateers. The commodore expressed the hope that Congress would give him the power to not only take deserters from privateers but to seize the entire crew when he found navy men on board. "That might make them more cautious in taking the Men out of the Service of the State," he declared.

Hopkins also discovered that some of Rhode Island's leading merchants, who were members of a committee overseeing the building of the frigates *Warren* and *Providence*, were diverting material and manpower from naval construction to work on their own privateers. He openly accused them of malpractice, thereby severing his relations with the most powerful element in Rhode Island. Because of this mismanagement, Hopkins later claimed, the two frigates "cost twice as much as the contract price." And as if he didn't already have enough headaches, the commodore was besieged by the Reverend Stephen Hopkins, a hell-fire preacher from Newport (who was not a relative), about the strong language used by sailors. "I did not enter the Navy as a Divine," Hopkins replied. "The Congress whom I serve made provisions for a Chaplain to perform that necessary duty, but to my Mortification I have not been able to get a single Man to act in that Character although I have applied to many. If you know of any that has the good of Mankind at heart Sufficient to expose himself to necessary Danger of that Service should be glad you would send him. . . ."

While Hopkins vied with the Rhode Island privateersmen for sailors, the Marine Committee bombarded him with suggestions for action. There was another plan for attacking the Newfoundland fisheries followed by orders that he proceed to Cape Fear in North Carolina to attack three British men-of-war lurking in the area. Unfortunately for the commodore, the orders usually arrived at a time when various segments of the fleet had managed to get to sea individually or in small groups. Either that, or the ships were undergoing necessary repair.

Before the general use of copper sheathing on the bottoms of wooden ships,[4] a vessel had to be hove down or careened every few months so it could be cleaned of a thick accumulation of barnacles and weeds that had become attached to the hull, slowing the ship down considerably. The vessel was run onto a smooth beach or a mud flat and guns, ballast, stores, and upper masts were removed. All openings in the hull, such as gunports and scuttles, were caulked tight. She was pulled over on her side by means of block and tackle attached to the masts. The crew fell to work scraping and burning the accumulated growth off one side of the bottom and it was coated with pitch and painted. Then the process was repeated for the other side and the ship was re-armed, re-rigged, and floated. Expert

---

[4] The practice of copper sheathing the bottom of ships began in the Royal Navy in 1758 but was not widespread until the middle of the American war.

handling was required in such an operation. If there was a mistake, the hull might dip under water and the ship would be flooded.

To the members of the Marine Committee, the failure of the fleet to move was simply blatant disregard of its orders. The ill feeling toward Hopkins intensified in Philadelphia. For example, John Jay sarcastically asked Edward Rutledge, a member of the committee: "What is your fleet and noble admiral doing?" Only "tenderhearted charity" could have prevented the dismissal of "that pretty genius," Jay observed.

The most successful of the independent cruises was made by Paul Jones in the *Providence*. On August 8, Congress confirmed his promotion to captain after ordering him to "take, Sink, Burn or destroy" all the enemy vessels he could find in the waters around Bermuda. The little Scot was nettled when he learned that his seniority in rank was not established as of the time that Hopkins had promoted him in May, but he got the *Providence* to sea with a minimum of delay. In the three months Jones had commanded the *Providence*, he had found her fast and maneuverable. He had a crew of about seventy men—the best he ever commanded, he was to say in later years—and they had been well-drilled in the use of the vessel's dozen 4-pounders.

A few days after putting to sea, Jones had taken several prizes and had escaped a British frigate. The *Providence* had been nipping at the heels of a group of merchantmen under convoy by the *Solebay*, 28, when the frigate turned and gave chase. After a day-long pursuit, she had drawn within musket shot of Jones's vessel. Until then, neither ship had shown its colors. "I now ordered ours to be hoisted and began to fire at them," Jones reported. "Upon this they also hoisted American colors and fired guns to leeward," which was the signal for "I am friendly." Jones did not swallow the bait, knowing the Continental Navy had no ship of this type at sea. Taking advantage of the nimbleness of the *Providence*, he quickly bore away after boldly crossing the frigate's bow. "Had he forseen this motion and been prepared to counteract it, he might have fired several broadsides . . . which would have done us very material damage," Jones said. "But he was a bad marksman . . . and did not touch the *Providence* with one of the many shots he fired."

After his encounter with the *Solebay*, several more prizes fell into Jones's bag, followed by a dry period. Jones decided that most of the British West Indiamen were homeward bound and out of his reach, as the hurricane season had begun, so he turned the bow of his sloop northward to replenish his supplies of wood and water. The run to Nova Scotia was stormy. A heavy gale forced him to dismount the ship's guns and "stick everything I could into the hold." The weather abated, and on September 20, as the *Providence* lay hove-to so the sailors could use the fishing tackle that Adams had ordered for Continental ships, a frigate was sighted. The man-of-war bore down on the *Providence* but the sloop danced away. A curious mock-engagement took place.

"I shortened sail to give him a wild goose chase and tempt him to throw away powder and shot," Jones related. "He excited my contempt so much by his continued firing at much more than twice the proper distance, that when he rounded to, to give his broadside, I ordered my marine officer to return the salute with only a single musket." Next morning, the frigate was seen standing toward Halifax. Accordingly Jones went to work with a will on the fishing fleet off Canso. Finally, repeated gales turned him toward the safety of Narragansett Bay. The *Providence* had taken sixteen prizes—half of them sent into port under prize crews and the other half lost or destroyed. The English fishing fleet in the area had been ruined.

Upon rejoining Hopkins, the exuberant Jones unveiled a plan for an expedition to the west coast of Africa with the aim of destroying Britain's African trade. Part of his plan included the capture of St. Helena, in order to take the East Indiamen that called there on their way home. The commodore had other plans. He ordered Jones to take the *Alfred*—Saltonstall having been appointed captain of one of the new frigates—and, in an attempt to put one of the plans broached by the Marine Committee into action, to return to Cape Breton to attack the fishery, capture the coal fleet, and to release about a hundred American prisoners forced to work in the Sydney mines.[5]

By taking all the able-bodied men from the *Providence* and from his prizes, Jones managed to get a complement large enough to work the *Alfred*. Accompanied by Hoystead Hacker in the *Hampden*, one

---

[5] The British were not the only ones to use mines for prisoners. Important Loyalists were imprisoned in the Simsbury copper mines in Connecticut where they were kept in cells more than a hundred feet below ground. Being sent to the mines was considered "a Shock Sentence —Worse than Death."

of the prizes he had taken, Jones put to sea on October 27. Unfortunately Hacker ran his command on a sunken ledge even before the ships had cleared Narragansett Bay, badly damaging her. The crew was transferred to the *Providence*, and a second start was made on November 1. On the way through Vineyard Sound, Jones sent a boarding party aboard the Rhode Island privateer *Eagle*, which he had reason to believe had enlisted deserters from the navy. Two deserters from the fleet and two from the army were discovered hiding behind a false bulkhead. Jones took them and twenty other men from the privateer's crew—a move that stirred a hornet's nest back in Rhode Island. The *Eagle*'s owners sued Jones for damages. Somehow Jones became convinced that Hopkins had disavowed his action although in reality the commodore had backed him to the hilt. "I can't but believe that Captn. Jones did as he thought best for the good of the Publick," he wrote the Marine Committee. When Jones returned from the cruise, Hopkins informed him that he had brought a countersuit against the *Eagle*'s captain for enlisting navy deserters. Eventually, both suits were dropped, but Jones's easy relationship with his commander was at an end. From this time on Jones's letters are bitterly critical of Hopkins.

Cruising off Louisburg, on Cape Breton Island, Jones took several rich prizes. On the morning of November 12, he fell in with the armed transport *Mellish* loaded with ten thousand winter uniforms and other supplies for the British army assembling in Canada for an invasion of the Northern states under General Burgoyne. "This prize is, I believe, the most valuable that has been taken by American arms," Jones told the Marine Committee. "She made some defense, it was trifling. The loss will distress the enemy more than can be easily imagined, as the clothing aboard her is the last intended to be sent out for Canada this season." She was too valuable a prize to risk the possibility of recapture, so Jones put a prize crew aboard and ordered the *Mellish*'s new skipper to remain within signaling distance of the *Alfred*.

Trouble had been brewing among the pick-up crew on the *Providence* even before the men had left Narragansett Bay. A week before sailing, a gunner had been court-martialed for having "collared and otherwise abused" Captain Hacker when they were still aboard the *Hampden*. Now officers and men were complaining that the sloop's leaky condition made her unsafe in rough weather. They believed she was too shorthanded to fight because so many seamen had been assigned to prize crews. Jones said he could "see no Just foundation" for the complaints and tried to inspire Hacker's crew "in our endeavours to relieve our Captive, ill treated Brethern from the Coal Mines." But it was all to no avail. During one stormy night, the *Providence* parted company with the *Alfred* and sailed back to Rhode Island alone. The "Epedemical Discontent" then spread to Jones's own ship. "The season was indeed Severe and everyone was for returning immediately to port," but Jones was determined to press on to the northward. Lying off Canso on November 22, he sent in armed boats that burned a grounded supply ship and an oil warehouse, and took away a small, fast schooner to serve as a tender.

Two days later, Jones's tiny squadron was moving through a thick fog when three strange sail were sighted. Alarm spread through the *Alfred* because a resident of Canso had informed Captain Jones that three British frigates had been dispatched to search for him following his cruise in the *Providence*. "Resolving to sell my liberty as dear as possible," Jones stood in toward the nearest of the ships only to find that they were colliers bound from Sydney to New York under convoy of a frigate which was out of sight in the fog. The colliers were taken without a fight. A crewman aboard one of them reported that the American prisoners working in the coal mines had enlisted in the Royal Navy. Scrubbing this part of his mission, Jones turned westward toward home. The next day, November 25, he took another valuable prize, the 10-gun British letter-of-marque *John*.[6] Putting a prize crew aboard under the command of Lieutenant Robert Sanders, Jones added the *John* to his flotilla.

With the *Alfred* in the van, the seven ships were crossing the northern edge of George Bank, east of Cape Cod, on December 8, when the squadron encountered the British frigate *Milford*, 28, one of the vessels sent in search of Jones. Luckily, it was getting dark. To throw the frigate off the scent while he saved his prizes, Jones sent a bright lantern aloft to the top of the *Alfred*'s mainmast to attract the attention of the *Milford*'s skipper as he tacked to the northeast in company with the *John*. At the same time, the prizes were ordered to maintain course to the southwest and they slipped by the frigate in the darkness.

---

[6] A letter of marque was an armed merchant ship authorized to take prizes. Unlike a privateer, however, her main duty was to carry cargo.

When daylight came, the *Mellish* and the other prizes had dropped below the horizon. Jones had not got a good enough look at the frigate the night before to determine her strength and ordered Lieutenant Sanders in the *John* to lay back and "make the Signal Agreed on if She was of Superiour or inferiour Force." Sometime later, the signal was made that the enemy ship was of "Superiour Force." The chase continued in squally weather. Because the *Alfred* was increasing her lead, the *Milford* halted the pursuit and turned to the *John*, which was lagging behind. She was forced to surrender with a few well-placed shots across her bow. Later, Jones berated Sanders for surrendering without a fight. A bitter Sanders got word to Commodore Hopkins from his captivity in Halifax that he felt Jones had left him in the lurch by not coming to his assistance. Looking back over the dispute, it seems fairly clear that Sanders had no choice but to haul down his colors or be blown out of the water. In addition, the *Milford*'s log states that the *Alfred* was twelve miles ahead when the frigate captured the *John*—too far away to be any help. The real unresolved question is why Jones did not signal Sanders to clap on all sail and make a getaway instead of lagging behind, or why Sanders didn't do so on his own initiative.

Be that as it may, the *Alfred* made it safely into Boston with only two days of provisions left. The *Mellish* and her valuable cargo of uniforms and most of the other prizes managed to avoid British cruisers and got into various ports. Luckily, none of them tried to make for Rhode Island, since a powerful squadron commanded by Commodore Sir Peter Parker had captured Newport on December 7 without opposition. This victory was the final blow to Hopkins's fleet. With British ships and British troops controlling the area about Newport, Hopkins's vessels were blockaded in Narragansett Bay without hope of escape before spring. The only service they could provide was to protect Providence from an attack up the bay. The fleet that had so proudly charted its course from Delaware Bay just a year before ended its life swinging idly at anchor in the Providence River.

IX

Architects of Defeat

Naval supremacy was the foundation of British strategy in America.[1] The Royal Navy gave British troops their mobility—what Washington called their "canvas wings." During 1776 alone, it enabled the King's forces to evacuate Boston safely, move south for an attack on Charleston, capture New York, and try to split New England off from the rest of the new nation. Command of the sea provided the British with the ability to concentrate superior forces at any chosen point along the coast. The Americans, restricted by primitive overland communications and lacking an adequate navy, could do nothing to thwart British troop movements. Throughout the long years of war, British maneuverability was a major problem for George Washington. Constant and irritating inability to cope with it turned the commander-in-chief into an ardent student of naval strategy. Within a month after the victory at Yorktown—a victory made possible only by a French fleet's momentary control of the Chesapeake Capes—he wrote Lafayette: "No land force can act decisively unless it is ac-

---

[1] The discussion of the operation of the British war machine in this and succeeding chapters is based upon Piers Mackesy's excellent account of the war from the British side, *The War for America 1775–1783* (Cambridge, Mass. 1965). Mackesy adopts a less critical attitude toward the British leadership than many scholars.

companied by maritime superiority. . . . For proof of this, we have only to recur to the . . . ease and facility with which the British shifted their ground, as advantages were to be obtained at either extremity of the continent, and to their heavy loss the moment they failed in their naval superiority."

The advantage of naval superiority was never applied intelligently. The mobility provided by seapower was often dissipated in raids and diversionary attacks. From the outset of the fighting, the British were committed to a division of their land and naval forces. The war for America is a tale of major operations combined with uncoordinated diversions. For the most part, the army was committed in "penny packets" and little use was made of the fleet to effect surprise. Despite their endless problems, the rebels were almost always able to adopt countermeasures in time to prevent disaster.

The direction of war emanated from London. The administrative machinery was substantially the same that had served the nation with varying degrees of success and efficiency during the earlier wars of the century. Throughout the American war, ministers displayed a consuming urge to control every movement of the troops and ships from their offices in Whitehall. The idea that long-range control of generals and admirals by political leaders is a product of our own era of instant communications is a fallacy. Exasperated by orders, counterorders, memorandums, and suggestions, General Sir Henry Clinton once exploded to a superior: "For God's sake, my Lord, if you wish me to do anything, leave me to myself!"

At the top of the administrative pyramid was a monarch. George III was thirty-seven in 1775 and had been king for fifteen years. He was a tall, awkward man with an oval face marked by thick, straight lips and vapid blue eyes set wide apart. In an age of easy morality, he was a family man who worked at being king with the dogged industry of his German ancestors. Fate had made him the ruler of Britain at a time when kings were still expected to govern, and he was determined to exercise the prerogatives of the Crown. He was not a soldier as his grandfather had been, but as the army's captain-general, he took a keen interest in its operations. If he did not actually choose his commanders, he insisted that they at least be acceptable to him. The King could not direct military affairs personally, but he could and did exert influence through his ministers, who controlled overall strategy and day-to-day operations.

The King's contribution to the war effort was moral. He tried to encourage his ministers, to stir their energies and to check the able and eloquent pro-American opposition. Most of all, he had to buoy up his boyhood friend, Lord North, who lacked the vitality to manage the war effort or lead his colleagues in the Cabinet. "Upon military matters I speak ignorantly, and therefore without effect," the Prime Minister confessed. Tormented by moods of depression and melancholia, he often talked of retiring. After 1778, when the power of France and Spain had begun to be felt in the war—if not before— he doubted the wisdom of continuing the conflict with the Americans. He was kept at his task only by the King who believed it easier to work with a man whose failings he knew rather than to chance another.

The Cabinet consisted of eight or nine chief ministers, with North presiding as First Lord of the Treasury. With him sat three Secretaries of State, the Lord Chancellor, the Lord President of the Council, the Lord Privy Seal, the First Lord of the Admiralty and, after 1778, the Commander-in-Chief of the Army. Business was usually conducted by convening the four or five members whose departments were most intimately concerned with the war, Mackesy notes. There were weekly Cabinet dinners. When they were over, those who could stay awake discussed the nation's business. In the heated political atmosphere of the period, it was common practice to seek full Cabinet authority for unpopular measures. "Every expedition in regard to its destination, object, force, and the number of ships is planned by the Cabinet, and is the result of the collective wisdom of all his Majesty's confidential ministers," Sandwich told the House of Lords. "The First Lord of the Admiralty is only the executive servant of these measures."

After the Cabinet made its plans, it was the task of the three Secretaries of State to carry them out by issuing "timely orders, to the Treasury, Admiralty, Ordnance, and Commander-in-Chief of the Army." One Secretary presided over the Northern Department and another over the Southern Department. Between them, they divided responsibility for the execution of foreign and military policy in Northern and Southern Europe. Until 1768, the jurisdiction of the Southern Secretary had extended to the American colonies. In that year, a Secretary was appointed[2] to head the American Department.

---

[2] Edmund Burke explained the creation of the American secretaryship by saying: "The two secretaries are doing nothing so a third was appointed to help them."

When war broke out in the colonies, the American Secretary became the center of the ministry's efforts to stamp out the rebellion. It was his responsibility to see the functioning of the war machine. What little coordination that occurred resulted from his efforts. If a well-provisioned striking force assembled on schedule with adequate naval support, it was due to the work of the American Secretary. Yet the other secretaries could and did make their influence felt. Specific orders to embark troops from Ireland to America could only be issued by the Southern Secretary, while the Northern Secretary was responsible for the hiring of mercenaries in Germany.

Supply and transport difficulties emphasized the ramshackle, chaotic state of the war machine. Every biscuit, every bullet, every man required by the British army in America, had to be carried across 3,000 miles of Atlantic Ocean—the most massive effort of its kind until the Twentieth Century. The officials responsible for formulating British policy failed to recognize the importance of this logistical problem. In the long run it cost them the war. Summing up the situation, Admiral James Gambier wrote: "Our army . . . is healthy, brave and zealous . . . [but] Twelve hundred leagues with its natural difficulties demand a solemn thought—the means and expense." Failure to understand the relationship between strategy, logistics, and shipping resources permeated almost every aspect of British conduct of the war. David Syrett, in a study of Britain's logistical and administrative problems, writes that campaigns were planned without attempting to determine whether the transports and the supply craft to carry out the movement were available. Few persons realized that the decision to stamp out the rebellion meant that large numbers of troops would have to be supplied from home and thousands of tons of shipping would be required.[3]

Provisions for the fleet were supplied by the navy's Victualling Board while the Treasury performed the same function for the army. The Board of Ordnance provided other stores and equipment for both services. While the Victualling Board gathered the navy's supply ships, the Navy Board, which operated independently of the Admiralty, hired supply ships for the Army after the Treasury relinquished the job in 1779. The Ordnance Board handled the transport

---

[3] David Syrett, *Shipping in the American War 1775–83* (London 1970).

of engineers and artillery to America; the navy furnished transport for infantry, cavalry, clothing, and other supplies. By July 1776, the Navy Board alone controlled 127,000 tons of shipping—no small amount in an era in which the average transport was of 250 to 450 tons displacement. Competition for shipping among the various agencies was rampant. There was hoarding and there were shortages of bottoms for charter.

Conditions under which the soldiers lived on board the transports were bad even by the standards of the time, reports Syrett. He quotes one account as stating: "The men were packed like herring. A tall man could not stand upright between decks, nor sit up straight in his berth. To each such berth six men were allotted, but as there was room for only four, the last two had to squeeze in as best they could." A Guards officer described transport life as "continued destruction in the foretops, the pox above-board, the plague between decks, hell in the forecastle, the devil at the helm." After a rough passage to America, a German officer declared: "It may be safely said that the most strenuous campaign cannot be as trying as such a voyage." Tempers frayed among the men herded together below decks during the long, tedious voyages. Some went mad. A duel was fought in the mid-Atlantic in 1776 in which a cousin of the Landgrave of Hesse was killed. There were two successful suicide attempts and one unsuccessful try among the Royal Welch Fusiliers on the way to the relief of Quebec that same year. Disease was rampant on the transports. Far more men and horses died at sea from sickness than were captured by enemy action.

Corrupt contractors profiteered on poor-quality provisions. Delays in shipping caused some supplies to go bad before the supply vessels sailed. Yankee privateersmen who captured British supply ships complained of the poor quality of the provisions. Moldy bread, wormy flour, rancid butter, and maggoty beef were often found. Admiral Thomas Graves, trying to revictual his fleet in New York in 1781, reported that the bread given him had been so long on the supply ships that "very little of it is fit to eat." Salt meat and rum had been so badly stowed that "the meat stinks and is seldom fit to eat [and] the rum casks damaged." Syrett observes that considering the conditions surrounding Britain's logistical operations, it is surprising that the British army in America received any supplies at all.

With the American Secretary controlling the war machine, it is easy to see why the King was eager to fill the post with a minister who favored "Roman severity" in dealing with the rebels. He found him in the person of Lord George Germain. On November 10, 1775, the indecisive and ineffectual Earl of Dartmouth was dismissed and replaced with Germain. He lost no time in setting out to be the "one great director" demanded by the King's supporters, a latter-day Pitt who could provide strong leadership in the Cabinet and energetic, vigorous conduct of the war. By gathering the full force of Great Britain in one mighty effort, Germain expected to end the war in a single campaign. According to his Lordship, 1776 was to be the year of decision. "Nothing is so much to be wished for as a decisive action," he declared. "One decisive blow by land is absolutely necessary. After that, the whole will depend upon the diligence and activity of the officers of the Navy."

Few British politicians have had so bad a press as Germain. He and Sandwich share the dubious distinction of being blamed for the prolongation and eventual loss of the American war. The common verdict of history is summed up in the statements that Germain was "probably the most incompetent official that ever held an important post at a critical moment" and that his tenure marks "the nadir of British military competence." Germain certainly had failures of character and shortcomings in the field of global strategy, but an impartial re-examination of the evidence against the haughty aristocrat indicates that he has been excessively condemned. He was very much a creature of the eighteenth century and it is unjust to judge him by the standards of a later age, Mackesy suggested.

Born Lord George Sackville in 1716, Germain was the third son of the Earl of Dorset and grew up in the great house at Knole, with its fifty-two staircases—one for each week of the year—and 365 rooms—one for each day. He became a soldier and through preferment quickly moved up in rank, becoming a lieutenant colonel at the age of twenty-five. He fought at the head of his regiment against the French at Fontenoy in 1745 and was badly wounded. By this time, young Sackville had acquired a lasting reputation for cold haughtiness. "He never had the art of conciliating affection," wrote Horace Walpole, who collected the gossip of the day. "His pride, which was naturally very great, grew into the most intolerable insolence."

Then came disaster. Lord George, by then a lieutenant general, had gone to Germany to command a detachment of British troops serving under Prince Ferdinand of Brunswick. At the battle of Minden on August 1, 1759, he delayed sending his cavalry forward after the retreating French infantry, preventing the almost certain destruction of the enemy force. Sackville was court-martialed at his own request to clear his name—foolishly as it turned out—unleashing long pent-up political animosities. He was found guilty of disobedience and "adjudged unfit to serve His Majesty in any military capacity whatever." It is said that George II struck him off the Army List and Privy Council books with his own hand. Sackville's treatment was considered unnecessarily vindictive by the public so it was not long before he made a successful entry into politics as a supporter of Lord North. In 1770, he assumed the name Germain, having inherited property from Lady Betty Germain, whose will had included this stipulation. That same year, his conduct in a duel caused by a slur from "a noisy politician" brought him public approbation. "In some eyes," commented Walpole, "Lord George Germain is a hero, whatever Lord George Sackville may have been."

The rebellion of what Germain called "the American peasants" was brewing and Lord George sensed in it the path back to power. He was shrewd enough to see that young King George III would sooner or later have to welcome anyone who championed the right of the monarch to rule the colonies by force. Germain offered the Americans only two alternatives: the sword or submission. Through the repeated statement of his views in Parliament, Germain came to be regarded as something of an expert on American affairs, although he had never visited the colonies. North, who looked upon the suppression of the rebellion as at best a regrettable necessity, was more and more impressed by Lord George's self-assured manner and strength of will.

When Germain came to power, he was sixty years old. A reserved and lonely man, he rarely dined out during the war except for the weekly Cabinet dinners. His unpopularity in some circles was increased by rumors that he was a homosexual. His association with Benjamin Thompson, a young American Loyalist who later became Count Rumford, created talk—especially after Thompson went to live in Germain's home. The American Secretary was vulnerable on other grounds. The "Ghost of Minden" was always being trotted out by the opposition, and he was scarcely a political asset to the ministry. There was considerable ill will between Germain and his three most important generals, Clinton, Howe, and Guy Carleton, the commander in Canada. Some of the bitterness extended back over the years to when Germain had been in the army. During his struggle to establish the "third" secretaryship on a par with the Northern and Southern Departments, he antagonized the other secretaries even though close cooperation was needed to manage the war. There was endless bickering over fine points of precedence and jurisdiction while important papers and orders were not written or delivered. Yet, a subordinate who saw him at work wrote that Germain "had all the requisites of a great minister, unless popularity and good luck are to be numbered among them."

The coolness between Germain and the other two Secretaries of State may have been damaging to the British cause, but the animosity that grew between him and Sandwich was fatal, according to Mackesy. The First Lord of the Admiralty was the one man in the Cabinet with whom a complete understanding was essential for the successful conduct of the war. It was all the more so in a ministry such as North's where the leader was wavering and undecided. Friction between Sandwich and Germain began early. It started with the American Secretary's biting criticism of the navy's unpreparedness for the war and its inability to protect transports and supply ships from Yankee cruisers. Soon it extended to its admirals and their operations. "I never could understand the real state of the fleet," an exasperated Germain once confided to Lord North. If the First Lord of the Admiralty approved a Cabinet proposal, there were always ships available, he noted. If Sandwich disapproved, the necessary bottoms could never be found.

Because the Royal Navy played such an important role in the loss of the American colonies, most of the blame has been assigned to John Montagu, Fourth Earl of Sandwich, who was its civilian head throughout the war. Sandwich has been wryly dubbed "the real father of American independence" because of his failure to prepare the navy for war and to fight energetically after the conflict had broken out. Unpopular enough in his own time to be described as:

> Too infamous to have friend,
> Too bad for bad men to commend,

he has been the victim of Whig historians who damned everyone associated with the North ministry. Even worse, Sandwich was a political apostate, having switched from the Whigs to the "King's Friends" when that became the road to power. On top of everything, his reputation for success with women created the picture of a dissolute rake and gambler. After all, the Earl did keep his mistress, by whom he had several illegitimate children, at the Admiralty, and he is supposed to have invented the sandwich so that he could spend more time at the gaming tables. Conventional historical wisdom depicts him as "a man entirely without nautical experience and far too much engrossed by his pleasures to concern himself with the disagreeable details of administration."

Recent research—including publication of Sandwich's papers—has disposed of the legend that Sandwich's regime at the Admiralty was a carnival of corruption and incompetence. No civilian politician had more experience in the post, and the truth appears to be that he was a first-rate administrator. He had already been First Lord twice before being re-appointed in 1771. Even such an unrelenting critic as Horace Walpole observed: "His passion for maritime affairs, his activity, industry, and flowing complaisance endeared him to the profession, re-established the marine, and effaced a great part of his unpopularity. No man in the Administration was so much master of his business, so quick or so shrewd." During his first tour in the post, in 1749, he instituted a system of inspecting the dockyards and other naval establishments to examine their condition and readiness. This seems an obvious step today but was considered a radical departure at the time. Important achievements of Sandwich's last administration were the dispatch of Captain James Cook on his second and third voyages, the coppering of the bottoms of all the navy's ships, and the introduction in 1779 of the carronade—a short-barreled heavy-hitting gun designed for smashing the sides of enemy ships.[4]

Sandwich's unpopularity stemmed from his participation in 1763 in the persecution of John Wilkes. Both Wilkes and Sandwich had been members of a notorious group known as the Monks of Medmenham, or more commonly as the Hellfire Club. The gossip of the time described it as a society in which the members dressed as

---

[4] The carronade was first cast at the Carron foundry in Scotland, hence its name.

monks and took part in bizarre religious rites. They were supposed
to have entertained lady friends who were masked and wore nuns'
habits at the house they had taken in the country. Some accounts say
the "nuns" were ladies of quality; others say they were prostitutes
imported from London for the entertainment of the "monks." The
club fell apart when political differences split the members—differences that were exacerbated by Wilkes when he began attacking
the government of which Sandwich and other "monks" were members, in his weekly newspaper, the *North Briton*, and in Commons.
There is a story that one day Wilkes encountered the Earl. "Wilkes,
you will either die on the gallows or of a pox," warned Sandwich.
"That depends," retorted the editor, "on whether I embrace your
Lordship's principles or your mistress."

Unable because of his Parliamentary immunity to have Wilkes
arrested for statements that the ministry considered libelous, the
government resolved upon a plan to strip him of it. The weapon was
an obscene parody of Pope's "Essay on Man" entitled "Essay on
Woman" that Wilkes had had printed in a very limited edition. It is
quite possible that Sandwich had read and chuckled over a copy at
Medmenham. One account states that it began "Awake my Sandwich." The Earl planned to read this "Essay" in the House of Lords
to destroy sympathy for Wilkes, paving the way for his expulsion
from Commons. The government's supporters reasoned that it would
be difficult to defend a man caught with a dirty book in his pocket.
So we have the curious spectacle of an outraged Sandwich in the role
of guardian of the public morals reading choice excerpts of the
"Essay" to the attentive peers. Also put into the record was an accompanying commentary—jokingly attributed to the Bishop of
Gloucester—that was if anything more obscene than the poem. To
add to the hypocrisy of the situation, Sandwich had been expelled
from the Beefsteak Club not too long before for blasphemy. It was
the first time, commented one Hellfire Club member, that he had
ever heard the devil preach.

Sandwich's strategy worked perfectly—except in one respect.
Although Commons voted to expel Wilkes, he had become a popular
hero. His constituents repeatedly re-elected him amid cries of
"Wilkes and Liberty!" Soon after the "Essay on Woman" affair, *The
Beggar's Opera* was presented at Covent Garden. When in the last
scene, Captain Macheath declared "that Jemmy Twitcher [a member

of his own gang] should peach me I own surprised me," the audience burst into laughter. The nickname of Jemmy Twitcher was immediately applied to Sandwich, who had "peached" on Wilkes—and it stuck to him for the rest of his life.

The Earl's personal appearance was also against him. Tall, shambling, and as weatherbeaten as any of his sailors, Sandwich had an odd look about him. Charles Churchill, a friend of Wilkes, once said that Sandwich looked as if he had been "half-hanged" and "cut down by mistake." Seeing him at a distance, one acquaintance noted, "I am sure it is Lord Sandwich; for, if you observe, he is walking down both sides of the street at once." Sandwich could joke about his appearance. Speaking of his French dancing master, he said "the man was very civil and on taking leave of him I offered him any service in London. 'Then,' replied he with a bow, 'I should take it as a personal favour if your Lordship would never tell anyone of whom you learned to dance.' " His wit sometimes appeared in his political dealings. Answering a letter from a critic, he replied: "Sir, your letter is before me, and will presently be behind."

"A legend persists that Sandwich was a slothful administrator," states Mackesy. "But his contemporaries and his own voluminous correspondence bear witness to his industry." He promised an immediate answer to any memorandum confined to a single sheet of paper. Even Admiral Lord Howe, no admirer, acknowledged that "to give him his due, he is seldom backward . . . in answering letters." Much of the criticism of Sandwich's work habits comes from Sir Charles Middleton, who succeeded the weak Captain Maurice Suckling, Nelson's uncle and first patron, as Comptroller of the Navy in 1778. "Unless . . . your Lordship gives your whole time to the business of the admiralty, the misapplication of the fleet will bring ruin upon this country," the Comptroller warned Sandwich. "Is it possible, my lord, that gentlemen who are at an office one day, and following their amusements or private concerns another, can carry on a line of business that requires not only great practical knowledge, but the closest application and attention?" There was certainly some merit in Middleton's criticisms and they were echoed by Germain, who found it difficult to work with the First Lord.

But Mackesy believes that Middleton had overstated the case. "Sandwich was the prisoner of an overcentralised and inflexible machine; and if he kept short office hours, he must be judged by the standards of the age," he has written. "In indicting Sandwich, Middleton was indicting the business methods of a class and a generation." Middleton later observed that while Sandwich "was called a jobber, they are all equally so, and indeed more so than ever I found him to be, though more secret in their manner."

Much of the blame for the shortcomings of the navy that is usually placed on Sandwich really belongs to Lord North. Yet the First Lord of the Admiralty could have resigned in protest against the disarmament policy imposed upon him if he had seriously opposed it. While the French were building a new and more powerful fleet to seek revenge for their defeat in the Seven Years' War, North was convinced that a strong navy was an unnecessary luxury. "I do not recollect to have seen a more pacific appearance of affairs than there is at this moment," he had said in 1772, pressing Sandwich to dismantle some of the guardships kept manned with skeleton crews in case of emergency. Low taxation and balanced budgets meant stable ministries and he looked to cuts in naval expenditures to reduce the national debt. North did not realize that many of the ships in reserve had been built in a hurry during the previous war using green timber. Half the fleet that existed on paper would soon be useless.[5] Vainly, Edmund Burke warned that "of all the public services, that of the Navy is the one in which tampering may be of the greatest danger . . . and of which any failure draws after it the largest and heaviest train of consequences."

Sandwich often told the Prime Minister the same thing privately, but he lacked the courage and loved the panoply of power too much to sacrifice himself for a principle. Like the King and George Germain, Sandwich was convinced that once the Americans had "felt a smart blow, they will submit." In the meantime, limited objectives called for limited efforts. To Sandwich, the safety of England was paramount. Ships of the line were not to be wasted in American waters. They were to be husbanded at home against the day when the Royal Navy might be forced to face the combined fleets of France and Spain—even if this policy eventually meant the loss of the American colonies.

---

[5] In 1782, the ship of the line *Royal George* plunged to the bottom as she lay at anchor at Spithead when her rotten hull gave way. Some eight hundred men, women and children went down with her. For years afterward, the tip of her mainmast showed above the surface, a pathetic monument to those entombed in her.

X

Uncombined Operations

The energetic Lord Germain lost no time in planning a British coun-
teroffensive in America. The rebellion had to be crushed before
France and Spain were tempted to take advantage of Britain's
difficulties and intervene in the struggle. The Yankees had had the
best of the opening phase of the war—forcing the British to evacuate
Boston and laying siege to Quebec. The time had come for them to
feel the full effect of British power. "As there is not common sense in
protracting a war of this sort," Germain declared, "I should be for
exerting the utmost force of this Kingdom to finish the rebellion in
one campaign." The plan called for attacks at three widely separated
points—Canada, New York, and the Carolinas. The objective of the
first was to drive the Yankee invaders out of Canada and separate
New England from the other colonies. The destruction of Washington's army as it gathered at New York was the target of the second
phase of the plan. The Southern operation was intended as a side-
show—both as a diversion and to provide support to Loyalists reported ready to flock to the Royal Standard as soon as it was raised.

To strike the enemy at three widely separated points was an appealing proposal. Unfortunately it entailed separating available

troops and ships into uncorrelated units, instead of combining them for one massive assault. The Southern operation was particularly ill chosen. Although the rebels had been strong enough to send the Royal governors fleeing to the King's ships for safety, these officials seemed to have had wondrous abilities to convince the ministry of the vigor of Loyalist sentiment in their colonies. The expedition was militarily unjustifiable because such operations are useful only when the troops and ships assigned cannot be employed in the major theater of action or when they force the enemy to divert a larger force from his main army. Neither Howe nor Carleton had enough men for the missions entrusted to them—and those diverted to the south under Clinton were badly needed elsewhere.[1] Such an expedition would be drawn away to convoy the transports. In all fairness to Germain, it must be pointed out that the planning for the Southern expedition had begun under Lord Dartmouth's administration. Germain was unenthusiastic, but failed to order the operation abandoned.

Germain's first task was to send a relief force up the St. Lawrence to lift the siege of Quebec by a ragtag rebel force commanded by Brigadier General Benedict Arnold. Canada had been a magnet to the Yankees from the very start of the conflict—a threat and an opportunity. It was a potential "fourteenth colony" where the inhabitants, supposedly restive under British rule, would welcome a liberating Continental Army. It was also the base from which the British might invade the United Colonies, severing New England from the rest of the nation. Memories were still fresh of the bloody use which the French and their Indian allies had made of the lake-and-river chain extending from the St. Lawrence to the Hudson. There was every reason to believe that the British would soon advance along the same route.

Two American columns had been sent north through the wilderness in 1775. The first, commanded by Brigadier General Richard Montgomery, followed the traditional route down Lake Champlain to the Richelieu River and on to the capture of Montreal.[2] The other was led by Arnold on an epic march across Maine to Quebec. When

---

[1] James, *The British Navy in Adversity.* Another reason advanced for the expedition was that Clinton was at odds with Howe, his superior. Detaching him solved a sticky problem of personalities.

[2] Because Lake Champlain flows into the Richelieu, north is considered down the lake.

supplies ran out, the men lived on roots and roast dog. Some tried to eat their shoes, leather breeches, and shot-pouches. "No one can imagine who has not experienced it, the sweetness of a roasted shot pouch to the famished appetite," recalled one trooper. Some six hundred survivors of the one thousand men who had started out burst upon the shore of the St. Lawrence where they were joined by the remnants of Montgomery's command and laid siege to Quebec. On the last night of 1775, in a howling blizzard, the Americans climbed the same path to the Plains of Abraham that Wolfe had taken sixteen years before and launched a surprise attack. The handful of British regulars and marines barricaded in the town under Carleton were alert, and the attack was beaten off. Montgomery was killed, Arnold was wounded and nearly half the men were killed, wounded or taken prisoner. The shattered force limped off to resume the siege.

Quebec was finally relieved on May 6, 1776, when advance ships of the squadron dispatched by Germain dropped anchor off Cape Diamond. Arriving at the mouth of the St. Lawrence almost a month before, Captain Charles Douglas, its commander, had found the ice extending nearly twenty miles out to sea. It was packed too closely to permit steering amid the pieces. Nevertheless, because of the urgency of the situation, he ran his ship *Isis*, 50, against the 12-foot-thick ice at a speed of five knots. Luckily the ice went to pieces. "Encouraged by this experiment," reported Douglas grandly, "we thought it an enterprize worthy of an English ship of the line, in our King and Country's sacred cause, and an effort due to the gallant defenders of Quebec, to make the attempt of pressing her force by Sail, thru the thick, broad and closely connected fields of ice." Decimated, by hunger, cold, and smallpox, Arnold's tiny besieging force retreated when the British squadron's sails were sighted. Once again, seapower had proven to be Britain's margin of victory.

While reinforcements and supplies for a strike along the river-lake line into the colonies poured in upon Carleton, who had been knighted for his defense of Quebec, plans went ahead for the Southern expedition. Leaving Boston on January 20, with about 1,500 men, Clinton sailed for the mouth of the Cape Fear River in North Carolina. There he was to rendezvous with a combined force of ships commanded by Commodore Sir Peter Parker and 2,500 troops under

Lord Cornwallis that was to have sailed from Ireland the month before. Clinton's orders were to restore the King's authority in the
southern colonies, re-establish the Royal governors, and rejoin Howe
for an attack on New York "as soon as the navigation of the northern coasts of North America became practicable." It took Clinton
until March 12 to arrive at Cape Fear—only to find that the "Irish
fleet" had not yet appeared.

The Southern expedition could well serve as a microcosm of the
logistical problems facing the British. Parker's ships were to have
been ready to sail by December 1, but they were delayed until mid-
month because of the difficulty in getting supplies aboard. Then the
wind intervened. Blowing steadily from the east, it held the ships in
the Thames until the end of the month. Not until four weeks after
the appointed sailing date was Sir Peter able to gather his convoy
and sail to Cork to pick up the transports. Another five weeks
slipped away before the expedition was ready to hoist anchor on
February 12. A few days out at sea, the convoy was scattered by a violent storm. Several disabled and distressed ships were forced to put
back into Cork. Yet Sandwich told the King, "I fear your Majesty
will never have a sea expedition that will be in readiness so near the
given time as this has been."

In the meantime, the Southern Loyalists, mostly Highland Scots
who hated the Lowlanders and Ulstermen prominent in the rebel
cause, had risen and been beaten in a series of sharp clashes. The
survivors scurried for the back country, pursued and harassed by
angry and merciless bands of rebels. Since one of the major reasons
for mounting the expedition was now gone, this would have been an
opportune moment for Clinton to abandon the operation and rejoin
Howe. Germain had foreseen just such an eventuality. He had given
Clinton latitude to make this move if he decided nothing important
could be gained in the South. Instead, Clinton did nothing but toy
with the idea of launching operations in Chesapeake Bay where
small, easily maintained outposts might support raids against the
Yankees and serve as havens for Loyalists.

While Clinton temporized, Parker, who had arrived at last on
May 3, broached an ambitious plan for an attack on Charleston, the
capital of South Carolina. As Clinton later told the story, a naval reconnaissance had disclosed that "the Rebel Work on Sullivan's
Island (The Key to Rebellion Road and Charles Town) was in so un-

finished a state as to be open to a *Coup de Main* and that it might be afterwards held by a small force under Cover of a Frigate or two . . . I thought Sullivans Island, if it could be seized without much loss of time, might prove a very important acquisition. Preparations were accordingly made . . . and on the 31st of May the Fleet sailed to the Southward."

The defenses of Charleston were stronger than they appeared. For months the South Carolinians had been throwing up earthworks, constructing fortifications, and mounting heavy cannon in both the town and surrounding areas. The principal works were erected on the low, sandy islands fringing the coast: specifically on Sullivan's Island to the north of the harbor entrance, and on James Island to the south. The bar at the main entrance to Charleston harbor is not directly at the mouth but some distance to the south, which meant an attacking fleet would need a southerly wind to come into action. Inside the bar the main channel turned to the northward, leading close in to the southern tip of Sullivan's Island. There, since January, the Rebels had been at work on a redoubt named Fort Sullivan, but popularly known as Fort Moultrie for its builder and commander. Colonel William Moultrie created the work from the material on hand: parallel walls of spongy palmetto logs were thrown up and the 16-foot space between them was filled with earth and sand. Thirty guns, ranging from 9- to 32-pounders, were emplaced on the south and east walls and in the two southernmost bastions, the only ones finished when the British attacked. The unfinished rear wall was defended by a half-dozen 12-pounders.

Fort Moultrie was not the only strong point. Between Sullivan's Island and Long Island [now known as the Isle of Palms] to the north ran a strip of water known as "The Breach." A British landing was expected on Long Island, so the Americans stationed a regiment at the tip of Sullivan's Island to guard the passage. To the south of the harbor entrance lay Fort Johnson on James Island, commanded by Christopher Gadsden. In addition, there were several gun emplacements within the harbor itself. All told, about a hundred guns and some 6,000 troops from all over the Southern colonies were in position.

Parker's fleet arrived off Charleston on June 1. The bigger ships and the transports were prevented by contrary winds from crossing the bar until June 7. Some of the guns of the *Bristol*, 50, the flagship, and other vessels had to be hoisted out so the ships could pass the shoals. While the fleet was getting into position, Clinton took a small sloop and made a reconnaissance of the area. Just as the Americans had predicted, he decided to land his troops on Long Island and support Parker's attack with an assault across "The Breach," hoping to trap the rebels on Sullivan's Island. After the troops had been landed, Clinton, to his "unspeakable mortification," found the ford, which had been reported to be only 18 inches deep at low tide, was pocked with holes 7 feet deep. He asked Parker for boats for an amphibious assault. The commodore, obviously convinced that the navy would be able to silence Fort Moultrie on its own, lagged in sending them. This breakdown in cooperation between the British commanders made it possible for a small American detachment in the scrub at the north end of Sullivan's Island to contain Clinton's entire force. Thus, the full thrust of the attack was made by Parker's fleet.

Awaiting a favorable breeze, the ships rocked in the greasy swells amid the heat and swarms of mosquitoes that infested the low-lying islands. Shortly before 11 A.M. on June 28, Parker hoisted a blue flag to the mainmast of the *Bristol*—the signal for his ships to go into action. Orders to fire swept along the sweltering gundecks. From the bomb ketch *Thunder*, a 10-inch mortar shell arched into the sky trailing a flickering fuse and dropped on Fort Moultrie. The frigate *Solebay*, 28, followed by the flagship, the *Experiment*, 50, and the *Active*, 28, moving under topsails, took up positions 400 to 800 yards—the estimates vary—from the fort. Three other ships, the *Sphynx*, 20, the *Actaeon*, and the *Syren*, both 28, moved to pass the fort and enfilade it from the westward. The *Thunder*, guarded by the *Friendship*, 22, anchored to the southeast and mechanically pumped shells into Moultrie.

Short of ammunition—the garrison had but twenty-eight rounds of powder for each of its guns when the action commenced—Moultrie ordered his men to take their time and make every shot count. The British ships took their places skillfully. Their fire was rapid and well-directed. But they were too far away from the fort to use grape shot to clear the walls effectively, either because of shoal water or because of fear of running aground. "The sides of ships being much weaker than those of shore works, while their guns were much more numerous, the secret of success was to get near enough to beat down the hostile fire by a multitude of projectiles," observed Admiral Mahan. The fort's gun crews returned the fire with a nervous rapidity that made alarming inroads in their powder supply. Eventually they steadied under Moultrie's command, and more powder was brought in. "Mind the Commodore; mind the two 50-gun ships," he directed. The gunners concentrated on the two big ships with a deadliness that became apparent as the bombardment stretched into the afternoon. "The Provincials reserved their fire until the shipping advanced within point-blank shot," a British officer reported. "Their artillery was surprisingly well served . . . It was slow, but decisive indeed. They were very cool and took great care not to fire except when the guns were exceedingly well directed . . . I can scarcely believe what I saw on that day; a day to me one of the most distressing in my life."

Everything seemed to go wrong for the British. The *Thunder* threw her shells with accuracy and most of them fell within the fort. But they had little effect. "We had a morass in the middle that swallowed them up instantly, and those that fell in the sand and in and about the fort were immediately buried so that very few of them bursted amongst us," Moultrie reported. Soon one of the *Thunder*'s mortars was overcharged by its crew, sprang loose from its mountings and became inoperative. The line of frigates that was to outflank the fort ran aground on a shoal known as the Middle Ground, where Fort Sumter was later built. Two of them fouled each other in the confusion. The *Sphynx* and the *Syren* managed to get clear after several hours, but the *Actaeon* was stuck hard and fast. Her crew set fire to her the next morning. "Had these ships effected their purpose," observed Moultrie, "they would have driven us from our guns."

Moultrie's men may have been short of ammunition, but they did not have to stint themselves on grog. "It being a hot day, we were served along the platform with grog in firebuckets which we partook of heartily," the Colonel said. "I never had a more agreeable draught . . . It may be very easily conceived what heat and thirst a man must feel in this climate, to be upon a platform on the 28th of June, amidst 20 or 30 pieces of cannon in one continual blaze and roar; and clouds of smoke curling over his head for hours together; it is a very honorable situation, but a very unpleasant one." The fort shook under the broadsides of the ships, but the British cannonballs buried themselves in the palmetto ramparts without throwing off showers of splinters or doing much damage. The earthen walls also served as a cushion. Of the twelve Americans killed and twenty-three wounded, nearly all were hit through the embrasures, rather than by cannon balls crashing through the fort's walls.

The rebel gunners played havoc with the men-of-war. Twice the quarterdeck of the *Bristol* was cleared of everyone except the commodore. Parker's breeches were blown off by a blast, and he was painfully wounded in the thigh and knee. An enemy roundshot sliced the flagship's cable. She swung stern-first to the fort's guns which poured their fire into her while she could make no reply. The *Bristol* took 70 hits and ended the engagement with 46 killed and 86 wounded, according to a British account. The *Experiment*, the other major target for Moultrie's gunners, sustained 43 killed and 75 wounded. Total British casualties were 91 killed and 170 wounded.

Throughout the sultry afternoon, hundreds of spectators watched the action from the steeples and rooftops of Charleston. Thick black clouds of smoke periodically engulfed the fort and the fleet. There was an anxious period when the staff flying the fort's flag—a blue banner bearing a crescent and emblazoned "Liberty"— was shot away. A young sergeant named William Jasper leaped through an embrasure after it, fixed it upon a sponge staff, and planted it upon the ramparts. At another point, the American guns fell silent for about an hour. This interval, said Moultrie, "was owing to the scarcity of powder which we had in the fort, and to a report that was brought me that the British troops were landed . . . I ordered the guns to cease firing, that we should reserve our powder for the musketry to defend ourselves against the land forces."

Despite Moultrie's concern, no attack came from that quarter. Clinton maintained that notwithstanding the problem of the ford "every Demonstration was accordingly made of an Intention to land on the Island, and every Diversion by Cannonade and other ways." Eventually he placed his troops and cannon for an attack, to be made the next morning, but it was called off when he learned of the battered condition of the ships. "About 9 P.M.," Parker reported, "being very dark, great part of our ammunition expended, the people fatigued, the tide of ebb almost done, no prospect from the eastward [meaning from the army], and no possibility of our being of any further service, I ordered the ships to withdraw to their former moorings." The troops spent an uncomfortable three weeks among the mosquitoes of Long Island before embarking to rejoin Howe in New York. "Nothing therefore was now left for us to do but to lament that the Blood of brave and gallant Men had been so fruitlessly Spilt," observed Clinton.

The assault on Charleston was a humiliating defeat for the British and a boost to rebel morale. The Southern expedition was shaky from the start because it depended on Loyalist military support. Yet something might have been gained if the commanders had shown speed and coordination in the conduct of operations. Clinton erred in accepting Parker's strategy to attack Sullivan's Island instead of running past the forts and directly storming or surrounding Charleston itself. Rather than attacking quickly, the British commanders spent leisurely weeks preparing the assault—while the Americans had time to bring in reinforcements and bolster their defenses. "Britain had worse defeats in the course of the war," writes one authority,[3] "but no more egregious fiasco."

On July 4, 1776, while Congress was proclaiming the independence of the British colonies in America, George Washington warned of an impending British attack on New York. He realized that the city was the key to a strategic plan aimed at splitting New England off from the Middle colonies. Pleading with Congress to send him all the men available, he told Hancock: "It now seems beyond question and clear to demonstration that the Enemy mean to direct their Operations and bend their most vigorous efforts against this Colony, and will attempt to unite their Two armies." One force was moving south from Canada under Carleton; the other was forming on Staten Island under Howe. The Hudson, navigable as far north as Albany, was the connecting link—and the navy would give the British control of it. A junction of forces would isolate rebellious New England and the northern colonies could be pacified immediately or be quarantined until the insurrection was quelled elsewhere.

By day, the white sails of 52 warships and 427 transports testified to British command of the waters about New York. At night the campfires of 34,000 troops—a large part of them German mercenaries—twinkled on Staten Island. They made up the largest British

---

[3] William B. Willcox, ed., *The American Rebellion: Sir Henry Clinton's Narrative* (New Haven 1954).

expeditionary force of the Eighteenth Century. Against them, Washington had 20,000 men, the biggest American army of the war but far from the most effective. New recruits filled most of the regiments. Their ignorance of elementary sanitation soon caused hundreds of men to be unfit for duty. "In almost every barn, stable, shed and even under the fences and bushes, were the sick to be seen, whose countenances were but an index of the dejection of spirit, and of the distress they endured," said Major General William Heath.

Political considerations played as much a part in the decision to defend New York as did military factors. In the spring of 1776, New York was still on the fence between the King and independence. Tories were everywhere. Many New Yorkers, expecting a British landing almost momentarily, held aloof, waiting to throw in their lot with whatever side showed signs of winning. Washington put his men to furiously preparing the city's defenses in hopes that this would stir support for the American cause. Surrounded by various bodies of water that gave the British fleet free play to maneuver and envelop the exposed American flanks with amphibious attacks, the city presented serious problems for its defenders. "What to do with the city . . . puzzles me," declared General Charles Lee. "It is so encircled with deep navigable waters that whoever commands the sea must command the town." Washington built forts on the shores of the Hudson to prevent enemy ships from outflanking Manhattan, ordered the forging of a huge chain to be extended across the river at West Point and dug in on Brooklyn Heights across the East River on Long Island. Although Brooklyn Heights dominated Lower Manhattan, just as Dorchester Heights dominated Boston, this position was strategically poor since Washington had no way of preventing the British from making a landing in his rear on Long Island or the fleet from taking up station in the East River. The Americans would then be trapped between the enemy army and navy.

Yet Howe, and his older brother, Admiral Richard Lord Howe, who now commanded the British fleet in American waters, delayed in delivering their attack. They waited until the last reinforcements had filtered in and until Parker's battered squadron limped back from Charleston. "We sleep upon the sea-shore, nothing to shelter us from the violent rains but our coats and the miserable paltry blankets," complained one Redcoat bivouacked on Staten Island. "There is nothing that grows upon this Island, it being a mere sand-bank, and a few bushes that harbour millions of moschitoes—a greater plague than there can be in Hell itself." [4] Except for a foray past the forts by two frigates that went up the Hudson to the Tappan Sea, there were no lightning strikes against the vulnerable American positions. No attempt was made to soften up the forts with a naval bombardment.

The admiral was obsessed with peace, not war.[5] Lord Howe had long been considered one of Britain's most respected seamen with a reputation for aggressive leadership and professional competence gained in thirty-five years service in the Royal Navy. Taciturn and swarthy, he was known to his sailors as "Black Dick." From the ships lying at Spithead to the House of Commons the same sentiments echoed: "Give us Black Dick and we fear nothing." Admiral Howe regarded the war in America as "a personal and national tragedy," observes Gruber. He wished to promote a reconciliation between Britain and her colonies rather than win a military victory. Sentiment played a role in his feelings because his family had close ties with the colonists. His brother, George Augustus, had been one of the most popular British officers in the colonies. When he was killed at Ticonderoga in 1758, the Massachusetts authorities appropriated funds to erect a memorial in Westminster Abbey.

As early as 1774, the admiral had offered to mediate the quarrel between the King and the colonists. But the ministry, putting its faith in coercive measures, consistently rejected his offers until late in 1775. By that time, the government was convinced that it could break the revolt by force of arms so it agreed to send him to America to accept what it confidently assumed would be an American surrender. Howe, however, held out for more responsibility. Lord North, to prevent the embarrassment of having such an important officer resign from the navy, finally acceded to his request that he be named

---

[4] Young Lord Rawdon, Clinton's aide-de-camp, left a different picture of British activities on Staten Island. "The fair nymphs of the isle are in wonderful tribulation as the fresh meat our men have got here has made them as riotous [as] satyrs. A girl cannot step into the bushes to pluck a rose without running the imminent fear of being ravished, and they are so little accustomed to these vigorous methods that they don't bear them with the proper resignation, and of consequence we have the most entertaining courts-martial every day."

[5] For a brief account of Lord Howe's motivations and operations see Ira D. Gruber, "Richard Lord Howe: Admiral as Peacemaker," in *George Washington's Opponents*, George A. Billias, ed. (New York 1969). A much fuller version is Gruber's *The Howe Brothers and the American Revolution* (New York 1972). This is now the definitive account of their mission to America.

both naval commander and peace commissioner. His brother, William, the military commander, was also named a commissioner. "These ministers who selected Howe solely for his ability as an admiral had no illusions about his views on conciliation," according to Gruber. They carefully hemmed him in with peace terms that made all but abject surrender impossible. The Howes were empowered to grant pardons and remove restrictions on trade—but first they must exact assurance from the Americans that the rebellion would be ended and Royal officers restored to their posts.

Admiral Howe arrived off Sandy Hook on July 12, 1776. Two days before, a New York mob had celebrated the signing of the Declaration of Independence by pulling down a 2-ton lead statue of George III that stood on Bowling Green and carting it away to be cast into bullets. The symbolism was lost on Lord Howe, who remained optimistic about the prospects for peace. Neither Congress's decision for "independency" nor his limited authority as a peacemaker dimmed his determination. He immediately attempted to open conversations with Washington, only to be rebuffed by the American commander-in-chief who refused to accept letters addressed to "George Washington, Esq., etc. etc." His aides archly informed the admiral that they knew of no such person in the American camp. When contact was finally made, Washington replied that he had no authority to work out any accommodation. He noted that the Howe brothers had nothing to offer but a pardon—which the Americans did not need.

By mid-August, the admiral concluded that force must be applied before the rebels would give serious consideration to his peace proposals. On the morning of August 22, the British finally began moving their troops to Long Island. Organized into ten squadrons, the landing craft pushed up on the beaches of Gravesend Bay as bands aboard the towering ships played marches. Within a few hours, General Howe had put 15,000 men ashore with cannon and equipment. Nevertheless the attack did not begin immediately. Until his older brother arrived on the scene, the General had repeatedly declared that he sought a decisive meeting with the Continental Army, adding that such an encounter was absolutely necessary for putting down the rebellion. Now he appeared to have abandoned this view for one more in keeping with the Admiral's. Although a force led by Clinton crushed the Yankee forces on August 27, Howe was apparently content merely to drive the American army from Long Island rather than to destroy it. He seemed more intent on occupying territory than seeking a decisive victory. The navy was not summoned to block the obvious rebel line of retreat across the East River. Not a single longboat patrolled the river.

Faced with disaster, Washington turned once again to John Glover and his Marblehead fishermen. During the night of August 29, he decided to withdraw the remnants of his troops from Brooklyn across the East River to Manhattan. Although the enemy positions were only 600 yards away, his men silently made their way to the beaches without alerting the British. They were ferried across the river in the dark in boats with muffled oars manned by Glover's men. The size of the rebel force trapped on Long Island shrank steadily. By dawn, these seagoing soldiers had managed to carry nearly 9,000 men across the river in a little less than nine hours. "In the Morning, to our great Astonishment, [we] found they had Evacuated all their Works . . . without a Shot being fired at them," wrote a surprised British officer. One authority has observed that the Long Island evacuation revealed a special aspect of Washington's generalship— his use of small-scale amphibious operations. "It is significant that Washington's desperate defensive move, the Long Island retreat, and his equally bold offensive stroke, the Trenton attack, were both fashioned around the same tactical device," writes George A. Billias, Glover's biographer.[6] "Using waterways in place of highways, Washington shifted his troops in small boats with such rapidity that he caught the enemy unaware on both occasions."

For two weeks after Washington's escape, the Howe brothers did nothing. The admiral engaged in a round of fruitless negotiations with a delegation from Congress while the Americans struggled to improve their defenses on Manhattan. Frustrated at the conference table once more, Lord Howe resolved to step up military pressure on the enemy. Under a barrage laid down by the guns of the fleet, General Howe landed a picked force at Kip's Bay, about midway between Lower Manhattan and Harlem. The raw Yankee troops fled

---

[6] *General John Glover and His Marblehead Mariners* (New York 1966). Some historians have compared the Long Island evacuation with Dunkirk in 1940, but Billias thinks the comparison poorly chosen. "Washington's forces were not under attack while the amphibious retreat was in progress, and the total number of troops involved in 1776 was only one-fortieth of the total evacuated in 1940."

for their lives. A leisurely chase followed in which the British drove the Americans from the island by frontal assault and flanking maneuvers better calculated to win territory than to bring on a decisive battle. By December, the British had driven the Continentals away from New York and into Pennsylvania.

Lord Howe's men-of-war, riding insolently in the waters off New York, were a constant irritation and challenge to the Yankees. The harbor was so crowded with ships that an observer noted that their masts looked like a pine forest with all the branches trimmed. The target was tempting, but the Americans could not strike at it. Lacking ships and effective shore batteries, they could only dream of finding some secret weapon that would blow the King's ships out of the water. Not too long before, a few members of Congress thought they had discovered just such a weapon. An old privateersman named John Macpherson had broached a mysterious scheme to John Adams for destroying the entire British fleet. "He proposed great Things," noted Adams in his diary. "Is sanguine, confident, positive, that he can take or burn every Man-of-War in America. It is a Secret, he says. But will communicate it to any one Member of Congress upon Condition, that it be not divulged during his Life at all, not after his Death but for the Service of his Country." The plausible old seadog persuaded Congress to advance him $300—and promptly faded into the mists of history along with his secret weapon.

While Congress chased will-o'-the-wisps, the world's first practical submarine took shape on the shores of the Connecticut River. It was built by David Bushnell, a Yale graduate with a taste for tinkering.[7] Until he was twenty-nine in 1769, Bushnell had helped work the family farm at Saybrook. That year his father died and he sold his interest in the estate to his younger brother, Ezra, and set out to fulfill a lifelong ambition by entering Yale. This was no easy task for an uneducated farmer. For two years he studied with a tutor and did not enter the college at nearby New Haven until 1771, when he was thirty-one. Most of the students were almost young enough to be Bushnell's sons. He had to work hard to keep up with them. Amid

---

[7] Much of the following is based on the most complete account of Bushnell's activities: Frederick Wagner, *Submarine Fighter of the American Revolution* (New York 1963).

his labors over the Greek Testament and Cicero's orations, rhetoric, ethics, arithmetic, and geometry, he found time to develop an idea that had long fascinated him.

Bushnell was convinced that he could make gunpowder explode under water. Gathering a group of friends together, he put on a demonstration at a neighboring pond. Two ounces of powder were placed in a container which was submerged and a fuse was lit. The underwater mine—the first to be developed so far as the observers knew—promptly sent a geyser of water climbing into the air. To prove that the explosion was no fluke, Bushnell later had the same success with a two-pound charge of powder. Since war with Britain was on the way, Bushnell was quick to realize that he had developed a weapon that could end the Royal Navy's domination of the American coast if a way could be found to deliver it. By the time of Lexington and Concord, he had not only perfected his mine but had produced plans for a submersible craft to transport it to a target.

While his classmates rushed off to join the army gathering outside Boston, Bushnell hastened home to Saybrook and began construction of his "sub-marine" in seclusion. The vessel, which took shape in a waterside shed, looked like no other craft. Two giant tortoiselike shells, built of oak staves like a barrel and reinforced internally against the pressure of the water, were clamped together with iron hoops. The seams of the craft, which was about six or seven feet long, were carefully caulked and the entire contraption was coated with tar. Because of its appearance, the craft was called the *Turtle*. The entry hatch at the top resembled the flattened crown of a round hat. There were eight small windows in this primitive conning tower to provide light for the operator. To provide stability, a nine-hundred-pound lead keel was attached to the bottom of the craft.

Two brass pipes admitted fresh air and exhausted stale air. To prevent flooding, these vents had check-valves in them similar to the snorkle air-intake devices on modern submarines. A foot-operated valve in the keel admitted water to submerge; a pump ejected it to ascend. The *Turtle* was driven forward and up and down by two sets of screwlike paddles which were manually operated by a series of cranks. A rudder, worked by a long tiller, guided the craft. As a safety precaution, two hundred pounds of the lead keel that was attached by a chain could be detached to enable the submarine to rise to the surface in case of emergency. It could also be let down forty or fifty feet for use as an anchor. Navigating instruments were rudimentary. Depth was shown by a calibrated glass tube leading to the water outside. Any change in water pressure forced the fluid up in the glass, along with a cork that bobbed against the graduated lines. There was also a compass. To illuminate the cork in the water-gauge and the points of the compass so that the operator could see them at night or when the *Turtle* was submerged, Bushnell attached fox fire, a wood that has a phosphorescent quality in the dark, to the cork and the compass points.

The mine itself was an egg-shaped cask containing one hundred fifty pounds of gunpowder and a clockwork timing device. It was attached to the rear of the submarine's shell by a long bolt, which when withdrawn not only released the mine but activated the timer. After about an hour, the charge would be exploded by a flint gunlock. To attach the mine to the keel of an enemy ship, Bushnell installed a long auger bit that passed through a socket in the top of the craft. After the bit had been screwed into the bottom of the target vessel, it would be detached from the *Turtle*. From this screw a short, strong line passed to the mine, holding it against the hull of the ship earmarked for destruction. All in all, the submarine was an ingenious piece of work considering the level of technology at the time. But it had a sizeable drawback. Once the vessel was submerged there was air for only thirty minutes work so it had to approach its target with the conning tower and air vents visible. This required that attacks be made at night or in periods of poor visibility.

Bushnell successfully tested the *Turtle* in the Connecticut River but he was too frail to operate her under combat conditions. His brother, Ezra, who had helped with the construction, was trained as captain, pilot, and crew. Plans were laid in late 1775 to bring "the famous Water Machine from Connecticutt" to Boston to attack the British ships lying there, but the need to replace and refine some of the craft's equipment delayed immediate action until spring. By then the British had departed for Halifax. When Lord Howe's fleet arrived off New York, Bushnell's craft was sent for. For months, the enemy had been receiving reports of an impending attack by some devilish product of Yankee ingenuity. "You may expect to see the Ships in Smoke"—one Loyalist informant had warned—but the British did not know precisely what to expect.

All was now ready for the launching of an attack that would

revolutionize naval warfare. Unexpectedly, Ezra Bushnell, the only man trained to operate the *Turtle*, was taken sick with one of the fevers that periodically decimated the Continental Army. It looked as if years of planning and hard work and all of Bushnell's money had gone for nothing. Where could a man be quickly found, who was, as Washington said, "hardy enough to encounter the variety of dangers to which he would be disposed; first from the novelty; secondly, from the difficulty of conducting the machine, and governing it under water, on account of the current; and thirdly, from the consequent uncertainty of hitting the object devoted to destruction, without rising frequently above water for fresh observations, which when near the vessel, would expose the adventurer to discovery and almost certain death." For several days Bushnell despaired of finding suitable volunteers until three men who had volunteered for service on the fire ships being prepared for launching against the British fleet were persuaded to fill the opening. One of them, Sergeant Ezra Lee, a twenty-seven-year-old Connecticut soldier, appeared the most promising and was hurried through a quick training course with the *Turtle* in Long Island Sound.

Shortly after midnight on September 7, 1776, the submarine bobbed off South Ferry Landing at the tip of Manhattan. The mine was placed in position above her rudder. Equipment was checked and rechecked. At last, Sergeant Lee squeezed through the hatch at the top of the conning tower and fastened it tight. Two whaleboats towed the *Turtle* through the darkness to as close as they dared to her target—Howe's flagship, the 64-gun *Eagle*—before casting off the lines. The current was swifter than Lee had expected and it swept him down the bay past the silent man-of-war. It took two-and-a-half hours of hard rowing to bring the submarine back into position to attack. By the time he was on target, the first glow of dawn was on the horizon. As Lee passed under the warship's stern, he caught a glimpse of sailors moving about on her deck above him and their voices came through the open portholes of the conning tower.

It was time to submerge. Making fast the portholes, he opened the valve that started the water flowing into the ballast tanks. To speed his descent he cranked the upper set of paddles rapidly to make full use of the brief half-hour that his air supply would last. When Lee was under the *Eagle*'s keel, he carefully raised the rod with the auger bit on the end to which the mine was attached and stuck it into her hull. Something went wrong. The screw would not enter. Each time he pressed it against the ship's bottom, the submarine seemed to rebound. Both Lee and Bushnell were later convinced that the bit had struck an iron bar connecting the ship's rudder with her sternpost. "Had he moved a few inches which he might have done. . . . I have no doubt he would have found wood where he might have fixed the screw; or if the ship were sheathed with copper, he might have easily pierced it," the inventor declared. With his hasty training, Lee was not as skilled in handling the *Turtle* as Ezra Bushnell. As he pulled along the *Eagle*'s keel to try again, the craft unexpectedly "rose with great velocity" and surfaced beside the ship before it "sunk again like a porpoise."

Daylight was breaking fast and the shaken Lee feared discovery by the small boats that would soon be active in the fleet anchorage. "I thought the best generalship was to retreat as fast as I could, as I had 4 miles to go before Governor's Island. So jogg'd on as fast as I could." Another accident soon befell the *Turtle.* Her compass went awry and Lee, not knowing in which direction he was heading, dared not submerge. Cranking away, he kept his vessel moving along on the surface. "The enemy's attention was drawn towards me from Governor's Island," and some of them set out in a small boat to inspect the strange craft. "I eyed them, and when they had got within 50 or 60 yards of me I let loose the magazine [the mine] in hopes that if they should take me they would likewise pick up the magazine, and then we should all be blown up together," the submariner said.

As soon as the mine was set adrift, the clockwork mechanism that would fire the gunlock in an hour started ticking. Spotting the strange-looking cask that had suddenly bobbed up in their path, the wary British seamen suspected some sort of Yankee trick. They rowed frantically back to Governor's Island to Sergeant Lee's "infinite joy." Lee finally came within sight at South Ferry and a whaleboat was dispatched to tow him in. When he staggered exhausted onto the wharf, Lee had been in the *Turtle* for five hours—and was alive to tell the tale. Less than a half-hour after he landed the drifting mine exploded, sending a vast column of water shooting into the air. Startled out of their beds by the ear-splitting roar and brilliant flash, crowds of people rushed from their houses. Was the town under bombardment? Had the magazines blown up? Panic broke out in the

British fleet. Cables were slipped and the ships drifted down the bay in great disorder. It was some time before they cautiously crept back to their anchorages. The first submarine attack in the history of warfare had been a failure, but only after it had come close to sounding the knell of British seapower.

Several other attempts were made to sink British ships in the Hudson but they were all unsuccessful.[8] Despite the best efforts of Bushnell, Lee, and the *Turtle*, British frigates retained control of the Hudson as far north as Tarrytown. The ease with which they ran past American forts and channel obstructions clearly demonstrated their ability to go all the way to Albany any time they wished to establish contact with Carleton's men descending from Canada.

---

[8] The *Turtle* was probably destroyed to keep it from falling into British hands later in the New York campaign. Bushnell soon began experimenting with floating mines that would explode on contact. In January 1778, he released about two dozen in the Delaware River above Philadelphia with the hope that they would float down and destroy the British fleet anchored off the town. One of the mines exploded prematurely killing several British seamen and setting off an alarm. The ships began firing at anything that floated—logs, kegs, bits of driftwood were all subjected to an intensive cannonade. Rebel newspapers gleefully reported the incident and "the Battle of the Kegs" was ridiculed in song and story.

XI

Fleets in the Forest

Guy Carleton's force—the other side of a great pincers designed to close about New England—was stalled on the shores of Lake Champlain. Stretching some 125 miles through the forest from north to south and ranging in width from 400 yards to fourteen miles, the lake was the vital link in the strategic waterway between the Hudson and the St. Lawrence. The absence of roads through the wilderness made undisputed control of the lake indispensable to Carleton's army in its pursuit of the disintegrating American expeditionary force. Bolting south across the Canadian border, the Yankees had quickly become a rabble—exhausted, panic-stricken scarecrows scratching for food on the countryside.

Infested with smallpox, without shoes, blankets, or warm clothes, the Americans peered anxiously over their shoulders with haunted eyes for the first sign of the Redcoats or their Indian allies. "I am heartily sick of this retreating, ragged, starved, thievish, pock-marked army in this unhealthy country," wrote one officer. Men struggled up to their armpits in water, pushing boats laden with the sick and whatever loot and stores they could salvage. Frenzied, famished, and plague-stricken, the Northern Army lost 5,000 casualties through death, disease, wounds, and desertion during the retreat from Canada. The flight did not halt before reaching Fort Ticonderoga at the junction of Lakes Champlain and George. So completely had the tables been turned, few believed that the British invasion could be stopped. Lake Champlain, which the Americans had regarded as the easy road to Canada, seemed a dagger aimed at the heart of their cause.

Due to Benedict Arnold's foresight, the Americans held temporary naval supremacy on the lake. The British would have to fight for it. The previous year, he had captured the schooners *Royal Savage* and *Liberty* and the large sloop *Enterprise*, all armed with an assortment of small guns. They were enough to keep Carleton from smashing up the lake for a lightning strike at Washington's rear. In addition, Arnold had seized the timbers, planks, and fittings of a partially built cutter on the ways at St. Johns on the Richelieu River and had ordered them numbered and carried south for reassembly. "We have, happily, such a naval superiority on Lake Champlain that I have a confident hope the Enemy will not appear upon it in this Campaign," declared General Philip Schuyler, commander of the Northern Department.

Arnold knew better. Fully realizing that Carleton would press both the skilled seamen of the British squadron at anchor in the St. Lawrence and the army's artificers into a massive shipbuilding program, he wrote Washington on June 25, urging the construction of a fleet:

> It now appears to me of the Utmost Importance, that the Lakes be immediately secured by a large Number of (at least Twenty or thirty) Gundaloes, Row Gallies & floating Batteries. The Enemy from, undoubted intelligence have brought over a large Number (it is said One hundred) Frames for Flat Bottom Boats design'd to be made use of on Lake Champlain, and from their Industry & Strength will doubtless become masters of the Lake, unless Every nerve on our part is Strained to exceed them in a Naval Armament. —I think it absolutely necessary that at least three hundred Carpenters be immediately employed.

General Horatio Gates, who had been given the job of reorganizing the shattered Northern Army, frankly confessed his ignorance of naval matters and gladly turned the problem over to the eager Arnold. "General Arnold (who is perfectly skilled in maritime affairs) has most nobly undertaken to command our fleet upon the Lake," he wrote John Hancock. "With infinite satisfaction, I have committed the whole of that department to his care, convinced he will thereby add to that brilliant reputation he has so deservedly acquired." Gates exaggerated Arnold's knowledge of naval matters. Nevertheless, at thirty-five, Arnold was at the height of his remarkable powers. A member of a prominent Connecticut family, the general had begun his career as a New Haven druggist and bookseller. Afterward, he became a successful merchant and started sailing his own ships to the West Indies and Europe—experience that was to serve him well on Lake Champlain. Tremendously energetic, Arnold was a thickset man of medium height, unusually strong and of great stamina. Ice-gray eyes were set off by black hair and a swarthy complexion. Overwhelming ambition, sensitivity to criticism, a volcanic temper, and a sharp tongue complete the picture of a man whose name has become synonymous with treachery. Yet he was one of the most courageous officers of the Revolution.[1]

Design as well as construction of the Champlain fleet is credited to Arnold. Four row-galleys were to be the capital ships of his battle line. Patterned after the galleys Arnold must have seen in the Mediterranean, they had two masts rigged with high-pointed lateen sails. Powered by seven pairs of sweeps, long oars, each worked by two or more men, the galleys were 72 feet long. The vessels were named *Washington*, *Congress*, *Gates* and *Trumbull*. They carried a variety of armament. The *Washington*, for example, was armed with two 18-pounders, two 12-pounders, two 9-pounders and four 4-pounders in her broadside, along with a pair of heavy guns in her bow and some swivels on her quarterdeck. Arnold's major reason for building such craft appears to have been that with a minimum of sails and rigging they would be simple to handle, an important consideration since they would be manned by untrained landsmen.

---

[1] Willard M. Wallace, one of Arnold's recent biographers, thinks the World War II officer that he most closely resembled was General George S. Patton. "Both these followers of fine fashions in clothes and weapons, loved the offensive, took great risks with calculation, hit swiftly and hard, and preferred the slam-bang of contact to the semi-academic cerebrations of staff work," he writes in *Traitorous Hero* (New York 1954). "Utterly courageous, each would have welcomed a soldier's death. In temperament there was a surprising similarity, for both were high-strung, impulsive, trigger-tongued and irascible . . . Both were beloved and hated by their troops, Arnold winning perhaps the greater degree of affection, which, however, turned to bitter detestation after his treason. In integrity of character the comparison ends; Patton was an honest man."

The mainstay of the fleet was the gundalow, or gondola. Nine were laid down—the *Boston, Connecticut, New Haven, New Jersey, New York, Philadelphia, Providence, Spitfire,* and *Success.* The *Philadelphia,* which was sunk in the ensuing battle, was raised from the bottom of Lake Champlain in 1935 in a good state of preservation. She is now on display at the Smithsonian Institution in Washington. Flat-bottomed and open, she is approximately 53 feet long and 15 feet in beam. The gondolas were propelled by two square sails on a single tall mast as well as eight sweeps to a side. They were armed with a 12-pounder in the bow and a pair of 9-pounders amidships. Crude brick hearths were built in the waist of the craft and 10-foot-long platforms for the officers and a helmsman were constructed on their sterns. Most of the vessels were painted barn-red—an apt color considering the crudeness of their design and construction.

Within hours of receiving orders to take charge of the fleet, Arnold dispatched the handful of carpenters available at Ticonderoga and Crown Point to Skenesborough (now Whitehall, New York) to repair the sawmill there and prepare ways for the hulls of the gondolas and row galleys. Located on Wood Creek, which empties into Lake Champlain about twenty miles south of Ticonderoga, Skenesborough was chosen not only for its sawmill but because it had everything needed for a shipyard. Philip Skene, the town's Loyalist founder, had also built a forge and foundry. There were iron deposits nearby, and the shore sloped gently down to water sufficiently deep to float the vessels after they were launched. A small stock of lumber was cut and seasoned but most of the oak and pine that would be needed was yet to be cut. Upon Schuyler and Gates, Arnold rained demands for carpenters—ship's carpenters or house carpenters, it made no difference—canvas, cordage, nails, needles, white lead, guns, powder, anchors, and hawsers.

Somehow the generals managed to deliver the men and supplies. Skilled shipwrights were so scarce that they could be lured away from the privateers building in the coastal yards only by promises of exorbitant wages. It was rumored among the troops that they were being paid $5 a day in hard money, given free food and promised a cow in return for their labors in the forest. Ironically, the British blockade of New York and Philadelphia helped divert labor and equipment to Lake Champlain because it cut off the frigates being built at those ports. Patiently Gates, stockless and coatless in the hot little rooms of Ticonderoga, forced through Arnold's incessant demands. Again and again, the General, "an old granny-looking fellow" at forty-eight, managed to come up with needed equipment and expedited it off to Arnold. "Where it is not to be had, you and the princes of the earth must go unfurnished," he added in one plaintive note.

Slowly, the fleet began to take shape. Down the forest paths, axemen felled great trees; steaming skid-horses dragged them to the saw-pits to be cut into timbers. The frames of the gondolas—built bottom-side up and planked and caulked with hot pitch before being turned over—were being shaped. Beyond them, row galleys were under construction, their sides towering over the smaller craft. By July 24, Arnold reported that four of the gondolas had been completed and were on their way to Ticonderoga. "Two others will be finished in five days & four more in Ten days . . . Thirty Carpenters are arrived from Connecticut & are Cuting Timber for a Row Gally . . . One hundred other Carpenters from Pensilvania & Massachusetts Bay will be here this evening, who will take in hand three other Gallies. The whole I expect will be compleated In three weeks. . . ."

Arnold still faced the problem of obtaining crews for the vessels. Gates put out a call for volunteers from the army. Quotas were established for each brigade, and a bonus of eight shillings a month in extra pay was offered for "service aboard the armed vessels." Some men stepped forward in hopes that pulling an oar would be less arduous than digging with a spade. Others were pushed out of the ranks by regimental adjutants eager to get rid of troublemakers and misfits. These landlubbers, about three hundred fifty in number, were sorted into seamen, gunners, and marines. They received their first lesson in seamanship on the row up the reed-lined channel from Ticonderoga to Skenesborough. There they were joined by another three hundred men scooped up along the Atlantic Coast. Arnold had to take his captains as well as his sailors where he could find them. Originally, he had written to five masters of his acquaintance offering them commands in his fleet. Only one accepted. Captain Seth Warner rode out of the woods one day in an ox cart, seated on his sea chest, his sextant in a wooden box on his knee. He was given command of the galley *Trumbull*, which still stood on the stocks. Warner rushed her to completion. The rest of the skippers came from the army or wherever Schuyler was able to recruit them along the seacoast. Immediately after their arrival, they were put to work supervising the construction of their commands with the hope they could cajole the workmen into showing more speed. Some, including Captain David Hawley, the Connecticut privateersman who had been a prisoner on the *Glasgow* during the night action with Hopkins's fleet, brought a few trained hands with them. Eager to strike back at the British after escaping from captivity in Halifax, Hawley was given command of the schooner *Royal Savage*, on which Arnold raised his flag in mid-August. As the vessels came off the ways, the officers quickly moved to instruct their raw crews in their new trade. The voyage to Ticonderoga and Crown Point for fitting out was used to drill the sailors in their duties aloft, how to set sail, the use of the long sweeps counted upon to give the vessels maneuverability, and the laying of guns to hit a moving target from an unstable deck. On August 24, little more than six weeks after construction began, Arnold was ready to take ten vessels down the lake to see what the British were up to.

As soon as Carleton realized it would be necessary to fight for control of Lake Champlain, he set about gathering a fleet that would overwhelm anything the Yankees put on the water. If the British did not face the same problems that had hampered Arnold—they had skilled manpower to build boats and then man them—they had others. The Richelieu River, which connects the lake with the St. Lawrence, was obstructed by shoals and ten miles of vicious rapids. Flat boats and barges could be dragged by oxen overland around the rapids, but any vessel big enough to match Arnold's galleys and schooners would have to be built at St. Johns, the northernmost point at which navigation of the lake could begin. Immediately after the last rebel had fled, two officers arrived in St. Johns to inspect what was left of the dockyard. Upon Lieutenant John Schank, of the Royal Navy, and Lieutenant William Twiss, an engineer officer, rested Carleton's hopes of beating the Americans in the shipbuilding race that he had to win if he were to force the Champlain gateway before winter came.

Fortunately for the British, both were able men. Schank was the inventor of what he called the "drop keel"—a board that could be raised and lowered in a slot set inside a boat along the center line. When lowered it served as a keel, permitting the boat to sail to windward; when raised, the craft could navigate in shoal waters. Twiss, for his part, had invented a new type of landing craft for infantry. It carried a flat shield across the bow, pierced with loopholes that could be lowered like a castle drawbridge to land assaulting troops with their boots and powder dry.[2] These inventions were considered too radical and were not used on Lake Champlain, so Twiss and Schank turned to the problem of bringing heavy vessels up from the St. Lawrence. Two of the ships were at anchor at the head of the Richelieu—the schooner *Carleton*, armed with twelve 6-pounders, and a large gondola carrying seven 9-pounders captured from the retreating Americans and renamed *Loyal Convert*. Stowed away in the hold of one of the British ships that had come out from England were the timbers of another schooner, the *Maria*, which was to be armed with fourteen 6-pounders. The most powerful vessel in Carleton's fleet was a two-masted, scow-like craft called a radeau, that was to be built at St. Johns. Named the *Thunderer*, she was a floating battery carrying six 24-pounders, six 12s and two howitzers —enough firepower to take on Arnold's entire fleet all by herself. To these craft were added a score of gunboats, each carrying a single 24-pounder in the bow and four longboats armed with smaller guns.

With this powerful armada under construction, Carleton was not afraid of any fleet the Americans could put together. Their source of seamen and supplies was 250 miles away on the seacoast while his own was only a few miles down river. Work would be finished on his fleet long before the Americans could construct more powerful craft that would again tip the balance in their favor. So Carleton settled down to build his fleet without regard to the urgency of the situation. No steps were taken to harass the Americans.

Soon weather and the forces of nature began to play havoc with the British commander's time schedule. It took a week to get the *Maria* and the *Loyal Convert* out of the water above the rapids and onto the rollers which Schank had set on the ground for the 10-mile haul to clear water at St. Johns. They had progressed only a few miles when it began to rain. The hulks bogged down and began to sink into the mud. The rollers they rested on began to give way. Heavy timbers had to be used to prop up the ships. And still it

---

[2] Similar craft were to be developed for use in World War II. It took another twenty years for the Admiralty to adopt Schank's idea for the "drop keel," or centerboard.

rained. Weeks of valuable time trickled away, along with Carleton's patience. The *Maria* and the *Convert* had to be cleared out of the supply route to the south. Consequently, Schank gave orders to have them taken apart and carried piece by piece to St. Johns where they could be reassembled. The attempt to move them overland had been a costly failure. The time lost on the road could be regained only by increasing the power of the British fleet to meet the row galleys Arnold had been given time to complete. To reinforce the fleet, the British decided to bring up the 180-ton sloop-of-war *Inflexible*, carrying eighteen 12-pounders, which was under construction at Quebec. She was knocked down into sections and hauled overland to St. Johns. Working day and night under Schank's direction, teams of shipwrights and riggers took just twenty-eight days to relaunch *Inflexible* on the lake. With her clouds of sails billowing against the sky, she was the most powerful ship that had ever been seen on America's inland waters.

Despite the size of the force being brought against him, Arnold kept up a bold front. To improve the morale of his men and to test the readiness of the British, he cruised down the lake to a narrow strait at Windmill Point, little more than 20 miles from the British base at St. Johns. There he taunted Carleton by drawing his fleet up in line of battle across the mile-wide channel in full sight of the enemy. Irritated by this display of insolence, the British dragged a battery of cannon up the cliffs overlooking the American anchorage and let fly a few ranging shots. Arnold merely danced away.

Arnold originally planned to meet the enemy in mid-lake. But when he learned of the existence of the *Inflexible*, which completely outclassed his entire force, he adopted a defensive strategy. Soundings were taken around Valcour Island, and on September 30 he moved his fleet into the narrow bay between the New York shore and the 2-mile-long island. There the hastily-outfitted galleys *Congress* and *Washington* joined him. Thickly wooded and rising about 180 feet, the island screened the American vessels from discovery by ships approaching from the north. A shoal at the northern end of the channel would also protect them from an attack in that direction.

For the most part, Arnold's captains, including his second in command, General David Waterbury, wanted to sail into the open channel and engage the British in a running fight to the south where they could take refuge behind Crown Point. Their argument was that the fleet could give battle—and then be preserved to fight another day. Arnold dissented. There was but one reason for the existence of the fleet—to fight the enemy and delay him, thereby giving the Northern Army time to counter the British thrust toward Albany and the south. Arnold's objective was not to preserve the fleet which, as a later generation would put it, was expendable. His judgment was sound. "A retreat before square-rigged sailing vessels having a fair wind, by a heterogeneous force like his own, of unequal speeds and batteries, could result only in disaster," according to Admiral Mahan. "Concerted fire and successful escape were alike improbable; and besides escape, if feasible, was but throwing up the game." Every day that he could delay Carleton brought winter and the end of the campaigning season that much closer.

Arnold correctly surmised that the British would wait for a stiff wind before proceeding south to hunt him down. He counted on them missing his fleet in its lair to the lee of Valcour and continuing on their way up the lake. Knowing that only a handful of the enemy vessels would be able to beat back against the wind, he noted that this meant that only a few "can attack us at the same time and those will be exposed to the fire of the whole fleet." To prevent Carleton and Captain Thomas Pringle, who had been named to command the British fleet, from dropping anchor and waiting for the wind to shift to the south, he would send a vessel or two out of his anchorage to fire a couple of shots before hurrying back to the line of battle.

At the time of the battle, Arnold, who had taken charge of the *Congress*, had fifteen vessels under his command.[3] These included the two other galleys, the *Washington* and *Trumbull*, the cutter *Lee*, and sloop *Enterprise*, and schooners *Revenge* and *Royal Savage* and eight gondolas, all manned by about seven hundred fifty men, mostly raw hands. Finishing touches were applied to some of the craft that had been rushed to completion as they lay in the cove. Tall, freshly-cut branches were tied along their sides to shield the men against sniper fire from the island itself. Although Arnold's fleet was sizeable and the numbers of men engaged were nearly equal, the

---

[3] The fourth galley, the *Gates*, was not finished in time for the battle and the schooner *Liberty* was detached on other duties. There has been considerable debate over whether the ninth gondola, the *Success*, was present for the action. The evidence indicates she was not.

British ships could throw about twice as much metal and were manned by trained sailors and marines under the command of experienced Royal Navy officers. Arnold called his own men "a wretched, motley crew. The marines, the refuse of every regiment, and the sailors, few of them ever wet with salt water."

Sails bellying in a chill northwest wind that stripped the lakeside trees of the last of their leaves, the British ships came in sight of Valcour Island early on the morning of October 11. Led by Carleton and Pringle, in the schooner *Maria*, they had sailed from St. Johns a week before. They proceeded cautiously up the lake, trailed by 400 flat-bottomed boats filled with troops. Ragged Vs of honking geese filled the lead-gray sky and accompanied them on the way southward. As Arnold had hoped, the British sailed past the entrance to his anchorage and went nearly 2 miles beyond the southernmost tip of the island before putting about. They would have to beat back against the strong wind that had been carrying them along. The first part of Arnold's plan had gone like clockwork. He gave the order to clear for action. Guns were loaded and run out. Additional powder and shot was brought from below. Wet blankets were draped about the magazines. Matches were lit. The decks were spread with sand to keep them from getting slippery with blood. The men worked with zeal, and Arnold undoubtedly hoped that the few weeks training they had received would have some effect.

With the *Congress* in the van, Arnold ordered the other galleys and the schooner *Royal Savage* to slip their moorings and move into the center of the lake. Whether he hoped to take advantage of the disarray of the British or to lure them into the channel where they would be targets for the entire American fleet is unknown. The British accepted the challenge. After firing a few shots, Arnold countermanded the order and withdrew into the crescent-shaped line. Unfortunately, the maneuver was not made without loss. Lacking the sweeps of the galleys, the *Royal Savage* could not head straight into the wind and was unable to return directly to the anchorage. "By some bad management," as Arnold put it, she ran aground on the southern tip of Valcour. Closing in rapidly, a group of British gunboats, which looked like so many crawling bugs with their single big gun in the bow and their oars slashing at the water, began to knock her to pieces. Hawley and his crew abandoned ship and were saved, but Arnold's papers and belongings that had not been transferred to the *Congress* were lost with the ship.

Because of the perverse wind, only the schooner *Carleton* and the gunboats came within range of the American fleet. The powerful radeau *Thunderer* and the flagship *Maria* never managed to get into action at all. The *Inflexible* brought her broadside to bear only after hours of clawing back down the lake. The *Carleton*, commanded by Lieutenant J. R. Dacres, finally came within musket shot of the Yankee line and dropped anchor. Dacres put a spring[4] on his ship's cable and had her pulled around until all his guns could play on the half-moon of rebel ships. By half-past twelve, "the engagement became general and very warm" as Arnold put it. "The cannonade was tremendous," declared Baron Riedesel, the commander of the German troops who was on the *Maria*.

The cliffs and the tall trees on both sides of the channel magnified the thunder of the guns to frightful proportions. On board the *Congress*, Arnold was everywhere. Smoke-blackened and hoarse, he moved from gun to gun, training, elevating, firing each cannon in her broadside. Pausing only to fire his pistols at the enemy as his inept gun crews reloaded, he shouted instructions and encouragement. The *Carleton* fired again and again into the American line, her shot dismounting guns and shattering the light wooden sides of the hastily built vessels. Arnold directed that the American fire be centered on the schooner. Hit by a flying splinter, Dacres was knocked unconscious. Another officer lost an arm. Then a lucky American shot severed the spring that was holding her broadside on target. The schooner's bow swung toward the Yankee line leaving her open to being raked. Anxiously, Pringle signaled the *Carleton* to withdraw but she was unable to move. Gaping holes appeared in her sides, and she began to sink low into the lake. The exultant American gunners poured shot after shot into her, sweeping her from end to end. Finally, nineteen-year-old Midshipman Edward Pellew, the *Carleton*'s only unwounded officer,[5] climbed out on the bowsprit to kick the jib over to the windward in hopes of bringing her around. With the help of two longboats she was finally towed out of range with two feet of water in the hold, eight men dead and another eight wounded on her deck.

---

[4] A spring is a rope taken from the quarter (one side of the stern) of a ship, to the anchor. By hauling upon it, the broadside is turned in the direction desired.

[5] Pellew later became Admiral Lord Exmouth, one of Britain's greatest sailors. Dacres also lived to hoist his flag.

In the meantime, Arnold continued to pound away at the gunboats, blowing up one manned by German artillerymen with a shot in its magazine. A pillar of smoke and flame rose from the spot where she had been a moment before. The American fire was so rapid, reported a British officer, that the boats dared not to come nearer than seven hundred yards, "as whenever they approached nearer they were greatly annoyed by grape shot." The *Carleton*'s place was taken by other British ships that had at last tacked up the lake. Slowly superior British firepower began to tell. The *Inflexible* arrived shortly before dusk—about five o'clock—and fired several broadsides into the American line, silencing most of Arnold's guns. As if to warn the Yankees there would be no retreat, the British had landed hordes of Indians on Valcour and the mainland. From the high ground, they blazed away at the decks of the American ships with muskets. Fortunately, the trees that Arnold had placed along his vessels' bulwarks provided an effective defense. As darkness fell, Pringle called off his ships and decided to wait until morning to finish off the American fleet.

Silhouetted against the flames of the *Royal Savage*—set afire by the British to prevent her recapture by the rebels—Arnold's captains arrived aboard the *Congress* for a council of war. Gathered in the galley's great cabin, smeared with blood and blackened by powder, they gave their reports. The flagship had at least twelve shotholes in her hull, some big enough for a man to put his head through, several at the waterline. The first lieutenant of the *Washington* had been killed, her captain and master wounded. Her mainmast had been shot through and would have to be replaced. All the officers of the *New York* except her captain had been killed. The *Philadelphia* had been so badly mauled that she sank at her mooring about a half-hour after the fighting had ceased. Several of the vessels had guns dismounted by enemy fire. All were leaking and badly in need of repair. Rigging and sails were in shreds. Ammunition was short. Arnold estimated that sixty men had been killed or wounded—with the dead being thrown unceremoniously overboard. It was obvious that the fleet could not take another day's battering. For the gloomy Americans there appeared to be no escape. The British fleet was lined up at the mouth of the channel; Indians and British troops bivouacked on Valcour and the mainland.

Arnold was always best in adversity. Fog began to set in, which gave him the opportunity he needed. With just enough sail set to maintain steerage way, oars muffled with rags, and the wounded covered so their groans would not carry across the black water, the remaining vessels were ordered to slip silently through the British fleet to the safety of Crown Point 35 miles away up the lake. At seven o'clock, with darkness complete and the mist hanging low over the water, the *Trumbull* led the way through the British line. The smaller craft followed at intervals while the *Congress* and *Washington* brought up the rear. Each vessel except the flagship, which was last, showed a dim lantern at its stern. Sliding along in the dark, the Americans could hear voices and hammering on the British vessels. About three hours after the *Trumbull* had started up the lake, the *Congress* was far enough away from the British for Arnold to order her noisy pumps manned.[6]

By dawn, when the British awoke to find the American anchorage was empty, Arnold and his fleet were at Schuyler's Island, a green mound in the lake about eight miles above Valcour. Enraged, Guy Carleton ordered an immediate pursuit without leaving orders for the troops that had been disembarked on the island. Pringle's vessels swept the waters around Valcour until the British were convinced that Arnold had made good his escape. An adverse wind slowed the pursuit to a crawl. Sending out scouts to locate the Yankees, Carleton returned to his anchorage.

"Most of the fleet is this minute come to an anchor," Arnold reported to Gates on the morning of October 12. "The Enemy's fleet is underway . . . and beating up. As soon as our leaks are stopp'd the whole fleet will make the utmost dispatch to Crown Point, where I beg you will send ammunition . . . On the whole, I think we have had a very fortunate escape." Attempts were made to plug the shot holes in Arnold's vessels and make them seaworthy, but the gondolas *Providence* and *New York* were too far gone to be salvaged. Arnold ordered their guns swayed out and placed at the extra ports of the remaining vessels. Skeleton crews took them out into 50 fathoms of water and chopped holes in their bottoms. A third gondola, the *New Jersey*, lay piled up on the rocks at the tip of the island where she rested because of the weight of the water in her. An attempt was

---

[6] Some historians contend that the Americans sailed around the lightly guarded northern end of Valcour rather than passing through the British line.

made to burn her but the vessel was too waterlogged for the flames to catch. The men had a hasty meal of boiled potatoes—their first food in twenty-four hours—washed down with a few swallows of rum. Then they went back to the sweeps.

Shortly before 2 P.M., what was left of Arnold's fleet was on its way south again. Sending the four remaining gondolas on ahead with the *Enterprise* and the *Lee*, he ordered the battered *Washington* to remain with the *Congress* as a rear guard. What followed must have been a nightmare for Arnold's men. Bucking contrary winds, pelted by cold sleet and rain, they bent and tugged endlessly at the sweeps, the pumps thumping endlessly in their ears. At any moment an enemy vessel might loom out of the heavy mist to unleash a broadside. When morning came, the Americans found they had come just six miles in sixteen hours. Crown Point was still twenty-eight miles away. The tall masts of the *Inflexible* were already in sight, only eight miles astern. The wind shifted and blew from the north, little comfort for the wretched Americans. It filled the sails of the British ships first, enabling the *Maria* to close the gap to little more than a mile before the first gusts reached the tattered sails of Arnold's vessels.

General Waterbury, in the *Washington*, said his craft was "so torn to pieces that it was almost impossible to keep her above water; my sails was so shot that carrying wind split them from foot to head." He asked Arnold for permission to run the galley ashore and to blow her up before she was overtaken. "I received for answer, by no means to run her ashore, but to push forward to Split Rock, where he would draw the fleet in a line and engage them again," added Waterbury. "But when I came to Split Rock, the whole fleet was making their escape as fast as they could and left me in the rear to fall into the enemy's hands." Cornered by the *Inflexible*, *Carleton*, and *Maria*, the wallowing galley absorbed a few broadsides before her flag fluttered down. Waterbury and 110 men were taken prisoner.

Stern chasers roaring defiance through the windows of her cabin, the *Congress* fought a stiff rear-guard action. The *Inflexible* lay under her quarter while the British schooners joined in pounding away at her. "They kept up an incessant fire on us for about five glasses [two-and-a-half hours] with round and grape shot, which we returned as briskly," reported Arnold. "The sails, rigging, and hull of the *Congress* were shattered and torn in pieces, the First Lieutenant and three men killed. . . ." Surrounded by seven enemy ships and with his own vessel being shot out from under him, Arnold resolved upon a final act of defiance. Signaling the gondolas to follow him to the windward where the enemy could not follow, he broke through the enemy line and herded the smaller craft upon the rocks of Buttonmold Bay, an inlet about ten miles north of Crown Point on the Vermont shore. The British stood offshore and pounded away at the American vessels at long range. Arnold ordered them set afire with their colors flying. He personally put the torch to the *Congress* and was the last to leap from her stranded hulk. After making certain there would be nothing left for the enemy to capture except a few charred wrecks, he marched the remaining 200 men—including 46 survivors from the flagship's original complement of 73—through the woods to Crown Point. "Very luckily," as he put it, "we escaped the savages who waylaid the road."

Who won the battle of Valcour Island? At first glance the answer is obvious. Of the fifteen vessels constituting Arnold's fleet during the fighting, all but four were lost. On the day of the battle, some 60 of his men were killed and wounded. Two days later, he sustained another 20 casualties. The *Washington*'s entire crew was captured.[7] In contrast, the British lost only one of their gunboats and fewer than 40 men were killed or wounded in the entire operation. Naval supremacy on Lake Champlain had passed to the British before the flames had consumed the shattered remnants of Arnold's fleet. Crown Point was hastily abandoned by Gates; the way to the Hudson and Albany lay open to Carleton's advancing troops. Only the fortifications at Ticonderoga blocked the British from rolling up Washington's crumbling army from the rear.

"The Rebel fleet upon Lake Champlain has been entirely defeated in two actions," Carleton wrote Germain on October 14. "The Rebels, upon the news reaching them of the defeat of their naval forces, set fire to all buildings and houses in and near Crown Point, and retired to Ticonderoga. . . ." So sure were the British that Valcour had been a victory that King George immediately made Carleton a Knight of the Bath. But hidden away in his dispatch was a

---

[7] Carleton immediately ordered the release on parole of Waterbury and his men. They arrived at Ticonderoga with such praise of their treatment by him that they were sent home to prevent them from lowering the will of the garrison to resist.

warning: "The season is so far advanced that I cannot yet pretend to inform your lordship whether anything further can be done this year." British troops were within sight of Ticonderoga, but Carleton hesitated to launch a final assault. A siege would take time, the terrible northern winter was coming on, and his supply line was overextended. With the American fleet out of the way, Carleton was convinced he could afford to wait until spring when siege operations would be more favorable. And so, he ordered a withdrawal down the lake to St. Johns, from where the army was dispersed into winter quarters in Canada. "If we could have begun our expedition four weeks earlier," observed Baron Riedesel, "I am satisfied that everything could have ended this year." Four weeks was exactly the time it had taken to launch the *Inflexible*.

The following year Burgoyne would move south to be met by a bolstered American army that would force his surrender at Saratoga. This victory brought French financial, military, and naval power to the aid of the struggling colonists. Without it, final victory would have been impossible. "That the Americans were strong enough to impose the capitulation of Saratoga," notes Mahan, "was due to the invaluable year of delay secured to them by their little navy on Lake Champlain, created by the indomitable energy, and handled with the indomitable courage of the traitor, Benedict Arnold."

XII

The Secret War

Britain's major failure in the opening years of the war was at sea. Success in putting down the American rebellion depended largely on the Royal Navy's ability to prevent Yankee and neutral ships from running the blockade with arms and ammunition that had been loaded in Spain, Holland, France, or the islands of the Caribbean. Even though the King's ships controlled the sea lanes, Washington's army was successfully equipped with supplies and munitions that could not be produced at home. Outgoing American and foreign vessels somehow managed to elude the blockading ships, carrying goods which were then exchanged for necessary supplies. Ninety percent of the gunpowder available to the American forces before the end of 1777—nearly 1.5 million pounds of it—was brought in by sea. Without this supply, the rebellion would have shriveled away.

From the very beginning of the conflict, the eyes of France and America had been directed toward one another. Sailors and travelers returning from France reported that the French were friendly to the American cause. As soon as the Treaty of Paris was signed in 1763 ending the Seven Years' War with the expulsion of France from her empire in the New World, French ministers began to think of revenge against England. The Duc de Choiseul, King Louis XV's foreign minister and a favorite of Madame de Pompadour, set out on a course to restore France to her traditional grandeur. No doubt the British colonies in America would soon tear themselves loose from England's tutelage. If France were to have her revenge, she must be ready to seize that moment. She must turn her back upon the dynastic struggles of Europe and in alliance with Spain be prepared to fight Britain for the supremacy of the seas. So, during the next few years, Choiseul dispatched an assortment of agents to America to sound out conditions. They sent back detailed reports on American defenses, trade patterns, and reactions to the Stamp Act and subsequent measures.

Choiseul was cheered by reports that the Virginians had declared that if trouble came with Britain, they would call upon France for help. Considering the revulsion of the colonists for Catholicism and their fears of France, this declaration showed desperation. Another French spy found a great spirit of liberty abroad in the land though he warned that the Americans desired possession of the French islands of Santo Domingo and St. Pierre and Miquelon in order to control the sugar market and fisheries. Perhaps the shrewdest assessment was made by Johann Kalb, a retired army officer, who toured the not-yet-independent colonies for several months.[1] The Americans were deeply attached to England and were angered only by the new taxes and restrictions, he reported. In a pinch, they would join the British to take the French islands. If they rebelled, their first inclination would be to be wary of foreign powers for fear of losing their own liberties. Choiseul preferred to believe the more optimistic reports. By 1766, he was convinced the time had come for the expected rupture. Rebellion had not yet ripened in America, however, and the years slipped away.

Choiseul fell from power—the victim of a court intrigue—and was followed in 1774 as foreign minister by the Comte de Vergennes. Vergennes brought to his post in the service of young King Louis XVI a passionate hatred of England and a desire to revenge France's humiliation. He proceeded, however, with considerably more caution than his predecessor. For the moment, Vergennes contented

---

[1] Kalb, an able soldier, was the son of Bavarian peasants but when he returned to America in 1777 with Lafayette he styled himself "Baron de Kalb." He was killed at Camden in 1780, without having received the recognition from Congress that he deserved.

himself with cultivating the Family Compact with Spain and enlarging his secret service. A French informant got himself elected to England's Parliament and reported on the secret debates. A secretary in the American Department, which supervised colonial affairs, was put on the payroll to the tune of 500 guineas a year. Other spies were at work in the War Office and the Admiralty.[2] Soon, Vergennes was extending a cautious hand to Benjamin Franklin, who was the agent for the colonies in London.

The Frenchman was perfectly willing to help the Americans if that hurt Britain. But he worried that England would turn her full power on any country that had interfered in her affairs if the conflict were settled peacefully. Vergennes knew the North administration was inept and was concerned that public pressure might drive it from power if the war went badly. If North fell, the King might be forced to recall the Earl of Chatham, the implacable architect of victory, to form a new ministry. Chatham might conciliate the Americans and summon them to join in renewing the war with France which had been ended against his judgment in 1763. Since the pick of French seamen were exposed in the Newfoundland fisheries and her colonies and trade were unprotected, Vergennes thought it best to be circumspect in his dealings with the Americans lest the British take alarm.

Franklin used the diplomatic weapon placed in his hands by France's interest in America with telling effect. He was under no illusion about the generosity of the motives behind it. Certainly, all Europe was sympathetic to the American cause, he wrote the Reverend Samuel Cooper, but he coolly analyzed the basis for this sympathy. "Europe has its reasons. It fancies itself in some danger from the growth of British power, and would be glad to see it divided against itself." This insight did not prevent Franklin from prophesying that foreign interference on behalf of the colonists would be the likely result if Britain allowed the situation to deteriorate. His friends among the Whigs, no doubt briefed by Franklin, amplified these warnings. Burke, Chatham, the Duke of Grafton, all pointed out that France might take the side of the Americans if rebellion broke out. Lord North joined them in dreading a new Anglo-French war, but his government did not alter its coercive policy in America.

---

[2] Helen Auger, *The Secret War for Independence* (New York 1955).

With the colonies drifting toward rebellion, gunrunning from the ports of the Bay of Biscay and the West Indies became big business. Henri Doniol, a French historian who searched the archives in Paris, claims that Franklin was instrumental in launching this secret war. If so, Franklin was successful in covering his tracks, for no documentary evidence has turned up to support Doniol's assertion. As Auger points out, it was unnecessary for Franklin to have taken a direct role in securing arms and powder for the American cause. The great trading houses of Europe—the Crommelins of Amsterdam, the Montaudoins of Nantes, the Guardoquis of Bilbao—were strong supporters of the American cause and quite capable of acting without prompting where there was money to be made.

Paradoxically, the slave trade served as the hook upon which to hang France's aid to the American colonists struggling for freedom. Nantes was the center of the French slave trade, which made the port an obvious center for clandestine operations, Auger observes. Since slavers sailing out to Africa were usually heavily armed, there was always a supply of munitions and arms in the town—which was slyly augmented by the ministry. The French merchants had also built up close contacts with American traders in the West Indies as a result of the trade in "black ivory." It was a fairly simple process to transform these illegal contacts into a gunrunning operation. Aside from the psychological gratification of revenge upon England, the trade gave the French merchants the opportunity to divert valuable colonial commerce from London and Bristol.

The French had their eyes set especially upon the tobacco trade, which amounted to about half the total colonial exports. On the eve of the Revolution, the American colonies were shipping about 99 million pounds of tobacco a year to Britain, which then re-exported 83 million pounds to other countries, earning a tidy profit for that service, notes one authority.[3] Obviously, the Yankees had something with which to pay for military supplies. The European merchants accordingly expanded their trade with the colonies. Under the terms of the Acts of Trade and Navigation, the Americans had been allowed to trade with the Continent only in certain restricted items. For example, an American merchant ship carrying salt fish to be exchanged for French wines and silks was required to call at an English port on

---

[3] Robert G. Albion, *Sea Lanes in Wartime* (New York 1942).

both legs of the voyage for a thorough check of the cargo as well as payment of duty. As war approached, Yankee ships omitted the duty calls. American merchants established their own agents abroad to help dispose of the forbidden cargoes and to see that ships returned directly across the Atlantic laden with goods that would not have passed British inspection. The illicit trade was so effective that by July 1775 a British diplomat stationed in Paris estimated that France had already furnished the colonies with military equipment worth at least $6 million.

Throughout the first summer of the war, Congress was torn over the question of throwing open American ports in exchange for foreign assistance. In 1774, it had adopted the so-called Continental Association by which Americans pledged themselves not to buy British goods or export American products to Britain. This policy was intended to present Britain with the choice of economic ruin or agreement to the demands of the colonies. The Continental Association, however, had proven to be a double-edged sword. British merchants were deprived of valuable markets and trade, but the Yankees were cut off from supplies of arms and ammunition. Franklin advocated as early as July 1775 that American ports be opened to any nation that would protect American shipping. For most members of Congress this step was too close to final independence. No other measure except independence itself would be more calculated to burn the last bridges of reconciliation. So it was not until April 1776 that American ports were opened to all nations and Yankee ships allowed to sail where they wished—British men-of-war willing.

Despite radical objections to making private profit the polestar of the new republic, the merchants were called in to provide the materials of war. They accounted for the great bulk of supplies that were brought into the country during the war. Some, like Robert Morris of the great Philadelphia merchant house of Willing and Morris, mixed public service and private profit. In 1775, for example, he entered into a contract with Congress to supply powder to the government. It ensured his firm a clear profit of $60,000 without risk of loss. Congress was obliged to pay a flat price of $14 a barrel, whether the powder reached America safely or not. At another point, Morris disclosed to an associate, with no apparent feelings of guilt, that he was withholding a recent shipment of powder from the market until prices improved, since Congress had no immediate need of it. Such deals merely sharpened the suspicions of the radicals that businessmen were unpatriotic and self-seeking.

On September 18, 1775, Congress resolved to systematize the procurement of military supplies—and as usual appointed a committee to deal with the matter. The Secret Committee, as it was known, was given wide powers and could draw upon large sums of money to be advanced to contractors. It conducted its business behind closed doors and destroyed most of its records. By November, it had been empowered to export produce to the West Indies in exchange for war materiel. By January 1776, its duties included the importation of supplies of all sorts: medicines, surgical instruments, blankets, cotton goods, and various metals. When privateering was formally authorized in April, the committee was given authority to arm and man vessels in foreign countries. For the duration of its life,[4] the Secret Committee was controlled by the firm of Willing and Morris—in fact, it was often operated almost as a subsidiary of the mercantile house. Thomas Willing was its first chairman, succeeded within a few months by his partner, Robert Morris. The original members included Franklin, Silas Deane, Robert R. Livingston, John Alsop, John Dickinson, Thomas McKean, John Langdon, and Samuel Ward—all men with considerable experience in foreign commerce.

The line between the public and private interest was often thin. Several committee members, especially Morris and Deane, had been heavily engaged in importing powder and arms both for Congress and on their own account before the committee was formed. After its organization, most of the contracts went to Willing and Morris, to Deane's friends and relatives, and to concerns connected with other committee members. At one time, Morris reported that his firm had twenty ships carrying supplies for the Secret Committee and five others in which it had an interest. In sorting out his public and private operations Morris was very hazy; he often shipped goods belonging to Willing and Morris in vessels whose charter and insurance were being paid by the Secret Committee. "There never had been so fair an opportunity of making a large fortune," he said.

Other merchants also found a good thing in the shipment of contraband. John and Nicholas Brown, of Providence, were given an

---

[4] The Secret Committee became the Committee of Commerce in July 1777.

advance of $20,000 in December 1775 to import munitions, with a commission of 2½ percent on their exports and their imports. On one voyage, they netted some 1,400 pounds. Many other merchants with close connections with the Secret Committee received juicy contracts. One of the committee's more questionable operations was launched in January 1776. Congress voted 40,000 pounds to import presents for the Indians. The contracting merchants were allowed a commission of 5 percent. The government insured their ships against seizure. Three of the four contractors were members of the committee: Morris, Alsop, and Francis Lewis, a new member. The fourth was Livingston's cousin. "Merchants experienced in foreign trade, with clever ships and captains ready to sail out on dangerous voyages, were the only ones meriting contracts," writes Auger, in explanation of the system. "There was profitmaking and profiteering, but the sinews of war were supplied. No real prejudice existed against a man entrusted with public business using it for the profit of himself and his family and friends."

While the Secret Committee was amassing supplies, Congress appointed on November 29, 1775, a Committee of Secret Correspondence "for the sole purpose of correspondence with our friends in Great Britain, Ireland, and other parts of the world." Under the chairmanship of Franklin, at seventy America's most experienced diplomat, this committee was to "probe sentiments abroad and to determine the intentions of the European powers—especially France—toward the rebellion." [5] These findings, in turn, would be used to influence basic decisions that had to be made by Congress.

Should the colonies send diplomatic and commercial agents abroad? Should they open American ports to trade with all nations except Britain and on what terms? Should they form alliances[6] with friendly powers? Should they declare for independence? Writing to Charles W. F. Dumas, a Swiss journalist long settled in The Hague who had sound political contacts, Franklin summed up the American position:

---

[5] The Committee of Secret Correspondence became the Committee on Foreign Affairs on April 17, 1777. It was the direct forerunner of the Department of State.

[6] By an alliance, the Americans of 1776 meant a pact of friendship and commerce, not a political agreement.

We wish to know whether, if, as seems likely to happen, we should be obliged to break off all connexion with Britain, and declare ourselves independent people, there is any state or power in Europe, which would be willing to enter into an alliance for the benefit of our commerce.

The Committee gained an inkling of France's intentions before the year was out. In December, a mysterious stranger named Julien Achard de Bonvouloir, who claimed to be a Flemish merchant, arrived in Philadelphia after a "terrible" voyage that had lasted a hundred days. Safely ashore, he put out feelers for a private meeting with the Committee of Secret Correspondence. The members—including the gout-ridden Franklin—had to go stealthily to the rendezvous selected, each one alone and by a different route at dusk. Bonvouloir maintained that he was a mere private citizen, in America only to explore the possibility of making a business deal to supply the Americans with munitions. Franklin immediately recognized the familiar aura of diplomatic intrigue, and surmised that the visitor was a French agent. This assumption is clearly apparent from the line of questioning followed by the Americans as reported by Bonvouloir to his superiors.

"They asked whether France would aid them and at what cost," he wrote. "I told them I thought France wished them well. . . . They asked me whether it would be prudent to send an empowered deputy to France. I told them I imagined this would be precipitous, even hazardous; that everything is known about London in Paris and about France in London, and that the step would singe the English beard." To a request for the dispatch of two engineers to help out the army, Bonvouloir replied: "France is well able to furnish you with two able engineers. All that is needed is to ask for them." And in reply to a query about the possibility of arms and munitions being procured in France in exchange for American commodities, the visitor blandly replied that "as this is a matter of merchant to merchant I do not see great inconvenience on the part of France."

The French archives have established the correctness of Franklin's assumptions regarding Bonvouloir. He had been employed as a secret agent by Vergennes at the recommendation of the Comte de Guines, the French ambassador to London. Bonvouloir was an adventurer who had traveled widely in America and the West Indies.

He had been instructed to gather information in the colonies and to give the rebel leaders unofficial assurance of French sympathy. Bonvouloir could not have arrived at a more opportune moment for the Americans. Montreal had just fallen, the British were besieged in Boston, and the conquest of Quebec appeared imminent. The wily Franklin saw to it that the stranger was well received and given all the information that would present the rebel cause in the best light. Bonvouloir was mesmerized and reported glowingly that "the troops are well clothed, well paid and well commanded . . . they have unbelievable spirit and good will. It is true that they are led by wise leaders."

At almost the same time, the Committee of Secret Correspondence had requested Arthur Lee, a member of the prominent Virginia family who had been acting in London as Massachusetts' agent, to serve as its correspondent. He was instructed to use "great circumspection and secrecy" in sounding out the attitude of the foreign powers to the American cause. Morris's Secret Committee also engaged in its own delicate negotiations for foreign assistance. Two more mysterious Frenchmen named Penet and Pliarne arrived at Philadelphia along toward the end of 1775 and immediately began discussing with the committee contracts for the supply of arms and munitions. They, too, denied any connection with the French government, saying they were only merchants from Nantes. But as one member of Congress wrote in his diary, they hinted "that our Ships may trade to that Kingdom by Connivance & that they are willing to send their Bottoms here."

On the strength of these intimations, the Secret Committee decided on March 3, 1776, to send an agent to France. The choice fell upon Silas Deane, perhaps because of his knowledge of commerce and the fact that he was available, having recently been replaced as a Connecticut delegate to Congress. A better selection might have been made, for Deane acknowledged in a letter to his wife that "people here, members of Congress and others, have unhappily and erroneously thought me a schemer." He was to go to Paris in the guise of a merchant supplying goods for the Indian trade, but his main task was to make contact with Vergennes and ascertain his intentions. Deane was to seek "clothing and arms for twenty-five thousand men, with a suitable quantity of ammunition and one hundred field pieces." The prospect of American independence was to be dangled before the French foreign minister as bait, with the explanation that "France has been pitched on for the first application, from an opinion that if we should, as there is great appearance we shall, come to a total separation from Great Britain, France would be looked upon as the power whose friendship it would be fittest for us to obtain and cultivate." And so Congress launched its first frail craft on the sea of international relations.

Fearful of British spies, Deane adopted the name of Jones, wrote his letters in invisible ink, and vowed that in the presence of English-speaking people he would use only the French language. This prompted Vergennes to remark: "He must be the most silent man in France, for I defy him to say six consecutive words in French." But before Deane even arrived in Paris, the French government had decided to take the plunge and provide what he was on his way to ask for—war supplies and money. Bonvouloir's optimistic report had gone a long way toward convincing Vergennes of the viability of the American cause. Fears that a reconciliation between Britain and her colonies was possible had been allayed by the North administration's decision to mount a full-scale offensive in America. The door to reconciliation had been slammed shut. Britain's military forces would be tied up by the attempt to reconquer the Americans. The immediate danger of a swoop on French and Spanish colonies in the Caribbean had receded. England could be left to dissipate her military and naval strength and exhaust her finances in a colonial struggle. The critical moment for France would come when the British gave up the struggle in America and withdrew. The degree of danger to France would depend almost entirely on the state of the British forces at the time. Vergennes was doing his best to ensure that they would not remain intact by broadening French support for the Americans.

An idea had been planted in his mind by Bonvouloir. If a sham commercial firm were established to supply munitions in exchange for American products, it might be possible for France to stir up trouble for her traditional enemy across the Channel without disturbing her official role as a neutral. If British protests were followed by threats, the French court could make a show of stopping the shipments without the risk of exposing its own involvement. The scheme was fleshed out and propelled by Pierre Augustin Caron, sometime watchmaker, man-about-town, and secret agent, who had added de Beaumarchais to his name when he had taken up playwriting. So eagerly did Beaumarchais push the cause of secret aid to the Americans that he sometimes gave the impression of being its instigator. Vergennes found in the ebullient dramatist a brilliant ally who helped convert King Louis XVI and the other ministers to the necessity of moving quickly to help the embattled colonists.

Beaumarchais had already carried out an intrigue for King Louis XV and Madame Du Barry as theatrical as any in his plays. The Chevalier d'Eon, a French secret agent who had undertaken the dual role of brother and sister at the court of Catherine the Great, had returned to France from Russia. D'Eon was a hermaphrodite whose feminine characteristics became dominant. He began to dress permanently as a woman and in his new role aroused jealousy. Banished from the court, the chevalier—who now preferred to be known as mademoiselle—went to England, taking with him some important state papers. As it was feared he might sell the documents to the British government, Beaumarchais was assigned to get them back. The playwright payed court to this "lady" who "drank and smoked and swore like a German trooper"—and carried off the papers in triumph.

On one of his trips to London, Beaumarchais met Arthur Lee, with whom he discussed the prospects for the rebellion. Ever prone to optimism, the playwright quickly convinced himself that Britain's colonial empire was breathing its last. He felt France's supreme opportunity had arrived to deliver the death blow. Beaumarchais worked on young King Louis to break down his scruples against making trouble for England on behalf of rebels. A drumfire of remonstrances and memoirs commenced. Beaumarchais wrote Louis in December that he appreciated, "the delicate conscientiousness of your Majesty . . . But, Sire, the policy of governments is not the moral law of their citizens. . . . It is the English, Sire, whom you need to humiliate and weaken, if you do not wish to be humiliated and weakened yourself on every occasion."

By January 22, 1776, Beaumarchais had worked out a dazzling scheme for funneling secret aid to the Americans. A fictitious firm to be called Roderique Hortalez & Company would supply arms. It would be financed by a subsidy of a million livres (about $200,000) each from the Bourbon Kings of France and Spain, backed by another million livres subscribed by French businessmen interested in trade with America. The firm would be allowed to draw military supplies from government arsenals and would replace them with modern equipment. The Americans would pay for the supplies in products such as rice and tobacco that the French government would help Beaumarchais sell in France at a profit. Through a dizzying pyramiding of figures, the playwright-turned-financier showed Louis how a million livres invested in munitions would result in profits of nine million livres. More important, the investment of a million livres in arms for the Americans "will cost the English 100 millions if they persevere in going 2,000 leagues from home to attack them."

A month later, Beaumarchais addressed another impassioned memoir to the King ominously headed "Peace or War." It warned of a Britain reconciled to her colonies, moving to capture the French sugar islands. "What shall we do in this extremity to win peace and save our islands?" he asked. "Sire, the only means is to give help to the Americans . . . Believe me, Sire, the saving of a few millions today may soon cause a great deal of blood to flow. . . ." Vergennes followed up with two papers arguing for a future war with England. He felt France's policy should be to deceive the British as far as possible, giving London a false sense of security. Such an approach would gain time for the Americans to be armed with French supplies while they were kept from making peace with Britain by vague promises of a military alliance. In the meantime, France and Spain would hasten preparations for the inevitable war with England.

The King wavered. There was strong opposition at court to the proposal, especially from Baron Turgot, the Controller General of Finance. Prophetically he warned that Vergennes's plan would lead to the bankruptcy of France. Alarmist arguments about the safety of France's colonies did not impress him. There was no need to go to war to secure the independence of the American colonies because all the colonies of the New World—including those belonging to France—were destined for freedom sooner or later. Only reluctantly did the hard-headed finance minister allow himself to be persuaded to support a limited policy of secret aid to the Americans.[7] When he

---

[7] Turgot was proven correct in the long run. The precarious financial condition of France after the American Revolution contributed at least indirectly to the outbreak of the French Revolution in 1789. If Louis XVI had followed the advice of Turgot rather than that of Vergennes and Beaumarchais, he might not have lost his head.

made a decision, Louis took the advice of Vergennes and Beaumarchais. On April 22, 1776, he issued a Royal command for the rebuilding of the navy and the supplying of new equipment to the army, thus releasing a great stock of surplus arms to Hortalez & Co. This instruction was followed on May 2 by an order directing that one million livres be furnished to Beaumarchais. To prevent English spies from linking the arrangement with the government, Vergennes had a note informing the playwright of the decision written by his fifteen-year-old son so his own handwriting and that of his clerks would not be recognized. Ten days later, Turgot resigned.

Establishing his home and business in a large building once used as the Dutch Embassy, Beaumarchais lost no time in accumulating enough supplies to fill a fleet of eight ships. An unresolved question was whether the supplies were intended as a gift or loan to the Americans. Arthur Lee, who either did not understand Beaumarchais's intentions or was misled by his own excitement, sent word to Philadelphia that the materiel was a gift. When Deane arrived, authorized to pay in promised goods for the arms and ammunition shipped to America, Beaumarchais made a contract with him on that basis. The suspicious Lee, who had been eased out of the arrangement after Deane came to Paris, immediately charged that the other two conspirators were trying to extract payment for what had been promised for nothing. For nearly two centuries attempts to disentangle the complexities of the intrigue have been largely unsuccessful. While it appears certain that the French government did not expect to be repaid, Beaumarchais almost as certainly intended to pocket whatever he could make on the deal—and for good reason. No matter what the King may have intended, the playwright and the French merchants had invested handsome sums in the venture. Eventually, the United States settled with his descendants for about $160,000.

Mountains of supplies began to pile up at Marseilles, Nantes, Bordeaux, Havre, and Dunkirk. But risks of the gravest sort had to be overcome before the contraband could be gotten to its destination. Lord Stormont, the British ambassador, was well informed by spies and periodically pressured the French to remember their neutral obligations. Once a vessel got to sea, it had to evade a line of British cruisers off the French coast and another in American waters. Mariners prayed for gales that would scatter the patrols in the Bay of Biscay and for fog to blanket their approach to the Yankee coast.

Under an assumed name, Beaumarchais went to Havre in December 1776 to get his first shipment to sea. Stored in neat piles along the waterfront, artillery, muskets, and powder from the French arsenals, together with thousands of uniforms and blankets were ready to be lightered aboard three ships lying out in the stream. Unfortunately, the flamboyant Beaumarchais could not resist the temptation to rehearse a group of actors in his popular new *Barber of Seville.* Of course, his identity quickly became known. The British ambassador raised such a storm at Versailles that Vergennes had to issue orders to hold up the sailing of the ships. Possibly, word of the order was leaked to Beaumarchais. In any case he made frantic efforts to get off at least one ship. Longshoremen worked for two nights in wild confusion to cram whatever they could on board the brig *Amphitrite.* The port authorities prevented the other two ships from sailing, but the brig slipped away with 15,000 uniforms, 10,000 muskets, and about 75 bronze cannon from the Havre forts and arsenal. The *Amphitrite* managed to elude the ships of the Royal Navy and reached Portsmouth, New Hampshire, safely.

Eight more of Beaumarchais's vessels are reported to have reached Portsmouth that spring. In March, for example, the *Mercury* arrived after a forty-day voyage from Nantes with a cargo of 1,000 barrels of gunpowder, 12,000 muskets, 11,000 flints, 1,000 barrels of powder, and 46 cases of cloth. Other merchant houses also plunged into the munitions business. One ship arrived with a cargo that had cost $90,000 in Nantes and sold for $240,000 in Boston. "Nine tenths of the military supplies that made the victory at Saratoga possible came from France or through foreign merchants whom she secretly encouraged," one historian has noted.[8]

A moderate amount of trade in contraband also developed with Spain and Holland. In the case of Holland, most of the trade was indirect because the sea route past England was dangerous. Dutch goods were usually sent to France or the Dutch West Indian island of St. Eustatius for transshipment to the mainland. A few shipments of Swedish iron came through safely from Gothenburg, but such crossings were the exception. As trade with Spain had always been allowed, with certain restrictions, even under the old colonial system, American merchants had close ties with the Guardoquis of Bilbao.

[8] Claude H. Van Tyne, *The War of Independence* (Boston 1929).

Salt figured prominently in the trade with Spain because, after powder, it was the commodity most seriously needed in America. Salt was essential for preserving meat and fish, and the old source at Turks Island in the West Indies had been cut off by the war.

Although Beaumarchais and the other European merchants were fairly lucky in getting their early shipments safely to America—only about one ship in nine being caught by the British—the Atlantic crossing was hazardous. Because of the danger of capture, for every vessel that went directly to America from Europe, scores shuttled back and forth to the French, Dutch, and Spanish islands of the Caribbean. From the islands, these cargoes were carried to America in the numerous small, swift vessels that the Yankees had long had in the island trade. The advantages of the divided voyage were emphasized by William Bingham, who made his fortune as agent for the Secret Committee at Martinique. "Very few French masters of vessels are acquainted with the coast of America, and admitting they were, large ships cannot take advantage of running into small inlets and harbors as lesser vessels may," he declared. "Besides all the Continental vessels sail with skilful pilots, which generally lessens the risk." Bingham carefully omitted the fact that he would lose a 5 percent commission on any cargo that went directly across the Atlantic.

The broken voyage also offered economic advantages as well as safety, states Albion. Most of the munitions were needed in the northern ports of America, while the most valuable exports—tobacco, indigo, and naval stores—were produced in the south. It would be dangerous for a vessel to unload war supplies at Boston and then try to make its way through cruiser-infested waters to Charleston to pick up a cargo. So the situation was perfect for turning the islands into flourishing supply depots for the Americans. The warehouses of Cap François and Port-au-Prince in Haiti, Martinique, St. Eustatius, Havana, and St. Croix were soon jammed with gunpowder and arms awaiting transshipment to the mainland and colonial products destined for Europe in exchange.

The French island of Martinique, known in those days as Martinico, was chosen to be a pivotal point in this network. Morris and Franklin wanted an agent there who not only knew trade and could procure arms, but who could also represent the colonies and gather intelligence. Together, they settled upon Bingham, the twenty-four-year-old secretary of the Committee of Secret Correspondence. A member of a well-to-do Philadelphia family, William Bingham had excellent contacts in the city's mercantile community and had shown a good head for business. "He is a young Gentleman of good Education, Family & Fortune," Morris wrote of his new agent. "His Correspondence has yet a good deal of the fanciful young man in it, but Experience will cure him of this, and upon the whole, I think he has abilities & merit, both in the Political and Commercial Line."

Morris told Bingham that, like Silas Deane in Paris, he was to go to Martinique as a private merchant interested only in moving goods to and from the West Indies. Under this arrangement, he would carry on a private business "in the mercantile line" with Willing and Morris for their mutual profit as a cover for his intelligence and diplomatic operations. Morris suggested two commercial ventures—the importation of powder and the purchase of linens which could be shipped back on the man-of-war that was to take him to his post. Bingham invested five hundred pounds of his own money in these operations, and like his mentor saw nothing wrong in using Continental vessels or business to make a profit. "We shall be ready to transact rich business," Morris cheerfully informed Bingham on June 13, 1776, shortly before the young man went down the Delaware to join the sloop-of-war *Reprisal*.[9]

Lying low in the water off Cape May, with three tall masts rising from her rakish black hull, the *Reprisal* looked more like a privateer than a ship of war. Armed with eighteen 6-pounders and carrying a crew of 130 men, she was commanded by Captain Lambert Wickes. Like Bingham, Wickes, a thirty-four-year-old native of Kent County on Maryland's Eastern Shore, may have owed his appointment, as a captain in the Continental Navy, to Robert Morris. He had previously been a master in the employ of Willing and Morris. The skipper must have enthusiastically welcomed Bingham. The orders Bingham brought meant an end to the seemingly endless patrol at the mouth of the Delaware, where with three other ships the *Reprisal* was trying to prevent British men-of-war from raiding up the Bay. The

[9] For Bingham's activities see William B. Clark, *Lambert Wickes, Sea Raider and Diplomat* (New Haven 1932) and Robert C. Alberts, *The Golden Voyage: The Life and Times of William Bingham* (Boston 1969).

strength of the Royal Navy in American waters had lately been increased so enough ships were now available to divert some of them to sealing Delaware Bay and other major arteries of colonial trade. Merchantmen plying to and from the West Indies were being nipped off with regularity.

Wickes did not sail for Martinique at once. For the better part of a month he waited for a dozen or so cargo vessels to arrive and form a convoy that was to be shepherded to a safe distance from the coast. Stormy weather was also being awaited to cover a dash past the blockading British ships. Unexpectedly, the delay provided young Mr. Bingham with the opportunity to witness one of those grim little incidents that make up so much of war. Late in the afternoon of June 28, the brig *Nancy*, which had been sent to St. Thomas by the Pennsylvania Committee of Safety to pick up a cargo of about 370 barrels of powder, was seen standing in toward Cape May with two British frigates in pursuit. Running his ship into shoal water, the brig's skipper obviously hoped to transfer her precious cargo to small boats and have it lightered ashore.

The *Nancy* needed help—and boats were sent from the American ships lying off the Cape. The *Reprisal*'s barge was filled with sailors and marines under the command of Lieutenant Richard Wickes, the captain's brother. Working throughout the night, the Americans unloaded all but about a hundred of the kegs of powder. At daylight, five boats loaded with British sailors and marines put out from the frigates. The Americans agreed it was time to retreat. Before abandoning ship, however, they stove in several of the powder casks, lit a long fuse, and hastily clambered over the side. The British took this for panic and let out a lusty cheer. A longboat with six marines and a master's mate bumped to the side of the *Nancy*. The party pulled themselves aboard. Suddenly, there was a flash of flame and a roar heard as far away as Philadelphia. A great fiery cloud rose a hundred and fifty feet into the air. When the smoke cleared the water was littered with shattered pieces of the ship and charred barrel staves. A gold-laced hat and a leg with a garter on it bobbed amid the debris. "The oars of the other boats were all knocked to atoms and two men had their ribs broke," reported a British officer. "Considering the whole, we were amazingly fortunate, as the pieces of the vessel were falling all round for some time." Bingham watched as the *Reprisal*'s barge returned. He saw the sailors gently lift out the body of Lieutenant Wickes, the only American casualty in the action.

Four days later, on July 3, with a brisk wind at her back, the *Reprisal* rounded Cape May and headed for the open sea with a convoy of thirteen merchantmen. Apparently the British blockading force had been withdrawn to take part in Howe's attack on New York. At twilight, well out of sight of land, the vessels scattered, each for itself. "I think they all got safely off," Wickes reported. But no sooner was his swift ship hull down over the horizon on its course to Martinique than the British snapped up three stragglers.

Sailing southeasterly in bright summer weather, Wickes whipped his crew into shape. Many of his men were inexperienced landsmen. The Captain worked them hard at the guns and at learning to sail the ship. To help the crew to overcome their fear of climbing the rigging, he may have used an old device: placing a cask of drinking water and a cup in the main top. If a sailor wanted a drink he had to climb for it. Benjamin Franklin is a witness of how well Wickes succeeded in instilling discipline and seamanship into his crew. Later that year, when the *Reprisal* carried him to France, Franklin called it "equal to anything of the kind in the best ships of the King's fleet." When he got to the Caribbean, Wickes evened the score with the British, capturing three merchantmen richly laden with island produce. Most of their crews accepted his offer to enlist in the Continental Navy.

On July 27, the green peaks of Martinique were sighted and the *Reprisal* soon lay off the town of St. Pierre. Wickes took a glass and swept the harbor, which lay bathed in late afternoon sunshine. A pretty picture except for the British man-of-war that rode at anchor with the Union Jack rippling in the breeze. She was the sloop-of-war *Shark*, armed with sixteen 9-pound guns. Captain John Chapman, her commander, was examining the new arrival. "I saw a Sail in the Offing with Colours which I was unacquainted with (being red & white striped with a Union next to the Staff)." He suspected the stranger to be "the property of his Britainnick Majesty's Rebellious Subjects in North America" so he stood out to intercept her. It was a tense moment for Wickes. The British vessel obviously outclassed the *Reprisal*, and his men were inexperienced and untried in battle. Besides, there were thirty-nine ex-British merchant seamen of questionable loyalty aboard his ship. Without hesitation, however, he decided to accept the enemy's challenge. Mindful of his duty to deliver his passenger safely, he ordered Bingham, his credentials and his baggage placed in a boat and rowed ashore as dusk was settling over the harbor.

The entire population of St. Pierre poured out of their homes, taverns, and shops to watch the dramatic scene as the two fighting ships squared away for battle. As the *Reprisal* crossed the mouth of the harbor, the *Shark* closed within hailing distance. "This is His Majesty's ship *Shark*. Heave to!" Chapman called out. Standing on his course, Wickes replied, "This is the ship *Reprisal*, from Philadelphia, belonging to the Honorable Continental Congress!" Her guns roared out a challenge which was accepted by the *Shark*. Soon a cloud of smoke enveloped both ships, hiding them from the spectators on shore. For nearly a half-hour, they dueled in the first naval engagement of the Revolution in foreign waters. Neither side sustained much damage. A bursting gun wounded a man on the American ship, and two men were hit on board her opponent. The adversaries were still maneuvering for position when one of the guns of the French fort lobbed two round shot at the *Shark*, neatly straddling her. Faced with this challenge, Chapman had no choice but to break off the engagement. He headed for the open sea.

Bingham and a wildly cheering crowd were on hand to greet Wickes when he came ashore about an hour later, the welcome making it completely clear where French sympathy lay. Taking advantage of the popular uproar, Bingham called that very evening upon the Governor, who told him he had ordered the *Shark* fired upon because her captain had committed a hostile act by challenging the *Reprisal* in French territorial waters. The governor also consented to receive Wickes. Thus Wickes became the first Continental naval officer to make a formal call upon a representative of a foreign government. To Bingham's surprise, the French were willing to go far beyond his expectations in cooperating with the Americans. Certainly, he was told, convoys would be provided for Yankee vessels until they were a short distance off shore. And the governor suggested that "if the American cruisers should bring any prizes into the ports of Martinico, he should not prevent their selling or disposing of them as they should think proper." Mr. Bingham might consider outfitting privateers at St. Pierre and Fort Royal (now Fort-de-France). Astonished by his good fortune, Bingham hastened to get Wickes off again with the news. Permission to bring captured ships into French ports meant that American captains operating in the Caribbean would not have to detail prize crews to take captured vessels into ports in the United States. This would avoid the risk of having prizes retaken on the way to the mainland.

So began William Bingham's profitable four-year stay on Martinique. The *Reprisal* sailed home after delivering him, not only with a cargo of 500 muskets and a small amount of powder, but also with the linens and other goods suggested by Morris. Bingham's share of the profits totaled about 750 pounds. Thereafter, Bingham bought supplies on the usual commission basis for the Secret Committee and often for the individual states, conducted an unofficial admiralty court to sell prizes, commissioned privateers and procured cargoes for sale for the private account of Morris and himself. Bingham also engaged in privateering ventures with Morris, although the older man had first hesitated to take part openly in such ventures. Nevertheless, when one of their ships was reported to have sent in nine prizes to Martinique, Morris allowed "we shall make a fine hand of it." One prize cargo brought almost 14,000 pounds; captured medicines taken on another ship were sold in Virginia "for the highest prices ever given." No one knows for certain how much Bingham realized from his stay in Martinique. When he returned to Philadelphia, he had massed enough of a fortune to marry the beautiful Ann Willing, daughter of Morris's old partner, Thomas Willing. He was also well on his way to becoming the richest man in America before he had turned forty.

But no matter how active the gunrunning and contraband trades may have been in the French islands, the center of this commerce was the tiny Dutch island of St. Eustatius, or Statia. Conveniently situated at the outer bulge of the Antilles, it was close enough to the colonies of several nations to be the perfect clearing house for contraband. Fully aware of the possibilities of neutral trade in wartime, the Dutch declared the island a free port and welcomed all comers. Statia was little more than a seven-square-mile rock jutting up out of the sea. It could scarcely produce enough sugar from its barren soil to fill a single fair-sized ship a year. Yet, during one thirteen-month period of the Revolution, 3,182 vessels are said to have cleared from the open roadstead that served as a harbor for Port Orange.

Traders from all over the world assembled along the mile-long single street of stone warehouses and shops that fronted the roadstead to exchange guns and munitions for American tobacco, indigo, flour, and naval stores. This street was a babel of English, French, Dutch, and Spanish. Even some British merchants maintained branch offices at St. Eustatius, and several hundred English and Scots businessmen, including a member of Parliament, were engaged in trading with the enemy under the shelter of Dutch neutrality. When British convoys reached the West Indies, it was not uncommon for some vessels to elude the convoying warships and make for the "Golden Rock." There they disposed of their cargoes at fancy prices. No law could restrain the "rapacity of merchants," Lord Sandwich observed bitterly. For its size, Statia was beyond doubt the richest island in the world. Every storehouse was crammed with goods and "every part of a very extensive beach covered with sugar, tobacco and cotton." As many as a hundred ships at a time might lay at anchor in the roadstead, and throughout the day and much of the night boats toiled through the surf with bags, boxes, and bales of goods.

Long before the firm of Hortalez & Co. had begun its operations, Washington's desperate shortage of powder was being eased by supplies from Statia. Although Holland's States General had officially banned the export of ammunition to the American colonies, the Dutch merchants could not abandon the opportunity to sell powder for six or seven times what it had cost them in Amsterdam. British secret agents reported that in the spring of 1776 at least eighteen shiploads of powder had gone out from Holland to be transshipped to the rebels. In 1780, Admiral Sir George Rodney, upon arriving to assume command of the Leeward station, observed: "This rock of only six miles in length and three in breadth has done England more harm than all the arms of her most potent enemies, and alone supported the infamous American rebellion."

Statia also influenced the development of the swift sailing craft that became known as the Baltimore Clipper, according to Robert Albion.[10] Abraham van Bibber, a clever merchant from Baltimore and Maryland's commercial agent on the island, urged both his home state and Virginia to concentrate their flour and tobacco

---

[10] *Sea Lanes in Wartime.*

shipments on Statia rather than spread them among the other islands. At the same time, he used his influence to direct returning cargoes to Baltimore, helping transform it from just another town on the Chesapeake into one of the new nation's leading seaports. The risks of capture on the long run up and down the Chesapeake Bay were a spur to the development of the fastest ships of the time. With speed at a premium, the ordinary ungainly merchantman was too vulnerable to capture by the Royal Navy. Baltimore shipbuilders found the answer by perfecting the fast little "clipper" schooner. Developed from the Bermuda sloop, the chief characteristics of these craft were tall, light and well-raked masts carrying an immense cloud of canvas. Designed to run rather than fight, they were soon in demand for use both as privateers and as slavers.

Statia is also credited with providing the first salute to the American flag in a foreign port.[11] On November 16, 1776, the *Andrew Doria*, then commanded by Captain Isaiah Robinson, dropped anchor in the roadstead. She fired a salute of eleven guns, which was returned by the fort with two guns less as if for a merchantman— which may have been fitting inasmuch as the brig had been sent there to load a cargo of military supplies. Angry over the continued disregard of the official Dutch embargo on the shipment of arms to the rebels, the British government made a diplomatic issue of this incident. To mollify London, the States General ordered Johannes de Graaf, the governor of St. Eustatius, home for explanations. The Governor, of whom van Bibber had once said, "We're well fixed with him," maintained it was all a mistake. He was not dismissed or even punished and in due course sailed back to his island in triumph.

The failure of Admirals Shuldham and Howe to stem the flow of supplies to the rebels produced carping criticism from Samuel Graves, who was in disgruntled retirement. "Judge if the small leaky half-manned squadron under my command did not as effectively serve their country and protect the trade as the numerous and well-appointed squadrons have done since I left America," he told Sandwich. Graves had a point. But even though the fleet in American waters had grown to fifty-nine substantial ships by May 1776, this was deceptive. Analyzing the disposition of these vessels,

---

[11] In reality, the first salute appears to have been given by the Danish fort at St. Croix in return to a salute from an American schooner several weeks before.

Piers Mackesy points out that fifteen were on Atlantic convoy duty or had orders to return to England, eight were detached to the ill-fated Charleston expedition, and the remaining ships were spread out between Quebec and Florida. Seamen had also to be provided for the flotilla on Lake Champlain and naval support furnished the army as it groped along the seaboard. Under the Howe brothers, complained some naval officers, the army was building an excessive dependence on the navy—and this left it unable to maintain a successful blockade of American ports.

Contrast this situation to that which prevailed when Britain next fought the United States, suggests Mackesy. At the outbreak of the War of 1812, she had a great fleet in commission that had been trained in twenty years of victorious combat. Only a small portion of the armada had to be deployed to the American coast because most foreign ports were either blockaded or under British control. There was no place for American vessels to exchange raw materials for ammunition and arms, and no neutral dared risk Britain's displeasure by trading with her enemy, Mackesy adds. Britain's command of the sea was absolute instead of being woefully lacking in authority as it was in 1775.

"Perhaps it was really impossible to combine major land operations with a successful blockade," Mackesy continues. "And yet a certain doubt persists." Cynics suggested that the navy allowed rebel ships to slip through the net "to encourage others to risk their property upon the ocean"—and increase the number of potential prizes. Others, including Lord Germain, were equally convinced that Lord Howe had failed to institute a rigorous blockade because he still hoped to reconciliate the Americans. When the admiral issued ambiguous orders regarding the blockade of the southern coast, Germain observed somewhat sardonically: "Lord Howe is the most disinterested man I know, in permitting the trade of Charleston to be carry'd on without interruption, when he might avail himself of so many rich prizes."

XIII

Of Ships and Seniority

Congress had planned to have the thirteen frigates authorized on December 13, 1775, ready for sea within three months, which would have provided the Continental Navy with a considerable array of strength in record time. For various reasons—including the political considerations which determined where the ships were to be built—this projection turned out to be wildly optimistic. Construction and outfitting proceeded with agonizing slowness throughout 1776. Indeed some of the vessels never got to sea at all. "It is astonishing to many of us here that after so long a Time for Preparation, not a single Frigate . . . has yet been made ready to put to Sea, while the British Frigates and Cruizers are distressing us everywhere," the Reverend Samuel Cooper wrote from Boston early in 1777. "There is Blame somewhere."

The pattern of delay was established early. The Marine Committee failed to settle immediately upon designs for the vessels and get them off to builders scattered along the Atlantic coast from Portsmouth to Baltimore. Three types of frigates were planned—of 32, 28, and 24 guns—all to be larger than similar ships in service with the British and French navies. Considerable debate has occurred over who should be credited with the basic designs. One authority believes they were the work of the Philadelphia ship designer Joshua Humphreys. Another disputes this finding and holds that the names of the designers have for the most part been lost to history.[1] In any case, plans for the ships were not ready for distribution until February 1776, and in New England, where six frigates were to be built, the builders tired of waiting. They had their own designs drawn up on the basis of the specifications already transmitted by Congress and pressed ahead with construction. As a result, only the four ships to be built in Philadelphia, the two in New York, and the one in Maryland appear to have been constructed from the official draughts.

Just as politics was the primary factor in deciding where the ships were to be built, it also determined who was to build them. Selection of the builders had been left to the member of the Marine Committee from the colony where the ship was laid down. They used the profitable contracts to reward political friends. John Langdon, a former delegate to Congress from New Hampshire, was placed in charge of the *Raleigh*, of 32 guns, at Portsmouth. Thomas Cushing, a political crony of John Hancock, was given the *Hancock*, 32, and *Boston*, 24, the ships to be built in Massachusetts. He chose a yard at Newburyport for construction of both. Rhode Island set up an eleven-member committee with Governor Cooke as chairman to oversee construction of *Warren*, 32, and *Providence*, 28, in two Providence dockyards. As we have seen, Esek Hopkins charged they turned it into what has been called "a political clambake." Silas Deane saw to it that the *Trumbull*, 28, was supervised by his brother, Barnabas, as she was built on the Connecticut River at Chatham. New York, Pennsylvania, and Maryland set up special committees to spread the gravy. Both New York ships, the *Congress*, 28, and *Montgomery*, 24, were to be built up the Hudson at Poughkeepsie. The four Pennsylvania frigates, *Randolph*, 32; *Washington*, 32; *Effingham*, 28; and *Delaware*, 24, were given to various yards in and near Philadelphia. Maryland's lone contribution, the *Virginia*, 28, was laid down in Baltimore.[2]

---

[1] For a pro-Humphreys view see M. V. Brewington, "The Design of Our First Frigates," *The American Neptune*, VIII (January 1948). The other side is summed up by Howard I. Chapelle in his *History of the American Sailing Navy* (New York 1949).

[2] Congress approved the names of the frigates on June 6, 1776.

The task imposed upon American shipyards by the building program was not as formidable as it appears. Colonial shipwrights had been turning out vessels of upward to forty-four guns for the Royal Navy since 1690 and had exhibited skill and knowledge in constructing frigates and smaller craft. Delays arose in the building of the new frigates primarily because of poor planning and shortages of material and skilled labor. Shipwrights were at a premium. They had been lured to yards where there were better paying jobs building privateers, just as seamen were enticed into shipping aboard these craft rather than in the Continental Navy. Some colonies had mustered shipwrights for militia duty without concerning themselves about the effect on shipbuilding. There was little preliminary planning which would establish priorities for the allocation of materials, armament, and supplies among the various ships. The records of the Marine Committee are filled with letters to its various agents pleading with them to shift equipment from one construction site to another. Messengers scurried from dockyard to dockyard ordering guns sent here, building material sent there.

The art of building large wooden men-of-war is now largely lost to the world. Eighteenth-century shipyards were without much machinery and most work was done with hand tools. Even sawmills powered by water were rare. Sawn timber and plank was produced by "saw gangs" of three or four men. Logs were rolled over a pit and two men worked a large ripsaw, one from above, the other below. The rest of the team placed the logs into position and then moved the finished work on. Four planks to the log was the usual product. There was much waste. The broadax and the adz—the latter cutting across the grain and the former with it—were used for shaping most heavy structural timbers. Other hand tools—augers, axes, hammers, chisels, and gouges—were used for detail work.

A shipwright combined the skills of a carpenter, caulker, joiner, and painter. He not only had to build a ship's hull but turned out masts, spars, and even blocks for the running rigging, as well. Crude lathes, usually operated by a foot treadle, like the sewing machines of a later era, were used to make turned work. Often there was a skilled woodcarver in the town who could make figureheads and other decorative work. The workday was long, from sun-up to sunset, six days a week with few holidays. When shipbuilding was slack, the men took a hand as carpenters, housebuilders, and furniture makers—anything that would pay a wage, for there was no unemployment compensation or social security to tide a man over until the next job.

English shipwrights swore by Sussex oak, saying it was the finest shipbuilding material in the world. Enormous quantities of it were used in construction of a man-of-war. For a 74-gun two-decker, about two thousand oaks were needed, all of them upward of a hundred years old. Large amounts of other woods were required for planking, masts, and spars. Trees with natural curves, known as "compass timber," were much sought after for the shaped parts of the hull. They were increasingly hard to come by. Originally, such wood had come from the gnarled oaks that grew in the English hedgerows but the supply was nearly depleted by the time of the Revolution. Less durable wood was being brought in from the Baltic to replace English oak. The shortage was due to the Navy's carelessness in maintaining the nation's timber reserves during the huge building programs of the Eighteenth Century.

The North American live oak which once grew along the coast of America from Virginia to beyond the Mississippi in a belt about twenty miles wide was later found to be superior to English oak in many respects, but the Royal Navy ignored its existence. White oak found in the northern part of the colonies was better known but was regarded as considerably inferior to English timber. The manner of shipment had something to do with this. While English oak was carried to the dockyards in lighters without touching water, American wood was usually floated down rivers in huge rafts and loaded dripping wet into the holds of the timber ships. During the passage to England, the wood steamed for weeks—the trip was usually made in the warmer months—and dry rot began to set in. Often logs were covered with fungi before they reached the dockyards. Theoretically, wood was to be seasoned for a year in the open air before being used in warship construction, but green timber was pressed into service in time of emergency. Ships built of unseasoned wood quickly deteriorated. The average life of a Royal Navy vessel during this period was only about ten years and few ships survived longer without extensive repairs or rebuilding.

The first stage in the construction of a wooden warship took place in a great shed called a mould loft. Master-shipwrights laid out the lines of the vessel in full scale on the floor. On the walls, which were of great height, they chalked out the side elevations. Orders were then given for the timbers to be cut and shaped to their designs. The ship itself was built in the open air and it was the custom in English yards to allow the frame to stand exposed to the weather for as long as a year before her ribs were planked. Although exposure was supposed to season the frame, the wetting and warping resulting from rain and sun triggered dry rot before the ship was launched. Some ships were said to be "as green as grass" from mildew and fungus even before their sides were covered over.

The keel, or backbone of the vessel, was laid down first upon oak blocks set four or five feet apart on ground that gently sloped to the water.[3] Several thick timbers, some measuring as much as two feet square, were joined together by "scarphs" to produce a keel of the required length. After the joints were cut to shape, they were fitted together with copper bolts which were found to have greater resistance to underwater corrosion than iron. The ship was built on this backbone. Two upright members, the sternpost and stempost, were raised into position on the keel, followed by the frames or ribs which were fixed at right angles to the keel and gave the ship her shape. Knees and beams to support the decks were added, and the frames were shored up by braces. The ship was ready for planking when the skeleton was complete. Planking was done in inner and outer layers, the inner layer being applied first.

Very little metalwork was used in ships constructed in the colonies because of the scarcity and expense. Usually there was more metal in a ship's anchors and guns than in all the rest of the vessel. Planking was fastened to the frames with treenails, or wooden pegs, driven into holes bored by augers. Treenails contributed to dry rot, but custom and thrift prescribed their continued use. Treenails had a tendency to shrink and admit water. The surrounding planking, once wet, began to rot, and the shrunken treenail rotted with it—until at last the sea poured in. This phenomenon was probably the cause of the loss of many wooden ships that disappeared without a trace.

When both layers of planking had been completed, the decks were added, the hull caulked, and the part below the waterline sheathed with copper to protect the ship's bottom against the ravages of the teredo worm. Copper also prevented the growth of weeds and

[3] See *The Anatomy of Nelson's Ships* by C. Nepean Longridge (London 1955) for a complete account of the building of a wooden man-of-war.

barnacles on a ship's bottom, which could reduce her speed by several knots. The resistance of copper was such that often the wood to which it was attached would become rotten, and the ship would be kept afloat by the protective covering of copper. Lord Collingwood, Nelson's second in command at Trafalgar, once said of his ship, "For the last six months we have been sailing with only a sheet of copper between us and eternity."

Once launched, the ship was brought alongside a sheer hulk, an old vessel that had been cut down and fitted with a single sturdy mast and blocks and tackle for stepping, or lowering, masts into newly built ships. The lower masts of a large man-of-war were massive—an inch of diameter to a yard of length being the general rule. The mainmast of a two-decker might be three feet in diameter. Other masts and spars were in proportion. Lower masts were made of a single tree trunk where possible. By the time of the Revolution such trees were hard to find even in the forests of North America. Perhaps one tree in 10,000 might be suitable for the mainmast of a ship-of-the-line. The slightest defect, such as a single rotten knot, would cause its rejection. Corrupt contractors often bored out the rotten knots, filling the holes with plugs to fool the inspectors. Sometimes the defect would not be discovered until the masts treacherously snapped in a gale. Because of the scarcity of satisfactory "great sticks," costs were high. In 1770, a tree trunk 36 inches in diameter and 36 yards in length—suitable for the mainmast of a 74—cost 110 pounds, considered an exorbitant price in that day. To make up for the shortage of satisfactory single trees, European shipbuilders began to build lower masts from several timbers bound together with iron hoops. Unlike wood destined for a ship's hull, which was left to season in the open air, masts were stored under water in mast ponds to keep them resilient. The great sticks were floated in upon the tide and were arranged in tiers, so that a mast pond could hold several sizable masts. Locks kept the water at a constant level. Nearby were mast houses, where mastmakers converted the sticks, which had arrived barkless, into proper proportions to meet current demands.[4]

After the lower masts and bowsprit, which jutted out from the bow of the ship, had been stepped and secured, the vessel received her rigging from the rigging-loft. To a landsman, the sails and rigging of a square-rigger were a hopeless tangle of canvas and rope, but

[4] Albion, *Forests and Sea Power.*

each line had a name and a purpose. A ship's rigging was set up by master riggers working with her officers. The shrouds, the rope ladders leading up the sides of the masts, and the stays which secured the masts, were made of hempen rope that had been laid in the rope walks that were a feature of every shipbuilding town and dockyard. After the lower rigging had been set up, the topmasts were sent aloft and rigged, followed by the topgallant masts. With the completion of the standing rigging, the yards, on which the square sails were set, were crossed on the masts. Ascending up the mast, the sails were called courses, topsails, topgallants, and royals. Staysails were set between the masts, a spanker on the mizzen mast, jibs on the bowsprit, and studding-sails at the extremity of the yards. They were furled and set with a network of running rigging. When ballast, guns, and stores were loaded aboard the vessel, she was ready for sea in a bravery of new paint and canvas.

Up and down the coast of America, the eyes of workmen, travelers, passersby, and sightseers were irresistibly drawn to the frigates as their skeletons began to rise along the major rivers. Overcoming shortages of material and skilled labor, builders pressed ahead with construction, and, one by one, the ships were launched. The *Warren* appears to have been the first to get into the water. She was sent down the ways into the Providence River on May 15, 1776. Three days later, the *Providence* followed her. The Rhode Island committee appropriated fifty dollars for the "entertainment" of the shipwrights who had worked on the vessels. On May 21, the *Raleigh* was launched at Portsmouth after only sixty working days "amidst the acclamation of many thousand spectators," states an enthusiastic contemporary account. She was "esteemed by all those who are judges that have seen her, to be one of the compleatest ships ever built in America . . . The good order and industry of the Carpenters deserve particular notice; scarcely a single instance of a person being in liquor, or any difference among the men in the yard during the time of her building."

The *Boston* was launched "in view of a great number of spectators" on June 3, and the *Hancock* slightly over a month later. The *Delaware* and *Randolph*, the only two of the four ships under construction at Philadelphia to be completed, slid down the ways in mid-July. The *Virginia* was floating off Fell's Point in Baltimore harbor by early August. The *Trumbull* was in the water the following month. Work on the two New York frigates, *Congress* and *Montgomery*, was delayed by the diversion of men and material to Arnold's fleet on Lake Champlain, and they were never completed. The capture of New York by the British and the closing of the Hudson made them useless in any case so they were burned in October 1777, to prevent their capture. Last to be launched were the Philadelphia frigates *Effingham* and *Washington*, which did not get into the Delaware until November. Both were scuttled the following year to prevent capture by the British. Only the *Randolph, Boston, Hancock*, and *Raleigh* were to get to sea in 1777.

Just how good were these ships? The designs were the product of different hands but in each case the builders were animated by the same idea—to produce a fast ship, a ship that would work well to windward and would be larger though somewhat more lightly built than similar craft in other navies. Howard I. Chapelle, a naval architect who made a study of the vessels based on surviving information and draughts made after the capture of some of the ships by the British, states that they were not copies of foreign models as sometimes believed. Rather, they were "the natural development of a previous search for speed under sail in craft smaller than frigates." At least in the case of the *Hancock*, her designer and builders succeeded so well that the British described her as "the finest and fastest frigate in the world." [5] Most of the frigates that did get to sea did good service—but mainly for the British, for they were soon captured. On the other hand, the *Trumbull* was not accepted into the Royal Navy after she was taken, indicating that she was either rotten or poorly built.

With most of the frigates fitting out at last, the Marine Committee set about establishing a naval administration and resolving the thorny question of relative rank among the captains. They tackled the administrative framework first. It had been quickly discovered that with thirteen members the Marine Committee was too un-

[5] The *Hancock* was taken into the Royal Navy as H.M.S. *Iris* and in this role captured the *Trumbull* in 1781. Later that year, she was captured by the French and incorporated into their navy. In her old age she was converted into a powder hulk in Toulon where she was found by the British when that port was taken in 1793—the last survivor of the Continental Navy then afloat. When the British evacuated Toulon, the old *Hancock* was blown up.

wieldly for efficient operations. Congress agreed that five of its members would constitute a quorum for the transaction of business. Like the Naval Committee which preceded it, the Marine Committee met in the evening after the daily session of Congress. Officers included a chairman, a vice chairman, and a secretary as well as several clerks. Rarely did more than half the Committee's members attend its sessions. Personnel were constantly changing, just as the membership of Congress was always in flux. The need for someone to receive and dispose of prizes soon led to the appointment of prize agents in the leading seaports of the country. Their duties were to see that prize cases were tried in the admiralty courts, to arrange for the sale of captured ships after they had been legally condemned, and to make an equitable distribution of the proceeds to the captors and to Congress. The same men who served as prize agents were also as a rule Continental Navy agents. In this role, they assisted the Marine Committee and the captains in purchasing, refitting, provisioning, and manning the navy's ships.

The increasing complexity of naval administration forced the Committee to provide some sort of permanent arrangement. Accordingly, on November 6, 1776, Congress created a three-member Navy Board to handle day-to-day operations. Five months later, John Adams persuaded Congress to establish a separate board for the New England states. Based in Boston, it became known as the Navy Board of the Eastern Department while the group at Philadelphia was called the Navy Board of the Middle Department. Both were subject to the Marine Committee. Writing to James Warren, one of the newly appointed members of the Navy Board at Boston, Adams outlined its duties as follows:

> You will have the building and fitting of all ships, the appointment of officers, the establishment of arsenals and magazines, which will take up your whole time; but it will be honorable to be so capitally concerned to laying a foundation of a great navy. The profit to you will be nothing; but the honor and the virtue greater. I almost envy you this employment.

The unresolved question is whether the Navy Boards helped clear up the confusion bedeviling naval administration or compounded it. Paul Jones, who was always free with advice on how the navy should be run, believed they added to the problems. What the

Navy really needed, he told Robert Morris and Benjamin Franklin, was "a man of Abilities at its head" to make decisions "so the small number of Ships we have may be constantly employed and not Continue Idle as they do at present." The decision to adopt that approach was still in the future. If Jones had known how the Marine Committee was planning to resolve the seniority question, he would have exploded. The list of twenty-four senior officers prepared by the Committee and accepted by Congress on October 10, 1776, was a monument to the powers of political patronage, favoritism, and sectional pressure. Here is the list with the vessels to which the captains were assigned as of that date:

1. James Nicholson of Maryland	Frigate *Virginia*
2. John Manley of Massachusetts	Frigate *Hancock*
3. Hector McNeill of Massachusetts	Frigate *Boston*
4. Dudley Saltonstall of Connecticut	Frigate *Trumbull*
5. Nicholas Biddle of Pennsylvania	Frigate *Randolph*
6. Thomas Thompson of New Hampshire	Frigate *Raleigh*
7. John Barry of Pennsylvania	Frigate *Effingham*
8. Thomas Read of Pennsylvania	Frigate *Washington*
9. Thomas Grinnell of New York	Frigate *Congress*
10. Charles Alexander of Pennsylvania	Frigate *Delaware*
11. Lambert Wickes of Maryland	Sloop-of-War *Reprisal*
12. Abraham Whipple of Rhode Island	Frigate *Providence*
13. John B. Hopkins of Rhode Island	Frigate *Warren*
14. John Hodge of New York	Frigate *Montgomery*
15. William Hallock of Maryland	Brig *Lexington*
16. Hoystead Hacker of Rhode Island	Brig *Hampden*
17. Isaiah Robinson of Pennsylvania	Brig *Andrew Doria*
18. John Paul Jones of Virginia	Sloop *Providence*
19. James Josiah	No ship assigned
20. Elisha Hinman of Connecticut	Ship *Alfred*
21. Joseph Olney of Rhode Island	Brig *Cabot*
22. James Robinson of Maryland	Sloop *Sachem*
23. John Young of Pennsylvania	Sloop *Independence*
24. Elisha Warner of Rhode Island	Schooner *Fly*

On the face of it, the list appears completely irrational. Nicholson had not even been commissioned in the Continental Navy until June 6, 1776—and now he was its senior captain. While Manley had commanded Washington's schooner fleet, neither he nor Hector McNeill had commanded a Continental ship at sea. Paul Jones was shunted to eighteenth place, and assigned to the old *Providence*, when he clearly deserved one of the new frigates, or at least the *Alfred*. If the list is examined closely, certain facts stand out. First of all, there is no mention whatsoever of Esek Hopkins, languishing with his blockaded ships in the Providence River. His absence indicates that the ways were being greased for another attempt at his ouster. No Rhode Islander ranked higher than twelfth on the list, making it obvious that there was considerable dissatisfaction with that state's past dominance of naval affairs.

The guiding principle of those who drafted the seniority list appears to have been what Admiral Morison aptly terms *"localitis."* The captains of the new frigates were almost all residents of the place where the ships were built. One reason advanced for this "favorite son" treatment is that seamen had to be recruited where a ship was fitting out. After the initial enthusiasm for the navy had died away, men would enlist only under a captain or other officer whom they knew.[6] Thus, Manley and McNeill, both well-known Boston skippers, got the ships building in Massachusetts. Biddle and Barry were given two of the Philadelphia-built frigates for the same reason. Thomas Thompson, appointed captain of the *Raleigh*, had been inspector of the ship while she was building at Portsmouth. Political influence may also have propelled Manley and McNeill to the top of the seniority list. John Hancock, the political boss of Massachusetts, was chairman of the Marine Committee; on the other hand, Silas Deane, brother-in-law of Dudley Saltonstall, the *Alfred*'s first skipper, was in Paris, which probably resulted in his ranking junior to the Bay State men.

The elevation of James Nicholson to the top of the seniority list was a political victory for Southern influence, that of Virginia's Richard Henry Lee in particular. As early as June 25, Nicholson's supporters in Baltimore were assured by Joseph Hewes, the North Carolina member of the Marine Committee, that "Capt. Nicholson has been strongly recommended, and Congress has a high opinion of his abilities and merit, and I have no doubt of his standing pretty high in rank." Samuel Purviance, Jr., chairman of the Baltimore Committee of Correspondence, beat the drum loudly for his fellow

---

[6] For example, the Rhode Island committee required the marine officers appointed to the two frigates under construction there to enlist specified groups of men before being given their commissions. Captains were required to bring in 40 recruits, lieutenants, 33, and second lieutenants, 27.

Marylander. He suggested to Lee that Nicholson would make an excellent commodore. The Virginian replied that Nicholson "will not be forgotten." But he cautioned that "it is not probable that the frigates will sail in fleets for some time; and therefore, 'tis likely that no higher appointment than that of Captain will soon take place." On October 11, the day after Congress approved the new seniority list, Lee wrote Purviance with evident pleasure that "the Congress have placed Captain Nicholson at the head, he being the first Captain."

The Continental Navy's new senior captain was the eldest son of a family prominent on the Eastern Shore of Maryland. Nicholson, forty years old at the time of his appointment, had been educated in England and had served in the Royal Navy at the capture of Havana in 1762. As captain of the *Defence* of the Maryland navy, he had won the praise of the communities along the Chesapeake by checking the advance up the bay of the British sloop-of-war *Otter*. He also recaptured several prizes she had taken. Nicholson was rewarded with the command of the frigate *Virginia* under construction at Baltimore. After the dismissal of Hopkins, he served as the senior officer of the Continental Navy until it was disbanded at the end of the Revolution. Nicholson's appointment, with its overtones of political favoritism and sectionalism, could not but help add to the bitterness and jealousy among the officers who had been commissioned earlier and who now found themselves junior to the latecomers. Paul Jones, for one, never forgot the slight.

Some months later, he wrote Robert Morris regarding the qualifications of naval officers and left no doubt of his feelings. "I cannot but lament that so little delicacy hath been Observed in the Appointment and Promotion of Officers in the Sea Service, many of whom are not only grossly illiterate, but want even the Capacity of commanding Merchant Vessells," he told the Vice Chairman of the Marine Committee. "I was lately on a Court Martial where a Captain of Marines made his Mark and where the President could not even read the Oath which he attempted to administer, without Spelling and making blunders . . . In my Judgement the Abilities of Sea Officers ought to be as far Superior to the abilities of officers in the Army as the nature of a Sea Service is more complicated. . . ."

By late 1776, the Marine Committee was growing impatient for its new ships to get to sea. Repeatedly, orders were issued to the captains to lose no time in preparing for action. Because of a shortage of crews, the failure to complete fitting out, and the British blockade, none of the frigates hoisted sail during the year. The *Warren* and *Providence*, probably the first of the frigates to be commissioned, were bottled up at Providence by the British blockade along with the *Columbus, Hampden*, and the sloop *Providence.* Esek Hopkins hoisted his pennant on the *Warren* early in December and looked for an opportunity to restore his tarnished reputation.

It came with the new year. On January 2, 1777, word was received on the flagship that the British frigate *Diamond* had run aground on the shoals halfway between Newport and Providence. If she could be taken, the commodore must have reasoned, the cloud that had hung over him since the *Glasgow* affair would be lifted. Because of the shallowness of the water—the *Gaspée* had met her fate in the same area five years before—Hopkins dared not risk his larger ships in an attack. Taking twenty-two men from the *Warren*, he added them to the crew of the old *Providence*, and with Abraham Whipple in command of the sloop, set off on the expedition.

Dropping down Narragansett Bay to where the *Diamond* lay, Hopkins was dismayed to find that capturing her would not be as easy as he had imagined. There was enough water under the frigate's keel to keep her from careening over on her side. Thus some of her guns could be brought to bear on the attacking force. A hot fight ensued with the *Providence* passing almost within musket shot of the *Diamond*, while a pair of 18-pounders emplaced on the shore pounded away at the British frigate. Twice during the engagement, Hopkins took the unusual step of going ashore to confer with the militia officer commanding the battery. On his second trip to the beach, the commodore's boat drifted away, leaving him ignominiously stranded for the rest of the night. When the tide turned in the early morning, the *Diamond* floated free and sailed down the bay. Hopkins later said no attempt was made to stop her because a 50-gun British man-of-war had stood a short way off during the engagement and could have come to the frigate's rescue if needed. A British account made no mention of the presence of this vessel and states that poor Yankee marksmanship saved the *Diamond*.

It was all too much of a reminder of the *Glasgow* affair. Hopkins's enemies in the squadron—no doubt egged on by the Providence privateersmen who had no cause to love him—lost no time in lampooning him for the loss of his boat and criticizing him for failure to use all the force at his disposal against the *Diamond.* Several of the *Warren*'s officers plotted to rid themselves of the commodore. On February 19, they drafted a petition to the Marine Committee blaming him for the failure in recruitment and charging that he had treated prisoners cruelly. Topping it off was their allegation that he had spoken disrespectfully of the Marine Committee to his officers. He was said to have called its members "ignorant fellows—lawyers, clerks—persons who don't know how to govern men." The *Warren*'s chaplain, John Reed, added a special touch, saying the commodore "is remarkably addicted to profane swearing. In this respect as well as in many other respects he sets his officers & men a most irreligious & impious example."

Hopkins had plenty to swear about, and he had never bothered to hide his impatience with some of the orders he had received from the Marine Committee—and the men who drafted them. His enemies took advantage of the old sea dog's irascibility, knowing full well the effect his disrespect for Congress would have on those thin-skinned gentlemen. The charges were enhanced with protestations of patriotism from the plotters. Piously, they claimed they had signed the petition solely because of "an earnest desire and fixed expectation of doing our country some service." Without waiting for permission from his superiors, John Granis, a marine captain, left the flagship and galloped off to Philadelphia to deliver the petition to Congress. It had the desired effect. Granis was immediately taken before a subcommittee to repeat the charges.

Since the elevation of Nicholson to the top of the seniority list, Hopkins's enemies had been waiting for the right moment to get rid of him—and now it was at hand. The Marine Committee laid the charges against the commodore before the whole body on March 25. This time no one rose to defend Hopkins. Without discussion, Congress the next day approved the following resolution: "That Esek Hopkins be immediately, and hereby is, suspended from his command in the American navy."

Certainly Hopkins was ill-suited for his post, and Paul Jones may well have been correct when he said, "The Navy would be far better without a Head than with a Bad one." But there is no disguising the fact that Hopkins was treated shabbily. He was given no hearing or trial. Granis had only to appear with his charges for the commodore to be ousted. Hopkins did not know the details of the charges against him until months later when Congress finally sent him a copy of the documents the marine captain had carried to Philadelphia. Bewildered but with dignity, the commodore wrote a friend shortly before going ashore for the last time: "I can assure you it gives me great Satisfaction that in my own Judgement I have done everything in my power (or would have been in any man's power in my place) for the Service of My Country. . . ."

Only one thing more was left to be done. After ignoring Hopkins all through 1777, the Continental Congress had this entry made in its *Journals* on January 2, 1778: "Congress having no further occasion for the service of Esek Hopkins, Esqr. who, on the 22 of December, 1775, was appointed commander-in-chief of the fleet fitted out by the Naval Committee, *Resolved,* That the said Esek Hopkins, Esqr. be dismissed from the service of the United States." Never again would the rank of commander-in-chief be bestowed upon an American naval officer.

XIV

Brave New Frigates

The *Randolph*, commanded by Nicholas Biddle, was the first of the new frigates to push her way into the Atlantic. On February 6, 1777, Biddle sailed out of Delaware Bay and for three or four days tested his ship's sailing qualities with a critical eye. With her sharp stem slashing through the water, Biddle tried the frigate before the wind, across the wind, and against the wind. He tested her under full canvas and with her sails reefed until he was convinced she was "the very best vessel for sailing that I have ever saw." The young captain had been ready to sail since November. He had studied the *Randolph*'s armament—twenty-six 12-pounders on her gun deck and six 6-pounders on the forecastle and quarterdeck—and decided she could carry more firepower. The Marine Committee quickly approved his suggestion to increase the frigate's armament to 36 guns by mounting four 6-pounders on the forecastle and six on the quarterdeck. The last details of fitting out were completed: the water casks were painted, magazine whitewashed, and wood for the galley stove cut and corded. Clothing for two hundred fifty men was ordered for the slop chest. "Captain Biddle's frigate *Randolph* . . . is now completely ready, except that she wants men which we hope to remedy," noted Richard Henry Lee.

Outside events intruded on the plans for recruiting a crew, however. Sir William Howe's attack on New York had not alarmed Congress about the safety of Philadelphia, but his movement into New Jersey set off panic in the capital of the new republic. At the urging of General Washington, the city's militia battalions marched north to join the Continental Army for a stand along the Delaware. Unable to man their ships, the five navy captains then in port in Philadelphia offered to join the army with whatever men they could scrape up. The Marine Committee accepted the offer and sent off John Barry, Thomas Read, and Charles Alexander, whose ships were still uncompleted, with two raw companies of seamen and landsmen detailed as volunteer artillerymen. Biddle and John Nicholson, skipper of the *Hornet* and younger brother of James Nicholson, were told to be ready to take their ships to sea with the crews they had.

Each day brought new reports of the approach of the enemy. Townsfolk began loading their belongings into carts and carriages. The roads into the back country were lined with fleeing refugees. "This City is alarmed with the News of Howe's army being at Brunswick, proceeding for this place," a diarist noted on December 2. "Drums beat; a martial appearance: the shops shut, and all business, except preparing to disappoint our enemies laid aside." Among the plans "to disappoint our enemies" were orders to Biddle and Nicholson to get ready for an immediate departure. Instructions were issued for burning the three uncompleted frigates if the British appeared likely to capture Philadelphia.

Where was Biddle to get the hands to man the *Randolph*? Congress empowered the Marine Committee to advance twenty dollars against prize money to every seaman who would sign on. Nothing happened. Sailors who might have been attracted by the offer had gone off with the militia. Five days later, on December 7, Congress passed the word that Biddle could secure recruits in the jails or among those prisoners of war who would volunteer for service in the Continental Navy. A jittery Congress offered Biddle a reward of $10,000 if he got his ship safely to sea. One nervous delegate worried that they would soon "hear the thunder of [British] cannon and mortars and feel the effects of shots and bombs." On December 11, Con-

gress voted dictatorial powers to Washington and abandoned the im-
periled city for Baltimore. Three members who refused to be
panicked remained behind—Robert Morris, George Clymer, another
Pennsylvanian, and George Walton, of Georgia. For all practical
purposes, the determined Morris, as vice chairman of the Marine
Committee, became the navy's head.

Congress had no sooner disappeared down the road to Baltimore than Morris began bombarding Biddle with orders. Biddle had
recruited from prison a few men of dubious loyalty but who were
well qualified as seamen, and he had added some landsmen to his
crew. "Seamen & Marines sufficient to work the Ship" were now
available, Morris believed. He thought it would be better to risk
sending her out shorthanded than "to let her remain & be destroyed." Biddle readily agreed and prepared for a dash into the
open sea in the company of the *Hornet.* Just as the two ships were
about to get underway, new orders arrived. A British blockading
squadron including the *Roebuck*, of 44 guns, had been sighted at the
mouth of the Delaware. There was nothing for Biddle to do but drop
anchor and wait for foul weather to drive off the British men-of-war.
On Christmas Day, Biddle and Nicholson resolved once again to try
to get to sea. Before the attempt could be made, the news of Washington's Christmas night victory at Trenton arrived, along with the
reports of his success at Princeton a few days later. The immediate
threat to Philadelphia was over. Winter closed in on the *Randolph.*
Ice gripped her wooden hull. Snowbound and windblown, she rode
at anchor with her deck deserted by all but a few marines posted to
keep her crew from deserting.

Throughout January 1777, Biddle impatiently awaited an opportunity to break out. Word was received from Silas Deane in Paris
that a large shipment of supplies had been sent from France to Martinique. Accordingly, Morris notified Congress, still in Baltimore,
that "Our River is now nearly clear of Ice and I propose pushing out
Capt. Biddle. I do think we cannot employ him & the small Vessells
better than to send them to Martinico for the Stores mentioned in
Mr. Ds letter." Apparently Biddle got him to change his mind. He
went to Philadelphia to point out that "the frigate had been designed
for fighting, not freighting," states William Clark, Biddle's biographer. Morris seems to have agreed. He issued new orders on January
30 for the *Hornet* and *Fly* to sail to Martinique while the *Randolph*

was to "proceed on a Cruize upon the enemies ships of war that are interrupting the commerce of the United States from the Harbour of Newport to the capes of Virginia." Morris now turned inspirational. "I must observe that there are no Cruizing Ships an over match for you except the two Deckers," he wrote Biddle. "What a glorious exploit it will be to add one of their frigates or 20 Gun Ships to our Navy."

Just before casting off on February 3, the *Randolph* received her last draft of men—nineteen British prisoners of war. Although they were listed as volunteers, one man later complained they were taken on board the frigate in irons. The consignment brought the frigate's complement to 240 officers and men. Three days later, the *Randolph* was at sea on a brief shakedown cruise, while the *Hornet* and *Fly* mustered the large convoy of merchantmen the warships were to guard until they were safely away from the coast.

No doubt Biddle took the *Randolph* to sea in an offshore breeze. The wind at her back propelled the frigate directly away from land. Under these circumstances, she would have gone out under jibs and topsails—the second lowest sails on the three masts. Normally, the first lieutenant would take a ship to sea, but any captain putting a new command through her paces for the first time would have been on the quarterdeck himself. Turning to his first officer, Biddle would have said, "You may set topsails, Mr. Barnes." William Barnes, the frigate's first lieutenant, would have taken up his speaking trumpet and bellowed out a string of orders: [1]

"Topmen lay aloft and loose topsails!"

"Man the topsail sheets and halyards!"

"Throw off the buntlines, ease the clewlines!"

"Sheet home!"

"Run away with the topsail halyards!"

Urged on by boatswain's mates wielding knotted ropes' ends, the topmen scampered up the shrouds and out onto the footropes hanging below the topsail yards. Following the age-old rule of the sea—"one hand for the ship and the other for yourself"—they lay

---

[1] The following account of taking a square-rigger to sea is based upon the Coast Guard Academy manual issued to cadets manning the *Eagle*, the school's three-masted barque, *Eagle Seamanship: Square Rigger Sailing* (New York 1969).

across the yards using one hand to claw at the lines holding the sails furled to the yard while hanging on with the other. This operation was difficult enough in good weather—in a heavy blow it became dangerous. For a sailor to loosen his grip on a spar when the ship rolled or pitched with a dizzying lurch meant going overboard to almost certain death, or plunging to the deck to be either killed or maimed.

"Man the topsail sheets and halyards!" would send the men on deck racing to the sheets, lines hanging from the corners, or clews, of the sails. Other men would grasp the halyards, lines running from the center of the yards through blocks to the deck below. "Throw off the buntlines, ease the clewlines!" was the signal for the men aloft to slacken the lines which kept the sails furled. "Sheet home!" called for the men manning the sheets to haul down on them so that the corners of the sail would touch the end of the yard below. "Run away with the topsail halyards!" would start the men manning these lines walking aft, lifting the topsail yards a short distance and making the sails taut. To set the triangular-shaped jibs or headsails, men would walk away with the halyards attached to them, which raised the sails. Bending sail took place amid a bedlam of shouted orders, twittering boatswain's pipes, curses, canvas cracking in the wind, and the stamp of dozens of feet.

As the wind freshened and the ship began to heel over, the captain might decide to set the rest of the sails—courses, topgallants, royals, and the spanker, the fore and aft sail on the mizzenmast. The topgallants and royals would be set the same as the topsails. Setting the courses, the biggest and lowest sail on each mast, would be done the same except that no halyards were involved. These yards were fixed in position; the sails were merely dropped from them. The spanker would be set by hauling it up to the top of the gaff with halyards.

Square-riggers were at their best running free, with the wind directly astern or blowing from the quarter. Sometimes, of course, the ship had to be sailed on a course against the wind. Naturally no sailing ship can sail directly into the wind though it is possible to sail at an angle to it. A frigate might sail to within six or seven points of the wind, or about 75 degrees.[2] So to reach an objective to the windward,

---

[2] There are thirty-two points to a compass circle, so each point would be equal to about eleven and one-half degrees.

the ship would sail a zigzag course, known as tacking or beating to windward. Beating to windward was a slow business involving much pulling and hauling on the braces, the tackle that swung the yards. It might take fifteen minutes before the vessel was settled on each new course, or tack. Sometimes, in passing through the eye of the wind to get from one tack to the other, the ship refused to complete the maneuver and ended up lying helpless, her bow directly in the wind. This was known as being "in irons" and caused the ship to drift backward. This could lead to disaster if a ship were near shore. If a ship got "in irons," the vessel had to be coaxed back into her original course until enough headway had been made to allow another attempt to get on the new tack. Smart sail handling was the mark of a competent officer. A fine judgment of wind power, direction, and a thorough knowledge of the capabilities and shortcomings of one's own vessel and crew were required. When a ship was in action, there was no time to plan maneuvers. Crews were drilled and redrilled in shiphandling so that when round shot whistled around their heads and the rigging and sails hung in tatters, they would do their duty automatically.

Pleased with the way the *Randolph* handled, Biddle put back to Cape Henlopen where a convoy of some forty to fifty merchantmen had gathered. The three largest carried tobacco for France. The smaller craft were bound for the West Indies. The frigate, in company with the *Hornet* and the *Fly*, guarded these ships for three days. On February 15, they parted company, the ships destined for the Caribbean turning south, the tobacco vessels continuing on their way to France. The *Randolph* swung her bow northward to the coast of New England where Biddle intended to seek out the 28-gun British frigate *Milford*, which had been playing havoc with Yankee shipping.

Just how far Biddle got on this mission is unknown. Within a few days after signaling farewell to the convoy, the *Randolph* sprung, or split, her foremast. The base was found to be rotten. The only practical course of action was to fish the mast out and rig a spare spar as a jury mast. Before this substitution could be made, a second and more serious accident befell the frigate. An ominous cracking from amidships was heard, and a startled officer on the quarterdeck cried a warning: "Stand clear the mainmast! She's going by the board!" There was just enough time for those nearby to leap to

safety. With a final splintering crack, the mast gave way, breaking off
at the deck. Held upright only by the standing rigging, it pitched and
rolled with the ship. "To see it stagger from side to side with the roll
of the vessel," Biddle said later, "was as unpleasant a sight as ever I
wish to behold."

The mast was ordered cut away before it capsized the ship.
Armed with axes, seamen frantically slashed at the rigging. After the
mast splashed into the sea, the carpenter examined the stump and reported it rotten to the core. A crewman told the captain that "he
knew those spars our masts were made of to have lain these 18 years
in the water at the mast yard." With his ship nearly helpless, having
only one good mast left, Biddle abandoned the cruise and decided to
make for a convenient port where his ship could be re-rigged. Fearing that the British blockading squadron had returned to the mouth
of Delaware Bay and knowing that the Chesapeake was being
scoured by enemy ships, he settled upon Charleston as the most
likely haven. The *Randolph* turned southward, buffeted by heavy
seas and wallowing under her jury rig. Lookouts manned the
mizzen masthead, straining their eyes for the sight of Lord Howe's
cruisers.

Ironclad discipline was maintained on the seriously damaged
vessel, for Biddle realized that the British prisoners of war recruited
in the Philadelphia jails might try to seize the ship. Indeed just such
an attempt was organized on the lower deck. Little is known about
the plot except for a brief account by Biddle's older brother, Charles,
who related the story as told to him. "While they were bearing away
for Charlestown, the British sailors with some others of the crew
formed a design to take the ship," according to this account. "When
all was ready, they gave three cheers on the quarterdeck. By the decided and resolute conduct of Captain Biddle and his officers, the
ringleaders were seized and punished, and the rest submitted without
further resistance." Probably the ringleaders were triced up at the
gratings and given a taste of the cat-o'-nine-tails.

To add to Biddle's troubles, a malignant fever swept the ship.
Half the crew were stricken. Fifteen men died before she reached
port. There are no details of the type of fever, but it may well have
been typhus, or jail fever as it was known in the Eighteenth Century.
The disease may have been brought aboard by the released prisoners
carrying lice from the pestilential jails where they had been confined.

The disastrous voyage finally came to an end on March 11, when the *Randolph* passed over the Charleston bar. Biddle surely breathed a sigh of relief at the completion of what he called "one of the most disagreeable passages that I have experienced."

The Marine Committee was bitterly disappointed at the unfortunate beginning of its major naval effort. But there was more bad news to come. Word was received that Dudley Saltonstall's command, the *Trumbull*, drew too much water to clear the shoals at the mouth of the Connecticut River. She was trapped. Whatever guns the frigate carried were removed to lighten her, leaving her defenseless. Benedict Arnold, who was home in New London at the time, thought a British raiding party which burned Danbury in April 1777 had the destruction of the *Trumbull* as its goal. This could be easily accomplished, he said, "as there is no Battery or Armed Vessell to Cover her." With his trained seaman's eye, Arnold suggested that with the aid of lighters and an easterly wind, the frigate could be safely shifted across the bar. But the *Trumbull* remained in the river, swinging idly at her moorings for more than two years, a symbol of poor planning and wasted resources.[3] A similar fate befell the *Virginia*. Despite repeated orders to James Nicholson to get her to sea, she was blockaded in Chesapeake Bay for the entire year, with the skipper being called "a Commodore snug in harbour."

Undaunted, the Marine Committee produced a multitude of schemes for making the best use of its fleet. For all the politics, sectional jealousies and factional feuding that dogged it, this body sometimes exhibited an inspired sense of naval strategy. Fully realizing that the American navy because of its weaknesses would be forced to adopt the tactic of commerce raiding, the Committee repeatedly sought to make certain this weapon was used with maximum effect. Enemy commerce would not be destroyed by individual captains seeking out isolated ships. To be really effective, squadrons must be sent to the major ocean crossroads to make them untenable for British shipping. During the early part of 1777 several bold plans were outlined that would have created panic among British ship-

---

[3] On April 12, 1777, Saltonstall informed the Marine Committee from "on board the Continental ship of war *Trumbull*" that he had captured two British transports after a sharp fight. As the frigate was bottled up in the Connecticut River at the time, this was a different vessel, possibly the 10-gun sloop *Trumbull*, a Connecticut privateer.

owners if they had materialized. In all cases, however, the scheme misfired because of the shortage of crews and the inability of the ships to break through the British blockade.

On February 1, Paul Jones was ordered to take command of the *Alfred, Columbus, Cabot, Hampden,* and the sloop *Providence* for what would have been a spectacular cruise. First he was to capture the island of St. Kitts in the West Indies where Robert Morris fancied he would find "considerably booty." Then Jones was to sail to Pensacola in West Florida where he was to deal with two or three British sloops that were making nuisances of themselves and to seize a supply of cannon in the town. The fleet was then to move on to the mouth of the Mississippi where Jones was to capture enemy vessels coming down the river with cargoes valued at 100,000 pounds. Finally, he was to make a choice between an expedition to the West African coast or to Barbados to capture British slavers. Morris explained the basic strategy as follows:

> It has long been clear to me that our Infant fleet cannot protect our own coasts; and the only effectual relief it can afford us is to attack the enemies defenceless places and thereby oblige them to station more of their Ships in their own Countries, or to keep them employed in following ours, and either way we are relieved so far as they do it.

This was sound strategic thinking. The trouble was that none of the American ships got to sea.

The Marine Committee came up with another strategic stroke on April 29. General orders were issued to the captains of a number of ships, including the *Randolph*, the *Andrew Doria*, and the *Columbus* to rendezvous off Abaco in the Bahamas on July 25. The intention was to capture the sugar fleet. This fleet, of upward of sixty sail, generally sailed from Jamaica about July 26 of each year, under convoy for England. "Our design is to intercept this Fleet, and take, sink burn and destroy as many of them as possible," the Marine Committee declared. Such a brilliant victory—along with the ample .
prize money it would provide—would make it considerably easier to enlist seamen.

When Biddle opened his sealed orders on July 10, he must have smiled grimly. He was not "cruizing near the Island of Hispaniola" as expected by the Marine Committee. Instead, the *Randolph* was still floating in Charleston Harbor. Although new masts had been stepped and rerigging had been completed by early June, the frigate's crew numbered a scant hundred officers and men. Recruiting efforts had been unsuccessful in the face of the lures of privateering, and during a late-spring storm a bolt of lightning had splintered the frigate's new mainmast from cap to deck. It had to be replaced. After reading his instructions, Biddle decided to get to sea immediately and make do with the hands available. Orders were given to bend sail. Ominously, summer lightning split the clouds as the ship began to make way and sheets of rain swept across the deck. Suddenly, there was a blinding flash—and the new mainmast was shattered like its predecessor. There was to be no rendezvous at Abaco for the *Randolph*, nor for any of the other Continental ships. Most of them remained bottled up in port.

The British blockade of Rhode Island made Boston the center of naval activity in New England. The frigates *Hancock* and *Boston*, which had been brought around to Boston from Newburyport where they had been built, finally stood out to sea on May 21, 1777, at the head of a flotilla that included nine privateers. They intended to destroy the troublesome *Milford*. Only a few weeks before, the British frigate had captured the *Cabot*, one of the Continental Navy's original four ships. She had driven the brig ashore on the coast of Nova Scotia after a two-day chase. The *Milford* had been so close behind the *Cabot* that Captain Joseph Olney and his crew barely had time to splash ashore and make their getaway in a stolen schooner. The first Continental vessel to be captured, the *Cabot* was taken into the Royal Navy. "There was a great day of general rejoicing" in Halifax where the vessel was taken, the Boston *Gazette* reported. "Guns firing, drums beating, colours displayed . . . Deluded creatures!— they think the fate of America depends on a single Brig."

The problems that had faced Biddle in manning the *Randolph* were multiplied for John Manley and Hector McNeill who were seeking an even greater number of men for the *Hancock* and *Boston*. Desertion was rife. In desperation, McNeill begged the Massachusetts authorities to establish regulations requiring travelers to identify themselves in the hope of detecting deserters. "This regulation would not be burthensome to honest Men but would Effectually stop all runaways." Manley offered personally to pay the army for any wages advanced or bounty given to sailors who had enlisted as soldiers if the men were turned over to him. Both officers had gone heavily in debt advancing money to their seamen for clothing and other needs. "The very Interest of Money which I have borrowed and advanced to Carry on the Service of this Ship would have maintained my Family in Credits," declared McNeill.

The unbridled operations of British cruisers off the coast ultimately led the Massachusetts authorities to provide some 2,000 pounds to the skippers so they could attract enough men to get their ships to sea. Nine privateers of mixed size accepted an offer of free insurance to join the two frigates in a twenty-five-day sweep of the area aimed at driving off enemy ships. As senior Continental officer, Manley was made commodore of the flotilla. With the *Hancock* in the van, a freshening spring breeze pushed the ships out onto the blue water. The wind hummed a low song in the rigging, and McNeill, for one, breathed a sigh of relief. "The long wish'd for hour is at last come in which I bid farewell to the sleepy Agents, disheartened Tradesmen and distress'd Seamen who frequent the Streets of Boston," he declared.

The prospects for the success of the squadron were limited. Trying to organize privateers was like harnessing seagulls, and it was common knowledge that there was bad blood between Manley and McNeill. Within six days, the privateers had run off, reducing Commodore Manley's flotilla to the two frigates. On May 29, the Americans picked off a brig straggling from a British convoy shepherded by the *Somerset*, a 64-gun warship, and sent her into Boston with a prize crew. At dawn the following day, the frigates sighted the *Somerset* with three large transports in her care. "Capt. Manley was not convinced of the size of our Opponent until she was within Shott of him," related McNeill with obvious distaste. "Very luckily for him the *Hancock*'s Heels saved his Bacon." The British ship pursued the Americans for six hours until nightfall. The *Hancock* and *Boston* cruised to the northeast in search of weaker prey. They saw nothing "except a few miserable Fishermen." Finally, on June 7th, they fell in with the British frigate *Fox*, 28.

The *Fox* tried to make a run for it, but the *Hancock* was a fast sailer and overhauled her. The two frigates lay broadside to broadside, pounding away at each other until the *Boston* came up. Both the *Hancock* and *Fox* were heavily damaged. Manley had his pumps going before the British ship, her wheel shattered and her masts

damaged, hauled down her colors. McNeill may have been late getting into action, but was prompt in reaching for the spoils. He sent
his first lieutenant over to the *Fox* to take command of the prize. The
angry Manley ordered McNeill to withdraw the lieutenant, which
was done "for the sake of peace."

Several days were spent refitting the battered *Hancock* and *Fox*
—a period in which McNeill urged Manley to sail southward to
Charleston. There, he said, they could clean the bottoms of their
ships and join Biddle in the *Randolph* for a West Indian cruise. He
maintained that Manley first agreed and then changed his mind.
"Nevertheless I follow'd him as the Jackall does the Lyon, without
Grumbling except in my Gizard." The breach between the two skippers widened after a near accident on the night of June 27. The *Hancock* changed course and in the darkness barely missed colliding
with the *Boston*. Charging that Manley had not shown the proper signal, McNeill wrote him a letter "and gave him my mind freely on his
misconduct which nettled the Commodore very much." Now it was
Manley's turn. "You commonly keep a considerable distance
astern," he wrote McNeill. "I should think . . . that we can Command our Ships to keep within hail of each other or so near as that
we can hear the bells strike." He caustically offered to let the *Boston*
take the van, so the ships could stay together. With that, Manley be-
moaned the fact that because of sickness "I am now laying upon my
beam ends & what is worse than that I cannot drink neither Punch,
Wine nor Grog."

In this unhappy fashion, the three frigates rolled homeward to
Boston. On the morning of July 6, they captured a sloop laden with
coal that was taken in tow by the *Hancock*. Toward evening, the *Fox*
signaled that two ships were astern, coming up fast. They were the
Rainbow, of 44 guns, and the brig *Victor*, 10, both under the command of Commodore Sir George Collier. Manley was not particularly concerned and towed the coal sloop all through the night, forcing the *Boston* and *Fox* to shorten sail to stay with him. When dawn
came, only about five or six miles separated the antagonists. At the
same time, a third British ship, the frigate *Flora*, 32, joined the chase.
Manley ordered the coal sloop put to the torch, and his ships cleared
for action. The *Flora*, running ahead of the other British vessels,
caught up with the *Boston* and exchanged broadsides with her. "Her
Shott was so well aim'd that some of them pass'd through our Ship,"

reported McNeill. His vessel fell off to make quick repairs. Manley, mistaking the *Rainbow* for a two-deck ship-of-the-line with 64 or more guns, chose "to try his heels." The Americans scattered, the *Hancock* to the southward, the *Fox* to the eastward, while the *Boston* kept to the northward with the wind behind her.

The *Rainbow* gave chase to the *Hancock*. She was identified by a British officer, recently a prisoner in Boston, who knew she was commanded by Manley "the Sea Officer in whom the Congress placed great Confidence and who is the Second in Rank in their Navy." The swift-sailing *Hancock* should have been able to make a clean getaway, but for some unexplained reason Manley shifted his water casks forward in order to alter her trim and make her sail faster. Instead, this forced the frigate down by the head, clipping some of her speed. The chase lasted throughout the night, and by four o'clock in the morning of July 8, the *Rainbow* had drawn close enough to open up on the *Hancock* with a bow chaser and "occasional Broadsides of Round and Grape" shot followed. At 8:30 A.M., Commodore Collier hailed Manley to warn him that if he expected quarter, he would have to strike his flag immediately. Manley made one last effort to draw ahead of the British ship. "I therefore fired into him, upon which he struck the Rebel Colours to His Majesty's Ship, after a Chace of upwards of 39 hours," Collier reported. The *Flora* had taken the *Fox* several hours before after a hot fight. Only McNeill in the *Boston* escaped, eventually running his ship up the mouth of the Sheepscott River on the Maine coast.

Manley was chagrined when he came aboard the *Rainbow* to discover that he had not surrendered to a ship-of-the-line but to a vessel only slightly stronger than the *Hancock*. He damned McNeill for not coming to his assistance, but the fault was pretty much his own. If he had exchanged a few shots with his adversary, he would have quickly learned that she was not a 64-gun ship but one well within the capabilities of his own vessel. Failing this, he would probably have escaped from the *Rainbow* if he had not foolishly altered the trim of his vessel. The British were delighted with having taken both Manley and the *Hancock*. "We have all long wished to get this man into our possession, from his talents and intrepidity, and fortunate it is that we have done so," Commodore Collier wrote Germain. "He was beginning to shew the Americans what they had not been accustomed to, the seeing of one of his Majesty's ships in their possession . . . Everybody here is overjoyed at the capture of Mr. Manley." The *Hancock*, taken into the Royal Navy as the *Iris*, fought only too well for her captors.

As for McNeill, he found his sanctuary left something to be desired. While British ships stood off the coast waiting for him to come out, the captain unburdened himself of a tale of woe: "In this present Situation I am much at a Loss what to do. My Ship's Company are so diminished by Manning the *Fox* & and the Men otherwise Lost since we Sail'd from Boston: my Ship is very Fowl . . . and besides that, we cannot make her Sail fast, trim which way we will." With unconscious humor, Captain Thomas Thompson, of the frigate *Raleigh*, still at Portsmouth awaiting men and guns, wrote McNeill congratulating him on his "safe arrival" in Maine. "If you can engage more men than you want should be glad to have them," he added.

In due time, McNeill managed to work his way down the New England coast to Boston without being caught by British cruisers. His reception was chilly. Public opinion held him responsible for the capture of the popular Manley. His reaction was to vilify the imprisoned officer. "I find myself involved in a chain of difficultys by his blunders and misconduct," he told the Marine Committee. "I must in justice to my self say, That he is totally unequal to the Command with which he has been intrusted, he being ignorant, Obstinate, Overbearing and Tyranical beyond measure." McNeill also got into difficulty with his own officers, who threatened never to go to sea with him again. The situation finally reached the point where the Marine Committee ordered the Naval Board of the Eastern District to suspend him from his command pending a court-martial. For the rest of the year the *Boston* lay idle at her mooring.

Realizing that he was not going to get command of the fleet that had been promised by Morris, Paul Jones went to Philadelphia and spent several weeks lobbying for a command of any kind. Jones's difficulty was twofold: He lacked roots in his chosen country and he had a querulous and sometimes overbearing manner that irritated both his superiors and his fellow officers, notes Admiral Morison. The first was overcome when the Marine Committee had tested his capacity and found him to be one of the ablest officers in its service. He never overcame the second. Although Jones could not have performed as successfully as he did without the help of brave officers and men, he very seldom mentioned any of them. Morison has observed that like Columbus, "he was a colossal egotist, seldom generous enough to share credit with his subordinates."

Part of his personality problem probably lay in his humble origins, which he was at great pains to hide. He had been born John Paul, Jr., the son of a gardener on the estate of William Craik at Arbigland, on the northern shore of Soleway Forth, a deep inlet on the western border of the Scottish lowlands and England. He was fascinated by the sea, and as soon as he was old enough, young John Paul spent his spare time out with the fishing boats and small coasters that plied along Soleway Forth. If there had been money in the family or someone with influence, he would probably have entered the Royal Navy as a midshipman. Instead he went into the merchant marine. In 1761, at the age of thirteen, he was apprenticed for seven years to a Whitehaven shipowner to learn the sailor's trade.

Three years of voyaging followed, to the West Indies and America—including Virginia, where his older brother William had set himself up as a tailor in Fredericksburg. When his employer went bankrupt and released young Paul from his apprenticeship, he drifted into the slave trade. Two voyages on a "blackbirder" were enough and John Paul left the "abominable trade," as he called it. He took passage home on a brig. During this trip, both the master and mate died of a fever and John Paul took command as no one else aboard could navigate. The vessel's owners were so pleased with his performance that they appointed him captain at the age of twenty-one. From cabin boy to master in eight years was quite a success story for a young man without family influence. Captain Paul adopted the manners and dress of the young gentlemen he had observed in the ports of the West Indies and in Virginia, rid himself of his Scots burr and took to carrying a sword. Although he had only a few years of schooling, he cultivated an interest in literature and wrote sentimental verse. If all had gone well, he would soon have been able to save enough to buy an estate in Virginia and fulfill his ambition to set himself up as a gentleman farmer.

But the whole course of his life was changed by an incident that occurred in 1773 while his ship was in port at Tobago. According to his own account, a mutinous seaman attacked him and Captain Paul ran the man through with his sword and killed him. For some reason, which has never been made clear, Paul claimed that his friends on the island advised him to flee. What he did for the next twenty months remains shrouded in mystery. Sometime during this period he adopted the name John Jones to conceal his identity while the murder charge hung over him, later changing it to John Paul Jones. He owed his appointment as a lieutenant in the Continental Navy to Joseph Hewes, a North Carolina congressman and shipowner, to whom he had applied for employment as a merchant captain.

While Jones was in Philadelphia in 1777, the *Amphitrite*, one of Beaumarchais's vessels, arrived in Portsmouth with a cargo of munitions. The Marine Committee decided to send Jones on her return voyage to France with orders to take command of "a fine frigate" to be purchased there by the American commissioners in Paris. A new commission was also sent relieving Jones of the *Providence*, a ball and chain to which he had been tied by the seniority list. Desperate for any command, Jones agreed to go to Europe. His orders were soon countermanded. On June 14, 1777, Congress approved his appointment as skipper of the 20-gun sloop-of-war *Ranger*, which was fitting out in Portsmouth. Almost symbolically, the next entry in the *Journals* of Congress reads: "*Resolved,* That the Flag of the thirteen United States be thirteen stripes, alternate red and white; that the union be thirteen stars, white in a blue field, representing a new constellation."

Jones arrived in Portsmouth to find his ship of secondary importance as far as local authorities were concerned. All efforts were being made to prepare the *Raleigh* for sea while the *Ranger* was being ignored. From the bewhiskered effigy of her namesake that formed her figurehead to the entwined vines and cherubs that decorated her stern and quarter galleries, the *Raleigh* was a pleasing sight as she rocked at anchor on the Piscataqua River. But behind her 36 gunports, most of the gun trucks were empty.[4] As there was no foundry in New Hampshire capable of casting cannon, John Langdon, the navy agent who supervised the *Raleigh*'s construction, had scoured Rhode Island and Massachusetts for guns. Prices were not only exorbitant, but locally-built ships were getting first call on the available weaponry. Anxious to get the frigate to sea, the Marine Committee had ordered Captain Thompson on April 29, 1777, to cruise against British vessels bound for New York. If he had to sail without suitable guns, his orders were to take his ship directly to

---

[4] *Raleigh* was rated for 32 guns but had extra gunports.

Brest, France, where he was to fill out her armament. He was particularly instructed to avoid large ships of war but to take merchant ships to be sold as prizes to defray the cost of the guns. At the same time, Thompson was warned not to "lavish away Money" because "frugality is an absolutely necessary [quality] in all men that are connected with the American Revenue."

As late as May 22, British intelligence agents informed Lord Howe that the *Raleigh* had only six or eight of her guns mounted. Shorthanded and despairing of obtaining cannon on this side of the Atlantic, Thompson finally decided to try in France. Accompanied by Captain Elisha Hinman in the *Alfred*, he sailed from Portsmouth in mid-August. Three days out, a small schooner was taken. Her captors found $4,390 in counterfeit Continental and Massachusetts currency aboard. The schooner was of little value so she was burnt along with the counterfeit money, except for a few bills preserved as samples. On September 2, another small vessel was taken. The day before she had straggled away from a West Indian convoy homeward bound under guard by four British warships—the *Camel*, a 22-gun converted merchantman like the *Alfred*, flying the pennant of Commodore William Finch, and the sloops of war *Weazel*, 16, *Druid*, 14, and *Grasshopper*. Thompson sent the prize off to an American port but took possession of the convoy's sailing orders and signals.

The convoy was sighted from the masthead of the *Raleigh* early the next morning. By sunset the two American ships were close enough to count sixty sail spread out over the horizon. To allay any suspicion, Thompson made a signal as if he were a member of the convoy that had been left behind. Then he trailed the rearmost elements. He hailed Hinman in the *Alfred* and told him he intended to run into the convoy at sunrise and destroy it. The *Alfred* was ordered to stay close astern of the *Raleigh* until they were both alongside the convoy commander's ship, where they would open their attack. During the night the wind shifted, carrying the convoy away from the Yankee vessels. They were forced to set all sail to catch up. While the *Raleigh* was a good sailer and was soon nipping at the heels of the fleet, the *Alfred* had proven to be "tendersided," or unable to carry a full press of sail. Thompson could not haul in sail without fear of being detected so he let his sails shake in the wind while awaiting the *Alfred*. When she fell further astern, he decided to "stand into the fleet and take my chance alone."

Pressing the captured signals into use, Thompson gave orders to the merchantmen, who thought the *Raleigh* was a British frigate that had just joined the escort. With gunports closed, she sailed within pistol shot of the *Druid*. "Then we up sails, out guns, hoisted Continental colours and bid them strike to the Thirteen United States," he reported. "Sudden surprize threw them into confusion and their sails flew all aback, upon which we complimented them with a gun for each State, a whole broadside into her hull . . . Our second broadside was aimed at their rigging, which had its desired effect . . . In about a quarter of an hour all hands quitted quarters on board the British man-of-war. We cleared her decks totally; not a man was seen nor a gun fired on board her for twenty minutes before we left. She lay like a log alongside of us entirely at the mercy of our shot." The first broadside fatally wounded the *Druid*'s captain and killed her master. Six of her crew were killed, five died later of their wounds, and 21 were hurt. During the forty-five-minute unequal struggle, the *Raleigh*'s loss was one man killed, two wounded.

A sudden squall had prevented the merchantmen from seeing the *Raleigh*, but the rumble of gunfire sent them scattering. The *Camel* and the other escort vessels were about five miles off when the firing started. They raced to the rescue of the shattered *Druid*. Fearing that he would be surrounded, Thompson broke off the action and dropped back to position near the *Alfred*. The British ships turned away and set to work rounding up the frightened merchant vessels. The *Druid* was leaking badly, but the crew managed to patch her up. She reached Spithead about a month later with her pumps clanking away. For three days and nights Thompson and Hinman dogged the convoy without success. Tiring of the chase, the Americans finally set a course for the French coast. They arrived off Lorient on October 7, with two rum- and sugar-laden prizes picked up after they had ceased to hound the convoy.

Thompson blamed the loss of his glittering opportunity to seize the convoy on the inability of the *Alfred* to keep up with his ship. "Had she been a stiff ship and sailed equally well with the *Raleigh*," he declared, "we should in all probability have destroyed the convoy and dispersed the whole fleet." His dash into the center of the convoy after the *Druid* showed a certain romantic élan as did his rhetoric: "I am determined never to war against merchantmen where I have an opportunity of waring against the King," he declared. Noble

sentiments indeed—but indicating a complete misunderstanding of
the nature of the struggle. The destruction of a rich convoy of sixty
heavily laden ships would have been a much more severe blow to
Britain than the capture of an insignificant sloop-of-war. Thompson's failure to cut out even one of the merchantmen is even more
glaring because he had been specifically instructed to avoid combat
with warships and concentrate on taking as many prizes as possible.
Every blow against the enemy's commerce helped turn the scale
against Britain. It is interesting to speculate on what might have happened if Paul Jones, who had put the *Alfred* to good use despite her
"tender sides," or Nicholas Biddle had been granted the once-in-a-
lifetime opportunity that was muffed by Thompson.

The unrelieved string of disasters that befell the Continental
frigates was at last broken by the *Randolph*. Once again a new mainmast had been stepped, and on September 1, the frigate put out to
sea. This time Biddle took no chances. Topping the mast was a thin
iron rod. Lightning rods that protected buildings were common in
Charleston, but to see one affixed to a ship "excited much attention."
Probably one of the persons Captain Biddle escorted around his ship
to show how the device worked was eighteen-year-old Elizabeth
Baker. During the long period of enforced idleness in Charleston,
Biddle had been introduced to Elizabeth by her brother, Robert. He
became a frequent visitor to the Baker plantation up the Ashley
River from the town. Before summer was over, he and Elizabeth
were engaged. The shattering of the *Randolph*'s masts had brought
him some good luck after all.

Biddle managed to fill out his crew by offering a $50 bonus to
any seaman who would sign on—$10 of it payable in advance.
Alarmed by the presence of British cruisers which were snapping up
American ships off the port, the South Carolina authorities had contributed to the bounty. In return, Biddle promised to cruise off the
Carolina coast and put an end to British commerce raiding. The size
of Biddle's bonus even attracted a few men from privateers that had
recently put into Charleston, an achievement in itself. When the
Randolph reached the open sea, it was found that she had lost some
of her fine sailing qualities. Due to her long stay in port, her bottom
had become fouled, reducing her speed considerably. No ships were
sighted for three days until, along toward twilight on September 3, a

lookout called from the masthead that he had spotted a distant sail. A midshipman, sent aloft with a telescope, soon informed the quarterdeck there were five ships plodding along toward the northward.

Throughout the night, the *Randolph* kept on their trail by means of the occasional lights they showed. Daylight revealed the *Randolph*'s quarry as two brigs, two ships, and one sloop, all bound for New York. Biddle ordered the Grand Union flag broken out and closed with the vessels. The larger ship opened fire. The sea around the frigate was peppered with shot. Biddle, however, withheld his broadside because he wanted all the vessels as prizes, not just one. While the *Randolph*'s broadside would have smashed the British ship to matchwood, the frigate would have had to turn to bring her guns into play. This meant the other British vessels would probably escape, especially since the *Randolph* had been slowed by her fouled bottom. Standing with Biddle on the quarterdeck, Captain Samuel Shaw, of the frigate's marine detachment, joked that he was too skinny to be hit by an enemy cannon ball. He was still laughing when an enemy shot cleanly parted a line at his back. He blinked, took one look at the dangling line and concluded his joke wasn't as funny as he had thought.

Drawing up to within pistol range of his adversary, Biddle ordered a single gun fired. It was enough. The vessel's colors were quickly hauled down. Without losing headway Biddle sent over a prize crew. Huddling together, the other ship and the two brigs were easily taken, but the sloop managed to get away. The vessel that had tried to resist proved a valuable prize. The *True Briton* was armed with twenty 6-pounders and loaded with rum for the British army. The other craft were also richly laden, bringing a total of 90,000 pounds in prize money. Many of Biddle's officers and men had been detailed off as prize crews and the *Randolph*'s bottom was badly in need of cleaning, so the captain decided to cut short the cruise and return to Charleston. In company with her covey of prizes, the frigate was greeted by cheering townspeople as she eased into her berth in the Cooper River. Biddle was doubly pleased by the outcome of the brief foray. It put 9,000 pounds of the prize money in his pockets and meant he would have no problem recruiting a crew when the time came to sail again. From now on, sailors would consider the *Randolph* a lucky ship.

XV

Debacle on the Delaware

For some superstitious folk, 1777 was the year of the hangman. Ever since the start of the year, they had seen in its last three digits a portent of the gibbets awaiting the leading American rebels. Gallows jokes were exchanged in the lobby and the great chamber of the State House in Philadelphia where Congress met. Toward mid-year, some of the humor faded. From the north came reports of the steady advance from Canada of a powerful new invading force led by "Gentleman Johnny" Burgoyne. Fort Ticonderoga, keystone of the American defense, fell to the British without a fight and the country lay open to the invaders. "I think we shall never defend a post until we shoot a general . . . and this event in my opinion is not far off," John Adams commented grimly. As if Burgoyne's invasion were not menace enough, Sir William Howe's still larger force threatened from New York. Although military practicality indicated a march up the Hudson to join Burgoyne, Howe's intentions were a mystery. Shortly after the fall of Ticonderoga, he had disappeared into the Atlantic with a large fleet of transports and men-of-war. So completely did the British dominate the sea, no American vessel put out to keep an eye on the armada.

Sir William had begun the year of the hangman with exceedingly ambitious plans. Undismayed by the setbacks at Trenton and Princeton and anticipating heavy reinforcements, he proposed to attack Boston, effect a junction on the Hudson River with the British army coming down from Canada, capture Philadelphia, and overrun South Carolina and Georgia. A large order indeed—but Howe had seemingly decided at last that nothing was to be gained by temporizing with the rebels. No doubt Lord Germain was delighted to see Howe display so much vigor, even if it were only on paper. Nevertheless, the American secretary was overwhelmed by the general's demand for 15,000 additional men and ten more ships of the line. There was a shortage of German mercenaries, England was producing a mere trickle of recruits, and the few regiments still at home could not be spared in the face of France's uncertain intentions. Germain ruthlessly pruned Howe's requests for men, horses and supplies, producing about half those sought. With these reduced forces went a tart lecture on the importance of living as much as possible off what resources could be found in America.

Piece by piece, Howe jettisoned parts of his plan due to the limited reinforcements available. First to go was the expedition against Boston. Shortly afterward, South Carolina and Georgia were dropped from the year's objectives. There remained only the proposed junction with Burgoyne and the invasion of Pennsylvania. Gradually, Sir William began to place secondary emphasis upon his role in the northern operation and put all his hopes for ending the war in 1777 on the attack on Philadelphia. Like all British generals during the war, he was hypnotized by the notion that certain areas of America were strongholds of Loyalism. He believed the mere presence of the King's forces would win them to the British cause. Howe thought Pennsylvania in particular was Loyalist. To seize it would divide the colonies and place the British in control of the leading metropolis of the continent. To take Pennsylvania would be easy. And by drawing Washington into Pennsylvania, he would be materially helping Burgoyne by dividing the enemy. He reserved for himself the opportunity to smash the American army.

Howe's decision to sail from New York on this mission in July, leaving Burgoyne to meet his fate at Saratoga, is usually pictured as a consummate piece of British blundering. One popular tale states that because of the laziness of Germain and the carelessness of his staff, orders to Howe to unite with Burgoyne were never sent.[1] The facts, however, are different. Germain approved the invasion of Pennsylvania on March 3, with the understanding that Howe's army would eventually cooperate with Burgoyne. On March 26, he sent Howe a copy of a dispatch to Carleton in Canada which said Burgoyne had orders to force his way to Albany and put himself under Sir William's command. What Germain apparently expected was that Howe would lead a land invasion of Pennsylvania which would be completed quickly and then march north to join Burgoyne. What he did not know until May 8 was that Howe contemplated an invasion by sea that would take considerably longer than planned when permission was given for the expedition. Upon learning of Howe's revised plan, Germain urged him to finish the campaign in plenty of time to cooperate with Burgoyne. By then it was too late to retrieve the situation. Howe did not receive the dispatch until mid-August when he was entirely committed to the Pennsylvania expedition.

Rather than risk another Trenton, Howe had decided to protect his lines of communication by conveying his army to Pennsylvania by sea. He hoped both to take the Americans by surprise and to give his troops the benefit of a healthful sea voyage during the hottest season of the year. Before Howe embarked his men, a month was wasted in meaningless maneuvering in New Jersey. Such dilatory tactics added sixty-five days to the campaign against Philadelphia and made any idea of cooperation with Burgoyne's army illusory. In contrast, Sir Henry Clinton evacuated Philadelphia the following year, proceeded across New Jersey by land, fought the Battle of Monmouth and arrived in New York all in a matter of seventeen days.

Early in July, Howe herded his men aboard the transports lying off Staten Island, but he was reluctant to sail until word was received of Burgoyne's progress. Sweltering aboard the transports, the troops consumed a large part of the fresh provisions intended for the voyage. Finally, on July 15, the General had word of Burgoyne's steady advance. Breathing confidence and showing the highest spirits, Burgoyne reported that Ticonderoga had been taken and that he was pressing on to Albany. This dispatch relieved Howe of concern for

---

[1] See George Bernard Shaw's *The Devil's Disciple* for one version of this legend.

the safety of the northern army. Two days later, he wrote Burgoyne he was proceeding with his campaign in Pennsylvania. Clinton was left with a skeleton force in New York and told to cooperate with Burgoyne as circumstances required. The astounded Clinton, learning of Howe's plans, did his best to dissuade him from the southern adventure. In Clinton's opinion, the best thing for Howe to do would be to go up the Hudson to meet Burgoyne. All the advantages of a move to the north were pointed out; all the disadvantages of operations to the south were emphasized. Sir William, however, had the last word. Coolly, he told Clinton that his Pennsylvania plan had the approval of the Ministry. Of course, Howe neglected to say that he had approval only for a lightning overland campaign—not for a drawn-out seaborne expedition.

Under the command of Admiral Lord Howe, a fleet of some 280 sail, including five ships of the line, put to sea on July 23. Loaded with perhaps 15,000 soldiers, hundreds of horses, innumerable pieces of field artillery, and tons of provisions and powder, the ships were an impressive sight. Just below Sandy Hook, the transports formed in two divisions. The flagship *Eagle*, 64, and the frigate *Liverpool*, 32, led the convoy. After them and on both sides of the transports came the *Augusta*, 64, and *Isis*, 50. In the rear were the *Nonsuch*, 64, with its couriers, the armed schooners *Swift* and *Dispatch*, both of 16 guns. Nine frigates "sailed around the fleet at some distance." One fifth of the strength of the Royal Navy in American waters was now committed to what turned out to be a two-month cruise with the storeships and transports. Elaborate steps were taken to deceive Washington as to the destination of the armada. They were unnecessary. Washington was more surprised than anyone else by a movement that seemed to defy sound military judgment in view of the well-known British plan for a junction at Albany. "Howe's in a manner abandoning Burgoyne is so unaccountable a matter that till I am fully assured of it, I cannot help casting my eyes continually behind me," he declared. Washington was so convinced that Howe could not be committing so supreme a blunder that he suspected the British intended to return to New York.

Even after Howe got underway, everything seemed to conspire against him, including the elements. The prevailing wind off the American coast in summer is south–southwest which slowed the

ships to a snail's pace. Twenty-four days were required to cover three
hundred and fifty miles. With a fair wind the fleet might have sailed
to Europe in less time. Sultry, windless days were followed by
breathless nights. Food and water for men and animals grew scarce
and the caulking between the deck planking melted. "Condemned to
broil in that Cursed Climate," the soldiers wilted in heat that veterans of service in the West Indies and Africa said was worse than anything they had experienced. Over three hundred horses—sorely
needed in what Howe planned as a campaign of movement—died at
sea. Those that survived were "mere carrion" by the time they were
unloaded.

Entirely in the dark about Howe's movements, Washington's
army was "compelled to wander about the country like the Arabs" in
search of the enemy fleet and army. On July 31, the British were
sighted off the mouth of Delaware Bay. Washington immediately ordered his troops across the Delaware from the vicinity of Trenton
where they had been standing by. The commander-in-chief galloped
south from Philadelphia to Chester "to look for a proper place to arrange his army" for the impending battle. Washington had no doubt
that the British would land their troops nearby and attempt to march
on Philadelphia. On August 2, he suddenly received word that the
fleet was gone. "A large ship which we took to be the Admiral fired a
gun and immediately the whole fleet backed and stood off . . . to the
eastward . . . about four o'clock p.m. they were [out] of sight;
whether they were bound for New York or Virginia is not in my
power to tell," wrote his informant. Nor was it in Washington's
power. He guessed that Howe had been "practising a deep feint,
merely to draw our attention and whole force to this point." The
British had to be returning to New York to advance up the Hudson.
"I shall return again with the utmost expedition to the North River,"
Washington declared. On reflection, however, he decided to wait before moving until he had word that the armada was actually off
Sandy Hook.

What had happened as the fleet lay off the Delaware capes?
Why had the Howe brothers decided not to land near Philadelphia?
The usual supposition is that they were the victims of faulty intelligence regarding the strength of the Yankee defenses and the difficulty of navigation up the Delaware for large ships. Upon arriving
off the capes, the fleet had been joined by the *Roebuck* and a small

squadron, which had been patrolling the area under the command of Captain Sir Andrew Snape Hamond. Hamond went aboard the *Eagle* to make his report and found Sir William still in bed at ten o'clock in the morning. A British officer later contended that Hamond "produced a chimerical draught of fortifications that were never erected and *chevaux de frise* that were never sunk. This intelligence caused us to bear away." Full blame rests on the Howe brothers, however. While Hamond did report that the Yankees had constructed fortifications further up the Delaware, he emphasized that there was nothing to prevent troops from landing on the lower river, by-passing the defenses and taking Philadelphia. Hamond pleaded "to no purpose." General Howe would not listen and his brother supported him. "To the astonishment of both Fleet and Army, the signal was made to turn away, and steer for the Capes of Virginia." [2]

While Howe was deciding to condemn his soldiers to another three weeks on the transports, Burgoyne committed a series of blunders that sealed his fate. After the fall of Ticonderoga, he had quickly taken Skenesborough. The next objective of his advance was Fort Edward about twenty-two miles to the south. The easiest route lay by way of Lake George, which was controlled by the invaders. Nevertheless, the British commander chose to strike overland from Skenesborough to Fort Edward, presenting the Americans with time to reorganize the resistance. Burgoyne made the decision for reasons that had nothing to do with military strategy. To go by water meant a short retreat over the route the British had already traveled. Burgoyne could not bring himself to turn his back upon the rebels, even for strategic reasons. He ordered an advance through the forest. As the troops sweated to get their wagons and artillery down the winding trail, Yankee axemen felled trees across their path, destroyed bridges, and dug ditches to create additional quagmires in the already boggy land. Twenty days were consumed in covering twenty miles. In every direction, the weary Redcoats saw smoke rising from dozens of fires. The defiant Yankees were putting the torch to their homes and crops so the enemy could not have them. When the

---

[2] Hamond claimed that the real reason Howe did not land the troops on the Delaware was an incorrect report that Washington was already across the Delaware and would be able to attack the flank of any force moving up the river. In actuality, points out Don Higginbotham in *The War of American Independence* (New York 1971), the Americans were a hundred miles away on the Jersey side of the Delaware, still seeking information as to Howe's whereabouts.

troops finally stumbled into Fort Edward on July 29, they had to wait for provisions. They waited for six weeks instead of plunging ahead the last few miles to Albany. Liquor and food ran short. "Pork at noon, pork at night, pork cold, pork hot," grumbled the troops. Worse was soon to come—no pork at all.

In the meantime, the British armada wallowed its slow way down the Atlantic coast, oblivious to the dangers engulfing Burgoyne. When told that the British were headed south, Washington allowed that he was "puzzled . . . being unable to account upon any plausible Plan. . . . why [Howe] should go to the southward rather than cooperate with Mr. Burgoyne." As late as August 21, Washington remained convinced that the British were making a feint before returning to either the Delaware or the Hudson. A council of war that day decided unanimously that Howe's most probable objective was Charleston. So certain were the American generals that they had unraveled the mystery of his intentions, that orders were given for the army to move "to-morrow morning towards Hudson's River." On that very day, an express rider arrived in camp with news that the British fleet was in the Chesapeake—"high up in the North East part of it." The orders to move northward were quickly cancelled.

The British fleet had rounded Cape Charles on August 14. It sailed majestically up the Chesapeake, the greatest naval force ever seen in those waters. The sight must have been breathtaking. If the full panoply of Britain's might could awe the Americans into abject surrender, as some British officers believed, this spectacle should have done it. Yet as the fleet sailed past Annapolis, an American flag flew defiantly from the rebel fortifications. Although this showed there would be no quick break in American resistance, a British officer said that "as it was an object of little importance, it was looked at with contempt, and passed without firing a shot." Early on August 25, "a distressingly hot, close morning," the van of the fleet dropped anchor at the northernmost reach of the Chesapeake at Head of Elk, near Elkton, Maryland. Flat-bottomed boats carried the first elements of the army ashore. They brushed aside a few companies of militia "without firing a shot." After all the hardships, all the delays, the British army was as far from Philadelphia as it had been when it had embarked more than a month before.

To impress the populace with its strength Washington marched his army of some 11,000 men through the streets of Philadelphia, as they moved to Brandywine Creek to make a stand. News of the defeat of a detachment of Burgoyne's army at Bennington on August 16 by a gathering of New England militia had sent morale in the army soaring. "I never saw men with Higher spirits," declared one trooper. With the commander-in-chief at its head, the Marquis de Lafayette at his side, and his mounted staff following, the column swung down Front Street and up Chestnut Street as the bands played a quick step. John Adams watched the procession and wrote his wife: "They marched twelve deep and yet took up above two hours passing by." The troops were "extremely well armed, pretty well clothed and tolerably disciplined," yet had not "quite the air of soldiers. They don't step exactly in time. They don't hold up their heads quite erect, nor turn out their toes exactly as they ought." Adams did not fear for the safety of Philadelphia. "I feel as secure here as if I were in Braintree," he told Abigail, "but not so happy."

A bitter battle was fought on the Brandywine. Although Howe succeeded in outmaneuvering Washington, the American general managed to extricate his troops in fairly good order. Harassing attacks were pressed against the British, but Philadelphia lay open to the enemy. "If Howe comes here, I shall run away, I suppose, with the rest," observed Adams. "We are too brittle ware, you know, to stand the dashing of balls and bombs." At three o'clock on the morning of September 19, Congress was warned by Colonel Alexander Hamilton, one of Washington's aides, that the city could not be held. Not a moment was to be lost evacuating the capital. Congress broke up precipitately, without adjourning. The streets were jammed with delegates, officials, and citizens scrambling for safety. "It was a beautiful, still moonlight morning and the Streets as full of Men, Women and Children as on Market day," reported Thomas Paine. Thus, said Eliphalet Dyer of Connecticut, "this plaguy fellow of an How" sent Congress on its travels again. Since it could not go to Baltimore because of the British fleet in the Chesapeake, Congress moved westward to York. With what may have been dry humor, Adams declared, "This tour has given me an opportunity of seeing many parts of this country which I never saw before." With bands playing, the British entered the town on September 26, to receive a warm reception. Howe settled in with a sigh of relief. Most Americans were disheartened by the loss of Philadelphia, but not the city's most distinguished citizen. Benjamin Franklin, then in Paris, was informed that Howe had taken Philadelphia and replied: "No, Philadelphia has captured Howe!" A week before, Burgoyne's tattered army had reached Stillwater on the west bank of the Hudson, just twenty miles from Albany. It went no further.

　　Having gained his objective, Howe discovered that the Yankee fortifications on the Delaware obstructed the passage of British ships and supplies to Philadelphia. The overland supply line from the Chesapeake to Philadelphia was too open to Yankee interference to be depended upon. Already Washington's army was choking off supplies from the back country. Reopening the river to British shipping was vital to the continued occupation of the city. No one appreciated this more clearly than Washington. If the river defense "can be maintained, General Howe's situation will not be the most agreeable," he noted, "for if his supplies can be stopped by water, it may easily be done by land . . . the acquisition of Philadelphia may, instead of his good fortune, prove his ruin." Having held his ships in the Chesapeake for as long as his brother needed them, Lord Howe began moving the fleet back to the Delaware on September 14. Head winds and heavy weather slowed the convoy, which did not arrive off the mouth of the Delaware until early October.

　　"This morning 36 Sail of the Enemies Ships went past this Town up the Bay, and this Evening 47 more were seen from the light House Standing in for the Cape," reported an American coast-watcher at Cape Henlopen on October 5. At this late date, the fleet began the ascent of the lower Delaware without difficulty, as it might have done two months before. By October 12, the ships were at Chester, ten miles below Philadelphia, where they halted until the river could be cleared of obstructions, rebel batteries, and rebel vessels.

　　The first line of American defense was at Billingsport. It consisted of a double row of *chevaux de frise* guarded by a small redoubt on the Jersey shore which was unfinished and only lightly held. On October 2, the 42nd Regiment were landed below the position and attacked the redoubt from the rear. The garrison spiked their few guns, fired the barracks, and escaped. With the *Roebuck* in the lead, six British ships maneuvered upstream through the obstructions only to find a more formidable obstacle facing them. Just seven miles downstream from Philadelphia was a triple line of sunken obstacles running clear across the channel from the New Jersey to the Pennsylvania side. The Pennsylvania side of the river lay under the guns of Fort Mifflin on Port Island while the Jersey side was guarded by Fort Mercer, about 1900 yards away at Red Bank. Upstream from the fortifications lay an American fleet that included the *Andrew Doria, Hornet, Wasp, Fly,* a pair of xebecs,[3] together with several row-galleys, two floating batteries, and a handful of fire ships and rafts belonging to the Pennsylvania State Navy. The frigates *Washington* and *Effingham,* still unfinished, were upriver from Philadelphia. The combined Continental and state flotilla was under the command of Commodore John Hazelwood, of the Pennsylvania navy, while the troops manning the forts were part of Washington's army. As there was no unity of command, the situation was made to order for misunderstandings.

The best ships the Americans possessed were lost before Howe's fleet even arrived. Immediately after occupying Philadelphia, the British had begun to erect batteries along the river front. On September 27, the new Continental frigate *Delaware* and the Pennsylvania ship *Montgomery* came down river to bombard the emplacements before they could be completed. Captain Charles Alexander anchored his frigate within 500 yards of the guns only to have her fetch up on the river bottom when the tide ebbed. Presented with this inviting target, the British gunners stepped up the cannonade. The *Delaware* caught fire. Alexander surrendered, and the British took possession of the strongest American ship on the river. The *Montgomery* was dismasted, and two schooners were lost when they also ran aground.

To harass the British as they worked at removing obstructions from the river bottom at Billingsport, the Yankees floated fire rafts and fire ships downstream. These craft, loaded with combustibles, were sailed as close to their objectives as possible. After trains of powder were laid and a flaming torch was thrown into the hold, the crew jumped into a waiting boat to make their escape. If all went well, the craft was an inferno before the enemy could board it and extinguish the blaze. The effectiveness of fire ships depended almost entirely on the courage and coolness of the crews. A fire ship ignited prematurely could usually be sighted in time to be coped with safely and effectively. On the night of October 14 alone, the Americans sent

---

[3] A xebec was a craft with lateen or triangular sails.

nine fire rafts down river. The British had little difficulty in getting grapnels on them and towing them ashore. Five days later the British had cleared and buoyed a wide channel through the lower tier of *chevaux de frise* at Billingsport. The upper row of obstructions was their next objective.

If either Fort Mercer or Fort Mifflin fell, it was obvious that the other could not be held. The British decided to attack Fort Mercer on the Jersey shore first. A combined sea and land attack was launched on October 22. A force of about 1,200 German troops and some artillery led by Colonel Carl von Donop were sent against the redoubt and several ships were assigned to support them with their guns. The garrison under the command of Colonel Christopher Greene, a cousin of General Nathanael Greene, consisted of about four hundred Rhode Island Continentals. A young French engineer, the Chevalier de Mauduit du Plessis, sent to assist Greene in bolstering the position, discovered that the Americans, inexperienced in the art of fortification, had overbuilt the works "beyond their strength" to man them. He reduced the size of the fort by building an interior wall across an extension on the river side. The walls of the pentagonal fort thus created were of earth and mounted fourteen guns. Fort Mercer was surrounded by a ditch containing an abatis, or a line of sharpened tree trunks pointed outward. After leisurely placing his men, von Donop sent one of his officers, with a flag and drummer, to demand the surrender of the fort. "The King of England orders his rebellious subjects to lay down their arms," the officer declared, "and they are warned that if they stand the battle, no quarter whatever will be given." The Americans accepted the challenge.

The Hessians attacked in two columns, supported by a battery erected to the rear of the fort. One column moved against the northern part of the structure, the section that had been abandoned and cut off. Led by Colonel von Donop, the other struck at the redoubt itself. With little difficulty, the first column swept over the wall, cheering and waving their hats—only to find themselves facing another breastwork. Von Donop's men moved forward at the same time. Meeting no fire, they penetrated the abatis and crossed the ditch only to be stalled under the parapet because they had no scaling ladders. At this point Greene gave the order to fire. His men aimed at the broad white belts of the Germans as they had been instructed. A tornado of grape shot and musket balls ripped through the bunched enemy ranks at point-blank range. Screaming men went down in rows and heaps. It was sheer butchery. Von Donop and his officers tried to rally their troops, but the Colonel was a conspicuous target. He fell with a leg wound that was to be fatal. The attack faltered and faded. The Hessian troops fell back and reorganized for another assault, this time against the southern side of the redoubt. They were stopped by fire not only from the fort but also from American row galleys on the river. Battered and broken, the Hessians finally withdrew to the shelter of the nearby woods, leaving the ground strewn with dead and wounded. Twenty men were left cowering under the parapet, driven half mad by fear. The Hessians lost 371 men killed, wounded, and captured, including twenty-two officers. Despite the threats of no quarter, the wounded and prisoners were well treated. Total American casualties were 14 killed and 23 wounded.

To support the Hessian attack, Lord Howe sent the *Augusta*, 64, the *Roebuck*, 44, the 32-gun frigates *Pearl* and *Liverpool*, as well as the sloop-of-war *Merlin*, 18, to deal with the American galleys. The *Augusta* had been stripped so that she could be brought close inshore to be used as a floating battery against Forts Mercer and Mifflin. Unknown to the British captains, the obstructions placed by the Americans had caused a shift in the channel. Both the *Augusta* and *Merlin* ran aground and they could not be refloated that day. Early next morning, October 23, the duel with the forts was renewed. The *Augusta* was steadily pouring round shot and grape into the rebel batteries, galleys, and fire rafts when suddenly she caught fire and blew up.[4] Despairing of getting the *Merlin* free, her crew abandoned her after setting the ship ablaze. The *Augusta* was the largest British ship to be lost in action with the Americans during both the Revolution and the War of 1812.

After this repulse, the British erected five new and more powerful batteries on Province Island, a low-lying mud flat just five hundred yards to the north of Fort Mifflin. Since the *chevaux de frise* had caused the river to be deflected into a new channel to the rear of the

---

[4] The exact cause of the explosion of the *Augusta* is unknown. J. Fenimore Cooper in his *Naval History of the United States* (Philadelphia 1840) states that some hay bales placed on the ship to make her shot-proof caught fire.

fort, a floating battery carrying twenty-two 24-pounders was swung into position only forty yards away from the fort. At 7:30 in the morning of November 10, the British opened a bombardment that lasted five days. Heavy guns, howitzers, and mortars poured shot and bombs into the redoubt. Defended by about 450 men commanded by Lieutenant Colonel Samuel Smith, Fort Mifflin was "unskillfully constructed." One observer described it as "a Burlesque upon the art of Fortification." The eastern side which faced the river had high, thick stone walls as did the southern face. But the rear and the northern side, which bore the brunt of the British attack, were defended only by ditches, a battery of ten 18-pounders, and palisades with four wooden blockhouses, each mounting four guns. The garrison was not half the size required to man the works adequately. " 'Twas a cursed little mud island," said Lord Cornwallis of Fort Mifflin. Yet its defense was one of the most obstinate and gallant actions of the entire war.

The Americans replied to the shelling as best they could. Ammunition was so scarce that the fort's single 32-pounder could be fired only by using British shot that fell within the walls. A gill of rum was offered for each shot recovered. Joseph Martin, a Connecticut soldier, saw "from twenty to fifty of our men standing on the parade [ground] waiting with impatience the coming of the shot. It would often be seized before its motion had fully ceased and conveyed off to our gun to be sent back again to its former owners." The shelling went on day and night. The barracks was battered into rubble. Great gaping holes were opened in the palisades. There was no shelter from flying splinters for the defenders. Periodically, British gunners swept the walls at random, breaking up repair parties working in the darkness. "Our garrison diminishes, our soldiers are overwhelmed with fatigue—they spend the nights in watching and labour without doing much on account of their weakness," reported Major André-Arsene de Rosset, a French engineer officer, who stayed to the end despite being wounded. Colonel Smith, injured by flying bricks, was evacuated to Fort Mercer across the river.[5] Major Simeon Thayer took over the command. After four days of shelling, all but two of the fort's guns had been dismounted. The beleaguered soldiers pleaded for help from the fleet, but Commodore Hazelwood,

---

[5] Samuel Smith later commanded the defenses at Baltimore in 1814 when a British invasion force was repelled and "The Star-Spangled Banner" written.

apparently concerned about the safety of his vessels, did not respond.

On November 15, the *Somerset*, 64, *Roebuck*, *Isis*, *Liverpool*, and *Pearl* were warped into position as close to Fort Mifflin as the obstructions would permit. The *Vigilant*, 16, towed another floating battery into the channel behind the fort. At a signal, all the British guns crashed out as one in the most intensive bombardment of the war. Over a thousand shot were fired every twenty minutes. American gun crews were wiped out, and the remaining cannon hurled from their carriages. The ships were so near that marines in their maintops shot down any man who showed himself. "The whole area of the Fort was completely ploughed as a field," said Martin. "Our men were cut down like cornstalks." By nightfall the walls had been demolished, the blockhouses destroyed. Fort Mifflin existed only in name. Thayer ordered his surviving men to set fire to what was left. Then they retreated over the river to Red Bank. Two hundred and fifty American defenders had been killed or wounded, their places being taken by replacements who had slipped in during the night. The British lost but seven killed and five wounded. With Fort Mifflin gone, the fate of Fort Mercer was sealed. Cornwallis carried two thousand men across the river to storm the redoubt, but Colonel Greene, realizing his position was hopeless, evacuated it on November 20.

The Delaware from Cape Henlopen to Philadelphia had fallen into British hands. The river squadron which Hazelwood had so carefully preserved was caught between the advancing British ships and the British batteries at Philadelphia. Although several of the Pennsylvania galleys managed to run by the city at night and escape up the river, the larger ships were destroyed by their crews. The *Andrew Doria*, *Hornet*, and *Wasp*, part of the first Continental fleet that had sailed so proudly out of those same waters less than two years before, drifted upstream on the tide while flames licked up their masts. Orders had already been given for the scuttling of the frigates *Washington* and *Effingham*. The disaster was complete. The soldiers blamed the sailors, and the sailors blamed the soldiers. Naval officers contended that the army could have attacked the shore batteries or neutralized them by erecting counterbatteries of its own. On the other hand, the soldiers maintained that Hazelwood had been too cautious in handling his flotilla. The vessels which he so carefully

preserved from harm during the fighting had to be destroyed when
the forts were lost. As Arnold had shown on Lake Champlain the
previous year, it was sometimes better strategy to sacrifice a fleet
than to save it. The British triumph was quickly marred, however, by
news from the north. Burgoyne had been run to ground at Saratoga
and had surrendered on October 17. Until the last moment, his men
had looked vainly down the Hudson for some sign of Howe's advancing forces.

Eager to get the news of Burgoyne's surrender off to Paris where
it would have immense impact, Congress sent two sets of dispatches
to Benjamin Franklin—the originals by the French merchantman
Penet and duplicates on Paul Jones's *Ranger*, which had been fitting
out in Portsmouth all summer. Preparing the sloop of war for sea
had been a trial for the energetic Jones. Although she had been
launched two months before he took command in mid-July, all available cordage, cannon, and sails had been turned over to the *Raleigh*.
Gracefully built and with a rakish tilt to her three masts, the sloop
had been named for Rogers's Rangers, a regiment in which many a
New Hampshire man had served, although Major Robert Rogers
was now fighting for the King. She was about 110 feet long, about
the size of a World War II submarine chaser, says Morison, and displaced some 320 tons. The *Ranger* carried twenty 9-pound guns, but
her new skipper, deciding she was overgunned for her dimensions,
reduced her armament to eighteen guns. "The ship *Ranger*, in the
Opinion of every Person who has seen her, is looked upon to be one
of the best Cruizers in America," Jones wrote in a handbill designed
to attract crewmen. Later, he discovered her shortcomings.

First of all, the *Ranger*'s masts, intended for a much larger ship,
were too tall and heavy. The quality of her sails also left something
to be desired. Instead of good canvas or duck, Jones had to accept
inferior sails made of a hemp-and-jute material generally used for
bagging. Topsails and studding sails were made of scraps of canvas
that were much too heavy for light sails. And she was short of rum—
the seaman's lifeline. The search for materiel brought the quick-tem-
pered Jones into open conflict with John Langdon, the Navy Agent
at Portsmouth. Exasperated by Jones's repeated demands for equipment, Langdon exploded that he knew as well as the Captain "how
to Equip, Govern, or Fight a Ship of War." Enraged, Jones com-

plained to the Marine Committee that Langdon "thinks himself my Master—and he, who was bred in a shop and hath been about a voyage or two at sea under a Nurse, had once the assurance to tell me that he knew as well as myself how to fit out, Govern and Fight a Ship of War!" Jones was unjust, as Morison points out, for Langdon had been master of four different merchant vessels before becoming a shipowner.

The *Ranger*'s officers were picked by a committee consisting of Langdon and William Whipple, a member of the Marine Committee from New Hampshire, with her skipper having little say. All the officers chosen with the exception of Marine Captain Matthew Parke, an old friend of Jones, were local men. None had served in the navy before; some were older than their thirty-one-year-old captain. Thomas Simpson, the first lieutenant, was Langdon's brother-in-law. To round up a crew, recruiting parties under the command of junior officers were sent off to nearby seaports. Because most of the seamen were gone—"in Halifax Gaol" as Whipple put it—many of the 140 hands enlisted were young landsmen dreaming of mountains of prize money. They included two free blacks. While Jones complained that "the outfit of this small ship hath given me more anxiety and Uneasiness than all the other duty which I have performed in the service," the *Ranger* had "the best disposed crew in the world."

The sloop sailed on November 1. Dirty weather followed her across the Atlantic and Jones found his ship to be "crank." Because her masts were oversized, the *Ranger* had a tendency to heel too much in a moderate wind, which meant that the guns on one side would fire into the air while the gunports on the other would be almost under water. As soon as Jones arrived in a French port, he resolved to obtain new spars, to replace her worn and baggy sails, and to have her bottom cleaned. Thirty-one days out of Portsmouth, the *Ranger* anchored off Nantes with two prizes that had been bound from Spain to England with fruit and wine. Two days before, the *Penet* had arrived with the momentous news of Burgoyne's surrender. On December 17, Vergennes informed Franklin that France had decided to recognize the independence of the United States.

And so the year of the hangman ended on a note of triumph for the American cause. However, the bright hopes held for the Continental Navy had faded. The physical and manpower resources for the creation of a navy were available, but no one knew how to bring them together. Only four of the thirteen frigates intended to challenge Britain's naval supremacy in American waters—the *Hancock*, *Boston*, *Raleigh*, and *Randolph*—had gotten to sea. One, the *Hancock*, had been captured. The *Delaware* was lost in the defense of Philadelphia. The *Washington*, *Effingham*, *Congress*, and *Montgomery* were destroyed to prevent their capture. The remaining four frigates were bottled up at their anchorages; the *Warren* and *Providence* in Narragansett Bay, the *Trumbull* in the Connecticut River, and the *Virginia* in the Chesapeake. Of the original Continental fleet, only the *Alfred*, *Providence*, and *Columbus* still survived—and the latter did not get to sea at all in 1777. The only British naval vessel captured during the year, the frigate *Fox*, had been retaken by the enemy. At the same time, the Royal Navy's strength in American waters was being augmented. Sandwich told the House of Lords that there were ninety-three warships in America, including six ships-of-the-line. This, of course, included the West Indian and Newfoundland stations, but seventy of the vessels, ranging from 10-gun cutters to 64s, were actively employed off the American coast.

While the thirteen frigates were building and fitting out, Congress had authorized on November 20, 1776, the construction of several additional men-of-war. These included three 74-gun ships, five 36-gun frigates and an 18-gun brig. Three sloops of war were authorized soon afterward, one of them the *Ranger*. Work proceeded very slowly on these ships. Two of the 74s, three frigates, and the brig were never completed. Shipbuilding materials, munitions, and congressional financing had been exhausted by the original building program. We find the Marine Committee writing to Congress about equipment for the *Confederacy*, one of the new frigates: "We have strained our credit to the greatest stretch and are afraid that the cable which is making for the *Confederacy* will not be delivered to us unless we can furnish money to discharge part at least of the great debt which we owe the rope-maker." Increasingly, twisting the lion's tail was becoming a task for privateers.

XVI

A Lust for Profit

"The spirit of privateering prevails here greatly," Joseph Warren said of New England in mid-1776. "The success of those that have before engaged in that business have been sufficient to make a whole country privateering mad." These observations could well have been applied to the rest of the country. Although Congress did not formally authorize privateering until March 23, 1776, the flood gates of free-lance commerce raiding had already been opened by the individual colonies. Massachusetts, for one, had begun issuing privateering commissions five months earlier. Some Yankee shipowners and seamen, mixing patriotism and a thirst for profits, had not even bothered to wait for legal authorization. Shrewdly assessing the weakness of the British force on the American coast, they hurried to sea in any craft that could mount a few guns—fishing smacks, coasting schooners, clumsy merchantmen, even open whaleboats. Often they ventured out with empty gunports and small arms, hoping by luck or bluff to capture vessels with guns that could be used. The idea was to make speedy captures before the Royal Navy instituted countermeasures.

When Congress finally decided to grant commissions, they

proved to be popular with potential privateersmen. Continental papers were taken more seriously as a defense against charges of piracy than those issued by the states. Although privateers were hardly timid men, it was only human to try to avoid any taint of piracy because pirates were summarily hanged. The British often threatened to hang captured American privateers from the nearest yardarm, and those taken prisoner were treated with savage brutality. While no one was executed the possibility remained, for the British government regarded American privateersmen as pirates. The validity of their commissions was unrecognized as they had been issued by a government which, itself, was not recognized.

The line between piracy and privateering in practice was a thin one. Privateers had a commission or letter of marque issued by a warring government that served as a license for the holder to seize or destroy vessels and property belonging to citizens of an enemy nation. Piracy, on the other hand, was the seizure of property without a license, in peace as well as in war. Simply stated, the privateer had a license to steal; the pirate did not. All privately owned vessels that operated with government licenses against the enemy are commonly called privateers, but there were two classifications. A privateer was a privately armed and licensed vessel fitted out to prey on the shipping of an enemy nation. An armed merchant vessel whose primary task was to carry cargo but which also had a commission to attack enemy shipping if she chose was known as a letter of marque from the legal authorization she carried.

Eleven days after Congress resolved "that the inhabitants of these colonies be permitted to fit out armed vessels to cruise on the enemies of these United Colonies," it enacted a law regulating the issuance of commissions. It was quite strict for a privateering law of the time and contained detailed provisions regarding the reporting of prizes and the care and treatment of prisoners. At least one third of a privateer's crew were required to be landsmen, an obvious—and unsuccessful—attempt to prevent the privateers with their higher wages, lax discipline, and bigger shares of prize money from draining away all the trained seamen. Bonds required of owners were steep: $5,000 for a vessel under a hundred tons and $10,000 for those over it. Nevertheless, this was no deterrent to those willing to gamble on a successful privateering voyage. One cruise—perhaps a single capture—might result in a small fortune.

Game was always plentiful because British seaborne commerce never ceased. The Royal forces in America were completely dependent on supplies and reinforcements from overseas, and it took time to organize an efficient convoy system. One authority[1] has estimated that at least 136 privateers—averaging less than 10 guns each—were fitted out by the colonists in the first two years of the war. There were probably others that didn't bother with commissions. Lloyd's of London has estimated that Yankee privateers captured five times as many British ships during this period as the number of American merchantmen and privateers that fell into British hands.[2] Even as late as 1778, when British privateers were becoming active and the Royal Navy was mopping up slow and inefficient privateering craft, the ratio was still running well in favor of the Americans. After the French alliance opened French ports to commerce raiders in 1778, the number of privateers with Continental commissions soared. In 1777, there were only 73 privateers active; by 1781, the number had reached 449.

Some shipowners had taken the long view right from the start of the war. They had foreseen a time when prizes would be harder to come by and the risks greater, when privateers might expect long voyages and substantial resistance. The speculative shipowner and his designer weighed the relative merits of the fore-and-aft and the square rig; the fighting qualities of British sloops-of-war and armed brigs were coolly assessed; a fine balance was struck between the size of a privateer's crew and her capacity for carrying shot and stores. Speed and handiness were the hallmarks of the new class of built-from-the-keel-up privateers—speed to overtake the quarry and handiness to avoid being taken by superior force. The ability to sail close to the wind was eminently desirable as it afforded the means of escape as well as the opportunity to snatch a prize from a convoy without interference from the escort.

Commerce raiders were not expected to fight—and did so only when absolutely necessary. The privateer's reason for going to sea was the plunder of fat merchantmen. Damage received in a broadside to broadside set-to might just cripple a privateer and send her limping back to port when a voyage was barely begun. Even worse, it might leave the privateer to the mercy of the first British cruiser to

---

[1] Edward S. Maclay, *A History of American Privateers* (New York 1899).
[2] See Mahan, *Major Operations of the Navies.*

come along. Eventually the increased presence of British privateers at sea as the war dragged on led to more powerful armament on Yankee privateers. By 1781, the average number of guns of the privateers at sea was slightly over fifteen. Some owners strengthened the sides of their ships to withstand all but the heaviest shot and mounted batteries of heavy cannon. These veritable ships of war were capable of standing up to the smaller King's ships in a free fight and winning.

The average privateer carried an extra-large crew to provide enough men to form prize crews for the ships which the privateer hoped to take. Once the capture had been made, a prize crew just large enough to work the craft was placed aboard in command of a junior officer (or a petty officer, if he could navigate) with orders to take her into the nearest port where she could be condemned and sold. Almost always, the prisoners outnumbered the prize crews, so great care had to be taken to prevent the recapture of the ship. Keeping the crew battened down below deck was the usual solution to the problem. Nevertheless, the history of privateering is filled with tales of prize crews being overwhelmed and made prisoner. Some vessels changed hands several times during a voyage as prisoners rose against prize crews only to be overwhelmed again later.

Once a prize had arrived at a friendly port, the vessel and her cargo were placed in the custody of the local authorities. The prize agent, who acted for the privateer's owners, would then file a libel against the ship and her cargo in the admiralty court. A hearing was held, and if the testimony and evidence proved that the prize was the property of the enemy, the court would order her sold at auction, together with her cargo. The proceeds would be turned over to the prize agent. If the court held that the prize was not enemy property, the vessel would be returned to her captain and crew. This rarely happened, and when it did, there was little or no chance of collecting damages for delaying the vessel's voyage. Should a sale be ordered, the proceeds were divided equally. One half went to the owners, to be further subdivided among them according to each man's interest in the privateer. The other half went to the officers and crew with shares handed out as specified in articles that had been signed at the beginning of the cruise.

One of the most favored hunting grounds for American privateers was in the Gulf of St. Lawrence. Often they were so numerous that they got in each other's way. Time and again, a privateer sighting a strange sail was forced to choose between fighting and running. If a ship chose to show its heels because the stranger looked stronger, the crew of the vessel being chased might jettison guns and stores to lighten her. In moments of extreme stress, the crew might be put to work sawing away the bulwarks, a process thought to help increase a ship's speed. If nothing else, it at least had the virtue of reducing the psychological tension of the chase. All too often, two vessels cleared for action only to discover that they were both Yankee privateers. Yet despite the difficulties, there was good hunting in the Gulf for the smaller privateers. They could capture fishing sloops and trading vessels without risk; if pickings were slim they could run into a helpless fishing settlement and plunder it. A ready excuse lay at hand: they were paying back the British for the burning of Falmouth. Of course, there was always the threat of British men-of-war based on nearby Halifax, but the menace was substantially reduced by intermittent fogs and storms. In bad weather, privateers often swept by the cruisers as they lay comfortably snugged down.

The other great hunting ground was the Caribbean. To cut down on losses to pirates and privateers that had haunted the area even before the American rebellion, the British had resorted to convoys and heavily armed merchantmen. Leisurely and publicly, outward-bound convoys were assembled in Portsmouth and Dublin. Their size, strength of the escort, destination, and sailing dates were common knowledge in an un-security conscious age. Several months were usually required for the ships to be collected for the voyage, so there was plenty of time for American agents to get the information home. With advance word, privateers could waylay the convoy, be ready to cut out a prize if the escort dropped over the horizon, or to pick up stragglers if a storm dispersed the fleet. Convoys numbering nearly a hundred merchantmen were not uncommon, and the privateers learned that by working in pairs or in "wolfpacks," they could rip the heart out of these fleets.

Exactly how many American privateers put to sea during the Revolution will never be known because many carried no commission from either the Continental or state governments. The records of the Continental Congress list 1,697 vessels to which letters of marque were issued, carrying 58,400 men and 14,872 guns.[3] Several of the states issued commissions to privateers as well—Massachusetts, New Hampshire, Rhode Island, Connecticut, Maryland, and South Carolina among them. Massachusetts is thought to have sent out perhaps a thousand ships under her own commissions as well as 626 with Continental documents. Probably some carried both commissions at one time or another. The American commissioners in Paris and the naval agents in the West Indies also commissioned privateers. Taking duplications into account, the best estimate of the total number of commissions issued is in excess of two thousand. These ships may have carried some 18,000 guns and 70,000 men. There seems to have been about the same number of British sailors engaged in privateering, most of them seduced from the Royal Navy. Speaking of the difficulty in manning the Navy's ships, former Governor Thomas Hutchinson of Massachusetts observed: "Some have proposed pressing the crews of all privateers." Not all the British privateers sailed from English ports. In 1779, it was reported that 121 were based upon New York and others at Jamaica in the West Indies.[4]

Just how effective were the American privateers? Estimates of the number of British merchantmen taken as prizes range all over the lot. Lloyd's reported 3,087 vessels were captured, while other sources say less. Breaking down the Lloyd's list shows that 879 vessels were retaken or ransomed, leaving a total of 2,208 in American hands. Eighty-nine British privateers were also captured, of which 75 remained in possession of the Americans. On the other side, the British captured 1,135 enemy merchantmen, of which 27 were retaken or ransomed. The British also took 216 privateers. At the same time, Maclay puts the number of British vessels captured by the Continental Navy at 196 ships. Between them, the privateers and Continental Navy may have taken as many as 16,000 British seamen as prisoners, which compares favorably with the 22,000 Redcoats captured by the army during the entire war.

---

[3] Charles H. Lincoln, ed., *Naval Records of the American Revolution* (Washington 1906). The record is incomplete as thirty ships did not list their armament and eighteen furnished no list of men.

[4] Gardner W. Allen, *A Naval History of the American Revolution* (Boston 1913).

What really mattered, however, was not the numbers but the effect of the privateers on Britain's economy. The House of Lords was told in February 1778 that Yankee privateers had, since the start of the war, captured or destroyed 733 ships with cargoes valued at more than two million pounds. From the West Indies came cries of anguish. The government was bombarded with demands for protection. "Within one week upward of fourteen sail of our ships have been carried into Martinique by American privateers," complained a Jamaican in 1777. A resident of Grenada reported the same year that of a fleet of sixty vessels that had sailed from Ireland with provisions for the island, only twenty-five arrived. "God knows, if this American war continues much longer we shall all die with hunger," he added. Insurance rates on cargoes skyrocketed. Rates on ships sailing in convoy soared by 30 percent over pre-war charges. Those sailing without convoy paid a 50 percent premium.

It is difficult, however, to reckon in monetary terms the value of the prizes taken. Maclay puts the figure at $18 million—probably a low estimate when it is noted that the privateer *Rattlesnake* took prizes worth over $1 million during a single Baltic cruise. Accepting the value of $30,000 for each prize (Maclay's figure) and applying it to the 2,200 British ships taken by the privateers, according to Lloyd's, the loss amounts to about $66 million. To an England suffering from depleted finances, engaged in mortal combat with France and Spain and with a large part of her own people unsympathetic to the war, these losses were a strong argument for ending the American conflict. Most of the many appeals for peace made to Parliament by the powerful British mercantile establishment emphasized the injuries to trade.

Arms and stores badly needed by the colonies were provided by the privateers. When a French fleet arrived at Boston in 1778, its requirements could not have been met except for the timely arrival of prizes taken by privateers. The privateers also provided luxury goods and a degree of prosperity seldom seen in America before. Not all of this new found prosperity was economically healthy, however. Inflation became a cancer gnawing away at civilian morale. Within a year after the Declaration of Independence, prices had doubled and tripled. "Four pounds a week for board . . . Shoes, five dollars a pair. Salt twenty-seven dollars a bushel. Butter, ten shillings a pound. Punch, twenty shillings a bowl," were some of the prices recorded by John Adams in Philadelphia late in 1777. He thought he had "never lived in my whole life so meanly and poorly as I do now." Privateering was one of the causes. Prize money was like finding cash in the streets. The crews spent their sudden riches with the traditional recklessness of sailors on what Benjamin Franklin called "Fineries and Fopperies." Luxury goods from captured ships were plentiful for those who had money. As the war went on, a surprising number of people were able to indulge new and extravagant tastes while Washington's army starved and went ragged in the field. Nathanael Greene reported news of the profits being made out of privateering had "distracted" the troops. "Were I at liberty, I think I could make a fortune for my family." Some of the great merchant families made tremendous fortunes from their fleets of privateers. Smaller investors tried to share in the profits. The people of the seaport towns gambled in privateering as later generations gambled in stocks. They used their shares as collateral and bought and sold futures. Privateer shares were reckoned in eighths and even smaller fractions—with one Hartford merchant having a one ninety-sixth share of a privateer. To hedge their bets, investors would take chances on several ventures at once.

In the beginning, the crews that shipped aboard privateers were mostly experienced seamen or men who worked about the harbors. As the war continued and normal activities were suspended, more and more people took up privateering for the sake of adventure and prize money. Clerks, farmers, lawyers, woodsmen, and doctors were caught up in the bonanza psychology sweeping the country. Advertisements for privateer crews played upon the thirst for easy money. In Wethersfield, Connecticut, a notice appealed to "All Gentlemen Volunteers who are desirious of making their fortunes in eight weeks." The Boston *Gazette*, soliciting recruits for a privateer, invited "all those Jolly Fellows, who love their country, and want to make their Fortune at one Stroke, to repair immediately to the Rendezvous at the head of His Excellency's Governor Hancock's Wharf. . . ."

Dr. Solomon Drowne, who went to sea on a brief cruise in the tiny Rhode Island privateer *Hope* in 1780, was typical of these "gentlemen volunteers." Facing financial difficulties on land, he signed on as surgeon of the 7-gun sloop. The first enemy he had to face was seasickness. "This is a sickness, that is indeed enough to depress the spirits even of the brave," he lamented as a storm raged about the ship. The raw hands took what comfort they could in the assurances of one of the few experienced seamen on board that "he never knew it more tempestuous." The topmast was unshipped, the guns stowed in the hold, and the hatches nailed tight to keep out the water. A detail was assigned to stand by with axes to cut away the mast if necessary to keep the vessel from capsizing. "A becoming fortitude predominates on board, though horror stalks around," the good doctor confided to his journal. Finally, the weather moderated, and the *Hope* began a seemingly fruitless cruise off the Jersey coast. On the twelfth day out, a heavily laden ship was sighted and everything was made ready to board her. "There seems something awful in the preparation for an attack and the immediate prospect of an action," Dr. Drowne noted.

Shortly after he had laid out his surgical instruments in the cabin and was awaiting the first of the wounded, "I hear the Huzza on deck in consequence of her striking." The *Hope*'s prize carried twenty hogsheads of sugar and enough rum to make all Rhode Island drunk. "We hardly know what to do with the prize," she was so large, reported Dr. Drowne. Her crew of ten men were brought on board the privateer and a prize crew detailed to the captured vessel. The rest of the cruise was called off and away they went to the nearest port with the Yankees apprehensive of sighting a sail because it might be a British warship. They were also worried about an attempt by the prisoners to take the ship. "Have our Pistols hung up in the Cabin, to be in readiness for the prisoners should they take it into their heads to rise upon the watch in the night," the doctor stated grimly. To the despair of the privateer's crew they lost sight of their prize during another storm but she turned up again as they entered the Providence River just nineteen days after the voyage had begun. Dr. Drowne realized enough from his share of the prize money to relieve his financial problems. He was careful never to go to sea again.

On the other hand, there are the adventures of Andrew Sherburne, who spent three years in various privateers and had nothing to show for it. He signed on the *Ranger* as a fourteen-year-old ship's boy after her return from France and was serving aboard her when she was taken by the British at Charleston in 1780. Most of her officers and men managed to escape and made their way to Portsmouth, where the citizens had formed a fund to replace the vessel. Instead of turning the new ship over to the Continental authorities, they decided to fit her out as the privateer *Alexander.* Most of the crew of the *Ranger* signed on, and although the *Alexander* cruised for several weeks, she failed to take a single prize. Back in Portsmouth, young Sherburne was approached by an officer of the privateer *Greyhound.* Since seamen were scarce, he was invited aboard, introduced to the other officers, told he was a fine lad and asked to sign on. Later, the privateer's officers invited several seafaring men to join them in "a jovial evening" in a local tavern.

A few days later Sherburne and some others found themselves on the *Greyhound* running toward the mouth of the St. Lawrence. Numerous sails were seen, but all turned out to be American privateers. Off Halifax what appeared to be a large merchantman was sighted, seemingly in distress. The privateer had drawn within gunshot before her captain realized that he was dealing with a British frigate. Only the heavy fog that enveloped both ships saved the *Greyhound* from capture. Several more weeks of aimless cruising followed in which only a few miserable fishing boats were taken. Young Sherburne was sent aboard one as part of a prize crew that was to take her into Salem. Not long after, they were overhauled by another vessel which fired heavily loaded swivels into them. The Americans heaved to, and twenty Newfoundlanders, greatly angered by the depredations of the privateers, sprang aboard. They had guns in their hands "loaded, cocked and primed and presented two or three at each of our breasts without ceremony, cursing us bitterly and threatening our lives." Only with difficulty did their captain persuade them to deliver the prisoners alive at a small Newfoundland village.

Once ashore the prisoners were surrounded by a mob of about a hundred inhabitants, among them "an English lady of distinction" who asked for papers. A copy of the *Greyhound*'s commission was presented which she read aloud. When she came to the clause authorizing the privateer to "burn, sink or destroy" enemy shipping, the crowd almost got out of hand and threatened to lynch the prisoners. The lady, however, managed to convince them that the Americans should be treated as prisoners of war and taken to a British post. Stripped of everything they had, including their shoes, the captives were marched overland to Morteer, a small port where the inhabitants fired a gun to celebrate the capture of the Yankees. The prisoners arrived at Morteer in May 1781 and remained in the guardhouse until September, when they were taken off in a sloop-of-war for delivery to England. The ship was wrecked off St. John's, and twenty of the 170 men aboard were lost. Sherburne and the remaining prisoners, who had endured considerable hardship, were placed on another ship bound for England. This vessel was commanded by a brutal old sea dog who delighted in having his men flogged "for very trifling faults, and sometimes when faultless." Sherburne resisted the captain's efforts to persuade him to join the Royal Navy, and he was sent to Old Mill Prison where he remained until the spring of 1782 when he was exchanged. Returning home, he spent only a few weeks ashore before signing aboard another privateer for a cruise to the West Indies. The vessel was quickly taken by a British frigate, and for the third time, young Sherburne found himself a prisoner of war. This time he was imprisoned on the notorious prison ship *Jersey* in New York harbor where he spent the remaining months of the war. He was released just after turning seventeen—with only empty pockets and a tale of misfortune to show for three years of misery and suffering.

Few vessels have as barbarous a history as the *Jersey* and the other British prison ships that lay anchored off New York during the American Revolution. Huddled on the mud flats of Wallabout Bay where the Brooklyn Navy Yard was later established, the hulks were synonymous with brutality. "What Andersonville was to the Civil War, the British prison ships were to the Revolution," it has been stated.[5] The cruelties that the British inflicted upon the men imprisoned on these vessels became stock horrors of American folklore, providing fuel for a century of atrocity stories and rampant Anglophobia. All prisons were horrible in the eighteenth century—crowded, filthy, and disease-ridden—and the normal conditions on men-of-war were only a little better. Nevertheless, the hulks set new levels of degradation. Conditions were so bad that two of the twenty ships at New York were destroyed by fires set by the prisoners who hoped either to escape in the confusion or to meet a quick death in the flames. Periodically, attempts were made to alleviate some of the

---

[5] Henry S. Commager and Richard B. Morris, eds., *The Spirit of 'Seventy-Six* (Indianapolis 1958).

worst evils, but the over-all record was bleak. While the lack of accurate records makes it difficult to determine the actual number of men who perished on these ships, the best estimate is that as many as 11,500 prisoners died—probably more than were killed by British muskets and bayonets. They were buried between high and low water around Wallabout Bay, and for years after the war the tides uncovered their bones.

Having run out of space in the local jails, warehouses, churches, and barracks at their major base in America, the British had hit upon the idea of using ships moored in the East River as prisons.

The first of the prison ships was the *Whitby*, a former transport, which received her first consignment of prisoners in October 1776. Within a few months, she was joined by several others, of which the *Jersey*, which arrived in February 1779, was the most infamous. Nicknamed "Hell Afloat" by those unfortunates condemned to imprisonment aboard her, the *Jersey* was a former 64-gun ship-of-the-line that had outlived her usefulness. She had been stripped of all spars and only her bowsprit and flagstaff remained, along with a derrick for hauling in supplies. Her decks and hull leaked and she soon rested on a mud bank. All her gunports were sealed, and along the sides of the hull two tiers of 20-inch squares were cut about ten feet apart and barred. They served to provide some air and light on the crowded lower decks where as many as twelve hundred men were herded at a time. A tent was set up on the quarterdeck for the guards and a 10-foot-high loopholed barricade protected them from the prisoners. The *Jersey*'s crew consisted of a captain, two mates, a steward, a cook, and a guard of forty soldiers and marines. At first, both captured American soldiers and sailors were imprisoned on the hulks but as time went on they became prisons for seamen exclusively.

Ebenezer Fox, a seventeen-year-old Massachusetts seaman imprisoned on the *Jersey* in 1781, recalled that as soon as a prisoner was brought on board, he was stripped of all valuables and immediately hustled below. "I now found myself in a loathsome prison, among a collection of the most wretched and disgusting looking objects that I have ever beheld in human form," he wrote many years later. "Here was a motley crew, covered with rags and filth, visages pallid with disease, emaciated with hunger and anxiety, and retaining hardly a trace of their original appearance." Rats scurried among the prisoners and the stench of dysentery was in the air. The sick and dying were sprawled on the bare deck without medical care. "The cries and supplications for water were terrible," said another prisoner.

Each morning the hatches were opened and the prisoners were called on deck with the baleful cry: "Turn out your dead!" Those who had died during the night were hoisted up by their comrades and sewn into their rags for burial in the nearby mud. The *Jersey* averaged about six bodies a day. The sick were carried on deck to get what benefit they could from the sunlight and fresh air. Working parties brought up the bedding for airing and washed the decks. The prisoners were divided into messes of six men each and received their rations at 9 A.M. These were set at two thirds of what were given British seamen. The bill of fare for Sunday was a pound of biscuit, one pound of pork, and a half pint of peas. For Monday, it was a pound of biscuit, a pint of oatmeal, and two ounces of butter; for Tuesday, one pound of biscuit and two pounds of salt beef; for Wednesday, one and a half pounds of flour and two ounces of suet. Thursday was a repetition of Sunday's ration, Friday of Monday's and Saturday of Tuesday's. No fresh vegetables were served, so scurvy was rampant.

"If this food had been of good quality and properly cooked, it would have kept us comfortable, at least from suffering," said Ebenezer Fox:

But this was not the case. All our food appeared to be damaged. . . . The cooking for the prisoners was done in a great copper vessel that contained between two or three hogsheads of water . . . and it was divided into two compartments by a partition. In one of these the peas and oatmeal were boiled; this was done with fresh water. In the other the meat was boiled in saltwater taken up from alongside the ship. All the filth that accumulated among upward of a thousand men was daily thrown overboard and would remain there till carried away by the tide . . . and in this water our meat was boiled.

Reports of the brutal treatment of American prisoners gave rise to long and tedious discussion in Congress but nothing was done about it. Early in 1777, Washington wrote Lord Howe "on the subject of the cruel treatment which our officers and men in the naval department, who are unhappy enough to fall into your hands, re-

ceive on board the prison ships in the harbour of New York." He
also told General Howe that some of the prisoners who had been exchanged "give the most shocking account of their barbarous usage,
which their miserable, emaciated countenances confirm." Unless
conditions improved, he warned, retaliatory measures would be
taken against British prisoners in American hands. Admiral Howe
replied that the reports of ill-treatment were exaggerated and that the
prisoners received the same rations and medical treatment as British
seamen. Over the next several years conditions on the hulks varied,
depending primarily on who was in command at New York. But the
plight of the privateersmen was particularly bitter. As civilians, they
were not prisoners of war, so when exchanges were finally agreed
upon, they were "at the bottom of the heap," points out historian
Jesse Lemisch. He goes on to suggest that their fate rested on
whatever arrangements their families and friends could make with
the British authorities.

Attempts to escape were frequent despite the hazards of being
shot in the act or flogged if caught. Some were successful. Faced with
death from starvation or disease, men were willing to accept the desperate gamble. Some managed to pull out the bars over the ports and
dropped into the water; others jumped over the side while on deck.
But this was only the first obstacle. An escapee had to be in good
enough physical condition to survive a perilous swim. He had to go
at least two miles to find a safe landing place because the shore was
patrolled near the ships. Once on land, he would have to make his
way through the British army on Long Island and dodge Tories on
the lookout for the reward offered for returning an escaped prisoner.
There was at least one mass breakout. One day a group of about
thirty-five prisoners rushed the sentries, disarmed them and made
good their escape in a small schooner lying alongside the prison ship.

There was one other way for prisoners to escape what appeared
almost certain death—to succumb to constant British pressure to
join the Royal Navy or to enlist in one of the British regiments stationed in the West Indies where they would not have to serve against
their own countrymen. "To an extraordinary degree, captured American seamen remained Americans," states Lemisch.[6] He estimates

---

[6] "Listening to the 'Inarticulate': William Widger's Dream and The Loyalties of America's
Revolutionary Seamen in British Prisons," *Journal of Social History* (Fall, 1969).

that even with death more likely than freedom if they refused to enlist in the British service, of every one hundred men who were imprisoned on the *Jersey*, only eight chose to join the King's forces. And of those who did defect, at least half may have been "old Countrymen," who had been born in the British Isles rather than America. The prisoners, according to Lemisch, called their companions who refused to defect "true sons of America" and "hooted at and abused" those who did not remain loyal to their country. In view of the harrowing conditions prisoners faced if they refused to enlist in the British army or navy, the continued loyalty of simple Yankee seamen is compelling testimony of their belief in the cause of freedom and independence.

Some privateer captains stood out above the rest. One of them was Jonathan Haraden, who began his naval service as a lieutenant on the Massachusetts brigantine *Tyrannicide*, 14, and later became her captain. On the vessel's first cruise in 1776, she captured a Royal Navy cutter, an 8-gun packet schooner and several other ships, some of them in lively engagements that taught Haraden the basics of sea fighting. In 1780 he was given command of the ship-rigged letter of marque *General Pickering*, 16, which carried a cargo of sugar to Bilbao, Spain. En route, the *Pickering* was attacked by a British cutter of 20 guns, but managed to beat her off after a desperate two-hour fight. Sailing into the Bay of Biscay, a few nights later, Haraden sighted a strange ship in the darkness. Running along silently, he made a quick estimate of her strength. She was schooner-rigged and apparently more heavily armed than the *Pickering*, but the Americans had the benefit of surprise. Haraden laid his ship alongside the stranger, proclaimed that she was a frigate of the largest class and threatened to blow the schooner out of the water. Since a squadron commanded by Paul Jones was on the loose in European waters, the British skipper was so alarmed that he surrendered his ship without a fight. She proved to be the English privateer *Golden Eagle*, 22. Not until the British captain came aboard the *Pickering* did he learn to his chagrin that he had surrendered to a ship of inferior force.

Followed by her prize, the *Pickering* was standing in to Bilbao harbor on June 3, 1780, when a large ship was observed working its way out of port. Haraden asked the captain of the captured privateer if he could identify her and was told—probably with a grin—that she was the 42-gun privateer *Achilles*, of London. The Yankees might well have steered clear of so powerful a craft, but Haraden, who had bluffed the *Golden Eagle* into hauling down her colors, wondered if his prisoner wasn't trying a little bluffing on his own. "I shan't run from her," he coolly replied. Darkness was falling but the Americans soon saw enough of their adversary to realize that she was indeed a powerful vessel. Apparently too powerful for the Americans. Before sunset, the *Achilles* had recaptured the British privateer though her captain decided to wait until daylight to make certain that the Yankee ship was within his grasp. Word quickly spread of the impending fight just outside the harbor. Bilbao took on a fiesta atmosphere. Thousands of Spaniards lined the shore, and the streets were crowded with spectators. They leaned out windows and huddled on rooftops. Some even pushed out in small boats for a better look. The English ship lost no time in beginning the attack shortly after dawn, but Haraden had chosen a position close in to some shoals so the British would be subjected to a raking fire as they approached him. For two hours, the *Achilles*, held up by light winds, was exposed to the American guns, before her captain swung her broadside into position. Haraden refused to close and from a distance subjected the British ship to a heavy fire concentrated at her waterline. "The *General Pickering*, in comparison to her antagonist, looked like a longboat by the side of a ship," said a witness. Running short of ammunition, the Yankee skipper ordered all the guns loaded with crowbars that had been taken from an earlier prize. This "flight of crowbars" tore the British vessel's rigging into tatters and drove gun crews from their stations. Obviously surprised by such resistance, the *Achilles*'s captain gave up the struggle and made for the open sea, abandoning the *Golden Eagle* and the prize crew left aboard her. With the *Golden Eagle* again following along in the *Pickering*'s wake, Haraden stood into Bilbao where the emotional Spaniards had gone wild with excitement. Waving and shouting, they wouldn't be satisfied until they had hoisted the victorious Yankee captain to their shoulders and carried him about the city in triumph.

On the return voyage, Haraden captured three armed merchantmen, two of 14 guns and one of 12 guns off Sandy Hook. Skillful shiphandling was the key. If the British ships had united, they could have cut the American privateer to ribbons. Haraden succeeded in separating them and then picked them off one by one.

On a later cruise he fell in with a Royal mail packet from the West Indies and they pounded away for four hours, heavily damaging each other. The ships had drawn away to make repairs when Haraden's gunner informed him that they had just one more round of ammunition for each gun. Instead of hauling off, Haraden ordered the remaining powder and shot rammed home and closed with the foe. Quietly, he told his adversary that he had five minutes to surrender or every man jack would be sent to the bottom. Running up the red flag—which signaled "no quarter"—Haraden coolly took out his watch and stood on the quarterdeck where he could be plainly seen from the British ship. "One minute!" he called out. Little more than an arm's length away, the British seamen stared into the muzzles of the shotted guns as a man with a lighted match stood by. Two minutes passed with no signs of surrender. Three minutes. As Haraden called out "Four minutes!" the British captain hauled down his colors. When the American prize crew went aboard to take possession of the packet, they found her deck covered with dead and wounded men. Blood oozed from her scuppers. In all, Haraden captured British ships carrying a total of 1,000 guns, before retiring to a prosperous life ashore in Salem. Few other seamen could say that they had outmaneuvered, outguessed, outshot, and routed an enemy ship which outgunned them by more than two to one.

Observing the great success the Yankees were having with privateers, the Tory merchants of New York and Newport fitted out some privateers of their own in 1778 and sent them out to prey on the coastwise trade. Within a short time, American commerce in Long Island Sound and off Rhode Island was almost annihilated. Under the prodding of George Washington, General Gates, the commander of the Northern Department, fitted out the 100-ton sloop *Argo*, armed her with twelve 6-pounders and placed her under the command of Lieutenant Colonel Silas Talbot with orders to stamp out Tory commerce raiding. Despite his military title, Talbot was an experienced sailor and the most versatile of American privateersmen. Born of poor parents in Massachusetts, he had gone to sea as a cabin boy on a coaster at the age of twelve. By the time he was twenty-one years old, in 1772, he had become master of a vessel and had accumulated enough money to build himself a house in Providence.

When war came, he was commissioned a captain in the army and took part in the operations around Boston.

After his regiment had been transferred to New York, he volunteered to command one of the fire ships being prepared to attack Lord Howe's fleet in the Hudson. One night several of the British warships moved above the city. Talbot chose the *Asia*, 64, the largest of the enemy vessels, as his target. To make certain that the fire ship would not be discovered until the last moment, Talbot ordered that the tar barrels and turpentine stowed aboard her not be set ablaze until the craft had fouled the *Asia*. The fire ship ran silently through the darkness but the British were on the alert. The alarm was given and round shot began to rip through the craft. Within a few minutes, the hulk crashed against the side of the man-of-war. Talbot ordered the trains of gunpowder fired and the crew abandoned their craft. Flames swept his vessel so fast that Talbot was severely burned before he could grope his way over the side. Shortly afterward, he was picked up by a small boat. Although frantic efforts by the *Asia*'s crew saved her from being consumed by the fire, the British were so alarmed by the attack that they hurriedly abandoned their mooring up river and dropped down below the city. Leading their blinded captain through the woods, the Americans sought help at several houses but no one would take him in. The people said "his appearance was so horrible he would frighten their children." Lodging and care for Talbot was finally found in the cabin of a poor widow. Slowly he regained his sight and recovered from his wounds.

Promoted to major, Talbot was twice wounded in the gallant defense of Fort Mifflin. Invalided home to Rhode Island, he soon evolved a plan to capture a heavily armed galley the British had stationed in the Sakonnet River, blocking the passage to Providence, the home port of many privateers. Loading sixty men, mostly volunteers from the army, on a tiny coastal schooner named the *Hawk*, which was armed with a pair of 3-pound popguns, he dropped down river in search of his quarry. He found her at anchor with her eight 12-pounders run out, ten swivels loaded and primed, and her sides protected by high nets to keep out boarders. With Yankee ingenuity, Talbot had ordered a large kedge anchor[7] lashed fast to the

---

[7] A kedge anchor was a heavy anchor used to shift a ship's position or to haul her clear if she ran aground. It was usually carried in a boat and dropped overboard some distance from the ship. The sailors on board the ship would then haul in on the anchor cable. If the anchor held, the ship would move.

bowsprit of the *Hawk* so that when she ran against the galley's side, the anchor would tear a wide hole in the nettings. A grapnel was ready to be thrown aboard the enemy craft to lock the vessels together.

As the schooner bore down on the floating fortress, the enemy hailed her. Silence. Another challenge, this time followed by a volley of musket fire. Talbot had ordered his men to lie down on the deck, so there were no casualties. Before the British could fire a single cannon, the *Hawk* had banged into the side of the galley. The kedge anchor ripped a gaping hole in the boarding nettings and the grapnel held the vessels together. "Boarders away!" shouted Talbot. Swinging cutlasses and brandishing pikes, the boarding party swept through the rip in the nettings and drove the surprised British sailors from the deck. Finally, only one man remained—Lieutenant Dunlop, the galley's commander. The Americans probably grinned from ear to ear as they surrounded him, for he was forced to surrender in his underwear. For this exploit, Talbot was promoted to lieutenant colonel.

Talbot then went to sea in May 1779 in the *Argo*, a clumsy-looking craft that steered with a long tiller rather than a wheel, and soon snapped up three enemy privateers, one with twelve 6-pounders, the same strength as her captor. Talbot's next prize was particularly gratifying—a 14-gun brig named *King George* commanded by one of the Rhode Island Hazards, who was a Tory. "Even the women, both old and young, expressed the greatest joy" when the ship was sent into New London as a prize. All of Talbot's early prizes were taken without a serious fight, but in August he ran afoul of the British privateer *Dragon*, armed with fourteen 6-pounders and packed with men. A bitter four-and-a-half-hour fight followed, often within pistol shot. Talbot's speaking trumpet was pierced in two places while he held it to his lips and the tail of his coat was taken off by a cannon ball. The *Argo* was in danger of sinking from several hits below the waterline when a lucky shot brought down the *Dragon*'s mainmast. She quickly surrendered.

No sooner had the *Argo*'s crew made their vessel shipshape again than another sail was sighted. She was the British privateer brig *Hannah*, armed with twelve 12-pounders and two 6-pounders. Even though his ship had been badly battered in the fight with the *Dragon* and the *Hannah* was twice her strength, Talbot attacked without hesitation. The fighting was sharp, but luckily for the

Americans, another Yankee privateer, the *Macaroni*, 6, joined in. The British ship struck. When the *Argo* reached port with her prizes, she was an object of curiosity. "She was so much shivered in her hull and rigging by the shot which had pierced her in the last two engagements that all who beheld her were astonished that a vessel of her diminutive size could suffer so much and yet get safely to port," noted a visitor. This time Talbot's reward was a commission as captain in the Continental Navy, but he stayed with the "army's privateer" for several more successful cruises, taking a total of twelve prizes and clearing the lower part of the New England coast of Tory privateers.

Talbot, however, apparently lacked the connections to get command of a Continental ship. During the summer of 1780, he was made skipper of the Providence privateer *General Washington*, a formidable vessel carrying twenty 6-pounders and manned by a crew of one hundred twenty men. Her first cruise began with Talbot's usual good fortune—two prizes were taken. Then his luck changed. Off Sandy Hook, the *Washington* stumbled into the midst of a British squadron and was pursued by the 74-gun *Culloden* and other ships. Normally, she should have been able to show her heels to her heavily built pursuers, but a storm came up. In blowing weather, a large, heavily sparred vessel could often carry sail while smaller craft had to reef their canvas. One of the British men-of-war lost her foreyard and fell behind, but the *Culloden* overtook the *Washington* and brought the privateer under her guns. Faced with the 74's double row of gun ports, Talbot had no choice but to strike his colors.

Talbot's varying treatment as a prisoner of war—ranging from courtesy to sheer barbarity—shows all the inconsistencies of the era. Taken aboard the *Culloden*, he was first treated kindly by his captors and then transferred to the *Jersey*. Early in 1781, he was among seventy-one American officers ordered transported to England on board the *Yarmouth*, 64, amid broad hints that they were going to be hanged as rebels. The treatment the Americans received convinced them that the British intended to cheat the gallows. They were crammed into the lower hold, five decks down, in a twelve-by-twenty-foot compartment with only three feet of headroom. There they were stowed without light or fresh air for fifty-three days during a stormy voyage. Eleven men died. The survivors lay in their own filth, unable to stand upright. No doctor visited them. Food was so

Admiral Thomas Graves
—*Courtesy of the Mariners Museum, Newport News, Virginia*

John Adams
—*Courtesy of Independence National Historical Park Collection, Philadelphia, Pa.*

(*Upper left*) Admiral Lord Rodney, by Sir Joshua Reynolds
—*Courtesy of The National Maritime Museum, London*

(*Upper right*) John Montagu, 4th Earl of Sandwich, by Thomas Gainsborough
—*Courtesy of The National Maritime Museum, London*

(*Left*) Admiral Sir Hugh Palliser, by Dance
—*Courtesy of The National Maritime Museum, London*

Admiral Sir Charles Hardy
—*U.S. Navy Photo*

Lord George Germain
—*U.S. Navy Photo*

Admiral de Grasse, from
portrait in the French Embassy
—*U.S. Navy Photo*

Admiral Lord Howe
—*Courtesy of the Mariners
Museum, Newport News, Va.*

Captain Abraham Whipple —*Courtesy of the U.S. Naval Academy*

(*Upper left*) Admiral Sir Samuel Hood
—*U.S. Navy Photo*

(*Upper right*) Captain Nicholas Biddle
—*Courtesy of Independence National
Historical Park Collection, Philadelphia,
Pennsylvania*

(Left) Comte d'Estaing
—*Courtesy of The White House
Collection*

(*Left*) Admiral Augustus Keppel
—*U.S. Navy Photo*

(*Lower left*) General Benedict
Arnold —*U.S. Navy Photo*

(*Lower right*) Captain Gustavus
Conyngham. From a
contemporary French caricature
—*Courtesy of the Mariners
Museum, Newport News, Va.*

GENERAL ARNOLD.

AUGUSTATUS KUNINGAM

Sea captains carousing in Surinam. Esek Hopkins is the man seated at the center of the table with the cocked hat. John Greenwood, the artist, painted himself into the picture in the doorway carrying a candle. —*Courtesy of the St. Louis Art Museum*

John Paul Jones. From a drawing done in May 1780 by Jean-Michel Moreau le jeune. Along with the Houdon bust, the best likeness of Jones
—*Courtesy of the Library of Congress*

GREAT
ENCOURAGEMENT
FOR
SEAMEN.

ALL GENTLEMEN SEAMEN and able-bodied LANDSMEN who have a Mind to distinguish themselves in the GLORIOUS CAUSE of their COUNTRY, and make their Fortunes, an Opportunity now offers on board the Ship RANGER, of Twenty Guns, (for FRANCE) now laying in PORTSMOUTH, in the State of NEW-HAMPSHIRE, commanded by JOHN PAUL JONES Esq; let them repair to the Ship's Rendezvous in PORTSMOUTH, or at the Sign of Commodore MANLEY, in SALEM, where they will be kindly entertained, and receive the greatest Encouragement.---The Ship RANGER, in the Opinion of every Person who has seen her is looked upon to be one of the best Cruizers in AMERICA.---She will be always able to Fight her Guns under a most excellent Cover; and no Vessel yet built was ever calculated for sailing faster, and making good Weather.

Any GENTLEMEN VOLUNTEERS who have a Mind to take an agreable Voyage in this pleasant Season of the Year, may, by entering on board the above Ship RANGER, meet with every Civility they can possibly expect, and for a further Encouragement depend on the first Opportunity being embraced to reward each one agreable to his Merit.

All reasonable Travelling Expences will be allowed, and the Advance-Money be paid on their Appearance on Board.

IN CONGRESS, MARCH 29, 1777.

RESOLVED,

THAT the MARINE COMMITTEE be authorised to advance to every able Seaman, that enters into the CONTINENTAL SERVICE, any Sum not exceeding FORTY DOLLARS, and to every ordinary Seaman or Landsman, any Sum not exceeding TWENTY DOLLARS, to be deducted from their future Prize-Money.

By Order of CONGRESS,

JOHN-HANCOCK, PRESIDENT.

DANVERS: Printed by E. RUSSELL, at the House late the Bell-Tavern.

(*Above*) The notorious prison ship *Jersey*. A wash drawing by R. Skerrett in 1908 after a sketch made by one of the prisoners
—*U.S. Navy Photo*

(*Left*) Recruiting poster used by Paul Jones to drum up a crew for the *Ranger*. This is the earliest American naval recruiting poster known to exist.
—*U.S. Navy Photo*

The British fleet setting sail from Sandy Hook for Philadelphia on July 23, 1777. The 64-gun *Eagle*, flying the flag of Admiral Lord Howe, is in the van. The armada, which consisted of 280 sail, carried some 15,000 troops, hundreds of horses and innumerable pieces of field artillery. —*U.S. Navy Photo*

H.M.S. *Augusta* ablaze off Fort Mifflin October 23, 1777. The 64-gun *Augusta* was part of the British fleet that had attacked Fort Mifflin the day before and had run aground in the Delaware River. She caught fire and blew up—the largest British ship to be lost in action with the Americans in both the Revolution and the War of 1812. Behind her, the sloop-of-war *Merlin*, which had also run aground, has been fired by her own crew before being abandoned. —*U.S. Navy Photo*

Rodney's flagship, *Formidable,* has just broken through the French line at the Battle of the Saintes on April 12, 1782, and is being followed by the remainder of the British fleet. —*U.S. Navy Photo*

The Continental frigate *Randolph* blows up during an action with H.M.S. *Yarmouth,* 64, off Barbados on March 7, 1778. Captain Nicholas Biddle and all but four of the *Randolph*'s 305-man crew were lost. —*U.S. Navy Photo*

The capture of the British armed schooner *Margaretta* by a party of Americans led by Jeremiah O'Brien off Machias on June 12, 1775. The Americans embarked on the lumber sloop *Unity*, chased, boarded and captured the *Margaretta* in a brief but bloody struggle. The encounter is often described as the naval equivalent of the Battle of Lexington. —*U.S. Navy Photo*

The gondola *Philadelphia,* sole survivor of Benedict Arnold's fleet on Lake Champlain. She sank after the battle on Oct. 11, 1776, but was raised from the bottom of the lake in 1935. She is now on display at The Smithsonian Institution surrounded by relics of the battle. One of the British cannonballs which helped sink the craft is still embedded in her side. —*Courtesy of The Smithsonian Institution*

A contemporary French engraving of the battle between the *Bonhomme Richard* and the *Serapis* off Flamborough Head on Sept. 22, 1779. The *Alliance* is shown firing into the *Richard*. The picture seems to be a variation on an engraving made by Richard Paton, an English artist, that was issued fifteen months after the battle but is more crude in execution. —*Courtesy of the Library of Congress*

The Continental sloop-of-war *Reprisal*, 18, vs. H.M.S. *Shark*, 16, off St. Pierre, Martinique, on July 27, 1776. The picture is in error in showing the *Reprisal* as a brig. In addition, the American vessel flew the Grand Union flag rather than the Stars and Stripes. —*U.S. Navy Photo*

short that when one of the prisoners died, the others concealed the
fact until the body began to putrefy so that they might continue to
get the extra rations. The water served out was so thick with slime
that the prisoners strained it between set teeth. When the *Yarmouth*
finally reached Plymouth, the prisoners were so weak they had to be
hoisted out of the hold with block and tackle. They were taken to
Old Mill Prison, where their treatment was little better than on the
Jersey.

Talbot was released after a few months. He made his way to
France and secured passage home on a Rhode Island brig. Two
·weeks later, she was captured by a British privateer. The privateer's
captain treated his prisoners with kindness. He remarked that Talbot
had been a prisoner long enough and transferred him to an English
ship bound for New York. From there, Talbot made his way home.
When Congress founded the United States Navy in 1798, he was
named as one of its first captains and commanded the frigate *Constitution.* The ex-cabin boy had come a long way.

Due to the shortage of commands in the Continental Navy and
the inability of many of its ships to get to sea, naval officers often
turned to privateering. John Manley and John Barry, among others,
served impartially in ships commissioned by the Continental Navy
and in privateers as the opportunities arose. During the war, about
sixty of the most formidable commerce raiders were skippered by
men who were, or became, captains in the navy. None had a more
fabulous career than Joshua Barney, described by one writer as "the
prince of privateers and adventurers." A native of Baltimore, he had
gone to sea as a boy. In 1775, at the age of sixteen, he found himself
the master of a wheat-laden merchantman on the way to France
after her captain died. Upon his return home, Barney shipped as a
master's mate on the *Hornet* which became separated from Esek
Hopkins's fleet during the cruise to New Providence. Later he served
as a master's mate on the *Wasp*, and as a lieutenant on the *Andrew
Doria* and *Virginia.* Twice he was taken prisoner, serving a total of
about five months before being exchanged.

On the beach in Baltimore in November 1778, he met Isaiah
Robinson, his old captain from the *Doria*, who was fitting out a new
privateer, the brig *General Mercer.* Robinson offered him the post of
first lieutenant. Barney, with no prospects of getting a berth in the

Continental Navy, accepted with alacrity. The *Mercer* was not impressive. She carried a mixed bag of guns of various sizes, a crew of thirty-five and a load of tobacco consigned to Bordeaux. However, she did present an opportunity to get back to sea. Three days out from the Chesapeake Capes, the British privateer *Rosebud*, armed with 16 guns and carrying a crew three times as large as the *Mercer*'s, was encountered. The Englishman demanded that the *General Mercer* surrender, but Robinson unleashed his broadside. The enemy's fore-topsail was carried away and her rigging much cut up. A running fight lasted through much of the night.

The British ship tried to keep astern of the *Mercer* and under her quarter when it was discovered she had no stern chasers. Under the cover of darkness, Barney had a gun port cut into the ship's stern and ran a 3-pounder out of it. The *Rosebud* drew up to the stern of the American ship the next morning, her forecastle packed with boarders. Barney double-shotted his gun with grape, topping it off with a crowbar. He waited until the enemy vessel was within point-blank range before firing. The hurtling crowbar and cloud of grape carried away the Englishman's headsails, broke up the boarding party and sliced the foreshrouds which supported the mast. The tangled wreckage would have taken the foremast over the side if the English captain had not quickly turned to reduce the pressure of the wind. This gave Robinson the opportunity he had been waiting for to rake the *Rosebud*. Staggering under the Yankee fire, the British privateer pulled away with half her crew either dead or wounded.

Selling off his cargo of tobacco in France at a sizeable profit, Robinson purchased eighteen 6-pounders and doubled the size of his crew to seventy men. After filling the *Mercer*'s hold with casks of brandy, he headed for home. Midway across the Atlantic, a British vessel was sighted and broadsides exchanged. Darkness put an end to the engagement. Next morning, the enemy ship was still in sight but was drawing away from the heavily laden brig. Robinson ordered the men to get out the sweeps. They sweated and strained at the clumsy oars until the *Mercer* was once more broadside to broadside with her opponent. The enemy ship quickly struck. The prize was an English privateer of sixteen guns, 6- and 9-pounders. Twelve of her crew had been killed and a number wounded by the *Mercer*'s fire, while the Americans sustained only one casualty. Barney took a prize crew aboard her and both vessels arrived safely at Philadelphia.

The proceeds of the voyage were enough for Captain Robinson to retire and for young Barney to get married.

Barney was soon at sea again, however. On a trip with his new wife away from their home in Philadelphia someone robbed his sea chest of everything he owned. Looking for employment, Barney accepted an appointment as first lieutenant of the newly commissioned Continental sloop-of-war *Saratoga*. Built by Joshua Humphreys, this trim craft was armed with sixteen 9-pounders and a pair of 4s. She was commanded by Captain John Young, twenty-third on the Marine Committee's list of captains. Running along the Jersey coast on October 8, 1780, the *Saratoga* took a sizeable British letter of marque, the *Charming Molly*, and Barney was detailed to take her into port as a prize. Three days later, he found himself a prisoner for the third time in as many years. Overawed by the 64-gun ship of the line *Intrepid*, Barney could do nothing but surrender meekly. He was one of the unfortunates carried to England in the hold of the *Yarmouth*.

Barney survived to escape from Old Mill Prison. He persuaded a friendly guard to provide him with a British naval officer's blue coat and to look the other way as he clambered over the prison wall. He made his way to the home of some Englishmen in Plymouth known to be sympathetic to the American cause, where arrangements were made to smuggle him across the Channel to France. At one point, Barney was in a coach that was halted for inspection by troops seeking him as an escaped prisoner. An officer thrust a lantern into the coach and began reading aloud the exact description of Barney and the clothes he had been wearing at the time of his escape without recognizing him. Securing passage on the Beverly privateer *Cicero* at Bilbao, he returned to America late in 1781. The Cabots, who owned the *Cicero* and a flotilla of other privateers, offered Barney command of a fine new ship of 20 guns then being fitted out. Instead, he took a sleigh over the snow-packed roads to Philadelphia to get his first glimpse of a son he had never seen.

Barney was on shore only a brief time. During the winter and early spring of 1782, local Tories, using barges and other small craft, began darting out of coves and creeks emptying into Delaware Bay to harass Yankee shipping passing to and from Philadelphia. When the Continental authorities were unable to provide protection, the merchants banded together and fitted out the cargo vessel *Hyder Ally* with four 9-pounders and twelve 6s, hired a crew of one hundred twenty men including a company of backwoodsmen to serve as marines and offered the command to Barney. On April 7, 1782, he was ordered to convoy seven merchantmen to sea and dropped down to Cape May to await a fair wind. The convoy was spotted by a British blockading squadron led by the *Quebec*, a 32-gun frigate. The British commander sent the 20-gun ship *General Monk*, which had been Silas Talbot's *General Washington* before her capture, and the privateer *Fair American*, which had also been taken from the Yankees, up the bay to reconnoiter. Barney ordered his convoy to flee, while he maneuvered the *Hyder Ally*, the only armed American vessel, to cover their retreat. The *Fair American* made straight for the convoy. In passing the *Hyder Ally*, she gave her a broadside to which Barney made no reply. The privateer, however, ran aground leaving the *Hyder Ally* and the *General Monk* alone to fight it out.

The British ship, carrying about double the metal of her adversary, sailed directly for the American vessel with the clear intention of unleashing her broadside at close quarters and boarding in the confusion. As she came on, Barney later recalled thinking "she would blow us to atoms, but we were determined she should gain her victory dearly." As the ships closed, Barney told his helmsman, "Follow my next order to the contrary." Then he shouted so as to be heard aboard the *Monk*: "Hard-a-port your helm!" The British vessel turned to port to keep abreast, but the Yankee helmsmen, following his cue, turned the *Hyder Ally* to starboard. The vessels fouled each other to the surprise of the enemy. Barney poured a raking fire into the *Monk* and it took but a minute or two to lash the ships together so the British could not make an effective reply.

The *Monk*'s crew tried to board but a devastating fire from Barney's backwoods riflemen swept her deck clean. One man called out to Barney: "Say, Cap, do you see that fellow with a white hat?" Barney looked in the direction indicated, and saw a man with a white hat on the enemy's deck jump at least three feet and fall. "Cap," called out the marksman as he reloaded his long-barreled rifle, "that's the third fellow I've made hop." At one point during the action, Barney stood on the binnacle on the quarterdeck to get a better view through the smoke, presenting an excellent target for enemy sharpshooters in the tops. A ball passed through his hat grazing the crown of his head. Another tore off part of the skirt of his coat. After half an hour of pounding by the Americans, the *Monk*'s decks were a shambles. More than half her crew had been killed or wounded, including every officer in the ship. Unable to get help from the *Quebec*, which was too far away, her captain surrendered. American casualties were four killed and eleven wounded.

Barney's prize was taken into the Continental Navy under her original name, and he was made her captain. Two years after his escape from Old Mill Prison, Barney visited Plymouth in the *Washington* and gave a dinner on board for all those who had helped him get away. Later, he served in the French Navy, skippered the Baltimore privateer *Rossie* during the War of 1812, taking prizes worth $1.5 million in a single cruise. In 1814 he commanded a handful of sailors and marines who made a stand against the British regulars at Bladensburg outside Washington, while the militia took to their heels, leaving the enemy to burn the Capitol and the president's home. He well deserves the title "sailor of fortune" bestowed by a biographer.

No discussion of privateering during the Revolution would be complete without mention of the Philadelphia privateer *Holker*, so fantastically successful in harvesting prizes that she was known as "the millionaire-maker." Blair McClenahan, her owner, had her built specifically as a privateer. She turned out to be a gold mine for him and a succession of captains and crews. The speedy brig first went out under Captain George Geddes as a 10-gun letter of marque in April 1779. She returned from St. Eustatius with a cargo of rum and sugar as well as the *Friendship*, a British vessel loaded with molasses, tobacco, and rice. Geddes's report on her performance was so enthusiastic that McClenahan increased her armament to 16 guns and transformed her into an all-out privateer. Before long, the brig was being called the "mischievious *Holker*" by the English newspapers as they recorded her triumphs. On her first cruise as a privateer, she captured six rich prizes, including one vessel loaded with 80 cannon for the British army. The proceeds of this voyage alone are said to have amounted to a million pounds. Geddes's share of the profits of this and of a following cruise were estimated at 100,000 pounds— enough to send him into retirement. He turned command of the *Holker* over to Matthew Lawler.

The third cruise, while not as spectacular, resulted in a satisfactory haul. In four months of cruising in the West Indies, three prizes were taken before the privateer returned to Philadelphia for an overhaul. A short time later, Lawler put to sea again, and this time the results were almost disastrous. The *Holker* fell in with the British privateer *Admiral Rodney*, which matched her in gun power, and they slugged it out until both ships were so badly damaged they had to break off the battle. The *Holker* returned to port for repairs and a new skipper, Captain Roger Keane. During her next cruise she was accompanied by the smaller privateer *Fair American*, also owned by McClenahan, and commanded by Stephen Decatur, whose son was to become a leading figure in American naval history. Their first prize was a valuable one—a brig with three hundred eight pipes, or huge casks, of fine Madeira wine. Numerous other prizes were taken in quick succession and McClenahan cleared nearly a million pounds on the voyage. Other successful cruises followed. The *Holker* also had some narrow escapes from British men-of-war sent out to put an end to her depredations. In April 1781, it appeared that they had succeeded. Word was received in Philadelphia that the *Holker* had been taken by a British frigate in the West Indies.

McClenahan shrugged off the loss as the fortunes of war. Besides, she had paid for herself many times over. Then on June 3, there was news from the Delaware capes—the *Holker* was standing in from the sea. The report of her capture had been false. She had been cruising among the islands taking prizes right and left. That winter she returned to the Caribbean and popped fourteen more British ships into her bag. Captain Keane became so rich that he quit the sea, turning command of the brig over to Captain John Quinlan. During the summer of 1782, the *Holker* lined his pockets with prize money, just as she had for his predecessors. Within a six-week period, she took sixteen prizes. She must have seemed a will-o'-the-wisp to the frustrated British cruisers seeking her.

The *Holker*'s luck finally ran out on March 2, 1783. The war had sputtered out on land but privateers still ranged the Caribbean. The *Holker* was scudding along the channel between St. Lucia and Martinique under dark and squally skies, when a lookout high above the pitching deck made out a distant ship, a British frigate. Captain Quinlan clapped on all sail, confident he could outrun his pursuer. The *Holker* leaped ahead with the frigate *Alcemene* in pursuit. From the warship's quarterdeck it was soon clear that the privateer, with its large spread of canvas, was drawing away. She was heeling well over under the press of the wind against her sails and the sea boiled along the top of her lee rail. Another squall bore down and the brig vanished into a thick curtain of rain. The *Alcemene* struggled ahead, her lookouts straining for a glimpse of the privateer. When the darkness lifted, the horizon was empty. The fury of the squall had kicked the *Holker* over on her beam ends, and she had capsized. The frigate's boats managed to snatch forty-seven survivors from the sea—less than half the privateer's crew of more than a hundred men.

Despite such disasters, privateering was so profitable that John Pickering, a member of a prominent Salem family, observed in 1783 that "there were many persons in Salem dejected by the return of peace." The privateers had rendered valuable service to the nation as well as lining the pockets of their owners and crews. Although commerce raiding did not directly protect the American coast and trade, it greatly decreased pressures upon them by forcing the British to scatter their fleets in escort work and trade protection. The raiders also slowed down the flow of trade to convoy speed, and sometimes interfered with the campaigns on land. For example, the fear of enemy privateers snatching up straggling troop and supply ships resulted in the late arrival of reinforcements for Canada in 1776. General Burgoyne later blamed the slowness of the convoy for the failure to cut off Arnold's retreat from Quebec that year. Prizes taken by the privateers also shifted from enemy hands to those of the Americans a great quantity of highly essential munitions and supplies that could not have been obtained in any other manner.

Of course, the Americans paid a price. As William Whipple wrote in 1778:

> The privateers have much distressed the trade of our Enemies, but had there been no privateers is it not probable there would have been a much larger number of Public Ships than has been fitted out, which might have distressed the Enemy nearly as much & furnished these States with necessaries on much better terms than they have been supplied by Privateers?

Other officials also constantly railed at the seduction of seamen from the navy by the privateers. William Vernon, a member of the Navy Board at Boston, for one, pleaded that "an Embargo upon all

Private Property, whether Arm'd or Merchant ships, may take Place thro' all the United States, until the Fleet is compleatly Mann'd." There is no question that privateering siphoned off men and energies that could have been applied to the navy. And even though the injury inflicted upon Britain was sizeable in the aggregate, it was not disabling. For these reasons, Admiral Mahan and other naval writers of his day were inclined to deprecate the services of the privateers in both the Revolution and the War of 1812. Speaking of commerce raiding as a military measure, Mahan argued: "It is doubtless a most important secondary operation of naval war, and is not likely to be abandoned till war itself shall cease; but regarded as a primary and fundamental measure, sufficient in itself to crush an enemy, it is probably a delusion."

Mahan's position must be viewed as a piece of special pleading, however. Writing at the turn of the century, he had an eye to the conditions of his own time. As an advocate of a strong navy, the admiral had his reasons to minimize the effects of earlier commerce warfare. From this, it was but a short distance to read into the naval failures of previous generations the necessity for a big navy. The commerce raiding activities of the U-boats in World Wars I and II and those of American submarines against Japanese commerce in the Pacific show that Mahan didn't have the last word. Considering the limited maritime resources available to the Americans at the time, John Adams shot closer to the mark when he said of commerce raiding: "This is a short, easy, and infallible method of humbling the English. . . ."

XVII

Sailing Against England

Benjamin Franklin put it best. "We have not the least doubt but that two or three of the Continental frigates sent into the German Ocean [the North Sea] with some lesser swift sailing cruisers, might intercept and seize a great part of the Baltic and Northern trade," he wrote Congress from Paris in May 1777. "One frigate would be sufficient to destroy the whole Greenland whale fishery, or take the Hudson Bay ships returning. . . . A blow might be struck that would alarm and shake Great Britain. . . ." From almost the moment he had arrived in France on Lambert Wickes's *Reprisal* near the end of the previous year, Franklin urged that the war be brought home to England. With his usual craftiness, he envisioned an attack upon Britain's commerce in her own waters as an instrument of diplomacy. If it could be so arranged that there was an appearance of French collusion in the raids, an outraged Britain could be forced into a war with France against her will. Franklin lived long before the age of psychological warfare, but he well understood its principles. Behind his benevolent smile lurked a master of intrigue, skillfully maneuvering the vacillating powers of Europe.

The orders issued to Wickes by the Marine Committee fitted in with this scheme.[1] After depositing the old gentleman safely in France, he was "to proceed on a cruise against our enemies." But instead of sailing to the usual haunts of the commerce raiders such as the West Indies or off Halifax, he was to "proceed directly on the coast of England, up the Channel." Having issued these momentous instructions, the Committee ended with an air of exultation: "Let Old England see how they like to have an active enemy at their own door; they have sent fire and sword to ours." The first captures of enemy ships in European waters had already occurred before the *Reprisal* nosed her way up the Loire to Nantes. The Newburyport letter of marque *Hawke* arrived at Bilbao on October 1, 1776, having captured five English vessels which had been sent home under prize crews. Captain John Lee, the *Hawke*'s skipper, released his prisoners in the Spanish port only to have them accuse him of piracy. He was arrested and his ship seized. Silas Deane, the first American commissioner in Europe, prevailed upon the French to intercede and Lee and his vessel were freed. Other privateers were also operating in European waters at the time and had taken several prizes.

The arrival of the *Reprisal* marked a new turn of events. She was the first Continental warship to appear in European seas, and she brought with her two English vessels that had been captured on the way across the Atlantic—the first American prizes to be taken into a French port. Lord Stormont, the vigilant British ambassador in Paris, was livid. He immediately sought an interview with the Comte de Vergennes, the French foreign minister, and said he expected that the *Reprisal*'s prizes would be "immediately restored to their owners." The French were quite properly reminded that the Treaty of Utrecht concluded between Britain and France in 1713 expressly denied the use of the ports of either power to the enemies of the other. "It was the General Interest of all civilized Nations to give no Refuge or assistance to Pirates," Stormont emphasized. Vergennes, still careful about open support of the American cause, replied that although France must be cautious about exposing her trade to the resentment of the Yankees, the treaty would be observed to the very

---

[1] For the most complete account of Wickes's activities, see William B. Clark, *Lambert Wickes.*

letter. While the diplomatic palavering continued, Wickes sold the prizes to French buyers under procedures that were to become standard in coming months. The vessels were sailed outside the harbor by their purchasers and given new figureheads and a hasty coat of paint, while their cargoes were placed aboard Dutch ships and taken to French ports less busy than Nantes. With the ships' names and descriptions altered, the records of the none-too-meticulous French Admiralty Courts made it all but impossible for their English owners to find them again. Lord Stormont could but fume.

As soon as the *Reprisal* was refitted, she sailed on January 24, 1777, on a cruise in the English Channel. With him, Wickes had a French pilot and several French sailors, strengthening the desired impression of France's collusion in the Continental Navy's first raid in European waters. Sailing off Land's End, Wickes kept an eye out for the Falmouth–Lisbon packet which might be carrying considerable specie. Four merchant ships were taken without difficulty before the packet *Swallow* sailed into sight. Although she was outclassed by the *Reprisal*, the packet put up a fight in which one American seaman was killed and two officers were wounded. Led by Wickes, a boarding party quickly subdued the British crew and put out a fire that had been started by the sloop's broadsides. The packet turned out to be in ballast, and carried no money. Wickes allowed her officers and few passengers to keep their possessions.

With the five British ships being worked by prize crews and nearly a hundred prisoners crammed aboard the *Reprisal*, Wickes sailed into the harbor of Lorient on February 14, raising the curtain on a ponderous diplomatic ballet. Hearing of the capture of the English ships, Stormont instantly lodged a strong protest with Vergennes. Soothingly, the Foreign Minister replied that the *Reprisal* had been ordered to leave French waters within twenty-four hours. From London, the American commissioners learned that "the prizes taken by Captain Weeks form the subject of every conversation." England seethed with outrage. A week later, the British envoy somewhat testily pointed out that the American ship was still in Lorient, and that far from the prizes being returned to their legal owners, two of them had been sold. There must be some mistake, replied Vergennes. "I assure you, sir, I know of no sale, and none has been permitted." Just about the same time, the sly foreign minister was being told by Beaumarchais: "I have missed at L'Orient the five laden vessels. They were sold when my agent arrived there. I confess to you the sin I was going to commit, because I am vexed that the others have committed it in my place." [2] Two weeks later, Stormont was complaining that the "American pirate" was still in port and all the prizes had been sold—"and sold to Frenchmen." This was "very extraordinary," allowed Vergennes. He would take the matter up with M. de Sartine, the Minister of Marine, who would, of course, make a full investigation. Stormont was playing with a deck well stacked against him—and what was worse, he realized it.

The American commissioners also took a hand in the game. Not wishing to make Vergennes's first test with the British too hard for him, they sent the minister a memoir carefully stating that they had not ordered Wickes to send prizes into French ports. "We learn his Cruize has been off the Coast of Spain and Portugal," they added, claiming that the prizes proved he had not been raiding off the French coast. After all, had not four of them been bound to Lisbon and Cadiz? In their report to Congress, Franklin and Deane noted that bringing prizes into French ports "has given some trouble and uneasiness to the court, and must not be too frequently practiced." Nevertheless, they also announced Wickes had been ordered "to make another Cruize before he returns to America."

Through all the maneuvering the *Reprisal* remained in Lorient. Although Wickes had received orders from the French to abandon the harbor, he had fallen back upon a clause in the Treaty of Utrecht permitting ships in distress to remain in port until they were fit again to go to sea. He told the port authorities that his vessel needed to be heaved down and repaired. Otherwise he could not answer for her safety. A carpenter and caulker were sent to inspect the *Reprisal.* Although they agreed that she needed work, they refused to sign a certificate saying the vessel would be in danger if she sailed unrepaired. The French authorities ordered Wickes to sail. Overnight something happened to the *Reprisal.* Next morning, Wickes asked the inspectors to examine her again. This time they found the vessel taking on water rapidly and eagerly signed the certificate. Not until long afterward did British agents learn that Wickes had had a hidden pump set up to fill the ship's hold with water.

---

[2] Beaumarchais said the five vessels and their cargoes were sold for 90 thousand livres, and were worth 600 thousand.

Ships and seamen were necessary for Franklin's plan to carry the war home to Britain. He had brought instructions from Congress to try to buy or borrow eight ships-of-the-line from France as well as a frigate and two cutters. Faced with the threat of war with Britain, the French initially refused to consider weakening their navy. Later, two ships were obtained. They were the 28-gun *Queen of France*, an old converted merchantman purchased from the French, and the *Deane*, a 32-gun frigate which was built at Nantes from French plans. The most important ship planned by the commissioners was *L'Indien*, a powerful 40-gun frigate built to a French design in Amsterdam. But the neutral Dutch were reluctant to get into trouble with Britain and delayed permission for the Americans to take possession of the vessel.

The commissioners lived within a web of intrigue. Franklin and Deane had agents in various ports along the French coast helping speed privateers and merchantmen on their way, keeping them posted on changes in French attitudes and regulations, helping recruit French seamen to fill vacant berths on these vessels and finding masters for ships and ships for masters. The British Secret Service, headed by William Eden,[3] surrounded the commissioners with a net of spies and double agents. While British agents spied on the Americans, the spies of Vergennes and Beaumarchais hunted for suspicious Englishmen in France, and the French police kept an eye on everyone. The most subtle of the double-dealers was Edward Bancroft, the secretary of the American commissioners, who also served the British. For 500 pounds a year, he furnished the names of ships and masters employed by the Americans together with details of their sailing and news of privateers and prizes. Writing his reports in invisible ink between the lines of fictitious love letters, Bancroft left them in a sealed bottle in a hole in a tree on the south terrace of the Tuileries. Promptly at half-past nine every Tuesday evening, they were picked up by a messenger who left another bottle containing any communications for Bancroft from the British. Neither Franklin nor Deane suspected Bancroft was transmitting their table talk to Lord Stormont. Arthur Lee, the third commissioner, who suspected

---

[3] Eden was a brother of Sir Robert Eden, last Royal Governor of Maryland and an ancestor of Anthony Eden, Lord Avon. His cover was an undersecretaryship in the Southern Department.

everybody but his own secretary, who was also a spy, was suspicious of Bancroft, but no one paid any attention to him. Thanks to Bancroft's information, Stormont could make accurate protests to Vergennes about French violations of neutrality. British cruisers also knew where to wait in order to pounce on ships and mail destined for America.

No longer daring to trust important papers to the careless masters of lumbering merchantmen, the commissioners decided to secure a swift-sailing cutter to carry their dispatches. Late in January, 1778, just before sailing on his controversial cruise, Wickes had sent Samuel Nicholson, a distant cousin and fellow Marylander, to Franklin with the recommendation that he be employed by the commissioners in their operations. Besides his relationship with Wickes, Nicholson had other credentials—he was the brother of Captain James Nicholson, who had been appointed the Continental Navy's senior officer only a few months before. Within a few days the commissioners asked Nicholson to procure a cutter. Although it was expected that he would have little difficulty in obtaining a vessel in one of the northern French ports, Nicholson's instructions also allowed him to cross the Channel to Dover and try his luck there if it were necessary. To command the craft, the commissioners settled upon Captain Joseph Hynson, Wickes's stepbrother, who was in London. He was instructed to meet Nicholson in either Boulogne or Calais. What the commissioners did not realize was that Nicholson had a mistress in London, Mrs. Elizabeth Carter, whom he wanted to visit.

Nicholson made only a perfunctory search for a suitable cutter in the French ports before dashing off to London, as much in quest for his mistress as a vessel. Even though the French ports were closely watched by Eden's agents, knowledgeable men moved back and forth with considerable ease. Smugglers operated freely between such ports as Deal and Dover, Dunkirk and Calais. It was a simple matter for a well-paying stranger to take his place among the barrels of brandy and bales of lace. No questions were asked at either end of the trip. Arriving at Mrs. Carter's house in Portland Street, Nicholson sent off a quick note to Hynson. "Take a coach and come immediately," he told him, because "my Business are of Such a Nature, won't bare putting to Paper." Hynson hastened to see Nicholson and was bedazzled when told that Franklin had selected him to carry the commissioners' dispatches to Congress. Although he was supposed to keep his mouth shut about the project, Hynson could not resist telling his landlady and good friend, Mrs. Elizabeth Jump.

Mrs. Jump's boardinghouse in Stepney had long been a snug harbor for seamen. She offered plenty of good food, grog, and company—including several unattached ladies. Hynson's attention was centered upon Isabella Cleghorn, and he could not resist letting her know what an important fellow he had become. Alarmed at what she and Isabella had learned, Mrs. Jump went off to see the Reverend John Vardill. Young Mr. Vardill, who was only twenty-five at the time, had been assistant rector of Trinity Church in New York before the Revolution and professor of natural law at King's College.[4] He had been in London at the outbreak of the war and in return for hints that he would be given an endowed chair of divinity at King's College after a British victory, he had joined the Secret Service. He specialized in spying on the American colony in London. Of course, Mrs. Jump was not in his social class, but he had cultivated her anyway because she was a good source of information about the comings and goings of Yankee shipmasters. The landlady unburdened herself of her fears to the sympathetic clergyman. At once, Vardill drove to Stepney and had a long chat with Hynson in his coach. "I expostulated with Him & found him disposed to be made of any use that might be thought expedient," Vardill told Lord North. Probably the threat of a charge of treason made the talkative Hynson more malleable.

Vardill and Eden planned to allow Hynson and Nicholson to purchase a cutter in England, take it to Havre where Hynson would receive the dispatches and then sail into the waiting arms of several British men-of-war. Mrs. Jump and Isabella were told nothing of Hynson's change of loyalties, and he continued to spout pro-rebel sentiments. Hynson rejoined Nicholson, and in company with Mrs. Carter they went to Dover in mid-February to search for a suitable cutter. Isabella was left in London. Hynson wrote her a careful letter about his travels with "my companion and wife. We have a fine time of it, nothing to do but Drive from one place to another." On the back of it, Isabella scrawled: "I have not Slept one hour since you left. For Gods sake write to me . . . I am wreatched." Nicholson was soon recalled to Paris leaving Hynson—and the Secret Service—to

---

[4] Now Columbia University.

provide the cutter. The vessel chosen was a discarded Customs vessel named the *Rochefort*, which could "neither fight nor run away," as Nicholson later observed. She was renamed the *Dolphin*. Hynson sailed her across the Channel to Havre on the night of February 22, arriving there five days later after a miserable voyage.

Seven British ships were stationed where they could easily pick up the cutter when she sailed out again. Day after day they relentlessly patrolled the area, waiting to spring the trap. Nerves grew taut at Eden's headquarters in Downing Street. What was wrong? Not until the end of March was word received from British agents in Paris that the plan was off. A schooner had arrived in Nantes from Baltimore, bringing news of Washington's victories at Trenton and Princeton. Deane and Franklin had decided against sending dispatches to America until they had more to report on French reaction to the victories. And then, the dispatches would go by the Baltimore schooner. Hynson and the *Dolphin* were to be held for other work. The whole elaborate plot had collapsed, leaving the rebels in possession of a cutter that had been placed in their hands by the British Secret Service. King George, who had been closely watching the conspiracy unfold, sent Eden a caustic memorandum: "I have ever doubted whether any trust could be reposed in Hynson; I am now quite settled in my opinion that He as well as every other Spy from N. America is encouraged by Dean & Franklin and only give intelligence to deceive."

The *Dolphin* was the newest addition to a rapidly growing American force in European waters. The Continental brigantine *Lexington*, commanded by Captain Henry Johnson, had already arrived off Nantes with a sheaf of privateer commissions for which Deane had been waiting for months.[5] A lugger, a type of small vessel much favored by the French for privateering, had been purchased in Dunkirk, named the *Surprise*, and given to Captain Gustavus Conyngham, another American skipper stranded in Europe. Samuel Nicholson was named captain of the *Dolphin*, which had been fitted out with ten 3-pounders. Thomas Bell, sent over by Robert Morris

---

[5] Johnson had been skipper of the privateer *Yankee* which had done good work until taken by the British. Johnson escaped from a prison ship in the Thames and made his way home. On the return voyage to Europe, he had taken two prizes.

on a privateering venture, was also recruited by the commissioners and a vessel sought for him.

With this small fleet at their disposal, the commissioners prepared a triple-pronged attack on British commerce. Lambert Wickes in the *Reprisal* was placed in command of a flotilla that was to include the *Lexington* and *Dolphin* for a raid through the Irish Sea as far north as the Orkney Islands with the valuable Irish linen fleet as the primary objective. At the same time, Conyngham was to take the *Surprise*, partly owned by Congress and partly by William Hodge, a Philadelphia merchant operating in Europe, out of Dunkirk on a cruise against British shipping. Bell was to secure a ship in Genoa for raiding in the Mediterranean. He was to sail out of Marseilles. Beaumarchais's agents purchased a ship for him with 90,000 livres supplied by Deane, but she never left Genoa. The authorities got wind of what the vessel was to be used for and forced her restoration to her original owners.

Conyngham was the first to get to sea, sailing on May 1, 1777. This "black" Irishman deserves more than passing mention. A member of the landed gentry of Ireland, Conyngham was well connected with Philadelphia's leading merchants. He had come to Europe from that city in September 1775 as master of the brig *Charming Polly* on a "powder cruise." As it turned out, he was blocked from taking on a cargo in France by the vigilance of British agents. So he sailed to the Texel in Holland where he loaded sixteen tons of powder. A gale had forced the brig into the Nieuport Canal and the wind held her there. Once more, the British interfered, and the Dutch allowed them to place a guard on the *Charming Polly*. When a favorable wind came up, Conyngham had the guards seized and started out of the canal. Unluckily, the wind turned, leaving the vessel stranded. Conyngham and his men took to the boats and fled to Dunkirk. The Nieuport fishermen quickly plundered the brig—and Conyngham was left to plot his revenge against the British.

The first mission assigned to the *Surprise*, which was armed with 10 small guns, was the capture of the British mail packet from Harwich to Holland. Then she was to attack enemy shipping in the North Sea. Three days after sailing, Conyngham took the packet *Prince of Orange*, as instructed, as well as a brig loaded with wine and fruit. Because the packet was carrying so many important-looking letters, Conyngham thought it advisable to return to Dunkirk with the prizes immediately. William Hodge, the part owner of *Surprise*, took the pouches to Paris before the expected diplomatic storm broke so they could be examined by the commissioners. An angry Lord Stormont descended on Vergennes, demanding the immediate release of the packet and the brig and the punishment of Conyngham. A raid on the English mails by a vessel sailing from a French port was too blatant a violation of French neutrality. The foreign minister immediately complied with the British envoy's demands. Two sloops of war were sent to Dunkirk on May 9 to seize the *Surprise* and arrest her captain and crew. Stormont expressed satisfaction. "The Success of my application with regard to the Dunkirk Pirate has been highly displeasing to Franklin and Deane," he reported. "They made strong Remonstrances, but were given to understand that there are some things too glaring to be winked at." British anger at France cooled—at least temporarily.

For his part, Vergennes told the Marquis de Noailles, the French envoy in London, that Conyngham's prizes had been restored to the British, not "for love of them, but only to do homage to the principles of justice and equity." Conyngham had shown a lack of discretion in taking the prizes into Dunkirk, where they could be seen by British spies. "There is a great distinction to be drawn," the minister emphasized, "between simply admitting in case of need, and for the moment, a privateer with her prize, and permitting that same privateer to lie, so to speak, in ambush in a neutral port; this latter case is precisely that of Mr. Cunningham." The British tried to get France to turn Conyngham over to them to be tried as a pirate, but the French wouldn't go that far. After about a month, he was released from prison, yearning for another chance to strike at Britain from the sea.

While Hodge set about procuring a new vessel for Conyngham, Wickes took his three ships to sea on May 28, with the aim of taking the rich Irish linen fleet. It was the first American squadron to cruise in European waters. Acting as commodore, Wickes instructed his captains not to separate "unless we should be Chased by a Vessel of Superior Force & it should be Necessary so to do for our own preservation." If the ships should become separated, they were to cruise in the Irish Sea or to the west of Ireland with the rendezvous off the Orkneys. Prizes were to be sent into French and Spanish ports only after the crews had been removed from them. "The Prize Master must not Report or Enter her as a Prize, but as an American Vessel from a port that will be most likely to gain Credit according to the Cargo she may have on board." To prevent the accumulation of prisoners, he recommended that captured seamen be placed on board neutral vessels. French sailors and officers made up a significant part of the crews of the ships. Fifteen of the *Dolphin*'s 35 men were French; 32 of the *Lexington*'s 80, and all but a handful of the seamen on the *Reprisal* had been recruited at Nantes and Lorient.

Contrary winds buffeted the tiny squadron for several days. They were chased by a British ship of the line which "fired several guns at the *Lexington*, but we got clear of her very soon," Wickes reported. Slowed down by the *Dolphin*, which proved to be a poor sailer due to the added weight of her guns, the ships were unable to make their way into the Irish Sea from the south and headed around the western coast of Ireland to enter it from the north. Before the cruise was over, the cutter sprung her mast and Wickes said "she was by no means fit for a Cruizer." That, at least, should have been some consolation for William Eden, who had presented her to the Yankees. Not until June 18 did the Americans take their first prize—the brig *Expedition* out of Whitehaven on England's west coast, in ballast for Norway. Her skipper probably was unalarmed by the approach of three strange sail because Wickes had ordered the ships to fly the Union Jack. Suddenly there was the thud of a cannon and a round shot hurtled across the *Expedition*'s bow. The brig hove to. Her captain was astounded to be told by a boarding officer that he was a prisoner of a Continental squadron commanded by Commodore Wickes. The British crew were hustled aboard the *Reprisal*, and the boarding party quickly scuttled the *Expedition*. That same day, four new names appeared on the muster roll of the *Dolphin*, indicating that some of the captured British seamen had been persuaded to switch sides.

Within a week, Wickes's pygmy squadron captured eighteen ships in the Irish Sea, almost all within sight of English shores. Eight were sent into port, three were released, and seven were sunk. No resistance was offered by these vessels except for a Scottish brig which fought off the *Dolphin* for about half an hour. Some of the prize crews sent off consisted entirely of Frenchmen, with the hope that this would convince the captain of any British cruiser that might re-take the ships that they were neutral vessels. Sailing along the Irish coast, Wickes conceived a plan to send the *Dolphin* into Dublin Bay to capture the Customs cutter stationed there. Unfavorable winds, however, caused cancellation of the expedition and also resulted in the failure of the squadron to take the linen fleet, its primary objective. It was held in port, unable to sail.

The number of prisoners on board the *Reprisal* had become formidable, almost exceeding the size of her crew, so Wickes ordered them into one of the prizes and sent it off to Whitehaven. With this problem taken care of, he instructed the squadron to turn southward for France. Shortly after dawn on June 26, the three ships were approaching the island of Ushant, where they would round the Brittany coast for the last leg of their voyage to Nantes, when a large ship was sighted far to the southwestward. Believing she might be a richly laden Indiaman, Wickes signaled his consorts to bear toward her. The capture of such a prize would be a grand culmination to a highly successful cruise. The vessel was the British *Burford*, 74. From her high poop, Captain George Bowyer correctly surmised that the on-coming vessels were "Rebel Privateers, who taking us probably for an India Man intended to attack us." He played along with the game, doing nothing to cause alarm. The *Burford* plowed along until about 9:30 A.M., when the Yankees realized their mistake. As the American skippers clapped on sail in the hope of making a getaway to the eastward, they could see a towering cloud of canvas billowing out on the tall masts of the two-decker.

Wickes quickly realized that the enemy vessel was gaining. If his ships remained together, they would all be captured, for the un-seaworthy *Dolphin* would slow them down. If they scattered, at least two of the vessels would escape. Signals fluttered from the *Reprisal*'s yardarm, instructing the other vessels to make their getaway as best they could. When Wickes issued the order, he knew the *Burford* would probably remain on his track because his ship was the largest of the trio. Just as he predicted, the British, ignoring the *Lexington* and the *Dolphin*, pressed on in pursuit of the *Reprisal*. Hour after hour the chase continued eastward along the coast of Brittany with the ship-of-the-line's log repeatedly recording "still in Chace of the Privateer." The 74 continued to gain—and at four o'clock tried a ranging shot from a bow chaser. It splashed just astern of the American ship. Periodically, the *Burford* punctuated the pursuit with shots which began to pepper the sea around her quarry. To present as small a target as possible, Wickes kept the *Reprisal*'s stern to the enemy. Still the *Burford* kept on, closing the distance between them. In a desperate attempt to avoid imminent capture, Wickes ordered his ship's battery of eighteen 6-pounders jettisoned. Sweating, straining seamen hoisted the guns over the side into the sea and followed them with anything else heavy enough to matter. The *Burford* was now only a musket shot away.

In the gathering twilight, Wickes saw the beckoning coast of France. Little by little, he steered his vessel closer into the shore. Her progress in this direction was slow because he could not afford to expose his side to the enemy ship, which would haul up and turn its broadside on him. Throwing the guns overboard had speeded up the *Reprisal*, but she was still unable to draw away. There was one more trick left in Wickes's bag. He put the ship's carpenter and his mates to work sawing through some of her beams, which was supposed to make the vessel more limber and lessen her resistance in the water. It was the last resort because this meant weakening the ship's structure to a point where a sudden storm might tear her to matchwood—and squally weather was blowing up. By now it was 8:30 P.M. The chase had been on for more than twelve hours. Darkness was closing in, and it looked all over for the Americans. Suddenly, they noticed the *Burford*'s masts separating—she was turning away. Captain Bowyer, alarmed at being so close to a rocky shore without a pilot and with darkness and a squall approaching, hauled in his studding sails and reefed his topsails. Wickes had won the chase by a hair. Hugging the coast throughout the night, he sighted the *Dolphin* the next morning. The two vessels sailed into St. Malo on the north coast of Brittany. They were received with open arms by a population that had made its living by privateering in every war against the British. The *Lexington* found refuge in the fishing port of Morlaix, about a hundred miles due west on the same coast.

Wickes's raid set off a great popular alarm in Britain. Up and down the coasts of England, Scotland, and Ireland, merchants demanded convoys for their ships. The Admiralty was assailed for failing to protect the nation's commerce. "For the first time since Britain was a maritime power," observed Silas Deane, "the River Thames and others of its ports were crowded with French and other ships taking in freight, in order to avoid the risk of having property captured." Some forty French ships were counted loading cargo in the pool of London while English ships lay idle. The great fair at Chester was cancelled. Marine insurance soared to unheard-of rates, even on such short hauls as from Dover to Calais. "It is true," states a contemporary chronicler, "that the coasts of Great Britain and Ireland were insulted by the American privateers in a manner which our hardiest enemies had never ventured in our most arduous contentions with foreigners." To placate the linen merchants, the Admiralty was forced to station four ships in the Irish Sea. "The sea is overspread with privateers," grumbled Lord Sandwich, "and the demands for convoys and cruisers so great that we know not how to supply them."

Stormont was instructed to warn the Court of Versailles that it must clearly understand that "Peace, however earnestly wished, cannot be obtained unless effectual stop is put to our just causes of complaint." Of course, King George and his ministers fully realized that the aim of the cruise had been to stir up trouble with France, but this only added to their anger. Putting his finger on the American purpose, Lord Weymouth, the Secretary of the Southern Department, declared: "The necessary Consequences must be a war, which is the object they have in view and they are not delicate in the choice of means that may bring about an end so much desired by them." Stormont made the strongest possible protest about the return of Wickes and his ships to French ports and demanded their immediate expulsion. Informed by his agents that a new cutter was being fitted out for Gustavus Conyngham at Dunkirk, he also added this to his list of grievances. Purchased by William Hodge, the cutter had been armed with fourteen 6-pounders and named the *Revenge*. She awaited an opportune moment to slip past the waiting British cruisers to sea.

Vergennes had reached the conclusion that war between Britain and France could not be postponed much longer, but he needed more time to prepare the way at Versailles for the decision. Once more he temporized and moved to placate the British. Yet, at the same time he had no desire to hand the American ships over to the British cruisers that prowled off the Brittany coast. So he resolved upon a novel solution. The Yankee ships would be "sequestered"— or refused permission to sail—until sufficient security was given that the vessels would not return to French ports. As for the *Revenge*, Stormont was assured the cutter would be sold to the French government, which would be the end of the matter. For the time being, the British were satisfied. In the meantime, France strengthened her fleet, re-equipped her army and awaited the return of her sailors from the Newfoundland fisheries.

The *Revenge* was sold as promised—but not to the French government. Hodge arranged a "sale" to Richard Allen, a British subject, who claimed she was to be sent on a trading voyage to Norway. A desperate game of cat-and-mouse took place at Dunkirk between Conyngham and the British agents watching him. The cutter's guns and powder were unloaded to lull the snoopers into complacency. On July 16, the unarmed vessel hoisted sail for her voyage to the north. But as soon as the cutter was out of port, she made for a secret rendezvous where under cover of darkness small boats brought out her guns and a number of French sailors. Conyngham was instructed by the commissioners to "retaliate in every manner in our power— Burn, Sink & Destroy the Enemy." Of his crew of one hundred six men, sixty-six were French, who according to an English report were "composed of all the most desperate fellows which could be procured in so blessed a port as Dunkirk." Shortly after sailing, the *Revenge* was "attackd, fired on, chased by several british frigatts, sloops of War & Cutters," her captain related. Nevertheless, she escaped into the open sea for a cruise that struck terror into the hearts of British merchants and shipowners.

Several troopships carrying German soldiers to England had been reported in the North Sea. Conyngham hoped to take them. But the delays which had postponed his departure from Dunkirk also prevented him from arriving off the mouth of the Thames in time to intercept the ships, resulting in the loss of what he called a "Glorious Opportunity." Five days after the *Revenge* sailed, Conyngham took his first prize—the schooner *Happy Return*, which was later burnt along with two other captured vessels when British men-of-war pressed too close. A two-month-long cruise carried the cutter around Britain into the Irish Sea and out into the Atlantic. Reporting to Robert Morris, Deane wrote:

> Our last accounts are, that they had taken or destroyed about twenty sail, and had appeared off the town of Lynn, and threatened to burn it unless ransomed; but the wind proving unfavorable, they could not put

their threats into execution. In a word, Cunningham, by his first and second bold expeditions, is become the terror of all the eastern coast of England and Scotland.

Conyngham's fourth prize caused trouble. On July 26, the brig *Northampton*, carrying a rich cargo of hemp and iron, was intercepted and proved so valuable a prize that it was decided to send her into port. On the way the vessel was retaken by the British and carried into Yarmouth where it was discovered that no fewer than sixteen of the twenty-one men in the American prize crew were Frenchmen. The British protested to the Marquis de Noailles. The French ambassador blandly replied that "in a great nation there were many turbulent spirits eager to run after adventures." An angry Stormont, who felt he had been duped by the French, faced Vergennes with the threat of war if restrictions were not placed on the activities of the American agents in France. He warned that orders would be given to British cruisers to attack the French fishing fleet due home momentarily from the Grand Banks. Vergennes realized that something would have to be done to appease Stormont —and done quickly. On August 11, he ordered the arrest of William Hodge as an obvious scapegoat, and had him confined in the Bastille because "it is a very serious matter to lie to a king, which he hath done." The unfortunate Hodge, the first American to be lodged in the Bastille, remained there until September 24. By then, the Newfoundland fishing fleet was safely in French ports.

In the meantime, Conyngham boldly continued to sweep the seas around Britain, where her supremacy had seldom been challenged. English ships were afraid to leave their harbors. English merchants were afraid to ship goods except in French or Dutch bottoms. Conyngham became one of the most dreaded men in England. Prints were struck depicting him as a ferocious-looking pirate with a brace of pistols stuck in his belt and a heavy sword in his hand. When a violent storm resulted in damage to the bowsprit of the cutter, he sailed into the small fishing village of Kinehead on the northwestern coast of Ireland to make repairs, obtain water and take on a few supplies. Realizing that he would be unable to send prizes to France, Conyngham ordered them into the Spanish ports of Coruña, Bilbao, and Ferrol. There they were disposed of by the mercantile houses of Guardoqui & Sons and Logoanere & Co., which had long acted as

American agents in Spain. Conyngham and the *Revenge* followed the prizes into Ferrol in mid-September.

Using the Spanish ports as bases, Conyngham cruised against British shipping in the Bay of Biscay, off the Strait of Gibraltar and as far out in the Atlantic as the Canary Islands. The Spanish government was not overly friendly to the American cause—obviously fearing an independent United States would be a danger to its colonies in America—but Conyngham's daring made him popular with the people. For example, a British officer on the ship of the line *Monarch* angrily complained that while the Spaniards at Cadiz procrastinated in delivering supplies to his vessel, Conyngham had no difficulty fitting out. "We had the mortification to see the usual honours paid to two Dutch frigates, and above all to the *Revenge*, American privateer commanded by Cunningham, who came swaggering in with his thirteen stripes, saluted the Spanish Admiral, had it returned, and immediately got product [supplies]; the Spaniards themselves carrying on board wood, water, fruit, and fresh provisions." The British planned a surprise attack on the cutter "in the dead of the night," but Conyngham, warned by a Frenchman, was on guard. The enemy "took Care to Keep their distance." The Spanish admiral, who had also heard the reports, offered a 74-gun ship to protect the *Revenge*, but the daring Irishman declined the offer, saying "it was our wish they would make the Attempt."

Conyngham's popularity made it difficult for the Spanish government to accede to repeated demands from the British that he be denied the use of Spanish ports. But it did not change his luck with his prizes once they were taken. More often than not, captured vessels did not get safely into port. For example, in January 1778, Conyngham cruised briefly along the Portuguese coast and took seven ships, only to have five of them recaptured. In some cases, unreliable prize crews sailed off in the vessels and independently sold them for their own profit. On several occasions, Conyngham was threatened with open mutiny when prize money failed to materialize. Motley crews formed of men of many nations were not amenable to discipline and sometimes were unwilling to abide by the laws of warfare when there was profit to be made. On May 31, 1778, the *Revenge* fell in with the Swedish brig *Henrica Sofia* bound from London to Tenerife with a cargo belonging to a Spanish subject. Conyngham attempted to restrain his crew, pointing out that the ship was a neutral vessel even if her cargo had been loaded in an English port. The men would not be denied their prize money and they put a crew on board with orders to take her to Boston. The crew even assumed responsibility for the act, giving their captain a paper attesting to the fact that "we have eng'd him to take her."

The greed of Conyngham's crew gave the British the chance they had been waiting for. Unable to deal with the swift-sailing *Revenge* on the high seas or to trap the cutter in port, they sought to close Spanish harbors to her. While the Court at Madrid had been cautious in making such a move because of Conyngham's popularity, the seizure of goods belonging to a Spanish subject provided the opportunity for action. The Spaniards were hoping to obtain Gibraltar from the British in exchange for their neutrality. To pave the way for a deal, Madrid ordered all Spanish ports closed to Conyngham. When he arrived at Coruña in midyear, the authorities formally told him he could not refit there. But one official quietly drew the Yankee corsair aside and made it known that he would be allowed to repair his ship this one time at a small port on the Galician coast.

With the ports of both France and Spain now barred to him, Conyngham decided it was time to seek new cruising grounds. On September 1, 1778, he hoisted sail for the West Indies, where the *Revenge* joined William Bingham's fleet of commerce raiders. For several months Conyngham cruised among the islands with only moderate success. "Kept the British privateers in Good order in those seas," he reported. "Captured two of them." One dispatch from Martinique credited the *Revenge* "with an engagement off Barbadoes with a King's Cutter of 28 guns . . . which would not have escaped had it not been for a high sea which prevented boarding her."

Shortly after the start of the new year, Conyngham sailed for Philadelphia, arriving there on February 21, 1779, with fifty chests of arms. Within a few weeks, the Marine Committee ordered the *Revenge* sold, and Conyngham turned to privateering. Much to his surprise, he soon found himself again on the quarterdeck of his old command. She had been purchased by a syndicate of merchants for use as a privateer. He became her captain and part owner. Not long after the cutter assumed this new role, she was deserted by her usual good fortune. Off New York, the *Revenge* ran afoul of the man-of-war *Galatea.* "I made an effort to escape, but in vain," Conyngham stated. "Her teeth were too many." Loaded down with 55 pounds of irons and threatened with the gallows, the man the British called "the Dunkirk pirate" was sent off to Old Mill Prison.

Few American naval officers of the Revolution were as successful as Gustavus Conyngham. In eighteen months of cruising in European waters, he captured twenty-seven British vessels and burned another thirty-three. Even though many of his prizes did not reach port safely, the sale of those that did financed the operations of the American commissioners in Europe—operations that were instrumental in bringing the European powers into the war on the side of the infant republic. Even more important, he had a significant role in upsetting the balance that kept France and Britain at peace. He was the perfect instrument of Franklin's plan to insult England, embarrass France, and make it impossible for the fiction of French neutrality to be maintained, declares one of his admirers.[6] Yet, very little is known today about Conyngham's exploits, perhaps because he lacked Paul Jones's knack for making his feats known far and wide. "Conyngham was inarticulate and modest, and he worked in a period of secrecy. By the time Jones arrived in France, the crisis was over and he could bask in the sudden sunshine of the Franco-American alliance. . . . But if, like Conyngham, he had taken sixty prizes and rocked the nations of Europe, the world would have heard about it."

Shortly after Conyngham sailed from Dunkirk, the British stepped up their efforts to pressure the French into turning the *Reprisal*, *Lexington*, and *Dolphin* out of the ports where they had taken shelter. On August 19, 1777, Lord Stormont gave Vergennes an ultimatum: The Yankee ships must leave French ports immediately "without convoy or escort of any kind" and must not be permitted to return. The Frenchman temporized with a plan to purchase the vessels from the Americans. Wary of such schemes after his unhappy experience with the *Revenge*, Stormont steadfastly refused even to consider the offer. Realizing that this time the British would accept nothing less than full compliance with their demands, Vergennes issued orders on August 31 for the expulsion of the American vessels. Franklin and Deane protested as a matter of form, but there are indications that they now believed the free-wheeling activities of the commerce raiders were in danger of becoming counterproductive. Soon the commissioners would be forced to send a circular letter to

---

[6] Auger, *The Secret War for Independence*.

the over-eager captains of all American armed vessels in European waters warning against the seizure of neutral vessels "contrary to the custom of civilized nations. . . ." They later told Congress: "We submit it to consideration whether it would not be better to forbear cruising [along the English and French] coasts, and bringing prizes in here, till an open war takes place."

In St. Malo, Lambert Wickes welcomed orders from the commissioners to return to America, but he stalled for time in hopes of making the unseaworthy *Dolphin* ready for the arduous voyage. Wickes stayed on, offering excuses. The winds were contrary; all his provisions were not on board; he would sail tomorrow. Finally, all the subterfuges were exhausted. Late on the afternoon of September 14, the *Reprisal* and the *Dolphin* hoisted sail. Tall-masted and rakish-looking, Wickes's ship seemed the same tight vessel that had sailed twice before from French ports to harass Britain's seaborne commerce. Shortly before leaving, Wickes dispatched a message to Captain Johnson of the *Lexington* at Morlaix suggesting that they join forces for the long voyage home. Unfortunately for both vessels, Johnson did not receive the message until too late to act upon it. To avoid patrolling British men-of-war, Wickes and his consort hugged the northern coast of Brittany where the *Reprisal* had been pursued by the *Burford*. Dawn found the two ships off Morlaix where they vainly awaited the *Lexington*. Later in the day, Wickes decided to resolve the problem of the *Dolphin*. He summoned the cutter close alongside for final instructions and told her skipper to take his vessel into Nantes under French colors and say she had just arrived from St. Eustatius. Even if she was interned, that would be better than having her founder at sea. The ships parted, and the *Reprisal* headed out into the Atlantic.

The *Lexington* actually cleared port on September 17 with a crew that included numerous Frenchmen who may not have been overly enthusiastic when they learned they were on their way to America. Two days later, she lay becalmed off Ushant, when daylight revealed a large British cutter a few miles away. She was the *Alert*, mounting ten 4-pounders, which made her inferior to the Yankee brigantine which carried fourteen 4-pounders and a pair of 6s. But the *Alert*'s skipper, Lieutenant John Bazeley, pressed home the attack. For two-and-a-half hours, the ships duelled, with the Americans intent on cutting up the British vessel's sails and rigging so they could get clear and continue their voyage. Johnson realized that he could not afford serious damage to his ship with an Atlantic crossing facing him. He seemed to have achieved his end as the *Lexington* was able to draw off. Bazeley, who seems to have been a skillful and energetic officer, soon managed to repair the damage to the cutter's rigging and set off in pursuit of the enemy vessel. The *Lexington* appears to have been cut up, too, in the first encounter. She was unable to bend all sail to take advantage of the freshening breeze so that the *Alert* caught up with her. After another hour's battering, Johnson hauled down his colors. The American ship lost seven men killed and eleven wounded while the *Alert* had only two killed and three wounded, one of them mortally. Johnson's casualties do not appear to have been serious enough to have caused the loss of his ship. One of his officers later stated that the *Lexington* had been short of ammunition, which may have accounted for her surrender to a ship of inferior force.

The pall of gloom that had descended over the American colony in Paris after the surrender of the *Lexington* was just beginning to clear when word was received of the loss of the *Reprisal.* She had gone down in a severe storm off Newfoundland on October 1. Lambert Wickes and his crew of one hundred thirty men had been lost except for the cook. The man and the ship that had carried Franklin to France, that had brought the Continental flag into European waters and had swept the seas around Britain were no more. If the capture of the *Lexington* had been a blow to Franklin and Deane, the loss of Wickes and his proud ship was a bitter shock. "This loss is extremely to be lamented," they wrote Congress, "as he was a gallant officer and a worthy man."

An era had come to an end—the era of clandestine commerce-raiding designed to embroil a reluctant France in a war with Britain. Within a few weeks, the momentous news of Burgoyne's surrender at Saratoga completely altered the entire aspect of naval operations abroad. France declared war with Britain. Ports which had been officially closed to American ships now welcomed them. The hard-pressed Royal Navy would have to spread its forces even thinner to guard Britain's vital trade routes from renewed assaults by Yankee privateers.

XVIII

Darkness Before Dawn

No other period of the war saw a more contrasting mixture of bright expectations for success at sea and the harsh realities of maritime conflict than the opening months of 1778. On February 6, treaties of alliance and commerce were signed between the United States and France, raising hopes for the speedy arrival of a French fleet off American shores to break the British blockade. Shortly afterward, the Continental Navy experienced a series of disasters that rolled in like a relentless tide. Within a single ninety-day period, the *Randolph*, *Alfred*, *Virginia*, *Columbus*, and *Independence* were lost, and the *Raleigh* ignominiously fled from a much weaker British force.

Nevertheless, the year began well for the navy. While Washington's army froze at Valley Forge and the commander-in-chief fulminated against those "who seem to have little feeling for the naked and distressed soldiers," a brilliant success was scored in the Caribbean. Just after the start of the year, Captain John P. Rathbun seized New Providence again—this time with but a single 12-gun ship and a handful of marines. Several valuable prizes were taken, the forts dismantled and some American prisoners released. "For sheer audacity,

304

the achievement is unrivaled in American naval history," states Rathbun's most recent biographer.[1] Yet Rathbun is almost unknown today and his exploits unrecognized. Rathbun had come to Philadelphia with Abraham Whipple from Rhode Island in 1775 to join Esek Hopkins's fleet. He served in the first expedition against New Providence and had been Paul Jones's first lieutenant in the *Alfred*. Singled out for promotion by Hopkins, he was, at the age of thirty-one, skipper of the sloop *Providence*.

Rathbun was in Charleston in December 1777, when the idea for a daring attack on the island first came to him. From a merchant skipper just returned from the Bahamas he picked up some interesting information. A 16-gun enemy brig, the *Mary*, was undergoing repairs at Nassau after having grounded on a reef. Rathbun recalled the *Mary* very well. She had escaped after an exchange of broadsides off New York in June in which the *Providence*'s sailing master had been killed. Rathbun's informant told him the *Mary* had been virtually stripped while she was undergoing repairs. Her guns and powder were stored in Fort Nassau overlooking the town. No regular troops were on hand. And, as in 1776, the forts were only lightly manned by local militia. Rathbun saw an opportunity for revenge—and prize money.

An audacious plan began to take shape in his mind. Relying on surprise, a landing party attacking under cover of darkness might seize Fort Nassau from its motley defenders, train the guns on the town, and make prizes of all the shipping in the harbor. The *Providence* would anchor off the town until the fort had been captured. It was a variation on Esek Hopkins's original plan of attack—but with a significant difference. Only a single ship would be involved.

Rathbun, who had been accompanied to Charleston by Lieutenant John Trevett, commander of the *Providence*'s marine detachment, outlined the plan to Nicholas Biddle, who was fitting out the *Randolph* for another cruise. Biddle and Trevett had served together in the *Andrew Doria* and were old friends. Biddle doubted the practicality of Rathbun's scheme, but the Rhode Islander was not to be dissuaded. Seeing that arguments would be useless in the face of

---

[1] Frank H. Rathbun, "Rathbun's Raid on Nassau," in *U.S. Naval Institute Proceedings* (November 1970). The author, a descendant of the captain, states: "Even in official records, his name is consistently misspelled Rathburne or Rathbourne, and both a World War II destroyer and a new ocean escort named in his honor were called *Rathburne*."

such determination, Biddle rose, said goodbye to his fellow captain and extended his hand to John Trevett. "I am very sorry, for I shall never see you anymore," he said.

The *Providence* was hardly out of sight of land before she was chased by a trio of British warships. Unable to draw away, Rathbun lightened his vessel by dumping his water, wood, provisions and extra spars. Still the British remained on his tail. When darkness fell, Rathbun gave up running. The *Providence*'s sails were hauled in and she lay completely silent on the black water. The British raced by on her original course. As soon as they were a safe distance off, up went the sloop's sails and away she went to Abaco. There, Rathbun refilled his water casks, secured fresh supplies and set to work building a tall ladder for scaling the walls of Fort Nassau. On January 27, the sloop, disguised as a trading vessel so she would not arouse suspicion, was on her way to New Providence. Her topmast had been sent down, her guns hidden and all crewmen not needed to work the vessel were ordered below. About midnight, her barge was put into the water. Trevett, who was in charge of the landing party, had already "picked out my lambs"—twenty-six marines and seamen—or half the sloop's complement. They filled their pockets with cartridges and got into the boat. All were "smart and active," Trevett said, except one fellow who claimed he was lame. "I cannot run," he declared. "You are the one I should choose," he was told and ordered into the barge.

Taking the scaling ladder with them, the Americans landed on the beach about a mile west of Fort Nassau. Silently, they made their way to the rear wall of the fort, which was surrounded by a fence of high, pointed wooden pickets. Trevett, who had taken part in the attack two years before, recalled that he had removed some of the pickets from the fence at that time, leaving a hole in it. As he said in his journal:

> So I left my men and went myself to see, and found it as I left it. I went through, and near the embrazures I heard talking in the fort, and instantly one of the sentinels came to the corner of the fort and cried "all is well!" and was answered from the other end of the fort, "all is well!" The ship that lay near the fort—her sentinel also cried "all is well!" I lay still a few minutes, as I supposed the sentinels were going their rounds. I then went back and we came on with the scaling ladder, and lay down near the fort until the sentry should come round again, for I

expected they gave the cry every half hour, and so it was. We had but a short time there before they came round and cried "all is well!" I waited a few minutes and then placed the scaling ladder near one of the embrazures and went over, every man following me. . . . As I was turning round the corner of the barracks I met one of the British senti-nels full [on]. I seized him by the collar, and ordered him in the first barrack door; he was much frightened, and exclaimed, "for God's sake, what have I done!" I examined the prisoner and found there was only one more sentinel, and he at the other end of the Fort. I soon put him in another barracks-room and examined them apart.

When the Americans expressed surprise that there were only two guards for such an important post, they were told that five hun-dred men could be summoned merely by firing one of the loaded cannon as a signal. Lighted matches sputtered near some of the guns, ready for use in an emergency. To pass the night, Trevett put some of his men to filling cartridge bags from the three tons of powder found in the fort's magazine. Others were ordered to shift a few of the heavy cannon about so they could be brought to bear on the ships in the harbor and the streets of the town spread out below. To allay suspicion, a marine was stationed on the seaward side of the walls to announce every half hour that "All is well!" Another re-sponded from the land side. They were answered by the watch on the anchored ship, who sensed nothing amiss.

"When daylight appeared we set our thirteen stripes flying at the fort," Trevett continued. Unhappily, there was no sign of the *Providence* in the harbor. She had been blown off by heavy winds,. and the landing party was on its own. As they had come ashore with-out food or water, Trevett sought provisions for them. One of his men was sent with a note summoning James Gould, a merchant who had once lived in Newport and was well known to the American officers. To keep Gould from learning the true size of the American force, Trevett met him outside the walls of Fort Nassau. The landing party consisted of two hundred men and thirty officers and was from a large fleet lying off Abaco under the command of Nicholas Biddle which was preparing to attack Jamaica, the marine declared. They had come to New Providence to take the *Mary* and had orders to leave private property alone if there was no resistance. Trevett also told Gould that while he had ample provisions for his men, he wanted a hearty breakfast for his officers. Suitably impressed, the merchant returned to the town and rousted out the bakers. Within a short time, he sent back a large supply of bread, butter, coffee and other provisions for the twenty-six hungry Americans. In the meantime, Lieutenant Michael Molten and two marines were sent to Fort Montague to demand the surrender of its two-man garrison. When told that Fort Nassau had been taken by two hundred thirty Americans, the pair opened the doors of the fort.

Trevett's next move was to take the *Mary*, which lay nearly ready for sea just a pistol shot from the fort. A midshipman and four heavily armed men were sent in a small boat to demand the vessel's surrender. But her captain was sick ashore and her lieutenant flatly refused to allow the Yankees to come aboard. Wearying of this palaver, Trevett "hailed him from the fort in hard language" and called him "some hard names." With the muzzles of the fort's 18-pounders pointed squarely at his craft, the officer saw the futility of further resistance. The *Mary*'s crew were sent to the fort as prisoners and several other ships in the harbor with rich cargoes were also taken. Some American seamen, who had been captured by a privateer and were seeking passage home, reinforced the boarding party.

There was still no sign of the *Providence*, so Trevett settled in for a long stay. To bluff the islanders into believing there was a large force in Fort Nassau, he may have adopted the old tactic of marching his men about to the sound of fife and drum. When Gould returned to ask if the breakfast he had sent up had been satisfactory, Trevett ordered an elaborate dinner of turtle meat. It was served on fine china and enjoyed by all—including Lieutenant Molten and his two men. Word had been passed to them to spike the guns of Fort Montague, smash the equipment and dump whatever powder had been found into the sea before rejoining the main body of invaders.

Shortly after 2 P.M., a lookout sighted the *Providence*, which had spent the night bucking headwinds. She was followed into the harbor by the British privateer *Gayton*. With her 16 guns, the privateer was more than a match for the *Providence*. Rathbun and Trevett hastily conferred and decided upon a ruse. They lowered their flag and quietly waited for the *Gayton* to come under the guns of the fort. Some of the islanders set about warning Captain William Chambers, the *Gayton*'s skipper, of the trap. "The devil was in the men, women and children," reported Trevett. "They turned out, covering the hills, men waving their hats, and women their aprons." Oblivious to his danger, Chambers took the signal as a greeting and sailed on into the clutches of the Americans. When some men rowed out to his ship and shouted a warning, Chambers finally got the point, and the privateer hastily put about. The Stars and Stripes were quickly run up and the fort's guns barked. The *Gayton* was hit by an 18-pound shot but little damage was done. Chambers skittered away and anchored off Fort Montague, where he presented no immediate threat.

The invaders spent a "tranquil and easy" night, but the inhabitants were "in very great consternation, moving their effects out of town," Trevett reported. Early the next day, work began on preparing the *Mary* and two other sizable ships for sea. All the powder and arms found in the fort and town were stowed aboard the *Providence.* But as the day wore on, the islanders began to show signs of resistance. "All the hills around [were] alive with them, their guns glistening in the sun," Trevett noted. When one group approached too near the fort, some of the marines were "anxious for me to order them to fire." Trevett, however, wished to avoid bloodshed. One of the islanders recognized the officer, who was standing on the parapet, from the previous raid on New Providence when he had led the marines who had captured Lieutenant Governor Montfort Brown. "See, there is that damned long-nose Buckerer come again, that carried away Gov. Brown!" the man shouted. "I paid no attention to such small stuff," allowed the officer.

Later, an informant told Rathbun that Captain Chambers had landed his men and guns and was preparing a night attack on Fort Nassau. Governor John Gambier was warned that if the men gathering on the hilltops behind the fort were not dispersed in fifteen minutes, a merciless cannonade would be unleashed upon the town. Quarter would be neither given nor asked. While this "polite billet doux" was on its way, Trevett ordered a spry young lad to shinny up the flagpole to nail the American flag in place. Gambier could see the youth at work and hear the ominous sound of hammering—signifying the intent to fight to the death. "In less than twenty minutes, there was scarcely a man to be seen on the hills," said Trevett. "During the evening, the whole town was as still as the grave."

The last of the booty was taken aboard the ships, several schooners set ablaze because there were not enough hands to man them and the guns of Fort Nassau were spiked. As the *Providence* stood by with her anchor short, Trevett had one last duty to perform. He ordered the heads of three casks of rice found in the fort broken open and distributed to the poor. "I kept laughing and talking with them [as] they filled their bags," he recalled with evident pleasure. Just as he was about to step into the barge to be rowed out to the *Providence*, a messenger arrived from Chambers with an invitation to join him in a bowl of punch at a local tavern. Although the Britisher promised no treachery, Trevett smiled and suggested that Chambers "come over the bar and take the sloop *Providence*, and then I would take some punch with him." Then he shoved off. With only a tiny sloop and fifty men, Rathbun had captured and held New Providence for three days, taken several valuable prizes and a large quantity of military supplies as well as releasing thirty American prisoners—all without bloodshed. "On the strength of this New Providence adventure alone," writes one authority,[2] "Captain John Peck Rathbun must be ranked as one of the most resourceful, skillfully audacious and successful captains in the Continental Navy."

Within a few weeks after his meeting with Rathbun and Trevett, Nicholas Biddle sailed in the *Randolph* for the last time. Was it fear for Trevett's safety or a premonition of his own fate that had inspired his final remark to his old friend—"I shall never see you any more"? Whatever the reason, on the day after the meeting, January 12, 1778, he made out his will. The bulk of his estate, which consisted of prize money, was left to his fiancée, Elizabeth Baker. Accompanying the frigate to sea were four ships of the South Carolina navy, three of them privateers temporarily taken into the state service. They were the ship-rigged *General Moultrie*, 18, and the brigs *Notre Dame*, 16, *Polly*, 16, and *Fair American*, 14. About one hundred fifty South Carolina officers and troops were assigned as marines. The squadron was ordered to destroy the British ships that had been blockading Charleston harbor, but when it got to sea on February 12, none of the cruisers were sighted. Shorthanded because so many men had been detailed off as prize crews, they had left their station to fill out their complements at St. Augustine. The *Randolph* and her consorts made for the West Indies in search of prizes.

Pickings were sparse. The only prize taken was a small schooner. On the afternoon of March 7, the squadron was sailing

---

[2] Morgan, *Captains to the Northward.*

about sixty leagues due east of Barbados when a distant sail was sighted. Signal flags fluttered at the yardarm of the *Randolph* ordering the smaller vessels to follow the flagship. As the stranger came up over the horizon. Biddle studied her intently through his telescope in the fading light. She appeared to be either a large merchantman or a British frigate. The enemy ship continued on her course toward them. The ship was obviously looking for a fight—and Biddle was ready to oblige. As the *Randolph*'s crew raced to their battle stations, her officers clustered on the quarterdeck and speculated whether the enemy vessel was a 20- or a 28-gun frigate. She ignored the other American ships and bore down on the *Randolph*, so Biddle decided to take in sail and await his opponent. In some confusion, the other ships followed suit, with the *Moultrie* lying in the path of the oncoming vessel.

Darkness had fallen and a quarter moon hung low in the sky. The stranger loomed out of the night and swept abreast of the *Moultrie*. She fired a warning gun and hailed: "Who are you?"

"The *Polly*," answered Captain Charles Sullivan.

"Where are you from?"

"From New York," replied Sullivan, as the enemy ship raced by his vessel.

"My God!" gasped Captain John Blake, one of the *Moultrie*'s marines. "A two-decker!"

She was the 64-gun ship of the line *Yarmouth*, carrying double the number of cannon mounted by the *Randolph*. Undaunted, Biddle watched as her huge bulk bore down upon him. The vessels were close—barely two ships' lengths apart—when a voice called out from the darkness:

"Who are you? Hoist your colors, or we'll fire into you!"

Biddle calmly turned to William Barnes, his first lieutenant, and said: "Give him an answer and open fire." Barnes's voice rang out, loud enough to be heard on board the nearby *Moultrie*. "This is the Continental frigate *Randolph*!" The Grand Union flag was broken out at the gaff as the frigate's 12-pounders spat out a sheet of flame. The *Yarmouth* shuddered under the impact before answering with a broadside. Both ships began firing together, the gun crews aiming at the muzzle flashes of each other's cannon. According to one eyewitness, "the *Randolph* appeared to fire four or five broadsides to the *Yarmouth*'s one." The ships were so close together the men could "throw their hand grenades from their tops to one another's decks." The *Yarmouth*'s mizzen topmast and bowsprit were shot away and one officer and four men were killed while another twelve were wounded by the frigate's murderous fire. The *Randolph* bore the brunt of the battle on the American side, although the *Moultrie* and *Notre Dame* got in a few shots. Some of the *Moultrie*'s shots, however, may have struck the frigate, as the excited Sullivan was firing indiscriminately into the darkness.

About a quarter of an hour after the battle started, Biddle was hit in the thigh by either a musket ball or a flying splinter. He fell, blood gushing from the wound. Refusing all attempts to carry him below, he ordered a chair brought to him and summoned a surgeon's mate from the cockpit to treat him on the quarterdeck. Propped up in the chair as his wound was being dressed, Biddle encouraged his men to keep up their fire. Steadily and rapidly, the frigate's guns were run in and out and her shot crashed into the *Yarmouth*'s tall sides. Suddenly, there was an explosion and the *Randolph* vanished in a flash of flame that towered above her masts.

The *Yarmouth* shivered as debris from the vanished *Randolph* rained down upon her. "A great piece of top timber, six feet long fell on our poop," reported the *Yarmouth*'s commander, Captain Nicholas Vincent. "Another large piece of timber stuck in our fore top-gallant sail. An American ensign, rolled up, [was] blown in upon the forecastle, not so much as singed." Only a column of smoke rose from the surface of the dark sea to mark the spot where Nicholas Biddle and his gallant crew had perished. The four remaining American ships scattered into the night.

On March 12, four days after the destruction of the *Randolph*, the *Yarmouth* was in pursuit of a ship not too far from the scene of the battle, when a lookout sighted an object in the water. Captain Vincent trained his glass on it and "discovered four men that seemed to be standing in the water, for what supported them was not at first visible." They were members of the crew of one of the *Randolph*'s quarterdeck 6-pounders—the only survivors of her three hundred five officers and men. Some freak of fortune had blown them over the side of the shattered ship in parallel arcs, and they found themselves as close together in the boiling sea as they had been on the frigate's deck. All were young and good swimmers. They fashioned a crude raft from the debris bobbing about them, and lashed it together with some broken lengths of rope. For four days and nights, they floated on the empty sea battered by periodic squalls. They had no food, although one of the men had salvaged a piece of blanket that retained rainwater which they sucked up through parched lips. The castaways were frantically waving their ragged shirts. A boat was lowered from the *Yarmouth*—and they were saved.[3]

The survivors could provide no clue as to the cause of the explosion of the *Randolph* and none was ever established. We will also never know what passed through Biddle's mind as he closed with the *Yarmouth*. On the face of it, his chances of victory over so powerful an opponent were slim even if his consorts had behaved well. Yet Biddle's conduct of the action indicates that he did not regard it as a suicide mission. Possibly he hoped to cripple the two-decker and carry her by boarding. As he had written to his brother, Charles, on June 16, 1776: "I Fear Nothing but what I ought to fear . . . And hope never to throw away . . . [a] Vessel and Crew merely to Convince the world I have Courage." Biddle's death at the age of twenty-seven deprived the Continental Navy of an officer with few superiors in the service. He had courage, intelligence, and professional skill, combined with the naval training that was so conspicuously lacking in nearly all the American officers of the period. "For so short a career, scarcely any other had been so brilliant," J. Fenimore Cooper observed in his *History of the Navy*.

Two days after the loss of the *Randolph*, the *Raleigh* and *Alfred* added to the growing list of disasters that plagued the Continental Navy during the opening months of 1778. Little more than a month after the two ships arrived in France, the American commissioners were anxious to see them homeward bound as the time was not considered propitious for a cruise in European waters. News of Burgoyne's surrender at Saratoga had not yet been received in Paris, and the French were under pressure from Britain to halt the

---

[3] The decision to stop and pick up the survivors carried with it an unexpected reward for the officers and men of the *Yarmouth*. The Admiralty allowed head money of 5 pounds for each man in the crew of a rebel vessel sunk or captured. Positive proof was required, which would not have been available without the testimony of the survivors. After they gave their statements, a 1,525-pound bounty was paid for the destruction of the *Randolph*.

activities of American cruisers operating out of their ports. Franklin wished at all costs to avoid embarrassing the French. Captains Thomas Thompson and Elisha Hinman were free to set their own course back to America though the commissioners pointed out that British commerce along the West African coast was unprotected. "By running along that coast you may greatly annoy and distress the enemy in that quarter and afterwards go for the West Indies," they were told. With a nod toward the touchy diplomatic situation, the officers were cautioned to "avoid giving any offense to the flags of the neutral powers."

Late in December 1777, as soon as a full complement of guns had been secured for the *Raleigh*—twenty-six 12-pounders and six 6-pounders—the two ships set sail for home by way of the African coast. They had little success, however. Only a wine-laden sloop was captured off Senegal before they turned toward the West Indies. Early on the morning of March 9, they were just to the east of the Windward Islands when two sails were sighted. Thompson ordered Hinman in the *Alfred* to look over the rearmost of the strangers. If she proved to be more powerful than his vessel, he was to make a signal. The *Raleigh* would come up and join him. By 10 A.M., four hours after the ships were first sighted, only five or six miles separated the vessels. It became evident to the Americans that the strangers were British warships.

Both groups began maneuvering for advantage. Once again, the *Alfred* showed herself a poor sailer. One of the British ships passed close to her and both vessels exchanged fire without damage. Thompson in the *Raleigh* moved to rejoin his consort about three miles away with the intention of combining forces before taking on the enemy ship. But, as he later reported, Hinman started to flee from his opponent before the frigate could join him. From Hinman's flight, Thompson surmised that the enemy ship was more powerful than the *Alfred*. He debated what to do. The sea was smooth, and the wind was light so it was obvious that the second British vessel would head off the *Alfred* before the *Raleigh* could come to her rescue. Instead of steering toward Hinman's ship to lend him a hand, Thompson hauled in sail. This unexpected action was taken, he later told a court of inquiry, with the hope of enticing one of the enemy vessels away from the *Alfred*. The British, however, refused to be decoyed from their prey. Thompson then ordered his ship ahead with the intention of running between the *Alfred* and the British vessels to distract the enemy and give Hinman a chance to escape. Just as the *Raleigh* was bending sail, he said, the *Alfred* hauled down her colors after only a ten-minute cannonade. Alone and faced with what he thought was a superior British force, Thompson took to his heels. The pursuit went on all day and all night. At daybreak, the enemy vessels appeared to be gaining. In a frantic effort to lighten ship, Thompson emptied his water casks and ordered all spare gear thrown overboard. Slowly, the *Raleigh* began to draw away. After nineteen hours, the British gave up the chase and stood off to the south with the *Alfred* as their prize.

The Continental Navy's first flagship was taken and the *Raleigh* put to ignominious flight by the *Ariadne*, 20, and the *Ceres*, 16. The *Raleigh*, with 32 guns and the *Alfred* mounting 20, should have been more than a match for the British ships—if they had been well handled. While Thompson dithered and Hinman panicked, the British captains acted with the skill and assurance that had made the Royal Navy the ruler of the seas. Recognizing that the American ships were stronger than their own, they teamed up to take on the Yankees individually. Contemptuously ignoring Thompson's gyrations, they captured the *Alfred* and then turned on the *Raleigh.* Only the frigate's speed saved her. Considering the fact that the *Raleigh*, alone, had almost the same gun power as both British vessels combined, it was not too much to have expected that the *Ariadne* and the *Ceres* should have been bagged by the Americans. Replying to his critics, Thompson maintained that he was making sail to rescue the *Alfred* when Hinman unexpectedly surrendered his ship. Hinman on the other hand flatly claimed that Thompson had deserted him. But Hinman was not without fault. His decisions to make a run for it, depriving himself of the protection of the *Raleigh* and then quickly surrendering after perfunctory resistance while there was still a chance that the *Raleigh* might come to his rescue, showed poor judgment. Both men were doubtlessly good seamen but they lacked the qualities for command.

Putting into Boston harbor early in April, Thompson found that the story of the disaster had preceded him. He was widely censured for failing to support the *Alfred*. William Story, the Clerk of the Eastern Navy Board, informed William Vernon, one of the members, that Thompson "is Condemned by every One and they are Crying

out why don't your board turn him out and hang him &c &c." The
public outcry grew so loud that the Marine Committee ordered a
court of inquiry on "the disagreeable business of the *Alfred*'s loss."
Inasmuch as the inquiry could not be held until Hinman and his
officers—imprisoned in England—could be heard from, Thompson
was relieved from command of the *Raleigh*. She was turned over to
John Barry.

If the destruction of the *Randolph* was a tragedy, the loss of the
Virginia was low comedy. Repeatedly, the Marine Committee had
urged and cajoled Captain James Nicholson to get the 28-gun frigate
out of Chesapeake Bay where she had rested since her launching. As
far back as January 24, 1777, when Congress was sitting in Baltimore, John Hancock, after a personal inspection, notified Robert
Morris that the vessel was ready to sail. In April, the Marine Committee ordered its senior captain to take the *Virginia* to Martinique.
He didn't move. Nicholson seemed a better politician than a seaman.
To all appeals for action, he had the same reply: he was short of supplies, short of men, short of officers. In June, he ventured down the
Chesapeake as far as the York River, but was chased back and did
not move again until the end of the year. On November 6, an exasperated Marine Committee wrote him: "The Committee having
wearied of the long delay of the *Virginia* in port . . . you shall proceed to sea at the first favorable opportunity." Shortly after the start
of 1778, Nicholson finally left his anchorage in Baltimore and started
down the Bay once more. By January 20, news of the frigate's departure had reached the Committee which wrote its agents in Baltimore
"we rejoice to hear that Captain Nicholson is off your hands." Unfortunately, the Committee had spoken too soon. That same day, the
Virginia, having almost reached the Chesapeake Capes, was sighted
by the British frigate *Emerald*, 36, and chased all the way back to its
sanctuary in Baltimore. Sadly, the Marine Committee told Nicholson: "Sorry your late attempt to get to sea was unsuccessful. Try
again."

Nicholson was none too eager to accept the advice. For three
months, the frigate rocked at her anchorage while her captain frit-
tered and fussed. Not until the end of March did Nicholson make
another attempt to run the blockade. This time, the prospects for
success were excellent. Propelled by a stiff breeze, the *Virginia* sailed

quickly down the Bay led by a brig with an experienced pilot aboard. The plan called for the frigate to slip past the British vessels at the Capes under cover of darkness. It appeared as if she were going to make it. Salt sea air from beyond the mouth of the Bay was already blowing fresh and the lights of the patrolling British frigates were stationary, indicating that they had not spied the swift-moving Yankee vessel in the gloom. Shortly after midnight, Joshua Barney, the *Virginia*'s first lieutenant, went forward with a group of hands to await the whispered command from the quarterdeck to shake out the fore courses. Suddenly, there was a grinding jolt. Barney and his men were flung into the scuppers. The pilot had put the *Virginia* on a shoal at the mouth of the Chesapeake.

Driven along by the wind and tide, the frigate lurched over the shoals, each bump threatening to rip open her hull. Finally, she passed into deep water where it was discovered her rudder had been torn away. There was nothing to be done except anchor. When daylight broke several British ships stood nearby. The moment Nicholson saw them, according to Barney, he ordered his barge hoisted out. Without explanation, without waiting to secure his papers and private signals, the Captain had himself rowed ashore to safety, as his officers and men gaped in astonishment. The eighteen-year-old Barney was left in command. He immediately gave orders for the anchor cables to be cut, estimating that given the direction of the wind, the ship would be blown ashore on Cape Henry. There she could be set afire to prevent her from falling into enemy hands and the crew could make their escape. Unfortunately, the other officers refused to agree. They were afraid they would be blown out to sea in an unmanageable vessel. Overruling Barney, they waited for the British to send a boarding party. Seeing the collapse of authority among their officers and realizing they would soon be British prisoners, the crew broke into the spirit room and got reeling drunk. The *Virginia* was lost without ever having fired a shot at the enemy. It was "All Fools' Day," Barney noted bitterly.

The following day, Nicholson came out to one of the British ships which had taken the *Virginia* under a flag of truce to inquire about obtaining his personal possessions. At the sight of his former commander, Barney exploded. Long afterward, he wrote: "I could not help upbraiding him with his conduct in quitting the ship . . . when if he had remained on board there was not the least doubt but we should have run the ship ashore where she might have been destroyed." Probably his remarks at the time were somewhat more heated, but Nicholson ignored them. Gathering his effects together, he returned ashore and made haste to turn his desertion into meritorious conduct. After the disabled *Virginia* had been forced to anchor under the guns of the British ships, Nicholson told the Marine Committee that he had abandoned her with "such of my crew as was inclined to run the risque of getting on shore." Since those able to contradict this tale were in the hands of the British, the Committee swallowed his excuse. A few days later, the Navy Board of the Middle District was informed that "Captain Nicholson and nine of his Crew, who were all that chose to venture in the barge, escaped to the shore." An inquiry was held into the loss of the *Virginia*, but Nicholson escaped a court-martial. He was given a clean bill of health—and was free to lose another Continental ship on another day.

Amid the gloomy reports rolling in on the Marine Committee, there were a few bright rays of hope. The frigates *Warren* and *Providence*, cooped up in Narragansett Bay since their launching, and the *Boston*, idle in the port for which she had been named since Hector McNeill's dismissal in November 1777, all managed to escape the British cordon in the early months of 1778. The *Boston*, under the command of Captain Samuel Tucker, who had been the skipper of the schooners *Franklin* and *Hancock* in Washington's tiny navy, was the first to break out. She carried a prestigious cargo. Tucker was ordered to take John Adams, newly appointed as one of the American commissioners in Europe, to France. Adams, however, was not merely a passenger. In its orders to Tucker, the Eastern Navy Board instructed him to "consult" with Adams "on all occasions with respect to your passage and general conduct." The civilian would, in effect, give orders to the captain. Accompanying Adams were his ten-year-old son, John Quincy Adams, who had persuaded his father to let him come, and the sons of Silas Deane and William Vernon, a member of the Navy Board. They left a vivid account of the horrors of an eighteenth-century Atlantic crossing.

The frigate weighed anchor on February 15, but Tucker did not proceed upon his voyage immediately. Short of hands, he put into Marblehead, where he hoped to recruit more men. Adverse winds and heavy snow held the *Boston* there for several days. Adams thought the "excursion to this place was unfortunate" because a large part of the crew were natives of the area. "Mothers, Wives, Sisters came and begged leave for their Sons, husbands, and Brothers to go on Shore." Tucker was forced to refuse most of the requests, out of fear that his ship, already short of hands, might lose more.

Although Adams sized up Tucker as "an able seaman, and a brave active, vigilant officer," he noted that "all was yet chaos on board" the frigate. The crew "were not disciplined: even the Marines were not. The men were not exercised to the Guns. They hardly knew the ropes." By the time the *Boston* was four days out at sea, however, Adams had other worries. The ship was battered by a gale which raged for three days. "No man could stand upon his legs; nothing could be kept in its place; an universal Wreck of every thing in all parts of the Ship, Chests, casks, chairs, Bottles &c.," observed Adams. The hatches were battened down and the air below was stifling. "Such was the Agitation of the Vessel that instead of sleeping it was with the Utmost difficulty that my little Son and I could hold ourselves in bed with both hands, and bracing ourselves against the boards, planks and timbers with our feet."

While the ship was rolling and pitching from the onslaught of the storm, "all of a sudden, We heard a tremendous Report." Adams was uncertain whether a British ship had overtaken them or the frigate's own guns had been discharged. "An Officer came down to Us and told Us that the Ship had been struck with lightening and the Noise we had heard, was a Crash of Thunder." The mainmast had been damaged and four men hurt, one of them dying within a few days. "In the midst of this terror and confusion I heard a Cry that the Powder room was open," Adams continued. "Cartridges, Powder horns, if not some small casks of Powder had been left rather carelessly in various parts of the Ship, near her guns. If a Spark of the lightening had touched any of these, the Consequences might have been disagreeable enough, but if it had reached the Powder room, it would have made an End of the Business . . . Sailors and Marines scampered away with their Lanthorns in such a hurry, that I apprehended more danger to the Powder room from their candles than from the Lightening." Before further damage was done, one of the ship's officers coolly took charge. He ordered the men to put down their lanterns while he went below to secure the magazine.

The storm finally abated, and in fair weather the *Boston* flew

along at nine knots, covering about two hundred miles in one
twenty-four-hour period. Soon Adams was complaining about the
boredom of an ocean voyage:

> The Life I lead is a dull Scene to me—No Business; no Pleasure; no
> Study. Our Little World was all wet and damp. There is nothing I can
> eat or drink without nauseating. We have no Spirits for Conversation,
> nor anything about which to converse. We see nothing but Sky, Clouds
> and Sea, and then Seas, Clouds and Sky. . . . There was I found, on
> board the Navy, the same general Inattention to Economy, that there
> was in the Army. There was the same general relaxation of order and
> discipline. There was the same inattention to the Sweetness of the Ship,
> and the Persons and Health of the Sailors, as there was at land of the
> Neatness of the Camp, and the health and cleanliness of the Soldiers.

Adams was not the least hesitant in exercising his official
prerogative, bombarding Tucker with suggestions for better management of the ship.

> I was constantly giving hints to the Captain concerning Order, Econ-
> omy and regularity. He seemed to be sensible to the necessity of them,
> and exerted himself to introduce them. He cleared out the Tween
> decks, ordered up the Hammocks to be aired . . . That Ship would
> have bred the Plague or the Gaol Fever, if there had not been great ex-
> ertions after the Storm to wash, sweep, Air, and purify Cloaths, Cotts,
> Cabins, Hammocks, and all other things, places and Persons. . . .

On March 10, the monotony of the voyage was broken when the
Boston sighted a 14-gun British letter of marque, the *Martha*. The
enemy vessel opened fire, cutting up the frigate's rigging, but her
captain had second thoughts when he saw the Yankee vessel's guns
run out. "Our sailors were all in a rage to sink her for daring to fire,"
Adams reported. "But Captain Tucker very promptly and prudently
ordered his Officers not to fire, for he wanted the Egg, without
breaking the Shell." The *Martha* proved to be a rich catch. Her
captain said her cargo of provisions and stores was insured by
Lloyd's for 72,000 pounds and was actually worth 10,000 pounds
more. A prize crew was placed aboard her, and she was sent off to
Boston.

The closing days of the voyage were marred by an unfortunate
accident. A French brig was sighted and Tucker ordered a signal gun
fired to bring her to. The cannon burst, shattering the right leg of

William Barron, the *Boston*'s first lieutenant. He was taken below where the surgeon amputated the leg. "I was present at this afflicting scene," said Adams, "and together with Captain Tucker, held Mr. Barron in our arms, while the Doctor put on a Turnequett and cutt off the Limb. Mr. Barron bore it with fortitude," but he died several days later. The officer was buried at sea in a chest weighted down with fragments of the gun that had caused his death. On March 30, 1778, six weeks after the *Boston* had weighed anchor, John Adams's turbulent taste of life at sea came to an end. The frigate slipped into the Gironde River and dropped anchor just below Bordeaux. Elated by news of the French alliance, Adams quickly gathered up his young charges and set off for Paris.

Early in March, Captain John B. Hopkins of the *Warren* took advantage of favorable weather conditions to elude the British cruisers which had kept his vessel bottled up in the Providence River. The night was "Exceeding Dark, and there was but little wind untill the Critecal time of Passing the Greatest Danger," the Eastern Navy Board was informed. Just as the frigate neared the British blockading squadron, the wind turned brisk, pushing the *Warren* out to sea. But she did not escape unscathed. During the chase, several shot passed through her hull, and some of her yards were carried away or damaged. The weather was still extremely severe and many of the *Warren*'s crew lacked warm clothes, so Hopkins decided to disregard his orders to go to New London and, instead, made a short cruise to the south. Two prizes were taken off Bermuda before the frigate headed homeward. She put into Boston on March 23—and remained there for the rest of the year as Hopkins vainly tried to round up a crew.

The frigate *Providence* ran the blockade of Narragansett Bay on the night of April 30. To end her long confinement in the waters in which she had been launched, the Eastern Navy Board had authorized the payment of a bounty of $90 to able seamen and $50 to ordinary seamen. It was hoped that these sums would attract enough men to get the vessel off to France to load cannon for several ships under construction. When about one hundred seventy men had signed on, Abraham Whipple resolved to wait no longer and weigh anchor with the first good wind. The night the *Providence* sailed was dark and the wind brisk. Nevertheless, she was detected by the British frigate *Lark*, which had been lying in wait for her. A bruising battle resulted. Whipple claimed to have badly cut up the enemy vessel and to have run the gauntlet of at least eleven British warships. Although the *Providence* had been severely handled, Whipple made repairs at sea and set a course for Nantes, where he arrived in twenty-six days to join the *Ranger* and *Boston*.

Shortly before the *Providence* escaped from "pergatory," the *Columbus* had also tried to get out. As there had been little prospect for success, her guns and stores had been unloaded and carried overland to New London. If the British captured her, they would get possession of nothing more than an old hulk. Hoystead Hacker, her skipper, chose the dark and windy night of March 27 to make his dash for freedom. That same evening, however, a merchant brig chose to try to run the blockade. She was discovered and the cruisers stumbled onto the *Columbus*. Unable to get away, Hacker beached her near Point Judith. She was stripped of everything of value and abandoned to be burned by a British landing party.

There was more to come. A month later—on April 24—Captain John Young, on the way home from France in the brig *Independence*, lost her on Ocracoke Bar off the North Carolina coast. Details are lacking, but the evidence indicates that the *Independence* was run aground by her pilot and battered to pieces. This latest in the seemingly unbroken series of disasters created a feeling of desperation about the Continental Navy. "Our Naval affairs have been conducted shockingly," said Colonel Timothy Pickering, the army's adjutant general. "From all that I can learn the conduct of the . . . commanders of our frigates has been generally shamefully bad." Few persons disagreed with his assessment.

XIX

Revolution Becomes World War

War between Britain and France did not erupt immediately upon the signing of the treaties of alliance and commerce between the French court and the upstart United States. For the moment the treaties were kept secret from the British, although the active British intelligence network in France had more than an inkling of what was going on. Not until March 13, 1778, did the French ambassador in London formally communicate the news of the signing to the British government with the remark that "the United States were in full possession of the independence proclaimed by their declaration of July 4th, 1776." That same night, Lord Stormont, weary of the long diplomatic duel in Paris, was recalled from his post. But war was not formally declared. Several months were to pass before the fighting actually began. Lord North fervently hoped that a conciliatory mission headed by the Earl of Carlisle that was being sent to America might persuade Congress against ratifying the treaties with France.[1] At the

---

[1] The Carlisle mission was empowered to negotiate with Congress and suspend, if necessary, all acts passed since 1763 considered offensive by the Americans. The commissioners were named on February 22, 1778, and were in America from June 6 to November 27. Their mission was a failure but if such concessions had been offered earlier they might have been accepted.

same time, the French were anxious to do nothing to endanger their defensive alliances with other European nations by appearing as the aggressor. So France and Britain waited with matches lighted for the other side to fire the first shot.

The entry of France into the war completely altered the entire nature of the Revolution. What had begun as a British attempt to suppress a colonial rebellion was transformed into a world war. During the first three years of the struggle, Britain's easy and absolute command of the sea had not been seriously challenged. Although the Continental Navy's handful of ships and the swarms of privateers had compelled the adoption of a convoy and escort system, most troop transports and supply vessels actually reached their destinations safely. This happy state of affairs was at an end. Britain now had to fight not only in North America, but would have to commit additional troops and ships to other theaters of operation—most notably in home waters and in the West Indies. The dangers of the naval war in American waters were also vastly increased. French ships unlike their American counterparts could completely isolate an army that relied on a 3,000-mile-long sea line of communications for reinforcements and supplies. So if the Royal Navy lost command of the coastal waters, British army garrisons could be destroyed—as eventually happened at Yorktown. British success, both on land and at sea, now depended on maintaining British superiority at sea.

But if the British had employed the same strategy that had served them so well in their previous wars with France, they would not have been threatened with the loss of command of the sea, in the opinion of William B. Willcox, a leading analyst.[2] During the Seven Years' War, Britain had blockaded French harbors to prevent French ships from getting to sea, while she had subsidized her European allies to distract the French with a military campaign on the Continent. But the prerequisites for such a strategy were lacking in 1778. Prussia, Britain's traditional European ally was disgruntled; Austria had gone over to the French camp; Spain was allied with France in the Family Compact; and the Dutch still smarted from having their toes stepped upon by the Royal Navy during the Seven Years' War. Far from hammering together an anti-French coalition,

----

[2] "Why Did the British Lose the American Revolution?" *Michigan Alumnus Quarterly Revue*, LXII (August 1956).

Britain found herself without a friend in Europe. In contrast, France not only had no Continental enemy but could count upon at least the good will, if not the support, of the European powers. At the same time, the ministry decided not to impose a blockade of the French coast on the ground that not enough ships were available. This decision—described by Admiral Mahan as "unpardonable"—was among the most disastrous of any made in London during the entire war. Its effects reverberated around the globe from the Chesapeake to the Indian Ocean. "The most the Admiralty could do, once a French squadron was known to have sailed," says Willcox, "was to have it followed in equivalent strength to its probable destination." But what was equivalent strength? he asks. How could the probable destination be accurately forecast? So, for the remainder of the war, Britain's fleets and armies operated "under the Damoclean sword of enemy seapower."

Britain might have been spared some of the worst humiliations of the next few years if France had not made a spectacular recovery as a naval power after the Seven Years' War. For the first time in almost a century, the French Navy was able to challenge British superiority and actually to win command of the sea. Immediately after 1763, the Duc de Choiseul had sparked a renaissance of the navy. Under his guidance, and that of his successors, popular support for the navy was skillfully aroused, discipline was restored to the fleet, and a new building program begun. Supporters of the naval revival were fortunate in that King Louis XVI took a direct interest in maritime matters and made a special point of visiting the ports and inspecting his ships. Gabriel de Sartine, the Minister of Marine, knew next to nothing about the sea but had the intelligence to surround himself with able advisors. Sartine deliberately prepared for war. By 1778, France possessed some sixty ships of the line and by 1780, the number had grown to seventy-nine.

The French naval revival was accompanied by a similar resurgence of naval activity in Spain. Like France, she smarted from the arrogance of Britain and lusted for revenge. An energetic program of naval expansion was launched and by 1779 Spain possessed forty-nine ships of the line. By comparison, the Royal Navy had seventy-three ships of the line at sea or in good repair in 1778.

French ships were also markedly superior in quality to those of

the Royal Navy. The French treated ship design as an imaginative
art. During the latter part of the Eighteenth Century, they produced
men-of-war which were more beautifully proportioned, faster,
stronger, and with more powerful batteries than anything built in
Britain during the period. A French 80-gun ship was usually bigger,
more roomy, faster and finer in every way than a British 98-gun ship.
Captured French vessels were highly prized by the British. They
were usually taken into the Royal Navy. British ship designers
seemed to have learned nothing from the captured vessels and
British men-of-war were so badly designed and proportioned that it
was said they were built by the mile and cut off as required. Often
their hulls were pierced for more guns than they could fight, and in
heavy weather the lower gun ports could not be opened.

Together with a building program, the French had established a
systematic plan of training in naval science. The British still held advantage in practical seamanship, and their gunnery was faster and
more accurate, but they were inferior in equipment and technique.
The French were far more advanced in tactics and signaling, and
officers spent time in special "evolutionary" squadrons which had
been established to teach the art of fleet handling in combat. At the
French Académie de Marine young cadets were instructed in mathe-
matics, hydrography, astronomy, naval architecture and instrument
construction, while British midshipmen learned the rudiments of
their profession on the quarterdeck and in the cockpit. To ensure an
adequate supply of seamen for the expanding French navy, a system
of classes was established in which all seafarers were registered. Each
year, a separate class was liable for service in the navy if needed.
This system was far more efficient than Britain's haphazard reliance
on impressment and the sweepings of the jails and gutters. Yet the
French navy had one great failing—it lacked a tradition of victory.
French admirals and captains were accustomed to playing a
defensive role and a century of inferiority to the Royal Navy had left
an indelible mark on the French naval mind.

Long and violent debates took place in Parliament over the
state of the navy when it became evident that war with France was
inevitable. As a result of the political animosities involved, it is all
but impossible to determine the Royal Navy's actual degree of pre-
paredness with any accuracy. Even the dispatches of the admirals on

the subject must be read with caution because some of them were prone to attribute the results of their own shortcomings to the conditions of their ships. A certain political animus must also be taken into account. Nearly all the ranking naval officers owed their appointment and promotion to the previous Whig administrations. Many of them were opposed to the war with America. Some, including Admiral Augustus Keppel, who was given command of the Channel Fleet, had even refused to serve on active duty until France entered the conflict.

As the warning signs of French intervention multiplied, the Earl of Sandwich had repeatedly urged Lord North to put the Royal Navy in a state of readiness. With his extensive experience at the Admiralty, Sandwich knew it would take time to fit out ships and provide crews. However, Lord North resisted efforts to speed mobilization on grounds that it would cost too much and might alarm the French court.

When the crisis eventually came, the opposition launched a furious attack upon the government. The Earl of Chatham charged in the House of Lords that the nation was in a "truly perilous" state. There were only twenty ships of the line manned and ready for service at sea, he declared. Sandwich replied that the navy had fifty-four ships of the line in service in home waters or fit for duty. Of these, thirty-five vessels were completely manned and seven more "in great readiness." "Our navy is more than a match for the whole House of Bourbon," he told the Lords. But Sandwich could not resist adding a flourish that was to be neither forgotten nor forgiven: "I should, my lords, be extremely sorry . . . if I permitted at any time the French and Spanish navy united, to be superior to the navy of this country; I should indeed be wanting in the discharge of my duty." Fortunately for Britain, her worst fears were not immediately realized—an attack by the combined fleets of France and Spain—because Spain did not enter the war for another year. Nevertheless, Sandwich's boast was quickly proven an empty one. A more accurate assessment of the strength of the grand fleets, provided by Sandwich for Lord North, gave the French and Spaniards sixty-five ships of the line in commission in European waters. The French fleet, containing thirty-three of the line, was divided into two units—one at Brest commanded by the Comte d'Orvilliers consisting of twenty-one ships of the line and thirty-five frigates; the other, at Toulon in the Mediterranean, had

twelve of the line and thirteen frigates under the command of the
Comte d'Estaing. So much for Sandwich's boast that the Royal Navy
could outmatch the combined fleets of the House of Bourbon. An
angry Edmund Burke, dissatisfied with the limp explanations as to
where the money for the navy had gone, hurled the heavy book of
navy estimates at the Treasury Bench during one heated debate. It
knocked over a candle and struck a government spokesman lolling
in his seat.

The major reason for the delay in getting ships ready for sea was
the Ministry's refusal to order an early mobilization. Sandwich's
pleas to place more ships on a war-footing before France entered the
war had fallen on deaf ears. Now the price was being paid. When
Admiral Keppel went down to Portsmouth to take command of the
Channel Fleet, he found only "six ships fit to meet a seaman's
eyes." [3] "It is not your Lordship's fault that our fleet is not in more
forwardness," Vice Admiral Sir Hugh Palliser, one of the Lords of
the Admiralty, told Sandwich. "It was no reasoning of ours that we
should not equip long ago for fear of alarming France . . . Thus they
have got the start on us." The chief difficulty facing the Royal Navy
was the lack of trained seamen. Admirals and captains cried out for
men so they could get their newly commissioned ships to sea before
the French were out. But American sailors who usually took up the
slack between the navy's manpower needs and the home-grown
supply were no longer available.

Prime seamen were at a premium, so the gap was filled with the
products of the press gangs and the prisons. Inexperienced landsmen
may have made up as much as half the crews of some vessels—which
were quickly decimated by disease and desertion. From 1774 to
1780, reports Christopher Lloyd, 175,990 men were recruited into the
Royal Navy. Of these, 1,243 were killed or died of wounds, 18,541
died of disease and 42,069 deserted. In these cold statistics, he states,
lies the basic reason for Britain's failure at sea during the American
War. Sickness and disease had a crippling effect on operations—particularly in the Channel Fleet, which received the largest proportion
of the unseasoned recruits. Because of the ravages of disease,
Admiral Keppel said his fleet could not remain at sea for more than

---

[3] The Opposition's hatred and suspicion of Sandwich was so strong that the Duke of
Richmond warned Keppel not to trust him "for a piece of rope yarn."

six weeks at a time. Yet the remedy for scurvy, the worst killer, lay unused near at hand. As early as 1747, Dr. James Lind had linked scurvy to a vitamin deficiency and prescribed a daily ration of lime juice as an antiscorbutic. Nevertheless, it took the Admiralty another forty years to adopt his recommendation.

The division of French naval power between Brest and Toulon created a serious strategic problem for the British. Everyone knew that d'Estaing was preparing to put to sea from Toulon.[4] Would he make a dash to America to overwhelm Lord Howe's squadron? Would he join d'Orvilliers at Brest? Would he go to Cadiz as the first step in Spain's entry into the war? Gerald S. Brown, who has made a detailed analysis of the Anglo-French naval crisis of 1778, thinks the strategic problem could have been quickly resolved if the ministry had shown resolution and judgment.[5] All that had to be done to end the uncertainty about d'Estaing's intentions and destination, he suggests, was to send a strong naval force to destroy the French fleet before it passed through the Straits of Gibraltar. To allow d'Estaing to get out to the open sea increased the complexity of the problem because defensive steps would have to be taken in both home waters and on the American station until his intentions were clear. Brown acknowledges that the Channel Fleet would have been temporarily weakened to send ships to the Mediterranean, but since it was known that d'Orvilliers was unready for sea, the Brest fleet was as yet no threat to Britain's security.

Throughout April, 1778, Lord North's cabinet was bitterly divided—and paralyzed—over the means to meet the threat posed by d'Estaing. Germain wished to send a fleet to intercept the French before they came out into the Atlantic. Energetic action should be taken to chasten the enemy early in the war, he declared. Risks were involved in the Mediterranean enterprise, but they were "trifling." Sandwich, however, was against the plan. "There are not ships enough as yet in readiness," the First Lord declared. He was supported by Keppel, who flatly opposed any suggestion that would weaken the Channel Fleet. Brown surmises that the underlying

---

[4] Paul Jones had suggested the dispatch of a French fleet to America as early as February 10, 1778, with the intention of attacking Lord Howe's ships in the Delaware.

[5] *The American Secretary: The Colonial Policy of Lord George Germain 1775–1778* (Ann Arbor 1963).

reason for the conflict was the differing strategic viewpoints of those involved. While Sandwich and Keppel were primarily concerned with the defense of Britain, Germain, as American Secretary, was for vigorous prosecution of the war in the colonies. Oblivious to the Channel Fleet's role in global strategy, Sandwich and Keppel were quite willing "to put to hazard the fortunes of the war in America" to ensure the safety of the home islands. Events, however, were to prove Germain correct.

So during the opening weeks of the war, the cabinet debated what to do—and nothing was done. Not until April 29, when news arrived that d'Estaing had sailed from Toulon sixteen days before with twelve ships of the line, five frigates and 4,000 troops, did the cabinet take action. Germain warned: "The fate of the country evidently depends upon the preventing of the Toulon Squadron from acting with success against our Fleet and Army and our possessions in North America." Lord Howe's fleet, which had only five of the line and three 50-gun ships, was endangered. Halifax, Quebec and Philadelphia might fall to the enemy. The British army in America might be cut off. Under the prodding of the King, Lord North issued orders for a fleet of thirteen ships of the line commanded by Vice Admiral John Byron[6] to be immediately prepared for service in American waters. This force was to seek out d'Estaing either on the American coast or in the West Indies and destroy him. A fleet was put together by shifting some of the vessels intended for Keppel to Byron's command.

The period of indecision and irresolution was not at an end, however. Sandwich and Keppel were still adamant in their opposition to any weakening of the Channel Fleet. They argued there was no clear evidence that d'Estaing was in fact headed for America. Keppel raised the specter of a British fleet beaten in a major engagement in the Channel and the home islands open to invasion if his fleet were deprived of an adequate number of ships. Poor North. He could not have been in an easy situation, trapped between Germain and Sandwich. Keppel's views were apparently decisive. As Brown notes, it was no small thing to disregard the professional advice of the admiral commanding the Channel Fleet. On May 13,

---

[6] Byron was the poet's uncle.

orders were issued to hold up Byron until further word was received of d'Estaing's intentions.

Three weeks of tortured anxiety followed. Reports reached London that the French fleet had not passed Gibraltar but had put back into Toulon—that d'Estaing was heading for Brest—that he had anchored at Cadiz. Finally, definite word arrived on June 2. The frigate *Proserpine* sped into Falmouth with the alarming news that d'Estaing's fleet had been sighted in the Straits on May 16. From the fleet's course and the great press of sail, the frigate's captain reckoned it was bound for America. Byron was now ordered to put to sea "without one moment's" loss of time. Contrary winds held him back and he did not sail until June 9. D'Estaing had more than a three-week head start.

Byron was known as "Foul-Weather Jack." The name was apt. From the moment his fleet entered the Atlantic, it was battered by gales and scattered. Alone and in groups of two and three, Byron's ships limped into ports along the American coast over the next two months. Because of the shortage of masts and in the haste to get the ships off to reinforce Lord Howe before he was attacked by d'Estaing, Byron's vessels had sailed with old spars and second-hand rigging. The experiences of his thirteen ships provide the most striking example of the influence of the timber problem on eighteenth-century naval operations.[7] When the storms struck, masts, yards, bowsprits, and booms, deprived of their elasticity by age, cracked throughout the fleet. If the injuries were not serious enough to send the masts over the side, ship's carpenters "fished," or repaired, them by binding them with anchor stocks or any other wood available to shore up the injured portion. Often these repairs were inadequate, and the masts later crashed into the sea or onto the deck. Even when spars remained in place, they were sometimes so weak that the ships could run before the wind only with reduced sail.

"The mainmast was sprung close to the gundeck, so much that it was expected to go with every roll," reported the captain of the 74-gun ship *Invincible* during the voyage across the Atlantic. "We cut it away on the quarterdeck to prevent the upper deck from being

---

[7] Albion, *Forests and Sea Power.*

torn up. [No sooner was this done] than the foremast went in three pieces, all of which fell on the forecastle and wounded several men but only one was killed. The bowsprit being sprung sometime before and now so bad, we had to cut part of that away." Byron's flagship, the *Princess Royal*, 90, crawled into Halifax after a voyage of sixty-seven days with her foremast splintered just above the main deck. One of his 64s did not appear in American waters until October. She had been dismasted and driven into Lisbon where she had been refitted. Other vessels followed in a crippled state. Their crews were exhausted.

Luckily for the British, the French took an astonishingly slow eighty-five days to sail from Toulon to the Capes of the Delaware. "Speed is the foremost of military virtues," d'Estaing had once proclaimed. "To surprise is almost to have conquered." He honored his own precept in the breach. Critics blamed the long voyage on the French admiral's insistence on putting his fleet through tactical drills during the passage. He claimed it was caused by the extreme slowness of some of his vessels and the necessity of keeping the fleet together. D'Estaing had begun his career as a soldier and did not switch to the navy until he was thirty years old. His rapid rise to the rank of Vice Admiral at the age of forty-nine had made him the object of jealousy among naval officers and this may have been part of the problem.[8] Whatever the reason, he missed a once-in-a-lifetime opportunity to bottle up Howe's fleet in the Delaware, where he could have destroyed it.

The failure of the French fleet to arrive quickly in American waters gave Lord Howe and Sir Henry Clinton, who had succeeded Sir William Howe as over-all military commander, time to meet the new threat. Philadelphia, as George Washington observed on learning of the French alliance, had become "an ineligible situation" for the British army in America. There was an inherent weakness in the division of the army between New York and Philadelphia with the sea the only link between them, especially now that this line of communication was no longer safe from attack by the French fleet. Clinton had been in the city only one day when on May 8 dispatches from

---

[8] D'Estaing had been captured by the British in India during the Seven Years' War and was accused of breaking his parole when released. The British commander, Admiral Edward Boscawen, threatened if he ever caught the Frenchman again, he would "chain him upon the quarterdeck and treat him like a baboon."

London informed him of France's official support of the rebels. He was instructed to evacuate Philadelphia, to detach an expeditionary force of five thousand troops for the capture of St. Lucia in the West Indies, and to send another three thousand men to Florida. The withdrawal from Philadelphia was a wise move. The capture of St. Lucia also made strategic sense as the Royal Navy was in need of a base close to Martinique. The Florida expedition, however, was another useless pursuit of the will-o'-the-wisp of Loyalist support that so hypnotized the British government.

Aware that a French fleet was probably on the way to American waters, Clinton decided to delay the departure of the southern expeditions until his own movement to New York was complete. It was impossible to furnish naval support for all the operations at once so the others would just have to wait. Fearing Washington might make a quick dash for New York before the British could arrive there if they went by sea, Sir Henry determined to quick-march his army overland to the Hudson through ninety miles of rebel-held country. Supplies and artillery were to be brought along by Lord Howe's ships. On June 18, the transports left the Philadelphia quays, and Clinton abandoned the city for which Sir William Howe had sacrificed Burgoyne the previous year. The long and vulnerable British column strung out over the back roads of New Jersey gave Washington an opportunity for which he had long prayed. With a force greater than Clinton's, he marched from Valley Forge and fell upon the British at Monmouth. Clinton took personal command as the disciplined Redcoats made good their retreat despite American attacks and suffocating heat. Meanwhile, frequent groundings, head winds, and calms had delayed the departure of Howe's ships; they did not get out into the open sea until June 28. Ten days later, d'Estaing's fleet arrived at the mouth of the Delaware.

The British had the narrowest of escapes. If Clinton had adhered to his orders and waited to send off the southern expeditions before leaving Philadelphia, his troops and ships would have been trapped between the anvil of the French fleet and the hammer of the American army—just as Cornwallis was to be caught at Yorktown. Had d'Estaing made "a passage of even ordinary length . . . Lord Howe with the British ships of war and all the transports in river Delaware must inevitably have fallen," observed Washington. "Sir Henry Clinton must have had better luck than is commonly dispensed . . . if he and his troops had not shared at least the fate of Burgoyne."

A fair wind carried Howe's vessels along the Jersey coast to New York, where the admiral planned to resign his command as soon as he had dispatched the expeditions to St. Lucia and Florida. These plans were quickly altered by the necessity of protecting his fleet from d'Estaing. Just before Howe's vessels dropped anchor off Sandy Hook on June 30, a packet arrived from England with news of the sailing of the Toulon fleet and the dispatch of reinforcements under Byron. To provide an early warning of the arrival of the enemy, Howe threw out a line of frigates to watch for the French fleet. He had no sooner begun his preparations when his cruisers announced d'Estaing's approach. On July 5, the French were sighted off the Virginia coast. Three days later they were at the mouth of the Delaware. On July 11, the sloop *Zebra* reported that twelve ships of the line and three frigates flying French colors were just outside the bar at Sandy Hook.

Black Dick Howe prepared as best he could for what promised to be a fight against hopeless odds. The men-of-war were short-handed so he called for volunteers from the transports. So many seamen came forward that there were barely enough hands left on these vessels to keep watch. The officers of the merchantmen in the harbor also offered their services; many of them took humble stations at the guns. In the time left to him, Lord Howe shrewdly assessed the strengths of his position. As the British had good reason to know, the shallow bar at Sandy Hook was hazardous to ships of the line. Several large vessels had struck on it during the course of the war. Under the best of circumstances, d'Estaing would not find it an easy task to feel his way into the harbor. Howe determined that if the Frenchman tried, he would have to do it under the concentrated fire of the British fleet.

The British commander stationed an advanced group consisting of one ship of the line and two frigates to harry the enemy as they sounded their way across the bar. Six ships of the line and a large storeship manned by volunteers and armed with artillery borrowed from the army were lined up inside the bar with their guns commanding the harbor entrance. Springs were placed on the anchor cables of the British ships so they could swing their broadsides to rake the French fleet as it passed over the bar. Clinton was equally active, erecting a battery near the tip of Sandy Hook and posting four regiments to guard against any attempt to land enemy troops. But no matter what Howe did to improve his position, d'Estaing had a marked superiority in firepower. One 90-gun ship, an 80, six 74s, three 64s, one 54, and five frigates were more than a match for six 64s, ten frigates, and an assortment of smaller craft.

For eleven days, the two fleets eyed each other across the bar. While awaiting a favorable wind and tide to carry him into the harbor, d'Estaing provisioned his ships from the shore and communicated with Washington, who enthusiastically welcomed the arrival of the French fleet. For the first time the British would be forced, as he had been for so long, to submit to the dictates of seapower. He sent Colonel John Laurens, a French-speaking aide, to the admiral with the promise of full cooperation in an attack upon New York. He also sent several experienced pilots to bring the French ships across the shoals.

Early on the morning of July 22, the French finally weighed anchor. Borne along by a flood tide and with a strong following wind at their back, they made for the bar. At the first sign that the French fleet was bending sail, Lord Howe ordered his men to their battle stations. Marine drummers thumped out "Hearts of Oak," and the decks of the British ships rumbled as the guns were loaded and run out. Anxiously, the sailors waited for their cannon to bear on the powerful enemy ships. "We . . . expected the hottest day that had ever been fought between the two nations," said one British seaman. "On our side all was at stake." The range shortened as the French bore in. Suddenly, they turned away and stood out to the open sea. The British gaped in surprise.

The American pilots were said to have flatly refused to take the French fleet across the bar. They warned d'Estaing that it was too treacherous for such heavy ships to try to cross the shoal because there was but twenty-two feet of water there. Only a perfunctory attempt was made to check out the accuracy of their statements. An officer was sent in a small boat to make a sounding, and when he, too, reported shoal water, the French fleet turned away. Yet the British reported that on July 22 a combination of a flood tide and a brisk northeast wind actually provided a depth of thirty feet at the bar. Howe's preparations for a stout defense also make it clear that he did not depend on shoal waters for protection. It appears likely that d'Estaing's reliance on the word of the pilots was a subterfuge for his own wavering doubts about the desirability of an attack in the light of France's uncertain naval policy. Mahan states that the Admiral "probably reasoned that the French had nothing to gain by the fall of New York, which might have led to peace between America and England, and left the latter free to turn all her power against his own country." The uncertainties of French naval policy were underscored by the orders King Louis XVI had given his admirals at the outbreak of the war. They were to "attack with the greatest vigor and defend themselves on all occasions, to the last extremity." Before a single ship had left port, however, these bold words were qualified with secret instructions imposing caution. But no matter what the reason for d'Estaing's failure, he had lost for the second time a splendid opportunity to annihilate the British fleet.

XX

Sea Fight—Classic Style

With the unruffled majesty of swans, the Channel Fleet of twenty-one ships of the line, three frigates and a pair of armed cutters put to sea for the first time on June 13, 1778. Byron had sailed a few days before on his tempestuous Atlantic voyage. War had not yet formally been declared, but Keppel, flying his flag in the newly commissioned *Victory*, of 100 guns, had secret instructions to prevent a junction of the Toulon and Brest fleets. Any French frigates that tried to shadow him were to be seized. If the French squadrons managed to join together, he was to attack the combined fleet if it was not overwhelmingly superior to his own force. While Keppel had expressed satisfaction with these very explicit instructions, his task was difficult. Not only were many of his ships undermanned and in poor repair, but their crews contained a high proportion of raw landsmen. In addition, his officers were unaccustomed to working together. Yet the future of Britain floated with Keppel's ships. If they were crippled or destroyed, control of the Channel would pass to the battle fleets of France and Spain. Not enough ships remained in reserve to form another British fleet—even if the time and materials were available for fitting it out.

Keppel's fleet worked its way down the Channel and was to the west of the Lizard on June 17 when a French squadron composed of the frigates *Belle Poule*, 30, and *Licorne*, 32, the 16-gun corvette *Hirondelle* and the lugger *Coureur*, 10, was sighted. Keppel had no wish to start a war, but he was concerned that information regarding his armada should not reach France. He ordered two frigates, the *Milford*, 28, and the *Arethusa*, 32, to intercept the French vessels and bring them into the fleet so he could speak with their captains. The French, however, crowded on sail and Keppel signaled a chase. Topmen scrambled aloft to shake out top gallants and royals. A little after six in the evening the *Arethusa* overhauled the *Belle Poule* and fired a shot across her bow with a demand that she heave-to. The French captain replied that he did not understand English. The order was repeated in French. By whose command was this order given, asked the Frenchman. When informed it came from Admiral Keppel, the French skipper said he didn't understand the order in any language and let fly with a broadside.[1] Soon the two frigates were engaged in a furious action that lasted into the night. After nearly four hours of intense firing, the magazines of both ships were about depleted. The British vessel's spars and sails were severely damaged while the *Belle Poule*'s hull was riddled with shot. The French frigate took shelter in a small bay on the Brittany coast. When the *Arethusa* attempted to follow, her shattered mainmast went by the board. Meanwhile, the *Licorne* and *Coureur* had been quickly taken and brought into the British fleet.

From captured documents, Keppel learned that the Brest fleet consisted of twenty-seven ships of the line ready for sea. Six more were fitting out.[2] Keppel decided it was his duty to avoid a fight until he had been reinforced. Turning homeward, the British fleet anchored off Spithead on June 27. The French regarded the *Belle Poule* affair as the long-awaited opening gun of the war. The frigate's crew were treated as heroes. They were feted and given medals and promotions. When King Louis formally declared war upon Britain on July 10, he fixed the time of the war's beginning as the date of the frigate action.

In Britain, frantic efforts were made to scrape together more

---

[1] The French claimed the British fired first.

[2] The French ships also carried orders from the Ministry of Marine that "Captain Cook, the useful navigator, was on no account to be molested."

ships, men and stores for Keppel. The timely arrival of the West India convoy enabled the crews to be impressed into the King's service without being allowed to set foot on shore. When the *Victory* led the fleet to sea again on July 9, there were twenty-four ships of the line flying Keppel's flag. Two days later, six more joined, bringing the Channel Fleet to thirty ships of the line. It was organized into three divisions. Vice Admiral Sir Robert Harland in the *Queen*, 90, commanded the van, Keppel the center. The rear was commanded by Vice Admiral Sir Hugh Palliser in the *Formidable*, 90. The presence of Palliser was unusual because he was still a member of the Admiralty Board. While he and Keppel had been friends in former years—Palliser had in fact been partially responsible for Keppel being named to command the fleet despite his links with the Opposition—political differences had grown between them. Keppel suspected that Palliser was a spy for Sandwich.

The Brest fleet had put to sea the day before under the command of the sixty-eight-year-old Comte d'Orvilliers, a seaman of considerable experience. It consisted of thirty-two ships of the line, but three of them—a 64, a 60 and a 50—were not considered in good enough shape to lie in the battle line. So the real strength of the French line was twenty-nine, including a 50-gun ship. D'Orvilliers was hampered by vacillating instructions. He was ordered to cruise for a month but with no special purpose. He was *not* to seek out the British fleet, and he was *not* to fight except under very favorable circumstances. Although d'Orvilliers's orders restricted him to the defensive, he found no lack of fighting spirit among his officers. Just before sailing, he reported that they had requested him to seek permission to "attack Admiral Keppel even in his anchorage if he does not put to sea."

It is worthwhile to take a brief look at the strategic conditions under which sea battles were fought during this period. To prevent ships of the same fleet from getting in each other's way, from blanketing the fire of their consorts, or, worse still, firing into them by mistake during the confusion of battle, the practice was to bring ships into action in line ahead. The vessels of a fleet trailed their leader in a single column, following the flagship's movements and signals. Each ship in the line was to place itself abeam of its opposite number in the enemy line—ships in the van against the enemy's van, the center against his center and the rear against his rear. So sacred had the line become that Paul Jones noted that a French fleet failed to attack a large British convoy because d'Orvilliers "would not break his line to give chase." Signals were primitive, often obscured by the smoke of battle, while the various vessels in a fleet had different sailing qualities. Some lagged behind while others shot ahead. Because of the difficulty of maintaining control of the fleet once an action had begun, admirals began to issue written fighting instructions before a battle for the guidance of their captains. Over the years, however, these instructions became encrusted with tradition. By the time of the American War, the Royal Navy's Permanent Fighting Instructions had become not an aid in fighting a battle, but an end in themselves. They pressed down on commanders with a dead hand, inhibiting originality and making a decisive encounter all but impossible. An admiral who followed the Fighting Instructions could not lose a battle, it was said. But neither could he win it.

Late on the foggy afternoon of July 23, Keppel sighted the French fleet about sixty-six miles from the island of Ushant just off the coast of Brittany. At once he formed a line of battle, and for the first of many times the *Victory* cleared for action. As the French were to the leeward of the British fleet, Keppel, anticipating a battle in the morning, took in sail "as action in the night is always to be avoided." D'Orvilliers used the darkness and Keppel's immobility to move his fleet around to the windward of the British. Daylight found him with the weather gage—the position closest to the wind—and the ability to force or refuse a battle that this position conferred. Wind and tide were of immense importance to the great fleets in the age of fighting sail, and the weather gage was an important tactical advantage to an aggressor. In the preliminary jockeying for position before a battle, an admiral bent on attacking an enemy tried to gain the advantage of the wind, or the weather gage. This meant he could steer straight for the enemy while the latter would have to tack against the wind. By gaining the weather gage, the aggressor gained considerable freedom of action. He could keep his distance or he could bore in quickly. An adversary in the leeward position could only claw his way slowly to the windward to make an attack and force a fight. When firing began, dense smoke from the exchange of broadsides rolled down on the leeward vessels, hiding their signals, complicating their maneuvers, and forcing them to aim their guns blindly. And if a stiff wind were blowing, the hulls of the leeward vessels heeled over, exposing their vulnerable undersides to enemy fire.

The French, following their orders, showed no inclination to engage. The position of the fleets was a reversal of their usual tactical dispositions. British admirals, in keeping with the Fighting Instructions and their traditions, sought the weather gage in order to bring about a decisive battle. The French, on the other hand, were usually committed to a defensive strategy based on avoiding a decisive struggle. By accepting the lee position they could stand off and rake the leading British ships as they bore down to attack in a formal line. And they could break off the engagement when desired. With this strategy in mind, French gunners were trained to fire on the upward roll with the object of crippling the rigging and sails of enemy ships so they would be unable to give chase. Nevertheless, Keppel was not entirely dissatisfied with his position. The movements of his opponent had placed the Channel Fleet between the French ships and their base at Brest. Two of the French vessels which had become separated from their fleet during the night were spotted by the British. Keppel sent ships to chase them, hoping to force d'Orvilliers to run downwind to their assistance, which would bring about a general action. The French admiral, however, was wary. He left the laggards to make good an escape on their own. This decision reduced the French line of battle to twenty-seven ships as compared to thirty for the British.

For the next three days, the fleets remained in sight of each other, with Keppel vigorously maneuvering to overcome the disadvantage of the lee position and attempting to force the French into battle. The morning of July 27 found the fleets about six miles apart. During the prolonged maneuvers, the British had lost formation because Keppel in his eagerness to engage the enemy had signaled a "General Chase." This meant that every ship was to do its best to catch up with the French instead of adhering to the formalized line as embodied in the Fighting Instructions. The British ships were scattered over ten miles of sea with Palliser's division furthest off. Keppel signaled for the ships to close up as the wind showed signs of turning favorable. Suspecting that this signal was the prelude to an attack on his rear, d'Orvilliers took advantage of a short squall which hid his ships and turned his fleet about into its own wake so as to put it on a parallel but opposite tack from the British. The aim of this maneuver was to bring about a "passing engagement" while the British fleet was still divided. Such an action with the two fleets firing as they moved past each other was rarely decisive, but in this instance, d'Orvilliers hoped to take advantage of the disorder in the British fleet to mass his fire on a few of the enemy ships while the rest were out of range. Keppel, readily perceiving the French admiral's intentions, had the option of falling off to reform his line in keeping with the Fighting Instructions. Without hesitation he rejected this alternative. Keppel realized if he opted for the conservative alternative he might lose the possibility of any engagement because the French might escape before the British could form a line and bring their fleet into action. So he decided to take the risk of forcing battle while his line was disarranged. "It was not the time for a drillmaster, nor a parade," says Mahan.

The three leading French ships passed the head of the British line well out of gunshot. Keppel barely had time to hoist the signal to engage before the *Victory* was firing into the fourth ship in the enemy line. It had all happened so suddenly that the battle was joined before either side had time to break out their national colors. Both fleets reduced sail. The ships slowly passed each other, wallowing so deeply in the heavy sea that the lower gun ports were awash on some of the vessels. The strong wind drove acrid banks of smoke down on Keppel's line, blinding the British gunners. In the choking darkness, some ships had to withhold their fire because they were unable to distinguish between friend and foe. Following their usual tactics, the French fired high to disable masts and spars, while the British fired on the downward roll, aiming at the enemy hulls and the men behind the guns. At one point during the three hours of action, d'Orvilliers's flagship, the *Bretagne*, of 110 guns, loomed out of the smoke and fought a sharp ship-to-ship duel with the *Victory*. The British flagship was badly cut up aloft and the *Bretagne* was hulled several times. One of the *Victory*'s broadsides chopped three gun ports into a single yawning chasm in her side. Then the vessels slowly drew apart upon their opposite courses, engaging the next ship in the opposing line. The British rear division was the most fiercely engaged. Palliser's own ship, the *Formidable*, wracked by an internal explosion, suffered the heaviest casualties in the Channel Fleet.

About 1 P.M., both the British van and center had passed clear of the French line and Keppel decided to put about, or reverse direction, and renew the action. But the severe damage to the rigging of the British ships prevented many of them from getting into station for some time. Four or five ships were so badly battered that they were unable to make headway. They simply drifted to the southward, away from the action. Spotting the cripples, d'Orvilliers turned the head of his fleet toward these vessels, hoping to cut them off. But one of his division commanders, the Duc de Chartres, either did not see the signal or chose not to obey it immediately. By the time the order was executed, the favorable moment had passed. As soon as Keppel saw what the French were up to he turned his fleet to the southward to protect the damaged ships. At 2 P.M. the *Victory* replaced the red battle flag with a signal to form a line of battle upon her. Harland, in the van, obeyed immediately and formed up at the head of the new line. But Palliser's heavily damaged ship did not come up in the rear. To make matters worse, it was the practice of the time for the ships of each division to conform to the movements of their own flagship. Instead of forming up astern of the *Victory*, Palliser's ships clustered about the crippled *Formidable*.

The two opposing fleets were once again converging. But Keppel found himself deprived of a large part of his force. Angrily, he made signals and then sent a frigate to Palliser with urgent orders for him to come up. Finally, he signaled each individual ship in Palliser's division to join the *Victory*. For some unexplained reason, he took four hours to resort to that particular signal. Darkness was falling when the rear ships filled their sails, and it was too late to renew the battle. Throughout the night, Keppel kept his men at quarters, for the French had given the impression that they were determined to fight a decisive battle the next day. During the night the British watched three widely spaced lights which they took to be the French flagships marking their positions for their squadrons. Dawn brought a surprise. Only three fast-disappearing French ships were still in sight—those which had shown the lights. D'Orvilliers had sailed off to Brest in the darkness. The remaining trio were already too far off to be overtaken.

Both sides claimed the victory in a battle neither had won. British casualties were 133 killed and 375 wounded, while the French lost 163 killed and 573 wounded. Neither side lost a ship, but there was a marked contrast in the state of the fleets at the end of the four days of maneuvering and cannonading. D'Orvilliers was still able to maneuver his ships while a number of Keppel's vessels were incapable of taking their places in the battle line. Moreover, the French enjoyed the unusual experience of bringing home all their ships after an encounter with the Royal Navy—no small success to veterans of the Seven Years' War. The French admiral, however, had shown a remarkable lack of offensive spirit. On the other hand, Keppel was handicapped in his efforts to attack by a hastily assembled fleet that had never worked together.

The indecisive battle off Ushant raged on in politics long after the two fleets had separated. Only a few days after the British ships returned to Plymouth for repairs, an article appeared in the *Morning Intelligencer*, an Opposition newspaper, alleging that it was solely Palliser's fault that a solid victory had not been achieved. Keppel was asked by Palliser to make a statement refuting the charge and refused. Charges and countercharges followed in the highly partisan press and in Parliament. Using his influence as a member of the Admiralty Board, Palliser demanded that Keppel be court-martialed on two contradictory charges: (1) that he had engaged the French without waiting to order his line as stipulated in the Fighting Instructions, and (2) that by halting to reform his line in the afternoon he had failed to "do his utmost" to resume the battle.[3] Passions were so aroused that the *Formidable* was kept at Spithead instead of being sent along to Portsmouth where the *Victory* was anchored because the Admiralty feared "the fatal consequences" should the crews of the two ships meet in the streets. The court-martial, held in Portsmouth, was a political carnival. Keppel's friends and followers, including a great many Opposition members of Parliament, crowded into the courtroom. The case dragged on for five weeks amid scenes of frenzied excitement. All other news was driven out of the newspapers. In the end, Keppel was acquitted, setting off wild anti-government demonstrations. He was carried through the streets of Portsmouth by a crowd singing "See the Conquering Hero Comes." Pandemonium broke loose when word of the verdict was received in London. "The sentence arrived at half an hour after nine," reported Horace Walpole, "and two hours later the whole town was illuminated." Palliser's house in Pall Mall was sacked by a mob and his effigy burned on Tower Hill. The admiral probably

---

[3] Admiral John Byng had been convicted of this second charge in 1757 and executed. As a captain, Keppel had sat on his court-martial. Voltaire commented that Byng had been shot in order "to encourage the others."

escaped with his life only because he had gone into hiding. The front gate of the Admiralty was torn off its hinges, and windows of Lord North's home were broken.

Now it was Palliser's turn to insist on a court of inquiry to clear his name. Although his conduct at Ushant was described as exemplary, the court observed that he had erred by not quickly informing Keppel that the *Formidable* was too seriously damaged to rejoin the line and by failing to promptly send the ships of his squadron to the Admiral. With the Whig Opposition searching for a Tory scapegoat to blame for Keppel's inability to win a decisive victory, Palliser's career was finished. At the same time, Keppel declared that he would not go to sea as long as Sandwich headed the Admiralty. Several other admirals supported him by declining to take command of the Channel Fleet when it was offered them. So the Royal Navy was forced to rely in time of peril upon a succession of elderly, worn-out commanders who were appointed for political rather than for professional reasons. Thus the nation was the loser because of the political affiliations and interests of its admirals.[4] The Keppel-Palliser Affair had one beneficial result, however. Keppel's acquittal was a clear sign that rigid and slavish conformity to the Fighting Instructions was no longer absolutely demanded. An admiral could now hope to conduct a battle according to his own best judgment and to the circumstances in which he found himself. The way was open to the free-wheeling tactics of the Nelsonian era.

After New York had been saved by a combination of Black Dick Howe's energy and d'Estaing's caution, the scene of action in American waters shifted to Rhode Island. While his fleet was hesitating off New York, d'Estaing and Washington had worked out a plan for a joint land-sea attack on the British garrison that had occupied Newport since the end of 1776. As early as July 17, Washington instructed General John Sullivan, who was then at Providence with 1,000 Continental troops, to recruit an additional 5,000 militiamen and to prepare for a descent upon Newport in company with the French fleet and the 4,000 soldiers aboard it. Nathanael Greene and Lafayette were also sent to Providence with two of the best brigades in the army—making a total of 10,000 men available to Sullivan. The

---

[4] The officers of the navy divided into two factions—jokingly referred to as the Montagus (since Montagu was Sandwich's surname) and the Capulets (or Keppelites).

part of Rhode Island occupied by the British was the island cut off
from the mainland by the Seaconnet Passage on the east, the Middle
or Narragansett Passage on the west, and a narrow strait to the
north. Newport, held by some 6,000 British troops under the command of Sir Robert Pigot, lay at the southern tip of the island.

Just as soon as the French fleet dropped over the horizon after
failing to cross the shoal at Sandy Hook, Lord Howe sent his frigates
to shadow them. Although the French fleet arrived off Point Judith
near the entrance to Narragansett Bay on July 29, there was little
d'Estaing could do except establish a blockade until the Americans
organized their forces. The delay was fatal to the enterprise. August
10 was selected as the date for the joint attack upon the British entrenchments at Newport. Two days before, the French fleet would
come up the Middle Passage and land the French troops on the west
side of the island. Sullivan's men, coming down from Providence,
would cross the Seaconnet Passage by ferry from Tiverton and land
on the east side. As a preliminary, on July 30, two small ships of the
line under command of the soon-to-be-famous Admiral Pierre-
André de Suffren de Saint-Tropez forced their way into the mouth of
the Middle Passage. One of them was hulled twice by the British
batteries on the small islands in the Passage as she passed. At the
same time, two frigates and a corvette entered the Seaconnet
Passage, forcing the British to burn the sloop-of-war *Kingfisher*, 16,
and some galleys to prevent them from being taken. On August 5,
Suffren moved further up on his side of the island, and the British set
fire to the remainder of their trapped fleet. The frigates *Cerberus*,
Lark, *Juno*, *Orpheus*, and *Flora*, all of 32 guns, the sloop *Falcon*, 18,
and several galleys were scuttled in Newport harbor to block the
entrance. Since this finished off most of the British vessels in the
area, the French were in unopposed command of the sea.

Relations between the French and Americans were good at the
start of the campaign—at least on the surface. On August 3, d'Estaing wrote Sullivan: "I fear that you left on my table a plan which I
have had the presumption to keep, because anything made by yourself is too precious a keepsake . . . I beg you, Sir, to be kind enough
to accept some pineapples and two barrels of fresh lemons." Despite
the fulsome compliments, friction between d'Estaing and Sullivan
quickly developed. The Frenchman considered the Yankee too brash

and direct and was unimpressed with the quality of the American troops provided for the expedition. D'Estaing, nevertheless, agreed to Sullivan's plans, and on August 8 the remainder of the French fleet began moving up the Middle Passage. Just as the position of the British, facing attack by a considerably superior force and blockaded by a strong fleet, seemed hopeless, Lord Howe appeared off Newport.

"The surprise was complete," lamented d'Estaing, who attributed the precision of Howe's timing to a conspiracy. Howe deserves more credit. The arrival of the British fleet was the result of intelligent deductions from the information provided the Admiral by his cruisers who were shadowing d'Estaing. While Howe had been waiting at New York for word of the destination of the French fleet, his force had grown stronger. A 50-gun ship had arrived from the West Indies, a 50 and a 64 had come in from Halifax, and on July 30 the first of Byron's ships had joined him—the *Cornwall*, 74. Her masts were "fished" and her hull leaking, but she was Howe's only 74. With these reinforcements, the admiral set off for Newport. Once more the fate of an army was to be decided by the timely arrival of a sea force.

Howe's was a bold move, for even with the new additions, he had only eight ships of the line to oppose the French twelve. The British fleet anchored off Point Judith hoping for the arrival of more of Byron's ships, but there was little it could do for the garrison. The next move was up to d'Estaing. Should he remain in position well up in the Middle Passage and be guided by the original plan? Or would he better serve the over-all strategic plan by putting to sea to deal with the immediate threat of Howe's ships? To the chagrin of the Americans, d'Estaing chose to fight at sea in defense of his own fleet. "Our ships would shortly have been battered . . . by a deliberate cannonade from the land," he later explained in a letter to Congress. ". . . We should in a short time have had to combat a squadron well protected, and provided with ketches, fire-ships and all the means which ensure the greatest superiority over ships that are destitute of them, and which are forced to engage at anchor, and between two shores in such an unequal combat." With equal plausibility, the Americans told d'Estaing that he needed only to defend the mouth of the harbor against a weaker adversary who would also be exposed to the fire of American and French shore batteries. If he could but curb his impatience, he had it within his power to bring about the surrender of the Newport garrison. Besides, any local fisherman could have told him that all signs pointed to the approach of an "August gale"—a hurricane racing up out of the West Indies. Of course, d'Estaing had the last word. On the morning of August 10—when he was to have landed his troops—his fleet put to sea, cutting its cables in its haste to be gone. The British forts at Newport and the surrounding islands opened up on the ships as they passed, and the French replied with a "prodigious fire." In two hours, d'Estaing was in open waters, steering for the British fleet.

With an inferior force Lord Howe could not chance an engagement without having the weather gage—and d'Estaing had the favorable position. For the better part of two days, the fleets maneuvered within sight of each other for advantage. The superior sailing qualities of the French ships were clearly evident. Along toward evening on August 11, darkness and heavy rain squalls enveloped the fleets. All thoughts of battle vanished in the struggle to survive the gale. Raging with unabated fury until the morning of August 14, the storm severely damaged and scattered the ships. In its wake, d'Estaing's flagship, the 90-gun *Languedoc*, dismasted and without a rudder, was attacked by the *Renown*, 50. The British vessel sailed under the stern of the helpless flagship and poured in several broadsides which were replied to by the few cannon able to fire aft. D'Estaing was so certain that he would have to strike his colors that all confidential papers were thrown overboard. "We were only a floating mass with nothing to steady us and nothing to guide us," the admiral said. At the critical moment, several French ships were attracted by the cannonade and drove off the *Renown*. The *Preston*, 50, took on the crippled *Marseillais*, 74, and was giving her a severe hammering when, once again, superior enemy forces sailed to the sound of gunfire to rescue a stricken French vessel.

The storm-battered fleets limped back to their bases—the British to New York and d'Estaing, with his flagship under tow, to Narragansett Bay. The land forces on both sides had been hard-hit by the storm. The Yankees lost men and horses by drowning and their powder had been drenched. The British were no better off, their tents "blown down and torn to rags." Both sides avidly scanned the horizon to see which of the fleets would return first since this would determine the outcome of the land campaign. When the corpses of five

French seamen drifted to shore along with some wreckage, the beleaguered British had dreams of being relieved, which intensified when sails were sighted off-shore on August 20. "We had great expectations of their being part of Lord Howe's fleet, and were not without hopes of his having engaged and defeated the French fleet," observed an officer. But the ships flew the fleur-de-lis—and the fate of the garrison appeared sealed.

It was not. The Comte d'Estaing, himself, reprieved the British from disaster. On the way back to Rhode Island, the French had learned that some of Byron's ships had arrived and the news gravely affected their judgment. Worried that the arrival of Byron meant he would be faced with a superior British fleet, d'Estaing fell back upon his orders, which required him to revictual his ships in Boston if he were faced with such an eventuality and to sail for the West Indies. The French Admiral told General Sullivan he sustained the decision of his officers that the safety of the fleet depended on a quick movement to Boston for refitting. The Americans were stunned. Newport lay within the grasp of the Allies if the French would only render the promised aid. Nathanael Greene and Lafayette were rowed out to the *Languedoc* to make a personal appeal for only two more days of cooperation. They were convinced that Newport could be captured within that time. "The devil has gotten into the fleet," Greene wrote bitterly to a friend.[5] "They are about to desert us." The admiral listened politely—and at midnight on August 21, sailed away. The departure of the French fleet ended the enterprise, for as Greene told Washington, it "struck such panic among the militia and volunteers that they began to desert in shoals." Indeed, Sullivan was lucky to make good a withdrawal before Lord Howe reappeared with thirteen ships of the line and 3,000 troops under Sir Henry Clinton.

Working at a furious pace with the limited facilities available in New York, Howe had repaired the storm damage to his ships and within eight days was back at sea. Learning of d'Estaing's departure from Rhode Island, he made a vigorous effort to overtake him. But it was too late to catch the French at sea, and the defenses of Boston harbor were too strong to be forced. Howe put back to Newport, supported a series of raids upon Yankee shipping in Buzzard's Bay

---

[5] Feeling was so high against the French among the Americans that Lafayette told Washington on August 25: "I am more upon a warlike footing in the American lines than when I came near the British lines at Newport."

and at Martha's Vineyard, and returned to New York. There he found six more of Byron's ships. British naval superiority in North America had been restored, providing the weary and frustrated admiral with the long-sought opportunity to strike his flag. He was succeeded by the ineffectual and unpopular Rear Admiral James Gambier.

Lord Howe's last two months in America were unquestionably his most successful. Commanding a much inferior fleet, he had shown imagination, boldness, and skill while waging a defensive campaign. He had saved New York, Rhode Island, and the British fleet and army—"an achievement unsurpassed in the annals of naval defensive warfare," according to Mahan. His accomplishment was in no small measure the result of d'Estaing's deficiencies. At the Delaware Capes, at New York, and at Newport, the French admiral had missed rare opportunities to destroy the British fleet. If d'Estaing had not taken so long to cross the Atlantic; if he had not been content with the pilot's stories about the depth of the water at Sandy Hook; if he had held his ground at Newport without venturing to sea, defeats of sizeable proportions would have been inflicted upon the British.

Salutes boomed out from the forts in Boston harbor and from the remaining few ships of the Continental Navy as the battered French fleet arrived on August 29 to repair the damage inflicted by British guns and stormy seas. Ironically, as soon as d'Estaing had been sighted off the Delaware Capes, the Marine Committee ordered all available vessels to be "immediately made Ready for sea . . . and dispatched . . . to join the Squadron of France." The Continental Navy, however, took no part in the fruitless maneuvers of the French fleet. Only the 10-gun brig *Resistance*, which had orders to search for the French, had sailed, and she was taken almost immediately by a British cruiser. Five ships were left at Boston—the frigates *Raleigh*, *Warren*, *Deane*, *Alliance*, and *Queen of France*. The *Deane*, built at Nantes and commanded by Samuel Nicholson, and the *Queen of France*, a converted merchantman, had recently arrived from France. The 36-gun *Alliance*, which had only lately been brought around from Newburyport where she had been outfitted, was under the command of a Frenchman named Pierre Landais. He had come to America as the skipper of a munitions vessel with no higher ambition than to obtain a post as a superintendent of ship construction. The burst of enthusiasm which greeted the alliance with his homeland had much to do with the Marine Committee's decision to give him a commission as captain of the finest frigate in the Continental Navy while American officers were begging for suitable berths.

When John Barry arrived on June 24 to take command of the *Raleigh* a dreary series of courts-martial were underway in the great cabin of the frigate. John Manley, fresh from British captivity, had been tried for the loss of the *Hancock* and was acquitted. Hector McNeill was dismissed from the service after being found guilty of abandoning the *Hancock* to her fate while he had been captain of the *Boston*. Thomas Thompson's trial on charges growing out of the capture of the *Alfred* ended with his dismissal. Last to convene had been a court of inquiry into Hoystead Hacker's misfortunes with the *Columbus*. He was absolved of all blame. Captain Barry, who had come to Boston buoyed by a successful series of small-boat operations against British shipping in the Delaware, anxiously awaited the moment when he could take possession of his new ship. Outwardly, the *Raleigh* appeared completely ready for sea as she lay moored to the Long Wharf. Nevertheless, many of the frigate's gun carriages were empty; her cannon lay at the bottom of the Atlantic where Thompson had heaved them in his flight from the British sloops-of-war. While awaiting delivery of new guns which had been ordered from a foundry at Providence, Barry tried to recruit a fresh crew.

He was still trying to deal with these problems when d'Estaing's fleet crept into Boston. At first the French were given a warm welcome. The admiral and his principal officers were feted by all the town's leading citizens and his seamen made themselves at home in the grog shops. Some of those encounters must have been strange affairs, for few of the Frenchmen spoke English and hardly any of the Bostonians spoke French. They often fell back upon Latin. Toasts were drunk—once it was seventeen toasts "at the interval of five minutes and accompanied by a discharge of Cannon." However, when news of the abandonment of Sullivan's army was received, the public mood turned ugly. Street fighting and back-alley brawls broke out. A young French officer was killed when he tried to stop a mob from pillaging a bakery established ashore to make crusty bread for the fleet.[6] The French were diplomats if nothing else and readily agreed with embarrassed American officials that it was the British who, in some mysterious way, had killed the officer. To put an end to the doubts cast against his courage, d'Estaing offered to land troops and lead them overland to Rhode Island to fight the British. Of course, Washington politely refused the offer.

Repair work on the French ships placed a considerable strain on America's meager naval and monetary resources which already were depleted by inflation and depreciation of the currency. Although Continental ships in the harbor went without supplies, the Eastern Navy Board managed to scrape up 35,000 pounds to pay for work and stores for the French fleet. The Continental Navy's turn came later. With her guns finally aboard and her crew fleshed out by stripping all hands from the frigate *Trumbull*, still lying useless in the Connecticut River, the *Raleigh* weighed anchor on September 25. Barry was ordered first to convoy two merchantmen out to sea and then turn southward to deal with some British vessels that were troubling shipping off the North Carolina coast. A few hours out, two British men-of-war were sighted. They were the *Experiment*, 50, commanded by Sir James Wallace who had raised havoc off the Rhode Island coast during the early part of the war, and the *Unicorn*, 22. Outgunned, Barry cracked on all sail. For sixty hours the chase continued along the coast of Maine. At one point, Barry thought he had lost his pursuers, but on the morning of September 27 they were once again visible from the quarterdeck of the *Raleigh*. Unable to outdistance them, Barry decided to engage the *Unicorn*, the leading enemy ship. If she could be disabled, then the *Raleigh* might be able to show her heels to the *Experiment*.

Shortly after the *Raleigh* and the *Unicorn* had exchanged their first broadsides, an ominous cracking was heard toward the bow of the American vessel. Her foretop mast pitched to starboard, carrying with it the main topgallant mast and several sails. The snarl of masts, yards, sails, and rigging dangled over the frigate's side, blanketing several of her guns and leaving her at the mercy of her smaller opponent. The *Unicorn* poured broadside after broadside into the crippled American vessel. Round shot and hurtling splinters cut down her

---

[6] As a conciliatory gesture, the Massachusetts House of Delegates resolved to promptly erect a monument over the grave of the Chevalier de Saint Sauveur. This was done one hundred and thirty-nine years later—on May 24, 1917.

crew. Thirty men were killed and wounded on the *Raleigh*—most of them as they struggled to free their ship of the tangle of wreckage.

It would take desperate measures to save his ship, Barry realized. His only hope was to board the *Unicorn* before the *Experiment* came up. In the descending darkness, he ordered his ship laid alongside the enemy vessel. The British captain sensed the purpose of the move and quickly sheered off. There was no hope of escape. The redoubtable Barry resolved that the British should not have his ship, and ordered the *Raleigh*'s bow headed for the rocky shore. For another hour, the running fight continued with the adversaries firing at the red muzzle flashes of each other's guns. Shortly before midnight, Barry reached his goal—a rocky island just to the south of the mouth of the Penobscot River. With a grinding shock, the *Raleigh* grated on the bottom and came to a halt. As the British stood offshore, Barry landed his crew, leaving a party behind to set fire to the ship. Either through treachery or negligence, the combustibles were not ignited. The next morning a British landing party took possession of the vessel and managed to haul her off the rocks. She was taken into the Royal Navy. About one hundred and thirty-five of the *Raleigh*'s crew were captured, but Barry and eighty-five of his men got away to the mainland. Several weeks later they arrived in Boston and were acclaimed for the stout defense of their ship. They were still there when d'Estaing, his ships repaired and revictualled, stood out to sea on November 4, bound for the West Indies. A storm blew up, hiding the fleet as it slipped past Byron's waiting cruisers.

Behind them, the French left six American ships—the *Deane, Warren, Providence, Boston, Alliance,* and *Queen of France.*[7] Only the latter was manned and ready for sea; the rest lacked crews and were described as being "in a most destitute and forelorn Situation." These half-dozen vessels were almost all that was left of the Continental Navy in American waters at the end of 1778.

---

[7] The *Boston* and *Providence* had recently returned from France after having taken a few prizes.

XXI

In Harm's Way

Rising and falling on the long swells, the *Ranger* plowed northward into the Irish Sea past a coastline familiar to Paul Jones from his boyhood. As he paced his quarterdeck, Jones may have brooded over the strange twist of fate that had returned the son of the gardener at Arbigland to these waters as captain of an avenging Yankee man-of-war. He had sailed this route on his first voyage as a thirteen-year-old apprentice, and he had often passed along these shores as a merchant skipper. The *Ranger* had sailed from Brest on April 10, 1778, and each mile she covered was bringing the war closer to Britain. "My first object was to secure an exchange of American prisoners in Europe," Jones said, "and my second to put an end, by one good fire in England of Shipping, to the burnings in America." He planned to raid an English seaport, destroy shipping, and kidnap some important personage to be held as a hostage to force the British government to free the prisoners.

Securing the release of American seamen held in British prisons was a project of considerable concern to Captain Jones. Although prisoners captured on land had been frequently exchanged, the British regarded those taken at sea as traitors, not prisoners of war. They stubbornly refused to exchange them for British captives. Thus, as of September 1, 1777, there were 123 American sailors jailed in Forton Prison near Portsmouth, and another 234 in Old Mill Prison at Plymouth. More had been captured since then. Jones reasoned that taking a hostage would force the British to adopt a more liberal policy of prisoner exchange. He had had plenty of time to work out the details of his plan.

From the moment Jones accepted command of the *Ranger*, he regarded it as a temporary assignment. As soon as he got to France, he expected the American commissioners to provide him with a larger vessel so he could carry the war home to Britain. Within a few days after his ship had anchored in the Loire on December 9, 1777, Jones was off to Paris to press his claim for *L'Indien*, a 40-gun frigate being secretly built for the Americans in a Dutch shipyard. A cloud hung over *L'Indien*, however. A month before Jones's arrival, British agents had discovered for whom the frigate was being constructed, and considerable pressure was placed on the Dutch authorities to prevent them from making delivery. Benjamin Franklin was sympathetic to Jones's claim, but he counseled patience. Delicate negotiations leading to the alliance between the United States and France were underway; final disposition of the frigate would have to wait until they were completed.

For six weeks, Paul Jones, on his first visit to Paris, savored the pleasures of the city. He was soon on excellent terms with Dr. Franklin, who never failed to encourage him. In return, Jones admired the old man and became a loyal follower. The captain was a constant visitor to the sumptuous Hôtel Valentois in suburban Passy where Franklin had taken up residence. This vast edifice was owned by Jacques Dontien Le Ray de Chaumont, a French shipowner and official who handled a large part of the unofficial aid sent to America before the alliance. He lived in the main part of the building with his young wife, while Franklin held court in a smaller pavilion. At Passy, Jones was an interested spectator as a colorful array of political adventurers, soldiers of fortune, diplomats, spies, bankers, scientists, and philosophers paid their respects to Dr. Franklin.

There were also Franklin's women friends. Most in evidence were Madame Helvétius, to whom Franklin proposed marriage at the age of seventy-two, and Madame Brillon, who allowed Franklin to play chess with her while she was in her bath.[1] Following either the advice or the example of the old man, Jones quickly discovered that the way to get things done in France was through the ladies. He launched an affair with Madame de Chaumont, whose husband was often away on business. The dashing sailor enjoyed this fling ashore—but, as Morison points out, it was later to prove rather embarrassing when he had to depend upon the lady's husband for supplies for his ships.

Realizing that no decision was to be reached immediately regarding *L'Indien*, Jones returned to the *Ranger* at the end of January 1778 with orders from the commissioners authorizing him to proceed "in the manner you shall judge best for distressing the Enemies of the United States, by sea or otherwise." This gave him a blank check for any action he planned. The immediate "scheem," as Jones described it, was a hit-and-run raid on an unsuspecting English port to destroy shipping. "When an Enemy thinks a design against them is improbable, they can always be surprised and attacked with advantage," he wrote the Marine Committee. "It is true, I must run great risk; but no gallant action was ever performed without danger."

Paul Jones was ready to take this risk, but the officers and men of the *Ranger* were more interested in prize money than in gallantry. While Jones was in Paris, the ship had been heaved down and her bottom scraped, her masts trimmed to make her more manageable and a new suit of sails cut to replace the makeshift canvas provided at Portsmouth. The men were kept busy until their skipper's return, but they were sullen and morale was low. They regarded Jones, always a perfectionist and a stickler for proper form, as a tyrant—and a foreigner to boot. This ill-tempered little Scotsman treated honest and patriotic Yankee seamen like dirt, or so they claimed. Thomas Simpson, the *Ranger*'s first lieutenant, had encouraged the men to believe that Jones would be gone as soon as the ship reached France and that he would take over as captain. Now Jones was back with some harebrained scheme that was not likely to provide any prize money. And speaking of prize money, where were the proceeds from the sale of the two vessels that had been captured on the way across the Atlantic? No one had seen a cent of it. Hard cash on the barrelhead was what the sailors understood—not promises of glory.

---

[1] Madame Helvétius once accused Franklin of having purposely put off a visit to her. "Madame," he replied, "I am waiting until the nights are longer."

Seven days after the signing of the treaties between France and the United States—on February 13, 1778—Jones took the *Ranger* and the brig *Independence* along the forbidding Brittany coast to familiarize himself with those dangerous shores. Along toward evening, he spotted a forest of tapering masts rising above the misty waters of Quiberon Bay where a powerful French squadron rode at anchor under the granite cliffs. Jones had been the first to unfurl the Grand Union flag over the fleet in the Delaware in 1775, and he had long coveted the opportunity to be the first Continental officer to exchange salutes with a French admiral. The moment appeared to be at hand. However, considerable haggling preceded the exchange of honors. Immediately upon anchoring, Jones sent a note to William Carmichael, Silas Deane's secretary, who was then at Quiberon, requesting him to inform the French commander that he intended to salute him with thirteen guns—"provided he will Accept the Compliment and Return Gun for Gun." Carmichael delivered the note promptly. That same evening, Commodore La Motte Picquet replied that he would be happy to return the salute with nine guns.

Jones had expected more. He wrote Carmichael the next day that "even the haughty English return Gun for Gun to foreign Officers of equal rank, and two less only to Captains by flag officers." Under this system, the French should return his salute with at least eleven guns. Nine was not enough. When it was pointed out that this was the salute authorized by the French for Dutch admirals and those of other republics, the testy little captain grudgingly accepted. With the Stars and Stripes whipping out from her gaff, the *Ranger* weighed anchor at 4 P.M. in "very Squaly weather" and sailed past the stern of the *Robuste*, the French flagship. Thirteen guns boomed out from the Continental vessel just as the sun was setting. Smoke wreathed the high sides of the French man-of-war as she answered with nine guns. The next morning, to make certain there had been no mistake—and perhaps with the hope, as Morison suggests, that "on second thought" the French commander might give him an extra gun or two—Jones had the *Independence* sail through the fleet and salute the *Robuste*. Once again, the French replied with nine guns. These were the first salutes to the Stars and Stripes by a foreign power.[2]

---

[2] Early in March, Admiral Sir George Rodney, who had taken refuge in Paris from his

For the next six weeks or so, the *Ranger* cruised off the Brittany coast, as her captain tried to persuade the French to detach a few ships to join him in a raid upon England. Meanwhile, trouble was brewing among his crew. Some of the men had kept copies of the recruiting poster which Jones had distributed back in Portsmouth—it promised "an agreeable Voyage in this pleasant season of the Year" —and now they were out in dangerous waters with snow covering the decks. The men were in a semi-mutinous state because their enlistments were to last as long as they were away from home, and no one knew when their mad captain would return to America. Prize money—or the lack of it—was so much in the mind of the *Ranger*'s officers that they objected to keeping Marine Captain Matthew Parke, the only man commissioned by Jones, on the rolls. They insisted that the Continental Navy regulations did not provide for an officer of his rank on ships of fewer than 20 guns. As the *Ranger* carried only 18 guns, it was not their intention to share prize money with Parke. To placate them, Jones was obliged to dismiss the officer, his only friend on the vessel. Finally despairing of obtaining support from the French for his plan, he put to sea on April 10 and boldly set a course for the west coast of England. The port of Whitehaven was to be his first target.

Lambert Wickes and Gustavus Conyngham had sailed around Britain into these waters the year before and taken many prizes, but they made no attempt to raid an English seaport. That was something no enemy had done since the Dutch had burned Sheerness in 1667. Jones selected Whitehaven not out of any animosity but because he knew the place. He had sailed from there on his first voyage and had often been in and out of the harbor. He knew that the wharves would be crowded with coasting vessels, fishing boats and colliers—and he could easily find his way in and out of the port either by day or by night.

Several small vessels were taken and burnt to prevent them from spreading the alarm as the *Ranger*, disguised as a merchantman, proceeded up St. George's Channel. When his disgruntled officers and crew protested that nothing was to be gained from burning prizes, Jones sent a large prize, the *Lord Chatham*, bound for Dublin with a

---

creditors, passed on the news of the exchange of salutes to Lord Stormont. He had picked it up while dining out with a group that included Edward Bancroft.

mixed cargo including a hundred hogsheads of ale, into Brest to placate them. On April 18, the revenue cutter *Hussar* hove in sight and Jones, pretending to be a merchant skipper, requested a pilot. When this was refused, the cutter's captain reported that "in an instant" the *Ranger*'s "ports were knocked open, her decks were filled with men and a tier of guns were run out." The *Hussar*, however, was a fast vessel and made her getaway. Two days later, a large British sloop-of-war was sighted at anchor off Carrickfergus in Belfast Lough. Some fishermen were picked up who identified her as the *Drake*, 20. Jones wished to sail directly into the Lough and capture the ship, but his skittish crew would have none of that. Instead they offered to try to surprise the *Drake* that night. The *Ranger* would cross her bow in the guise of a peaceful merchantman, rake her and then anchor alongside and carry her by boarding. Due to drunkenness and ineptitude, the plan misfired. The *Ranger*'s anchor caught on its cathead, and she quickly overshot the *Drake*. Jones held his breath, waiting for the enemy to open fire. Nothing happened. Lulled by the innocent appearance of the *Ranger*, the *Drake*'s watch ignored her. Nevertheless, the opportunity for a surprise attack had been lost. With dirty weather blowing up, an angry and disappointed Captain Jones was forced to abandon his attempt to capture the sloop. But he carefully filed her away in his mind to be dealt with later.

Steering due east across the Irish Sea to the English coast in a snow storm, the *Ranger* headed for Whitehaven where Jones intended to carry out his plan to burn all the shipping in the harbor. Once again, he had to deal with mutinous behavior. Tipped off that some of the crew—urged on by the officers, according to Jones— were planning to throw him overboard and sail the ship home, Jones quashed the plot by putting a pistol to the head of the purported ringleader and daring the rest to make a move. That ended the rebellion. When the captain asked for volunteers to man the boats that were to go into Whitehaven, about forty men stepped forward. But both his lieutenants, Simpson and Elijah Hall, begged off, claiming they were "overcome with fatigue." Very well, Jones replied coolly, he would go himself. He took charge of one of the boats, choosing Lieutenant Jean Meijer, a Swedish army officer who had volunteered for service on the *Ranger*, as his second in command. Lieutenant Samuel Wallingford, of the Marines, commanded the other boat. With Jones acting as his own pilot, the sloop moved slowly up the funnel-shaped Solway Firth toward Whitehaven on the night of April 22. The wind grew faint and finally died long before the sloop reached the point of planned embarkation for the raiders. When the boats pulled away from the *Ranger* at midnight, the ship was still a considerable distance from the port.

For three hours, the men rowed against a strong tide. Since the sun rises early along the Scottish border at that time of the year, dawn was already breaking when they finally reached Whitehaven. But Jones decided it was too late to change plans. A stone pier divided the anchorage into two sections, each protected by a battery. Jones estimated that there were about 150 vessels on the north side and from 70 to 100 on the south. Most of them were aground at low tide, which meant they would burn more easily. Wallingford's party was assigned to fire the shipping to the north of the pier while Jones's group would take care of the rest. First off, he seized the southern battery. "We took the fort by storm," the Captain reported. "Lacking ladders, we had to climb [the wall] by mounting upon the shoulders of our largest and strongest men, and entered it in this manner through the embrasures." Jones was the first man in the fort. The sentries, huddled in the guardhouse against the cold, were quickly overpowered, and the guns spiked. Taking only a midshipman with him, Jones then spiked the cannon in the north battery. In the meantime, Lieutenant Meijer stood by the boat to make certain that the men did not abandon their captain on the beach. Apparently the Swedish officer had heard some muttering among them.

Anxiously Jones awaited the sight of flames pouring from the ships that were to be burnt by Wallingford. "To my great astonishment, I saw that the boat sent to the northern part had returned without having accomplished anything," he declared. Immediately after landing, Wallingford and his men had headed for the nearest ale house and "made very free with the liquor, etc." They later told Jones that they had been frightened off by strange noises. The Captain observed "that these noises existed only in their imagination." Worse yet, one of Jones's volunteers turned out to be a traitor. An Irishman named David Freeman, who had enlisted on the *Ranger* in Portsmouth under the name of David Smith in order to get home, dashed off to arouse the town against the raiders. Shouting and banging on doors, he ran from house to house warning the occupants to turn out to prevent their homes and property from being destroyed. Hundreds of confused people poured into the streets. While they were still trying to puzzle out what was happening, Jones went steadily about his work. Fire bombs made of canvas dipped in brimstone were hurled aboard a large collier and a barrel of tar was rolled into the conflagration to help it spread more quickly.

"The sun was a full hour above the horizon and as sleep no longer ruled the world it was time to retire," Jones reported poetically, but he could not resist one final gesture of defiance. Even though his men, cursing him under their breaths, were frantic to be off, he remained alone on the wharf "to observe at my leisure the terror, panic, and stupidity of the inhabitants." They "remained motionless like statues or ran hither and thither like madmen as they tried to quell the flames." Some recognized him as the John Paul who had sailed out of Whitehaven many years before. The *Ranger*'s boats had drawn off before a few of the inhabitants pulled themselves together enough to pepper the raiders with inaccurate gunfire from cannon taken from one of the anchored vessels. During the night, the sloop had managed to get in closer to the shore, and by 6 A.M. the landing party was safely back aboard. There were no casualties.

Aided by a rain storm, the people of Whitehaven soon managed to put out the fire. The damage was slight—costing only from 250 to 1,250 pounds, according to various British estimates. But the psychological effect was something else again. Not for a century had an enemy been bold enough to land on the shore of Britain. Where was the Royal Navy? Panic struck the coastal towns, and the militia was turned out. Opposition newspapers howled about the "defenseless" state of the seaports and the "inexcusable" laxness of the government. Several men-of-war were diverted from convoy duty to search out the Yankee "pirate." "What was done," Jones later observed, ". . . is Sufficient to show that not all their boasted navy can protect their own coasts, and that the scenes of distress which they have occasioned in America may soon be brought home to their own door." But he also noted that if the crew of the *Providence* had been with him, all the vessels at Whitehaven "would have been laid in ashes."

Captain Jones was no sooner back on his quarterdeck than he ordered a course set for St. Mary's Isle, a peninsula jutting out into Solway Firth, about two hours' sail away. No doubt angry and disappointed at the failure of his raiders to start the holocaust that he had planned at Whitehaven, he decided to put the other part of his project into immediate effect before the countryside was aroused. He would kidnap the Earl of Selkirk from his home overlooking Kirkcudbright Bay and hold him hostage in order to force the British government to exchange prisoners. Morison suggests that the Earl may have been a guest at Arbigland where Jones's father had been gardener. Based upon this boyhood memory, he may have naïvely assumed that Selkirk was a great lord for whose freedom the British government would barter the American seamen it held captive. In reality, the Earl was a minor Scots peer.

Shortly after ten o'clock on April 23—the same morning as the raid on Whitehaven—the *Ranger* anchored in shallow waters that were familiar to her skipper. Jones, David Cullam, his sailing master, and Lieutenant Wallingford were rowed ashore by a dozen well-armed sailors. Leaving a few men to guard their boat, the party marched up the path to the Selkirk mansion. Along the way they met the head gardener, who was alarmed by the sudden appearance of a gang of rough-looking men carrying muskets and cutlasses. Jones told him they were a Royal Navy press gang in search of likely hands for the King's ships. When this word spread, the Captain knew that all the able-bodied men in the neighborhood would go into hiding. From the gardener, he learned that the Earl was away, taking the waters at Buxton in England. As far as Jones was concerned, that was the end of the raid. He started back to the cutter.

But Cullam and Wallingford insisted that the men be allowed to loot the mansion. They had returned empty-handed from Whitehaven, and there was little in the way of prize money to show for a dangerous voyage. Besides, many of the crew had friends in New England whose homes had been burned by British raiders, and they demanded revenge. Jones was in a quandary. To give in to this demand would degrade himself in his own eyes to the level of banditry; to deny the men would incite even more insubordination. He had but a moment to make a decision. The Captain yielded and gave his officers permission to go to the house and demand the family silver, while he would remain behind at the boat. Only Cullam and Wallingford were to enter the mansion while the men remained outside. Lady Selkirk was to be treated with "the utmost respect" and the house was not to be looted or damaged.

The Countess had just finished breakfast when she saw some "horrid-looking creatures" surrounding her home. She took them for pirates. Several female guests fled to the top floor while Lady Selkirk, who was "well advanced in her pregnancy," remained in the parlor to meet the leaders of the landing party. "Of the two officers, one was a civil young man in a green uniform," she later told her husband. "The principal [Cullam] one was in blue . . . and had a vile black-guard look." Demanding the family plate, Cullam declared: "Produce it directly. We are masters of this house and everything in it." Lady Selkirk quickly decided to do what was wished. She went to the pantry where the butler was trying to hide the silver in a maid's apron and told him to hand over the lot. The Americans called for sacks—proof that Jones had not originally set out to gather plunder, according to Morison. When the bags had been filled, Cullam asked for an inventory to make sure it was all there. "Where are the coffee pot and the teapot?" he asked after a quick glance at the list. They were produced upon Lady Selkirk's order by the butler who had hidden them. The teapot was still filled with wet leaves from the morning's breakfast. Although all this took only fifteen or twenty minutes, the Americans "appeared in consternation most of the time," recalled Lady Selkirk's son, and were so anxious to get away they made no demands for items on the inventory that were in other parts of the house.

When Lady Selkirk asked for a receipt for the stolen items, young Selkirk said Cullam "seemed not able to write or read; so he gave the inventory of the plate to the other, and bade him write a receipt." Wallingford, described as "naturally well-bred and not to like his employment," got only as far as writing "This is to cert—" when something went wrong with his pen. Cullam brusquely told him to forget about the receipt. The men tossed the sacks over their shoulders and marched off to the beach where they found Captain Jones, appalled that any officer would stoop to pilfering silver, waiting with the cutter. The *Ranger* had already put out to sea when a group of volunteer defenders, aroused by a servant, arrived at the Selkirk mansion. From them the Countess learned, as she wrote to William Craik, that her assailants were under the command of John Paul, who was "born in your grounds." To her husband she wrote, he was "as great a villain as ever was born."

Jones was not happy about this adventure. It did not square

with his own image of himself as a gentleman and man of honor. He composed a lengthy letter to Lady Selkirk upon his return to Brest which he dispatched to the British Postmaster General for delivery to her. "It cannot be too much lamented that in the profession of Arms, the Officer of fine feeling and of real Sensibility, should be under the necessity of winking at any action of Persons under his command, which his Heart cannot approve," this long exercise in bombast began. Jones promised to purchase the silver himself when it was placed upon sale and see that it was returned to the Countess at the first opportunity. It was a promise that he kept—paying for the plate out of his own pocket.[3] But it is just as well that Jones never saw the Earl of Selkirk's reply to his letter. "It certainly was fortunate both for Lady Selkirk and me that I was from home, and it was also fortunate for you, Sir, that your officers and men behaved well," he wrote, "for had any of my family suffered outrage, murder or violence, no quarter of the Globe should have secured you . . . from my vengeance."

With the alarm being sounded all along the coast and British cruisers being sent in pursuit of the *Ranger*, Jones had plenty of excuse to return to Brest without delay. Instead, he headed back to Belfast Lough to deal with the *Drake*. At daybreak on April 24, she was sighted standing out to sea, word having been received the night before of the raid on Whitehaven. Uncertain as to whether the strange sail was the Yankee "pirate" or a peaceful merchantman, the *Drake*'s captain sent a lieutenant in a gig to reconnoiter. Through skillful seamanship, Jones kept the *Ranger*'s stern toward the officer's boat so he could not count her gunports. The lieutenant was invited aboard. No sooner had he set foot upon the quarterdeck than he was informed that he was a prisoner of war. This deception and the prospect of prize money "tickled the caprice" of the *Ranger*'s crew, who had, only minutes before in a "town meeting" presided over by Lieutenant Simpson, debated whether or not to fight. Jones later charged that Simpson had "held up to the crew that being Americans fighting for liberty, the voice of the people should be taken before the Captain's orders were obeyed." If the capture of the

---

[3] The market was poor in France for "old-fashioned" English silver so Jones had it valued as Bullion. It was estimated to be worth $600. Fifteen percent of this was the captain's share so he paid $510 for the set.

Drake's boat had not "Soothed [the men] into Good Humour," he charged, a mutiny might have occurred. As it was, the crew sprang to the guns to make "a truely Gallant" fight.

Several guns boomed out from the *Drake* impatiently signaling the gig to return. Sensing that a battle was about to start, small boats crowded with spectators who had come out to see a fight drew off to a safe distance. Alarm fires were lit on both sides of the Lough. The *Drake* had to buck an ebbing tide and freshening headwinds so Jones awaited her offshore. With the *Ranger*'s yards set aback and the courses clewed up, the Captain watched his adversary slowly come out to meet him. Something about the *Drake* reminded him of the *Alfred*, his old command. Later, according to Morison, he learned that like the *Alfred*, the *Drake* had been built in Philadelphia a few years before the war for the merchant service and had been taken into the Royal Navy. The *Drake* and the *Ranger* were evenly matched. The *Drake* carried twenty 6-pounders and perhaps one hundred and seventy-five men, while the *Ranger* mounted eighteen 9-pounders and was manned by a crew of about one hundred and twenty-five. Many of the *Drake*'s hands, however, were raw volunteers, and she was short several officers.

The distance between the ships lessened very fast. An hour before sunset the *Drake* raised the Union Jack, and the *Ranger* broke out the Stars and Stripes. "What ship is that?" demanded the British captain. "The American Continental ship *Ranger!*" was the reply, followed by a broadside that swept the deck of the *Drake*. The English vessel had been astern of the *Ranger* so Jones suddenly turned his craft to place her across the bow of the enemy ship and raked her. Round shot smashed through the *Drake* from stem to stern. "The action was warm, close and obstinate," said Jones. Because the British ship carried a larger crew, he decided to stand off at pistol shot to prevent the *Ranger* from being grappled to the *Drake*'s side and boarded. The American gunners were ordered to cripple the English vessel so she could be taken as a prize by concentrating their fire on her sails and rigging rather than pounding away at her hull. A torrent of grape and chain shot sliced up the *Drake*'s top hamper. Soon she was unmanageable. Her masts were splintered, some of her yards were carried away and her sails hung in tatters. A musket ball killed her captain early in the fight, and her first lieutenant was mortally wounded. Within an hour and five minutes of the *Ranger*'s first broadside, the *Drake*'s sailing master, her senior surviving officer, cried "Quarter! Quarter!"

A boarding party was sent over in the *Drake*'s own boat. They found her decks running with blood and rum. A keg of spirits had been brought up on deck to celebrate the coming victory, and it had been smashed by a round shot. Forty-two men were reported killed and wounded during the brief struggle. The vessel's head sails and fore-and-main topsail yards had been shot away. The spanker gaff appeared ready to fall at any moment and the British flag trailed over the side in the water. The *Ranger* suffered three men killed, including Lieutenant Wallingford, and another five were wounded. The ship, itself, was only lightly damaged.

With about two hundred prisoners battened down in the hold—about one hundred and thirty from the *Drake*, including the cook's wife, and the rest from a half-dozen other vessels taken and burned earlier in the cruise—the *Ranger* headed north and west around Ireland with her course set for Brest. Before leaving Belfast Lough, Jones set ashore the fishermen who had been taken prisoner a few days before, but not before giving them a gift of money. "The grateful fishermen were in raptures, and expressed their joy in three huzzas as they passed the *Ranger*'s quarter," Jones reported. A prize crew under the command of Lieutenant Simpson was placed aboard the *Drake* and she was taken in tow by the *Ranger*. All went well enough until May 4. They were off Ushant when a ship was sighted that looked like it would make a good prize. Jones cast off the towline after hailing Simpson and instructing him to follow along in the chase. Shouted from quarterdeck to quarterdeck, the order was apparently misunderstood on the *Drake*. Simpson's partisans later claimed that the instructions were so indistinct that the prize master hailed the *Ranger* and asked if he were to make his way alone to Brest. Lieutenant Hall was supposed to have answered in the affirmative. The *Drake* turned away to the south while Jones cracked on all sail in pursuit of the strange vessel which was traveling to the northward. She turned out to be Swedish and neutral. Furious that Simpson had disobeyed his orders—or so he was convinced—the restraint that Jones had maintained in the face of the officer's near-mutinous conduct finally collapsed. The *Ranger* overhauled the *Drake* and Jones ordered her to heave-to. Hall was sent over to take command and Simpson was placed under arrest for insubordination. On this discordant note, the cruise ended.

Jones confidently expected that a cruise which included a raid on an English seaport and was climaxed by the capture of the first British man-of-war taken in European waters would be rewarded by the American commissioners with a more important command. Instead, he was confronted with problems that turned the next nine months into a period of bitter frustration. As Morison has so aptly put it, he was "in irons"—like a ship that had lost headway and was drifting backwards. Some of his worst character traits came to the fore: vanity, oversensitiveness, and unpredictable outbursts of bad temper. Immediately after the *Ranger* dropped anchor, the Captain visited the Comte d'Orvilliers on his flagship, seeking a place to keep his prisoners until they could be exchanged for Americans held in England. Hostilities had not yet been declared between France and Britain, so the Admiral advised Jones to ship his captives to America in the *Drake* to forestall an order by the French government for their release. As a favor to Jones, whom he liked and respected, d'Orvilliers agreed to say nothing to the government about the prisoners, and ordered them confined on a prison hulk in the harbor for safekeeping.

Benjamin Franklin had been trying for months to arrange an exchange of prisoners without success. At one point Lord Stormont had coldly informed him: "The King's Ambassador receives no applications from rebels but when they come to implore His Majesty's Mercy." Life was severe for American prisoners. Charles Herbert, a young seaman who spent nearly two years in Old Mill Prison, reported: "Many are strongly tempted to pick up the grass in the yard and eat and some pick up old bones . . . that have been laying in the dirt a week or ten days . . . and suck them. . . . Many are driven to such necessity by want of provisions that they have sold most of the clothes off their backs for the sake of getting a little money to buy some bread." The prisoners hunted for rats and if a dog or cat was unlucky enough to stray into the prison, it was immediately eaten by the famished men. Even so, the death rate was low when compared with the New York prison ships.[4]

---

[4] The American prisoners were given a food allowance less than a third of that provided French, Dutch, and Spanish captives. A proposal to put the Americans on the same rations as

The captives brought in by Paul Jones gave Franklin new leverage in his attempts to free American prisoners. For the first time, the Americans held enough enemy seamen to make such a trade worthwhile to the British. To emphasize this, the American commissioners let it be known that henceforth British prisoners would be treated in the same fashion as the Americans in England. This was enough to spur an exchange in March 1779. The 164 prisoners taken by Jones, including the wife of the *Drake*'s cook and about 60 men captured by the French after the declaration of war, were exchanged for 228 Americans. Regular exchanges took place thereafter, although Parliament did not formally authorize the arrangement until early in 1780. By then, some 1,100 American seamen were languishing in British jails.[5]

At the same time, Jones's men were clamoring for their prize money and unjustly blamed the Captain for the delay, though he was, in fact, doing everything he could to get the money. Just a few days after the *Ranger*'s arrival, Jones cashed a draft on the American commissioners for $4,800 so he would have funds to distribute "among the officers and Men to whom I owe my late success." This was quite generous but highly irregular. The first word he heard from Paris after his return from the cruise was not praise for capturing the *Drake* but news that the draft had not been honored. Jones was caught so short of cash, he complained, "I know not where to find tomorrow's dinner for the great number of mouths that depend on me for food." He was finally forced to depend upon the charity of

---

the others was defeated in the House of Lords by a 47 to 14 vote. During the course of the debate, it was stated "that the diet of prisoners, as persons in a state of inactivity, ought to be sparing . . . if more than enough was allowed, it would render the prisoners unhealthy. . . ."

[5] Franklin's concern about the plight of American sailors imprisoned in England did not end with this exchange. He quietly commissioned three small cutters—the *Black Prince*, *Black Princess*, and *Fearnot*—as privateers and gave them the mission of capturing British seamen to be exchanged for hapless Americans held in Forton and Old Mill prisons. The cutters were active for about a year, from mid-1779 to mid-1780—and captured 114 enemy vessels. A total of 287 British prisoners were taken, of which 161 were brought in. The rest were paroled at sea and allowed to go off in their ships which had been ransomed.

The *Black Prince*, first of the cutters to be commissioned, had a curious history. She was manned by Irish and English smugglers who had broken out of prison in Dublin, recaptured their ship which had been taken by revenue agents, and sailed to Dunkirk. Using an American captain as front man, they obtained a privateering commission from Franklin. By the time the old man found out that he had been tricked into granting the commission to foreigners, they had been so successful that he overlooked the subterfuge. The complete story of the cutters was related for the first time by William Bell Clark in *Ben Franklin's Privateers* (Baton Rouge 1956).

the French authorities for provisions. Franklin sent a soothing letter on June 1, but to a proud and sensitive man such as Jones, he had been placed in "a Deplorable & disgraceful Situation in the sight of the French Fleet." When the prizes were finally sold after a protracted delay, they brought only a fraction of what had been expected—and the *Ranger*'s crew blamed him.

The case of Lieutenant Simpson also turned out to be more of a headache than Jones had anticipated. Simpson had been relieved of his command and placed under arrest without having had an opportunity to explain his actions. Jones wanted to have him court-martialed, but there were no senior American naval officers in Europe to constitute a tribunal. So Simpson remained under arrest. His confinement was not rigorous. He had a cabin on the *Drake* and the run of the ship until Jones became convinced he was undermining the discipline of the prize crew. When the Captain came on board the *Drake* "they became so insolent as to refuse duty and go below." At the suggestion of Admiral d'Orvilliers, Simpson was removed to a ship where the French confined officers awaiting discipline. He caused so much trouble there that the French commander had him transferred to a naval prison ashore. Jones paid his expenses out of his own pocket. The prison was described by some members of the *Ranger*'s crew as "a Lousey, Dirtey french Gaol" unfit for a "Faithful, true & Fatherly Officer."

So declared seventy-seven sailors, who called themselves "the Jovial Tars Now on board the Continental Sloop of War *Ranger*" in a petition sent to the commissioners. Twenty-eight warrant and petty officers signed another petition charging that Captain Jones was "arbitrary, his temper and treatment insufferable, for the most trivial matters threatening to shoot the person or persons whom he in sallies of passion calls ignorant and disobedient." Elijah Hall also told the commissioners that Jones was "the sole cause of the Disorder on board the ship" because "his mode of Government is so far from ours that no American of spirit can serve with Cheerfulness under him." For his part, Jones contended "my treatment of the officers and men in the *Ranger* has been strictly consistent with the laws of hospitality and humanity; I am ready to justify every measure which I have adopted towards them, though some of them were measures I should have wished to avoid."

Paul Jones was no sadistic martinet or sea-going tyrant. But he was a perfectionist, always criticizing and nagging his subordinates, damning them in fits of temper for which he was later apologetic. According to Midshipman Nathaniel Fanning, who served on the *Bonhomme Richard*, Jones became angry one day with one of his lieutenants and ordered him below. As the officer descended the ladder, Jones "kicked him on the breach several times." Shortly afterward, the Captain sent the officer an invitation to dine with him. This, said Fanning, was typical of Jones—"passionate to the highest degree one minute, and the next ready to make a reconciliation." Like many self-made men, Jones was extremely self-centered, neither inspiring complete loyalty nor attracting abiding friendships. He took good care of his men—but not out of sympathy or consideration. To him, they were like his cannon and ships—a means to an end.

　　The American commissioners, impressed by the support given Simpson by his shipmates and worried about the long-term effects of the conflict with Jones, persuaded the Captain to free the lieutenant on parole. Simpson rather than Jones had the full support of two of the commissioners, John Adams and Arthur Lee. He returned to the *Ranger* on July 27 "to the joy and Satisfaction of the whole Ship's Company," according to Dr. Ezra Green, the surgeon. A few weeks later, on August 21, Simpson took the *Ranger* to sea under orders to sail her home to America, where, much to Jones's chagrin, Congress promoted him to captain. No doubt John Langdon, his influential brother-in-law, helped ease the way. Jones remained behind in France. He was lucky to have seen the last of the *Ranger*, her malicious officers and her unreliable crew, although it is doubtful that he viewed it in this light at the time. He relinquished command only after having received assurance from Franklin that he would be given *L'Indien*. The powerful frigate now lay at Amsterdam almost ready for sea. On June 10, the old man had written Jones that it was all "settled" and Jones hastened to Passy to pick up his commission. Once there he was forced to wait another two months for a decision on the disposition of the ship, growing increasingly exasperated as prospects for obtaining command of her gradually faded. The frigate was finally sold to the French. Madame de Chaumont probably provided some consolation during the long summer afternoons while her husband was away, but Jones grew increasingly frustrated as a result of his inability to secure a command.

Sartine, the Minister of Marine, invited the Captain to unveil his plans for action against Britain—and bold schemes poured from his pen. He suggested a sweep directly up the Clyde to Glasgow; an expedition to the west coast of Africa to intercept homeward-bound British East Indiamen; an attack on English convoys to the Baltic; a raid on the Newfoundland fisheries. All had one common denominator—Paul Jones was to be placed in command of three or four French frigates and given a free hand. All very interesting, said Sartine, but he promised nothing. Numerous ships were mentioned as possible commands for the American captain, but none materialized. Several British prizes were brought into Brest and Jones was offered his pick of them. All were rejected in disgust. "I wish to have no Connection with any Ship that does not sail *fast,* for I intend *to go in harm's way,*" he told Chaumont.

"Have patience," counseled Benjamin Franklin, but Jones's patience was at an end. "The Minister . . . after possessing himself of my schemes," he wrote a friend, "has treated me like a Child five successive times by leading me on from Great to little and from little to less." So passionate and intemperate had the Captain become in denouncing the insults to his "sacred honor," that Franklin and Chaumont considered bundling him out of France. In his anger, Jones probably forgot that obtaining a ship for him was not the only problem with which the American commissioners had to deal. Yet when all allowances are made for the difficulties which beset the commissioners, it was "the height of folly," as Morison says, to have kept a man of Paul Jones's character on the beach for nearly a year —and this while he was on the enemy's doorstep. "A little more pressure on the part of the Americans at Passy could probably have got *L'Indien* out of neutral waters and under Jones's command," he points out. Fortunately, a command was found for Jones at the end of 1778. She was nothing like the swift and powerful *L'Indien,* but Jones described her as "the only Ship offered for sale in France that will answer our purpose." She was the *Duc de Duras*, a tired old East Indiaman of some 900 tons. To compliment his patron, Dr. Franklin, whose almanacs translated into French as *Les Maximes du Bon-homme Richard* were all the rage in Paris, Jones re-christened the vessel the *Bonhomme Richard.*

For so famous a ship, little is known of the *Bonhomme Richard.*

Launched in 1766, she was a typical French Indiaman of the period
—sturdily built but clumsy and slow. She was purchased for Jones
by the French government at a cost of about $42,000, and King
Louis XVI underwrote the expenses of fitting her out. Despite Royal
sponsorship, Jones had considerable trouble obtaining proper guns
for his ship. The Captain thought she was sound enough to carry a
battery of twenty-eight 18-pounders on her covered gun deck, which
were ordered cast. But none of the guns arrived in time. He had to
settle for what he could wheedle from French arsenals that were giving priority to arming French ships. Twenty-eight 12-pounders—sixteen of them new guns and the rest second-hand—were mounted on
the *Richard*'s gun deck. Six 9-pounders were placed on the forecastle
and quarterdeck, and a half-dozen old 18-pounders of questionable
worth were mounted in the gun room or junior officer's mess under
the gun deck. New ports for them had to be cut in the *Richard*'s sides
just above the waterline. They were so low that in all but a flat calm
these guns would be useless.

    With every available seaman needed to man King Louis's ships,
Jones was barred from enlisting French sailors. He had to take his
men where he could find them. Those who signed on were "so un-
governable that I found the sole expedient by which I could control
them was to divide them into two parties and to place one knave
under the eye and guard of the other," declared Jones. The *Richard*
put to sea with a polyglot crew of almost a dozen different
nationalities that made her a floating Foreign Legion. There were
even two East Indians. Despite Jones's comments, most of his men
were competent, experienced seamen, and this crew turned out to be
one of the best he ever commanded. Accounts vary as to the exact
makeup of the 380 officers, men and boys who shipped aboard the
Richard. Morison states that there were 20 officers, most of them
Americans—and unlike those on the *Ranger* all had been hand-
picked by the Captain. There were 43 petty officers, more than half
British deserters and prisoners of war and the remainder Americans,
and 144 seamen and boys, of whom 46 were American, 54 British,
and the rest from seven different countries. There were also 137
French marines and 36 French "landsmen," mostly raw peasants
and fishermen from Brittany.

    Many of the Americans, including Richard Dale,[6] a twenty-two-

---

[6] Dale had been captured in the *Lexington*. He served as a captain in the Quasi-War with
France in 1798 and later was Commodore of the Mediterranean squadron.

year-old Virginian who was named the *Richard*'s first lieutenant, had escaped from British prisons, while the rest had been released from captivity primarily through Jones's efforts. They were eager volunteers. "Revenge sometimes is quite pleasing to man," noted John Kilby, one of the former prisoners who had been captured in a Maryland privateer and spent twenty-two months in Forton Prison. "We believed that . . . Jones would not disappoint us in our great wish and desire." The former prisoners received a quick introduction to their new skipper's methods of maintaining discipline. "The first sight presented to our View was 13 men strip'd and tied up on the larboard side of the quarterdeck," Kilby later recalled. "The boatswain's mate, Commenced at the first nearest the gangway, by giving him one Dozen lashes with the Cat o nine Tails. . . ." The men being flogged were the crew of the Captain's barge who had deserted their boat and gotten drunk ashore, leaving the angry Jones to hire a fishing boat to return him to his ship. When the boatswain's mate reached the coxswain of the barge, Kilby reported, First Lieutenant Dale said: "As he is a bit of an officer, give him 2 Dozen." After punishment had been administered, Jones addressed the volunteers. "Well gentlemen & my lads, I well know where you have all been for a long time. I know you are true to your Country, and as my ship has got a severe name, if any of you want any liberty that's not allowd by the Rules of the Ship, you are to come into my Cabon [cabin] and let me Know."

John Adams, who visited the *Richard* at Lorient before returning to America, left a lively impression of Paul Jones, whom he did not like very much. The Captain, he said:

> . . . is the most ambitious and intriguing officer in the American Navy. Jones has Art, and Secrecy, and aspires very high. You see the Character of the Man in his uniform, and that of his officers and Marines—variant from the Uniforms established by Congress. Golden Button holes for himself—two Epauletts—Marines in red and white, instead of Green. Eccentricities and Irregularities are to be expected from him—they are in his Character, they are visible in his Eyes. His voice is soft and still and small, his eye has keenness and Wildness and softness in it.

Adams was probably nettled to see that Jones and his officers had abandoned the dingy blue uniforms with red trimmings decreed by Congress for the Continental Navy on September 5, 1776. They

wore blue coats with white lapels, waistcoats and breeches patterned
after the uniform of the Royal Navy.[7] The design was smarter than
the blue and red ordered by Congress and was an aid in using
deceptive tactics at close quarters.

While Jones was fitting out his ship and arguing with Chaumont
about money and supplies—he believed the French official was
taking revenge for Jones's affair with his wife—there was much
discussion of how the *Richard* was to be employed. The first plan
called for a raid on a major English port such as Liverpool or Bristol
by a combined naval and military force. Jones would be given
command of a small squadron while the troops would be led by the
Marquis de Lafayette, who had returned to France in February 1779
to urge King Louis to send more French soldiers and ships to
America. With two such ardent officers in command, this operation
would have had interesting results. But the project fell through. The
next scheme called for Jones's ships to be sent on a cruise off
Scotland and northern England to divert some of Britain's scanty
naval forces from barring the way to an intended invasion of
southern England.[8] The invasion never occurred, and Jones was
finally dispatched with his squadron on a commerce-destroying
voyage around the British Isles with orders to return to the Texel, the
port of Amsterdam.

Besides the *Bonhomme Richard* with her forty ill-assorted guns,
Jones's squadron consisted of the fine new American frigate *Alliance*,
36, commanded by Pierre Landais, who had been made an honorary
citizen of Massachusetts; the French frigate *Pallas*, 26; the brig *Vengeance*,
12; and the fast cutter *Cerf*, armed with 18 small guns. All
except the *Alliance* were outfitted and maintained by the French
Navy, but the French officers were given Continental commissions
and the ships sailed under the American flag. From the moment
Jones hoisted his pennant as commodore, he had trouble with
Landais, who turned out to be dangerously unstable. Suspicious,
jealous, and incompetent, Landais was unable to get along with his
officers and men. During the *Alliance*'s voyage across the Atlantic,
on which Lafayette had been a passenger, Landais claimed he had

---

[7] Dissatisfied with the uniform decreed by Congress, a number of captains including Paul
Jones had met in Boston in March 1777 and agreed upon the blue and white one as a substitute.

[8] See Chapter XXII for the story of the attempted invasion of Britain in 1779.

only narrowly put down a full-scale mutiny.[9] Adams, who saw much of the French captain, wrote in his diary that "his face is small and sharp so that you form a mean opinion of him from the first sign. . . . He knows not how to treat his officers, not his passengers, nor any Body else. . . . He is bewildered—an absent bewildered man—an embarrassed mind." It did not take long to confirm Adams's insight. No sooner had the squadron put to sea for a shakedown cruise on June 19, 1779, than the *Alliance* and the *Richard* collided in a squall. The flagship's bowsprit was so badly damaged it had to be replaced, and the *Alliance* lost her mizzenmast. Paul Jones was convinced that Landais had caused the accident by refusing to grant the right of way, but the *Richard*'s officer of the watch was made the culprit and dismissed from the service. A topman also fell to his death, Kilby reported. "As he fell he struck the Cock of Jones hat, but he did no Injury to Jones." Besides his problems with Landais, Jones also had difficulties with his crew. Some of the French and American volunteers came to blows, and a plot was detected among the British prisoners to seize the ship and take her to Britain with Jones as a captive. The suspected mutineers were dealt with according to the age-old law of the sea. The ringleader was given two hundred fifty lashes and thrown into a French prison.

Discipline restored, repairs made, and with two French privateers accompanying the squadron, Jones got underway on his historic cruise early in the morning of August 14, 1779. It was just one week short of a year since the day the *Ranger* had left for America without him. Shortly before the ships slipped away to sea, the commodore issued written instructions to his captains ordering them to pay careful attention to all signals from the flagship, to avoid losing company with her, and to proceed in an emergency to places previously arranged as points of rendezvous. It quickly became apparent, however, that none of the captains took Jones's authority very seri-

---

[9] According to the confessions of the ringleaders, Landais was to be cast adrift in a small boat without food or water; the lieutenants would be forced to walk the plank unless they agreed to navigate the ship to England, the surgeon and marine officers were to be hanged and their bodies tossed overboard while the sailing master was to be tied to a mast and "cut into pieces and hove overboard." Lafayette was to be put in irons and carried to England as a prisoner.

ously. On a leisurely voyage under easy sail around the southern tip of Ireland, one of the privateers took a prize, but the French skipper refused to allow the commodore to send a prize crew over to the captured vessel. The next day the privateers deserted the squadron, taking the prize with them. Because of the lack of discipline of his captains, Jones said later that during the cruise, "I did not sleep three hours in the twenty four from Lorient to the Texel."

Several rich prizes were taken off the western approaches to Ireland, then as now a great highway for British commerce. And the commodore's problems with Landais increased. When Jones signaled the *Alliance* to cease chasing a vessel near a dangerous shore, the Frenchman stormed on board the *Richard* in an ugly mood. In the presence of several of her officers, he addressed the commodore "in the most indelicate manner and language," Jones said. "He told me he was the only American in the squadron"—no doubt due to his honorary Massachusetts citizenship—"and was determined to follow his own opinion in chasing where and when he thought proper. . . ." Shortly afterward, all the ships except the *Vengeance* separated from the flagship without permission. The *Cerf* returned to France, and the *Pallas* and *Alliance* rejoined the *Richard* from time to time at various points of rendezvous. Even when the *Alliance* was in sight, Landais refused to obey orders or to acknowledge signals. Off the Shetland Islands, the Frenchman, in defiance of Jones's orders, sent two valuable prizes into Bergen, Norway, where the authorities promptly turned them over to the British consul.

In mid-September, the squadron was sailing along the east coast of Scotland. "Though much weakened and embarrassed with prisoners," reported Jones, "I was anxious to teach the enemy humanity, by some exemplary stroke of retaliation, to relieve the remainder of the Americans from captivity in England." In the absence of the *Alliance*, the commodore summoned the captains of the *Pallas* and *Vengeance* to his flagship. He unfolded a daring plan for a landing at Leith, the all-but-defenseless port of Edinburgh, and setting fire to it in reprisal for British attacks on American ports. At first the French captains flatly refused to participate in such an adventure. The arguments went back and forth throughout the night. "They made many objections and difficulties to the project," Jones related. At last, he hit upon a proposition that appealed to them—to hold the town for 200,000 pounds' ransom as an alternative to burning it. Jones "was now heard with attention," and the Frenchmen entered into the plan with enthusiasm. On September 17, the three ships sailed boldly into the Firth of Forth, striking terror into the hearts of the citizens of Leith and Edinburgh. Women, children, and old folks were hustled into the countryside, drums beat and the young men, armed with fowling pieces, pikes, and claymores, gathered on the waterfront. Three banks packed up their money and readied it for shipment inland.

This grim scene had its lighter moments, however. One of the loyal lairds of Fifeshire, fearful of the approach of the dreaded Paul Jones, trundled out a brass cannon to defend his mansion but found he had no gunpowder. So, according to Morison, he sent his yacht in search of the British frigate *Romney*, which was in the neighborhood, to ask for the loan of a barrel of powder. Unable to find the *Romney*, the yacht's skipper hailed the first ship he saw. With her officers wearing blue and white uniforms and her marines scarlet coats, the ship could only be a Royal Navy man-of-war, he thought. She was the *Bonhomme Richard*. Without cracking so much as a smile, Jones furnished the powder and retained one of the yacht's crew as a pilot. Let John Kilby relate what happened next.

"What was the news on the Coast?" asked the commodore.

"Why, very great & bad news," answered the pilot. "That Rebel Paul Jones is Expected every day to land."

The commodore then asked him what he thought of this Jones.

"He is the greatest Rebel & pirate that Ever was," answered the pilot, "and aught to be hanged."

After asking the man if he knew to whom he was talking, the commodore said: "I am Paul Jones."

Dropping to his knees, the frightened pilot "begged for his life." Laughing, Jones ordered him to get up and declared: "I won't hurt a hair of your head, but . . . you are my prisoner."

The American squadron lay within gun shot of Leith, and the boats had been hoisted out for a landing, when a sudden, severe gale blew up, driving the ships out of the Firth of Forth back into the North Sea. Having lost the advantage of surprise, Jones abandoned the project. On September 19, he proposed a raid on Newcastle-on-Tyne, with the objective of cutting off London's winter coal supply. With no promise of ransom to tempt them, the captains of the *Pallas* and *Vengeance* refused to take part in the expedition and threatened to desert the squadron for good unless Jones abandoned the coast of England. If the commodore obstinately insisted on remaining in these waters, they told him, it was only a matter of time until a superior British squadron would corner them all. Separating, the ships sailed southward along the Yorkshire coast, taking several prizes on the way.

On the morning of September 22, the *Richard*, flying the British flag, was off the mouth of the Humber River. Jones hoisted the signal for a pilot. Two boats came out, and both men were taken prisoner. The wind was too light for the *Richard* to move up the Humber estuary in pursuit of a merchant convoy that had taken shelter there so Jones turned northward toward a rendezvous with the rest of his ships off Flamborough Head, a chalk-cliff headland jutting out into the sea. From there, the squadron was to proceed to Holland. During the night the *Pallas*, *Vengeance*, and *Alliance*, which had not been seen for more than two weeks, rejoined the flagship. Along toward three o'clock the following afternoon—September 23—lookouts at the *Richard*'s masthead sighted numerous sails standing in from the north and moving in their direction. To Jones's delight, one of the captured pilots told him it was a convoy from the Baltic, forty-one ships loaded with valuable naval stores and timber for the Royal Navy. Cracking on all sail, the squadron went in chase of the merchantmen who had put about and fled northward to the protection of the batteries of Scarborough Castle on the seacoast. The two escorting men-of-war hastened to interpose themselves between the fleeing convoy and the enemy ships since the British captains had been informed of the identity of the strange ships by boats that had come out from the shore.

From the captured pilots the commodore learned that the escort vessels were the new frigate *Serapis*, rated at 44 guns but actually carrying 50, under the command of Captain Richard Pearson, and the sloop-of-war *Countess of Scarborough*, 22. Jones quickly realized that to get at the convoy, the escort would have to be eliminated as quickly as possible. But since the wind was light, the squadron made little headway, taking more than three hours to cover the ten or eleven miles that separated it from the British vessels. The sun was setting when at 6 P.M. Jones ordered his men to quarters and hoisted the signal "Form Line of Battle." None of his captains paid the slightest attention to it. The *Alliance*, which had been in the lead, sheered off leaving the *Richard* to shoot ahead to engage the *Serapis* alone; the *Pallas*, which had been astern of the flagship, also turned away though she later engaged the *Scarborough*; the *Vengeance* took no part at all in the action. Still showing British colors, the *Richard* came about, and soon she and the *Serapis* were sailing side-by-side, a pistol shot apart as they headed westward away from Flamborough Head. The American ship was to the south and to windward of her adversary.

Darkness was falling, but Jones made out the double row of stubby black guns run out of the ports of the British vessel and the men with lighted matches behind them. On her lower gun deck the *Serapis* mounted a main battery of twenty 18-pounders compared with the six unreliable cannon of that weight stowed in the *Richard*'s gunroom. The *Serapis* also carried twenty 9-pound guns on her upper covered gun deck, compared with the *Richard*'s main battery of twenty-eight 12-pounders. On her spar deck, the *Richard* had six 9-pounders, and the *Serapis* ten 6-pounders. The British vessel also had the advantage of a homogeneous crew and was new, with a copper-sheathed bottom that prevented fouling and improved her speed. As the ships closed, "the moon was rising with majestic appearance, the weather being clear, the surface of the great deep perfectly smooth, even as in a millpond" recalled Midshipman Fanning.

"What ship is that?" called out Captain Pearson.

"The *Princess Royal!*"

The creak of yards and masts and the squeak of ropes in their blocks sounded louder than usual as the ships ran silently side by side through the darkness. Jones stood by with a speaking trumpet in his hand but remained silent.

"Where from?" asked the British captain with irritation. "Answer directly or I'll fire into you!"

Instead of replying, Jones struck the British ensign flown by the *Richard* and raised a flag with red, white and blue stripes. Broadsides erupted from both ships. "The battle being thus begun, was continued with unremitting fury," reported Paul Jones. "Every method was practised on both sides to gain an advantage and rake each other." At the first or second salvo, there was a burst of flame from the *Richard*'s gunroom. The ship shook from stem to stern. The air was filled with agonized screams and the smell of burnt powder and seared flesh. Two of the old 18-pounders had exploded, killing most of their crews, shattering the battery and blowing a gaping hole in the deck above. In an instant, the weight of the American vessel's broadside was cut to 195 pounds as compared to 300 pounds for the *Serapis*.

After an exchange of only a few broadsides, Jones quickly realized that he could not win a gunnery duel with the *Serapis*. His only hope lay in grappling the British vessel against the *Richard*'s side and killing off her crew. Otherwise, his ship would be shot to pieces at long range. But the *Serapis* was the more manageable and faster vessel. Every attempt to lay the *Richard* alongside the British ship was fended off by Captain Pearson. Early on in the battle, Jones let the *Richard* drop behind the *Serapis* and then ran her across the British ship's wake and into her starboard quarter in an attempt to board. The boarders were repulsed by a curtain of fire, and Jones sheered off. Now it was Pearson's turn. The *Serapis* shot ahead of the *Richard* and the British captain tried to place her in a position to sweep the deck of the American vessel with raking fire. Turning to avoid being raked, the *Richard* ran her bow into the *Serapis*'s stern and hung there, unable to bring a single gun to bear upon her adversary. Pearson, having clearly demonstrated his ship's superior firepower and maneuverability, thought Jones might be ready to surrender. At this point—not later in the battle as is commonly assumed—he confidently called out: "Has your ship struck?" From out of a cloud of smoke came the defiant answer: "I have not yet begun to fight!" [10]

The *Richard* backed off, and soon the ships were again broadside to broadside. The American vessel absorbed some heavy punishment. Blood stained the scrubbed planks of her deck. Men were butchered and timbers shattered as British round shot plunged through her hull. Great sections of bulwarks were torn away, scattering rolled up hammocks that had been stowed in the nettings about the deck. Gun crews frantically kicked them out of the way of their guns which were jumping back and forth to the limit of their breechings. Silhouetted in the fading light, the *Serapis* stood off,

[10] The first account which included this statement was given in 1825 by Richard Dale, the *Richard*'s first lieutenant, to an early biographer of Paul Jones. Jones did not mention having said it in his report of the action.

black and menacing, her sides methodically spouting sheets of flame. Taking advantage of a sudden gust of wind that reached the *Richard* first because she had the weather gage, Jones tried to surge ahead and cross the bow of his opponent. The maneuver "did not exactly succeed to my wishes," he acknowledged. Some of the *Richard*'s braces had been shot away and the yards could not be trimmed quickly enough for her to successfully complete the turn. The two ships crashed against each other. The *Serapis* ran the tip of her bowsprit into the *Richard*'s mizzen rigging, their yards became entangled and the vessels pivoted in the wind until they were locked together bow to stern. A fluke of the *Serapis*'s spare anchor hooked onto the bulwarks of the *Richard*'s starboard quarter, sealing the embrace and jamming the muzzles of their guns against each other. This was the moment Jones had been waiting for. "Well done, my brave lads!" he cried. "We have got her now!" Grappling hooks were thrown on board the *Serapis* to bind the vessels together. With his own hands, Jones seized one of the British vessel's forestays, which had been parted by a shot and fallen across his quarterdeck, making it fast to the *Richard*'s mizzen mast. Samuel Stacey, the sailing master, worked with him, cursing heavily under his breath as British shot whistled about them. "Mr. Stacey, it's no time to be swearing now," the commodore reproved him. "You may by the next moment be in eternity."

Captain Pearson struggled desperately to break the *Richard*'s deadly embrace so he could bring his superior firepower to bear. He ordered the grappling irons cast off or severed, but any British sailor who showed himself in the open was cut down by sharpshooters stationed in the fighting tops of the American vessel. When Pearson ordered an anchor dropped, hoping this would pull his ship clear, the wind and tide caused the ships to swing about in a half-circle, still gun muzzle to gun muzzle. They were so close that the gunners on the *Serapis*'s starboard side, coming into action for the first time, found that they could not raise the lids of the gunports. They blasted them apart with a salvo through the lids. To use their rammers, gun crews on both ships had to thrust them into the enemy's ports. Fires broke out in several places on both ships and periodically it was necessary to break off combat to subdue them. Several times the flames licked "within a few inches of the magazine," said Dale. Attracted by the thunder of the cannonade, hundreds of Yorkshiremen huddled on the heights of Flamborough Head to watch the battle, which was illuminated by the flash of gunfire and by moonlight glowing intermittently through the clouds.

Despite the clinch holding the ships together, the *Serapis*'s two decks of 18-pounders soon shattered or overturned all of the *Richard*'s main battery of 12-pounders. Her gun deck was a shambles. The sea poured in through several shot holes below the waterline, and one of her pumps was knocked out. Each broadside ripped through the old Indiaman, turning her into a mass of splinters and shattered timbers. When the battle ended it was found that only a few stanchions prevented her main deck from crashing down into the wreckage below. By 8:30 P.M., three quarterdeck 9-pounders were the only guns on the *Richard* still capable of firing. The commodore helped trundle one of them over from the unengaged port side and served her himself, concentrating on bringing down the *Serapis*'s mainmast with double-headed shot. Jones's sole advantage outside his own courage was the marksmanship of the French marines and seamen in the tops. They concentrated their fire on the men in the *Serapis*'s tops, picking off the snipers stationed there. The ships were so close "we could with ease go from our maintop into the *Serapis*'s maintop," said Fanning. His men swept the upper deck of the British vessel clean. No man could remain alive there, and the battery of ten 6-pounders was quickly deserted. Jones's decision to grapple the *Serapis* prevented the British gunners from bringing down his masts and yards, which continued to support the men in the tops even though their ship was a battered hulk. "During this time," Pearson reported, "from the Great Quantity and Variety of Combustible Matters which they threw in upon our Decks . . . we were on fire not less than ten or twelve times in different places." But the *Serapis*'s 18-pounders continued to spew out death and destruction.

Suddenly, the *Alliance* loomed out of the darkness and bore down on the *Richard*. A ragged cheer greeted her appearance but it was drowned out by the frigate's broadside. "To my utter astonishment he discharged a broadside full into the stern of the *Bonhomme Richard*," said Jones. "We called upon him for God's sake to forbear firing into the *Bonhomme Richard*," but Landais put about and unleashed another broadside into her forecastle before disappearing into the darkness. Several men were killed as they screamed curses at the *Alliance*, and the *Richard* was repeatedly hit below the waterline.

"Every tongue cried that he was firing into the wrong ship," reported Jones. There was "no possibility of his mistaking the enemy's ship for the *Bonhomme Richard*," he added. Jones had his night recognition signals lit, the moon was up and, despite the confusion, the yellow sides of the *Serapis* should have been clearly distinguishable from the *Richard*'s black topsides. The commodore, for one, was convinced that Landais's action was deliberate. After the battle, the Frenchman confided to an intimate that his purpose was to sink the *Richard*, then board and capture the British vessel and thus become the hero of the battle. Later, when Captain Pearson faced a court-martial for the loss of the *Serapis*, he maintained that he had been attacked by two frigates—and this belief may have played an important role in his eventual decision to surrender. The fact of the matter, however, is that the *Alliance* was more of a danger to the *Bonhomme Richard* than she was to the *Serapis*.

Powder-blackened and weary, his ship shattered and sinking, Jones fought on. "My situation was really deplorable," he said. At one point, resting from his work at the 9-pounder, he sat down on a broken timber. A frantic marine officer dashed up and exclaimed: "For God's sake, Captain, strike!" Jones leaped to his feet and declared: "No, I will sink, I will never strike!" While the sharpshooters in the tops kept the *Serapis*'s deck clear of men—Captain Pearson on his quarterdeck alone was spared, probably at Jones's orders—other marksmen concealed on the *Richard*'s gun deck fired through shot holes and ports picking off the British gunners. The gun crews were so decimated that the powder monkeys were soon bringing up cartridges from the magazines faster than they could be used. The frightened boys simply dropped them on the deck near the guns and ran for more. Aloft, William Hamilton, an enterprising Scotch seaman, took a basket of hand grenades and a lighted match out to the end of one of the *Richard*'s yardarms that hung directly over an open hatch on the *Serapis*. He carefully dropped a lighted grenade through the hatch, and it fell among a pile of loose cartridges. They went up in a searing flash, killing at least twenty British seamen and horribly burning others. Some, their clothing afire, jumped screaming into the sea. "Many stood with only the collars of their shirts upon their bodies," reported Lieutenant Dale.

Unnerved, Pearson was about to strike his colors when three of the *Richard*'s ranking petty officers, fearing that their ship was sinking beneath them, decided to surrender. The gunner ran aft to haul down the colors, but, as Jones wrote, "fortunately for me, a cannon ball had done that before by carrying away the ensign staff." "Quarters! Quarters, for God's sake!" bawled the man. "Shoot them! Kill them!" shouted Jones. He yanked a pistol from his belt and hurled it at the gunner, bringing him down in his tracks, giving birth to the legend that Jones had shot one of his own men. Having heard the cry, Pearson hopefully called out: "Sir, do you ask for quarter?" Jones shot back: "No, sir, I haven't as yet thought of it, but I'm determined to make you strike!" Pearson ordered "Boarders Away!" Armed with pistols, cutlasses, and pikes, the boarding party swarmed onto the *Richard*'s bulwarks. Jones's men were "lying under Cover with Pikes in their hands ready to receive them," and the sharpshooters in the tops redoubled their deadly fire. The boarding party quickly retreated in disorder to their own ship.

Water was rising fast in the hold of the *Richard*. It was already sloshing around the feet of the several hundred prisoners that had been taken during the cruise when the master at arms rushed below and freed them. Properly organized, they might have been able to seize the ship. But the prisoners were frightened and were quickly shoved and prodded to the pumps. If they valued their lives, they were told to bear a hand. One man, the captain of one of the prizes taken a few days before, managed to slip away and clamber through a gunport to the *Serapis*. He told Pearson that if he could hold out just a little longer, Jones would have to strike or sink. The *Richard* was on fire in several places, she was leaking badly, and all her cannon had been silenced except the trio of 9-pounders on the quarterdeck. The battle settled down to a war of nerves between the two captains. Which one would give way first?

Jones could feel his vessel settling beneath him. Yet with single-minded determination he continued to bang away at the *Serapis*'s mainmast with his 9-pounder. Shortly before 10:30 P.M., the mast began to totter. For Captain Pearson, this was the final blow. The *Countess of Scarborough* had already struck to the *Pallas* so he could expect no help from that quarter; the *Alliance* was undamaged and might return at any moment to attack him; his ship was on fire. Four of his 18-pounders were still firing, but he decided to surrender. "I found it in vain and in short impracticable from the situation we were in to stand out any longer with the least prospect of success," he later explained to the Admiralty. With his own hands, Pearson tore down the ensign which he had ordered nailed to its staff.

The battle—one of the bitterest ship-to-ship actions in naval history—had lasted for almost three and a half hours and the "butcher's bill" was heavy. Jones put his own losses at one hundred and fifty killed and wounded, without specifying the proportion of each. Pearson stated that the *Serapis* had forty-nine killed and sixty-eight wounded, but Jones, after checking with the English surgeon, estimated that at least a hundred men had been killed on the British vessel. Both ships suffered severely. Pearson had just been brought over to the *Richard* to surrender his sword and to share a glass of wine with his conquerer when the mainmast of his ship toppled into the sea, taking the mizzen topmast with it. The *Serapis* was as badly cut up aloft as the *Richard* was wrecked below. The old Indiaman's rudder was almost torn off, her stern was completely shattered, her quarterdeck was in danger of falling into the hold and she was taking on water at a prodigious rate. The timbers of the lower deck, "from the mainmast to the stern, being greatly decayed with age, were mangled beyond my power of description," observed Jones. The dead and wounded were lying about in heaps, and Midshipman Fanning reported that the blood was "over one's shoes."

Quite naturally Jones did not want to lose the *Richard.* For a day and a night the crews of the American ships and their captives— now well over five hundred men—were put to work trying to salvage her. The fires were put out and the pumps clanked and thumped constantly in an attempt to hold the sea at bay. But on the evening of September 24—the day after the battle—the commodore recognized that the *Richard* was doomed. The wounded were taken off as Jones reluctantly transferred his flag to the *Serapis*—nicknamed the "Sea Raper" by the American sailors. From her deck the next morning, he "saw with inexpressible grief, the last glimpse of the *Bonhomme Richard*" as she plunged bow first below the bubbling waters of the North Sea. She had not been much of a man-of-war, but she had served him well.

Pearson had lost two warships, but he provided time for the Baltic convoy to escape without loss to the protection of the guns of Scarborough Castle.[11] With the *Serapis* and *Countess of Scarborough* crippled, Jones dared not make an attempt to cut out some of the merchantmen and turned his squadron eastward toward Dutch waters in accord with his orders. As soon as word was received of the battle, the Admiralty sent ships scurrying in search of Paul Jones. Semi-hysterical reports that his ships had been sighted off Scotland, off Norway, and off the western approaches to Ireland poured into Whitehall. "Paul Jones resembles a Jack o'Lantern to mislead our marines and terrify our coasts," commented the London *Morning Post* on October 1. "He is no sooner seen than lost." Two days later, the American squadron anchored off the Texel to the cheers of the Dutch. The reaction to Jones's victory in France and America was ecstatic. His feats stood out in bright contrast to the failure of the combined fleets of France and Spain to invade England that summer and to the dismal tide of events in America.

---

[11] Pearson was tried before a court-martial for the loss of his ship and acquitted. He was later knighted. When Jones learned of this, he said: "Let me fight him again . . . and I'll make him a lord!"

XXII

Times to Try Men's Souls

There was a storm coming. Gray winter seas surged about the two fleets—one British, the other French—which were sailing just over the horizon from each other on parallel courses toward the islands of the Caribbean. Clouds of stinging rain swept across their decks and a turmoil of angry water boiled about them. Sail had been taken in and the tangle of men-of-war, transports, and supply ships rolled along under bare masts. Unknown to their commanders, both fleets had left port the same day. The Comte d'Estaing, ignoring American demands that his twelve ships of the line help to clear the coast of the British or to attack Quebec and Halifax, had slipped out of Boston past "Foul Weather Jack" Byron's fleet on November 4, 1779. He intended to commence operations against the British West Indian islands. With New York safe and command of the sea restored to the Royal Navy, Sir Henry Clinton felt secure enough to dispatch the long-delayed expeditionary force charged with the capture of St. Lucia. Accordingly, Commodore William Hotham put out with five ships of the line and 5,000 troops under the command of Major General James Grant. Shifting these forces to the Caribbean raised the curtain on a new theater of the war.

387

The furious gale that struck the fleets in the latitude of Bermuda did more damage to the French ships, but some of Hotham's supply vessels lost contact with their convoy. At least one fell into d'Estaing's hands, providing the first news that a British fleet was at sea. The French admiral guessed that the British were heading for either Barbados or Antigua—and settled upon the latter because the main British base in the Caribbean was there, at English Harbour. Arriving off Antigua on December 6, d'Estaing spent two days fruitlessly cruising for Hotham's ships before making sail for Martinique, the major French base in the area. On December 10, the British fleet arrived instead at Barbados, joining two ships of the line already there under the command of Rear Admiral Samuel Barrington. Giving orders that the troops were to be kept on the transports, Barrington sailed immediately for St. Lucia. He had spent a frustrating summer awaiting reinforcements from America and was anxious to be on the offensive. Barrington had come out to the Caribbean in May, before the war with France had been formally declared, with orders to make no move until he had received further instructions. After that, the Admiralty seemed to have completely forgotten his existence. No fast-sailing frigate was sent to inform him of the official declaration of war, which he learned of only after the French had seized the initiative.

British policy required that all their islands in the Caribbean be held against all odds. "Our [West Indian] Islands must be defended even at the risk of an invasion of this Island," King George declared. "If we lose our Sugar Islands, it will be impossible to raise money to continue the War. . . ." Today, it is difficult to envision the significance attached to these tiny islands. But in the Eighteenth Century the commercial importance of the West Indies was so great that purely military considerations gave way to the protection of trade. Rich and exotic, the West Indian islands flash across the scene leaving an impression of wealth and decadence. The overriding reason for this phenomenon is that these colonies meshed well with the pattern of trade of the era. By producing cotton, cacao, coffee, indigo—and most important, sugar, molasses and rum—they supplied the mother country with raw materials that she could not produce at home. At the same time the islands were a ready market for British manufactured goods, creating a great expansion of trade and industry.[1]

Behind the dazzling white beaches and tall palms lay extensive plantations. The average estate contained about nine hundred acres and was worked by slaves directed by the owner, or more frequently his agent. Food was ordinarily not produced on the plantation and was imported from the British colonies on the American mainland. For example, salt fish taken on the Grand Banks rather than fresh fish from local waters was the staple of the slave diet. Despite the limited amount of good land available, agricultural production was extremely wasteful. The same crops would be planted over and over again on the same ground until it no longer provided a profitable return. The unproductive fields would then be abandoned and new tracts pressed into use. Agriculture on this grand scale required considerable capital and the small planter who had originally worked the Caribbean islands soon gave way to the magnate. The bubble burst early in the next century. Sugar production had become so profitable that it had been extended to other parts of the world, resulting in overproduction and a catastrophic drop in prices, while overcropping finally exhausted the soil. The emancipation of the slaves gave the economy of the West Indies a *coup de grâce* from which it has never recovered. When, in 1833, Parliament voted 20 million pounds to compensate the West Indian planters for the loss of their freed slaves, they were so deep in debt that most of the windfall went to their creditors in London and Bristol.

The Eighteenth Century, however, was a prosperous time for the Caribbean planters. Steadily rising standards of living in England transformed sugar and coffee, which were once considered luxuries, into necessities. More and more land was put into use, more and more slaves were imported to increase production to meet still greater demands for tropical products. Yet, at the same time, the islands were being drained of their white population. "Few proprietors continue to live in them who think themselves able to remove to Britain," observed a traveler. The plantations were placed in the hands of agents and overseers while the owners went to England to spend their wealth and cut a figure in society. The increased value of

---

[1] Seeing the elaborate carriage of a West Indian planter on a London street, George III turned to one of his ministers and declared: "Sugar, sugar, eh? All that sugar! How are the duties, eh, Pitt, how are the duties?"

the islands, along with their vanishing white population, meant the protection provided by the mother country was vital to prevent the ever-present threats of foreign invasion and slave revolts. Simultaneously, British governments became increasingly aware of the power of the absentee West Indian planters. Joined by the merchants trading to the Caribbean, the planters exerted considerable influence on British politics. One of the primary reasons that Britain finally chose to retain Canada rather than Guadeloupe at the end of the Seven Years' War in 1763 was the opposition of the British planters to the threatened loss of their sugar monopoly.

It was inevitable therefore that the defense of the Caribbean islands should be basic to British strategic policy. Squadrons were sent out to the Caribbean to escort the immensely rich convoys upon whose safe passage the economy of the nation largely depended. The movements of the fighting fleets were tied to those of the West Indian trade—sometimes with unhappy results. Sailings of men-of-war were delayed until the convoys were formed and the fleets were often slowed by the necessity of protecting the merchantmen. The islands also loomed large in the eyes of the enemy. It has been estimated that a third of French imports and exports were accounted for by this trade. France hoped that by a successful war it could add most of the British islands in the Caribbean to its possessions. This objective was to cause a fatal flaw in French naval strategy because French admirals tended to regard territorial conquest as their primary objective and the destruction of the enemy fleet as secondary. They completely ignored the fact that the conquest of the West Indian islands would be an easy matter after the destruction of the hostile fleet.

Despite the importance of the islands, the entire British military force in the area consisted of just 1,600 men and only about 1,000 of them were fit for duty because tropical sicknesses had ravaged the garrisons. Although this force was useless unless it was kept together, the West Indian planters insisted the detachments be scattered about the various islands to thwart slave uprisings and attacks by the indigenous Caribs in the southern islands. Jamaica, the largest and richest of the islands, had 440 troops but there were only a hundred on Grenada, thirty on Tobago, and but sixty men on Dominica, which was surrounded by a closely knit group of French islands.

Thus, the safety of the British islands depended almost exclusively on the Royal Navy. And the operations of the navy were governed by the wind, resulting in serious defensive problems. From the end of July to the beginning of November, the Caribbean is subject to severe hurricanes. During that part of the year it was customary for sailing fleets to leave the area for either North American or European waters. Strategic positions during the months when the fleets operated in the Carribean were dictated by the trade wind, which blows, roughly speaking, from east to west. The British West Indies islands were divided into two groups: the chain of small eastern islands, known as the Lesser Antilles, running 600 miles from St. Kitts on the north to Tobago on the south,[2] and Jamaica, a thousand miles to the west. A ship might sail with the wind from Barbados or Antigua to Jamaica in about a week, while the return voyage against the wind could take as long as two months. Thus, ships assigned to Jamaica could not be expected to beat back to defend the Lesser Antilles in case of emergency. The Admiralty was faced with a difficult choice. It could try to maintain two strong fleets in the Caribbean—one based upon Port Royal, Jamaica, and the other at English Harbour on Antigua. Or it could keep a strong force in the Lesser Antilles and hope that it would not be necessary to send ships to defend Jamaica. Because of the shortage of vessels and crews, the latter policy was settled upon. Nevertheless, British admirals were haunted by the fear that Jamaica might be surprised and captured before word of the attack was received at Antigua or Barbados—especially after Spain entered the war. In practice, however, the danger was slight. The Spaniards did not mount an attack and the French were as reluctant to lose the windward position as the British. So the two great fleets fought out their campaigns among the Lesser Antilles.

The French drew first blood. While Barrington fretted at Barbados awaiting orders, the Marquis de Bouillé, the Governor of Martinique, launched an attack on Dominica, which lay just to the north of his own island. On September 7, 1778, he landed a force of about 2,000 men from a makeshift flotilla of sloops and schooners escorted by a few French frigates and privateers. The heavily outnumbered

---

[2] This was known in the Royal Navy as the Leeward Station, because of its position vis-a-vis Jamaica. The Lesser Antilles are divided into two sections—the Windward Islands to the south and the Leeward Islands to the north.

British garrison quickly surrendered, turning over the one hundred sixty-four cannon in the decaying fortifications. Immediately on hearing of the attack on Dominica, Barrington hurried to the rescue with all the force he could muster. He was too late. The French were firmly established ashore and Barrington had no troops to make a landing. He could do nothing but return to Barbados. With the capture of Dominica the French islands formed a solid block extending from Guadeloupe on the north to St. Lucia on the south, severing the line of British islands. The Royal Navy was also deprived of a fine anchorage for watching the French.

During his long and frustrating wait for Hotham, Barrington had had plenty of time to lay plans for the capture of St. Lucia. Lying within sight of Fort Royal, the main French base on Martinique, St. Lucia had several good anchorages. It was an excellent position from which the British fleet could watch the French and intercept their reinforcements as they made their landfalls. Within three days of Hotham's arrival at Barbados, the British expedition lay off St. Lucia. The two days spent by d'Estaing in his futile search for Hotham's fleet at Antigua had been enough to give the British momentary control of the sea. On the afternoon of December 13, the British fleet anchored in the Grand Cul de Sac, an inlet on the western side of St. Lucia. Hotham, who had organized the efficient landing on Long Island in 1776, put General Grant's troops ashore with the smoothness of experience. The next day, white flags heralded the surrender of the French garrison distributed about the Carenage, a bay leading to the town of Castries, the Vigie Peninsula running along the northside of the harbor, and the height known as Morne Fortune.

The British had just assumed control of these positions when the frigate *Ariadne* approached under a cloud of canvas flying the signal "Enemy in Sight!" Her captain was soon aboard the flagship, the *Prince of Wales*, 74, reporting to Barrington that a French fleet of twelve ships of the line and a number of frigates and transports were in the offing. It was d'Estaing. He had arrived at Martinique on December 9, the day before Hotham's arrival at Barbados, and had found enough troops on hand to bring the French land force to 9,000 men. With a fleet far superior to anything the British could bring against him, he planned to capture the British islands of Barbados, Grenada, and St. Vincent in that order. The armada was on its way to Barbados when d'Estaing heard of Barrington's attack on St. Lucia from an American privateer. Elated at the opportunity to crush the entire British sea and land force with one blow, he immediately shifted course for St. Lucia.

To oppose the overwhelming power of the French, Barrington had just seven ships of the line, including three of only 50 guns, while Grant had little more than half the number of troops at the disposal of the enemy. But neither British commander yielded to despair. In fact, they considered themselves lucky to have completed the capture of St. Lucia so quickly. If they had delayed, d'Estaing would have caught them at Barbados or on the open sea. They decided to meet the French threat as Howe and Clinton had met it at New York. Barrington herded the transports into the Cul de Sac and placed his line across its mouth with their broadsides pointed seaward as Howe had done at Sandy Hook.

On the morning of December 15, d'Estaing stood in toward the Carenage, and was surprised when his fleet came under fire from the batteries. He then decided to attack Barrington's ships anchored across the entrance to the Cul de Sac. Twice the French fleet sailed in to deliver a cannonade against the British ships. It had little effect and Barrington's line remained unbroken.

Frustrated at sea, d'Estaing decided to put his experience as a soldier to work and take the British defenses from the rear. The following morning, some 5,000 French troops were landed near the northern tip of the island and marched overland to attack the three British brigades totaling about 1,300 men. The Redcoats that were holding La Vigie Peninsula were veterans who had been fighting in America since the outbreak of the war. They dug in on a low, scrub-covered hill. With d'Estaing bravely leading the way, the French swept forward to attack the British bastion. They were repulsed with heavy losses. It was Bunker Hill all over again—but this time with the British holding the defensive position. Twice again, the French charged with great courage but were unable to dislodge the stubborn British troops. In three hours of fighting over 400 French soldiers were killed and no fewer than 1,200 wounded. British losses totaled 13 killed and 158 wounded. After the grim lesson of La Vigie, d'Estaing's subsequent efforts to recover St. Lucia were little more than perfunctory. Chagrined by his inability to dislodge the British, he wrote Sartine, the Minister of Marine: "From failure to failure, and from one misfortune to another. The King's fleet, collected here, ready to conquer, has not been able to defend or even retake St. Lucia." On December 28, the admiral decided to abandon the enterprise and return to Martinique. Shortly after the first of the new year, Byron, still in pursuit of d'Estaing, arrived with ten ships of the line to shift the balance of naval power to Britain. The first round of the struggle for the West Indies had gone to the British.

During the next six months both the French and British reinforced their fleets in the Caribbean. By the end of May 1779, Byron had twenty-one ships of the line. D'Estaing's fleet had grown to twenty. Since there was no blockade of the French home ports, reinforcements reached him without difficulty. Nevertheless, the British fleet, operating from its new base at St. Lucia, had managed to keep the French bottled up at Martinique. Sickness, however, was a problem and took a heavy toll of British soldiers and sailors. Of the some 5,000 troops fit for duty when Grant had landed on the island, 1,400 were sick or dead by April 1. By the middle of May, the total had risen to over 1,800. The fleet was so shorthanded that two army regiments were detailed as marines. Late in May, Byron was alarmed to learn that a large French convoy that would tip the balance in favor of the enemy had left Brest for the West Indies. It was vital that it be prevented from joining d'Estaing. For five days he sailed to the west of Martinique in search of the enemy ships. Finally he was compelled to leave this station in order to protect a British convoy forming at St. Kitts for the homeward voyage. Profiting by Byron's absence, d'Estaing sent 400 troops southward past St. Lucia and captured the tiny British island of St. Vincent.

On June 27, the French convoy got safely to Martinique with desperately needed provisions and reinforcements. Commodore La Motte Picquet brought with him five ships of the line—giving d'Estaing twenty-five such vessels. "The convoy has arrived," reported the elated admiral. "These four words tell everything." D'Estaing immediately set to work on his next project, sailing on June 30 with his entire fleet and 5,500 troops. The French objective was Barbados but adverse winds caused a change of plans. On July 2, d'Estaing anchored off Grenada. The island's garrison of some 160 regulars and 300 militia surrendered the next day to the overwhelming enemy force, presenting the French with the richest British sugar island in the Lesser Antilles. Thirty heavily laden English merchant vessels and a small armed sloop were also taken in the harbor.

At daybreak four days later, Byron appeared off the island with twenty-one ships of the line and a convoy of twenty-eight vessels carrying troops and equipment. After escorting the merchantmen beyond the reach of French cruisers he had returned to St. Lucia on July 1 to learn of the loss of St. Vincent. Grant had just got his troops aboard the transports when a frigate came in to report that the French had been sighted steering for Grenada. Byron sent a frigate to look into Fort Royal on Martinique but the enemy's cruiser screen prevented her from making a careful inspection. The frigate's captain incorrectly told the Admiral that thirteen French ships of the line were still in port. From this, Byron concluded that only a weak detachment had gone to Grenada. He sailed for the island on July 3, confident that he could handle the slim force he supposed d'Estaing had with him. Two days later, a French frigate sighted the British fleet. On receiving the report, d'Estaing, whose ships were moored in St. George's Harbour, prepared to weigh anchor.

Byron, who was short of frigates, was forced to weaken his line by detailing three of his ships to guard the transports while he sailed ahead to the entrance of the harbor with the rest of his fleet. Soon after sunup on July 6, the French fleet, slowed by a morning calm, started coming out. Ignorant of the enemy's strength and quick to seize the opportunity to attack before d'Estaing could form a line of battle, Byron signaled a "General Chase." Just as at Ushant the year before, the British ships entered battle in disarray. Rushing pell-mell upon the French, the faster ships plunged ahead and were badly battered by the combined fire of the French van and the shore batteries. The rest of the British fleet straggled into action. Shortly after the first contact was made the wind freshened, permitting the entire French fleet to draw out of the harbor in good order. For the first time, Byron realized that he was faced by superior numbers. This did not deter him. The three ships guarding the transports were called up, and the British fleet was ordered into a line parallel with the French. The battle moved to the westward away from the island. The rigging of several of Byron's ships was severely cut up. Four were disabled and drifted off from the action. D'Estaing, however, did not forget his strategic purpose was to cover the French force on Grenada. About 3 P.M., he ordered his fleet to come about and headed back to the island and, incidentally, in the direction of the dismasted British ships. Byron followed. Instead of capturing the damaged vessels, the French admiral was content to cannonade them in passing. The cripples could do nothing except helplessly accept the heavy punishment. Satisfied by what he regarded as a tactical victory, d'Estaing slipped back into St. George's Harbour during the night. The next day, the battered British fleet withdrew to St. Kitts, its tactics having again proven inadequate against an enemy who systematically avoided close quarters.

Neither side lost a ship during the day-long Battle of Grenada, as it was called. As usual the French suffered greater casualties, but they retained control of Grenada. Once again, however, d'Estaing's inability to profit from an advantageous position saved the British from disaster. After the three British ships had left the convoy undefended, it was easy prey for the French frigates. If d'Estaing had set them among the convoy, nothing could have saved the troop-laden transports. Byron's heavy ships could not have broken off the action and dashed to the rescue in time to prevent their destruction. And with four crippled British ships lying dead in the water before him awaiting the *coup de grâce,* d'Estaing was content to fire a few broadsides into them, leaving the vessels to stagger away to fight another day. Even Byron had not expected this. "To my great surprise no ship of the enemy was detached," he reported. Pierre de Suffren, who commanded one of the French ships, lamented: "Had our Admiral's seamanship equalled his courage, we would not have allowed four dismasted ships to escape." Nevertheless, despite d'Estaing's shortcomings the second round of the war in the West Indies had gone to the French. They had added St. Vincent and Grenada to their possessions and had regained command of the sea.

The onset of the hurricane season cleared the board in the West Indies. Toward the end of August, first Barrington and then Byron left the Caribbean for England with most of their ships. At the same time, the French fleet turned westward for a feint at Jamaica before steering toward the American coast. D'Estaing's orders required him to return to France when the hurricane season restricted naval operations in the West Indies, but he decided instead to heed American pleas to aid them in repelling British attacks against South Carolina and Georgia before proceeding home. Following the collapse of the

Franco-American attempt to oust the British from Newport, the war in the North had settled down into a stalemate, and the scene of action had shifted to the South. British troops, dispatched from New York and Florida, scored an immediate success, easily taking Savannah, the capital of Georgia, from the rebels on December 29, 1778. In May of the following year, Commodore Sir George Collier, the temporary British naval commander in America, carried out a devastating raid in the Chesapeake that cost the Americans great quantities of supplies, ordnance, and tobacco. At least 137 vessels were captured or destroyed and two million pounds worth of damage inflicted without the loss of a man.

To the strategists in London, the South seemed the most vulnerable part of the United States. Weakened by the presence of thousands of black slaves, with powerful Indian tribes menacing its frontiers, and possessing far less in the way of military resources than the Northern states, the South invited attack. As long as the British held New York, Washington would be unable to send troops below the Susquehanna River to aid the inhabitants against invasion. The British based their decision to move southward on two assumptions: Tory sentiment was still strong in the South, and command of the sea could be held by the Royal Navy. Despite the disastrous failure of the Southern expedition of 1776, which had been based upon an expected Loyalist uprising, the British clung to this will-o'-the-wisp as if it were a fetish. The Southern colonies could only be recovered if the Loyalists proved to be numerous and energetic. Such support, however, required a long-term commitment of British troops because the army could not conquer the area and leave again without betraying all the King's supporters to the enemy. Success in the South also required that Britain remain superior by sea as well as land. This superiority would be difficult to maintain because the French had unhindered access to the American coast. The British army would be divided between New York and the South, with the sea the only link between its parts. The entire plan depended upon the ability of the Royal Navy to control the waters adjacent to the Southern States.

So unexpected was the arrival of the French fleet off Savannah on September 1, 1779, with twenty-two ships of the line, eleven frigates and transports carrying some 4,000 troops, that a 50-gun ship carrying the payroll of the British army in Georgia fell into d'Estaing's hands. So did a frigate and two storeships. While the French and their American allies, commanded by Major General Benjamin Lincoln, dug in around the city, word of the return of the French fleet spurred action in the North. Both Sir Henry Clinton and George Washington were surprised by the news. Washington immediately wrote the French admiral suggesting a move against New York, where Vice Admiral Marriot Arbuthnot, the new British naval commander-in-chief, had but five ships of the line. Fearing just such a move, Arbuthnot desperately prepared to repeat the defensive performance of Lord Howe at Sandy Hook. Clinton ordered Newport evacuated to concentrate all available troops at New York. This decision is usually portrayed as a disastrous error. Admiral Sir George Rodney, who was then maneuvering for a ranking command, called it "the most fatal measure that could possibly have been taken." His probable motive was to discredit Arbuthnot, according to Piers Mackesy. The British had never used Newport as a base for their fleet and the strongest argument for retaining it was the negative one of denying it to the enemy. Later, a French fleet and army did indeed find a secure base there from which they contributed to the victory at Yorktown. But Arbuthnot and Clinton had to face the immediate reality that some 3,000 troops and a half-dozen warships were tied up at Newport when they were badly needed elsewhere.

There was no real foundation, however, for Washington's hopes and Clinton's fears. After d'Estaing's initial good fortune, his luck changed. Relations between the French and Americans quickly deteriorated and a massive six-day bombardment of the town by sixty-seven cannon and mortars had little military effect. Meanwhile, the admiral was under pressure from his captains to abandon the expedition. The ships were in dire need of repairs, the hurricane season was approaching, they were vulnerable to attack by a British fleet while their guns were ashore and the men were dying of scurvy at the rate of thirty-five a day. After a council of war, d'Estaing decided to cut short the siege by storming the British works.

Unforeseen delays held up the attack, and it was daylight on October 9 before the troops finally pushed forward. Lincoln and d'Estaing, still a soldier at heart, personally led the main attacking column. In the face of withering fire, the combined French and American force fought its way across a ditch surrounding the key British redoubt and planted its standards upon the parapet. But a second column failed to support them, and d'Estaing was badly wounded in savage hand-to-hand fighting. The Allied force was finally hurled back with heavy casualties by a counterattack launched by a handful of British grenadiers and marines. In only two hours, the French and Americans lost more than 800 men killed and wounded, of whom about 650 were French. Estimates of British losses vary, but are usually put at less than 200 men killed and wounded.

Lincoln urged d'Estaing to continue the siege, but the Admiral's nerve was apparently shaken by the heavy casualties, his wounds and the dangerous position of his fleet. He gave up just as he did at New York, at Newport, and at St. Lucia. The Comte de Grasse, one of his commanders, wrote of the Savannah expedition: "Good God! It would have to be seen to be believed, and if we told half we would be taken for exaggerators. . . . The Navy will feel the effects for a long time." Troops, stores, and guns were hastily reembarked on the French ships amid the same bitter recriminations that had followed the misadventure in Rhode Island the year before. Before the end of October, the French had left the coast of America for the second time, leaving frustration, disappointment, and a retreating American army in their wake. A small squadron was detached to the West Indies and the rest of d'Estaing's fleet returned to France. Once again, the Americans had seen the great strategic promise of French seapower dangled before their eyes only to have it withdrawn.

For Britain, the worst crisis of the war was brewing near home.[3] Englishmen were confronted in mid-1779 by the specter of invasion —this time by the combined fleets of Spain and France. Spain declared war on England on June 16, but preparations for the break had been moving at a rapid pace for some time. Hard bargaining preceded the Spanish entry into the conflict—not as an ally of the rebellious American colonists but in partnership with its sister Bourbon kingdom of France. Before the formal declaration of hostilities, France agreed, in exchange for Spain's promise to enter the war, to aid her in recovering Gibraltar, Minorca, Jamaica, and the coast of Honduras from Britain. No peace would be concluded without Gibraltar. This agreement meant that the United States,

[3] For a detailed account of the invasion threat see A. T. Patterson, *The Other Armada* (Manchester 1960).

already bound not to make peace without the approval of France, now found itself obliged, without having been consulted or having given its consent, to remain at war until Spain won Gibraltar. Yet the haughty Spaniards declined to recognize American independence in a vain attempt to insulate their colonies in the New World from the dangerous virus of rebellion.

Successive French ministries had examined plan after plan for the invasion of Britain over the past century. All had one common factor—success depended on securing command of the English Channel. This objective had never been obtainable. In 1779, however, the combined fleets of France and Spain were overwhelmingly superior to any force that Britain could gather. A fleet of no fewer than a hundred French and Spanish ships of the line was available to secure command of the Channel, while the Royal Navy could muster less than half that number of vessels. Once the fleets were united, the armada was to move up the Channel, sweeping all before it. In the meantime, two armies totaling nearly 40,000 men were to be poised at Le Havre and St. Malo, ready to embark the moment the English fleet was eliminated or immobilized. The troops were to seize the Isle of Wight and bombard and destroy the adjacent naval base at Portsmouth. Subsidiary operations might be launched against Bristol and Liverpool, the ports that sent out most of Britain's privateers. If the troops were not exhausted they would then be ferried over to attack the victualling depot at Cork, on the southern tip of Ireland.

Time was a vital factor in the plan. The Spaniards insisted that the expedition be concluded by the end of August, before the weather made navigation hazardous in the Channel. This deadline gave the Allies four months from the beginning of May to concentrate their fleets, train them in combined maneuvers, win control of the Channel, and bring off the invasion. The strategy was sound enough in theory, but it rapidly fell apart. Interminable haggling broke out between Paris and Madrid over the roles each power should play. In the end, the French provided thirty ships of the line and the Spanish thirty-six—"a force," observed a contemporary, "unheard of 'til now in history." The two fleets were to rendezvous twenty miles off the Spanish port of Coruña in early May and spend some time operating together to coordinate their movements. No secret was made of the preparations. The prospects of carrying the war to the shores of "Perfidious Albion" inspired volunteers to flock to the army assembling on the coast of Normandy and the fleet fitting out at Brest under the command of the Comte d'Orvilliers.

Supplies and men were short and the weeks dragged on without the French fleet taking to the sea. Not until June 4 did d'Orvilliers leave Brest, five weeks behind schedule, and then only because he feared the British might impose a blockade. He arrived at the rendezvous six days later to find no sign of the Spanish fleet that was supposed to be awaiting him. For six weeks the French fleet impatiently awaited the arrival of the Spaniards, sailing aimlessly about, wasting the finest weather of the year. "All these delays make me fearful that your projects will not be carried out and that the campaign will be abortive," the admiral warned Sartine. "It is sickening . . . to be dependent on foreigners." The effect of the delay soon began to be felt among the French. The ships had been hustled to sea with their complements short 4,000 men, without their full supply of water and provisions and many ships were without surgeons or adequate medical supplies. Before the Spanish came in sight on July 23, the fleet had consumed half its provisions. Fever and smallpox were stalking the decks. When the Spaniards finally arrived, it was found that although French signal books had been sent to Spain, they had not been issued to the fleet. Another week was wasted in translating the signal codes and agreeing on orders. Don Luis de Cordoba, the Spanish commander, was seventy-three years old and had seen little active service at sea. He was distinguished only for his piety. It was his custom to devote a portion of each day to his prayers, and there were strict orders that he was not to be disturbed. When a staff officer ignored this rule to report some disaster, the aged Admiral merely looked up from his rosary and murmured, "It is God's will." Not until early in August did this unwieldy mass of ships start to sail up the Channel—with less than a month left to fulfill its mission.

The British had had no illusions about the attitude of Spain and had been preparing to meet the onslaught of a combined French and Spanish fleet since early in the year. In this crisis, George III sought to rally his kingdom by recalling that "the vigour of mind shown by Queen Elizabeth and her subjects," aided by "Divine Providence," had saved Britain from the Spanish Armada two centuries before. Others, including Lord North, did not share the King's faith in the workings of Providence. There were but thirty ships of the line in the

Channel Fleet, which had put to sea only hours before the Spanish ambassador delivered his country's declaration of war. These ships and a few thousand regular troops were all that was available to defend the home islands. So much for Sandwich's boast the previous year that the Royal Navy was a match for the combined fleets of the Bourbon powers.

Because the Whig admirals refused to serve under Sandwich in the wake of the Keppel-Palliser affair, command of the Channel Fleet had devolved almost by default upon Admiral Sir Charles Hardy, the sixty-four-year-old governor of the old sailors' home at Greenwich. Hardy had been a distinguished officer in the Seven Years' War, but had not been afloat for nearly twenty years and his health was poor. The best that could be said for him was that he was acceptable to all factions in the strife-torn navy. To lend some competence to direction of naval operations, Richard Kempenfelt, an officer of great ability, was named as Hardy's Captain of the Fleet, or chief of staff.[4] No sooner was he on board the *Victory*, than Kempenfelt was appalled at what he saw. "There is a fund of good nature in the man, but not one grain of the Commander-in-Chief," he wrote of Hardy to his superiors. "My God, what have you great people done by such an appointment?" Intra-service feuding had also had its effect upon the fleet. Discipline was poor and the level of efficiency low. Upon one occasion Hardy ordered a signal to be made to form a line of battle and a string of flags was run up to the *Victory*'s masthead. The admiral was amazed to see some of his ships promptly heave-to and begin to lower their boats. It was then discovered that the signal had been sent for the captains of the fleet to send their weekly reports on board the flagship. This fiasco may well have spurred Kempenfelt to hurry his work on an improved system of signals which he produced the next year.

As usual, there was also a shortage of experienced seamen. In March 1779, the fleet had been 5,600 sailors and marines short of its full complement. Toward the end of May, there was still a shortage of 1,500 men, although exemptions protecting seamen serving on colliers and in the fishing fleets from impressment were being disregarded. Troops and press gangs were sent out to capture men for the

---

[4] Kempenfelt, later promoted to Rear Admiral, drowned in 1782 when the rotten bottom fell out of his flagship, the *Royal George*, while she lay at anchor at Spithead.

Royal Navy. Everyone who could be caught was taken, although legally only seamen were liable. Soldiers sometimes surrounded churches during services and as the congregations filed out ruthlessly seized likely looking men. Those who protested that they were not sailors were told they would make good seamen after they had smelled salt water. As one authority has said, "It was unsafe for any able-bodied man to venture abroad unless he had on him an undeniable protection or wore a dress that unmistakably proclaimed the gentleman."

In the throes of the crisis, Sandwich suffered a personal loss that distracted him from official business. On the evening of April 7, Martha Ray, the First Lord's mistress for nineteen years, was murdered by a jealous lover. James Hackman, an obscure young man who had developed a passion for her, decided that if he couldn't have the lady, no one else would. Carrying a brace of pistols, he accosted Miss Ray at the colonnaded entrance to the Covent Garden Opera House and shot her in the head. Then he turned the other pistol on himself, but succeeded only in inflicting a slight wound. He was tried and hanged after a sensational trial that set tongues clacking. Sandwich was overcome with grief at his mistress's death. He had taken her from a milliner's shop when she was sixteen and he was forty-three. She had lived in his house, sang at his parties, and bore him five children who were brought up as if they had been members of Sandwich's legitimate family. Even the King, who was often aghast at the loose living prevalent in the era, sympathized with him. "I am sorry Lord Sandwich has met with any severe blow of a private nature," he wrote. ". . . This world scarcely contains a man so void of feeling as not to compassionate your situation."

The tragedy indirectly resulted in one of the few bright rays of generosity to pierce the political miasma of the day. "Robbed of all comfort in the world," as Sandwich expressed it, he was forced to beg a critic to delay a debate on a motion in the House of Lords demanding his removal from the Admiralty. The Earl of Bristol graciously used a touch of the gout as a convenient excuse to comply. When the vote was finally taken, Sandwich managed to survive by a 78 to 39 margin. Lord North had stepped into the breach with the assertion that a vote of censure against one member of the Cabinet involved all, for the entire Government accepted responsibility for every measure taken by the First Lord of the Admiralty.

All through June and July, Hardy's ships cruised at the far western end of the Channel, off the Scilly Islands, waiting for the Combined Fleet to make its appearance. Alarm was spreading. On July 9, a Royal proclamation was issued commanding the people of the Southern counties to drive all their horses and cattle from the coast in case of invasion. Volunteer militia companies sprang up everywhere. "Even this little village is grown a camp," wrote Horace Walpole from his home at Strawberry Hill. "Servants are learning to fire all day long." The Cornish gentry sent bands of tin miners to work on the fortifications of Plymouth. Even smugglers offered their services. A boom was placed at the entrance to the port and orders were given to sink hulks across the mouths of other harbors. To add to the anxiety of the Government, a convoy of 200 ships was expected shortly from Jamaica, and a number of vessels with rich cargoes were due in from the East Indies. Only one thing was certain. The Combined Fleet was far superior to any British force that could be collected to bar its way if it came up the Channel.

Just how could Britain hope to defeat such an armada? Thirty or perhaps forty ships of the line, at best, could not be expected to beat sixty-six warships. Some Englishmen may have trusted in Providence to repeat the experience of the Spanish Armada—believing that as before the enemy would be destroyed by their own mistakes and the anger of the elements. Nevertheless, there were more positive grounds for hope. Specifically, d'Orvilliers and Cordoba had been given a most difficult task. Unless they brought Hardy to bay and destroyed or immobilized his ships, the invasion would be militarily impossible because the British fleet would constitute a permanent threat to the invasion force. Swift-sailing British cruisers could dart in and out of the armada and play havoc with the defenseless transports. Another ground for British hopes was that they had scored a technological breakthrough of immense importance. By July, the Channel Fleet could boast of seven two-deckers with copper bottoms that could remain at sea for considerable lengths of time without fouling their hulls. More were on the way. Just when Spain's entrance into the conflict put the Royal Navy at a decided numerical disadvantage, it became possible to increase the efficiency of British ships by keeping them at sea longer. "Twenty-five sail of the line, coppered, will be sufficient to hazard and tease this great unwieldy combined armada, so as to prevent their effecting anything," observed Kempenfelt. The whole enemy force would have to escort the transports "and even then it would be impossible to protect them entirely from so active and nimble a fleet."

And where was d'Orvilliers and his armada? Bucking head-winds, ravaged by disease, and short of supplies, his undisciplined fleet had clawed its way up from the Spanish coast to the Channel. On August 15, the *Marlborough*, 74, was on her way to join Hardy off the Scillies when a large number of ships were sighted. Six . . . then eight . . . and finally a whole armada was spread out across the horizon "like a wood on the water." At first the British captain thought this was the Channel Fleet until he came so close as to be in imminent danger of capture by the Combined Fleet. Crowding on all sail, he made haste to inform Hardy of what he had seen. During the last week in July, the British fleet had been forced into Plymouth by dirty weather. At the time the enemy had entered the Channel, Hardy was on his way back to his station at the western approaches. By the time Hardy learned of d'Orvilliers's position, the enemy was far inside his guard, riding unchallenged within sight of Plymouth. The two fleets had passed one another unknowingly in a game of blind-man's bluff.

The worst had happened. For the first time since the Dutch wars, an enemy fleet was in possession of the Channel, and the very safety of the Realm was in jeopardy. And an easterly wind was driving Hardy's fleet before it, sending it out into the Atlantic. "Never at any other time in history," writes a French historian, "not even when Napoleon's army lay encamped at Boulogne, was the French navy so near its oft-dreamt goal, the invasion of England." Panic spread among the civilian population of Plymouth. The ships of the Combined Fleet could be plainly seen riding off shore. Their fears were increased when, on August 17, the thud of gunfire was heard. The British 64, *Ardent*, on her way down the Channel to join Hardy, mistook the enemy fleet for his. She sailed right into it and was quickly forced to surrender after a brief exchange of fire. When d'Orvilliers followed this up by standing in toward the Sound, a bombardment of the town was believed imminent. All business ceased, shops were quickly closed and houses shut up. The inhabitants began to flee inland. "I did not think . . . that I should be Master of the Dockyard

[for] ten hours longer," declared one official. But nothing happened. By daybreak on August 19, the enemy fleet had vanished, leaving behind anxious speculation about its destination.

If the frightened populace of Plymouth could have known what was taking place on the French admiral's flagship, the *Bretagne*, they would have breathed considerably easier. The shortage of provisions and water was now desperate, there were surprisingly few pilots who knew the English coast despite its proximity to France, and the epidemic was making such terrifying progress that many of the vessels were little more than hospital ships. D'Orvillier's son, a young lieutenant, was among those carried off by the fever. So many dead were thrown overboard while the enemy ships were off the Devon coast that the people refused to eat fish for a month. D'Orvilliers was still waiting for a wind to take him up the Channel in the hope of finding the British fleet—which was actually astern of him—when he received new orders on August 16. The whole plan of operation was changed. Portsmouth and the Isle of Wight were no longer the primary objectives. Instead, there was to be a landing at Falmouth on the southern coast of Cornwall. The French army would establish a bridgehead that was to be held throughout the winter. Water and provisions to keep the fleet at sea for several more months were to be supplied by a convoy from Brest.

D'Orvilliers was considerably upset by these orders. The prospects for revictualling at sea were not very bright, despite the promises. He faced the grim prospect of months of cruising off a dangerous shore during the worst weather of the year without adequate provisions or water. The admiral made a final appeal to his superiors, begging that the entire operation be called off. "I cannot persuade myself that the project contained in my last instructions . . . can subsist when it has been sufficiently considered," he declared. "The condition of the Navy alone—devastated by disease, without water and soon without food—make it imperative to abandon it." Only one way remained to salvage the campaign. The British fleet must be found and defeated in battle to release the Combined Fleet from being forced to conduct a winter blockade. On August 25, the admiral called a council of war on his flagship in which it was agreed to make one more effort to bring the English to battle. Whatever provisions remained were divided among the various ships, extending the fleet's cruising time until September 8.

Six days later, on August 31, the two fleets at last came within sight of each other. The wind had shifted, allowing Hardy to come back up the Channel from the Atlantic. The fleets were off the Lizard, near the southern tip of England, when after intermittent sightings through patches of fog or mist over the previous two days, the armada was plainly seen from the masthead of the *Victory*. Hardy had thirty-nine ships to his opponents' sixty-six. But the Combined Fleet was so spread out that it was doubtful that many of the enemy ships could get into action if the British chose to fight. Hardy decided to risk an action—but only after trying to draw the enemy further up the Channel where the narrow waters, the proximity of friendly ports to receive damaged ships and the possibility of more reinforcements might further reduce the Franco-Spanish margin. He ordered his fleet to continue along to the eastward away from the enemy, ignoring their presence. D'Orvilliers hoisted a signal for a chase, but his fleet was straggling so badly—especially the Spaniards, who were described as able "to overtake nothing and run away from nothing"—he was unable to close. By the next morning, the British were well to the east of the enemy, who had been distracted to the southward by another concentration of ships, which turned out to be a fleet of Dutch Indiamen.

Many of Hardy's officers and men felt deeply humiliated by his "retreat"—which they regarded as running away from the enemy. Captain Adam Duncan of the *Monarch* spoke of his "indignation and shame at being unable to do more than stand looking over the stern gallery" of his ship. A Major Floyd, of the flagship's marine detachment, wrote that "the British fleet fled before the enemy, and the seamen hung their hammocks before the *Victory*'s [figure] head, that she might not see such days." Nonetheless, Hardy had scored a tactical success—he had again placed his fleet between the enemy and the southern ports, covering them from invasion.

Everyone assumed that a battle was inevitable. "I hope soon to hear of an action," declared King George on September 2. That same day, Sandwich wrote Hardy: "I need not tell you that the eyes of the whole world are upon you and that no man in this kingdom ever had such an opportunity as yourself of serving his country." The dockyards were scoured and every ship available was pressed into service. Some were scarcely able to float but everything capable of carrying sail and firing a gun was to be sent to join Hardy. In the first three days of September, six ships of the line joined the Channel Fleet, bringing its total strength to forty-five. Unknown to the British, d'Orvilliers received orders on September 3 to abandon the project and return to Brest. There was to be no resounding sea victory. A month later, the army camps at St. Malo and Le Havre were disbanded.[5]

Since the invasion failed to materialize and not a single French soldier had been even embarked, the campaign can be considered a defeat for France and Spain and, in consequence, a victory for Britain. The sole result of the immense effort put forward by the Bourbon powers was the inadvertent capture of one British warship, the *Ardent*. Hardy's fleet had not fired a shot, but its mere presence at sea—constituting what Mahan called "a fleet in being"—had prevented the enemy from putting the invasion plan into execution. As Marie Antoinette said, the expedition "cost a great deal of money to do nothing." On the other hand, British strategy was defective. The entire invasion could have been nipped in the bud if the Channel Fleet had been stationed off Brest as soon as it was known that the French were preparing for sea. The British fleet was superior to the Brest fleet and could have prevented it from sailing to make a junction with the Spaniards.

Hardy was also dangerously lax in not maintaining contact with d'Orvilliers after the two fleets had sighted each other and parted. Instead, he continued to sail calmly up the Channel to Spithead, although for all he knew the Combined Fleet might well be at his heels. Even if it were assumed that the armada was returning to its base, one cannot imagine Nelson or Paul Jones—if they had been in Hardy's place—failing to even shadow the enemy. Not only would they have done this, more than likely they would have pursued and fallen upon the stragglers as the fleet withdrew. Confronted with this lack of audacity, King George firmly declared: "We must risk something, otherwise we shall only vegetate in this war. . . . I wish either to get through it with spirit, or with a crash to be ruined."

For the Continental Navy, 1779 was a year of mixed blessings. While the fleets of Britain, France, and Spain contended for suprem-

---

[5] D'Orvilliers, grieving over the death of his son, entered a monastery upon his return to France.

acy in the Caribbean and in the English Channel, it struggled to maintain itself as a fighting entity. The six frigates in Boston at the start of the year—the *Alliance, Deane, Warren, Providence, Boston,* and *Queen of France*—rocked uselessly at their piers as their captains labored to recruit crews and obtain supplies. As usual, manning was a trial. By early February, the *Boston* and *Warren* had but seventy men each and the *Providence* only thirty. The *Confederacy,* at New London, was having so much trouble getting a crew that Captain Seth Harding impressed some French prisoners being exchanged by the British. The French authorities entered a vigorous objection, and Harding and other skippers who had resorted to this means of filling out their crews were forced to release the bewildered Frenchmen. So low had the navy's prestige sunk that it was looked upon as a place to dispose of the dregs of the army. Sending Washington the court-martial proceedings upon one of his soldiers convicted of desertion and theft, General Elias Dayton said the man deserved the death penalty. "But as he is the son of a good Whig who begs that we only spare his life, perhaps your Excellency could order him aboard a frigate, it might answer as good a purpose as to execute him."

The Eastern Navy Board also contemplated an embargo on privateering until the Continental ships had obtained crews. William Vernon warned that it would be impossible to recruit men "unless some method is taken to prevent desertion" to the privateers. "I wish, I hope and pray for an Embargo . . . thro' all the United States, until the Fleet is compleatly Mann'd." But nothing came of the proposal. Supplies—especially flour—and funds were also short. The Navy Board complained: "We are at present wholly destitute of money, have stop'd the payment of Bills for Sometime. . . ." Only the contribution by the army of fifty hogsheads of rum from its stores kept the navy afloat. Repeated demands for funds from the nearly moribund Marine Committee to meet the mounting pressure from creditors and suppliers were all but ignored. To save the credit of the navy, the members of the Eastern Navy Board were finally forced to borrow $20,000 on their own personal notes.

The *Queen of France,* commanded by Captain Joseph Olney, was the ship in the most advanced state of readiness. On February 10, Olney was ordered to make a cruise to the south to deal with British privateers playing havoc with the trade of Maryland and Virginia. Few American merchant vessels sailing out of Chesapeake Bay escaped them—which contributed to the flour shortage in New England. With Richard Henry Lee, a Virginian, presiding over the Marine Committee, the appeals of the Baltimore merchants for Continental Navy protection fell upon receptive ears. There was also widespread dissatisfaction in the rest of the country over the tendency of Yankee captains to regard the navy as solely a New England defense force and to send their prizes into northern ports. In view of this, Lee carefully stipulated that Olney was to remain at sea as long as his provisions held out, and he was to return to Philadelphia or one of the Chesapeake ports, not to New England.

The *Queen* did not get to sea until March 13, which allowed time for Captain John B. Hopkins to secure a crew for the *Warren*, and for Thomas Simpson to bring the *Ranger* down from Portsmouth where she had remained since returning from France the previous year. They received orders similar to Olney's. With Hopkins in command, the squadron was cruising off Cape Henry at the mouth of the Chesapeake early on April 7 when a convoy of ten British ships was sighted. Seven of the vesssels, store ships and transports, bound from New York to Georgia, were taken along with the *Jason*, 20, their escort. There were no troops aboard but the ships were loaded with provisions and complete equipment for a cavalry regiment. Elated by this success, Hopkins violated his instructions by not continuing the cruise. He ordered his ships and their prizes to put about for the north, later claiming the decision was based on "intelligence of a large number of armed vessels, being off Chesapeake and Delaware Bays."

The flour shortage was at least temporarily eased by the captured provisions, and the sight of the prizes flying the Stars and Stripes they sailed into Boston boosted morale. The Marine Committee was so pleased with the outcome of the cruise it sent Captain Hopkins a congratulatory letter. But like his father upon his return from New Providence in 1776, the younger Hopkins was to have only a brief triumph. As soon as the *Warren* and *Queen of France* had been sighted, the Eastern Navy Board, fearing that if the frigates tied up to a pier at Boston, their crews, which had taken months to recruit, would probably desert, warned the captains to remain at Nantasket Road. The directives were ignored and, as predicted, the men quickly melted away, leaving the vessels useless.

The reason for the failure of Hopkins and Olney to keep their ships out of the harbor soon became clear. They had been named prize agents for their crews, which the Navy Board found to be "very injurious to the service . . . as well as dishonorable." Thus, they would receive not only a captain's share of the prize money but also a commission on each man's share—which averaged about $2,000.[6] "We must inform you by Appearances and their Conduct that they are more attached to their own Interest and Emoluments than to the honor & benefit of the United States," a disgusted Navy Board informed the Marine Committee. ". . . No men were ever more asiduous in Search of gain than those two Captains have been." The Committee approved the suspension of Olney and Hopkins. With more captains than ships available, this ended their service in the Continental Navy. John Rathbun was given the *Queen of France* and Dudley Saltonstall was moved over to the *Warren* from the *Trumbull*, still stranded in the Connecticut River.

On July 18, a squadron consisting of the frigate *Providence*, under the command of Abraham Whipple, the *Queen of France* and the *Ranger* lay-to wrapped in a dense Newfoundland fog. Nothing could be seen, but the sounds of ship's bells and an occasional signal gun were heard. When the fog lifted, the Americans discovered they had stumbled into a Jamaica convoy of some sixty ships bound for London under escort by a two-decker and several smaller vessels. The *Queen* found herself alongside one of the lumbering merchantmen. Rathbun, an old hand at deception, played the part of an escort vessel and requested the English skipper to come aboard his ship. As soon as he was on the frigate's quarterdeck, he was made a prisoner. A boarding party went over to the merchantman to make her a prize. Whipple and Simpson followed Rathbun's example and the Americans remained in the convoy throughout the day, plucking eleven ships in all from it. Three of the prizes were later retaken by the British, but the remaining vessels, loaded with rum, sugar, cotton, and spices, were brought safely into port. As the line of strange ships stood into Boston harbor, the citizens anxiously gazed seaward from the rooftops, fearing they were a British squadron bent on bombarding the town. When the American colors were seen

---

[6] It was also suspected, according to Morgan's *Captains to the Northward*, that Olney and Hopkins had bought up their seamen's shares at a fraction of their true worth. Sailors usually sold their shares at a discounted price rather than await the completion of the lengthy legal process that preceded the payment of prize money.

streaming out from the ships, joyful salutes were fired by the forts and church bells were rung in wild celebration. The value of the prizes and their cargo was over a million dollars, making this the Continental Navy's most lucrative cruise of the war.

Bostonians were concerned about the arrival of a British fleet off their town because the enemy was known to be building a base on the Penobscot River in Maine, some 175 miles to the north and east. This project had a double-barreled objective. It was to provide a home for the dispossessed Loyalists who had fled to Nova Scotia and was also to serve as a base for British cruisers preying on the New England coast. The site selected was Bagaduce,[7] a bootlike peninsula jutting out into the waters of Penobscot Bay. In June 1779, about seven hundred British troops sailed southward from Halifax under Brigadier General Francis McLean. They were accompanied by three sloops commanded by Captain Henry Mowat, who had burned Falmouth in 1775. The British wasted no time. As soon as they landed on June 17, the silence of the Maine woods was broken by the sound of axes and the crash of falling timber. A small redoubt named Fort George began to take shape on cleared ground at the top of a high bluff. Provisions, artillery, and equipment had to be manhandled about a quarter-mile from the shore up to the fort, making construction so difficult that a month later work was still continuing.

Northern New England had been free of enemy troops since Sir William Howe evacuated Boston in 1776, so news of the occupation of Bagaduce caused considerable shock and alarm. Something had to be done about the "designing and artful wretches" encamped just two days sail from Boston. Without consulting the Continental authorites, the Massachusetts General Court authorized an expedition to dislodge the invaders. A call was issued for twelve hundred militiamen to serve under Brigadier General Solomon Lovell, a veteran of the Newport campaign the previous year. Lieutenant Colonel Paul Revere was called from his silversmith's bench to command the artillery. Abigail Adams noted that in Braintree more than half the men between sixteen and fifty were already in the army so the Penobscot expedition had to rely on the sweepings. About nine hundred men

---

[7] Now part of Castine, Maine.

volunteered. One officer reported that a sizeable number were "small boys and old men unfit for service." Most had arms, but many of them needed repair.

The army was to be transported to Maine by water so the plan of operations included support by a sizeable naval force consisting of state-owned vessels and privateers. Permission was granted for the three remaining Continental ships at Boston to join the expedition. They were the frigate *Warren*, now under command of Dudley Saltonstall, the "lucky" sloop *Providence*, which had been given to Hoystead Hacker after Rathbun moved on to the *Queen of France*, and the 12-gun brig *Diligent* recently captured from the British and skippered by Lieutenant Philip Brown. Saltonstall, the senior Continental officer, was named Commodore of all the naval elements. Besides the Continental ships, these included three 14-gun brigs of the Massachusetts Navy, the *Hazard*, *Active*, and *Tyrannicide*; New Hampshire's contribution was the 20-gun *Hampden*, a dozen privateers and twenty-one transports and supply ships. They carried a total of some three hundred guns of varying power and about three hundred marines—half Continental and the rest from Massachusetts. This was the largest naval expedition mounted by any of the states during the war.

There was considerable delay in getting the flotilla to sea. To muster enough seamen for the expedition, the Massachusetts authorities took the unusual step of impressing men for service on the ships and laying down a forty-day embargo on merchant shipping. Since the embargo prevented seamen from securing other employment, it was easier to enlist sailors for the fleet.[8] It was expected that this particular service would be brief, easy, and triumphant. Saltonstall's instructions were to "Captivate, Kill or destroy the Enemies whole Force both by Sea & Land, & the more effectually to answer that purpose, you are to Consult measures & preserve the greatest harmony with the Commander of the Land Forces, that the navy & army may Cooperate & assist each other." All would have gone well if this injunction had been heeded. But cooperation depended upon understanding between the commanders of the sea and land forces—and as in many other combined operations, it was lacking at Penobscot.

---

[8] When Continental officers pleaded with the local authorities for such action, it was usually flatly rejected.

The Americans arrived in Penobscot Bay on July 25, to find the British prepared for them. It was impossible to keep such a sizeable undertaking secret. The delay in starting and the breaches of security were so serious that Marine Lieutenant John Trevett, who had long served on the *Providence*, begged off going to the Penobscot. As Trevett predicted, as soon as General McLean, the British commander, heard of the expedition, he hurried a messenger off to New York to seek help. Then he set about preparing his defenses. Work on Fort George was pushed and secondary batteries were established on the Bagaduce peninsula and nearby Nautilus Island. Captain Mowat moored his three sloops, with a total of fifty-six guns, closely together at the entrance to the harbor with the transports huddled behind them. As soon as the Americans arrived, nine of their ships stood in toward the British line. Brisk fire was exchanged for more than two hours with little effect. That same evening, General Lovell tried to establish a beachhead on Bagaduce. A strong wind blew up and forced him to call off the landing because he feared the first wave might be stranded on the beach.

Early on July 26, about one hundred fifty marines led by Captain John Welsh, of the *Warren*, landed on Nautilus Island under the cover of gunfire from the ships and drove off the Redcoats. Two 18-pounders and a 12-pounder that commanded the British anchorage were mounted by Paul Revere's artillerymen. Mowat moved his vessels further up the harbor to get them out of range. The next day was spent in reconnoitering the British position, an unnecessary delay in the opinion of some of Saltonstall's officers, who said it gave the enemy more time to prepare to meet an attack. On July 28, an assault was launched on Bagaduce under cover of a naval bombardment. Light was just breaking when the guns of the ships sent a rain of shot pouring into the woods surrounding Fort George, smashing trees and digging up the ground. The battery on Nautilus Island dueled with Mowat's sloops at long-range. Firing slackened and died away when the small boats carrying the Yankees nosed up on the beach. They landed in three divisions, with the marines on the right meeting the stiffest resistance. To keep from falling as they clambered up the bluff, the men clung to trees and shrubs, while the British fired down upon them. Despite heavy casualties, the marines swept the heights. Reinforced by the militia, they drove the Redcoats back from their outlying positions to the safety of the fort.

At this critical point, the tenuous cooperation between the American land and sea forces completely collapsed. Although his men had smashed to within six hundred yards of the British defenses, Lovell refused to order another assault. He insisted that Saltonstall's fleet deal with the enemy's ships before the troops attacked the bastion. With the British protected by their entrenchments, he declared that his force was insufficient to storm the enemy stronghold as long as it was supported by Mowat's warships. In turn, Saltonstall refused to launch an attack even though he had overwhelming naval superiority. He argued that Fort George should be taken before he moved against the ships. When a militia colonel told the commodore the vessels could be silenced in a half-hour, Saltonstall looked down his nose at him and replied: "You seem to be dam knowing about this matter! I am not going to risk my shipping in that dam hole!"

Arguments see-sawed back and forth. Days stretched into weeks and an operation that should have been quickly completed turned into a dreary siege. Fort George, little more than a crude breastwork when the Americans arrived, grew into a formidable structure. Some of Saltonstall's captains, worried about being cooped up at the head of the bay and haunted by the threat of a British squadron appearing from over the horizon, pleaded with him to launch an immediate attack. News of the commodore's inaction drifted back to Boston, and on August 12 the Navy Board sent him a stinging rebuke. "We have for sometime been at a loss to know why the enemy's ships have not been attacked. . . . It is agreed on all hands that they are at all times in your power," the Board declared. "It is therefore our orders that as soon as you receive this you take the most effectual measures for the capture or destruction of the enemy's ships. . . ." In fact, it was already too late. Early the very next day, two American vessels that had been patrolling the mouth of Penobscot Bay sighted a cluster of strange ships standing in under full sail. A powerful British squadron had come to the rescue of the beleaguered British garrison.

Flying his flag in the *Raisonable*, 64, Commodore Sir George Collier had left New York on August 3 in company with the 32-gun frigates *Blonde* and *Virginia*, the latter presented to the Royal Navy through the incompetence of James Nicholson the year before; a 28, two 20s and a 14-gun sloop. Fog had slowed their progress, but be-

cause of the blunders of the rebel commanders, they arrived in time
to rescue the garrison. The Americans were demoralized by the long
rows of gunports on the British ships. The troops piled onto the
transports, abandoning their cannon and equipment. Saltonstall's
captains reported aboard the *Warren* for orders where panic and
confusion reigned. At a frantic meeting some of the more resolute
officers argued that the fleet should make a stand with the ships
drawn up to rake the British men-of-war as they came up the bay in
single file. Enough damage might be done to their top hamper to
allow some of the American ships to escape. Saltonstall appeared to
agree—and then lost his nerve. About noon, he signaled his captains
that it was every man for himself. Discipline disintegrated, and a
mad rush for safety began. All the American vessels, armed ships,
and transports tried to run up the river with Collier's vessels in hot
pursuit. Not a shot was fired by the Americans as they fled for their
lives.

Ships were run aground and set on fire to keep them from falling into enemy hands. Terrified seamen and soldiers fled into the
surrounding woods. By nightfall, towers of smoke and flame soared
above the trees. "To attempt to give a description of this terrible Day
is out of my Power," Lovell wrote in his journal. ". . . Transports
on fire. Men of war blowing up . . . and as much confusion as can
possibly be conceived." All the expedition's forty vessels were destroyed except for two captured by the British. Among those lost
were the *Warren* and the little *Providence*, the last of Esek Hopkins's
original squadron. Barefoot and in rags, a mob of dispirited soldiers,
sailors and the marines plodded through the northern wilderness
toward Portsmouth and Boston. It was a long, heartbreaking walk.

Few military disasters were as complete. Nearly five hundred
Americans were killed or taken prisoner while the British lost only
fifteen men; nineteen armed ships were lost and about $7 million
wasted. There was nothing to show for it except sore feet, mosquito
bites, and ruined reputations. The expense was "not so great as the
disgrace," said one officer. The militia blamed the fleet for the failure
of the expedition, and the sea captains blamed the militia. Several of
the leaders—including Paul Revere—were court-martialed for misconduct. Perhaps with the motive of establishing a claim on
Congress for the cost of the expedition, the Massachusetts authorities   saddled   Saltonstall   with   most   of   the   blame   for   the

fiasco.[9] "The principal reason for the failure was the want of proper spirit and energy on the part of the Commodore," declared an investigating committee. Some angry New Englanders said he ought to be shot. A court-martial was quickly convened, and Saltonstall was dismissed from the Continental Navy. He had presided over one of the sorriest episodes in American naval history.

---

[9] The Massachusetts authorities succeeded in persuading Congress to reimburse them for $2 million of the cost of the expedition.

XXIII

Britain on the Offensive

Shortly before noon on the day after Christmas, 1779, the two-decker *Europe*, an admiral's flag snapping at her foretopmast, poked her way through a field of bobbing ice and headed out past Sandy Hook to sea. From her quarterdeck, Sir Henry Clinton, a notoriously poor sailor, was already feeling queasy as he surveyed a fleet of ninety transports and supply vessels stretched out along the pitching horizon as far as the eye could see. Crammed below decks on the transports were about 8,000 men, the backbone of the British Army in America. Some of them had been aboard ship for weeks, awaiting the order to sail. The transports were escorted by five ships of the line, under the command of Vice Admiral Marriot Arbuthnot, that deliberately plowed through the choppy sea while nine frigates,[1] dashing about like sheep dogs nipping at the heels of their charges, tried to keep the convoy in order.

Following the bloody repulse of the French and Americans at Savannah and the hasty departure of d'Estaing, Clinton had decided that the time had come to subdue the Southern colonies. The cam-

---

[1] Including the *Raleigh* and *Virginia* which had been captured from the Americans.

paign was to begin with the capture of Charleston, which had successfully resisted his efforts to take it in 1776, go on to pacify the Carolinas, and end on the shores of Chesapeake Bay. Thus, the vital link between the Northern and Southern colonies would be severed and everything from Georgia to Virginia subjugated to British control. The Chesapeake had long beckoned Clinton. For some time he had wished to establish an outpost athwart the main rebel line of communication and create a rallying point for Loyalists. The new operation provided an added incentive—to hinder the Americans from moving supplies or men southward. "The Chesapeake, in short, was the place to clamp a tourniquet on the artery of American supplies," states one historian.[2]

Every circumstance was favorable to the expedition. Washington's army, spending the worst winter of the war at Morristown, New Jersey, was in no condition to send help to the South. A few ragged regiments might be detached, perhaps, but not much more. Although Valley Forge has gone down in history as a synonym for privation, the army's suffering was considerably greater during the winter of 1779–1780. "Our prospects are infinitely worse than they have been at any period of the War," George Washington gloomily reported to Congress at year's end. ". . . Unless some expedient can instantly be adopted a dissolution of the army from want of substenance is unavoidable." Dr. James Thacher, a military surgeon, wrote in his journal that "the sufferings of the poor soldiers can scarcely be described . . . the soldiers are so enfeebled from hunger and cold, as to be almost unable to perform their military duty." At the same time, General Lincoln's garrison at Charleston was desperately weak. The Carolinians were disheartened by the defeat at Savannah, discouraged by the belief that they had been left to face the enemy alone, and distraught at the possibility of a Tory uprising. "The fleet cannot have a finer offing," observed one officer as the ships left New York.

Gales, cold weather, and mountainous seas lashed the convoy during its voyage southward. An ordnance vessel loaded with cannon sprang a leak and sank and a transport was blown clear

---

[2] William B. Willcox, "The British Road to Yorktown: A Study in Divided Command," *The American Historical Review*, LII (October 1946). This article and Willcox's *Portrait of a General: Sir Henry Clinton in the War of Independence* (New York 1964) are the foundation for my account of British land operations in the final years of the war.

across the Atlantic, finally coming to rest in Cornwall. Not until the end of January did the battered vessels reach the safety of the Tybee River, near Savannah. "We had a dreadful voyage to this country, with loss of almost everything, baggage, horses, etc., and came to Tybee pretty much in a state of nature," grumbled the wretched Clinton. After repairing their fleet, the British groped toward Charleston, landing troops on Johns Island, thirty miles south of the city, on February 11, 1780.

Charleston, America's fourth largest city, occupied the broad tip of a peninsula between the Ashley River on the west and the Cooper River on the east. These streams flowed into Charleston harbor, which was bounded on the south by James Island where Fort Johnson was situated, and on the north by Sullivan's Island, the site of Fort Moultrie, which had withstood Clinton's attack nearly four years before. Since then, however, the Charlestonians had become lax as years of relative peace, prosperity, and privateering had banked the fires of patriotism. When the time came to defend Charleston, only about a third of those who fought were from South Carolina. The city's fortifications had been allowed to deteriorate and were too weak to repel a determined attack. Charleston was also vulnerable from the land. The broader part of the peninsula on which the city was located was connected to the mainland by a long, narrow isthmus which was only lightly fortified. Determined not to repeat his mistakes of 1776, Clinton decided to envelop the city from both the land and sea and soon controlled the entire western shore of the Ashley River across from Charleston. The British commander-in-chief waited until the fleet had passed over the bar and was in the lower harbor before crossing to the mainland, so the British did not get into position to break ground for a complex of siege works until April 1.

At the time the delay seemed to aid the Americans. It gave Lincoln time to strengthen his defenses and summon reinforcements. In the long run, however, it proved their undoing. The false sense of security resulting from the reinforced defenses convinced the Americans to gamble everything on being able to hold Charleston until a French or Spanish fleet came to the rescue. Some 2,000 Continental troops and a slightly larger number of militia were drawn into the town, along with the Continental Navy's last squadron. To aid in the defense of Charleston, the Marine Committee, in one of its final acts,[3] ordered Whipple to take the frigates *Providence, Queen of France*, and *Boston* as well as the sloop *Ranger* southward and "there persue the orders of the Commanding officer of that place." For once, the Continental Navy had little difficulty manning its ships— the happy result of the sizeable prize money won during the squadron's last cruise. The ships arrived at Charleston at the end of 1779 after a stormy voyage in which they were severely damaged. "I believe if the gale had continued twelve hours longer she would have foundered," Whipple said of the *Providence*. A survey of the *Queen of France* convinced the commodore that the frigate would be unable to go to sea again "without more repair than she is worth." Shortly before the British fleet appeared off the bar, the *Providence* and *Ranger* got out on a brief cruise in which they captured a 14-gun brig and two small sloops, before being chased back into port. This was the squadron's last sortie.

Unlike Lovell and Saltonstall at the Penobscot, Lincoln and Whipple worked together without friction, acting with zeal and determination to defend Charleston with the resources at hand. The local authorities granted the commodore the power to impress all idle seamen and placed four ships of the South Carolina navy at his disposal. They were the *Bricole*, 44, and *Truite*, 26, which had been purchased from the French, the *General Moultrie*, 20, and *Notre Dame*, 16. With the American ships now blockaded in the harbor, Lincoln hoped to use them as floating gun platforms to guard the entrance to the channel. They were to be moored broadside-on so as to rake any vessel trying to force a passage across the bar, much in the same way Lord Howe had deployed his ships against d'Estaing at Sandy Hook. To determine the feasibility of the plan, soundings were made of the waters about the bar and the adjacent shoals. Genéral Lincoln was profoundly disturbed by the report of Whipple's captains. They said such an arrangement was impractical because

---

[3] The Marine Committee, which had been under fire for some time for alleged inefficiency, was replaced at the end of 1779 by a Board of Admiralty. The Board of Admiralty was to consist of five members—two members of Congress and three appointed from outside the body. Because of the low ebb in the fortunes of the Continental Navy, few men were willing to serve on the board. Francis Lewis and William Ellery accepted their appointments, but the third outside vacancy was never filled. Congress was not disposed to grant much independence to an agency that contained non-Congressional members and the board found itself even more dependent on Congress than had the Marine Committee. Ellery and Lewis served reluctantly until 1781, when they resigned. For the administrative history of the Continental Navy see Paullin, *The Navy of the American Revolution*.

the swells would be too strong for a ship to ride across the current when conditions of wind and tide would be just ripe for the British to attempt the passage. This was indeed bad news for the defenders. It meant that there would be no possibility of stopping the British from crossing the bar and making a combined land and sea attack on Charleston. A few small vessels were left to harass the British as best they might while the remainder of the squadron was withdrawn to a line extending from Fort Moultrie on Sullivan's Island to the Middle Ground shoals.

On March 4, Admiral Arbuthnot appeared off the bar with the British fleet. For the next sixteen days, the British busied themselves with lightening their heavier ships by removing guns, provisions, and water so the vessels could pass over the shoals. Several small rebel vessels tried to interfere with the operation but were brushed away. When the enemy started across the bar, Whipple summoned his captains for a council of war on the *Providence*. Plans were discussed for an attack on the British ships before they had time to replace the guns that had been removed from the heavier ships but nothing was done. The American squadron withdrew up the Cooper River. To protect it, a line of eleven ships was sunk across the river from the lower tip of town to a small island called Shute's Folly. South Carolina's vessels, several merchantmen, and the decrepit *Queen of France* were sacrificed in this cause. They formed the foundation for a boom of logs and chains connected to the protruding masts of the sunken hulks. The guns of the rest of the ships were removed, and their crews joined the army as artillerymen. "We then bent our whole force and strained every nerve for the defense of the town," said Whipple.

While Clinton's sappers were pushing their siege works closer to the city, the British fleet sealed the fate of Charleston in little more than an hour. Three ships of the line and the same number of frigates ran past the guns of Fort Moultrie on the afternoon of April 9. Several vessels were hit and a transport which followed them had to be burned after running aground on a shoal, but most of the vessels sustained only minor damage. This unexpected achievement stunned the Americans, who had expected that the fort's 32-pounders would guard the inner harbor, just as they had during the previous attack. The moment Washington heard the news, he apparently gave up hope of saving Charleston. ". . . The propriety of defending the town depended on the probability of defending the bar, and that, when this ceased, the attempt ought have been relinquished," he declared.

Clinton demanded the garrison surrender the next day. The British force had grown to 14,000 men, including the sailors who were now manning shore batteries, and the city was completely surrounded by land and sea. Although General Lincoln was having second thoughts about his decision to defend the city, the local authorities stubbornly refused to consider surrender. The shelling of the town commenced. After a few days the British gunners and sailors were tempted to cut short the siege by burning Charleston to the ground. "Send twenty-four pound shot into the stomachs of the women," joked some of the naval officers, "to see how they will deliver them." Soon the town was ablaze, but the flames were put out. Clinton angrily laid down strict orders against a recurrence. It was absurd, impolitic, inhuman to burn a town you mean to occupy, he declared. So the siege went on. Charleston held out for a month, capitulating on May 12. The capture of Charleston was the greatest British victory of the war and the most severe defeat suffered by an American army until Bataan in 1942. An estimated 5,000 prisoners were taken and the booty included the *Providence, Boston,* and *Ranger,* which were taken into the Royal Navy.[4] The loss of these four ships along with those burned on the Penobscot all but eliminated the Continental Navy as an effective fighting force. Only five vessels were left in mid-1780—the *Trumbull* and *Deane* in New England waters; the *Confederacy* undergoing a refit at Philadelphia after being dismasted in the West Indies; the new sloop-of-war *Saratoga,* which was also in the Delaware; and the *Alliance,* in Europe.

The *Trumbull* had at last been added to the navy's active list in August 1779. After Dudley Saltonstall had been transferred to the *Warren,* the Eastern Navy Board had passed custody of her on to Captain Elisha Hinman, who had been freed by the British and absolved by a court-martial from any responsibility for the loss of the *Alfred.* Within two months, Hinman accomplished what Saltonstall

---

[4] The *Boston* became the *Charleston* and the *Ranger* the *Halifax;* only the *Providence* retained her name.

had failed to do in three years—he managed to get the *Trumbull* over the bar that had trapped her in the Connecticut River. A number of casks containing water were tied along her sides and after they were pumped out, the resulting buoyancy was enough to carry her over the shoals. Hinman took the frigate to New London where he began recruiting a crew and fitting her out for sea. Pleased with Hinman's efficiency and spirit, the Navy Board recommended that he be given command of the frigate. The Marine Committee had other plans. To the surprise of the local authorities, who had already assured Hinman of the appointment, James Nicholson was named her captain. The Marine Committee maintained that as the navy's senior officer, Nicholson had first call on any available vessel. Political influence probably played a large part in this appointment, as it had when he was originally given his rank.

Exhibiting the same lethargy that had infuriated Congress while he was in command of the *Virgina*, Nicholson did not take the *Trumbull* to sea until May 1780. The frigate's crew, most of them "green country lads," according to their skipper, had not gotten over their seasickness when on June 1 the solid-looking Liverpool letter of marque *Watt* was sighted about 200 miles north of Bermuda. Hoisting British colors, Nicholson edged up on the enemy vessel and counted her gunports. She carried twenty-six 12-pounders and from six to ten 6-pounders, making her a match for the *Trumbull*'s twenty-four 12s and half-dozen 6s. The ships maneuvered for position with the American frigate, fresh from the dockyard and her bottom clean, having the advantage. Suspecting that the strange vessel might be a Yankee cruiser, the *Watt*'s captain raised a private recognition signal. When this was not immediately answered, he ordered several guns fired into the *Trumbull* and made off, apparently with the idea of avoiding battle.

Nicholson clapped on sail and easily brought his ship up with the enemy. The *Trumbull* was about a hundred yards away from her, when the *Watt* fired a broadside. Still boring in, the American captain waited until the range had closed to pistol shot before ordering the Stars and Stripes broken out. Then the *Trumbull*'s guns roared. "A furious and close action commenced," reported Nicholson. For the better part of two-and-a-half hours the ships dueled yardarm-to-yardarm. Fires were started on both vessels, but their crews managed to extinguish them. The ships were badly battered in what developed into one of the hottest actions of the war. "We were literally cut to pieces," said Gilbert Saltonstall, captain of the marines on the *Trumbull*. "Not a shroud, stay, brace, bowling, or any other of our rigging standing." The *Watt* also suffered heavily. "Our hull, rigging and sails cut to pieces," Captain John Coulthard wrote. "Very leaky from a number of shot under water, one pump fit to work, the other having been torn to pieces by a twelve-pound shot." But the fighting continued. Despite the shattered condition of his ship, Nicholson was confident that the enemy vessel could be taken when one of his officers informed him that the mainmast was tottering. To make quick repairs he drew off, only to have this mast and the mizzenmast, as well, go by the board. The *Watt* limped off, licking her wounds. Before she was out of sight, her main topmast was seen to fall. In what was regarded as a drawn battle, Nicholson reported that eight of his men had been killed, ten later died of wounds and another twenty-one were wounded. The British reported eleven killed, two dead of wounds and seventy-nine wounded. These were heavy casualties considering the size of the crews involved.

Eight days later, on June 9, there was another savage ship-to-ship encounter—this one off Newfoundland between the 26-gun Massachusetts frigate *Protector*[5] and the English letter of marque *Admiral Duff*, of 32 guns. Emerging from an early morning fog, the American vessel spotted a sizeable ship under British colors bearing down on her. "Looked as large as a 74," Midshipman Luther Little recalled many years later. "All hands piped to quarters. Hammocks brought up and stuffed in the nettings, decks wet and sanded," his account continues. "Our captain [John Foster Williams] ordered a broadside. . . . She replied with three cheers and a broadside. Being higher, they overshot us, cutting our rigging. A regular fight within pistol range. In a half hour a cannon shot came through our side, killing Mr. Scollay, a midshipman who commanded the fourth 12-pounder from the stern. His brains flew over my face and gun, which was the third from the stern.

"In a half hour all their topmen were killed by our marines, 60 in number and all Americans. Our marines killed the man at their wheel and the ship came down on us, her cat-head staving in our quarter-gallery. We lashed their jib-boom to our main shrouds. Our

[5] The *Protector* had not been ready for sea at the time of the Penobscot expedition and escaped destruction.

marines firing into their port holes kept them from charging. We were ordered to board, but the lashing broke. . . ." One of the *Duff*'s sails caught on fire, and the flames raced down the rigging, touching off a pile of cartridges on her quarterdeck. Wracked by explosions, "the *Duff* sunk, on fire, colors flying." Only about fifty-five of her crew, about half of them wounded, were saved. One of those rescued had been down with fever in the sick bay and had floated out of his hammock to safety, according to Midshipman Little. On her way back to Boston, the *Protector* had a run-in with the British frigate *Thames*, 32, but escaped after a running fight that lasted several hours. The remaining Continental Navy ships made a few brief cruises during the year without accomplishing much. For the most part, the ships lay idle at their moorings without crews and without money to attract them.

Elsewhere events were moving at a fast clip. As soon as the Combined Fleet had dropped over the horizon, the British and the Bourbon powers laid plans for future naval operations. The Franco-Spanish grand strategy included the siege of Gibraltar, the maintenance of token forces in American waters and the Indian Ocean, and an offensive against British possessions in the Caribbean. For Britain, the danger of invasion was over but the enemy's plans embodied threats that were just as menacing. The war in America was a constant drain on British resources and her sprawling empire was vulnerable around the globe. Gibraltar, Minorca, the West Indies, India—all were threatened and no one could tell where the next blow would fall. Gibraltar, under siege by the Spaniards since July 1779, was running short of supplies and had to be relieved; the West Indies, source of a large portion of the nation's wealth, had to be strengthened; seaborne trade, the lifeblood of the British economy, had to be protected. Accordingly, Sandwich evolved a plan to meet all these contingencies at once. A great convoy consisting of three separate elements would be dispatched. It would carry supplies to Gibraltar, include ships of the line to reinforce the Leeward Station and escort the outward-bound Jamaica merchant fleet in whose holds room had been found for troops for the conquest of the French West Indian Islands. Command of this important expedition was entrusted to Admiral Sir George Bridges Rodney.

Rodney's name, according to his most recent biographer, David Spinney, "has always evoked a curious mixture of admiration and antipathy." [6] He was never liked by his fellow officers even though his success forced respect. They railed against his efforts to impose stricter discipline upon them. Some pointed to his rapacity for prize money, which at times robbed his victories of their full military impact. Others contended these triumphs were the result of luck rather than ability. And there were those who resented his fervid Toryism and unbending aristocratic arrogance. So delicate in appearance as to be almost effeminate, he was vain, selfish, and given to blaming subordinates for his failures. Nevertheless, Rodney was the most successful British admiral of his day, twice returning victorious to Britain from the West Indies.

The admiral, sixty-one years old at the time of his appointment, had entered the Royal Navy at the age of fourteen. The Eighteenth Century was above all an epoch of "interest" or political patronage, and Rodney's career was propelled by the breezes of aristocratic influence. Assisted by a recommendation from the Duke of Chandos, a relative, he had been sent to sea as a "King's letter boy," a mode of entry into the navy instituted by Samuel Pepys, when he was secretary to the Admiralty. Under this system, boys entered the Service under Royal patronage, which assured them a rapid rise in their profession. Rodney was the last to enter by this method. In his own latter years, he himself adopted an imperious view of patronage, promoting his son to captain at the age of sixteen. Rodney had not reached that rank until the ripe old age of twenty-four. By the end of the Seven Years' War he was a rear admiral, a member of Parliament and wealthy from his share of prize money.

Politics and gambling were Rodney's passion—and undoing. The faro bank and whist tables at White's Club where thousands of pounds changed hands on the turn of a card held a fatal fascination for him. Rodney lost heavily and was plunged over the brink of financial disaster in 1768 by a heavily contested election for the Northampton seat in Commons. It cost the Admiral a cool 30,000

---

[6] Until recently, there was no adequate biography of Rodney. This has now been admirably filled by Spinney's *Rodney* (London 1969), upon which much of the following is based. For a shorter account, see Christopher Lloyd's sketch in *George Washington's Opponents*, or Donald Macintyre, *Admiral Rodney* (London 1962). Although the Admiral's middle name is usually given as "Brydges," he spelled it with an "i".

pounds to win the seat by a two-vote margin. Faced with ruin as a
result of the expense of the campaign, harassed by his mounting
gambling debts, and with no golden flow of prize money to refill his
coffers, Rodney resorted to loans at exorbitant rates of interest in
order to hold his creditors at bay. Debt piled upon debt. A period as
commander of the Jamaica Station, intended to restore his financial
health, turned out to be a disappointment. The haughty admiral also
managed to alienate the powerful West India planters and merchants with his cool, insolent manner. Unlike his predecessors, he refused to wink at violations of the trade and navigation acts, going so
far as to seize several ships that were supposedly violating the law.

   Upon his return to England, Rodney's financial condition was
so desperate that he was forced to flee to Paris to escape his creditors. And there the old sea dog sat out the opening years of the
American Revolution. From the French capital, he repeatedly wrote
Sandwich asking for a command, and his wife and friends lobbied
for him in London. Not until war broke out with France did he get
his opportunity. When it came, apparently through the efforts of
Germain, Rodney was almost prevented from grasping it by his numerous French creditors, who threatened to have him arrested if he
tried to leave Paris. Rodney's rescue came from an unexpected quarter. The Marshal de Biron, one of the great soldiers of France and an
old friend of the admiral, "ransomed" him from his creditors by
paying off the debts he had piled up in France.

   The appointment of Rodney to the command of the Leeward
Station was a gamble for Sandwich. The accumulated mistakes of
the past—Keppel's failure at Ushant, Byron's blundering in the Caribbean, the unopposed appearance of an enemy fleet in the Channel
—had been compounded by the refusal of many ranking naval
officers to serve the government for political reasons. The First Lord
had no other choice than Rodney. He at least supported the King's
policy in America and was eager to serve. This outweighed his
weighty liabilities. Gout and a kidney complaint sometimes incapaci-
tated him for days on end, and he had not commanded a squadron
in wartime in seventeen years. Looming over all else was the admiral's tangled finances. In an attempt to placate the King and the
West India merchants who remembered Rodney's freebooting ways
with a shudder, Sandwich made certain that he would not be subjected to the temptation to restore his fortunes at the public expense.

A special commissioner was appointed to remain at the admiral's elbow during the purchase of stores and equipment for the expedition.

To ensure the success of the mission, a good portion of the Channel Fleet was temporarily diverted to Rodney's command. He was given twenty-two ships of the line, a 44, and seven frigates. With this force, he was to escort a convoy of some three hundred transports, supply vessels, and merchantmen until they were well away from the French ports on the Bay of Biscay. Then the West Indies ships, with a small escort, would part company and head for Barbados where Rear Admiral Sir Hyde Parker was awaiting their arrival. The rest of the fleet would lift the Spanish blockade and relieve the British garrison of some 5,000 men under siege at Gibraltar. Then the ships belonging to the Channel Fleet would immediately put about for home, those destined for Minorca would continue on into the Mediterranean, while Rodney in his flagship *Sandwich*, 90, and three other ships of the line would proceed to the Caribbean. Speed and secrecy were vital to the success of the expedition. Since it was impossible to conceal the huge number of storeships and transports being assembled at Portsmouth from prying eyes, the orders given their skippers made no mention of Gibraltar or Minorca. Dockyard clerks scribbled instructions for Barbados and Jamaica, so that as far as anyone realized, the entire armada was bound across the Atlantic. Only Rodney knew the true destination of all the vessels.

During his enforced idleness in Paris, the admiral had had plenty of time to analyze the drawbacks of the Fighting Instructions and had linked them to the inability of the Royal Navy to win a decisive battle against a French fleet. Rodney's solution was to increase the firepower and the weight of the attack against a particular section of the enemy's line. To accomplish this, he wrote an entirely new article of the Fighting Instructions, which he distributed to his captains before sailing. When a special signal was hoisted, the heaviest ships of the British line were to leave their assigned positions and form up in the van or in the rear of the fleet as instructed in order to concentrate their fire power upon a single sector of the enemy line. The remaining British ships would close up and fill their places. In essence, this was the application of the long-established military principle of concentration of firepower to naval operations, notes Spinney.

Slackness in the dockyards at Portsmouth and adverse winds delayed the departure of the fleet. "For God's sake get to sea without delay," fumed Sandwich as an impatient monarch breathed down his neck. Not until December 23, 1779, did Rodney's ships, flying the flag of an Admiral of White, manage to weigh anchor and begin their momentous voyage. Within a week, the armada had passed out of the danger zone off the French coast and the vessels destined for the Caribbean were sorted out for the long voyage to the westward. The remainder plowed on through rough seas toward Gibraltar. Shortly after daybreak on January 8, 1780, a covey of strange sails crept up over the horizon. Much to Rodney's delight, they turned out to be a Spanish convoy of about twenty ships guarded by a two-decker and several smaller craft. It was obvious that the admiral's luck had begun to turn. The British warships were quickly among the Spaniards, lashing out in all directions. "They hauled down their colours as fast as our ships came up with them," exulted one of the British captains. The two-decker, the *Guipuzcoana*, 64, was a new and well-built ship, so Rodney ordered her name changed to *Prince William* in honor of King George's third son,[7] who was serving as a midshipman in the fleet, and incorporated her into the armada along with a dozen of the Spanish provision ships. The rest were sent off under prize crews to England.

Eight days later, on the afternoon of January 16, a Spanish fleet was sighted off Cape St. Vincent. With nine ships of the line and a pair of frigates, the Spanish admiral, Don Juan de Langara, had been cruising off the Strait of Gibraltar, confident that he could deal with any force sent to relieve the Rock. The intelligence reaching him was that the heavy British ships had already parted company with the Gibraltar convoy and were now well out into the Atlantic. The admiral's failure to put out a screen of frigates to reconnoiter the enemy cost him his squadron. Langara's reaction when he saw a seemingly endless line of British ships rounding the Cape can only be imagined. By the time he gave orders to flee, it was too late. Rodney, who was in bed suffering from a painful attack of gout, had already signaled for a general chase, beginning what was to be known as the "Moonlight Battle."

Although Rodney had nearly twice as many ships as Langara,

---

[7] Afterward King William IV.

the conditions under which the battle was fought "were such that only a gambler would have taken the risk," notes Christopher Lloyd. The wind was blowing at near gale force, a high sea was running, which prevented the British three-deckers from using their lower guns, darkness was closing in and the British ships ran close in along a lee shore to prevent the Spaniards from escaping into their ports. Oblivious to the dangers, the admiral summoned his sailing master to his bedside and commanded: "Lay me alongside the biggest ship you can, or the admiral if there be one." One by one the Spanish ships were caught by the much faster, coppered-bottomed British vessels and battered into submission. The 70-gun *Santo Domingo*, under attack by three British ships, blew up with a tremendous roar. It was "a most shocking and dreadful sight," young Prince William wrote his father. "Being not certain whether it was an enemy or a friend, I felt a horror all over me." Within moments, all that was left was a fragment of her mast with a Spanish sailor clinging to it—the only survivor of a four-hundred-man crew. The chase went on into the night, with the British fleet pounding along after the Spaniards in the dim light cast by the battle lanterns. Dawn found the British ships clustering about their prizes, as they rolled in the heavy sea. Five enemy ships of the line were captured including the Spanish flagship, one had blown up and only two escaped. The prizes were incorporated into Rodney's fleet—"as fine ships as ever swam, now completely refitted, manned and put into the line of battle," the admiral reported.

In the mellow afterglow of the battle, Rodney paid generous tribute to his officers, especially his Flag Captain, Walter Young. He did not know that Young was in correspondence with Sir Charles Middleton, the comptroller of the navy, claiming credit for the victory because he had urged "the ailing and irresolute admiral" to make the signal for a general chase. While Rodney was unaware of Young's backbiting, he was too experienced a commander not to sense that all was not well among his officers. Writing to Sandwich, he said: "It is with concern that I must tell your Lordship that my brother officers still continue their absurd and illiberal custom of arraigning each other's conduct. . . . The unhappy difference between Mr. Keppel and Sir Hugh Palliser has almost ruined the Navy." And to a friend, the admiral lamented the passing of "the Old Good, Necessary Discipline of the British Navy."

Rodney's arrival at Gibraltar could not have been more timely. Since the Spaniards had begun the siege, the British had received nothing in the way of reinforcements or supplies except for an occasional shipload of cattle that managed to sneak through the blockade. General George Elliott, the governor of the outpost since 1777, had worked hard and well at improving its defenses so that the artillery kept the enemy at a respectful distance. One of the major feats performed by the garrison was the mounting of a 24-pounder at the highest point of the Rock. This had to be accomplished by hacking a road out of its precipitous sides. But as weeks and months had passed, the feeling grew that the British government had decided to leave Gibraltar to its fate. As early as November, bread was beginning to run short. "Thistles, dandelions, wild leeks, etc., were for some time the daily nourishment of numbers," one of the besieged officers noted in his journal shortly before the arrival of Rodney's fleet. ". . . Famine began to present itself with its attendant horrors."

The fleet was given a triumphal welcome. Troops, stores, and provisions poured ashore. Frigates were dispatched to Tangier to hasten fresh provisions to the fortress. "Great Britain was again Mistress of Straits," Rodney declared. Elliott kept the troops intended for Minorca but the stores were forwarded to the island before Rodney sailed out onto the broad Atlantic. As it turned out, the run of successes was not yet complete. On their way home, the returning ships of the Channel Fleet fell in with a French convoy bound for Mauritius in the Indian Ocean. Several transports and a 64-gun escort carrying 60,000 pounds sterling were captured. This exploit brought the number of prizes taken in the Gibraltar expedition to six ships of the line and about three dozen merchantmen. Another three battleships were destroyed or wrecked by storms. The victories were greeted with great enthusiasm in London. Public buildings were illuminated and salutes fired. Rodney was granted the freedom of the city, the thanks of Parliament, and a 2,000-pound-a-year pension by the King. "You have taken more line-of-battle ships than had been captured in any one action of either of the last preceding wars," wrote Sandwich, basking in the reflected glory of having selected Rodney for his command. There was however a small cloud on the admiral's horizon. As he pursued his lonely course toward the West

Indies with four ships of the line, he lamented that none of the coppered vessels had been allowed to accompany him.

While Rodney's fleet was being fitted out for its momentous voyage, Paul Jones and his squadron, fresh from the battle off Flamborough Head, were at the center of a three-cornered diplomatic duel between France, Holland, and Britain that lasted through the autumn of 1779. Jones's ships had no sooner dropped anchor at the Texel, than Sir Joseph Yorke, the British ambassador, lodged a vehement protest with the Dutch government. He demanded "that these ships and their crews may be stopped and delivered up with the pirate Paul Jones of Scotland, who is a rebel subject and criminal of state. . . ." The Dutch moved with deliberate slowness. Discreetly supported by the French and remembering that they, too, had once been rebels, Dutch officialdom engulfed the irate envoy in a flood tide of notes and aide-memoires. In the meantime, Jones repaired his ships and anxiously eyed the movements of a squadron of British cruisers that lay off the port waiting for him. This game of cat and mouse continued for the rest of the year.

One of the commodore's first acts had been to inform Benjamin Franklin of Pierre Landais's irrational conduct during the battle. "Either Captain Landais or myself is highly criminal, and one or the other must be punished," he declared. "His conduct has been base and unpardonable." Franklin summoned Landais to Paris to explain his conduct. Four of the *Alliance*'s officers, including her first lieutenant, submitted statements contending they had "told Captain Landais at different times that he had fired upon the wrong ship." Franklin fully realized that the political climate in Paris made it imprudent to take strong action in France against a French officer, even though he held an American commission, so the whole matter was referred to the Continental Congress. "If . . . I had 20 ships of war at my disposition, I should not give one of them to Captain Landais," Franklin observed. He managed either to induce Landais to step down from his command or suspend him from it, for Jones soon raised his pennant on the *Alliance*. But he had not heard the last of Pierre Landais.

Jones's situation was fast becoming intolerable. His crew was restless and angry over the delay in selling the prizes. The men had received only one ducat each, which some of them contemptuously tossed overboard "in a fit of rage," said Midshipman Fanning. The Dutch were showing signs of collapsing under British pressure and were beginning to insist that he sail as soon as possible. And there were those pesky British frigates off shore, patiently cruising back and forth. "If you can take Paul Jones," Sandwich had told one of his captains, "you will be as high in the estimation of the public as if you had beat the Combined fleets." Jones was unafraid. "The ship is well manned and shall not be given away," he assured Franklin. To protect Jones's squadron, the French ambassador claimed all the ships were French and ordered the Stars and Stripes replaced with the French ensign. He knew that the Dutch authorities would think twice before ordering a French squadron out to face the guns of the Royal Navy. But Jones refused to have any part in this subterfuge. The American flag remained flying on the *Alliance* although the commodore was persuaded to turn the *Serapis* and *Countess of Scarborough* over to the French so they could carry the British prisoners he had taken to England for exchange. As part of the disguise, the French offered Jones a commission as a privateer—which he considered a gross insult. The touchy little Scot's anger at his allies increased when he learned that his prisoners had been exchanged for Frenchmen, not Americans.

Toward the end of the year, foul weather drove the British blockading squadron off its station, which was the opportunity Jones had been waiting for. With high winds singing in the rigging of the *Alliance*, he took her to sea. Characteristically, he chose to ignore the long and safe route around Scotland and sailed directly down the Channel. By the time the frigate's bell had tolled out the old year and ushered in the first day of 1780, she had safely passed through the narrow seas and was off Ushant. The *Alliance* was not a happy ship. There was considerable bad blood between her original officers and men and those from the *Bonhomme Richard*. Fist fights flared among the crew and threats of duels were hurled among the officers over the part both ships had played in the battle off Flamborough Head. "Our ward-room . . . exhibited nothing but wrangling, jangling and a scene of discord among our superior officers," reported Midshipman Fanning. And John Kilby, from his vantage point on the gun deck, said that the *Richard*'s men "always insisted that the Crew of the *Alliance*, both officers and men, were Cowards." The crew, claiming that Jones had promised to take them to Lorient where they would receive their pay and prize money, refused to work when he ordered a cruise off the Spanish coast. They were eventually routed out by an armed party led by Lieutenant Dale and persuaded to return to duty but the search for prizes was unsuccessful. Some of the men contracted a venereal disease when the ship put into Coruña to take on wood, water and provisions.[8] So it must have been with a sigh of profound relief that Jones anchored in Lorient on February 19.

While Jones had been on his fruitless cruise, Franklin had received instructions from the Board of Admiralty to get the *Alliance* off as quickly as possible with a cargo of arms, uniforms, and other supplies for Washington's army. As soon as he heard of the frigate's return, he wrote Jones urging him to load and sail immediately. He was also to take Arthur Lee, one of the American commissioners in Europe, as a passenger. Paul Jones probably knew that the quarrelsome Lee was the sworn enemy of Dr. Franklin and anyone considered close to the old man—and that included himself. Even so, he welcomed him to the ship and assured Franklin that he would quickly get the *Alliance* ready for sea. Relations between Jones and Lee rapidly turned stormy. Lee demanded that a huge coach he had purchased be shipped along with the large amount of personal baggage he and his servants had accumulated. Pointing out that a frigate had very little extra room for cargo—and that had already been filled by arms and provisions—Jones refused to carry Lee's property. This affront inflamed Lee's enmity, and he nourished his grudge until he was ready to strike.

Without pay or prize money, the crew of the *Alliance* became even more discontented. Franklin managed to scrape up enough to provide a month's pay for each man—the first in almost a year—but their prize money was still held up for a number of reasons. As naval agent for the American commissioners, Chaumont had control of the money, and he was deeply involved in various speculations. The men, themselves, also contributed to the delay. The French government wished to purchase the *Serapis* and *Scarborough* at fixed prices

---

[8] Jones dropped Gustavus Conyngham, who had been a passenger on his vessel, off at Coruña, where he took a ship for America. Conyngham had tunneled out of Old Mill Prison near the end of 1779 and had made his way to Holland where he met Jones. He was unlucky enough to be captured again on his way home and ended the war a prisoner.

of so much per gun, the method customarily used by the French to pay for warships taken as prizes. The crew of the *Alliance* "raised a clamor at this," however, and insisted that they could get more for the ships if they were auctioned off to the highest bidder. That took time, and when the vessels were finally sold they brought less than if the original proposal had been accepted.⁹ "Unless the prize money is paid," warned Jones, "my throat will assuredly be cut." To try to speed up the process of payment he went to Paris in mid-April.

The next six weeks were the happiest time in Paul Jones's life. Having won the only important Allied naval victory of the previous year while the Combined Fleet had accomplished nothing, he found himself the social lion of the Paris season. Franklin took him to the French Court where he was introduced to King Louis XVI and Queen Marie Antoinette, whom he described as "a sweet girl." He was inducted into the Order of Military Merit by the King with the rank of Chevalier and presented with a gold-hilted sword. Great men invited him to dine. Beautiful women, ranging from high-priced courtesans to the great ladies of the Court, threw themselves at him. The stamp of the quarterdeck did not follow Jones into the salon and boudoir. "From the intrepid character he justly supported in the American Navy, I expected to have seen a rough, stout, warlike Roman," said Abigail Adams. "Instead of that I should sooner think of wrapping him up in cotton wool, and putting him in my pocket, than sending him to contend with cannon balls."

Jones's return to the *Alliance* was postponed from day to day, week to week. Not all his time in Paris was spent in playing the social lion, however. He kept up the pressure on the Ministry of Marine to sell the prizes and for Chaumont to come up with the overdue funds. He also tried to persuade the authorities to allow him to repeat the cruise of the *Bonhomme Richard* on a larger scale. Because the French navy had lost so many men to disease during the abortive expedition against Britain, there was a shortage of crews to man its frigates. Jones suggested a remedy. He would sail home in the *Alli-*

---

⁹ The *Scarborough* was finally sold as a merchantman and the *Serapis* was purchased for the French Navy. She was razeed, or cut down, and sent out to the Indian Ocean where she was destroyed by fire in 1781. Jones eventually received $2,658 in gold as his share of the prize money and no other American officer got more than $818—and the men even less—not much even by the standards of the day considering the risks they took.

ance, obtain command of the *America*, the 74-gun ship of the line being built at Portsmouth, and return to France with double crews. Enough men would be provided to man several of the idle French frigates, which would be turned over to his squadron. Sartine, the Minister of Marine, expressed an interest in the proposal, but nothing came of it.

While Jones was enjoying himself in Paris, Arthur Lee, smarting at his treatment by Jones, encouraged Landais to claim command of the *Alliance*. Stirring the discontent among the frigate's officers and crew, the conspirators promised to get them their long overdue pay and prize money. Near the end of May, one hundred fifteen officers and men signed and sent to Franklin a document written by Landais stating that they would not sail until they had received six months' pay, all their prize money, and Landais, "their legal captain," had been restored to command. Fourteen officers, including those who had originally stated that Landais had deliberately fired on the *Richard*, also signed a statement maintaining that the Frenchman's conduct had been above reproach. Upon receipt of the documents, Franklin wrote Jones, who had left Paris before they arrived, that "you are likely to have great trouble. I wish you well through it."

Instead of returning directly to his ship, Jones dallied in Nantes where he was feted by his fellow Masons. He did not arrive at Lorient until June 9. Even then, he did not go directly on board his ship, but lodged ashore with one of his mistresses. Landais and Lee picked this time for their coup.[10] On June 13, the Frenchman boarded the ship at a time when virtually all the officers who had served under him were on the quarterdeck and Jones's officers were either ashore or below at dinner. He was greeted with cheers. Those officers who did not accept his authority were summarily ordered ashore, although none of the crew were allowed to leave. John Kilby said fifty-two men, all survivors of the *Richard* including himself, were put in irons. When Jones learned that he had been outwitted, Midshipman Fanning said, "his passion knew no bounds; and in the first paroxysm of rage, he acted more like a mad man than a conquerer." But instead of storming aboard the frigate and confronting Landais, as might have been expected, the normally impetuous Jones

---

[10] In recounting the Landais affair, I have relied upon the account given by Richard B. Morris in "The Revolution's Caine Mutiny," *American Heritage*, XI (April 1960).

returned to Paris to seek fresh authority from Franklin and Sartine. The French Minister issued a warrant for Landais's arrest.

Lee's carriage and baggage were hoisted aboard the frigate and supplies that were badly needed by Washington's army were dumped on the wharf to make room. Jones returned to Lorient on June 20 to discover that the *Alliance* had been warped out of Lorient harbor to nearby Port Louis which was closer to the sea. The port officials, however, had placed a boom across the mouth of the harbor to block Landais's escape, a gunboat armed with three 24-pounders was ordered to stand by to prevent the boom from being cut and the commander of the citadel was instructed to fire on the frigate if she attempted to get away. Similar instructions were given to three French warships in the port, and boats were readied to board the *Alliance*. But the command to attack was never given. To the surprise of those who knew him, Jones had the order to fire upon the *Alliance* reversed and the boom lifted. He justified this strange shift in a letter to Robert Morris: "My humanity would not suffer me to remain a silent witness of bloodshed between Allied Subjects of France and America." It was not a very convincing statement. Morison speculates that Jones was secretly glad to be rid of the *Alliance* and hoped to obtain command of a larger ship. Publicly, he blamed the French officials for his loss of the frigate, but Franklin had no patience with Jones's excuses. "If you had stayed on board where your duty lay, instead of coming to Paris, you would not have lost your ship," he declared.

With the boom removed, Landais lost no time in slipping out to sea on July 8, with Philadelphia his destination. The *Alliance* carried no other cargo than 76 chests of small arms, 216 barrels of powder and a battery of 18-pounders that had originally been ordered for the *Bonhomme Richard* but had been cast too late to be of use. To find room for them in the hold, Landais had ordered Lee's carriage put back on shore but the commissioner did manage to cram a large amount of his own goods on board. The passage to America was one of the maddest on record. Landais quarreled violently with his crew, his officers, and his passengers. Officers who refused to swear allegiance to him were placed under arrest. No one, including Arthur Lee, was exempt from his moods. One day at the dinner table. Landais slammed down a carving knife on Lee's fork as that gentleman was helping himself to some meat on the serving dish. Richard

Morris relates what happened next: "I'll let you know I am captain of this ship and I shall be helped first at the table," the Frenchman cried. "You shall not pick the liver out of the dish. You shall take the first piece that comes to hand as I do." Lee was confounded and declared he had always acknowledged that Landais was the captain of the ship. "I was never so used in my life," he added.

"When you get ashore," replied Landais, "you may load your pistols as soon as you please."

Upon one occasion when the frigate was sailing before a fair wind, the Captain ordered the sails reefed, to the anger of the men who wanted to get home as quickly as possible. At another time, Landais started chasing one of his officers up and down the deck after accusing him of disobeying orders. When the *Alliance* reached the Grand Banks and the crew wished to fish in order to add to their meager rations, Landais refused permission. Fearing that the frigate might be taken if she continued on to Philadelphia, the men insisted that she put into Boston which was closer. The Captain refused. Finally, the officers and passengers banded together and forced Landais, who was pretending to be sick in his cabin, to give up command of the ship to Lieutenant James A. Degge, her first officer. Earlier he had been placed under arrest by the Captain. Degge took the *Alliance* into Boston, arriving on August 19. After receiving Landais's incoherent report, the Eastern Navy Board ordered John Barry to relieve him. The Frenchman refused to quit the ship and three husky marines had to drag him kicking and screaming from his cabin. He then turned up at the Navy Board's office and demanded to be allowed to sleep on the floor as he had no place to go. At the court-martial that followed, most of the witnesses, including Arthur Lee, contended that Landais was insane. He was ordered dismissed from the navy—and so was the unfortunate Lieutenant Degge, who had been charged with mutiny.

To replace the *Alliance*, the French placed the 20-gun sloop-of-war *Ariel* at the disposal of the Americans to carry the arms and equipment that Landais had dumped on the quayside. Although Franklin pressed Jones to get the ship loaded and on her way, she did not sail for another four months. In order to find room for even part of the military supplies awaiting shipment—11,000 muskets, uniforms for 10,000 men, 800 barrels of gunpowder, and 120 bales of cloth—the sloop had to be re-rigged and her armament reduced to 16 guns. Even so, there was not enough space. Jones persuaded Franklin to charter two merchant vessels to carry the overflow. He attributed the delay in sailing to contrary winds and the loading of the ships, but in all probability Jones was not dismayed. Until the very last, he hoped for a more powerful command and another opportunity to go on a raiding voyage against England. Jones also kept up his shore activities. Upon one occasion, relates Fanning, the captain "had some business with a lady of pleasure" and went to a house of assignation where he forgot his gold watch. Shortly afterward, a midshipman assigned to the same room found the watch and recognized it. He showed it to several other youngsters, including Fanning, and they decided to pawn the watch at a coffeehouse in exchange for a dozen bottles of fine Bordeaux. The pawn ticket was surreptitiously returned to their commanding officer, who was probably more careful about where he left his watch in the future.

The *Ariel* sailed at last on October 7, only to run into a terrific storm that nearly carried her onto the rocky coast of Brittany. Almost buried under towering seas, she was dismasted and was lucky to limp back to port. Everyone was astounded that the vessel had survived, for, as Jones reported, "the tempest had covered the shore with wrecks and dead bodies." Richard Dale said he had never seen "such coolness and readiness in such frightful circumstances as Paul Jones showed in the nights and days we lay off the Penmarque Rocks, expecting every moment to be our last." So terror-stricken were the French seamen who made up much of the crew that they were kept at the pumps only by officers with drawn swords who threatened them "with instant death if they quit their duty," reported Fanning. But the damage resulting from the gale caused another two months' delay in her departure. Not until mid-December did the sloop again hoist sail for America. Because the *Ariel* was so heavily laden with military supplies and carried important dispatches, Jones hoped to avoid contact with other vessels. But a few hundred miles to the east of the West Indies, a distant sail was sighted. The stranger, whom Jones guessed was British, gave chase. Jones tried to escape during the night, but the enemy vessel stayed with him. It was obvious that the British ship was more heavily armed than the *Ariel* and faster. To deal with her, Jones settled upon a stratagem. The sloop was cleared for action but her gunports were kept closed, the French marines sent below and the Union Jack raised to the gaff. The *Ariel* had been a British ship that had been captured by the French, so Jones was confident that the disguise would fool the skipper of the British vessel until he got alongside her. When the stranger came up, Jones, wearing his blue-and-white uniform and swaggering like an officer of the Royal Navy, bluffed her captain into giving an account of himself. His vessel was the 20-gun privateer *Triumph*. She had originally sailed from Newburyport under the command of Captain John B. Hopkins and had been captured a few months before. Jones tried to persuade the English captain to come aboard. When he refused, five minutes was allowed him to change his mind. At the end of that time, up went the American flag and out went the *Ariel*'s guns. She swooped across the stern of the *Triumph*, firing broadside after broadside.

Within ten minutes the Englishman had struck his colors and was begging for quarter. Jones's crew were still cheering when the enemy captain suddenly crammed on sail and made his getaway from the slower *Ariel*. An angry Jones called the British captain "a knave" and considered his ruse as "contrary to the laws of naval war and the practice of civilized nations." Given the fact that Jones had masqueraded under British colors until the very moment he opened fire, the *Triumph*'s skipper was well within his rights to use any trick to save his ship, as Morison points out. So ended Paul Jones's last battle under the American flag. A few weeks later, on February 18, 1781, the *Ariel* dropped anchor off Philadelphia, just over three and a quarter years since Jones had departed from the shores of America in the *Ranger*.

Fresh from their triumphs in Spanish waters, Rodney's four ships of the line arrived at Barbados on March 17, 1780. The admiral was astonished to find the anchorage at Carlisle Bay completely empty. Sir Hyde Parker had sailed off with his seventeen ships leaving not a scrap of information as to his intentions. The British fleet could be anywhere on the blue Caribbean for all the angry Rodney knew. To add to his problems, he was suffering from gout and had to be carried ashore from the *Sandwich*. The local merchants informed him that his second-in-command was at St. Lucia watching the French at nearby Martinique. More ominously, the merchants reported that a large French convoy, escorted by four ships of the line under the command of the Comte de Guichen, one of France's abler admirals, was expected momentarily. In fact, unknown to Rodney, the French had been sailing across the Atlantic on a course nearly parallel to his own. The admiral immediately detached one of his 74s to inform Parker of his arrival while the others were ordered to cruise in the area in search of the French convoy. On the same day that these ships were ordered to sea—March 22—de Guichen brought eighty-three transports and merchantmen into the harbor of Fort Royal, Martinique. Instead of only four big warships, as reported, he had sixteen ships of the line with him.

Within five days, Rodney was back on his feet, and his tiny squadron had joined Parker at Gros Islet Bay, the British base at the northern tip of St. Lucia. The arrival of Rodney and de Guichen at their respective bases brought the two fleets almost face-to-face across only about thirty miles of open water. In numbers they were roughly equal—twenty-three French ships of the line against twenty-one British. A distinct advantage lay with the French, however. Not only were their ships of a superior design, but almost all of them were fresh from home, completely refitted and with clean bottoms. With the exception of the ships that Rodney had brought with him, the British fleet had been in the West Indies for some time. Few of the vessels were coppered, and five had fought under Byron at Grenada. They had been battered by hurricanes and their seams had opened under the heat of the tropical sun. One ship, the *Fame*, 74, could scarcely keep afloat. The fleets were commanded by two of the most skillful naval tacticians of the day, and the greatest sea battle of the era seemed in the offing.

But de Guichen had his hands tied by ambiguous instructions. Battle was not to be offered and he was specifically ordered only "to keep the sea . . . without too far compromising the fleet intrusted to him." Rodney, on the other hand, was eager to offer battle, confident that his skill in maneuver would nullify the enemy's numerical advantage. The admiral allowed himself five days after his arrival at St. Lucia to instill a sense of organization and esprit into his raggle-taggle fleet, to make his instructions and battle signals known to his captains and for wooding and watering his ships. Unfortunately, he did not have the time or the inclination to give much information about his tactical and strategic ideas, and his captains did not instinctively know what was required of them. On April 2, the signal to weigh anchor was raised to the masthead of the *Sandwich*, and the fleet bore away to Fort Royal under a rain of orders, exhortations and reprimands from the irascible commander-in-chief. Shortly after his arrival, de Guichen had paraded his fleet off St. Lucia as a challenge to the British. Now Rodney returned the visit. For two days his ships cruised off the French base "near enough to count all their guns and at times within random shot of some of their forts." The French refused to pick up the gauntlet so the British fleet returned to Gros Islet Bay after several fast vessels were deployed to keep an eye on the enemy.

De Guichen and the Marquis de Bouillé, the Governor of Martinique, had in the meantime developed their own plans for action. Troops were to be embarked and the fleet would put to sea, compelling Rodney to follow them to the leeward. Then they would come about and recapture St. Lucia or take Barbados before the slower British ships could catch up. On the night of April 13, twenty-two French ships of the line and five frigates with 3,000 soldiers on board slipped out of Fort Royal. With them went a convoy that was to be covered part of the way on its voyage to Haiti. As soon as word reached Rodney that the French were at sea, he headed northward in pursuit with twenty ships of the line, one 50-gun ship and five frigates. The *Fame* was in such bad shape she was left behind. The speed of the French fleet was held down by the convoy, so along toward noon on April 16 its sails were sighted by the leading British vessels.

This was the moment Rodney had been waiting for. He broke out the signal "General Chase" at the masthead of the *Sandwich* and his fastest ships surged ahead. By dusk the distance between the two fleets had dropped to only a few miles, but Rodney called off the chase. He fully realized that he was not dealing with an inferior force in full flight. Faced with a fleet superior in numbers to his own and commanded by one of the ablest naval tacticians of the time, he had no desire for a melee in the dark such as the one with Langara three months before. The British ships were ordered into a line ahead for the night and two frigates were stationed between the fleets to keep the commander-in-chief informed of the enemy's movements. In the darkness, the fleets matched maneuver for maneuver, but Rodney kept the weather gage.

Dawn broke on April 17 with the fleets running along parallel but opposite courses—the British going north and the French, who had come about during the night, heading south. The leisurely pace and the cumbersomeness of fleets in the age of fighting sail can be judged by the fact that with the ships sailing about two cable lengths apart, a distance of some 400 yards, the British line extended over six miles of sea and the French fleet was strung out for nearly twelve miles. As his ships were propelled along by gentle, early morning breezes, Rodney made final dispositions for the battle to come. His plan was to concentrate his attack upon the enemy rear. A signal to this effect was made at 6:45 A.M. To make certain that there was no mistaking his intentions, Rodney ordered the distance between his ships closed up to a single cable length. The signal was acknowledged by every ship in the fleet so the admiral assumed all his captains understood his plan. This turned out to be a false—and costly—assumption.

For the next hour-and-a-half, the two long lines of stately ships passed each other on opposite tacks. Their crews, soon to be exchanging devastating broadsides, had nothing to do but gaze at each other across the intervening patch of tropical sea. Guns had been loaded and run out, matches lit, and ample supplies of shot and powder brought up from the magazines. Partitions and screens below had been taken down, and loose gear was thrown overboard. Until the admirals issued their next set of orders there was nothing to be done except to haul occasionally on the braces or trim the set of a sail to keep a ship in its designated place in line. Old salts hid their fears in rough mockery of those who had never been under fire and coolly commented on the enemy's trim or the way he handled his sails. By 8:30 A.M. Rodney believed that the time to strike had come. The French line was strung out with its van well beyond the rearmost British ships and his own fleet was compact and concentrated. The *Sandwich* hoisted a signal that was repeated up and down the British line by the frigates stationed for that purpose on the side away from the enemy. Yards were squared around and helms were put up. The line ahead slowly became a line abreast and the distance between the two fleets narrowed rapidly. The British were ready to deal a devastating blow to the French rear.

Suddenly, the whole plan went awry. The French fleet, instead of keeping majestically on its course to the south, came about and headed north. It was as if de Guichen had fathomed Rodney's intentions. In reality, he had given the order to wear, or pivot 180 degrees, before the British fleet began to bear down on him. Rodney's plan was foiled. If he persisted, his ships would come up against what had been the comparatively well-organized French van rather than the straggling rear. He called off the attack. For the next two hours, the admirals again maneuvered their fleets, ending up in the same relative positions they had been in earlier, with both sailing north. During the maneuvers, Rodney also had trouble with several of his officers, especially Captain Robert Carkett, of the *Stirling Castle*, 74, which was in the British van. On several occasions, Carkett was either lax in obeying signals from the flagship or ignored them, prompting an exasperated Rodney to signal him individually. Carkett was a brave officer—he had risen from the lower deck through conspicuous gallantry—but he was apparently confused by the commander-in-chief's elaborate maneuvers.

Shortly before noon, all again appeared ready to Rodney's eye. With twenty of his ships concentrated against about fifteen at the rear of the enemy line, the signal flag ordering No. 21 of the Fighting Instructions into effect was broken out on the *Sandwich*. On quarter-decks throughout the fleet, signal books were hastily thumbed for the proper order. It stated: ". . . Every ship in the squadron is to steer for the ship of the enemy, which from the disposition of the two squadrons, it must be his lot to engage. . . ." The signal for close action quickly followed.

As his ships held their fire and bore down on the French line, Rodney's thoughts can be imagined. After hours of maneuvering, he had brought his fleet to the point where he could deliver a massive blow to a portion of the French line. All his captains had to do was to bear down on the enemy ship directly opposite them and a good part of the French fleet would be overwhelmed. "At about noon the French fleet began to attack as is their usual custom at a distance (what seamen term playing at long bowls), our fleet remaining quiet," said a midshipman on the *Intrepid*, 64, quoted by Spinney. "Not even one Bull Dog opened its mouth till the proper time. Our captain, the Hon. Henry St. John, said he would not fire a shot till we could see the buckles on the men's shoes, and on account of our near approximation we opened our fire with a hearty good will. We peppered away briskly, taking as much care as we could that our shot might tell; but we had not been long engaged before we discerned that some of the ships ahead of us were remiss in their duty. . . ."

To Rodney's utter astonishment, the *Stirling Castle*, the fleet's leading ship, did not engage the French vessel immediately opposite her. Instead she slanted off along the enemy line to open fire on the leading French ship. One by one, the ships of the van division, commanded by Sir Hyde Parker, followed along, stretching out the British line. Rodney's plan for a knock-out blow on the French rear was ruined. It was too late to make a new signal and the Battle of Martinique, as it was to be known, was turned into an old-style formal battle—exactly what Rodney had been trying to avoid. Habit had triumphed over imagination. Battles had always been fought by ships seeking out their opposite numbers in the van, center and rear, and some of Rodney's officers were so conservative they could not envision any other way of fighting an action. Unfortunately, Parker and Carkett were such men. Not only did Parker's whole division follow Carkett's lead, but in the confusion, the *Grafton*, 74, leading the center, pressed on with misguided zeal, widening the gap from the next ship astern. On the quarterdeck of the *Couronne*, 80, the French flagship, the breakdown of the British attack was greeted with cheers. Too late, de Guichen had realized that he had been outmaneuvered by Rodney. He had fully expected the British attack to be devastating. "Courage!" cried one of his officers. "The English desert their commander!" To Rodney, this appeared to be only too true.

The only alternative left to him was to attack with his center and rear squadrons. Setting an example, Rodney drove the *Sandwich* into the French line slightly to the rear of the *Couronne*. Fighting ferociously, the 90-gun flagship—in tune with the frustrated fury of her admiral—battered the 64-gun *Actionnaire*, which was no match for her. Then she turned her guns on the *Intrépide*, 74, which had come up to take the other vessel's place. She, too, felt the onslaught of the aroused gunners of the *Sandwich*. Without realizing it, Rodney had fought his way through the French line and lay to the lee of it, virtually cut off from support. Spotting the *Sandwich*, de Guichen first feared that his line had been broken and his rear cut off. When he realized that the British flagship was alone, he brought the *Couronne* and two 74s that were unengaged because of the gap in Rodney's line down to deal with her. For ninety minutes, it was three ships against one. When Rodney looked around for help, he looked in vain. Both his van and rear had drawn off, and the center was engaged. The *Sandwich*'s foretopmast crashed over the side taking a tangle of rigging and sails with it. Heavy shot was tearing through her hull. The ships were so close together that hand grenades were hurled onto each other's decks. The *Couronne* was set afire. A terrified dog swam across from the French ship to the *Sandwich* and was picked up to become the admiral's pet. Finally, help appeared to have arrived. The 64-gun *Yarmouth* loomed out of the smoke and was cheered by the *Sandwich*'s crew. Inexplicably, she did not join in the melee. Instead, the two-decker lay about a quarter-mile off, her sails backed as if she were hove-to. A preemptory signal to make more sail brought an acknowledgment and nothing more. Rodney angrily ordered a shot fired into the *Yarmouth* to make her obey the signal, but none of the flagship's guns would bear. This strange behavior lasted for almost an hour before the ship came up to support the *Sandwich*.[11] Eventually, the British flagship fought her way clear of the ring of enemies. She had fired 3,260 round shot and burned up 160 barrels of powder—and was barely afloat.

Shortly after 4 P.M., the action ended. Despite the tactical mistakes that marred the battle, several British ships, including the *Stirling Castle*, had given a good account of themselves. The French drew off and disappeared in the gathering dusk. Too badly damaged aloft to give chase, the British remained where they were to plug shot holes and repair rigging. Neither side had lost a vessel in a battle that would probably have been decisive if Rodney's plans had not been disregarded by his own captains. The British lost 120 men killed and had 354 wounded; the French losses were 222 killed and 537 wounded. Both sides claimed a victory, but the French had little to base their claim upon. De Guichen abandoned his plan for an attack upon St. Lucia and retreated to Basseterre, on the island of Guadeloupe, where he received supplies from neutral St. Eustatius and debated what to do next. Leaving a few frigates to keep an eye on the French, Rodney returned to St. Lucia.

---

[11] The *Yarmouth*'s captain was later court-martialed and dismissed from the Navy when he could give no satisfactory explanation for failing to come to the support of the *Sandwich*.

While shipwrights, carpenters and riggers sweated under the blazing tropical sun to patch up the British fleet, Rodney sat at his desk in the *Sandwich*'s great cabin composing his official dispatch on the action. It was a blistering document that paid tribute to the courage and skill of the French while ignoring Rodney's own officers. So acidulous were some of his comments that the First Lord of the Admiralty suppressed a paragraph that claimed "the British flag [ship] was not properly supported" during the engagement. Another Keppel-Palliser controversy with its appalling effects on discipline and professionalism was too dangerous to risk, reasoned Sandwich. Rodney had already made his stinging views known to the offending officers in letters and personal statements, however. To Carkett, he wrote that only his conviction that the captain's actions had resulted from an error of judgment restrained him from ordering Carkett dismissed from his ship. Not even Hyde Parker, his second-in-command, was protected from the flood of reprimands that Rodney poured down upon the West Indies fleet. Nevertheless, the ultimate responsibility for the failure lay with Rodney, himself. Undoubtedly, the signaling system in use at the time was inadequate and some of his captains had little imagination. In the final analysis, however, the major reason for the failure was that the captains had had little time to learn what was in Rodney's mind, and in his aristocratic arrogance he had made hardly any effort to communicate his thinking to them.

On May 6, word was received that de Guichen was again at sea and Rodney put out after him. Four days later, the French were sighted to the east of Martinique. French intentions were a mystery, but whatever they were, they could not be realized until their tenacious British pursuer was shaken off. Despite the battering the French ships had received, they were still faster and in better condition than those under Rodney's command. Captain Young wrote Middleton that "the Fleet is in a shattered condition. For God's sake and our country's send out copper-bottomed ships to relieve the foul and crippled ones." Holding the weather gage and confident of their superiority, the French danced about the plodding British fleet, always threatening but always staying just out of reach. Nearly every day at 2 P.M.—after the French sailors had been given their wine ration, joked one of the British captains—the enemy would bear down as if to attack. Having tantalized their opponents, they would draw away. Rodney used this frustrating period to drill and instill discipline into his fleet. Transferring his flag to the frigate *Venus*, 36, he kept a sharp eye on everything. Any captain whose ship was not on station or who was slow in obeying signals drew an instant reprimand from the commander-in-chief. "My eye on them had more dread than the enemy's fire and they knew it would be fatal," Rodney wrote his wife. ". . . In spite of themselves I learnt them to be what they had never been before, *officers*."

On May 15, he succeeded in luring the French closer than usual by simulating a withdrawal. De Guichen swallowed the bait, and Rodney, aided by a fortuitous shift of the wind, moved to cut off part of the French line. Unfortunately for the British, the wind again shifted and the French bore away after an indecisive brush that caused little damage on both sides. For four more days the fleets continued to maneuver at a respectful distance in variable winds. There was another brief but sharp engagement on May 19. In Rodney's opinion, "the fire of His Majesty's ships was far superior to that of the enemy who must have suffered great damage. . . ." He appeared to be right, for de Guichen decided he had had enough. He sailed away to his base at Fort Royal on Martinique, the victim of the fatal French doctrine of trying to achieve strategic advantages without accepting tactical risks. As for Rodney, he had fought three battles, held his own with ships that were inferior in numbers and quality to the French fleet, and had not lost an island to the enemy.

Rodney was to have no time to rest on his laurels. The British fleet had barely come to anchor at Barbados when a frigate raced in with the alarming news that a powerful Spanish fleet was on the way. Don José Solano had left Cadiz at the end of April with twelve ships of the line and eighty-three transports carrying some 11,000 men. They were expected in the Caribbean momentarily. Rodney quickly realized that the situation confronting him would be desperate if the Spaniards joined de Guichen. His seventeen battered ships of the line would be confronted by thirty-six battleships. A cruiser screen was immediately thrown out to watch for the Spanish while Rodney again pushed his fleet out to sea on June 7. By then, however, Solano had evaded Rodney's frigates and had joined the French in the lee of Dominica. Thus, for the British, the month of June was critical. All homeward-bound convoys were canceled to keep them from falling into enemy hands. Warnings were sent to every British island to strengthen its defenses. Rodney prepared to meet an attack on St. Lucia. But nothing happened. After sending the Spanish convoy on to Havana, the Combined Fleet dropped down to Martinique, where it remained under the vigilant eye of several British frigates.

As July began, Rodney breathed easier for a number of reasons, Spinney points out. He was reinforced by five 74s that had been long-promised by the Admiralty. The campaigning season was drawing to a close with the approach of the hurricane months, for, as the old salts said, "July—stand by." If the enemy did not strike soon, the weather would make it impossible. And unknown to the British, serious dissension had broken out in the Combined Fleet. The Spaniards refused to cooperate in any of the French schemes to capture the British-held islands. Solano only wished to obtain supplies from his allies before moving on to defend Spanish possessions in the western end of the Caribbean. Sickness was wiping out his crews, and provisions were running short. Tempers flared among the proud French and Spanish officers, and there was more than one fatal duel. With the passing of each day, the danger of a concentrated attack lessened.

On the night of July 5, the Combined Fleet, showing no lights and making no signals, slipped silently out of Fort Royal to the westward. Rodney's frigates trailed them, somewhat mystified as to the enemy's eventual destination. The Spanish fleet was bound for Havana, and Solano had insisted that the French accompany him at least part of the way to provide protection. De Guichen, under strict orders to leave the Caribbean at the onset of the hurricane season and return home, agreed and went as far as Cap François (now Cap Haitien), a major French base on the north coast of Haiti. There he found letters from Lafayette and the French minister in Philadelphia imploring him to come north and begin operations in American waters. Worn out from his exertions and mourning the loss of his son in one of the engagements with the British, de Guichen ignored the request and on August 16 sailed for Europe. Rodney, facing the onslaught of bad weather and suspecting that de Guichen had, in fact, gone to America, prepared to follow. His fears were confirmed when he received the disquieting news that a French fleet and transports loaded with soldiers had already arrived at Newport. The admiral divided his fleet—sending the ships in the poorest condition to Jamaica to escort the September convoy home while keeping those in best repair with him. "Without a moment's hesitation," as Rodney put it, he sped off to New York with ten sail of the line.

The French fleet and troops that so alarmed Rodney were the results of Lafayette's flying visit to Paris in 1779, during which he had begged King Louis and his ministers to send a strong expeditionary force to America. Vergennes had come to the conclusion at the same time that little could be expected of the Americans unless France took an active part in the war. The necessity of naval superiority in North American waters had been emphasized, and Vergennes was now prepared to act upon this advice. The shelving of the invasion of Britain had made it imperative that an effective strike be launched somewhere against the British to keep them off balance. Finally, in February 1780, the French government decided to take the steps recommended by the ardent young Marquis. A substantial fleet was ordered to America along with a sizeable number of troops, who were to be placed directly under the command of George Washington.

The choice of the Comte de Rochambeau, a veteran soldier with almost forty years service, to head the expedition was a fortunate one. Although he spoke no English, he was tactful and judicious in temperment, and unlike d'Estaing, had no difficulty cooperating with his strange new allies. Rochambeau sailed from Brest on May 2 with some 5,500 troops under the escort of seven ships of the line and five frigates flying the commodore's pennant of the Chevalier de Ternay. Their destination was Newport, abandoned by Clinton the previous autumn. A second detachment was scheduled to follow, bringing Rochambeau's total force to about 8,000 men. These reinforcements never sailed because the Ministry of Marine was lax in providing transports, and by the time enough shipping was found, the British had finally clamped a blockade on Brest.

The sailing of de Ternay's squadron did not go unnoticed by the British. At once the Admiralty dispatched a warning of his approach to Clinton and Arbuthnot, who were still at Charleston. Six ships of the line with coppered bottoms were sent racing across the Atlantic under Rear Admiral Thomas Graves with the hope that they would arrive in American waters before the French. If Graves arrived in time, his ships, added to the five that Arbuthnot had, would maintain British naval superiority. The two British squadrons might then intercept de Ternay at sea and give him a warm reception. If the French eluded them and Rochambeau's troops were landed, they would be highly vulnerable for some time to a quickly launched British amphibious attack. On the way across the Atlantic, de Ternay, following a southerly course, had a brush with four small British ships of the line off Santo Domingo on June 20. Both sides pounded away at each other at long range, but the French commander, sticking quite properly to his main objective of safeguarding the convoy, ignored the opportunity to take on an inferior enemy force. On July 10, his squadron dropped anchor off Newport. Graves arrived at New York just three days later to join Arbuthnot, who had hurried up from Charleston with Clinton and about 4,000 troops. The remainder of the British army, some 8,000 men, had been left behind in the south under Lord Cornwallis, who had instructions to maintain control of South Carolina and avoid risky operations.

As soon as he learned of the arrival of Rochambeau, Washington sent Lafayette to Newport with a carefully worked out plan for a combined land-and-sea attack on New York, an operation of high priority with him. For the first time, a French army was firmly established on American soil, and the control of American waters that the Royal Navy had exercised almost unchallenged for more than five years was in jeopardy. Washington looked to the future with gleeful anticipation. The very first message he sent Rochambeau outlining his proposals underscored his belief in the influence of seapower upon military operations. "In any operation, and under all circumstances, a decisive naval superiority is to be considered as a fundamental principal, and the basis upon which every hope of success must ultimately depend," he declared. Rochambeau and de Ternay probably agreed. The junction of Arbuthnot and Graves had deprived them of precisely this superiority.

Speed was essential if the British were to dislodge the French before they had time to dig in at Newport. Everything depended on getting the ships and troops into position to strike. Under the pressure of the crisis, cooperation between the land and sea forces collapsed. Bad blood had existed between Clinton and Arbuthnot at Charleston, but they had managed to suppress their personal animosity until they came north. Both Sir William Howe and Cornwallis had found Clinton a notoriously difficult colleague, and Arbuthnot, a prickly character of sixty-eight and in failing health, lacked tact in dealing with him. Neither understood the problems nor respected the views of the other, so the result was suspicion and hatred. "I am sure he is false as hell, and shall behave in consequence," said Clinton of the admiral. "The fellow is a vain, jealous fool," said Arbuthnot of the general. Delay followed delay. While the British commanders bickered at cross purposes, de Ternay placed his squadron in a strong defensive position in Newport harbor and Rochambeau, reinforced by New England militia, hurriedly rebuilt the old British fortifications and threw up shore batteries. The state of the American troops was a shock to the French general, used to the disciplined, well-supplied armies of Europe. The half-starved, scarecrow look of the men, their battered hats, patched coats and britches, stained hunting shirts, and broken shoes shook him. "Send us troops, ships and money," he wrote home five days after landing. "Do not count on these people nor on their resources. . . ." The strife among the British commanders gave him valuable time to improve his position for they were not ready to mount an attack until July 27. Rochambeau might have found himself in trouble with 6,000 British troops supported by eleven ships of the line moving against him had not Washington descended from the Hudson highlands for a feint against New York. The diversion achieved its aim. Clinton scampered back to the city at once to meet the threat to his base of operations—relieving the pressure on Rochambeau. No further effort was made to dislodge the French although Arbuthnot maintained a loose blockade of Newport from Gardiner's Bay, about twenty-five miles away on Long Island Sound.

Well into the autumn Washington and Rochambeau continued to plan for an offensive as soon as the French troops left at Brest arrived at Newport and de Guichen answered the urgent appeals sent him to come northward. Once the ships were on hand, a decisive naval superiority would be regained, making offensive operations possible. Not until long afterward was it known that the reinforcements had been blockaded at Brest and de Guichen had gone home. In September, Washington and Rochambeau arranged a face-to-face meeting at Hartford, midway between their respective camps, to plan joint strategy. Word of unidentified sails moving over the horizon filled the American commander with happiness as he rode through the autumn foliage to the conference site. "It seems very likely that the Comte de Guichen is really approaching the coast," he declared. Rochambeau's reluctant pledge to attack New York as soon as reinforcements had arrived was secured. Not until the meeting was well underway did Washington learn that the strange ships were not French at all, but British. Rodney had arrived from the West Indies, dashing any lingering hope of a Franco-American offensive in 1780. The sea was more completely in enemy hands than ever before.

The Allies were fortunate that the British did nothing with their naval superiority. Rodney anchored at New York on September 14, increasing the number of British ships of the line to over twenty, more than double those under de Ternay. Nevertheless, his coming only resulted in the addition of a new factor to the quarrel among the British leaders. No attack was launched on Newport. Without inspecting the situation himself, Rodney, again suffering from gout, accepted the word of Arbuthnot and Clinton about the difficulties of getting at the French squadron. As senior officer on the station, he temporarily displaced Arbuthnot as commander-in-chief, creating deep and implacable resentment on the part of the older officer. Prize money played a major role in the disagreement. The new commander insisted on maintaining a tight blockade of Narragansett Bay and sent out frigates to harass Yankee commerce and privateers. As senior officer, Rodney, with his creditors in London always in mind, insisted on a share of the "loaves and fishes," much to the anger of Arbuthnot who was the loser. The acrimonious dispute raged until November 16, when Rodney sailed for the Caribbean.

The year closed with the French locked up in Newport—"like an oyster in his shell" was the way one observer described their situation. Unlike Washington's army, however, they were adequately supplied—hard cash had a way of bringing supplies to camp while the Americans lived from hand to mouth. Yet they missed their "mistresses and the pleasures of Paris; no theaters, no balls; they are in dispair," declared an officer. "Only an order to march upon the enemy will console them." No such order came, and the troops settled into the tedium of winter quarters.

The abortive campaign of 1780 provides a basic lesson in the vital role of seapower in the American Revolution. Without naval superiority, the armies of France and the United States could do little more than fight a defensive war—and defense would not win the war. Without command of the sea, the French force in which Washington had placed such high hopes turned out to be nearly useless. Writing to Benjamin Franklin at year's end, he declared: "Disappointed . . . especially in the expected naval superiority, which was the pivot upon which everything turned, we have been compelled to spend an inactive campaign, after a flattering prospect at the opening of it. . . ."

XXIV

The World Turned Upside Down

Gloom shrouded the American cause as the curtain rose on the fateful year of 1781. "I see nothing before us but accumulating distress," despaired George Washington. "We have been half our time without provisions and are like to continue so. We have no magazines, no money to form them, and in a little time we shall have no men. . . . We have lived upon expedients until we can live no longer." In London, Lord George Germain saw the light at the end of the tunnel. "So very contemptible is the Rebel Force now in all Parts and so vast is our Superiority everywhere," he declared, "that no resistance on their Part is to be apprehended that can materially obstruct the Progress of the King's Army in the Speedy Supression of the Rebellion." Even many die-hard English supporters of the American cause were compelled to agree that Germain's assessment of the military situation appeared correct.

Hopes built upon the arrival of the French expeditionary force at Newport had crumbled. The squadron rocked uselessly at anchor consuming valuable supplies. Rochambeau's troops were idle. No reinforcements had arrived from France, and de Guichen had not even replied to the appeal for assistance from the West Indies fleet.

A British army under Lord Cornwallis was raising havoc in the Carolina back country. Inflation had reached the point where a captain's pay for an entire year was not enough to buy a pair of shoes. For all practical purposes, the Continental Navy hardly existed as a fighting force. Treason and suspicion seemed everywhere. A plot by Benedict Arnold to betray West Point, the key to the American position on the Hudson, had misfired only at the last moment. And on New Year's Day, 1781, the veteran soldiers of the Pennsylvania and New Jersey Lines mutinied with a demand for back pay and discharges to which they were entitled after three years' service. A despondent Washington confided to his journal that he saw no prospects for success "unless we receive a powerful aid of ships, land troops and money from our generous allies."

To help secure this aid, the commander-in-chief, acting at the suggestion of Congress, sent his young French-speaking aide, Colonel John Laurens, on a special mission to Paris in February. He was to seek a sizeable loan and appeal for a fleet of sufficient strength to ensure French naval supremacy in American waters. "Next to a loan of money, a constant naval superiority upon these coasts is the object most interesting," Washington told Laurens. "This superiority, with an aid in money, would enable us to convert the war into a vigorous offensive." Without this help, he warned that the struggle would soon be over. "If France delays a timely and powerful aid . . . it will avail us nothing should she attempt it hereafter. . . . We are at the end of our tether."

With these somber words ringing in his ears, Laurens rode off to Boston with Thomas Paine, the Revolutionary pamphleteer, to board the *Alliance*, which was to carry them to France. To his dismay, Laurens found that the frigate was not ready to sail. There was no money to fit her out, and the only men John Barry, her new skipper, had been able to recruit were unreliable former British prisoners of war and some riffraff from the dockside ale houses. With Laurens's mission before him, Barry asked the Massachusetts General Court to grant him authority to impress seamen to balance the excessive number of British sailors in his crew. The value of the ship and the importance of her mission were temptations that might lead to a mutiny by the English hands, he declared. Laurens supported him, for he had no desire to join his father, Henry Laurens, who had been captured at sea the previous year while on his way to Holland, and was now languishing in the Tower of London. Barry's plea was rejected, although Laurens managed to persuade the authorities to put up enough money to pay a bounty to a few militiamen who volunteered for service on the frigate.

Described as "barely in condition to go sea," the *Alliance* sailed on February 11. Only the emergency nature of the voyage persuaded Barry to put out with such a crew. There were not, he said, ten men, officers included, "that could steer her" and "no seamen aboard but disaffected ones." As soon as the ship was at sea, the former prisoners began plotting to seize her and kill all the officers except one who would be offered the choice of taking the frigate into an English port or being put to death. Dark oaths were sworn on a Bible and a round robin, a popular means of sealing such a compact, was circulated secretly among the crew. With no illusions about the reliability of his men, Barry ordered his officers to remain alert. Marines patrolled the decks day and night. Padlocks were placed on the arms chests. These precautions were enough to deter any action by the conspirators, though mutiny continued to smoulder on the lower deck all the way across the Atlantic.

An advance copy of Laurens's instructions had been sent to Benjamin Franklin. While he awaited the arrival of the special emissary, the old man started to lay the groundwork for the appeal for a fleet. He wrote Vergennes on February 13: "By several letters to me from intelligent persons it appears, the great and expensive exertions of the last year . . . was rendered ineffectual by the superiority of the enemy at sea; and that their successes in Carolina had been chiefly owing to that superiority." If enough ships were sent to America, the entire course of the war would be changed. The pressure exerted by Franklin came at a critical moment. Vergennes was convinced that the struggle had dragged on too long and had become costly beyond the calculation of the government. If France were not to be bankrupted, the war must be ended quickly. The coming campaign must be decisive, Vergennes said in a memorandum for the Spaniards. "Everything urges us to end the war; the means for waging it daily decrease, and the European situation may change at any moment."

A plan of operations was finally settled upon. No attempt would be made to strengthen Rochambeau's detachment, which would remain an auxiliary force under Washington. Instead, the Americans would be given enough supplies and money to field an army of from

10,000 to 15,000 men, and a French fleet under the command of the Comte de Grasse would be sent to the Caribbean. De Grasse was to cooperate with the Spaniards if they had any plans for action. When the hurricane season approached, he was to sail north to join de Ternay's squadron at Newport. What he would do there was left to circumstances. If the worst happened and the American army disintegrated—the French believed this a strong possibility after the mutiny of the New Jersey and Pennsylvania troops—the admiral was to evacuate Rochambeau's force and return to the West Indies. Orders for de Grasse's fleet to sail were issued on March 7, and Franklin was informed of the decision five days later.[1]

De Grasse had fought the British since boyhood. On one occasion he had been taken prisoner and had spent three months under lenient jailors studying the Royal Navy. He had fought as a subordinate under d'Estaing and de Guichen, and had been promoted to flag rank only a little while before. Haughty and with a ferocious temper, he was noted for his severity, and some of his captains were cowed by his very appearance. At six feet two inches, he was one of the tallest men in the French Navy—and it is said of him that he was "six feet six on days of battle." Opinions conflicted as to his abilities. One young officer said that although de Grasse had a "brutal character," he was "a good seaman and known for his bravery." Others said he was "over-cautious" and "a timid tactician." Flying his flag in the 104-gun *Ville de Paris*, the world's most powerful battleship, he sailed from Brest on March 22 with twenty ships of the line and a convoy of one hundred fifty sail. With him went French hopes for a quick victory.

Trouble was brewing for Britain in other quarters as well. She had united the maritime powers of Europe against her by her highhanded treatment of neutral shipping. Finding the British contention that a belligerent power had the right to seize goods destined for an enemy even if it were carried on neutral ships an intolerable burden, the maritime nations of Northern Europe formed the Armed Neutrality. Conceived by the Danes, proclaimed by the Empress Catherine of Russia, and subscribed to by Sweden, this was a defensive treaty for the protection of neutral shipping. All the European bellig-

---

[1] Laurens did not arrive in France until March 10, 1781.

erents—France, Spain, and Britain—were invited to accept its principles, which can best be summed up in the maxim "free ships make
free goods." France and Spain, who had nothing to lose, quickly ac-
quiesced; Britain chose to disregard the whole matter. Holland, desperately trying to find a way to protect its commerce from the increasing interference of the Royal Navy, was the first non-Baltic
nation to embrace the Armed Neutrality. Matters had reached the
point where a British captain had gone so far as to fire upon a Dutch
man-of-war that had resisted a search of merchantmen in its convoy.
Casting an appraising eye over the rich but weakly defended Dutch
colonies in the Caribbean, Britain used Holland's decision to ignore
an Anglo-Dutch treaty of alliance and enroll in the Armed Neutrality as a pretext for a declaration of war at the end of 1780.

At the same time, Cornwallis's campaign in the south was not
going as well as expected. This was the direct consequence of his decision to disregard the instructions given him by Clinton. When Sir
Henry had been forced to leave Charleston for New York to meet
the threat presented by the arrival of Rochambeau, he had left orders for his successor to maintain control of South Carolina and
avoid risks. To Clinton, Charleston was the key to the occupation of
the Southern colonies because it was the ideal base for an army that
depended on supplies and reinforcements brought in by sea. As he
departed for New York, he reported: "I leave Lord Cornwallis here
with sufficient force to keep it against the world—without a superior
fleet shows itself, in which case I shall dispair of ever seeing peace restored to this miserable country."

Sir Henry's goal had been to pacify the areas already theoretically under British control and then to slowly and systematically en-
large this territory to include North Carolina and Virginia. If control
were solidified over the captured territory, Loyalists would be more
likely to be coaxed out into the open to take an active role in subju-
gating the South without fearing they would be left behind at the
mercy of their rebel neighbors once the British Army was gone.
Moreover, Clinton, with his eye always upon the sea link that bound
the British armies in North and South together, proposed that the
invasion of North Carolina, when it came, follow along the east
coast by way of the Cape Fear River. Thus, the British army would
always be in contact with the Royal Navy. Later, troops might be
sent to Virginia as a diversion to Cornwallis's operations.

Restless and ambitious, Cornwallis had more dashing ideas. The cautious approach to the conquest of the South as expounded by Clinton was not for him. He held a dormant commission to succeed Clinton as commander-in-chief in case of Sir Henry's death or resignation, and relations between the two had been tense before Clinton left for New York. Tall and awkward and with a cast in one eye from a childhood injury, Cornwallis was regarded as one of the most promising of the younger British generals. "A good officer," wrote one of his subordinates, "devoted to the service of his country . . . beloved by the Army." Although he had supported the American cause in Parliament, he was now all for striking a deathblow to the rebellion. As a result of the ill-will between the two generals, Cornwallis began to ignore Clinton and to report directly to Germain in London. The British began to fight two different wars, with each commander regarding the other as failing to give proper support to his command. Under these unpromising circumstances, the fateful Southern campaign was launched.

Cornwallis's operations opened with a triumph. In August 1780, he destroyed an American army led by Horatio Gates at Camden, in upper South Carolina. One fourth of the rebel force was either killed or wounded, and Gates, who escaped only after hard riding, left behind the reputation he had gained at Saratoga. Having scored this victory, Cornwallis concluded that the South Carolina back country was sufficiently pacified to make Charleston secure. He struck out to the northward. Instead of moving along the coast as Clinton had suggested, he marched into the rugged North Carolina piedmont, saying the coastal plain was too unhealthy for major military operations. He paid a heavy price for this decision. Because Cornwallis chose the inland route, he was out of touch with the navy and sacrificed all hopes of supplies and reinforcements from that quarter, as William Willcox has pointed out. Because he was short of supplies, he could not remain in one place long enough to attract Loyalist support. Because he was unsupported, he could not hold the territory he had conquered. Because he could not hold territory, he could not force the Americans into a showdown battle while he still had the strength to win it. The similarity of his plight and that of Burgoyne in 1777 is startling. Like Burgoyne, Cornwallis was a boxer swinging at empty air.

For sheer savagery and brutality, the struggle in the Carolinas matched anything in the history of warfare. Atrocities were commonplace on both sides. Prisoners were shot after surrendering and some were hanged by their captors. Harassed by merciless guerrilla bands operating against his flanks and rear, and with his army decimated by sickness, Cornwallis stumbled along in pursuit of General Nathanael Greene, the ablest American general after Washington. A series of bloody encounters followed, which were climaxed by a drawn battle at Guilford Courthouse, North Carolina, on March 15, 1781, in which a fourth of the British army was killed or wounded. Cornwallis's great adventure was over. No longer able to continue his conquests and short of provisions, he fell back to Wilmington, on the Cape Fear River, to nurse his wounds. Confidence unimpaired, he informed Clinton of his arrival after a "uniformly successful" campaign—in which three quarters of his army had melted away.

In the meantime, Rodney had returned to Barbados in December 1780 after his foray to America to find his bases leveled by a ferocious hurricane that had lashed the Caribbean islands in October. Supplies had been destroyed, dockyard facilities wrecked, and several of the ships left behind severely damaged or sunk. As his fleet moved silently into the anchorage at Carlisle Bay, the admiral was horrified by what he saw. The warehouses were crumbling, the trees stripped, the beaches piled with debris. "The most beautiful island in the world has the appearance of a country laid waste by fire and sword," he reported to Sandwich. The men looked about them with awe. Nearly every building at the naval base and in Bridgetown had been unroofed or completely flattened by the storm's violence.

Awaiting Rodney were dispatches from the Admiralty with promises of reinforcements and a new second-in-command to replace the troublesome Hyde Parker. Rear Admiral Sir Samuel Hood[2] was on his way with eight copper-bottomed ships of the line. To find a suitable second to Rodney had been a trying experience for Sandwich. "It has been very difficult, very difficult to find out proper flag-officers to serve under you," he wrote. "Some are rendered unfit from their factious connections, others from infirmity or insufficiency, and we have at last been obliged to make a promotion to

---

[2] Later Lord Hood, a patron of Nelson, who called him "the greatest sea officer I ever knew."

do the thing properly." The appointment of Hood should have been pleasing to both officers. Their friendship extended back to the time when Hood had served as a midshipman under Rodney, then a young captain. Until Hood's appointment in the Caribbean, his naval career appeared over at the age of fifty-six. He had been serving ashore as commander of the Portsmouth dockyard, normally considered a final appointment before retirement. Sandwich's search for the right second-in-command for Rodney resulted in Hood's being given flag rank and another tour of active duty.

Impatiently awaiting Hood's arrival—his fleet having been reduced to nine ships of the line—Rodney thought he saw an opportunity to strike a blow at the French, who had also been battered by the great hurricane. Word had reached him that the storm had severely damaged the enemy's defenses at St. Vincent. Embarking troops under the command of General John Vaughan, the admiral prepared to put to sea to pick up an island cheaply. But, for some unexplained reason, he hesitated for several days—Fleet Captain Young claimed "an unsteady fit" had seized him—and the French were warned of his coming. The garrison was reinforced while the British delayed so that when Vaughan's troops landed, the enemy's defenses were too strong to be assaulted. The project was abandoned with Rodney blaming the West Indian colonists for passing the word of the expedition on to the French. For now, he let his anger simmer, though the opportunity to vent it fully soon came.

The arrival of Hood's squadron set off a torrent of activity at Gros Islet Bay, the British base at St. Lucia. With fresh stores and new materiel brought in by Hood's convoy, Rodney's ships were feverishly refitted for battle. Sails and rigging were repaired, empty provision rooms restocked, and magazines replenished with shot and powder. By the end of January, the fleet consisted of twenty-one ships of the line ready for sea. At this point, a sloop raced in from England with the news that war had been declared with Holland. Rodney was ordered to attack the Dutch West Indian islands of St. Eustatius and St. Martin immediately. The Admiral must have chortled in anticipation as he again loaded Vaughan's soldiers on shipboard. Ever since he had taken command of the Leeward Station, he had regarded St. Eustatius with loathing. The mile-long row of stone warehouses that fronted along the sea was crammed with the produce of America to be traded for the manufactured goods of Europe, all in defiance of Britain's attempts to put down the rebellion. So unscrupulous were the West India merchants that it was suspected that two thirds of the goods sent out from England and Ireland under convoy were shipped off to Statia, from where they found their way to America and the French base at Martinique. Without these supplies, the French could but barely keep a fleet at sea, declared Rodney. If the Dutch were villains for permitting the trade, the English merchants who participated in it were traitors. He would deliver a blow "like a clap of thunder" against this "nest of vipers."

Leaving six ships cruising off Fort Royal to keep an eye on the four remaining French battleships, Rodney and Hood slipped away to the northward to St. Eustatius. Late in the afternoon of February 3, the islanders were just awakening from their post-luncheon siestas when they saw a British fleet standing into the roadstead with its guns run out. The shore batteries and a Dutch frigate, the only warship present, were covered. Completely overawed, the Dutch, who had not yet learned of the declaration of war, quickly surrendered. Informed that a convoy had sailed for Europe just thirty-six hours before, Rodney sent two of his fastest ships of the line and a frigate in hot pursuit. They soon caught the convoy, and after a brief engagement with a Dutch two-decker, brought the ships back to the island. Rodney was astonished by what he found. "The riches of St. Eustatius are beyond all comprehension," he wrote his wife. "One hundred and thirty sail of ships in the road, with one Dutch man-of-war of thirty-eight guns and five other ships of war, from fourteen to twenty-six guns, belonging to the Americans,[3] and more than one thousand American prisoners." Proof that some British merchants were putting profit above patriotism was provided by the capture of twelve vessels from the convoy that had come to the Caribbean with Hood. The Dutch flag was kept flying for nearly a month after the capture to decoy unsuspecting vessels into the port and another seventeen ships were added to the plunder. "Not a night [passes] but an American arrives loaded with tobacco," the jubilant admiral declared. The neighboring islands of St. Martin and Saba were also captured, sending the total value of the booty to over three million pounds.

For the British commander, this was the opportunity of a life-

---

[3] These were privateers rather than ships of the Continental Navy.

time. The Dutch claimed the English sailors "acted like robbers, searching, digging, confiscating." After years of money troubles, Rodney was rich beyond his wildest dreams, and the sudden change in his fortunes went to his head. The admiral's long-standing anger with the West Indian merchants robbed him of all caution and their goods were summarily confiscated. The merchants claimed that the seized goods were part of their legitimate trade with the Dutch that had been permitted by law, but Rodney brushed such appeals aside with a sailor's contempt for pettifogging. *"Delanda est Carthago,"* he wrote to one of his correspondents with a classical flourish. He appears to have been particularly highhanded in dealing with a group of about one hundred Jewish traders who, he said, "will do anything for money . . . and had been deeply concerned in supplying the enemy with provisions." At his orders, the Jews were stripped and their garments searched. After 8,000 pounds in notes had been found, they were ordered to leave the island on one day's notice without their wives and children. The English merchants, at least, were to have their revenge. They dragged the admiral through the courts over a period of a decade, from law suit to law suit, nearly bankrupting him.

The splendor of what one writer has called "the Aladdin's Cave" into which Rodney had stumbled blinded him to the immediate tactical realities. Although there were plans to send Hood to capture the Dutch colonies of Curaçao and Surinam, no attempt was made to complete the bloodless conquest. The disgruntled Hood blamed Rodney, commenting that "the Lares of St. Eustatius were so bewitching as not to be withstood by flesh and blood." [4] To such charges, Rodney later replied that within a few days after the capture of the island, he had received word—later proven false—that a large French fleet was on the way. Because Curaçao was so far to the leeward that it might take several weeks for any ships sent there to beat back should an emergency arise, the expedition was dropped. Instead, Hood was ordered to take eleven ships of the line, and along with the half-dozen cruising off Fort Royal, station himself to the windward of Martinique to surprise the approaching French fleet.

---

[4] *Webster's New Collegiate Dictionary* defines "lares" as "household effects." But Daniel A. Baugh, in an essay on Hood in *George Washington's Opponents*, states that Hood wrote "lures," which was mistakenly transcribed by the editor of the admiral's letters.

Rodney remained behind at St. Eustatius in the *Sandwich* to oversee the loading of the convoy that was to carry the captured treasure to England. Hood, according to Spinney, maintained that the negative decision on Curaçao was made sometime before the false report of the approach of the French was received.

This conflict, to prove so costly, was apparently based on a clash of personalities. Hood owed the sudden rise of his fortunes to his friendship with Rodney. Nevertheless, within a few months of his arrival in the Caribbean he was severely criticizing his chief behind his back. Just what caused the alteration of their relationship is unknown. Rodney was a difficult man—as Sandwich acknowledged in making his search for a suitable second—and perhaps his icy manner in dealing with subordinates froze any warmth that had existed between the two men. On the other hand, Hood was not suited to be a second-in-command. "Subordination was not his forte," states one of his biographers.[5] ". . . He carried no oil for troubled waters in his locker." Strong willed and outspoken, he was well aware of his own considerable abilities and harshly critical of his superiors.

For the next five weeks Hood cruised an empty sea to the east of Martinique. In view of the fact that if the French squadron that was supposed to be approaching joined with the vessels already at Fort Royal, the British would be outnumbered and the initiative lost, Hood pressed Rodney to leave St. Eustatius and take command of the fleet. The admiral, however, was busy putting the final touches on the prize convoy. His only reaction to his second-in-command's pleas was to order him to switch station from windward of Martinique to the leeward. The change in plan was influenced by a number of considerations. Rodney wished to keep the four French ships of the line at Fort Royal bottled up so that they would not menace the weakly-defended St. Eustatius convoy.[6] He also wished to blockade the island, which was known to be short of provisions. Moreover, with the threat of a French squadron no longer imminent, Hood's ships could be revictualled and watered one by one at St. Lucia while the rest patrolled in the lee of Martinique. Hood pleaded, protested,

---

[5] Dorothy Hood, *The Admirals Hood* (London 1942).

[6] The plunder was loaded aboard thirty-four merchant ships which were guarded by two ships of the line and three frigates. Off the Scilly Islands, a French squadron captured twenty of the merchantmen.

and argued against his new orders. Although the reports of a French squadron had been a false alarm, he emphasized that sooner or later an enemy fleet would be sent to the Caribbean. Such a force could not be intercepted from the leeward. "Should an enemy's fleet attempt to get into Martinique, and if the commander of it inclines to avoid a battle, nothing but a skirmish will probably happen," Hood warned, "which in its consequences may operate as a defeat to the British squadron, though not a ship is lost and the enemy suffer most." Nevertheless, Rodney, falling back upon his experience in the waters around Martinique, remained adamant. Hood was ordered to continue his lonely patrol. Beating back and forth against wind and current, it proved impossible to detach ships to run into Gros Islet Bay for fresh provisions. Scurvy soon broke out among Hood's exhausted crews.

Along toward mid-day on May 3, a battered two-decker limped into the St. Eustatius roadstead with her pumps working to keep her afloat. She was the *Russell*, 74, of Hood's squadron, bringing grim news. Five days before, on April 28, de Grasse's fleet of twenty ships of the line and a large convoy had arrived in the Caribbean. The French had brushed past Hood's poorly placed ships and had anchored safely in Fort Royal. Although the British commanders had expected a French fleet sooner or later, the arrival of de Grasse came as a complete surprise. No frigates had been stationed off Brest to carry a warning of de Grasse's departure to them, and no squadron had been sent racing after the French as in the past. The entire Channel Fleet was engaged in escorting another relief convoy to Gibraltar, and there were no ships left to reinforce Rodney in the West Indies. In the long run, the price of Gibraltar was the loss of the American colonies.

Driving his ships relentlessly and towing his slower vessels to increase speed, de Grasse had made a thirty-six day passage across the Atlantic, a swift one for the time. Coming in with the wind at its back, the French fleet rounded the southern tip of Martinique on April 29. The convoy hugged the coast and the battleships stood out to the leeward as a protective screen. As soon as Hood abandoned his station off Fort Royal to meet the threat, the four ships that had been blockaded in the harbor came out and joined de Grasse. They increased his fleet to twenty-four ships of the line. Against them, Hood mustered eighteen ships, including a 64 manned by volunteers that had come up from St. Lucia at the last minute. In both number of ships and in gunpower, the British fleet was inferior. Unable to beat up to the French from the leeward, Hood could only hope that de Grasse, with the advantage of the weather gage, would accept his challenge to battle.

The Frenchman, however, had no intention of coming to close quarters. As the protection of the convoy was his major interest, he was content to bang away at the British at long range. "I believe never was more powder and shot thrown away in one day," Hood later told Rodney. Shortly before noon, the fleets came about and headed south toward the tip of the island. Both vans began to run out of the lee of the land, and the freshening breeze caught four of Hood's ships, drawing them away from the rest of his line. They were carried along into contact with eight French vessels and badly knocked about. The *Russell* was the most shattered. Her magazine was flooded and the sea was gaining on her pumps, so she was ordered to St. Eustatius to carry the news of the encounter to Rodney.

All during the next day, April 30, the two fleets maneuvered within sight of each other without closing. Several of Hood's ships were now leaking so badly their captains reported that they could not keep up with the rest of the squadron. Finally the admiral broke off contact and headed north to join Rodney, and de Grasse followed his convoy into the harbor of Fort Royal. Hood's prophecy of the consequences of stationing his squadron to the leeward of Martinique had been fulfilled with a vengeance. Several British ships had been badly damaged with nothing gained while the French had won naval supremacy in the Caribbean. As far as Hood was concerned, the blame rested squarely on Rodney's shoulders. "There never was a squadron so unmeaningly stationed as the one under my command," he declared.

As soon as Rodney received news of the engagement, he hurried to sea with the *Sandwich* and the *Triumph*, 74. But it was too late to do anything but gather up the scattered pieces of Hood's squadron. The various elements of the British fleet made a junction at Antigua on May 12, where with ships and crews in a bad state, it was allowed two days to take on provisions and water before moving on to defend Barbados. While Rodney was trying to restore his fleet, the French were taking advantage of their naval superiority. An attack was launched on the British base at St. Lucia on May 10, but the defenses proved too strong to be assaulted. The enemy withdrew only to strike elsewhere. On May 23, the same day that Rodney's fleet arrived at Barbados, French troops went ashore at Tobago, about 200 miles to the south. First reports reaching the British commander put the enemy force at only two ships of the line and some nine hundred men. Not daring to risk the loss of Barbados to the French main force if the attack on Tobago were a feint, Rodney dispatched Rear Admiral Francis S. Drake, a descendent of the Elizabethan sea dog, with a relief force of six ships of the line carrying reinforcements for the garrison. Shortly after Drake departed, de Grasse's fleet of twenty ships of the line was sighted standing to the southward. Luckily, Drake managed to escape and rejoin Rodney, who ordered his entire force to weigh anchor and proceed to Tobago. It was already too late. By the time the British fleet arrived off Tobago, the island had surrendered. The defense collapsed after the French issued orders for four plantations to be burned every four hours until the garrison surrendered.

Fearful for the safety of Barbados, Rodney retraced his course. Late in the afternoon of June 5, de Grasse's fleet, now twenty-three ships of the line, was sighted off the Grenadines also steering north. Rodney, who held the weather gage, resisted the temptation to attack. To the anger and disgust of Hood, who accused him behind his back of avoiding battle, the fleet continued to plow on to Barbados. Rodney did not want to gamble on a melee in the dark which could result in serious damage to his fleet and leave the main British base in the Caribbean exposed to the enemy. "I gave orders that all the lights of the fleet should be particularly conspicuous to the enemy, that in case they chose an action, they might be sure their wishes should be complied with the next day," he reported. De Grasse had no intention of giving battle, however, and the two fleets soon lost sight of each other in the night.

All remained quiet for the next several weeks as the fleets lay idle—the British at Barbados; the French at Martinique. Nevertheless, the time for a decision on further operations was approaching rapidly. The hurricane season was due shortly, and Rodney's health was deteriorating. He wanted to go home, but complaints about his freebooting actions at St. Eustatius were already being heard in England and there would be embarrassing questions about the loss of Tobago and his apparent refusal to attack de Grasse. He received little sympathy from Hood as he agonized over what should be done. "It is quite impossible from the unsteadiness of the Commander-in-Chief to know what he means three days together," he wrote. "One hour he says his complaints are of such a nature that he cannot possibly remain in the country and is determined to leave the command to me; the next he says he has not thought of going home."

The problem resolved itself on July 5, when de Grasse put to sea with twenty-seven ships of the line and a convoy of nearly two hundred merchantmen. Rodney surmised that they were bound for Cap François, Haiti. From there, he expected that the convoy would be sent home to France with the produce of the French West Indian islands while de Grasse would sail to reinforce the French forces in America. Fast-sailing ships were sent to warn the British commanders at Jamaica and New York of the latest developments. Rodney's own fleet was to follow, but without the admiral because he had finally decided his health would not permit it. Hood was ordered to take fourteen ships of the line, convoy some British merchant ships to Jamaica and then go to New York. It was believed that this force, combined with the ships already in North American waters, would be sufficient to deal with de Grasse because he would undoubtedly detach some of his ships to escort the valuable West India convoy to France and leave others behind to protect the islands. Rodney sailed for home on August 1, needlessly taking three ships of the line with him. They were to be sorely missed, for his erroneous strategic estimate of de Grasse's intentions was to be a fatal contribution to the coming British debacle. Ten more days passed before Hood left for the American coast. While the British were making their new dispositions, de Grasse arrived at Cap François on July 16, to find dispatches from Rochambeau urging him to come north with ships, men and money. Twenty-five pilots familiar with the American coast had been sent to bring him in safely.

In early 1781, a land-sea campaign had unfolded on the American coast that was almost a dress rehearsal for the final operations that led to the British surrender at Yorktown. In December 1780, Clinton had sent his newest brigadier general, Benedict Arnold, to Virginia with a force of some 1,600 men to create a diversion. Operating with his usual energy and efficiency, Arnold led his men, mostly American Loyalists, on a broad swath of destruction through the Old Dominion. With almost no opposition, he swept from the shores of the Chesapeake to Richmond, burning, looting, and terrifying the populace as he went. When Arnold finally withdrew to his poorly protected base at Portsmouth, Washington saw a chance to trap him between an American army and a French fleet. Lafayette was sent marching overland with some twelve hundred troops. A great storm had temporarily scattered Arbuthnot's ships that had been blockading Newport and a quick move by the French to the Chesapeake would neatly bag the arch-traitor. If Arnold fell into American hands, Washington ordered Lafayette "to execute the punishment due his treason and desertion in the most summary way." With that, Washington turned to persuading the French naval commander to cooperate.

The Chevalier de Ternay had died during the past winter and command of the Newport squadron had passed to the Chevalier Destouches, who turned out to be an extremely conservative and unimaginative officer. Ignoring the opportunity to get his entire fleet to sea that had been presented by the weather, he sent only one ship of the line and two frigates south to cooperate with Lafayette. The three ships sailed on February 9, 1781, and accomplished almost nothing in Virginia. The vessels supporting Arnold drew less water than they did and had withdrawn up the Elizabeth River out of reach. The French quickly returned to Newport, their only success the capture of the *Romulus*, a British 44. Angered at this half measure, Washington personally went to Newport early in March to persuade the French to move against Arnold. He was received with the honors of a Marshal of France, but despite all the assurances of cooperation, the fleet showed no signs of sailing. For two days it remained at anchor while Washington fretted about the loss of the opportunity to strike an important blow against the British. He was gratified on March 8 to see the French squadron finally disappear into the cold winter sunset.

Two days later, Arbuthnot, informed that the French had left Newport and acting with unaccustomed vigor, gathered his fleet "in the hope of being able to fight the enemy before their entry to the Chesapeake or if practicable to attack them there." Although the French had a head start, the wind favored the British and their copper-bottomed ships were faster. Early on March 16, the fleets, evenly matched at eight ships of the line each, sighted each other about forty miles off Cape Henry at the mouth of the Chesapeake. The British ships had more firepower and the British had the weather gage, but with the wind blowing up and a high sea running, this was a disadvantage. Heeling over in the wind, the ships were unable to open their lower gun ports on the engaged side for fear of causing the ships to flood. Thus the British were unable to use their superior weight of metal.

The ensuing action was fought strictly according to the book, with both fleets banging away as they passed each other's battle lines. Arbuthnot was so concerned about maintaining his line that he kept the signal to form a line of battle flying from his masthead throughout the engagement without hoisting the signal for close action. The two vans battered each other and drew apart. Destouches then came about and brought the remainder of his fleet into action against the crippled British ships, inflicting considerable damage. Having done just enough to satisfy his honor, he headed out to sea and back to Newport. Arbuthnot limped into Lynnhaven Bay behind Cape Henry to protect Arnold. The French had had the best of the exchange, but they failed to take advantage of it. Had Destouches persisted, he probably would have won control of the Chesapeake.

Washington's scheme for the entrapment of Arnold was ruined. Ten days after the sea battle, on March 26, the turncoat's safety was further insured when transports bearing some two thousand reinforcements arrived under General William Phillips, who took over command of the British forces in Virginia. For the next two months, this army ravaged the countryside at will. British gunboats ranged up and down the rivers, putting landing parties ashore to wreak havoc and then whisking them away before resistance could form. Even Washington's own Mount Vernon was laid under tribute, which was paid to keep a raiding party from destroying it. The only opposition to the British came from a few ragtag regiments, most of the men "poor fellows, almost naked" under the command of Lafayette. Marching overland from Baltimore, he arrived at Richmond just in time to save Virginia's new capital from Phillips and Arnold. Early in May, Lafayette observed that the British were concentrating their force at Petersburg, to the south of Richmond, for some as yet unfathomed purpose. Not until later did he learn that Cornwallis, unknown to Clinton, had informed Phillips that he was abandoning

Wilmington and would join him in Virginia rather than return to Charleston.

Cornwallis seems to have had an obsession that the Carolinas could not be subdued as long as the rebels were supplied from Virginia. If Virginia could be pacified, so he thought, then all the provinces to the south would fall due to a lack of supplies. Cornwallis's fixation upon Virginia as the major theater of operations prompted him to go so far as to suggest to Clinton that he abandon New York and bring his army south where the rebellion could be finally crushed. Sir Henry was astounded and regarded the suggestions as nonsense. "It would certainly have been the speediest way to finish the war," he wryly commented, "for the whole army could have been annihilated in our campaign." Cornwallis arrived in Virginia on May 20 to take command of a combined force of some seven thousand men from Arnold, who had succeeded Phillips when the latter had died the week before. Surprised that Cornwallis was not returning to South Carolina, Nathanael Greene turned away and struck deep into the South, rolling up the British garrisons that had been left behind. But the junction of the British columns in Virginia placed Lafayette's force in considerable danger. "I am not strong enough even to get beaten," he wrote Washington, while Cornwallis boasted, "The boy [Lafayette] cannot escape me." The stage was set for the climactic campaign of the American Revolution.

After depositing Laurens and loading supplies for Washington's army, the *Alliance* sailed from Lorient on March 29. Shortly after sail was hoisted, a splash was heard and the cry "Man overboard!" came from aloft. The ship was hove-to and a boat was hoisted out to search for the missing sailor, a topman named Patrick Duggan. There was no sign of him. Duggan's death cast a shadow over the group of former British prisoners of war who had been plotting to seize the ship. He had been one of the ringleaders and his disappearance seemed an ill omen to many of the superstitious sailors. Some demanded that the plot be ended and the round robin that they had all signed on the outward voyage be destroyed because it was a death warrant. The paper was torn up and thrown overboard.

The next day, one of the seamen, an American Indian, came aft with a request to see John Barry. He told the Captain as much as he knew of the plot to seize the ship and identified three of the leaders.

Acting quickly, Barry armed his officers and the men thought to be loyal. A detachment of marines was sent below to the berth deck to arrest the ringleaders and place them in irons. Throughout the night, no one slept. Armed men patrolled the ship and the crew wondered what the morning would bring. At dawn on March 31, a twittering boatswain's pipe called all hands on deck. They found marines drawn up across the quarterdeck with their muskets leveled at them. The three prisoners were brought up and unshackled. Barry told them that they were charged with mutiny. If they confessed the names of their accomplices, their punishment would be eased. Only the snapping of the flag at the gaff could be heard as the grim-looking captain awaited an answer. After a few moments of sullen silence, Barry motioned to the boatswain and his mates.

Strong hands seized the prisoners who soon were dangling by their thumbs from a yardarm. A boatswain's mate took the cat-o'-nine-tails from its red baize bag and laid it on the backs of the men. Again and again, the whip whistled through the air. How many lashes were inflicted before the leaders named their fellow plotters is unknown.[7] Midshipman John Kessler reported that the prisoners "underwent a very severe whipping" before they talked. "The names of 25 of their accomplices were obtained from them before the whipping was discontinued." As each man was named, he was called to the quarterdeck, stripped of his shirt, tied to the hammock nettings "and the whipping continued until it was thought all were disclosed that could possibly be obtained." This brutal process was typical of eighteenth-century sea law. If the conspirators had been successful, they would have—by their own confessions—killed all the officers except for the one who had been selected to navigate the frigate to an English port. Later, Barry was to show mercy. The three ringleaders were court-martialed and condemned to death but he did not exact this penalty.

The punishments quickly restored discipline to the ship, for when the *Alliance* fell in with a pair of well-armed British privateer brigs on April 2, the crew sprang cheerfully to the guns. Both enemy vessels were easily taken and sent off under prize crews. Shortly after this success, the sea turned boisterous, and the frigate was badly bat-

---

[7] Continental regulations specified that a captain could order only a dozen lashes but Barry ignored the prohibition.

tered. With her masts and rigging damaged, she was greatly slowed and Barry was apprehensive when, off Cape Sable on the evening of May 27, he sighted two strange sails standing toward him. They were the British sloops-of-war *Atalanta* and *Trepassey*, armed with a total of thirty 6-pounders and spoiling for a fight. The wind had died down and the *Alliance* was lying "like a log" on a sea that was as quiet as a mill pond. Seizing their opportunity, the captains of the lighter enemy ships ordered out long sweeps and had their vessels rowed around to safe positions off the frigate's stern quarters. As a result of this maneuver, the British could stand off and knock the American vessel to pieces without having to worry about her twenty-eight 12-pounders and eight 9s. "We could not bring one-half our guns, nay, ofttime only one gun astern to bear on them," reported Midshipman Kessler.

The *Alliance*'s deck was swept by grape and her hull shattered by round shot fired at close range. The men cursed and prayed for the merest puff of a wind so they could bring their guns into action. Barry, who was moving among his men trying to encourage them, was felled by a grape shot in the shoulder. Although blood was streaming from the wound, he stayed on deck to direct the battle. There he remained until, almost fainting from loss of blood, he was taken below to the cockpit. As the captain was carried from the deck, a shot carried away the frigate's colors. The few guns that could be fired were reloading, so in the lull the British thought she had struck. Powder-grimed men leaped onto the bulwarks and into the shrouds of the enemy vessels to cheer. Their jubilation was short-lived. Another American flag was quickly broken out, and the guns began to fire again. At one point, Hoystead Hacker, the *Alliance*'s first lieutenant, went below to ask Barry for permission to surrender before the ship was sunk. "No sir!" thundered the Captain. "If the ship cannot be fought without me, I will be brought up on deck!" Before Barry could carry out his threat, what was left of the frigate's sails began to fill in a light breeze. Here at last was the wind for which the Americans had prayed. Hands leaped to the braces and the *Alliance*'s broadside swung around to bear on her tormentors. Fourteen 12-pounders crashed out, smashing into one of the British ships. In a moment, the guns were run in, reloaded, and run out again. After only a few salvos, both the *Atalanta* and *Trepassey* hauled down their colors. Down in the cockpit, John Barry heard his men cheering and sank back exhausted and happy. Nine days later, on June 6, the *Alliance* sailed into Boston—sixty-nine days out from Lorient.

At the time Barry had been in France, Seth Harding in the *Confederacy*, Samuel Nicholson in the *Deane*, and John Young in the *Saratoga* had been cruising with small success in the Caribbean. In mid-March they headed for Philadelphia, loaded with stores for the Continental army and escorting a convoy of about three dozen merchantmen. The other two men-of-war became separated from the convoy during a storm so the *Confederacy* proceeded along alone. On April 14, near the Delaware Capes, Harding sighted a sizeable enemy ship bearing down. The merchantmen were ordered to scatter, and the *Confederacy* cleared for action. Although the cargo of supplies greatly interfered with the working of his ship, Harding steered for the enemy vessel. Unexpectedly, another ship came up over the horizon and broke out the Union Jack. She was the *Roebuck*, 44, and her consort was the *Orpheus*, 32. Harding surrendered to this superior force without a fight. So ended the brief and lackluster career of the *Confederacy*. She was taken into the Royal Navy and renamed the *Confederate*. While the *Deane* had made her way safely into Boston, the *Saratoga* was never sighted again. Apparently she had foundered during the storm with all hands.

The *Trumbull* did not get to sea again after her battle with the *Watt* for more than a year, and then only because James Nicholson had accepted about fifty British prisoners of doubtful loyalty to fill out his crew. Escorting a convoy of twenty-eight merchantmen, he sailed from Philadelphia on August 8, 1781, only to run into a storm the next day that carried away the frigate's fore-and-main topmasts. The convoy pressed on, leaving the *Trumbull* behind to repair the damage. While she was wallowing along, two British ships were sighted. Nicholson ordered his men to their battle stations but "instead of coming, three quarters of them ran below." The remainder put up a fight, but the frigate was quickly battered into submission. Her captors turned out to be former American ships—the *Iris*, 32, which had been the frigate *Hancock* and the *General Monk*, formerly the 18-gun privateer *General Washington*. The *Trumbull* was in such bad shape that she was towed into New York by the *Iris*. She was not taken into the Royal Navy, indicating that the last of the Continental Navy's original thirteen frigates was either poorly built or rotten.

As the Continental Navy dwindled into insignificance, with the *Alliance* and *Deane*—the only ships left—lying in port unable to recruit crews, the members of the Board of Admiralty decided there was no longer any need for their services and resigned. The dissolution of the Board left the Navy without a head during the summer of 1781. Finding someone qualified to accept the post proved as difficult as it had been to get members for the Board of Admiralty. Earlier in the year, Congress had decided to centralize some of the government operations under single executives and a Secretary for Foreign Affairs, a Superintendent of Finance, a Secretary of War, and a Secretary of Marine were to be appointed. The Navy secretaryship fell to Robert Morris by default. Already the custodian of an empty treasury as Superintendent of Finance, he had assumed the duties of the defunct Board of Admiralty until someone was chosen to fill the vacancy. On September 7, 1781, Congress made the appointment official, naming him as Agent of Marine, a post he held until November 1784. The position was analogous to the First Lord of the Admiralty in Britain. The appointment was probably the best that could have been made because Morris was not only one of the ablest administrators in the new nation, he was familiar with maritime affairs as a merchant and privateer owner.

One of Morris's first appointments—made while he was filling the post temporarily—was to name Paul Jones as captain of the 74-gun ship of the line *America*, which had been on the stocks at Portsmouth, New Hampshire, since 1777. Jones was now the commander of the most powerful warship in the Continental Navy—if he could get her finished and to sea. He might also have had flag rank if it had not been for the jealousy of James Nicholson. Before going to sea on the *Trumbull*'s final cruise, Nicholson had learned that a congressional committee was considering making Jones an admiral and vigorously lobbied against it. "I immediately took my Hat and with very little Ceremony waited on the President of Congress at his house & informed him what I had heard," Nicholson wrote Barry. He protested that to promote Jones would be an injustice to the captains who were senior to him and spiced his objections with "many things pretty severe of the Chevalier's private as well as

Public Carrector too odious to mention." That ended Jones's chance for promotion to admiral.[8] Having coped with the *America*, which Jones found "half-built" while the dockyard was short of material to finish her, Morris sought to get the *Alliance* and *Deane* out on a cruise. The lack of crews kept them in port until after the fall of Yorktown, however.

The perfectly coordinated allied land and sea campaign that resulted in the surrender of Cornwallis was the product of circumstances rather than that of a carefully worked out strategy. It began with the arrival of the French frigate *Concorde* in Boston on May 6 with two important passengers aboard—the Comte de Barras, the newly appointed commander of the squadron at Newport, and the Vicomte de Rochambeau, the general's son. They brought the news that Laurens and Franklin had succeeded in obtaining a sizeable loan from France and that de Grasse's fleet was on the way to the West Indies. Even more important, Rochambeau received a letter from the admiral "for himself alone" informing him that the fleet would come north in July or August to liberate the squadron bottled up in Newport. In view of these developments, the French commander sought a strategy conference with Washington. It took place on May 21, at Wethersfield, near Hartford, Connecticut.

Without actually revealing that de Grasse was expected off the American coast later in the summer, Rochambeau raised the question of what should be done if such an eventuality did occur. Washington favored an all-out attack on New York—which he argued had been weakened to send reinforcements to the South—while the French general regarded such an operation as too hazardous. To him, the Chesapeake appeared a much more profitable field of endeavor—especially after some captured British dispatches indicated that the enemy's strategy was to concentrate on the subjugation of the Southern states. Washington contended, however, that a blow against New York would force the British to withdraw troops from the south, taking pressure off Lafayette and Greene. In arguing against making Virginia the major theater of operations, the commander-in-chief said that without naval supremacy it would be impossible to move troops by sea, an overland march would be too haz-

---

[8] David G. Farragut became the first American admiral in 1862.

ardous, and the men would arrive too late in the campaigning season
to be effective. Pending the arrival of the French fleet—if it were to
come—the two armies should be concentrated on the Hudson. "The
force thus combined may either proceed to the operations against
New York or may be directed against the enemy in some other quarter as circumstances dictate," the minutes of the meeting declared.

Soon the French army was on the move in obedience to the decision reached at Wethersfield, although Rochambeau maintained a
healthy skepticism about the wisdom of an attack on New York.
Countryfolk lined the roads of Connecticut as some four thousand
French soldiers swung by in spotless white uniforms piped with
crimson, dark green, rose, and violet to distinguish the various units.
Artillerymen wore blue coats lined with white, and a corps of light
troops appeared in sky-blue coats and red britches. Even the names
of the regiments had a romantic ring—the Royal Deux-Ponts, the
Soissonais, the Saintonge, the Bourbonnais, and the Auxerre. The
junction with Washington's army of some 4,500 men which had
come down from the Hudson highlands took place on July 6 at
White Plains, within striking distance of the British lines north of
Manhattan. But the concentration failed to bring about the object
for which Washington had called the armies together. The British
positions were too strong to assault, so there was little the allies
could do but settle in and make tentative probes.

Clinton had been bracing for an attack on New York since a
dispatch from Washington to Lafayette outlining the decisions of the
Wethersfield conference had fallen into his hands. Paradoxically, the
fact that the entire allied plan was known to the British had fatal
consequences for the British rather than the Americans and French.
Clinton, always apprehensive about the safety of New York, was
thrown into near panic by the prospect of a joint assault that might
be supported by a French fleet. His reaction had an important role in
bringing about the downfall of Cornwallis. Off to Virginia went a series of peremptory dispatches ordering Cornwallis to go on the defensive and to send as many of his men as could be spared to reinforce New York. This demand came as the strategic underpinnings
were being knocked out from under the Virginia campaign. Cornwallis, who had once considered Virginia so important that he suggested Clinton abandon New York and join him there, now wished
to return to Charleston to defend his outposts in South Carolina.

And Clinton, who had deplored Cornwallis's advance into Virginia, now told him that Admiral Thomas Graves, who had succeeded Arbuthnot as naval commander, wanted a winter base in the Chesapeake for his ships. Portsmouth, Old Point Comfort, and Yorktown were suggested as possible sites to be occupied by Cornwallis.

All this took place amid a tangle of orders and counterorders in which Clinton tried to direct Cornwallis's operations from New York, while Lord Germain tried to direct both of them from across the Atlantic. For example, Cornwallis had no sooner received Clinton's order to send reinforcements to New York than he received a letter from Germain prohibiting the withdrawal of a single man from the Chesapeake. Slowly, Cornwallis withdrew down the York Peninsula, beating off harassing attacks by Lafayette and trying to decide where to dig in. Portsmouth was regarded as too difficult to defend; Old Point Comfort was ruled out by his engineers. Cornwallis finally settled upon Yorktown although he thought it exposed to attack. It was a sunny little town of fewer than two hundred houses. "Great part of the houses form one street, on the edge of a cliff which overlooks the river," wrote an English visitor to Yorktown. Looking down on the town and harbor, the traveler admired the tranquil jumble of rooftops, shady trees and twisting lanes. Into this peaceful haven Cornwallis marched his footsore army on August 1. Reporting the move to Washington, Lafayette added wistfully, "If we should have a great fleet arrive at this moment, our affairs would take a happy turn."

Such a fleet was on the way—almost as if it had been planned. The dispatches from Rochambeau which de Grasse found awaiting him at Cap François on July 16 all but requested him to come to the Chesapeake rather than to New York. Written after the Wethersfield conference, the letters outlined the discussions between Washington and Rochambeau but in such a way that operations in the south were made to appear more attractive. "There are two points at which the offensive may be made against the enemy: Chesapeake Bay and New York," the general informed de Grasse. "The southwesterly winds and the state of distress in Virginia will probably make you prefer Chesapeake Bay, and it will be there where we think you may be able to render the greater service." Rochambeau also implored the admiral to bring as many troops and as much money as he could get his hands on.

De Grasse moved with daring and vision. He immediately informed Washington and Rochambeau that he had chosen the Chesapeake as "the point . . . from which the advantage you propose may be most certainly attained." Then he set about getting the troops and money. Obtaining men was a comparatively easy task for there were three French regiments at Cap François—some 3,500 men—under the command of the Marquis de Saint-Simon. They had been detailed to join the Spaniards in offensive operations in the western Caribbean but had spent most of their time in garrison duty. Saint-Simon and his officers were eager for action. They persuaded the Spaniards to allow them to embark with de Grasse after promising that the regiments would return to San Domingo by November. Within twelve days after the receipt of Rochambeau's dispatches, the troops had been loaded aboard the men-of-war and the fleet was ready to sail. Obtaining money was a more difficult problem. De Grasse appealed to his Spanish allies for gold, but the authorities were evasive. He pleaded with the local merchants who demanded security for a loan. The admiral offered to pledge his own plantation on the island as well as his chateau in France, both of which were worth far more than the sum sought. The merchants agreed to furnish the money but delayed so long in producing it that de Grasse angrily broke off the negotiations. He then turned to the Spanish director of customs, a Señor de Salavedra. So persistent was de Grasse in his demands that the official agreed to go to Havana to obtain the money. He was sent ahead on the frigate *Aigrette*, while the fleet prepared to follow.

Freak accidents cost de Grasse two of his ships before he left Cap François. Just after dawn on July 23, a clerk on the *Intrepide*, 74, went below to draw the morning issue of *tafia*, a strong brandy served the crew at breakfast. Someone handled a lantern carelessly and the volatile liquor flashed into flames that swept the ship. Nearby vessels in the crowded harbor sought frantically to get away from the burning *Intrepide*. Finally, her "stern sprang into the air with a majestic rumble," reported a spectator. It was "a horrible sight." Flaming brands and splinters showered the other vessels and injured people and damaged houses ashore. Twenty sailors were

killed. At almost the same time, the 40-gun frigate *Inconstante* fell
victim to a similar accident as she sailed off the coast of San Domingo. She too caught fire and exploded while brandy was being
drawn. There were only eighty survivors of her crew of two hundred.
As a result of these catastrophes, de Grasse ordered tighter restrictions on the distribution of brandy. Sickness was also a problem. The
fleet had been forced to leave 1,800 sick men at Martinique and the
admiral feared he might have to leave as many more at Cap François
if he did not get away soon.

The French fleet sailed on August 5. With the powerful *Ville de
Paris* in the van, de Grasse's twenty-six ships of the line were an imposing sight as they stood out to sea. Some of the seamen had decorated their ships with tropical plants and the greenery combined with
the multi-colored signal flags fluttering from mastheads and
yardarms to give the vessels a festive air. It took a long time for them
to pass out of the harbor and vanish over the northwest horizon.
Two more 74s and the frigate carrying de Salavedra joined the armada at sea. The official had good news. The Spanish authorities
claimed they had no money but the citizens of Havana raised 1.2
million livres in little more than six hours. Some ladies had even
given their diamonds to the cause. One caustic Frenchman, however,
described the money as "an excuse for the seventeen Spanish men-
of-war not to accompany de Grasse. Is it not a shame for these vessels to lie rotting two years in port?"

De Grasse took a bold gamble in ordering all his ships to accompany him to America, leaving none to escort the merchant convoys or to protect the islands. The gamble succeeded only because
Rodney had not even dreamed the French would take it. He assumed that de Grasse, after detaching a number of his ships for convoy duty and to protect the French islands, would go north with
about a dozen ships. Therefore, Hood had been left with only fourteen ships of the line. De Grasse quickly saw that the projected new
campaign was worth the risk, writing Rochambeau: "I believe myself authorized to take some responsibility on my own shoulders for
the common cause." Afterward, a British naval officer commented:
"If the British Government had sanctioned or a British admiral had
adopted such a measure . . . the one would have been turned out
and the other would have been hung. No wonder that they succeeded and we failed." De Grasse also took another audacious step

in setting his course through the Old Bahama Channel between the north coast of Cuba and the Bahama banks, a route which was usually avoided because of treacherous reefs and unpredictable storms. It was the one course on which he could avoid being sighted by British cruisers as he approached the mainland.

Away to the north and unknown to de Grasse, Hood was also racing toward the American coast. He hoped to join Admiral Graves's squadron at New York and give battle to one of the French fleets—either that of de Grasse or the one commanded by de Barras that was still at Newport—before they combined forces. The British ships were copper bottomed and Hood was sailing on a direct course so he arrived off the coast before the French. On August 25, he sent a frigate to look in the Chesapeake, and when she reported no trace of the enemy, he hurried on to New York. Hood arrived off Sandy Hook on August 28 and was furious at the lack of urgency he found among the British commanders.

Unlike his predecessor, Arbuthnot, Graves managed to get along with Clinton. Yet this did little for the British cause. While the net was being drawn tight about Cornwallis, they concentrated on de Barras's squadron at Newport. Although neutralized by superior British forces, the eight French ships were regarded as a constant menace to the far-flung British supply lines, for they could break out again into the Atlantic as they had in March 1781. Clinton was eager to pull this thorn from his side. When the French troops were withdrawn from Newport, the opportunity seemed to have presented itself for an attack on de Barras's anchorage. Clinton and Graves knew that de Grasse was on the way from the West Indies—followed no doubt by a British squadron—with the strong possibility that the blockade of Newport might be lifted. This would add de Barras's ships to the French fleet, making it unbeatable. To forestall such a disaster, it was agreed that an attack would be launched against Newport.

But Graves, a brother-in-law of Lord North, was a plodder who lacked the strategic foresight demanded by the fast-moving events on the American coast.[9] Throughout the summer, he acted as if no

---

[9] He was only temporarily in command and was awaiting the arrival of Admiral Sir Robert Digby, who was to assume control of the North American Station.

threat from the West Indies existed. In mid-July, he wasted precious weeks in which Newport might have been taken in a fruitless search for a French supply convoy reported off the coast. The fleet groped about in a fog near Boston, accomplishing nothing except to put new strains on the ships, still suffering from the damage inflicted earlier in the year during the battle off the Chesapeake. Even after Graves received definite word from Rodney that de Grasse was on the way to America with Hood in his wake, Graves remained oblivious to the threat of French seapower. Instead of heading out to sea to make contact with Hood at the Chesapeake Capes so Cornwallis would be protected, he and Clinton calmly continued planning their attack on Newport.

Immediately upon his arrival, Hood had been appalled by an example of Graves's lackadaisical planning. Pilots had been sent to Sandy Hook to bring his ships across the bar so they could be revictualled in the harbor. Hood objected because he realized that this would cause considerable delay in getting to sea again. Learning that Graves and Clinton were conferring on Long Island, Hood had himself rowed ashore and appeared at the meeting to the surprise of his superiors. "You have no time to lose," he told them. "Every moment is precious." The British fleet should get to sea immediately either to attack Newport or to search for de Grasse. Word was received later that night that de Barras had already sailed on August 25—he had been ordered to carry Rochambeau's artillery to Virginia—so Graves agreed to put to sea immediately with the hope of falling on de Barras with the overwhelming superiority provided by the arrival of Hood's ships.

Nevertheless, while Hood fretted off the bar, it took another three days before Graves could get his five seaworthy ships of the line ready to sail. Five more had to be left behind. As usual the ships were in poor repair and shorthanded, though just a few weeks before, a press gang had swept over New York, dragging away four hundred men to serve in the fleet. Lieutenant Bartholomew James, one of its leaders, reported that some citizens were even snatched from their homes:

> The business . . . furnished us with droll yet distressing scenes—taking the husband from the arms of his wife in bed, the searching for them when hid beneath the warm clothes, and, the better to prevent delay taking them naked, while the frantic partner of his bed, forgetting the

delicacy of her sex, pursued us to the doors with shrieks and impreca-
tions, and exposing their naked persons to the rude view of an unfeel-
ing press gang.

With his ships manned through such desperate measures,
Graves put to sea on August 31 with nineteen ships of the line. The
British had no accurate information regarding the whereabouts of de
Grasse and de Barras except that they were both somewhere at sea.
A course was set for the Chesapeake only because it was believed
that de Barras was headed southward.

Washington and Rochambeau were also on the way south with
their armies. They had received word from de Grasse on August 14
that he was bound for the Chesapeake, with the admonition that
they join him as soon as possible. Whatever was to be accomplished
would have to be done quickly, for the admiral intended to leave for
the West Indies by October 15 because of the commitments he had
made to the Spaniards in exchange for Saint-Simon's troops. "Employ me promptly and usefully that time may be turned to profit," he
told Rochambeau. Within four days, the armies were on the march.
Orders were hurried off to Lafayette telling him to keep Cornwallis
from escaping from the York Peninsula. While the main body of
troops was slipping away on the long march to Virginia, every effort
was made to deceive Clinton as to the allied intentions. A small force
was left to hold the lines before New York, bake ovens were built,
and roads were improved as if a siege were planned. Despite persistent reports that the enemy was on the move, Clinton, suffering
from spells of temporary blindness, stolidly awaited an eventual attack on New York. After all, the enemy's strategic plan had fallen
into his hands. Besides, he had been assured by the admirals that the
Royal Navy would be able to match any fleet brought to North
America by de Grasse, retaining command of the sea. Like Rodney,
Sir Henry was a prisoner of his own failure of imagination. He could
not believe that his opponents would risk their entire force in a bold
gamble for a decisive victory.

Still, there were enough possibilities of failure in such a complicated operation with its reliance on timing and coordination of land
and sea forces that the march south was a period of intense anxiety
for Washington. The army had not been paid for months, and there

was considerable muttering among the men about taking their grievances directly to Congress when they reached Philadelphia. Washington thought it prudent to march his men through the capital without stopping. At the same time, he had received a report that a
British fleet—actually Hood's ships—was off Sandy Hook. There
was real danger that de Barras's squadron carrying the French siege
train might be intercepted. A British fleet might also enter the Chesapeake before de Grasse arrived. And where was the French admiral?
To Lafayette, Washington confided: "I am distressed beyond expression to know what is become of the Count de Grasse."

On September 5, Rochambeau and his staff were nearing the
waterfront at Chester, Pennsylvania, after an inspection of the Delaware forts, when they saw a tall officer in Continental uniform jumping up and down, waving his hat in one hand and his handkerchief in
the other. As Rochambeau's small boat approached the shore, the jubilant figure seemed to be George Washington. But, of course, that
was impossible. The French knew the commander-in-chief as a cold,
austere figure. Yet it was Washington. And he was not only jumping
up and down and waving his hat, but shouting. The Frenchmen
heard the name "de Grasse!" The admiral and his fleet had arrived
in the Chesapeake on August 30, Washington shouted. "A child
whose every wish had been gratified, would not have experienced a
sensation more lively," said one of the French officers. The trap had
snapped shut on Cornwallis.

Early that same morning—September 5—twenty-four French
ships of the line swung at anchor in Lynnhaven Bay behind the hook
of Cape Henry, smoke curling from the breakfast fires in their galleys. De Grasse was not prepared for action. Three of his larger vessels had been sent to blockade the mouths of the York and James
Rivers, and several of his lighter vessels had been ordered to sail up
the Chesapeake to Head of Elk and bring back the allied army.
Many of de Grasse's men were absent from their ships, ferrying
Saint-Simon's troops ashore or gathering wood and water for the
fleet. Shortly after 8 A.M., the frigate *Aigrette*, on patrol at the entrance to the Bay, sighted a cloud of sails coming down from the
north. There were three . . . five . . . then eight ships. Apparently de
Barras's squadron had arrived. There was laughter and cheering in
the French fleet. Ominously, the distant sails continued to appear.

The count increased to twelve ships . . . fifteen . . . and finally nineteen. It could only be the British. The great ships began to stir. Urgent signals were hoisted, and guns were fired to summon the working parties back to their vessels. The galley fires were doused. Men were sent forward with axes to cut the anchor cables in case the ships had to get out quickly.

Plowing along at little more than three knots, Graves's fleet had taken more than four days to cover the distance between New York and Virginia. Several of Hood's ships had turned out to be in poor condition. They were "the shadow of ships more than the substance," according to the angry Graves, who had been assured by Hood that his fleet was in fighting trim. The *Terrible*, 74, was in the worst condition with five pumps working. Other ships were leaky, or had their masts sprung, or were short of water and provisions. At one stage of the voyage, the fleet was forced to lay-to off the Jersey coast, wallowing in the swells for hours, as emergency repairs were made to some of the cripples.

From ten miles out, a lookout on the British frigate *Solebay* reported a forest of masts within the Chesapeake. Convinced that a mistake had been made, the vessel's captain went aloft himself. Training his glass in the direction indicated by the lookout, he made out several warships. At first, Graves thought they were de Barras's squadron. But as the British drew nearer, the count of ships mounted grimly to twenty-four. Unable to conceive that de Grasse would bring his entire fleet from the Caribbean, Graves surmised that a junction of the two French fleets had taken place. Nevertheless, the admiral was undaunted. He realized the immediate danger to Cornwallis if the French were not defeated or at the very least forced to withdraw. Graves ordered his ships cleared for action and bore down upon the enemy with a brisk northeast wind at his back. The curtain had risen on the Battle of the Chesapeake Capes.[10]

Although de Grasse had overwhelming superiority in the number of ships and guns, he was confronted with serious tactical problems. His fleet was held fast by the tide, and when it turned he would have to get to sea in the face of a strong northeasterly wind. Although the mouth of the Chesapeake is ten miles wide, the channel

---

[10] The most detailed and readily available account of the battle is in Harold A. Larrabee, *Decision at the Chesapeake* (New York 1964).

for large ships between Cape Henry and the Middle Ground, the shoal where James Nicholson had lost the *Virginia* in 1778, is only three miles wide, leaving little room for maneuver. Some of his best officers and about 1,600 men were ashore helping the army. One of the French 74s, the *Citoyen*, lacked two hundred seamen and most of the other vessels were shorthanded too. Under the circumstances, de Grasse could have placed his ships in a defensive line across the entrance to the bay and awaited the British attack. By venturing to sea he assumed a double risk—of being defeated or having Graves slip into the Chesapeake behind him after he had sailed. On the other hand, remaining in the bay would condemn de Barras's squadron to almost certain destruction or capture, with the loss of the army's siege artillery. Besides he did not need a victory, only control of the Chesapeake which would result from even an indecisive battle. After weighing his options, de Grasse decided to put to sea to engage the enemy.

As soon as the tide began to turn, at about noon, the admiral ordered his ships to cut their anchor cables. Signal flags shot up to the masthead of the *Ville de Paris*, instructing the fleet to form a line of battle in the order of speed in getting to sea without regard to their usual fighting stations. One by one the ships scrambled around Cape Henry to the open sea, some of them having difficulty because they were so short of men. First out was Commodore Louis-Antoine de Bougainville in the 80-gun *Auguste*, the chief of the fleet's rear division, who assumed command of the van. The first four ships came out in good order but the rest of the fleet straggled in their wake. De Grasse's flagship was twelfth in line, well behind Bougainville, while the last French ship was more than three miles back.

The British fleet swept down upon the French from the windward in a tight line-ahead formation, the ships a cable-length apart. Hood in the *Barfleur*, 90, commanded the van, Graves was in the center in his flagship *London*, 98, and the rear was commanded by Admiral Drake, in the 70-gun *Princessa*. "Graves was in a position almost beyond the wildest dreams of a sea-commander," observed one authority.[11] "His whole fleet was running down before the wind, and his enemy was . . . working slowly out of harbour. He had only to fall on their van with full force and the day was his." But Graves

---

[11] James, *The British Navy in Adversity*.

ignored the opportunity. As his fleet neared the French van, he gradually altered course to the west. This maneuver placed the two fleets on approximately parallel but opposite courses. Graves was an unimaginative formalist who believed in adhering to the regular line of battle, ship-to-ship from van-to-rear. What he had in mind was the standard naval engagement provided for in the Fighting Instructions—an exchange of broadsides between two parallel lines of ships. He muffed a golden opportunity to overcome de Grasse's superiority and secure a decisive victory that would have brought a different outcome at Yorktown. Summing up after the battle, Hood declared: "The British fleet had a rich and most plentiful harvest of glory in view, but the means to gather it were omitted. . . ."

Shortly after 2 P.M., Graves noticed that his ships were coming perilously close to the Middle Ground shoals. A signal was hoisted for the fleet to wear together, or pivot 180 degrees, until the line had come about and was heading east to the open sea in the same direction as the French. The order of the British line was now reversed. Hood's ships, which had been in the van, were now in the rear and Drake's vessels, which had been in the rear, were now in the van. As a result, Graves was leading from weakness. The *Terrible* and several of the other ships that had come from the Caribbean in poor condition would make the first contact with the French van, which was considerably stronger.

While these maneuvers were taking place, de Grasse was frantically trying to get all his ships out from behind Cape Henry. He was saved from disaster by Graves. Instead of bearing down on the still disorganized French line and pinching off de Grasse's leading vessels with a determined attack, Graves waited for the enemy center and rear to come up. This aberration presented de Grasse with a gift of valuable time—Hood later claimed it was "a full hour-and-a-half"—to close up his line. At about 2:30 P.M. Graves gave the order for his leading ships to edge down to the starboard toward the French line, approaching it at an angle from the north. But he signaled them to attack in line-ahead, which meant the British vessels would come up against the French in piecemeal fashion. A basic rule of naval tactics for an attack by an inferior fleet was thus violated, notes Larrabee—all elements must strike together to bring maximum firepower into play. Not until 3:46 P.M., when the opposing vans and centers were roughly parallel, did Graves hoist the signal for close action—while keeping the signal for line-ahead still flying. The vans were within pistol shot while the centers were a greater distance off and the rears were still miles apart, when the first broadsides thundered out. Eight hours had elapsed since the *Aigrette* had sighted the British fleet.

Heavy fighting raged between the vanguards of the two fleets. Although there were originally eight British ships against four French before Bougainville was reinforced, the British had the worst of it. The 74-gun *Shrewsbury*, which led the British line, was hammered so badly by the *Pluton*, 74, that her first lieutenant and thirteen crewmen were killed and her captain and forty-six men wounded. The *Intrepid* tried to cover the crippled *Shrewsbury* and was also roughly handled. She received sixty-five shot holes on her starboard side alone and had twenty-five men killed and thirty-five wounded. The *Terrible*, weakest ship in the British line, was badly battered. She began to take on water at the rate of two feet every twenty minutes, and there were doubts that she could be kept afloat. The action was so hot that Bougainville brought the *Auguste* close enough alongside the *Princessa* to give the impression that he intended to board. His aggressiveness brought praise from de Grasse, who said: "Now that's what I call combat!" After the first hour, the battle extended down to the leading ships of the center divisions of the two fleets. Yet even though Graves was outnumbered and his van was taking a beating, the seven ships in Hood's rear division scarcely fired a shot.

The reason was the contradictory signals that Graves flew during the action—line of battle and close action. There was a complete collapse of communication because the admiral had not had the time or the inclination to instruct his captains in the interpretation of his signals. The result of flying the signal to close while displaying the signal to maintain a line ahead was utter confusion. The line of battle signal took precedence and as long as it was flying, no vessel could deviate from its position in the battle line. Hood did not bring his rear division into the fight until it was too late, and he was subsequently criticized for a lack of initiative as strongly as he had criticized Graves.

For the ships in the van, the simultaneous signaling of line ahead and close action caused no confusion. They were near enough to the enemy to abide by the signals. For the vessels in the rear under

Hood's command, it was an altogether different matter. These ships were at such a distance from the enemy because of the angle upon which the British had attacked the French, that they could not close without at least temporarily disrupting the line ahead. Obeying the Fighting Instructions to the letter, Hood and his captains regarded the signal for line of battle as the controlling one. Graves contended that this signal was flown only intermittently after the signal for close action was given—and then it was hoisted merely to call some ships back into line that had become bunched up on the *London*'s beam. The flagship's log bore him out. He maintained that it had been his intention for Hood to attack immediately. Hood, on the other hand, contended that two signals were flown simultaneously until about 5:25 P.M. when the line of battle signal was lowered, and other witnesses supported him. At this point he tried to bring his rear division into action but it was already too late. Although the vans remained within pistol shot of each other, firing died away at sundown because the crews were exhausted. As the British naval historian Michael Lewis has remarked, Graves had maintained his line—and lost America.

Night fell with the fleets still cruising in parallel lines about ten miles off Cape Henry. Graves sent a frigate to gather reports on the damage to his van and the news was grim. Not only was the *Terrible* sinking, but several of the other ships were badly cut up and in danger of losing their masts. The British van was in no condition to resume the fight until spars and rigging had been replaced. Graves began to lose hope that he would be able to attack the French the next day—his original numerical inferiority having risen from five to ten or eleven ships because of the battering his lead vessels had taken. Otherwise, casualties had been comparatively light in the brief, furious action. The British had ninety men killed and 246 wounded against total French casualties of 209. Graves's major problem was the loss of speed and maneuverability he had suffered as a result of the skill of the French gunners in disabling masts and rigging. During the night, the crews of both fleets remained at quarters within sight of each other with matches glowing and lights lit.

The first view that Graves had of de Grasse's fleet as dawn broke on the morning of September 6 was not reassuring. The

French "had not the appearance of near so much damage as we had sustained," he said. With his fleet unable to attack, Graves had no plan of action to meet the new situation. He called upon Hood for his advice, even though he was critical of his second-in-command's failure to support him during the battle. Graves was convinced that only Hood's delay in launching his attack had cost him a victory over de Grasse's larger fleet. Writing to Sandwich, he said that if he had been properly supported, several of the French ships "must have been cut to pieces." Perhaps uneasy about his own less than heroic part in the battle, Hood blamed Graves for the failure. When a frigate captain came on board the *Barfleur* to deliver the admiral's message, Hood was in his cabin composing a scathing denunciation of the conduct of the battle for his friends at the Admiralty. "I dare say Mr. Graves will do what is right," was his frigid reply to Graves's request for counsel. Throughout the remainder of the day, the two fleets continued making repairs, with Graves reporting that his ships were in too "mutilated a state" to bear down for an attack. He seems to have given no thought to what should have been his primary mission—the relief of Cornwallis. A lookout on the *Citoyen* reported that at least five British ships were replacing topmasts and one had a badly damaged mainmast. That evening, Graves summoned Hood and Drake to the *London* for a council of war that broke up with recriminations over the way the battle had been fought.

"Why didn't you bear down and engage?" Graves demanded of Hood, according to an account published the following year.[12]

"You had up the signal for the line," Hood replied.

Graves turned to Drake and asked: "Why did you bear down on the enemy?"

"On account of the signal for action."

"What say you to this, Admiral Hood?" said Graves.

"The signal for the line was enough for me."

In this fashion the two fleets moved on to the southeast with the commanders warily watching each other's maneuvers while seeming to have forgotten they were contending for control of the Chesapeake. By September 9—four days after the battle—Bougainville confided to his diary that he was "very much afraid" that the British might put about and seize control of the bay. That night de Grasse

---

[12] Quoted in Larrabee, *Decision at the Chesapeake.*

came to the same conclusion. Contact was broken off with the enemy and all sail was set for the Chesapeake. Just as Bougainville had been more concerned about fulfilling the French fleet's mission than his superior, Hood was more upset by the sudden disappearance of the French than Graves. He implored the admiral to hurry back to the Chesapeake to prevent de Grasse from "giving most effectual succor to the rebels." But Graves did not immediately give the order to put about and the fleet was further delayed by the agonizingly slow death of the *Terrible*. She was now making six feet of water an hour and her pumps were worn out. On the evening of September 10, she was set afire—the only ship lost in the battle by either fleet. With this painful duty out of the way, Graves finally set a course for Cape Henry and sent the frigate *Medea* on ahead to scout the situation.

Three days later, the *Medea* returned under a full press of sail with momentous news. The French had already entered the Chesapeake. Unknown to the British, the fleets of both de Grasse and de Barras lay within the shelter of Cape Henry—a total of thirty-two ships of the line. While de Grasse and Graves had been fruitlessly sparring to the southward, de Barras and his eight ships of the line and a convoy bearing the allied army's siege guns had slipped into the bay. Uncertain about what to do next, Graves turned once again to Hood. "Admiral Graves presents his compliments to Sir Samuel Hood," he wrote, "and begs leave to acquaint him that the *Medea* has just made the signal to inform him that the French fleet are at anchor . . . in the Chesapeake, and desires his opinion what to do with the fleet. . . ." Hood's answer was cutting. ". . . Sir Samuel would be very glad to send an opinion, but he really knows not what to say in the truly lamentable state we have brought ourselves."

Nothing remained but for the distraught Graves to call another council of war to face the fact, as Hood had pointed out, that "we should have barred the entrance [to the Chesapeake] to de Grasse: now he has barred it to us." The gloomy meeting attended by Graves, Hood, and Drake in the great cabin of the *London* ended with a decision that sealed the doom of Cornwallis's army. Because of "the position of the enemy, the present condition of the British fleet, the year so near the equinox, and the impracticability of giving an effectual succor to General Earl Cornwallis in the Chesapeake, it was resolved that the British squadron . . . should proceed with all dispatch to New York." [13]

A week later, on September 19, the crippled fleet arrived off Sandy Hook, rumors of its defeat having raced ahead. The New York Loyalists needed only to look at the battered condition of the ships and the grim faces of the officers and men to determine what had happened. Hundreds of Tory families began packing their belongings in preparation for a move from the city. Clinton agreed that as soon as the fleet had been repaired, 6,000 troops would be embarked in an attempt to relieve Cornwallis. Operating on the assumption that de Barras had already joined de Grasse before the battle of September 5, Clinton and Graves throught Britain's loss of command of the sea was only temporary. They believed the French had but twenty-four ships of the line which would be matched by Graves's fleet when it received reinforcements. Three ships were being brought from England by Admiral Digby, Graves's successor, two were due in from Jamaica and two were undergoing repairs at New York. When added to the eighteen survivors of the battle, they would give Graves parity with de Grasse. "I was inclined to hope [that these additions to the British fleet] would soon turn the scale in our favor," declared Sir Henry.

This illusion was shattered on September 23, when it was learned that the French fleet actually consisted of thirty-six ships of the line. Even Clinton now realized the significance of the few hours of gunfire off the Chesapeake capes. "All depended on a fleet," he declared. "Sir Henry Clinton was promised one, Washington had one." Only desperate measures could save Cornwallis now. The British commanders were trapped between their desire to save Cornwallis and the grim reality of the strategic situation. They promised Cornwallis rescue, but time after time the date of sailing was postponed. The dockyards were blamed for delays in repairing the ships and Digby was cursed for his tardiness in arriving. Plans were dis-

---

[13] Taking a less critical view of Graves than that adopted by most historians, Mackesy argues that had the British fleet sailed into the Chesapeake, it might have been blockaded and destroyed. "The French would have commanded the sea and been at liberty to shift their troops at will against Charleston or even New York." While the surrender of Cornwallis was to break Britain's will to continue the war, the destruction of Graves's fleet would have had greater repercussions, according to Mackesy. "The Leeward Islands and Jamaica would have fallen, New York would have been assaulted or starved. India could not have been defended. And if the French had permitted it, Nova Scotia and Canada would have passed to American rule."

cussed for a diversionary attack—perhaps on Philadelphia—in hopes of drawing de Grasse away from the Chesapeake. But the underlying reason for delay was the realization among the admirals that to rescue Cornwallis they would have to battle their way through a vastly superior fleet, embark the troops at Yorktown, and somehow fight their way out to sea again. Only Hood seemed eager to take the chance. "Desperate cases require bold remedies," he declared. He proposed that three or four fireships be sent into the Chesapeake and when the enemy fleet was in confusion, there would be "a favorable opening for pushing through it." The others were skeptical, but in the absence of another proposal it was reluctantly accepted.

On October 19, a rescue fleet of twenty-three ships of the line commanded by Graves finally shook out their sails and set a course for the Chesapeake. Clinton, who was aboard the *London*, wrote Germain to assure him that the fleet would arrive at Yorktown well in time to rescue Cornwallis. But it was already too late. Shortly before 2 P.M. that same day, Cornwallis surrendered. Some 7,000 Redcoats marched out of their redoubts and passed between a long line of white-coated French troops and an opposite rank of Continentals who had cleaned and mended their tattered uniforms as best as they could. As the British trudged along, a band struck up a melancholy tune that went:

> If buttercups buzzed after the bee,
> If boats were on land, churches on sea . . .
> Summer were spring and the t'other way round,
> Then all the world would be upside down.

XXV

The Storm Subsides

"Oh God! It is all over!" cried Lord North upon learning of Cornwallis's surrender. The news had arrived about mid-day on November 25, 1781, and came first to Lord Germain. He immediately dispatched a messenger to the King and went himself to Downing Street to inform the Prime Minister of the disaster. The Sunday stillness of Whitehall was broken only by the random clip-clop of horses' hooves. From time to time, distant church bells tolled the hour. North received the news "as he would have taken a ball in the breast," said Germain. He flung up his arms and paced the room exclaiming over and over again that all was lost. In contrast, George III accepted the disaster with scarcely a tremor. Germain was entertaining guests at dinner that night when he received a reply to his message from His Majesty. Looking up from the paper, the American Secretary said: "The King writes just as he always does, except that I observe he has omitted to mark the hour and minute of his writing with his usual precision." It was the only sign of the effect of the catastrophe on this precise man.

Washington would have been greatly surprised by North's reaction. To him, Cornwallis's surrender was merely "an interesting

event that may be productive of much good if properly improved."
No one in the Continental Army, from the rawest private to the commander-in-chief, believed for an instant that the Yorktown campaign
was the end of the war in America. The British still controlled New
York, Wilmington, Charleston, Savannah, and St. Augustine. True,
they had lost a quarter of their North American army, but their remaining forces were several times larger than Washington's, and
there was nothing to prevent the ministry from sending more troops.
The French had won a momentary naval superiority on the American coast, although de Grasse was already sniffing the breezes and
planning his return to the West Indies. When he did, the British
would again control the sea lanes. Under these circumstances, it was
inconceivable to most Americans that so dogged an adversary as
Britain would halt the long struggle to retain her colonies.

The last British prisoner had barely stacked his arms at Yorktown before Washington set about trying to convince Admiral de
Grasse to follow up the smashing victory with a joint expedition
against one of the remaining British garrisons. The great strategic
lesson of Yorktown, as far as Washington was concerned, was that
"no land force can act decisively unless it is accompanied by a maritime superiority." Now that he had this long-sought naval superiority, he was eager to keep the pressure on the British. An immediate
attack on Charleston was proposed, but de Grasse resisted the
suggestion, remembering that he had promised the Spaniards to return to the Caribbean at the end of the hurricane season to attack Jamaica. Washington assured him that the Charleston project would
not interfere with his timetable. "This capture would destroy the
last hope which induces the Enemy to continue the war," he declared.

When the admiral flatly refused to support the Charleston expedition, Washington came up with an alternative—an attack on Wilmington, which could be taken more speedily. Command of the
American troops had been given to Lafayette, so the persuasive
young Marquis went aboard the *Ville de Paris* to sell de Grasse on
the proposal. He returned to headquarters on October 23 with a
promise from de Grasse to ferry some 2,000 men to Wilmington.
Preparations were immediately begun to embark two brigades of
Continental infantry with their supplies and artillery. Unfortunately,
the admiral soon had second thoughts about the expedition. While

he told Washington his ships would be too overcrowded if he had to carry Lafayette's troops and the French regiments which were to go with him to the Indies, he had actually become convinced that an attack upon Wilmington would take longer than expected and that favorable winds for a return to the Caribbean would be lost.

Disappointed at the prospect of losing naval superiority, Washington used, as he put it, "every argument" to persuade de Grasse to remain. "A constant Naval superiority would terminate the War speedily," he declared. "Without it I do not know that it will ever be terminated honorably." Yet in the end, Washington was forced to "submit" to de Grasse's desire to be gone. Taking de Barras's squadron with him, de Grasse sailed with thirty-three ships of the line on November 5. Six days later, Hood left New York with eighteen ships of the line. Only a few French frigates were left behind to protect Rochambeau's troops who went into winter quarters at Williamsburg where the officers spent many a pleasant hour over their punch in the Raleigh Tavern. The Americans returned to the Hudson highlands to keep an eye on Sir Henry Clinton in New York. Before the French fleet vanished from the American coast, Washington had wrung from de Grasse only tentative and none too enthusiastic consent to join operations against the British the following May either at New York or at Charleston. The admiral declined to commit himself firmly without further instructions from France. It was just as well— for within a few months the *Ville de Paris* was a battered hulk and de Grasse a British prisoner for the second time.

Defeat after defeat rolled in upon the British in the closing months of 1781, and Lord North's days in power were drawing to a close. The ministry was bankrupt. It offered no realistic analysis of the situation, no reforms, no changes—just more of the same. To everyone, it was clear that the war in America had been lost. The French, now freed of the necessity of supporting their American allies, would concentrate on ejecting Britain from her tottering empire. In America, Yorktown had been taken, and West Florida had been captured by the Spaniards. In the West Indies, Tobago had fallen, the British fleet outnumbered, and Jamaica was ripe for plucking. In the Mediterranean, Minorca was about to fall, and Gibraltar was still besieged. In India, rebellion had flared on land, and the French had won control of the sea.[1] At home, a combined French and Spanish fleet again paraded unchallenged at the entrance to the Channel. Lord North would be remembered by history, declared the Whig opposition, for having "in seven years, dismembered the most powerful state in the modern world."

With her empire crumbling into ruin, with the national debt nearly doubled by the war, with taxes rising, with the army and navy undermanned, Britain seemed to have little choice but to abandon the struggle. Only the King retained a Crusader's unshaken faith in eventual victory. Never, he declared, would he buy peace by granting independence to America. "The prosecution of the war can alone preserve us from an ignominious Peace," he warned his disheartened countrymen. George III had always counted on the bulldog tenacity of his people to ensure victory, and nothing disturbed him more than to see Englishmen bending and breaking under the burden of defeat. As far as he was concerned, his subjects were no longer cast in the heroic mold of the Elizabethans.

Once more the ministry turned to Rodney for salvation. "The fate of the empire is in your hands," declared an anguished Sandwich. Recuperating at Bath from a bladder operation, the old admiral immediately responded to the appeal to return to the West Indies even though his gout was so severe he could not hold a pen. Rodney stopped off in London only long enough to defend himself successfully in Parliament against charges growing out of the capture of St. Eustatius. By early December, he was aboard his flagship, the 90-gun *Formidable*, at Plymouth, straining to get away with twelve ships of the line. Contrary winds and the usual dockyard inefficiencies held the fleet in port while the admiral fumed about "neglect, unwillingness and disobedience."

---

[1] One of the brightest chapters in French naval history was written during this twilight period by Admiral Pierre-André de Suffren de Saint-Tropez on the other side of the world in the Bay of Bengal. Without a base and without adequate supplies or ships, he maintained his fleet in fighting trim. In a series of five savage battles during 1782–1783, he fought a British fleet commanded by Vice Admiral Sir Edward Hughes to a standstill. Unhappily for the French admiral, he was given only indifferent support by his officers and was never able to win a clear-cut victory. When the opportunity for a knock-out blow appeared to have arrived, news of the end of the war reached the fleets. Suffren was unique among French naval officers in believing that the objective of the fleet should be to sink the enemy and gain control of the seas rather than to husband its own ships or support other actions. As Mahan pointed out, "attack not defense was the road to seapower in his eyes."

The delay had its fortunate aspects, however. Rodney was able to obtain as his Captain of the Fleet Sir Charles Douglas, a noted gunnery expert and commander of the squadron that had relieved Quebec in 1776. Quickly Douglas set about making a number of technical changes aimed at improving the fleet's gunnery. The rate of fire was speeded up by installing flintlocks on the guns of some of the ships in place of the matches heretofore used. A system of blocks and tackle was devised so that the broadside guns could fire as much as forty-five degrees fore and aft. Most of the ships were also outfitted for the first time with carronades on their upper decks. Carronades were short-barrelled cannon which were light for their caliber, permitting 32-pounders to be mounted on quarterdecks and forecastles, increasing the weight of the broadsides. At short range, these weapons possessed tremendous smashing power. Ships carrying them had a considerable advantage over those not so fitted—and the French had not yet adopted carronades.

French plans to send reinforcements to de Grasse were upset by the same storms which had held Rodney in port. For weeks the dockyards of Rochefort and Brest worked overtime fitting out warships and merchantmen destined for the West Indies, Gibraltar and the Indian Ocean. On December 12, nineteen ships of the line under the command of the Comte de Guichen and a large convoy were sighted about 150 miles southwest of Ushant by a British squadron of twelve ships of the line flying Kempenfelt's flag. The British admiral had bitterly criticized the orders which had sent him to sea in thick and squally weather with an inferior fleet. But when the sky suddenly cleared, he found that the French warships had been caught to leeward of the convoy. Nothing separated his ships and the hapless French merchantmen. They tried to scatter, but before night fell, Kempenfelt had swooped up fifteen under the eyes of the helpless de Guichen. If he had had enough frigates, Kempenfelt said, de Guichen would have suffered "a most ridiculous disgrace—that of having all his convoy taken from him." A few days later, a storm completed the work begun by the British. The French armada was scattered and crippled, with only two ships of the line and five transports limping across the Atlantic to join de Grasse. The rest put back into Brest.

Rodney's fleet finally sailed on January 14, 1782, well ahead of de Grasse's reinforcements. This advantage appeared likely to have little influence on the outcome of the struggle, and did little to help British morale. Dismal, humiliating failure had turned public opinion against the war. The ministry's majority in the Commons was steadily melting away and its most unpopular members were being jettisoned to prolong its life. Germain was the first to go. He resigned as American Secretary late in January, receiving as his reward the title of Lord Sackville. The caustic Edmund Burke was prompted to remark: "What has the American war produced? What but peerages and calamities." Sandwich was not one to depart so quietly. Unlike Germain, he had never lived within his means and had been forced to seek—and hold—office by financial necessity. Sandwich was nothing if not a fighter, and he stoutly resisted all attempts to make him the scapegoat for Cornwallis's defeat. A motion laying the surrender to "the want of a sufficient naval force to cover and protect" the army was defeated by a handsome majority. But the struggle was in vain. On February 27, Parliament approved a motion against the continuation of the war in America by a margin of nineteen votes—a staggering defeat for the Government.

That should have spelled the end of the North ministry. Yet King George clung to his old friend with a desperation that confounded even the Prime Minister. Weary of the struggle and despairing of victory, North repeatedly asked his Royal master to allow him to step down. But the monarch struggled against the inevitability of a Whig ministry until March 20, when he at last permitted Lord North to hand over the seals of office. On March 27, the jubilant Whigs took office with the Marquis of Rockingham as Prime Minister. Rockingham, who had long opposed the King's coercive policies toward America, was best known for repealing the Stamp Act in 1766. Reshuffling the cabinet, he entrusted colonial affairs to the Earl of Shelburne, European affairs to Charles James Fox, and the Admiralty to Keppel. Rockingham then set about liquidating the war and making peace. Orders were sent to Clinton relieving him of command and instructing Sir Guy Carleton, his successor, to concentrate all British forces at New York prior to an evacuation. Richard Oswald, a British merchant who had spent considerable time in America, was placed in charge of the negotiations with the American Commissioners in Europe. He arrived in Paris to begin talks with

Franklin on April 12—the same day Rodney won the most smashing naval victory of the war.

After a fast but stormy voyage, Rodney had arrived at Barbados on February 19 to find British bastions in the Caribbean falling on all sides. The situation had deteriorated so badly that it looked as if the West Indies would go the same way as the American colonies. Only Jamaica, Barbados, St. Lucia, and Antigua remained in British hands. The energetic Marquis de Bouillé, the French governor of Martinique, had recaptured St. Eustatius, along with 250,000 pounds intended for the pay of the British army in North America. The settlements at Demerara and Essquibo on the mainland of South America (now part of Guyana) had been taken without a fight. When Rodney dropped anchor at Carlisle Bay, he learned that Hood had gone to the relief of the garrison at St. Kitts, which was hard pressed by a combined French land and sea force. Stopping only long enough to water, the admiral sailed off to join Hood. Sir Samuel had been kept extremely busy by the French since his return from New York on December 5, 1781. Counting the ships he had brought with him and those he found on the station, he had twenty-two ships of the line—many in poor condition. "We have several vessels here that are not of much use," Hood reported. The captain of the *Alcide*, 74, painted a vivid picture of the condition of his ship: "We cannot wash the Lower Deck, the seams are so open over the Bread Room, Sail Room and Store Rooms. . . . While we wash the Main Deck the people cannot lay in their Hammocks." The fleet was so short of bread that the crews were issued yams instead. Only adverse winds and currents had prevented de Grasse from bringing his armada of thirty ships against the main British base at Barbados.

De Grasse had turned his attention to St. Kitts. On January 11, 1782, some six thousand troops were landed on the island and Basseterre, the capital, was quickly seized from its 700 British defenders. Instead of surrendering, the British retired to Brimstone Hill, one of the highest points on the island, and dug in to await help from the Royal Navy. As soon as Hood received word of the attack, he hurried north to St. Kitts with his entire fleet, stopping only to embark about five hundred soldiers at Antigua. He arrived off the island on January 23 with a daring plan. The British fleet would attack de Grasse's twenty-five ships of the line and two 50s at daybreak as they lay at anchor in the Basseterre roadstead. Departing from the usual practice of the day as exemplified by Rodney and Graves, Hood summoned his officers to the great cabin of the *Barfleur* where he explained what he had in mind and what was expected of them. Because of the Admiral's foresight in notifying his captains of his intentions, they felt they had been placed on their mettle rather than left to obey blindly the flagship's signals. This expression of mutual confidence resulted in what has been called "one of the most masterly tactical displays of naval history." [2]

On the way into the roadstead that night, two of Hood's ships, the *Alfred*, 74, and *Nymphe*, 36, collided. The ensuing confusion threw the time schedule of the attack off so the French spotted the approaching British well in time for de Grasse to get to sea. The two fleets remained in sight of each other throughout the next day as they drew away from the island while maneuvering for position. At this point, Hood decided to put into action the plan he had suggested to Graves after the Battle of the Chesapeake Capes. He would come about and run his fleet into the roadstead which had been abandoned by the enemy that morning. "I thought I had a fair prospect of gaining an anchorage," Hood declared, "and well knowing it was the only chance of saving the island, if it was to be saved, I pushed for it."

Daylight on January 25 found the two fleets west of Nevis, the island just to the south of St. Kitts. The British were headed north close inshore while the French were several miles to the leeward, heading south. Moving along under easy sail, Hood gave every impression of intending to give battle while de Grasse confidently awaited an attack by the inferior British force. Shortly after noon, when the French were abreast of his ships, Hood suddenly broke out a signal at the masthead of the *Barfleur* that was repeated up and down his line. Full sail blossomed on the British ships, and they began to surge ahead toward the Basseterre roadstead, twelve miles away. Although de Grasse quickly realized what was happening, it took two hours to bring his ships about in chase of Hood. By then,

---

[2] Macintyre, *Admiral Rodney.*

Hood had ordered his fleet to swing into the anchorage in line ahead. As his van anchored it was covered by the center and rear, which had yet to come about into their position in the new line.

The critical moment came when the French van caught up with the British rear, which had yet to make its turn into the anchorage. Hood's last four ships were in trouble as the French finally came up. The *Ville de Paris* attempted to cut them off by pushing through a gap between the laggards and the rest of the British line. But Hood's faith in his captains was justified. The three ships ahead of the gap saw the danger and reduced sail enough to close it. The rear now followed the van and center into the anchorage. Although the rear ships were somewhat shot up by French fire, Hood's masterly maneuver had been a brilliant success. There was nothing the chagrined de Grasse could do except sail along the British line and pound away, which he proceeded to do twice the next day. Hood had foreseen this maneuver, so springs had been placed on the anchor cables of the British ships. When the French came along, the British vessels swung to bring all their guns to bear on the enemy. By the end of the day, the French had been so badly mauled that they withdrew.

While Hood's seizure of the roadstead from under the nose of the furious de Grasse raised British morale, there was little he could do to help the defenders of Brimstone Hill who faced the overwhelming numerical superiority of the French invaders. He hoped that the garrison would be able to hold out until Rodney arrived with enough reinforcements to drive off the French fleet or until de Grasse wearied of the siege and sailed away. But the garrison, with many men sick and exhausted and weakened by heavy casualites, surrendered on February 12. Hood realized it would only be a matter of time until the French dragged the large cannon and mortars that had fallen into their hands to the shore to make his anchorage untenable. But to get out he had to evade the French fleet waiting offshore, which had grown to twenty-nine ships of the line. Once again, Hood resolved upon a bold stratagem to save his fleet. Shortly before midnight on February 13, the British cut their cables and silently slipped away. Small boats carrying lanterns were left behind to deceive the French. The next morning de Grasse gazed with amazement at an empty roadstead. While historians have uniformly hailed the tactical brilliance of Hood's actions at St. Kitts, Rodney regarded them sourly. He maintained that Hood, instead of lingering in the anchorage accomplishing nothing, should have remained at sea and attacked de Grasse while he had the weather gage. "What a Disgrace to Britain!" he later wrote a friend. "What Encouragement to France and her Fleet! What Discouragement to the Officers and Men of the British Fleet. . . ."

Hood and Rodney rejoined forces off Antigua on February 25, ending French naval supremacy in the Caribbean. Between them they had thirty-four ships of the line while de Grasse had thirty-three, including a pair of 50-gun ships. With the French reportedly lingering in the north to add Nevis and Montserrat to their spoils, Rodney immediately set a course for Martinique with the hope of cutting de Grasse off from his base. He was disappointed to find that the French admiral was already safely at anchor in the harbor of Fort Royal. Leaving a few frigates to watch the enemy, he dropped down to his own base at Gros Islet Bay on St. Lucia to refit and provision Hood's ships. Intelligence reaching Rodney indicated that it was de Grasse's intention to escape from Martinique, make a junction with the Spanish fleet at either Havana or Cap François and then attack Jamaica, the richest of Britain's islands in the Caribbean. The French were short of supplies so they had to await the arrival of a convoy bringing reinforcements and badly needed stores before the expedition could sail. Rodney and Hood agreed that the convoy must be intercepted before it joined de Grasse. But once again they quarreled—as they had the previous year in a similar situation—over the best method to meet the threat. And once again, Hood turned out to be correct.

Sir Samuel suggested that the British fleet, now numbering thirty-six ships of the line including reinforcements from England, be split into two squadrons. One should cruise to the north and windward of Dominica, the island immediately above Martinique, in case the French convoy sailed in from the north. The other would guard the traditional southern approach between Martinique and St. Lucia. Rodney, however, flatly refused to divide his fleet, arguing that this might allow de Grasse to escape from port. He saw no reason to doubt that the convoy would pass between St. Lucia and Martinique and restricted his subordinate's cruising to that area. As a result, the British missed the convoy. Shepherded by the two ships of the line that had survived Kempenfelt's attack and the Atlantic storms, it came down from the north at the end of March as Hood had predicted and slipped safely into Fort Royal. "How Sir George Rodney could bring himself to keep his whole force to guard one path . . . and to leave another . . . without any guard at all, is a matter of the utmost astonishment to me," was Hood's bitter comment. ". . . Nothing short of a miracle can retrieve the King's affairs in this country."

De Grasse now had thirty-five ships of the line and sufficient troops for the capture of Jamaica. He needed only a fair wind for the proper moment to sail. Unceasing vigilance was maintained by the British, stung by the failure to prevent the arrival of the convoy. A line of frigates patrolled the waters off Fort Royal day and night, ready to bring Rodney word that the French had sailed. The possibility of a decisive battle seemed to rejuvenate the old admiral. For the moment, his ailments had ceased, and he acted with the vigor of a much younger man. On the other hand, Hood was taken sick with a liver complaint compounded by anxiety over what his capricious chief would do next. Rodney paid him a visit aboard the *Barfleur* and outlined his plans, which relieved his subordinate's mind to some degree. "I never found him more rational and he gave me very great pleasure by his manner of receiving what I said respecting future operations," declared Hood. The British commanders were still enjoying this unusual state of harmony when the frigate *Endymion* hurried into Gros Islet Bay on the night of April 7 to report that the French fleet was putting to sea.

In addition to his warships, de Grasse took a hundred and fifty merchantmen with him. The vessels were to sail for France as soon as they were out of reach of marauding British cruisers. Hopeful of avoiding battle, the admiral's major concerns were to join the Spanish fleet and to protect his convoy. He planned to sail close to the chain of islands that paralleled his passage to the west so the merchantment could take shelter in case of attack. With his head start, he tried to outdistance the British, but the slow speed of his clumsy armada soon wrecked this plan. By nightfall on April 8, the French fleet was clearly in sight from the mastheads of Rodney's thirty-six pursuing ships of the line.

Straining to catch any gust of wind, more than a hundred warships, British and French, took part in a ponderous ballet in the lee of Dominica. Shortly after daybreak on April 9, about half the

French fleet had worked its way clear of the island and began to draw away from the rest. The British had a similar experience. Eight ships of Hood's van division drew away from the center of the British fleet, an inviting target for the French. Seeing an opportunity to crush or disable part of the enemy force, de Grasse sent his convoy into the nearby harbor of Basse-Terre on the island of Guadeloupe while his van and part of his center, commanded by the Marquis de Vaudreuil, were ordered to come about and deal with Hood. De Vaudreuil ran down alongside the British ships, which were lying almost stationary in the water, their yards aback to keep from pulling too far ahead of the rest of their fleet. Then de Vaudreuil put about so that he was again sailing north. Fifteen French ships were ranged against eight British vessels, but fear of the British carronades kept the French at a distance. Even so, four of Hood's ships were severely battered before the rest of the British fleet caught a breeze and came up. Although the damaged British ships managed to maintain their stations, a French 64, the *Caton*, which had been roughed up in the skirmish, had to be sent into Guadeloupe for repairs. De Grasse had muffed a great opportunity. He failed to make full use of the advantage offered him by the fitful wind and Hood's impetuous advance out of the reach of support by detaching too few ships for the attack. If he had sent in more, as Hood wrote, "he might have cut us up by pouring a succession of French ships upon us as long as he pleased."

While the fighting had been in progress, the French admiral had sent word to Guadeloupe for the convoy to leave the island for Cap François. Guarded by two 50-gun ships, it was out of sight by nightfall, and de Grasse pressed on to the windward in its wake. Rodney crept after the French throughout the next day. During the evening, a signaling error brought the British van to a halt for a short time—a delay that might have been fatal had it not been for a collison that night in the French fleet. The *Zelé*, 74, damaged the 64-gun *Jason* so badly that the smaller vessel was sent limping into Basse-Terre. Added to the loss of the *Caton*, this reduced the French line to thirty-one ships and slowed it down enough to allow Rodney to keep the enemy in sight. The next morning, the damaged *Zelé* and an escort vessel were seen to have dropped away to the leeward of the French fleet. The British commander ordered a general chase with the hope of snapping up the stragglers. By late afternoon, about a half-dozen British vessels were close enough to the laggards to force de Grasse to bear down to protect them. With his fleet already greatly reduced in strength, he felt he could not lose two more ships. There was no fighting, however, because Rodney recognized the odds facing his leading ships and recalled them. Nevertheless the French lost much of the advantage they had gained to the windward.

During the night, at about 2 A.M. on April 12, the luckless *Zelé* rammed the *Ville de Paris*. It was her fourteenth collision in thirteen months—testimony to the declining standards of seamanship in the French fleet. All that night the British fleet pressed on under full canvas in hopes of catching the French. Dawn presented Rodney's crews with a thrilling sight. The bulk of the French fleet was spread out in some disorder only a few miles away to the windward while off to the leeward the *Zelé*, her foremast gone and bowsprit snapped short, was being towed by a frigate in the direction of Guadeloupe. This left de Grasse with only thirty ships of the line to face Rodney's thirty-six. The fleets were now in a basin of blue tropic water between the northern tip of the Dominica and a clutch of islets known as the Saintes. The towering peaks of Grande Soufrière and Morne Diablotin looked down as the curtain rose on the last major action of the war in the Caribbean—the Battle of the Saintes.

Shortly before 6 A.M. Rodney ordered Hood to send four of his fastest ships against the *Zelé* and her consort in an effort to entice de Grasse to abandon his position to the windward—and with it the weather gage—to come to their rescue. As Rodney had hoped, his adversary accepted the challenge and turned to aid the crippled vessel. While waiting for the action to begin, Rodney ordered his crews to breakfast, for it was a tradition in the Royal Navy to send sailors into battle with full stomachs. On the quarterdeck of the *Formidable*, Sir Charles Douglas, the Captain of the Fleet, watched the slow unfolding of the preliminary maneuvers in the scant early morning breeze. Suddenly, he snapped his long spyglass shut and went to Rodney's cabin, where the admiral was resting from the rigors of four sleepless days and nights, to make a somewhat theatrical announcement: "I give you joy, Sir George," he said with a sweep of his gold-laced cocked hat. "Providence has given you your enemy broad on the lee bow." Douglas was premature in his estimate of the situation, but de Grasse, in his effort to rescue the *Zelé*, had come so far to the leeward as to make a battle inevitable. Rodney had at last brought his enemy to bay.

Signals were broken out at the masthead of the British flagship at about 7 A.M. to recall the four ships in chase of the *Zelé* and to order a line of battle one cable's length apart. Hood's damaged ships were shifted to the rear of the British line and the van came under the command of Admiral Drake in the *Princessa*. The heart-stirring throb of the drums beating to quarters resounded throughout the British fleet as the ships cleared for action. Galley fires were extinguished, cabin bulkheads were dismantled, cockpits were rigged as casualty stations, marines were sent aloft to the fighting tops, and cartridges and round shot were brought up from the magazines. Finally, there was an ominous rumble like thunder as the guns were loaded and run out. For the first time during the war, a British fleet was about to go into battle with more ships and guns than the enemy.

To maintain the weather gage, de Grasse pressed on to the south, running close into Dominica with the aim of passing along the British line at a safe distance and avoiding a serious action. On the other hand, Rodney urged his van ahead in a desperate race to cross the head of the French line and seize the wind. The silent fleets drew near each other with the British in a well-ordered and compact line while the French straggled into position with sizeable gaps in their formation. Some of the French ships were as much as ten miles away from the main body. But as the heads of the two lines crept toward each other, it soon became clear that the French would hold the weather gage. Stripped to the waist, the British gun crews stood by, waiting for their weapons to bear on the enemy vessels.

At about 7:30 A.M., the leading French ships passed across the bows of Drake's vessels, firing ineffectually at long range. The captain of the *Marlborough*, 74, at the head of the British line, pressed on. Shortly before eight o'clock, he reached the French line at the ninth ship from the van, the 74-gun *Brave*. Turning parallel to the enemy vessels but running on an opposite course, the *Marlborough* unleashed the first broadside of the battle. The rest of Drake's division followed in stately succession, their sides exploding in a thunder of gunfire. The center came next with Rodney's flagship, the *Formidable*, firing her first broadside at 8:08. The fleets, thirty-six British vessels and thirty French, moved slowly along on opposite tacks, periodically hidden in clouds of flame and smoke as they passed each other. To prevent the action from turning into an indecisive replica

of the Battle of Ushant four years before, Rodney kept the signal for
close action flying and reinforced it with an order to alter course to
the starboard—closer to the French. The spirit of his officers was
typified by Captain Henry Savage of the *Hercules.* Slightly wounded
early in the battle, he sat in a chair on the quarterdeck of his 74
shaking his fist at each enemy ship as it passed and urging his
sweating gunners "to sink the French rascals!"

The French suffered far more severely than the British during
the cannonade. Their ships were crowded not only with large crews,
but were crammed with 5,500 soldiers for the invasion of Jamaica.
The effect of the British carronades was murderous at the short
range maintained by Rodney. Douglas's gunnery reforms also had
their effect. The classical rule of naval warfare had been "two or
three quick broadsides in passing," but the special tackle fitted at the
order of the Fleet Captain enabled British gunners to train their
weapons well ahead or astern of their vessels. The British ships fired
two or three broadsides both before and after a French vessel could
bring her guns to bear. And while the ships were opposite each other,
the British were able to fire more rapidly because of the flintlocks that had been fitted to some of their guns. So great was the
number of bodies cast overboard from the French ships that the sea
boiled about them with the thrashing of schools of sharks that had
been attracted by the blood.

Although de Grasse's fleet was absorbing severe punishment,
the battle was going well enough for the French. As long as they held
the weather gage they were committed to nothing more formidable
than the usual "passing" engagement. Within an hour or so they
would be free to make repairs and continue on to the west. Yet there
was cause for alarm. De Grasse saw that his course was leading him
into the still waters off Dominica, where there would be little wind
and where he could not hope to thwart Rodney's determined attempts to fight at close range. He tried to break off the action. Twice
he signaled his fleet to wear, or pivot 180 degrees, so his ships could
steer back in the direction from which they had come. But with the
foe little more than a pistol shot away to the leeward, there was simply no room to wear without colliding with the British ships, so the
French captains ignored their admiral's frantic signals.

Fate now played into Rodney's hands. Just after 9 A.M., a badly
battered French 74, the *Glorieux,* drifted alongside the *Formidable.*

She shuddered under the full fury of the British three-decker's broadsides, and her rigging and masts hung in a crazy tangle. Suddenly, there was a shift in the wind which caused great confusion among the French. Some vessels were taken aback, or were pushed astern; others were forced to turn toward the British line to maintain headway. Ships fouled each other and fell away to the leeward, opening a great gap in the French line.

Here was the chance of a lifetime—and Rodney seized it. Altering the flagship's course to starboard, he thrust her into the gap looming before him. The French line was broken. The credit for the maneuver has been claimed for many people, and there has been considerable debate over whether it was premeditated or taken on the spur of the moment. Some writers claim that once, while dining with Lord Germain, Rodney had stated his intention to break the enemy line the next time he met the French and demonstrated with cherry stones how it would be done. Others say he borrowed the idea from a book on naval tactics written by John Clerk, an Edinburgh merchant. And there are those who say Sir Charles Douglas persuaded the admiral to take the move. Only one fact really matters— Rodney issued the order, which paid off. "As the blame, had it failed, would certainly have had to be borne by Rodney, so must the credit, when it succeeded, go to the same man," is the judicious summation of one British naval historian.[3]

Unlike the Battle of Martinique when Rodney, in the *Sandwich*, had fought his way through the enemy line but was not supported by the rest of his fleet, five British ships followed the *Formidable* in among the French even though no signal had been made for breaking the line. In fact, no signal existed for such a maneuver as it was not even contemplated in the Fighting Instructions. Raking the French ships on both sides of them as they forged into the gap, the British quickly reduced them to shattered wrecks. To the *Formidable*'s starboard, the *Glorieux* lost all her masts and was transformed into a mere hulk filled with the dead and dying. The flagship's journal reported that "not a single shot missed and dreadful must have been the slaughter" aboard her. The *Diadème*, which was to the port of the British ships, also suffered severely.

As soon as his ships had fought their way through the French

---

[3] Michael Lewis, *The Navy of Britain* (London 1948)

line and seized the weather gage, Rodney took stock of the situation. He was pleased at what he saw. Captain Alan Gardner, of the 98-gun *Duke*, the vessel just ahead of the *Formidable*, had seen what the admiral had done and followed his example by crashing through the enemy line at another point. And in the rear, Commodore Edmund Affleck had led Hood's entire squadron into the French line and to the windward. The French fleet was cut into three separate divisions and never reformed. In the melee that followed, the superior fighting qualities and firepower of the British crews and ships quickly asserted themselves. Several French ships were almost torn apart by the volume of fire poured into them from both the windward and leeward. Yet the French had suffered less aloft than the British, and most of de Grasse's ships were in better condition to catch the light and fitful airs that were barely filling the sails of both fleets. Even though some of the French men-of-war were battered wrecks, his fleet managed to drift downwind clear of the British. The dismasted *Glorieux*, her decks a shambles but with her flag defiantly nailed to the stump of a mast, lay motionless between the two fleets, a mute witness to the effectiveness of British gunnery. So ended the first phase of the Battle of the Saintes—an action in which Rodney had broken his own line, the enemy's line and the whole formal system of fighting naval battles.

The fruits of victory were yet to be harvested. For the next few hours, both fleets were almost becalmed. Their crews spent the time in knotting and splicing rigging and repairing the damage to their ships. By 1 P.M., the smoke had drifted away to reveal the French making off to the leeward in several disorganized groups. The dismasted *Glorieux* wallowed along under tow by a frigate. British ships were moving in for the kill, with Hood having put his boats into the water to pull the *Barfleur* into the wind. On the *Formidable*'s quarterdeck, Douglas declared in his orotund fashion: "Behold, Sir George, the Greeks and Trojans contending for the body of Patroclus." Still uncertain as to the outcome of the battle, Rodney snapped "Damn the Greeks and damn the Trojans. I have other things to think about." Later, with victory assured, he was all affability. "Now my friend, I am at the service of your Greeks and Romans," he told Sir Charles, "for the enemy is in confusion and our victory is secure."

All that afternoon, the British fleet followed at the heels of the shattered French ships. Rodney's cautious insistence that they conduct the pursuit as a unit provoked the usual scathing criticism from Hood who wanted a general chase with every stitch of sail set. The *Glorieux* was the first enemy vessel to be snapped up. Her senior surviving officer, a lieutenant, had courageously ordered the frigate to cast off the tow line so she would not be captured too. Next to be taken were the *César* and *Hector*, both 74s that along with the *Glorieux* had borne the brunt of the British attack. The *Ardent*, 64, which had been taken by the French off Plymouth in 1779, was also captured. She quickly hoisted the Union Jack for there were some British prisoners aboard. The *Ardent* was a particularly valuable prize because she carried most of the French siege artillery destined for Jamaica.

Nevertheless, the greatest prize was yet to be taken. Limping off under a few ragged sails, de Grasse's flagship, the great *Ville de Paris*, lagged behind the rest of the enemy fleet. Abandoned by his officers, short of ammunition, his scuppers running with blood, de Grasse gallantly tried to fight his way out of the ring of hostile ships surrounding his flagship. But the *Ville de Paris* had been stripped of her sails, and no longer answered her helm. Shortly before sunset, de Grasse, one of the three men left standing on her upper deck, surrendered to the *Barfleur* after a few guns were fired for the sake of honor. The battle was over. Elated by the capture of the enemy commander-in-chief and the world's greatest battleship, Rodney made the signal to break off action and lie-to in the gathering darkness.

Hood was thunderstruck. Not only would he have pursued the fleeing enemy with more vigor during the afternoon, but he would have continued the chase during the night to finish off the disorganized French fleet the next morning. Hood later claimed that had he commanded the fleet, "upwards of twenty sail of the enemy's ships of the line" would have been captured rather than the mere five bagged by Rodney. He accused Rodney of having been so overcome with childish delight in capturing the *Ville de Paris* that he lost sight of reality—just as he had when he had been exposed to the riches of St. Eustatius.

Rodney later acknowledged that he may have displayed too

much caution, but, as Spinney points out, his ships had been seriously damaged aloft, there was a shortage of ammunition, and without a moon it was dangerous to chance a night action where British vessels might fire into each other by mistake. And the French may not have been as disorganized as Hood contended. Commodore Affleck, who had not seen the signal to break off action and pressed on after the enemy with a half-dozen ships, found at daylight that they had outdistanced him. The only sails visible on the horizon belonged to the British fleet. In his cabin, Rodney was writing the opening words of his dispatch: "It has pleased God, out of His Divine Providence, to grant His Majesty's arms a most complete Victory over the fleet of his enemy. . . ."

The aftermath of the battle was grim. "The carnage on board the prizes is dreadful," reported Sir Gilbert Blane, the Physician of the Fleet, after an inspection. "The *Ville de Paris* has nearly three hundred men killed and wounded. . . . The *Glorieux*, when boarded, presented a scene of complete horror. The numbers killed were so great that the surviving, either from want of leisure, or through dismay, had not thrown the bodies of the killed overboard, so that the decks were covered with the blood and mangled limbs of the dead, as well as the wounded and dying." [4] Even greater horrors were to come. On the *César*, the French crew broke into the spirit room and got roaring drunk. Someone upset a candle, and within a few minutes the ship was ablaze from stem to stern. Everyone aboard, some 400 Frenchmen and a 60-man British prize crew, died when her magazine exploded or met death among the sharks. More men were killed on the French flagship than in Rodney's entire fleet. Total French casualties from the battle were estimated at over 3,000 soldiers and sailors, while the British losses were comparatively light—243 men killed and another 816 wounded.

For four days, the British fleet lay-to repairing damage. During this period, Rodney entertained de Grasse on his flagship and was favorably impressed with his equanimity and bearing in the face of adversity. Dr. Blane noted that the French admiral laid his misfortune not on the inferiority of his force, "but to the base desertion of his officers." De Grasse was said to have taken particular notice of the "superior discipline, neatness and order" prevailing in the British ships and stated that the French navy was a

---

[4] Quoted in Macintyre, *Admiral Rodney*.

century behind the Royal Navy in these matters.[5] By April 17, Rodney was ready to proceed to Jamaica. Hood, who had been impatiently champing at the bit, was allowed to take ten ships of the line and sweep ahead of the fleet. Two days later, he was in the Mona Passage between Puerto Rico and Santo Domingo when several sails were sighted. Giving chase, Hood overtook and captured the two French 64s, *Caton* and *Jason*, that had put into Guadeloupe for repairs after the first brush between the fleets. From his prizes, he learned the disappointing news that the Marquis de Vaudreuil, who had inherited command of the French fleet, had passed through the passage the day before on his way to Cap François.

Rodney dropped anchor at Port Royal, Jamaica, on April 29 with his prizes and those of his ships most needing a refit. Hood had been sent with twenty-five ships of the line to cruise off Cap François to keep an eye on the enemy. Despite Rodney's victory at the Saintes, the combined Franco-Spanish fleet was considerably stronger than the British and they had an army of some 8,000 men. Still bitter about Rodney's failure to follow his advice after the battle, Hood sourly commented: "Had Sir George done what he might and ought, we should all most probably have been peaceably at home by our firesides. . . ." But Rodney turned out to be the better prophet. He correctly forecast that the French and Spanish would never face the British in the West Indies again. The damage inflicted upon the French fleet, the inherent hostility between the allies, and the spread of disease among the troops all combined to stifle any enemy initiatives.

In the meantime, Rodney, who had received no news from London in months, grew anxious about the strange silence. July and the hurricane season were at hand, and the time was near for taking his ships to North America for safety. And what had been the reaction to his victory? On July 9, he wrote the Admiralty: "Their Lordships may imagine my concern in not having received any dispatches." The following day, he received his answer. The frigate *Jupiter* arrived at Port Royal flying the flag of Admiral Sir Hugh Pigot and carrying orders for Rodney's replacement as commander-in-chief.

---

[5] De Grasse was a pioneer in the use of public relations. No sooner had he been taken prisoner than he began writing denunciations of his subordinates contending they had disobeyed orders and deserted him, etc. While in London, he wrote a series of pamphlets in his own defense, which he had published and distributed throughout Europe.

Keppel, the new First Lord, had held out as long as he could against the demands of his political associates that Rodney, an old Tory, be dismissed from his command. Although he and Rodney did not see eye to eye on political affairs, Keppel resisted because they had long been friends. On May 2, still unaware of the victory in the West Indies, he succumbed to pressure and issued an order for Rodney's recall. Pigot, who was sent out to replace him, had not held a sea command since 1770 and was chiefly known for the assiduity with which he played for high stakes at the faro bank operated by Charles James Fox, one of the new Secretaries of State. He was said to be indebted to Fox to the tune of 17,000 pounds—and his new command was given him to allow him to pay off his losses. Rodney's dispatch was not received at the Admiralty until May 15—the same day that Pigot sailed. When news of the victory was released, the public made the most of one of the few opportunities it had been given to celebrate during a long and disastrous war. "All London was in an uproar," Rodney's daughter, Jane, wrote her father. Church bells were rung, and the Tower guns roared out salutes. The government quickly reversed itself, for it would be impossible to recall a national hero in disgrace. A King's messenger was sent in pursuit of Pigot to stop him before he sailed, but he was too late. A fast cutter was then ordered out to catch the *Jupiter* but failed to find her.

Rodney knew nothing of this. Pigot's arrival at Port Royal must have created gnawing doubts in the mind of the old man as to how the outcome of the Battle of the Saintes would be received at home. Would it be accepted as an overwhelming victory or would he be pilloried for failing to have taken more of the enemy's ships? He did not have long to wait for an answer. Shortly after Pigot had hoisted his flag, a packet arrived with a new set of dispatches. The first to be opened addressed Rodney as "My Lord." To make amends for its hasty action in relieving the captor of the redoubtable Comte de Grasse, the ministry had rewarded him with an English peerage, an additional pension of 2,000 pounds a year, and the thanks of Parliament. There were also honors for his subordinates. Hood received an Irish peerage, and Drake and Affleck were knighted. Sandwich, for whom the victory had occurred too late, told the admiral, "I am sure your being recalled in the height of your glory will be the most fortunate event that ever happened to anyone."

And so the curtain came down on the war in the West Indies. Pigot and Hood took most of the British fleet to American waters in pursuit of de Vaudreuil, who had switched his base to Boston for the hurricane season. Thomas Graves, who had been at Jamaica, escorted the prizes and several ships that needed repairs to England.[6] Rodney sailed home for the last time with his retinue in the *Montagu*, 74, to receive a welcome not seen again until Nelson returned from the Nile. The old sailor cruised no more, although there were still battles to be fought in the law courts, arising from the claims of the West India merchants. He died in 1792, a relatively poor man.

Rodney's victory at the Saintes was not a victory of annihilation, but it had a profound impact on the outcome of the peace negotiations that ended the American Revolution. It was decisive in that it made Jamaica safe from attack and permitted the step-by-step reconquest of the British islands in the Caribbean. More important, the victory restored the confidence of the British people, who had been fed a steady diet of half-hearted actions and solid defeats. Peace with honor was now possible. With public esteem re-established, American independence could be recognized, and such hotly debated points as the rights of American fishermen to dry their catches on the shore of British North America—which more than once threatened to wreck the negotiations—could be gracefully conceded. In order to obtain the most favorable terms, the British deliberately set about to divide their enemies. They found a receptive audience in Franklin, who had been convinced by Rodney's victory of the desirability of making a separate peace.

Britain's retention of Gibraltar in the face of repeated Spanish attempts to capture the fortress also played an important role in creating disarray among the allies. A secret article in the Franco-Spanish treaty of alliance had committed France to fight until the Spaniards conquered Gibraltar. When the Rock was relieved once more in October 1782 by a fleet commanded by Lord Howe, who had been recalled to duty by the new ministry, the French despaired of its conquest. Frantically searching for a morsel that might be offered Spain in place of Gibraltar, Vergennes suggested that the Spaniards might have the American territory between the Appalachians and the Mis-

---

[6] Most of the prizes, including the *Ville de Paris*, were destroyed during a storm on the voyage home. As many as 3,500 men may have been lost.

sissippi. Charging duplicity, the American commissioners used this to justify their own separate negotiations with the British. France, at odds with her allies, facing financial ruin, and with her main fleet defeated, was forced to reconsider the Carthaginian terms which she had offered the British. Thus, supported by the defensive victories of the Royal Navy, Lord Shelburne, who had become Prime Minister after the death of the Marquis of Rockingham, was able to conclude a satisfactory peace.

Rumors of impending peace had been circulating for some time in Havana when John Barry put to sea in the Continental frigate *Alliance* early in March 1783, but he was taking no chances of running into a British cruiser. Every stitch of canvas had been set and the vessel bowled along at top speed off the coast of Florida. Stowed away in the skipper's cabin was a chest containing more than 100,000 Spanish milled dollars—a fabulous sum in Continental currency—which was sorely needed by Congress to placate its creditors. Sailing in company with the frigate was the 20-gun *Duc de Lauzun*, which had recently been purchased in France for the navy. The specie had been originally loaded aboard the smaller vessel, but Barry thought that with British ships infesting the area, the money would be safer on the better-armed and speedier *Alliance*. Several distant sails had been sighed, but so far the voyage had been largely uneventful.

The *Alliance* and the *Lauzun*, along with the *General Washington*, which had been retaken from the British by Joshua Barney the previous year, constituted the entire active Continental Navy. For the most part, the craft were being used as dispatch vessels and commerce raiders rather than fighting ships. As for the remainder of the Navy, the *Deane*, renamed the *Hague* after Silas Deane came under suspicion of treachery, lay idle at Boston, and the frigate *Bourbon* was still uncompleted on the stocks at Middletown on the Connecticut River. The 74-gun *America*, completed under the supervision of Paul Jones at Portsmouth, had been launched the previous November but she never broke out the Stars and Stripes at sea. Much to the disgust of Jones, who had hoped to command her, Congress ordered the *America* presented to the French as a replacement for the *Magnifique*, one of the Marquis de Vaudreuil's 74s, which had been lost when her pilot ran her aground on a shoal in Boston harbor.[7] Everyone was too polite to mention it, but the gift had really been made because Congress was unable to pay the cost of outfitting a ship of the line. So low had the Continental Navy fallen that the only duty that could be found for Jones was to send him to sea as an observer on de Vaudreuil's flagship during a fruitless cruise to the West Indies that preceded the end of the war.

Early on the morning of March 10, three strange sails were sighted from the masthead of the *Alliance*. Through his telescope, Barry contemplated the strangers as they bore down on the American vessels. Snapping the glass shut, he ordered all sail set. The ships were the British frigates *Alarm*, 32, *Sybil*, 28, and the sloop-of-war *Tobago*, 18. They were on the lookout for a Yankee vessel reportedly carrying specie from Havana to Philadelphia. Barry signaled Captain John Green, the *Lauzun*'s skipper, to stay as close to the *Alliance* as possible, but it soon became obvious that the smaller vessel could not keep up with the swift-sailing frigate. The gap was widening between her and the *Lauzun*, while the *Alarm* was coming up fast with her consorts close behind. Splashes could already be seen where the British had tried a few ranging shots with their bow chasers. Unwilling to leave Green to his fate, Barry ordered the *Alliance*'s mainsail clewed up to slow her down enough for the *Lauzun* to draw alongside. Barry urged Green to throw his guns overboard to lighten his vessel. With that, he cracked on sail, and the *Alliance* again shot ahead. The *Lauzun*'s guns, except for her stern chasers, splashed into the sea. Jettisoning them had no effect, however, for the British continued to narrow the distance between the ships.

Barry was searching for a way to aid Green without endangering his own vessel when help arrived unexpectedly. From over the horizon there appeared a large ship, which seemed to be standing in the direction of the American vessels. The captain of the *Alarm* had apparently spotted her, too, for he veered away. Both skippers identified her as a 50-gun French ship that had been at Havana. On the assumption that she would join the fight, Barry decided to take on the enemy. If the *Alliance* engaged the *Sybil*, which was now closing in on the *Lauzun* and firing rapidly, he believed Green would have an opportunity to escape. Orders were issued to bring the frigate

---

[7] The *America*, which had been built of unseasoned timber, became so rotten that she was ordered broken up in 1786, after only three years' service.

between her consort and the attacking, oncoming British vessel.

"Captain Barry went from gun to gun on the main deck, cautioning against too much haste," and warning his gunners not to fire "until the enemy was right abreast," reported John Kessler, one of his officers. The range began to shorten. A shot from the *Sybil* struck the *Alliance*'s cabin, smashing it to splinters and mortally wounding a man. Still, Barry held his fire. The frigate's gun crews tensely awaited the command to unleash their broadside. Coolly measuring the dwindling distance between the two vessels, Barry waited until the British ship was within pistol shot. Then he gave the order to fire. The *Alliance*'s broadside smashed into the *Sybil*, ripping long splinters from her sides and tearing her sails and rigging. Again and again, the frigate's guns hurtled in and out, firing much faster than the stricken British vessel. One of the *Sybil*'s officers was killed and several men were wounded. Her foretop mast tumbled over the side, and her ensign was shot away. Within a half-hour, said Kessler, all the British vessel's guns "were silenced and nothing but Musketry was fired from her." Transformed into a battered wreck, she sheered off to rejoin the *Alarm* and *Tobago*, which, like the French ship, had taken no part in the action.

Barry inspected the damage to the *Alliance* and, finding it slight, moved off with the *Lauzun* to meet the oncoming Frenchmen. Why, he angrily demanded, had not the two-decker come to his support? The French captain explained that he had seen Barry's signal, but since he was carrying a half-million dollars in gold, he had feared the American vessels had already been taken by the British who were using them to decoy him into their clutches. "His foolish idea thus perhaps lost us the three frigates," Kessler remarked. To make amends, the Frenchman suggested a chase of the fleeing enemy vessels. For several hours the pursuit continued, but the British had too much of a head start. Along toward evening, the *Alliance* and *Lauzun* turned away and headed for the Delaware capes. British cruisers were too thick off the estuary to make Philadelphia, so Barry sailed on to Newport, where he dropped anchor on March 20. Three days later, momentous news was received. Britain had proclaimed the end of hostilities on February 4, 1783. After nearly eight years of arduous warfare, the United States was at last a free and independent nation. John Barry and the *Alliance* had fought the Continental Navy's final battle.

Epilogue

Seapower had helped make America a nation—but the new nation could not afford a navy. Hard pressed to meet the government's financial obligations, Robert Morris, the Agent of Marine, decided to sell off the remains of the Continental Navy. One by one, the ships went on the block. First the *Hague* and then the still uncompleted *Bourbon* were sold. The *Duc de Lauzun* was sent to Europe with a load of tobacco and both ship and cargo were disposed of in France. Next, it was the turn of the *General Washington* to go under the hammer. Finally, only the *Alliance* remained. Some members of Congress wished to keep her "for the honor of the flag of the United States and the protection of its trade and coasts from the insults of pirates." But the expense of repairs precluded even this gesture. The frigate was auctioned off for $26,000 at the Merchants' Coffee House in Philadelphia on August 1, 1785. The Continental Navy had sailed into history. Thirteen long years were to pass before Congress—pressed by the insults of Revolutionary France—laid the foundations for the United States Navy. At its birth, the new service's only possession was the fighting spirit bequeathed it by Paul Jones and Nicholas Biddle . . . Lambert Wickes and John Rathbun . . . Gustavus Conyngham and Silas Talbot. No other legacy could have been of more value.

Chevy Chase, Maryland
September 1970–July 1972

Appendix I
Rules for the Regulation of the Navy of the United Colonies

The Commanders of all ships and vessels belonging to the thirteen United Colonies, are strictly required to shew in themselves a good example of honor and virtue to their officers and men, and to be very vigilant in inspecting the behavior of all such as are under them, and to discountenance and suppress all dissolute, immoral, and disorderly practices, and also such as are contrary to the rules of discipline and obedience, and to correct those who are guilty of the same, according to the usage of the sea.

The Commanders of the ships of the thirteen United Colonies, are to take care that divine service be performed twice a day on board, and a sermon preached on Sundays, unless bad weather or other extraordinary accidents prevent it.

If any shall be heard to swear, curse, or blaspheme the name of God, the Commander is strictly enjoined to punish them for every offense, by causing them to wear a wooden collar, or some other shameful badge of distinction, for so long time as he shall judge proper. If he be a commissioned officer, he shall forfeit one shilling for each offence, and a warrant or inferior officer six pence. He who is guilty of drunkenness, if a seaman, shall be put in irons until he is sober, but if an officer, he shall forfeit two days' pay.

No Commander shall inflict any punishment upon a seaman beyond twelve lashes upon his bare back, with a cat of nine tails; if the fault shall

---

[1] From *Naval Documents of the American Revolution*, Vol. II.

deserve a greater punishment, he is to apply to the Commander in chief of the Navy, in order to the trying of him by a court-martial, and in the mean time, he may put him under confinement.

The Commander is never by his own authority to discharge a commission or warrant officer, nor to punish or strike him, but he may suspend or confine them, and when he comes in the way of a Commander in chief, apply to him for holding a court-martial.

The Officer who commands by accident of the Captain's or commander's absence (unless he be absent for a time by leave) shall not order any correction, but confinement, and upon the captain's return on board, he shall then give an account of his reasons for so doing.

The Captain is to cause the articles of war to be hung up in some public places of the ship, and read to the ship's company once a month.

Whenever a Captain shall inlist a seaman, he shall take care to enter on his books the time and terms of his entering, in order of his being justly paid.

The Captain shall, before he sails, make return to, and leave with the Congress, or such person or persons as the Congress shall appoint for that purpose, a compleat list of all his officers and men, with the time and terms of their entering; and during his cruize shall keep a true account of the desertion or death of any of them, and of the entering of others, and after his cruize, and before any of them are paid off, he shall make return of a compleat list of the same, including those who shall remain on board his ship.

The men shall, at their request, be furnished with slops that are necessary by the Captain or purser, who shall keep an account of the same, and the Captain, in his return in the last mentioned article directed to be made, shall mention the amount delivered to each man, in order to its being stopped out of his pay.

As to the term "inferior Officer," the Captain is to take notice that the same does not include any commission or any warrant officer, except the second master, surgeon's mate, cook, armourer, gun-smith, master at arms, and sail maker.

The Captain is to take care when any inferior officers or volunteer seamen are turned over into the ship under his command from any other ship, not to rate them on the ship's books in a worse quality, or lower degree or station, than they served in the ship they were removed from; and for his guidance he is to demand from the commander of the ship from which they are turned over, a list under his hand, of their names and qualities.

Any officer, seamen, or others, entitled to wages or prize money, may have the same paid to his assignee, provided the assignment be attested by the Captain or Commander, the master or purser of the ship, or a chief magistrate of some county or corporation.

The Captain is to discourage the seamen of his ship from selling any part of their wages or shares, and never to attest the letter of attorney of any seaman, until he is fully satisfied that the same is not granted in consideration of money given for the purchase of his wages or shares.

When any inferior officer or seaman dies, the Captain is forthwith to make out a ticket for the time of his service, and send the same by the first safe conveyance to the Congress, or agents by them for that purpose appointed, in order to the wages being forthwith paid to the executors or administrators of the deceased.

A convenient place shall be set apart for sick or hurt men, to which they are to be removed, with their hammocks and bedding, when the surgeon shall advise the same to be necessary, and some of the crew shall be appointed to attend and serve them, and to keep the place clean.

The cooper shall make buckets with covers and cradles, if necessary, for their use.

All ships furnished with fishing tackle, being in such places where fish is to be had, the Captain is to employ some of the company in fishing; the fish to be distributed daily to such persons as are sick or upon recovery, provided the surgeon recommend it, and the surplus, by turns amongst the messes of the officers and seamen, without favour or partiality and gratis, without any deduction of their allowance of provisions on that account.

It is left to the discretion of Commanders of squadrons, to shorten the allowance of provisions according to the exigence of the service, taking care that the men be punctually paid for the same.

The like power is given to Captains of single ships in cases of absolute necessity.

If there shall be a want of pork, the Captain is to order three pounds of beef to be issued to the men, in lieu of two pounds of pork.

One day in every week shall be issued out a proportion of flour and suet, in lieu of beef, for the seamen, but this is not to extend beyond four months' victualling at one time, nor shall the purser receive any allowance for flour or suet kept longer on board than that time, and there shall be supplied, once a year, a proportion of canvass for pudding-bags, after the rate of one ell for every sixteen men.

If any ships of the thirteen United Colonies, shall happen to come into port in want of provisions, the warrant of a Commander in chief shall be sufficient to the Agent or other instrument of the victualling, to supply the quantity wanted, and in urgent cases where delay may be hurtful, the warrant of the Captain of the ship shall be of equal effect.

The Captain is frequently to order the proper officers to inspect into the condition of the provisions, and if the bread proves damp, to have it aired upon the quarter deck or poop, and also examine the flesh casks, and if any of the pickle be leaked out, to have new made and put in, and the casks made tight and secure.

The Captain or purser shall secure the cloaths, bedding, and other things of such persons as shall die or be killed, to be delivered to their executors or administrators.

All papers, charter parties, bills of lading, passports, and other writings whatsoever, found on board any ship or ships, which shall be taken, shall be carefully preserved, and the originals sent to the court of Justice for maritime affairs, appointed or to be appointed by the legislatures in the respective colonies, for judging concerning such prize or prizes; and if any person or persons shall wilfully or negligently destroy or suffer to be destroyed, any such paper or papers, he or they so offending, shall forfeit their share of such prize or prizes, and suffer such other punishment as they shall be judged by a court-martial to deserve.

If any person or persons shall embezzle, steal, or take away any cables, anchors, sails, or any of the ship's furniture, or any of the powder, arms, ammunition, or provisions of any ship belonging to the thirteen United Colonies, he or they shall suffer such punishment as a court-martial shall order.

When in sight of a ship or ships of the enemy, and at such other times as may appear to make it necessary to prepare for an engagement, the Captain shall order all things in his ship in a proper posture for fight, and shall, in his own person, and according to his duty, heart on and encourage the inferior officers and men to fight courageously, and not to behave themselves faintly or cry for quarters, on pain of such punishment as the offence shall appear to deserve for his neglect.

Any Captain or other officer, mariner, or others, who shall basely desert their duty or station in the ship, and run away while the enemy is in sight, or, in time of action, or shall entice others to do so, shall suffer death, or such other punishment as a court-martial shall inflict.

Any officer, seaman, or marine, who shall begin, excite, cause, or join in any mutiny or sedition in the ship to which he belongs, on any pretence whatsoever, shall suffer death, or such other punishment as a court-martial shall direct. Any person in or belonging to the ship, who shall utter any words of sedition and mutiny, or endeavour to make any mutinous assemblies on any pretence whatsoever, shall suffer such punishment as a court-martial shall inflict.

None shall presume to quarrel with or strike his superior officer, on pain of such punishment as a court-martial shall order to be inflicted.

If any person shall apprehend he has just cause of complaint, he shall quietly and decently make the same known to his superior officer, or to the captain, as the case may require, who will take care that justice be done him.

There shall be no quarreling or fighting between shipmates on board any ship belonging to the thirteen United Colonies, nor shall there be used any reproachful or provoking speeches, tending to make quarrels and disturbance, on pain of imprisonment, and such other punishment, as a court-martial shall think proper to inflict.

If any person shall sleep upon his watch, or negligently perform the duty which shall be enjoined him to do, or forsake his station, he shall suffer such punishment as a court-martial shall judge proper to inflict, according to the nature of his offence.

All murder shall be punished with death.

All robbery and theft shall be punished at the discretion of a court-martial.

Any master at arms who shall refuse to receive such prisoner or prisoners, as shall be committed to his charge, or having received them, shall suffer him or them to escape, or dismiss them without orders for so doing, shall suffer in his or their stead, as a court-martial shall order and direct.

The Captain, officers, and others, shall use their utmost endeavours to detect, apprehend, and bring to punishment, all offenders, and shall at all times readily assist the officers appointed for that purpose in the discharge of their duty, on pain of being proceeded against, and punished by a court-martial at discretion.

All other faults, disorders, and misdemeanors, which shall be committed on board any ship belonging to the thirteen United Colonies, and which are not herein mentioned, shall be punished according to the laws and customs in such cases at sea.

A court-martial shall consist of at least three Captains and three first lieutenants, with three Captains and three first lieutenants of Marines, if there shall be so many of the Marines then present, and the eldest Captain shall preside.

All sea officers of the same denomination shall take rank of the officers of the marines.

Every Member of a court-martial shall take the following oath, viz:

"You _____ swear that you will well and truly try, and impartially determine the cause of the prisoner now to be tried, according to the rules of the Navy of the United Colonies. So help you God": which oath shall be administered by the president to the other members, and the president shall himself be sworn by the officer in said court next in rank.

All witnesses, before they may be admitted to give evidence, shall take the following oath:

"You swear the evidence you shall give, in the cause now in hearing, shall be the truth, the whole truth, and nothing but the truth. So help you God."

The sentence of a court-martial for any capital offence, shall not be put in execution, until it be confirmed by the Commander in chief of the fleet; and it shall be the duty of the president of every court-martial, to transmit to the Commander in chief of the fleet, every sentence which shall be given, with a summary of the evidence and proceedings thereon, by the first opportunity.

The Commander in chief of the fleet, for the time being, shall have power to pardon and remit any sentence of death, that shall be given in consequence of any of the afore mentioned Articles.

There shall be allowed to each man serving on board the ships in the service of the thirteen United Colonies, a daily proportion of provisions, according as is expressed in the following table, viz:

Sunday, 1 lb. bread, 1 lb. beef, 1 lb. potatoes or turnips.
Monday, 1 lb. bread, 1 lb. pork, ½ pint peas, and four oz. cheese.
Tuesday, 1 lb. bread, 1 lb. beef, 1 lb. potatoes or turnips, and pudding.

Wednesday, 1 lb. bread, two oz. butter, four oz. cheese, and ½ pint of rice.

Thursday, 1 lb. bread, 1 lb. pork, and ½ pint of peas.

Friday, 1 lb. bread, 1 lb. beef, 1 lb. potatoes or turnips, and pudding.

Saturday, 1 lb. bread, 1 lb. pork, ½ pint peas, and four oz. cheese.

Half pint of rum per man every day, and discretionary allowance on extra duty, and in time of engagement.

A pint and half of vinegar for sick men per week.

The pay of the officers and men shall be as follows:

Captain or commander,	32 dollars,	Cooper,	15 do.
Lieutenants,	20 do.	Captain's or Com-	13⅓ do.
Master,	20 do.	mander's clerk	20 do.
Mates,	15 do.	Steward,	6⅔ do.
Boatswain,	15 do.	Chaplain,	26⅔ do.
Boatswain's first		Able Seaman,	18 do.
mate	9⅓ do.	Captain of marines,	8 do.
Ditto, second ditto	8 do.	Lieutenants,	7⅓ do.
Gunner,	15 do.	Serjeants,	7⅓ do.
Ditto mate,	10⅔ do.	Corporals,	7⅓ do.
Surgeon,	21⅓ do.	Fifer,	6⅔ do.
Surgeon's mate,	13⅓ do.	Drummer,	
Carpenter,	15 do.	Privates or marines,	
Carpenter's mate	10⅔ do.	15 dollars,	

PER CALENDAR MONTH.

Appendix II
Vessels of the Continental Navy

Alfred, 24	Ship	Purchased 1775	Captured 1778
Columbus, 20	Ship	Purchased 1775	Destroyed 1778
Andrew Doria, 14	Brig	Purchased 1775	Destroyed 1777
Cabot, 14	Brig	Purchased 1775	Captured 1777
Providence, 12	Sloop	Purchased 1775	Destroyed 1779
Hornet, 10	Sloop	Purchased 1775	Destroyed 1777
Wasp, 8	Schooner	Purchased 1775	Destroyed 1777
Fly, 8	Schooner	Purchased 1775	Destroyed 1777
Lexington, 16	Brig	Purchased 1776	Captured 1777
Reprisal, 16	Brig	Purchased 1776	Lost at sea 1777
Hampden, 14	Brig	Purchased 1776	Sold 1777
Independence, 10	Sloop	Purchased 1776	Wrecked 1778
Sachem, 10	Sloop	Purchased 1776	Destroyed 1777
Mosquito, 4	Sloop	Purchased 1776	Destroyed 1777
Raleigh, 32	Frigate	Launched 1776	Captured 1778
Hancock, 32	Frigate	Launched 1776	Captured 1777
Warren, 32	Frigate	Launched 1776	Destroyed 1779
Washington, 32	Frigate	Launched 1776	Destroyed 1777
Randolph, 32	Frigate	Launched 1776	Lost in action 1778
Providence, 28	Frigate	Launched 1776	Captured 1780
Trumbull, 28	Frigate	Launched 1776	Captured 1781
Congress, 28	Frigate	Launched 1776	Destroyed 1777
Virginia, 28	Frigate	Launched 1776	Captured 1778

---

[1] Based upon lists in George F. Emmons, ed., *The Navy of the United States* (Washington 1853), and Allen, *A Naval History of the American Revolution* (Boston 1913).

Effingham, 28	Frigate	Launched 1776	Destroyed 1777
Boston, 24	Frigate	Launched 1776	Captured 1780
Montgomery, 24	Frigate	Launched 1776	Destroyed 1777
Delaware, 24	Frigate	Launched 1776	Destroyed 1777
Ranger, 18	Ship	Launched 1777	Captured 1780
Resistance, 10	Brigantine	Launched 1777	Captured 1778
Surprise	Sloop	Purchased 1777	*
Racehorse, 12	Sloop	Captured 1776	Destroyed
Repulse, 8	Xebec	Pennsylvania State gunboat lent to Continental Navy—1777	Destroyed 1777
Champion, 8	Xebec	Pennsylvania State gunboat lent to Continental Navy—1777	Destroyed 1777
L'Indien, 40	Frigate	Built in Holland 1777	Sold to France; later acquired by South Carolina Navy as *South Carolina*— Captured 1782
Deane (Later *Hague*), 32	Frigate	Purchased 1777	Sold 1783
Queen of France, 28	Frigate	Purchased 1777	Sunk 1780
Dolphin, 10	Cutter	Purchased 1777	*
Surprise, 10	Lugger	Purchased 1777	Seized by France
Revenge, 14	Cutter	Purchased 1777	Sold 1779
Alliance, 32	Frigate	Launched 1778	Sold 1785
General Gates, 18	Ship	Purchased 1778	Sold 1779
Retaliation	Brigantine	Purchased 1778	*
Pigot, 8	Schooner	Captured 1778	*
Confederacy, 32	Frigate	Launched 1779	Captured 1781
Argo, 12	Sloop	Purchased 1779	Sold 1779
Diligent, 12	Brig	Captured 1779	Destroyed 1779
Bonhomme Richard, 42	Ship	Purchased 1779	Lost in action 1779
Pallas, 32	Frigate	Lent by France 1779	Returned
Cerf, 18	Cutter	Lent by France 1779	Returned
Vengeance, 12	Brig	Lent by France 1779	Returned
Serapis, 44	Frigate	Captured 1779	Sold 1779
Ariel, 20	Ship	Lent by France 1780	Returned 1781
Saratoga, 18	Ship	Launched 1780	Lost at sea 1781
America, 74	Ship of the line	Launched 1782	Given to France
General Washington, 20	Ship	Captured 1782	Sold 1784
Duc de Lauzun, 20	Ship	Purchased 1782	Sold 1783
Bourbon, 36	Frigate	Launched 1783	Sold 1783

* Disposition unknown

Bibliography

THE MOST IMPORTANT WORKS ARE DESIGNATED WITH AN ASTERISK.

* Adams, John, *Diary and Autobiography*, ed. by L. H. Butterfield (New York 1964).
———, *Life and Works of John Adams*, ed. by C. F. Adams (Boston 1850–56).
Ahlin, John H., *Maine Rubicon* (Calais, Maine, 1966).
Alberts, Robert C., *The Golden Voyage: The Life and Times of William Bingham* (Boston 1969).
* Albion, Robert G., *Forests and Sea Power: The Timber Problem of the Royal Navy 1652–1862* (Cambridge 1926).
———, *Sea Lanes in Wartime* (New York 1942).
Alden, John R., *The American Revolution* (New York 1954).
Alderman, Clifford L., *The Privateersmen* (Philadelphia 1965).
* Allen, Gardner W., *A Naval History of the American Revolution* (Boston 1913).
Auger, Helen, *The Secret War for Independence* (New York 1955).
Barrington, Shute, *The Political Life of William Viscount Barrington* (London 1814).
Baynham, Henry, *From the Lower Deck* (Barre, Massachusetts, 1970).
Beatson, Robert, *Naval and Military Memoirs of Great Britain* (London 1804).

* Beck, Alverda S., ed., *The Letter Book of Esek Hopkins* (Providence 1932).

* ———, ed., *The Correspondence of Esek Hopkins* (Providence 1933).

Bemis, Samuel F., *The Diplomacy of the American Revolution* (Bloomington, Indiana, 1967).

* Billias, George A., *General John Glover and His Marblehead Mariners* (New York 1966).

* ———, ed., *George Washington's Opponents* (New York 1969).

Bliven, Bruce, Jr., *Under the Guns: New York 1775–1776* (New York 1972).

* Boatner, Mark M., *Encyclopedia of the American Revolution* (New York 1966).

Bolander, Louis H., ed., "The Log of the *Ranger*," *United States Naval Institute Proceedings* (February 1936).

Bowen, Catherine Drinker, *John Adams and the American Revolution* (New York 1950).

Brady, William, *The Kedge-Anchor; or Young Sailors' Assistant* (New York 1848).

Brewington, M. V., "The Design of Our First Frigates," *The American Neptune* (January 1948).

Bridenbaugh, Carl, *Cities in Revolt: Urban Life in America 1743–1776* (Oxford 1955).

* Brown, Gerald S., *The American Secretary: The Colonial Policy of Lord George Germain, 1775–1778* (Ann Arbor 1963).

Bryant, Samuel W., *The Sea and the States* (New York 1967).

Burnett, Edmund C., ed., *Letters of Members of the Continental Congress* (Washington 1921–1936).

———, *The Continental Congress* (New York 1941).

Burt, Struthers, *Philadelphia, Holy Experiment* (New York 1945).

* Chappelle, Howard, *The History of the American Sailing Navy* (New York 1949).

Chidsey, Donald B., *The American Privateers* (New York 1962).

Clark, William B., *Ben Franklin's Privateers* (Baton Rouge 1956).

* ———, *Captain Dauntless: The Story of Nicholas Biddle of the Continental Navy* (Baton Rouge 1949).

———, *The First Saratoga* (Baton Rouge 1953).

* ———, *Gallant John Barry* (New York 1938).

* ———, *George Washington's Navy* (Baton Rouge 1960).

* ———, *Lambert Wickes, Sea Raider and Diplomat* (New Haven 1932).

* ———, and Morgan, William J., eds., *Naval Documents of the American Revolution* (Washington 1964).

Cobbett, William, ed., *The Parliamentary History of England*, Vols. XIX and XX (London 1806–1828).

Coggins, Jack, *Ships and Seamen of the American Revolution* (Harrisburg 1969).

Commager, Henry S. and Morris, Richard B., eds., *The Spirit of 'Seventy-Six* (Indianapolis 1958).

* Conyngham, Gustavus, *Letters and Papers Relating to the Cruises of Gustavus Conyngham*, ed. by Robert W. Neeser (New York 1915).

* Cooper, J. Fenimore, *Naval History of the United States of America* (Philadelphia 1840).
Corbett, Julian S., ed., *Fighting Instructions 1530–1816* (London 1905).
* Dandridge, Danske, *American Prisoners of the Revolution* (Charlottesville 1911).
Deux-Ponts, William de, *My Campaigns in America* (Boston 1868).
Dictionary of American Biography.
Dictionary of National Biography.
Dowdell, Vincent S., Jr., "The Birth of the American Navy," *United States Naval Institute Proceedings* (November 1955).
Drowne, Solomon, *Journal of a Cruise in the Fall of 1780* (New York 1872).
East, Robert A., *Business Enterprise in the American Revolutionary Era* (New York 1938).
Einstein, Lewis, *Divided Loyalties: Americans in England During the War of Independence* (Boston 1933).
Eller, Ernest M., "Sea Power in the American Revolution," *United States Naval Institute Proceedings* (June 1936).
Emmons, George F., ed., *The Navy of the United States* (Washington 1853).
Fanning, Nathaniel, *Fanning's Narrative* (New York 1912).
Farmer, Edward, "Skenesborough: Continental Navy Shipyard," *United States Naval Institute Proceedings* (October 1964).
Fenwick, Kenneth, *H.M.S. Victory* (London 1959).
* Field, Edward, *Esek Hopkins* (Providence 1898).
Flexner, James T., *George Washington in the American Revolution* (Boston 1967).
Footner, Hulbert, *Sailor of Fortune: The Life and Adventures of Commodore Barney U.S.N.* (New York 1940).
Forbes, Esther, *Paul Revere and the World He Lived In* (Boston 1942).
* Force, Peter, ed., *American Archives* (Washington 1837–1853).
Fortescue, J. W., *A History of the British Army*, Vol. III—1763–1793 (London 1902).
Fox, Ebeneezer, *The Adventures of Ebeneezer Fox in the Revolutionary War* (Boston 1847).
Freeman, Douglas S., *George Washington: A Biography*, 7 vols. (New York 1948–1957).
* French, Allen, *The First Year of the American Revolution* (New York 1968).
Gammell, William, *Life of Samuel Ward* (Boston 1846).
Graham, Gerald S., *Empire of the North Atlantic* (Toronto 1966).
Graves, Thomas, *The Graves Papers and Other Documents Relating to the Naval Operations of the Yorktown Campaign*, ed. by Francis E. Chadwick (New York 1916).
Green, Ezra, *Diary of Ezra Green, M.D.* (New York 1971).
* Gruber, Ira D., *The Howe Brothers and the American Revolution* (New York 1972).
Herbert, Charles, *A Relic of the Revolution* (Boston 1847).
Higginbotham, Don, *The War of American Independence* (New York 1971).
Hood, Dorothy, *The Admirals Hood* (London 1942).

Hood, Samuel, *Letters of Lord Hood*, ed. by David Hannay (London 1895).

Howard, James L., *Seth Harding, Mariner* (New Haven 1930).

Hubbard, Timothy W., "Battle at Valcour Island: Benedict Arnold as Hero," *American Heritage*, XVII (October 1966).

James, Bartholomew, *Journal of Rear-Admiral Bartholomew James*, ed. by J. K. Laughton (London 1906).

* James, William M., *The British Navy in Adversity* (New York 1926).

Jameson, J. Franklin, "St. Eustatius in the American Revolution," *The American Historical Review* (July 1903).

Jenrich, Charles H., "The Old *Jersey* Prison Ship," *United States Naval Institute Proceedings* (February 1963).

* *Journals of the Continental Congress, 1774–1789*, 34 vols. (Washington 1904–1939).

Kilby, John, "Narrative of John Kilby," *Maryland Historical Magazine* (Spring 1972).

* Knox, Dudley, *The Naval Genius of George Washington* (Boston 1932).

———, *A History of the United States Navy* (New York 1948).

Langley, Harold D. *Social Reform in the United States Navy, 1798–1862* (Urbana, Ill., 1967).

Larrabee, Harold A., *Decision at the Chesapeake* (New York 1964).

* Lemisch, Jesse, "The American Revolution Seen From the Bottom Up" in *Towards a New Past: Dissenting Essays in American History* (New York 1969).

* ———, "Jack Tar in the Streets," *The William and Mary Quarterly*, XXV (July 1968).

———, "Listening to the 'Inarticulate': William Widger's Dream and the Loyalties of America's Revolutionary Seamen in British Prisons," *Journal of Social History* (Fall 1969).

Lewis, Charles L., *Admiral de Grasse and American Independence* (Annapolis 1945).

Lewis, Michael, *A Social History of the Navy* (London 1960).

* ———, *The Navy of Britain* (London 1948).

Lincoln, Charles H., ed., *Naval Records of the American Revolution* (Washington 1906).

Lloyd, Christopher, *The British Seaman* (London 1968).

* ———, and Coulter, Jack L. S., *Medicine and the Navy*, Vol. III—1714–1815 (Edinburgh 1961).

———, *The Nation and the Navy* (London 1965).

Longridge, C. Nepean, *The Anatomy of Nelson's Ships* (London 1955).

Lorenz, Lincoln, *John Paul Jones: Fighter for Freedom and Glory* (Annapolis 1943).

Lovette, Leland P., *Naval Customs, Traditions and Usage* (Annapolis 1939).

McCusker, John J., Jr., "The American Invasion of Nassau in the Bahamas," *The American Neptune* (July 1965).

———, "The Tonnage of the Continental Ship *Alfred*," *Pennsylvania Magazine of History and Biography* (1966).

McGuffie, T. H., *The Siege of Gibraltar* (Philadelphia 1965).

Macintyre, Donald, *Admiral Rodney* (London 1962).
* Mackesy, Piers, *The War for America 1775–1783* (Cambridge 1965).
McLarty, R. N., *The Expedition of Major-General John Vaughan to the Lesser Antilles, 1779–1781* (Unpublished doctoral dissertation, University of Michigan 1951).
* Maclay, Edgar S., *A History of American Privateers* (New York 1899).
———, *A History of the United States Navy* (New York 1901).
* Mahan, Alfred T., *Major Operations of the Navies in the War of American Independence* (Boston 1913).
———, *Types of Naval Officers* (London 1902).
* ———, *The Influence of Seapower Upon History 1660–1783* (New York 1957).
Marcus, G. J., *A Naval History of England: The Formative Centuries* (Boston 1961).
Martelli, George, *Jemmy Twitcher* (London 1962).
Martin, Joseph P., *Private Yankee Doodle*, ed. by George F. Scheer (Boston 1962).
* Masefield, John, *Sea Life in Nelson's Time* (New York 1925).
Maurer, M., "Coppered Bottoms for the Royal Navy: A Factor in the Maritime War of 1778–1783," *Military Affairs*, XIV (1950).
Melville, Phillips, "Eleven Guns for the Grand Union," *American Heritage* (October 1958).
Metcalfe, Clyde A., *A History of the United States Marine Corps* (New York 1939).
Metzger, Charles H., *The Prisoner in the American Revolution* (Chicago 1962).
* Middlebrook, Louis F., *Maritime Connecticut During the American Revolution* (Salem 1925).
Middleton, Charles, *Letters and Papers of Charles Lord Barham*, ed. by J. K. Laughton (London 1906).
Miller, John C., *Origins of the American Revolution* (Boston 1943).
* ———, *Triumph of Freedom 1775–1783* (Boston 1948).
Montross, Lynn, *Rag, Tag, and Bobtail* (New York 1952).
———, *The Reluctant Rebels* (New York 1950).
* Morgan, William J., *Captains to the Northward* (Barre, Massachusetts, 1959).
* Morison, Samuel E., *John Paul Jones: A Sailor's Biography* (Boston 1959).
———, *The Maritime History of Massachusetts* (Boston 1961).
Morris, Richard B., *The Peacemakers* (New York 1965).
———, "The Revolution's Caine Mutiny," *American Heritage* (April 1960).
Mowat, Henry, "Captain Henry Mowat's Account," *Magazine of History*, Vol. III, Extra No. 11 (1910).
Namier, Lewis B., *England in the Age of the American Revolution* (London 1930).
Norton, William, ed., *Eagle Seamanship: Square Rigger Sailing* (New York 1969).
Pares, Richard, *King George III and the Politicians* (Oxford 1953).

Patterson, A. Temple, *The Other Armada* (Manchester 1960).

* Paullin, Charles O., *The Navy of the American Revolution* (Cleveland 1906).

* ———, ed., *Out-Letters of the Continental Marine Committee and Board of Admiralty* (New York 1914).

Postgate, R. W., *That Devil Wilkes* (New York 1929).

Potter, E. B., *The Naval Academy Illustrated History of the United States Navy* (New York 1971).

———, and Nimitz, Chester W., *Sea Power: A Naval History* (Englewood Cliffs, New Jersey, 1960).

Powers, Stephen T., *The Decline and Extinction of American Naval Power 1781–1787* (Unpublished doctoral dissertation, University of Notre Dame 1964).

Pratt, Fletcher, *The Compact History of the United States Navy* (New York 1967).

Rathbun, Frank H., "Rathbun's Raid on Nassau," *United States Naval Institute Proceedings* (November 1970).

Robertson, Eileen A., *The Spanish Town Papers* (New York 1959).

Rodney, Lord, *Letter-book and Order-book of George, Lord Rodney* (New York 1932).

* Sands, Robert C., *Life and Correspondence of John Paul Jones* (New York 1839).

* Sandwich, Earl of, *The Private Papers of John, Earl of Sandwich*, ed. by G. R. Barnes and J. H. Owen (London 1932).

Seitz, Don C., *Paul Jones: His Exploits in English Seas during 1778–1780* (New York 1917).

Sherburne, Andrew, *Memoirs* (Utica 1828).

Sherman, Andrew M., *Life of Capt. Jeremiah O'Brien* (Morristown, New Jersey, 1902).

Shuldham, Molyneux, *The Dispatches of Molyneux Shuldham, Vice Admiral of the Blue* (New York 1913).

* Smith, Philip C. F. and Knight, Russell W., "In Troubled Waters: The Elusive Schooner *Hannah*," *The American Neptune* (April 1970).

* Spinney, David, *Rodney* (London 1969).

———, "Sir Samuel Hood at St. Kitts: A Reassessment," *The Mariner's Mirror* (May 1972).

Sprout, Harold H. and Sprout, Margaret, *The Rise of American Naval Power, 1776–1918* (Princeton 1967).

Stewart, Robert A., *The History of Virginia's Navy in the Revolution* (Richmond 1934).

* Stout, Neil R., "Manning the Royal Navy in North America, 1763–1775," *The American Neptune*, XXIII (July 1963).

———, *The Royal Navy in American Waters 1760–1775* (Unpublished doctoral dissertation, University of Wisconsin 1962).

* Syrett, David, *Shipping and the American War 1775–83* (London 1970).

Tornquist, Carl G., *The Naval Campaigns of Count de Grasse during the American Revolution* (Philadelphia 1942).

* Trevett, John, "Journal of John Trevett," *Rhode Island Historical Magazine*, Vols. VI and VII (1885–1886).

Uhlendorf, Bernhard A., trans. and ed., *The Siege of Charleston* (Ann Arbor 1938).

Valentine, Alan C., *Lord George Germain* (London 1962).

Van Doren, Carl, *Benjamin Franklin* (New York 1938).

Vernon, William, "Papers of William Vernon and the Navy Board" in *Publications of the Rhode Island Historical Society* (January 1901).

Wagner, Frederick, *Submarine Fighter of the American Revolution* (New York 1963).

Wallace, Willard M., *Appeal to Arms: A Military History of the American Revolution* (New York 1951).

———, *Traitorous Hero: The Life and Fortunes of Benedict Arnold* (New York 1954).

* Ward, Christopher, *The War of the Revolution* (New York 1952).

Washington, George, *Writings of George Washington*, ed. by John C. Fitzpatrick (Washington 1931).

Watson, J. Steven, *The Reign of George III 1760–1815* (Oxford 1960).

Wells, David F., *Trial of Admiral Keppel* (Unpublished doctoral dissertation, University of Kentucky 1957).

White, Thomas, *Naval Researches* (London 1830).

Willcox, William B., ed., *The American Rebellion: Sir Henry Clinton's Narrative of His Campaigns, 1775–1782* (New Haven 1954).

* ———, "The British Road to Yorktown: A Study in Divided Command," *The American Historical Review* (October 1946).

* ———, *Portrait of a General: Sir Henry Clinton in the War of Independence* (New York 1964).

* ———, "Why Did the British Lose the American Revolution?" *Michigan Alumnus Quarterly Review* (August 1956).

Yeager, Philip, "Last in the Hearts of His Countrymen," *United States Naval Institute Proceedings* (October 1968).

INDEX

Index